Political Economics

Zeuthen Lecture Book Series
Karl Gunnar Persson, editor

Modeling Bounded Rationality
Ariel Rubinstein

Forecasting Non-stationary Economic Time Series
Michael P. Clements and David F. Hendry

Political Economics: Explaining Economic Policy
Torsten Persson and Guido Tabellini

Political Economics
Explaining Economic Policy

Torsten Persson and Guido Tabellini

The MIT Press
Cambridge, Massachusetts
London, England

This book was set in Times Roman by Interactive Composition Corporation.

Printed and bound in the United States of America.

Library of Congress Cataloging-in-Publication Data

Persson, Torsten.
    Political economics : explaining economic policy / Torsten Persson and Guido Tabellini.
        p.   cm. — (Zeuthen lecture book series)
    Includes bibliographical references and index.
    ISBN 0-262-16195-8 (hc)
    1. Economic policy.   I. Tabellini, Guido Enrico, 1956–   II. Title.   III. Series.
HD87.P468   2000   00-028245
338.9—dc21

To Christina, Johanna, Jenny, and Julia
To Giovanna, Marco, and Anna

Contents

Series Foreword

The Zeuthen Lectures offer a forum for leading scholars to develop and synthesize novel results in theoretical and applied economics. They aim to present advances in knowledge in a form accessible to a wide audience of economists and advanced students of economics. The choice of topics will range from abstract theorizing to economic history. Regardless of the topic, the emphasis in the lecture series will be on originality and relevance. The Zeuthen Lectures are organized by the Institute of Economics, University of Copenhagen.

The lecture series is named after Frederik Zeuthen, a former professor at the Institute of Economics.

Karl Gunnar Persson

Foreword

Political economics has become one of the most active research areas in the last decades. Building on earlier work of the public choice school, rational expectations macroeconomics, and game theory, political economics has taken the next step by including rational voters, parties, and politicians in the models. In political economics, rational agents populate the markets and participate in politics. The assumption of rational behavior allows an adequate description of complicated incentives and trade-offs, and has contributed to a substantial increase in the understanding of the finer workings of the economic system. Similarly, taking the incentives of politicians into account allows a better understanding of the formation of policy and the role of different political institutions in shaping economic policy.

An authoritative survey of this body of research is long overdue. A survey should draw the big lines, compare and evaluate the different contributions, and point toward new directions for research. It should be an exposition that simplifies, cuts to the bone, and renders the basic structure of the arguments visible to the reader. The present book does this. It goes even further, as new ideas are developed and explored.

But books are finite in length, and authors inevitably have to make selections of which areas to cover. The focus here is on democratic societies and on important economic problems where the viewpoint of political economics seems particularly apt. The uninitiated reader will enjoy the first section of the book, where the basic issues and tools of modeling political equilibria are discussed. Armed with Condorcet winners, median voter theorems, Downsian and partisan parties, and so forth, the reader is ready for the subsequent parts.

Part 2 is devoted to redistributive politics. This is an important area where the traditional assumption of a benevolent planner seems most at odds with reality. The focus is on how the interplay between democratic institutions and self-seeking individuals, lobby groups, and parties determines the degree of redistribution. In the background is the possibility of explaining the huge cross-country differences in redistributive policies.

In part 3 the focus is on comparative politics. Can we explain differences in fiscal policies by alluding to differences in democratic institutions? For instance, will a European-style parliamentary system provide different outcomes than an American-style presidential system? What are the consequences of different electoral systems? Is there a rationale for the separation of powers?

Part 4 discusses intertemporal issues: debt, pensions, capital taxation, and growth. When policy takes place over time, new strategic dimensions arise and expectations are important. Present governments can influence the alternatives available for future governments. This may explain excessive public debt levels. The interplay between inequality and growth has been the subject of long debates. A possible link is provided by the redistributive policies chosen by the median voter and their effect on savings. The final part of the book is devoted to the topical area of monetary policy institutions.

The authors have made an impressive effort in providing a unified framework for large parts of the exposition. This makes the book particularly appealing; it makes assessments of different contributions much easier. Furthermore, the arguments have been made as simple and transparent as possible. Torsten Persson and Guido Tabellini are masters in "economizing on the modeling." They have another virtue: an eminent ability to maintain perspective and relate to the important issues. The text never wanders off into inessential technical details.

This book will become the standard reference for researchers in the area and the backbone of graduate courses around the world—certainly in Copenhagen.

Christian Schultz
Institute of Economics
University of Copenhagen

Preface

This book is written for the professional economist or political scientist who wants to become familiar with the recent research on political economics. We especially target students taking graduate courses in economics or political science, but some of the material could also be used in advanced undergraduate courses. Although the book is self-contained and most concepts and methods are developed gradually, the reader should have a good background in microeconomics, macroeconomics, and applied game theory.

Part 1 of the book introduces the analytical tools and is a prerequisite for the remainder of the book. Parts 2 to 5 deal with substantive economic policy issues; each of these can be read independently. Each part begins with a separate introduction, where we highlight a number of empirical regularities, put the following chapters in context, and provide a detailed road map. We comment on the original literature both as we go along and in separate "Notes on the Literature" at the end of each chapter. All chapters (except the first and the last) include a number of problems, constructed by Isabelle Brocas, Micael Castanheira, Ronny Razin, and David Strömberg. These problems have educational value for the student, but they also extend some of the results and ideas in the text. A separate exercise book by the same authors (published by MIT Press and made available electronically) reproduces the problems and suggests solutions.

The project leading up to this book has developed gradually. We were gaining a perspective on this body of research, while writing a number of surveys, for the *Handbook of International Economics,* Vol. 3 (Persson and Tabellini 1995), the *Handbook of Macroeconomics,* Vol. 2 (Persson and Tabellini 1999a), and the *Handbook of Public Economics,* Vol. 3 (Persson and Tabellini 1998). We are grateful to North-Holland and the editors of those volumes for letting us use some of the ideas in these surveys, and conversely—since the last of those *Handbooks* is still forthcoming—to MIT Press for letting us use some of the material in this book.

A final impetus for writing the book was the invitation to deliver the Zeuthen Lectures at the University of Copenhagen in June 1998. We are deeply grateful to the organizer of those lectures, Karl-Gunnar Persson, for his stimulus and warm hospitality during our two-week stay. More generally, we would like to thank the economics faculty at the University of Copenhagen for their comments and criticism at a crucial stage of the project. Without those comments, that friendly working environment, and the subsequent deadline, the project would have dragged on much longer.

When the book was almost completed, we had the opportunity to present its detailed contents, in July 1999, at "Encounters with Authors," organized by the Center for Basic Research in the Social Sciences at Harvard University. We are grateful to Jim Alt, who organized the event, and to all participants in this ten-session workshop for listening carefully to our arguments, reading the book in draft form, and sharing their thoughts and comments with us. That feedback came right when we needed it most and was an essential input in improving the quality of the final product.

The material underlying the book was used in various courses and lectures that we gave separately or together in the recent past: the Seventh Summer School in Economic Theory at the Hebrew University, Harvard University, the Kiel Institute for World Economic Studies, the London School of Economics, the NAKE Lectures in the Netherlands and, naturally, at our home institutions, Stockholm University and Bocconi University. We are grateful to students in those classes for their comments and their help in spotting mistakes or clearing up confusion.

Some of the material in the book draws on our joint published work with Gérard Roland. We are deeply grateful to him for his collaboration and for the inspiration he provided while we were working together. Many of the ideas appearing in chapters 9 and 10 owe much to his involvement in those joint projects.

We want to express our thanks to many colleagues for their comments and feedback. These were invaluable in gaining a better understanding of the subject matter, finding better ways of organizing the presentation, and improving the exposition. Our greatest debt is to the authors of the companion exercise book. Isabelle, Micael, Ronny, and David read the entire book carefully and helped us to improve the exposition and correct mistakes.

We are grateful for comments on single chapters or the whole book by Jim Alt, Carlos Boix, Francesco Daveri, Francesco Giavazzi, Giovanni Favara, Paul Klein, Assar Lindbeck, Eric Magar, Michele Polo, Gérard Roland, Ken Shepsle, and Fabrizio Zilibotti. We would also like to thank a number of people for useful discussions, guidance to the literature, and specific comments on the *Handbook* chapters, in particular Alberto Alesina, Alan Auerbach, David Austen-Smith, David Baron, Roel Beetsma, Tim Besley, Francesco Daveri, Daniel Diermeier, Mathias Dewatripont, Avinash Dixit, Barry Eichengreen, Jon Faust, Raquel Fernandez, Fabio Ghironi, Rex Ghosh, Elhanan Helpman, Dale Henderson, Peter Kenen, Jean-Jacques Laffont, Francesco Lippi, Roger Myerson, Maury Obstfeld, Per Pettersson, Adam Posen, Ken Rogoff, Gérard Roland, Howard Rosenthal, Andrei Shleifer, Lars Svensson, John Taylor, Jean Tirole, and Gisela Waisman.

At different stages of the project, we benefited from excellent research assistance by Fabio Ghironi, Paolo Dudine, and Alessandra Bonfiglioli.

Writing a book is a long and tiring process. It was made considerably easier by the outstanding administrative and editorial assistance we received from Christina Lönnblad and Alessandra Startari through many revisions. Christina made a truly heroic effort in the last month of work, checking language and references and editing and assembling the final version of a long and complicated manuscript, while managing to remain her usual cheerful self.

Last but not least, we want to thank our editor, Terry Vaughn, for being so kind and accommodating to our requests and helping us put an end to this enterprise.

Finally, we are grateful to a number of institutions for giving us financial support. During the course of the project, our research was supported by the Axel and Margaret Ax:son Johnson Foundation, the Bank of Sweden Tercentenary Foundation, Bocconi University, the Centro Nazionale Ricerche, the London School of Economics, Harvard University, and the Swedish Council for Research in the Humanities and Social Sciences, and by a TMR grant from the European Commission.

1 General Introduction

Economic policies vary greatly across time and place. In the late 1990s total government spending as a fraction of gross domestic product stood at more than 60% in Sweden and well above 50% in many countries of continental Europe, but around 35% in Japan, Switzerland, and the United States. Striking variations are also evident in the composition of spending: transfers are high in Europe, but low in Latin America. Among the fifteen members of the European Union, spending on the unemployed ranged from 2% to 17% of total public spending, whereas the replacement rate in unemployment insurance ranged from 20% to 90%. At the same time, public debt was less than 40% of GDP in Norway but more than 120% in Italy and Belgium. Inflation has taken a different time path over the last thirty years in many industrialized countries, resulting in an average inflation rate of roughly 8% in the United Kingdom but 3% in Germany. Available measures of corruption vary a lot, even across countries with comparable levels of development and similar economic structure.

Despite these differences, we observe some common patterns. Virtually all industrial countries saw the growth of government take off in the mid-1930s and again in the late 1960s, whereas it slowed down, or turned negative, after the war and toward the late 1980s. Public pensions have grown rapidly in the last three decades to become a dominant component of public spending in all European countries. During the same period, public investment has been hovering around 3% of GDP. Inflation accelerated everywhere in the developed world in the 1970s and came down again in the 1990s, though earlier in some countries than in others.

How can we explain the variations in the data? And what are the sources of the common patterns? Do these outcomes covary systematically with other aspects of economic policy or with the economic and social environment? Can alternative political constitutions and legislative procedures explain part of the policy outcomes? Are the observed patterns of spending and taxation likely to reflect socially optimal policies—given some normative criterion? Do they even reflect the preferences of a majority? If not, how can we account for the deviations? Are they reflections of political failures due to imperfections in the political process?

Goals

This book explores how such questions might be answered. We want to explain economic policy in modern democracies: what determines the size and form of redistributive programs, the extent and type of public goods provision, the burden of taxation across alternative tax bases, the size of government deficits, the extent of corruption by public officials, the structure of labor market regulation, the stance of monetary policy during the course of the business cycle or the electoral cycle? When searching for an answer to these questions, we reach the boundary between political science and economics. As in political science, we study collective choice and political institutions. We want to understand how policy decisions are made, what shapes the incentives and constraints of the policymakers taking those decisions, and how conflicts over policy are resolved. But as in economics, we are ultimately interested in the outcomes of policy decisions. We also want to understand how the economic consequences of policy feed back into private agents' policy preferences and how these preferences are aggregated back into public policy.

It is popular to refer to research in this area as "political economy." Sometimes that term is used to suggest an alternative analytical approach, as if the traditional tools of analysis in economics were not appropriate to study political phenomena. This is definitely not our view and not our approach in this book. On the contrary, we borrow the main tools of analysis from economics, modeling policy choices as the equilibrium outcome of a well-specified strategic interaction among rational individuals. Hence, the title of the book.

Roots

Alt and Chrystal published a book with a similar title more than fifteen years ago (1983). Since then, research in political economics has expanded rapidly; it now transcends several traditional fields. The roots of this research can be traced back to at least three different traditions in economics and political science.

The most recent tradition, from which we come as economists, is the *theory of macroeconomic policy,* dating back to the work by Lucas in the mid-1970s. Lucas taught us to study the consequences of economic policy by contrasting systematic policy rules. Only when policy is formulated as a rule can we give precise content to private expectations, through the assumption of rational expectations. As suggested by Kydland and Prescott (1977) and Calvo (1978), however, not all policy rules are equally plausible. Only those rules that the policymaker has no incentive to abandon become credible, or "time-consistent." This idea gave rational expectations a game-theoretic foundation. Rational individuals reason strategically and base their expectations on their perception of the policymaker's incentives. A complete theory must thus include specific hypotheses about what governs those incentives. From this insight it is only a short step to a political approach to macroeconomic policy. Since that step was taken in the mid-1980s, a rapidly growing literature on macroeconomic policy has attempted to build more solid foundations for the hypotheses on the policymakers' incentives. Because of its starting point, research in this tradition has always insisted on solid underpinnings in economic theory and maintained the assumption of individual rationality. It has also paid particular attention to intertemporal policy choices and economic dynamics. At the same time, however, this research has often relied on rather superficial assumptions about political institutions and political conflict and tended to shy away from empirical, applied analysis. Early contributions to this tradition were surveyed in Persson and Tabellini 1990.

A second, older and more established tradition in the positive analysis of economic policy is *public choice,* which goes back to the classic contributions by Buchanan and Tullock (1962) and Olson (1965). This school has focused on public finance, trade policy, and regulatory policy. Moreover, the agency problem between the government and citizens at large has always held center stage in this line of research. The public choice school emphasized many ideas that are still highly relevant in today's research on economic policymaking. One of these is the crucial importance of interest groups, especially the importance of lobbying by organized interest groups and the pervasiveness of rent-seeking activities. Another long-lasting contribution is the idea that many agency problems in politics originate in the public's being imperfectly informed about the details of specific policy programs. The public choice school also stressed the importance of the constitution and the constraints it imposes. Researchers in this tradition were reluctant, however, to use formal game-theoretic tools or to impose strong notions of individual rationality. As a result, the initial work sometimes relied on weaker theoretical or microeconomic foundations. The voluminous literature on early public choice is surveyed in several places and with particular clarity and completeness by Frey (1983) and Mueller (1989).

A third fundamental tradition for research on political economics is the formal analysis in political science. This tradition goes back to works such as Riker 1962 and is often referred to as *rational choice.* Results in the spatial theory of voting and axiomatic social choice theory, following the publication of Arrow's (1951) impossibility theorem, disillusioned many researchers about the prospects for a general theory of collective choice based on individual preferences alone. Since the early 1980s, however, formally oriented political science has changed its emphasis, turning to the study of collective choice within specific political institutions. This approach models the institutional details, exploiting the tools of noncooperative game theory. For example, alternative political systems differ in the way politicians are elected, how agenda-setting powers are allocated, and how the legislative process is structured. Such differences can be formally represented by alternative extensive form games. Researchers in the rational choice tradition have mainly focused on political institutions as such, paying little attention to specific economic policy issues. Ordeshook (1986) and Inman (1987) survey some of the early literature, whereas some of the contributions in Mueller 1997 contain more up-to-date surveys.

Ten to fifteen years ago, these three traditions largely developed in parallel without too much contact with each other. Integration among the three has been increasing over time, however. In this book, we try to combine the best of all three traditions.

As in the macroeconomic tradition, we take a general equilibrium approach. With only a few exceptions, the models we analyze have explicit microfoundations. Economic behavior as well as political behavior are thus derived from the same individual preferences. Given equilibrium policies, economic behavior is aggregated into economic outcomes in well-specified markets. Given equilibrium economic outcomes, political behavior is aggregated into policy decisions under well-specified political institutions. In an overall equilibrium, economic and political outcomes are mutually consistent.

As in the public choice tradition, we stress the ability of interest groups to influence the political process. We also highlight the agency problems in politics, namely the conflict between political representatives acting in their own interest but against that of voters at large. Furthermore, constitutional issues play an important role throughout the book.

As in the rational choice tradition, we pay close attention to the structure of collective decision making, modeling specific institutional features as well-defined delegation games. We also borrow a number of specific ideas and tools of analysis from this tradition, particularly in our modeling of electoral competition and legislative decision making.

In simplified form, our approach can thus be summarized as follows: we adopt the equilibrium approach of the macroeconomic theory of policy and exploit the tools of rational choice in analyzing some of the classic problems in public choice.

Positive versus Normative Analysis

The book always conceives economic policy as the equilibrium outcome of a well-defined noncooperative game under primitive assumptions about economic and political behavior. The rules of that game reflect the nature of the political institutions. We thus take these institutions as given and see them as important determinants of economic policy (though institutions are certainly not the only determinants of policy in these models). But we refrain from seeking positive explanations for the structure of these institutions. Nor do we seek to explain how political institutions have evolved over time. Implicitly, we view institutions as inherited by history and difficult to change. To some extent, this is really our view: political institutions have a great deal of inertia, and when institutional change takes place, it is often in the midst of dramatic social events or profound and radical changes in society. To understand the evolution of institutions, pure and abstract analysis should thus be integrated with a historical approach. Such a positive analysis of how institutions evolved is certainly an interesting area of research. But we are also trying to simplify our task, and it is easier to study one problem at a time.

The book asks positive questions about policy: we primarily want to know why policy is the way it is, not what it ought to be. Nevertheless, in many instances we contrast the positive predictions against a normative benchmark. Without much discussion, and in the absence of clearly superior alternatives, our normative benchmark throughout the book is a Benthamite utilitarian optimum, namely the policy maximizing the sum of individual utilities. If the analysis has normative implications, these typically concern the design of institutions, such as the structure of budgetary procedures, the degree of central bank independence, or the form of the electoral rule. Once more, this raises the question of why institutions are what they are. The normative implications are relevant only insofar as ideas, not just political expediency, help shape institutional reform. Otherwise, the institutions ought to be endogenous as well, and normative analysis could only deal with the rules for constitutional change. But then, these rules might also be endogenous; the argument easily runs into an infinite regress, and we do not have much to add to this philosophical discussion.

Limitations

Taking institutions as given is certainly a limitation in the book's approach. But there are other limitations. First, we confine our analysis of political institutions to a relatively narrow set. When discussing electoral competition, we analyze only two-party or two-candidate elections. As a consequence, our treatment of electoral politics misses an important part of reality in countries with proportional elections and several parties. This reflects the current state of formal modeling. It is hard to model the outcomes of multiparty competition, particularly when the policy space is multidimensional (see Schofield 1997 and Myerson 1999 for recent reviews). Our treatment of legislative decisions also entails drastic simplifications, particularly when it comes to modeling the process of government formation and dissolution in parliamentary democracies. Again, the existing literature is small and at an early stage (see, however, Laver and Shepsle 1996 and Diermeier and Merlo 1999 for recent interesting work). Furthermore, we never analyze the role of the government administration in shaping the details of economic policy, which means that we do not consider large literatures on the private agenda of the bureaucracy, going back to the classical work by Niskanen (1971), and on the organizational design of government agencies, as in the seminal work by Wilson (1989).

Second, we are selective in our choice of economic policy problems. We study policy problems that belong to public finance (public good provision, different kinds of redistribution, taxation), macroeconomics (fiscal policy, including public debt issue), and monetary economics (aggregate demand management, international policy coordination). But the level of our examination is quite abstract, and the discussion of specific applied policy programs is quite limited. Moreover, we entirely neglect other important policy issues belonging to trade policy or regulation; contributions to politics and trade policy are surveyed by Hillman (1989) and critically discussed by Rodrik (1995), while Laffont (1999) summarizes some recent promising work on the politics of regulation from the perspective of agency theory. Furthermore, we pay only limited attention to questions in local public finance; the literature on fiscal federalism is surveyed by Inman and Rubinfeld (1997).

Third, we omit some important theoretical topics. In particular, our treatment of informational issues is, at best, superficial. We largely ignore a large literature on asymmetric information in politics. Some of this research is surveyed by Calvert (1986). We also ignore a growing literature on information aggregation through voting and other political institutions (see Piketty 1999 for a recent survey). Another topic where we only scratch the surface is the literature on economic and political reform. Important contributions to this literature are collected in Sturzenegger and Tommasi 1998; Drazen 1999 also deals at length with this material.

Finally, the book does not include any new empirical analysis. Our policy problems have a strong empirical motivation, and throughout the book we seek to provide references to existing empirical research. However, it is fair to say that, for a research program with a strong positive motivation, the bridge linking theory with data is way too fragile. Fortifying this bridge is a task that ought to be addressed with urgent priority. Two volumes on electoral cycles by Alesina and Rosenthal (1995) and Alesina, Roubini, and Cohen (1997) are steps in this direction, as are many papers discussed in the chapters to follow.

In the remainder of this introductory chapter, we provide an overview and a road map to the book. To help the reader gain a better perspective, we try to view the contents from two different angles. First, section 1.1 summarizes the main economic policy issues that we will analyze. Then section 1.2 discusses the main ingredients of the political models on which we build our analysis. Section 1.3 offers some concluding remarks.

1.1 Economic Policy

The book is divided into five parts, each dealing with a different economic policy problem. To a large extent, the underlying economic model is kept very similar within each part. Part 1 is designed to provide a toolbox; its four chapters introduce virtually all the political models we will be using in the rest of the book. Whereas this part is a prerequisite for all the others, each of the subsequent parts can be read more or less independently. Part 2 deals with the determinants of redistributive programs aiming at broad or narrow groups of the population. Part 3 investigates the effect of alternative constitutional features, such as the electoral rule or the political regime, on the broad design of fiscal policy. Part 4 discusses policymaking in an intertemporal economic setting. Part 5 focuses on monetary policy.

Throughout the book, the private sector is assumed to contain a large number (a continuum) of heterogeneous individuals. Markets are generally assumed to work well; there are few elements of imperfect competition or other market failures. Exceptions include the usual free-rider problem in the provision of public goods, externalities, the absence of nondistorting tax instruments, and—in the context of monetary policy—some nominal rigidities. We keep our economic models as simple as possible to focus on the political determinants of policy choices. But except in the case of monetary policy, the models are always formulated as general equilibrium models with explicit microfoundations (even though we make heavy use of simplifying assumptions about preferences and technology to obtain closed-form solutions).

Government Spending and Redistribution

The general topic of parts 1 to 3 is static (or one-time) choices of fiscal policy, such as the provision of public goods and the design of redistributive programs. The government raises taxes and spends the resulting revenue in three alternative ways: (a) on general public goods—like defense—or broadly targeted redistributive transfer programs (such as social insurance or pensions) benefiting a large number of individuals; (b) on narrowly targeted redistribution to well-defined groups, through specific programs, like agricultural support or local public consumption, benefiting only a narrow constituency; (c) on rents for politicians or their close associates. Different economic agents or groups in society evaluate each of these policies differently. As a result, each type of policy instrument induces a specific kind of economic conflict.

Large groups of beneficiaries evaluate broadly targeted programs and general public goods in a similar fashion. Moreover, because of their broad nature and universalistic design, these programs cannot easily be tailored to the specific demands of well-defined groups of voters. Hence conflict in evaluating such programs tends to be unidimensional, running from the left to right. Benefits might be roughly the same for large groups of individuals, whereas costs are proportional to income. Rich individuals carry a larger share of the tax burden and favor smaller programs, while poor individuals pay less taxes and thus have an interest in more generous programs. We refer to this traditional conflict over the vertical (size) distribution of income as an instance of *general-interest politics*. Prime examples of policies involving this type of conflict are discussed in chapter 6. They include a number of the programs that constitute the modern welfare state: redistributive taxation, pensions, unemployment insurance, and regional transfers. We ask how the generosity of these programs depends on a number of socioeconomic factors. General-interest politics reappear in several other chapters.

Narrowly targeted programs, on the other hand, induce a multidimensional conflict. Because the benefits are concentrated among small groups of beneficiaries, whereas everyone shares the costs, each small group would like to funnel a lot of money in its own direction while restraining spending on other groups. We refer to this kind of conflict as *special-interest politics*. Chapter 7 introduces the analysis of such programs by asking which groups are likely to benefit the most. Here we stress the ability to get organized into a lobby, having a large number of ideologically neutral voters willing to swing their vote, and being represented in the legislature by powerful politicians as determinants of political success. Special-interest politics are studied in many of the subsequent chapters.

Whereas broadly or narrowly targeted programs induce conflict among voters, rents for politicians are at the core of the agency problem pitting voters at large against politicians (or other government officials). Voters may be unanimous in their desire to limit the rents extracted by politicians, but may lack the necessary means to do so. Rents can take various forms, depending on specific economic circumstances: literally, they are salaries for public officials or financing of political parties. Less literally, one can think of various forms of corruption and waste in connection with public projects as ultimately providing rents for politicians. The resources appropriated by spending of this type might be small in most modern democracies, compared to the overall size of tax revenues. But since these resources directly benefit the agents in charge of policy decisions, the political struggle to appropriate these "crumbs" can nevertheless exert a strong influence on other policy decisions. This agency conflict is introduced in chapter 4 and reappears in many other chapters.

Parts 1 and 2 study different spending programs in isolation. We ask how the size of such programs is determined and thus impose implicit restrictions on the policy tools available to the government. In part 3, we relay these restrictions, and the government can allocate spending however it wants among the three alternative uses outlined above. Throughout most of part 3, we keep the economic model very general and the analysis centers on a set of questions that we label *comparative politics*. How do different political institutions or constitutional features shape the broad design of policy when there are no restrictions on the policy instruments? We contrast majoritarian and proportional elections, as well as presidential and parliamentary regimes, and find clear predictions regarding the size and composition of government spending in different political systems. Asking how well different political systems handle the agency problems between voters and politicians, we find a formal rationale for the classical idea of separation of powers.

Dynamics and Sequential Policy Choice

In part 4, we study *intertemporal* fiscal policy choices, such as capital taxation, fiscal deficits, and public investment. These policies are formulated sequentially over time and affect state variables like debt or capital. Time adds important new channels to the analysis of economic policy.

On the one hand, private agents making intertemporal choices must anticipate the future course of policy. Expectations of future policies become a crucial determinant of private behavior, and the analysis highlights the strategic interaction between the government and private agents. Chapter 11 provides a general methodological discussion of how to model policymaking in a dynamic environment. In chapter 12 we apply these methods to several questions, including what forces determine how the tax burden is levied on different factors of production, such as capital and labor. We then show how credibility problems and political forces tend to raise tax rates on capital relative to labor, whereas tax competition between jurisdictions over mobile tax bases might depress them.

On the other hand, the government itself chooses policy sequentially. This adds another form of strategic interaction, namely that between policymakers holding office at different points in time. We apply the general methodology, showing how debt or public capital create "facts," influencing the policy choices of future governments or politicians. In chapter 13, we argue that these forces may explain seemingly myopic behavior by governments, such as excessive budget deficits, or insufficient government investment in infrastructure.

Finally, chapter 14 draws on these insights and asks to what extent endogenous policy choices can explain the enormous differences in economic performance across countries. This takes us to the nexus between politics, policymaking, and economic growth.

Monetary Policy

Part 5 of the book turns to monetary policy. It leaves public finance aspects of monetary policy aside and focuses on aggregate demand management. We study monetary policy in a simple Phillips curve model with rational expectations, in which nominal contracts or rigidities generate a temporary trade-off between output and inflation. Since aggregate demand policies affect many individuals in the same way, we mostly disregard the conflict among voters, assuming that all economic agents evaluate policy in a similar fashion. Nevertheless, conflicting interests remain between the monetary authority and private agents, either because of implicit externalities or other distortions or because of an agency problem between politicians and voters at the time of elections. Because of nominal rigidities, private expectations of future policies play a key role in this setting as well. Much of the analysis in this part centers on the strategic interaction between the central bank and the private sector.

In chapter 15 we deal with the prospective credibility problems in monetary policy. We show how such problems lead to suboptimally high and variable inflation and suboptimal employment fluctuations, despite a well-meaning monetary authority. Chapter 16 turns to the politics of aggregate demand management. Here we demonstrate how political forces might create electoral and partisan cycles in policies and macroeconomic outcomes. The topic of chapter 17 is institution design. Can institutional reform help address the policy failures identified in the two previous chapters? We show that multilateral exchange rate regimes, central bank independence and various accountability mechanisms might go some way toward that goal. Chapter 18, finally, deals with the international coordination of monetary policy. Here selfish national objectives and a temptation to pursue beggar-thy-neighbor policies generally lead to collectively irrational outcomes. Moreover, domestic credibility problems complicate the strategic interactions between countries.

1.2   Politics

The book includes a variety of models of political behavior. But all of these respect two fundamental principles. First, all individuals—voters, as well as politicians—act rationally, though not always under full information. Second, we study representative, rather than direct, democracy: policy choice is delegated to elected representatives. All political models in the book are thus delegation games in which the principals are the citizens at large and the politicians act as their agents.

Citizens interact with politicians in two ways: through voting at the elections, and through lobbying by organized interest groups. We neglect other forms of political participation, such as protests. Protests are certainly important in the real world, and we wish we had more to say about them. But they have rarely been studied formally by economists or political scientists (an exception is the interesting work by Lohmann (1994, 1998)).

These assumptions are not sufficient to model a political delegation game, however. We also need to take a stance on two questions. First, what motivates politicians? Second, is policy effectively chosen before or after the elections (that is, during the electoral campaign through binding electoral promises, or once the elected politicians have taken office)? Depending on how we answer these questions, we are led to very different models of political behavior. Indeed, the answers provide a way of classifying models of political equilibrium, both in the existing literature and in this book.

The Motivation of Politicians

How should we model the motivation of politicians? We have two basic options, not necessarily mutually exclusive. On the one hand, we can assume politicians to be purely self-interested: they care about being in office per se, or about the rents they receive. They choose policy so as to further these goals, but otherwise do not care about what policy is implemented. In this case, we say that politicians are *opportunistic*. When we need to be more precise, we distinguish between "office-seeking" politicians, who care only about winning the elections, and "rent-seeking" politicians, who also care about extracting tangible rents for themselves. Chapters 3 (office seeking) and 4 (rent seeking) introduce different models with these assumptions. On the other hand, we can assume that politicians care about the well-being of particular groups in society and choose policy so as to maximize a social welfare function that puts disproportionate weight on these groups. In the book, we refer to objectives complying with this assumption as *partisan* (following the terminology coined by Hibbs (1977) and used by Alesina (1987)). Chapter 5 introduces different models of this type.

Both assumptions have their pluses and minuses. Opportunism is the standard assumption in the public choice literature. From a methodological point of view, it is perhaps the most appealing. There are many ways of being partisan, but only one way of being self-interested.

The results of the analysis may thus be less sensitive to arbitrary assumptions if politicians are deemed to be opportunistic. Moreover, this assumption is more consistent with the way we usually treat individual agents. Most formal modeling assumes voters to care about their own economic well-being, with no altruism in their political behavior. This may well be the wrong assumption, but once it has been made, it seems natural to assume that politicians are no different. A politician's well-being depends disproportionately on his rents and the outcome of elections, whereas policy outcomes may not affect him much on an individual basis. Although this is not true for dramatic decisions—such as declaring a war or closing the borders of a country—it is certainly a good approximation for most marginal decisions in economic policy.

Nevertheless, individual political behavior, by voters as well as politicians, often seems to be driven by ideological considerations that transcend individual benefits, by a sense of what is just or legitimate, or by a particular view about the consequences of economic policy or the role of the state. Political opportunism assumes all of this away and is thus unable to explain why different politicians sometimes enact very different policies, or why they make seemingly unpopular policy decisions. Furthermore, parties are important actors in the political system. As we do not yet have an accepted model for the internal workings of political parties, it may be a necessary shortcut to assume that they represent the preferences of a particular group in the electorate.

We do not seek to argue that either opportunism or partisanship is always the better assumption. To some extent, this may depend on the problem at hand. Moreover, these two assumptions are not necessarily mutually exclusive: politicians may be opportunistic but also motivated by a particular ideological view of the world. Or perhaps more realistically, they may be forced to act according to a consistent ideological view in order to preserve their voters' loyalty. We therefore exploit both assumptions, though we try to keep them distinct and emphasize when they make a difference.

Preelection Politics

Consider the second crucial modeling question, namely the timing of policy choices. If we regard electoral promises as binding and enforceable, perhaps through an implicit reputation mechanism, we are driven to study electoral competition. Candidates propose policies to maximize their chances of winning elections, perhaps also taking into account their desire to extract rents or to implement policies consistent with their partisan view of the world. Citizens evaluate the policy platforms on the table and cast their votes for the candidate they deem best. The essential political action thus takes place in the electoral campaign, and the role of the election is to select a particular policy. Once elected, an incumbent politician just implements his preannounced policy. For this reason, we refer to models incorporating this timing as models of *preelection politics*. They are really models of electoral competition.

Throughout the book, we study two different models of preelection politics (as mentioned above, we always confine ourselves to electoral competition between two parties or candidates). These two models differ in their assumptions about voters' behavior. If citizens vote exclusively on the basis of their economic policy preferences, electoral competition is like the choice of location in Hotelling 1929, or Downs 1957. In equilibrium, the two candidates propose the policy preferred by the *median voter*. Such an equilibrium may not exist, but when it does, it is simple to characterize and robust to other assumptions. In particular, the assumption about the politicians' motivation becomes unimportant, as all candidates are forced to do the same thing to win the elections. Existence of equilibrium is much more likely when disagreement over policy choice is one-dimensional, as in the case of general-interest politics. For this reason, median-voter equilibria are used in chapter 6 to analyze the determinants of broad welfare state programs.

Voters may not always vote for their preferred economic policy, however. They might abstain or let their vote be influenced by other (fixed) attributes of the competing candidates, such as their ideology. If this is the case, we are driven to models of *probabilistic voting*. In these models, voters are not all alike in the eyes of the competing candidates: some voters are more important than others because they are more likely to reward policy favors with a vote. Electoral competition now leads to a very different equilibrium, with both candidates maximizing a particular social welfare function. Different voters are weighted by their "responsiveness," that is, how likely they are to reward policy favors with a vote. But the politicians' motivation now matters crucially for the outcome, and different politicians may choose different policies. Probabilistic voting models are very flexible. For one thing, an equilibrium exists under general conditions, irrespective of the dimensionality of policy. For another, these models can easily be extended to include other political activities, such as lobbying. They are used in chapters 7 and 14 to analyze special-interest politics, in chapter 8 to contrast policymaking under different electoral rules, and in chapter 13 to analyze strategic public debt accumulation.

Postelection Politics

An alternative assumption is that electoral promises are not binding or are too vague to matter. Then all the action in policymaking takes place once elected politicians have entered office. We refer to models incorporating this assumption as models of *postelection politics*. These models view a political constitution as an incomplete contract: politicians are appointed to office without a clear and enforceable mandate (see Dixit 1996a for an interesting discussion of the constitution as an incomplete contract). Thus the role of elections is very different than in preelection models. Rather than directly selecting policies, voters select politicians on the basis of their ideology, competence, or honesty, or more generally, their behavior as incumbents.

In this case as well, we propose two classes of models. The simplest ones are built on a winner-takes-all assumption: only one politician or party holds office and is free to set policy. To win the next election, however, this incumbent needs to please at least a majority of the voters. The opposition plays only a passive part, providing the voters with an alternative to the incumbent at the elections. With partisan politicians, the theory generates a simple prediction of policy divergence. It also naturally draws the attention to the entry stage in the political race: what type of politicians (in terms of ideological preferences) have stronger incentives to participate as candidates in elections? Models of this type are used in part 4 to analyze intertemporal policy choices, where the prediction of policy divergence has interesting implications and where issues of strategic delegation from the voters to a particular policymaker arise naturally.

We also extensively use winner-takes-all models of postelection politics with opportunistic politicians. Here the contrast between theories of pre- and postelection politics is particularly stark; once in office, rent-seeking politicians have an incentive to abuse their power, designing policy for their own benefit. In this case, postelection politics suggest a role for retrospective voting: voters can discipline an incumbent by voting against him if he misbehaved or acted against their particular interest when in office. In chapter 9, we ask which electoral rules make this kind of voters' control most effective. Retrospective voting rules, based on the incumbent's performance, have another interesting implication: the incentives to perform well (or to appear to perform well) are at their strongest just ahead of the elections. This naturally leads to a theory of electoral cycles, which is introduced in chapter 4 and exploited in chapter 16 in the context of monetary policy.

The second class of postelection politics models is richer in that it relaxes the winner-takes-all assumption and studies policy formation in legislatures. Several politicians are in office and bargain over policy according to well-specified procedures. These incumbents are, again, accountable to the voters at a subsequent electoral stage. Using the analogy with incomplete contracts, the constitution assigns specific control rights over policy (power to propose, veto, amend, or approve) to different offices. The specific allocation of control rights determines the rules of the game, namely the extensive form within which legislators or office holders bargain among each other. Models of postelection politics are more likely to capture important aspects of the functioning of modern democracies. They are quite complex, however, and their use in the literature is still in its infancy. Models of legislative bargaining among partisan politicians are used in different parts of the book, especially in chapter 7 with reference to special-interest politics.

An important point that comes up in chapters 7, 9, and 10, is that bargaining among politicians is complicated by the fact that they act as agents for the voters. The principal-agent structure of politics thus exerts a strong influence on policy outcomes. Alternative voting rules or lobbying practices have very different effects when directed at political representatives bargaining among each other, rather than at a single policymaker. In the first case, we get surprising interaction effects between the specific rules of legislative bargaining and the behavior of voters or interest groups. This suggests a rich and promising research program on comparative politics investigating how economic policy choices are affected by the political system, including the rules for legislative bargaining, but also the electoral rules, or the allocation of tasks in a federation. Part 3 is devoted entirely to these questions. Much more remains to be done, however, both theoretically and empirically.

In choosing between models of pre- and postelection politics, the latter are more appealing on the grounds of realism and novelty. Electoral promises are clearly not enforceable, and they are often too vague to be binding after the elections. Nevertheless, what happens in the course of the electoral campaign is also important, particularly when it comes to party formation and the entry or selection of political candidates. We return to the tension between the two assumptions in the course of the book.

1.3   Concluding Remarks

A reader of this book expecting to find a general positive theory of economic policy will be disappointed. We already know from the general results in social choice and voting theory that some compromises must be made, and the present approach in the field is still quite dispersed. Our goal is more modest. We seek to provide a unified approach, where possible, and to identify the best ingredients for a successful positive theory of economic policy.

But the best ingredients may differ, depending on the specific policy issues. An important distinction is that between narrowly targeted programs, providing benefits to small interest groups, and broadly targeted programs, providing benefits to large groups of voters. Because these policy instruments induce rather different conflicts among the voters, it is only sensible to expect their political determinants to be quite different.

In this chapter, we have identified two important modeling choices that researchers in this field must make, given the current state of knowledge. One concerns the politicians' motivation: opportunistic versus partisan. The other concerns the relevance of electoral promises: binding versus unimportant. Existing research has not produced a clear consensus on these issues, and we will pursue different lines of attack. But progress in the field depends on our finding a way of resolving some of these tensions, building a bridge between pre- and postelection politics, and gaining a better understanding of what motivates political candidates. We return to these challenges in the final chapter.

1 TOOLS OF POLITICAL ECONOMICS

The purpose of this first part of the book is mainly methodological. It introduces almost all of the modeling tools that we will use in subsequent parts when analyzing the politics of policy choice. In keeping with the general approach outlined in chapter 1, we prefer to introduce these tools not in the abstract, but in the context of specific policy examples. Introducing the tools of the trade also means surveying a number of approaches used to model political equilibria in the existing literature.

We begin in chapter 2 by giving a selective account of some of the most salient results in the theories of social choice and voting. Our ambition is not to survey these vast literatures here. But we do want to paint a rough background to the approach we will take in the book. As does much of the literature, we focus on the question under what conditions pure majority rule is capable of selecting an equilibrium policy and how we may overcome nonexistence of such a policy, often called a Condorcet winner. We report on some useful conditions and illustrate their meaning in a sequence of different policy examples. These examples and our discussion of them stress two sets of assumptions. One concerns the economic environment that determines the form of individual policy preferences. If we can reduce policy conflict to a single dimension—either because the policy is unidimensional, or because individual heterogeneity is unidimensional—we can find conditions that guarantee the existence of a Condorcet winner. But when conflict is multidimensional, such a policy does not exist. Another set of assumptions concern the precise institutions within which decisions on policy are made. Alternative institutional assumptions select a well-defined policy when a Condorcet winner does not exist. But institutions go far beyond guaranteeing existence of an equilibrium policy. Even when a Condorcet winner exists, reasonable assumptions about policymaking institutions often imply a different equilibrium policy. We use the results and discussion in this chapter as a stepping-stone for our main task, namely, the positive modeling of policymaking in representative democracy.

In the next three chapters, we move closer to our main task by surveying different models of elections and political equilibria. Surveying these models is a natural starting point for modeling policymaking in representative democracies, where elected politicians constitute the most obvious filter between individual policy preferences and policy outcomes. As discussed in chapter 1, different branches of the literature have developed different traditions, relying on different basic assumptions, regarding the objectives and other attributes of the political candidates and their ability to commit themselves to electoral promises. It is therefore useful to investigate the implications of alternative assumptions and to collect them in one place, particularly as we know of no other survey with the same scope.[1] To give

---

1. Osborne 1995 contains a very useful and up to date survey of spatial models of electoral competition, as does Ordeshook 1997. Mueller 1989 is an excellent survey covering some of the same material in textbook form, but it does not cover the most recent contributions and focuses on a broader set of issues.

some structure to this analytical survey, we stick to a common economic model in which a society populated by heterogenous voters has to make a choice on how much public consumption to finance through a redistributive income tax. Even though our main purpose is methodological, the analysis will help us think about basic political forces that might lie behind one of the stark, stylized facts discussed in chapter 1, namely, first-order differences in the size of government.

In chapter 3 we start out by setting up a simple model of public finance and deriving a normative benchmark. We study how policy is determined in different versions of the traditional Downsian model of electoral competition. This model assumes that two opportunistic, purely *office-seeking* candidates (or parties) can commit themselves to electoral platforms that are simply promises of a specific economic policy program. For each version of this model we ask two questions: what are the determinants of equilibrium policy, and is the policy socially optimal? We begin by discussing the properties of standard "median-voter equilibria." Then, by changing the assumptions regarding candidate attributes, we consider probabilistic voting leading to what we call "swing-voter equilibria." Finally, we allow some groups of voters to be organized in lobbies that contribute to the candidates' campaign chests, attempting to tilt the election outcome toward their favored candidate. In each of these models of preelection politics, elections serve the purpose of resolving policy conflict among different voters.

Chapter 4 in contrast deals with the same positive and normative questions in the case of opportunistic and *rent-seeking* politicians. These politicians actively try to divert some resources for their own benefit that could otherwise have been used to cut taxes or boost public consumption. We first discuss whether or not the Chicago school is right in its optimistic view that political competition is conducive to socially optimal outcomes. The benefits of such competition hinge on two features of the political environment: whether candidates are perfect substitutes for the electorate and whether candidates can make binding commitments to electoral platforms. The commitment issue is related to concepts well known from contract theory, such as enforceability, verifiability, and observability. The chapter also demonstrates how elections can work as a disciplining device, even in the absence of credible policy commitments. In one setting, labeled the "electoral accountability model," voters reelect only incumbents maintaining sufficiently good performance. In another setting, the "career concern model," they reelect only incumbents having sufficiently high expected competence. The chapter thus illustrates two other functions of elections, namely, to select politicians on the basis of either good behavior or high competence.

In chapter 5, we introduce partisan candidates, who are motivated by policy outcomes as such. Because of this motivation, we can derive their behavior from the same kind of utility function as that of the citizens. Partisan preferences that differ between politicians are, however, immaterial for the policy outcome if competing "citizen candidates" can indeed commit themselves to electoral platforms. When commitment is possible, centripetal political forces are strong enough to make the candidates converge on the same platform, even though they have very different innate policy preferences. But a tension arises after the elections: if candidates are really outcome motivated, they want to pursue very different policies ex post. Absent credible commitments, the policy program will therefore be chosen after the election according to the preferences of the winning candidate. Given such postelection policy choices, we illustrate the working of the "citizen-candidate model." Here, the set of candidates standing for election is endogenous: any citizen can enter as a candidate at a cost. Finally, we study the outcome when a set of partisan incumbents select the policy program in legislative bargaining. This simple model abstracts from elections, altogether. Later on in the book, however, we embed legislative bargaining games in more complete models of the political process.

2 Preferences and Institutions

In this chapter we outline—in a very simple way—some of the important tenets of social choice theory and spatial voting theory. We ask when a voting equilibrium exists under pure majority rule, how to cope with problems created by the nonexistence of such an equilibrium, and, more generally, how majority rule aggregates individual policy preferences.

The discussion is first cast in a general framework, which we then specialize into simple policy examples as we proceed. Thus in section 2.1, we formulate a general policy problem and the policy preferences of individual voters, setting the stage for the subsequent analysis.

Then in section 2.2 we discuss different restrictions on individual policy preferences sufficient to guarantee the existence of a Condorcet winner. We also show that this policy constitutes a majority-voting equilibrium under certain assumptions about voting behavior and the process of voting. Essentially, these assumptions confine disagreement among the voters to a single dimension, a condition that is possible only if policy itself is unidimensional, or if individual voter heterogeneity is unidimensional.

In section 2.3, we discuss the consequences when these restrictions on preferences are violated: voting cycles may occur, and incentives for agenda manipulation and strategic voting obtain. To guarantee existence of a political equilibrium, we therefore need to impose additional structure on the collective choice problem by restricting the institutions that govern how policy decisions are made. In this context, we illustrate the ideas behind models of probabilistic voting, structure-induced equilibrium, and agenda setting.

Finally, in section 2.4, we take stock of the chapter's main conclusions and discuss their implications for our main purpose: the modeling of equilibrium economic policymaking in a representative democracy.

2.1 A General Policy Problem

Many positive analyses of the politics of economic policy share the same general structure. Consider thus a set of citizens affected by some vector of policies $\mathbf{q}$. (Throughout the book we denote vectors with boldface letters, whereas scalars are denoted with italics.) This set of citizens can be small (as in a committee) or large (as in the electorate). For now we allow for a small set, although the plausible set is large (and often approximated by a continuum) in most policy applications. These "voters" are indexed by their individual attributes. Introducing a notational convention that will also be followed throughout the book, we use superscript is to denote variables specific to individuals of type i. Thus, let α^i (possibly a vector) denote the specific features of voter i, capturing his idiosyncratic preferences, endowments, risks, technological opportunities, or other socioeconomic attributes. The α^is are assumed to be distributed among the citizens according to some given distribution. Individuals have utility functions defined over bundles of consumption c^i; they could also have some other well-defined economic objectives, such as profit functions.

In his role as an *economic agent,* an individual chooses his consumption bundle so as to maximize his utility function $U(c^i, \mathbf{q}, \mathbf{p}; \alpha^i)$, subject to some (budget or time) constraints $H(c^i, \mathbf{p}, \mathbf{q}; \alpha^i) \geq 0$, where $\mathbf{p}$ is some vector of market-determined data (prices or quantities). We can thus define the *indirect utility* of individual i as

$$\widetilde{W}(\mathbf{q}, \mathbf{p}; \alpha^i) = \underset{c^i}{\mathrm{Max}} \; [U(c^i, \mathbf{q}, \mathbf{p}; \alpha^i) \mid H(c^i, \mathbf{p}, \mathbf{q}; \alpha^i) \geq 0]. \tag{2.1}$$

Any *policymaker* setting $\mathbf{q}$ must respect the market-determined value of $\mathbf{p}$ and some further constraints, such as a balanced government budget or a resource constraint, that an atomistic private agent can neglect. Let us summarize these various constraints by $G(\mathbf{q}, \mathbf{p}) \geq 0$. Typically, the constraints will be binding, in which case the implicit function theorem allows us to write $\mathbf{p} = P(\mathbf{q})$; that is, the market outcomes depend on policy and parameters.

In his role as a *political agent,* individual i engages in voting, lobbying, or some other form of political activity. His *policy preferences* govern his actions in these activities. We obtain these policy preferences from his indirect utility function $\widetilde{W}$, taking into account the equilibrium constraints as summarized by $P(\mathbf{q})$. Let us define these reduced-form policy preferences by

$$\widetilde{W}(\mathbf{q}, P(\mathbf{q}); \alpha^i) \equiv W(\mathbf{q}; \alpha^i).$$

Using this notation, we can define the *preferred policy,* or the bliss point, of voter i as

$$\mathbf{q}(\alpha^i) = \underset{\mathbf{q}}{\mathrm{Argmax}} \; W(\mathbf{q}; \alpha^i). \tag{2.2}$$

Because of differences in α^i, different individuals typically have conflicting policy preferences.

In this general setting, a positive analysis of economic policymaking amounts to specifying an institution and asking how it aggregates political actions, based on individual policy preferences, into equilibrium policies. Unfortunately, one of the most famous results in the social sciences demonstrates that the search for a general answer to this question is a futile exercise. Arrow's (1951) ingenious impossibility theorem shows that no general rule enables a democracy to consistently aggregate individual preferences into policy choices. One implication of this theorem of particular interest for our purposes is that majority rule—despite its apparent predominance in real-world politics—does not generate well-defined equilibrium policies, unless we restrict its applicability either to individual policy preferences of a specific form or to political institutions of a specific type. Exploration of such restrictions has been the subject matter of a great deal of subsequent research, in social choice as well as in the spatial theory of voting.[1] In the next two sections, we point to some of the most celebrated results from this endeavor. Many of the general results are illustrated by specific policy examples.

2.2   Restricting Preferences

The aim of this section is to study preference aggregation by pure majority rule. We define pure majority rule by the following three assumptions:

A1. *Direct democracy.*   The citizens themselves make the policy choices.

A2. *Sincere voting.*   In every vote, each citizen votes for the alternative that gives him the highest utility according to his policy preferences (indirect utility function) $W(\mathbf{q}; \alpha^i)$.

A3. *Open agenda.*   Citizens vote over pairs of policy alternatives, such that the winning policy in one round is posed against a new alternative in the next round and the set of alternatives includes all feasible policies.

We will certainly not maintain these assumptions in subsequent sections and chapters, when we go on to study policy choice in a representative democracy. They are useful, however, for explaining the logic of some basic theoretical results.

The Marquis de Condorcet, a French mathematician and philosopher, had pointed to the prospective problems of finding a stable outcome from majority rule already in the eighteenth century, by demonstrating how pairwise voting over policy alternatives may fail to produce a clear-cut winner. In other words, majority rule may not lead to a transitive binary relation between policy alternatives. Below, we give examples of this failure of majority rule to produce a clear winner, which is often referred to as the Condorcet paradox. In this section, however, we state and discuss sufficient conditions for existence of a well-defined majority winner.

2.2.1   One-Dimensional Policy

Let us make the following definition:

DEFINITION 1.   A **Condorcet winner** is a policy q^* that beats any other feasible policy in a pairwise vote.

Suppose now that the policy space is unidimensional, so that q is a scalar. In this case, a simple way to rule out the Condorcet paradox goes back, at least, to Black's seminal (1948)

---

1. Inman 1987 includes a very nice survey of work in these areas and how they relate to Arrow's theorem. Mueller's (1989) textbook and the contributions in Mueller 1997 also provide useful perspectives on this vast body of work.

study of decisionmaking in a committee. Following Black, the policy preferences defined in (2.2) are said to be *single peaked* for voter i if his preference ordering for alternative policies is dictated by their relative distance from his bliss point, $q(\alpha^i)$: a policy closer to $q(\alpha^i)$ is preferred over more distant alternatives. Specifically:

DEFINITION 2.   Policy preferences of voter i are **single peaked** if the following statement is true:

If $q'' \leq q' \leq q(\alpha^i)$ or, if $q'' \geq q' \geq q(\alpha^i)$,   then
$$W(q''; \alpha^i) \leq W(q'; \alpha^i).$$
(2.3)

We have a simple, but useful, first result:

PROPOSITION 1.   If all voters have single-peaked policy preferences over a given ordering of policy alternatives, a Condorcet winner always exists and coincides with the median-ranked bliss point.

To prove this *median-voter theorem,* we can rely on a simple "separation argument." Fix the parameter vector at some value, order the individuals according to their bliss points $q(\alpha^i)$, and label the median-ranked bliss point by q^m.[2] Suppose that q^m is pitched against some other policy $q'' < q^m$. By (2.3), every individual whose bliss point satisfies $q^m \leq q(\alpha^i)$ prefers q^m to q'', since it is closer to his bliss point. By A2, these individuals also vote for q^m. The coalition voting for supporting q^m thus constitutes a majority. Applying an analogous argument to $q'' > q^m$ we obtain the result that q^m is a Condorcet winner.

Under direct and sincere voting by individuals (i.e., A1–A2) and the additional assumption of an open-agenda process (i.e., A3), we have the following:

COROLLARY 1. q^m is the unique equilibrium policy (stable point) under pure majority rule, that is, under A1–A3.

The reason is simple: q^m beats any previous winner the first time it comes up and cannot be beaten in any subsequent vote.

From a general perspective, unidimensionality and single-peakedness are very strong assumptions. Unidimensionality of q severely restricts the available policy instruments, which may be implausible in many applications. If private agents make no economic choices, single-peakedness of W is fulfilled by the innocuous assumption that private utility is concave (in the single policy instrument). But interesting economic policy problems do

---

2. Let us assume either that the set of voters describes a continuum, or that it is finite but odd in number. The median bliss point is then unambiguously defined. An even-numbered finite set of voters requires a slight technical variation in the present and the following arguments that keeps track of odd and even numbers.

include endogenous private choices and market outcomes. When private choices depend on policy, concavity of the primitive utility function U is no guarantee of a well-behaved indirect utility function W, as is well known from the analysis of optimal taxation. In particular, problems may arise when market outcomes, which themselves depend on policy instruments, enter individual policy preferences, say through externalities, indivisibilities, or government budget constraints. Our model represents this possibility formally by allowing $P(q)$ to enter as an argument of W.

There are, however, more general sufficient conditions. One such general condition is the single-crossing property formulated by Gans and Smart (1996). An essentially equivalent condition, order-restricted preferences, was formulated by Rothstein (1990). Both conditions impose restrictions on the character of voter heterogeneity rather than on the shape of individual preferences. Specifically, suppose that in addition to the policy variable q, the individual parameter α^i is also unidimensional with a domain on the interval $\mathcal{V}$. The interval $\mathcal{V}$ thus denotes the set of voters. The Gans-Smart condition can be stated as

DEFINITION 3.   The preferences of voters in $\mathcal{V}$ satisfy the **single-crossing property** when the following statement is true:

If $\quad q > q'$ and $\alpha^{i'} > \alpha^i$, $\quad$ or if $\quad q < q'$ and $\alpha^{i'} < \alpha^i$, $\quad$ then

$$W(q; \alpha^i) \geq W(q'; \alpha^i) \Rightarrow W(q; \alpha^{i'}) \geq W(q'; \alpha^{i'}). \tag{2.4}$$

In other words, single crossing enables us to project preferences over q on the set of voter types, $\mathcal{V}$. This condition is distinct from single-peakedness but has similar implications. Specifically

PROPOSITION 2.   If the preferences of voters in $\mathcal{V}$ satisfy the single-crossing property, a Condorcet winner always exists and coincides with the bliss point of the voter with the median value of α^i.

To prove this proposition, label the critical value of α^i as α^m. Then, by (2.4), every voter with $\alpha^i \geq \alpha^m$ prefers $q(\alpha^m)$ to any $q < q(\alpha^m)$. Similarly, everyone with $\alpha^i \leq \alpha^m$ prefers $q(\alpha^m)$ to any $q > q(\alpha^m)$. In other words, $q(\alpha^m)$ wins a pairwise vote against any conceivable alternative. Clearly, the argument is related to the separation argument applied above, in the case of single-peaked preferences where the voters were ranked according to their individually preferred policies. But here, the monotonicity of policy preferences instead allows us to rank voters according to their individual types.

It is easily verified whether the single-crossing condition is satisfied, since it is closely related to the familiar Spence-Mirrlees condition on marginal rates of substitution. Specifically, suppose that preferences are defined over a two-dimensional choice variable, but policy is effectively one-dimensional because of a budget or resource constraint. Single crossing as defined above is then equivalent to the Spence-Mirrlees condition that marginal rates of substitutions can be ordered by individual type.

Evidently, single crossing, like single-peakedness, is capable of generating the existence of a political equilibrium under pure majority rule.

Example 1. Redistributive distortionary taxation. Consider a simplified version of the well-known model of redistribution financed by distortionary taxation, formulated by Romer (1975), Roberts (1977), and Meltzer and Richard (1981). We provide a more extensive treatment and several extensions of this model in chapter 6. In our version, the ith individual has quasi-linear preferences:

$$w^i = c^i + V(x^i),$$

where c^i and x^i denote individual consumption and leisure, respectively, and $V(\cdot)$ is a well-behaved concave utility function. The private budget constraint is

$$c^i \le (1 - q)l^i + f,$$

where q denotes the income tax rate, l^i the individual labor supply, and f a lump sum transfer. The real wage is exogenous and normalized at unity. Individual productivity differs, such that individuals have different amounts of "effective time" available. That is, individuals are subject to the "time constraint"

$$1 - \alpha^i \ge x^i + l^i, \tag{2.5}$$

where $-\alpha^i$ is individual productivity. We assume that α^i is distributed in the population with mean α and median α^m. It is easy to verify that optimal labor supply satisfies

$$l^i = L(q) - (\alpha^i - \alpha), \tag{2.6}$$

where $L(q) \equiv 1 - \alpha - V_x^{-1}(1 - q)$ is decreasing in q by the concavity of $V(\cdot)$.[3] A higher tax rate thus distorts the labor-leisure choice and induces the consumer to work less. Furthermore, more-productive consumers work more at every tax rate. Let l denote average labor supply. Since the average of α^i is α, we have $l = L(q)$. The government budget constraint can therefore be written:

$$f \le ql \equiv qL(q).$$

Let q be the policy variable with f determined as a residual. By straightforward substitution

---

3. Maximize the utility of individual i's subject to the budget and time constraints. The first-order condition implies $1 - q = V_x(1 - \alpha^i - l^i)$, where a subscript denotes a derivative. Take the inverse of $V_x(\cdot)$ and simplify to get the expression for l^i in the text. Note that $L_q = 1/V_{xx}(x^i) < 0$.

into the individual utility function, we can express the policy preferences of individual i as

$$W^i(q; \alpha^i) \equiv L(q) + V(1 - L(q) - \alpha) - (1 - q)(\alpha^i - \alpha). \tag{2.7}$$

It is easy to see that the indirect utility function in (2.7) fulfills the single-crossing condition (2.4). Suppose that the average labor supply $L(q)$ were convex enough to imply non-single-peaked preferences $W^i(q; \alpha^i)$. Then monotonicity of individual labor supply in α^i is still sufficient to guarantee the existence of a well-defined Condorcet winner, namely the tax rate preferred by the voter with median productivity and income.

Problem 2 of this chapter gives an example of a policy problem with similar properties.

2.2.2   Multidimensional Policy, Unidimensional Conflict

What if the policy is instead multidimensional? From a general point of view, the existence problem gets significantly worse (the following section explains why in more detail). Nevertheless, we can still find monotonicity restrictions on the policy preferences that guarantee the existence of a majority winner. The single-crossing property defined above can be generalized to multidimensional policies, but in that case it may be harder to verify whether it is satisfied. A simple sufficient condition can be found, however, that again ensures the existence of a Condorcet winner. This condition is less general than single crossing, but it relies on a very similar idea: voter heterogeneity is limited in that voters' preferences for a multidimensional policy can be projected on a unidimensional space in which different voters can be ordered by their type. Following Grandmont (1978), we label this condition "intermediate preferences" (even though Grandmont's definition is slightly more general).

Specifically, let $\mathbf{q}$ be a vector of policies and $W(\mathbf{q}; \alpha^i)$ be the policy preferences of a voter of type α^i. As before, the parameter α^i is unidimensional, with a domain on the interval $\mathcal{V}$. Thus, although policy is multidimensional, voters differ only in one dimension, namely with regard to the parameter α^i. Then we can state:

DEFINITION 4.   Voters in the set $\mathcal{V}$ have **intermediate preferences,** if their indirect utility function $W(\mathbf{q}; \alpha^i)$ can be written as

$$W(\mathbf{q}; \alpha^i) = J(\mathbf{q}) + K(\alpha^i)H(\mathbf{q};), \tag{2.8}$$

where $K(\alpha^i)$ is monotonic in α^i, for any $H(\mathbf{q})$ and $J(\mathbf{q})$ common to all voters.

Clearly, it is easily verified whether the voters' preferences satisfy this condition. If so, we have a very useful result. Let $\mathbf{q}(\alpha^m)$ be the policy preferred by the median value of α^i in the set $\mathcal{V}$. Then once more:

PROPOSITION 3.   If voters in $\mathcal{V}$ have intermediate preferences, a Condorcet winner exists and is given by $\mathbf{q}(\alpha^m)$.

The proof is again a simple separation argument, which relies on the assumed monotonicity. As $\mathbf{q}(\alpha^m)$ is a maximum, we have that

$$K(\alpha^m) \lesseqgtr \frac{J(\mathbf{q}(\alpha^m)) - J(\mathbf{q})}{H(\mathbf{q}) - H(\mathbf{q}(\alpha^m))} \quad \text{as} \quad H(\mathbf{q}) \gtreqless H(\mathbf{q}(\alpha^m)),$$

for any $\mathbf{q} \neq \mathbf{q}(\alpha^m)$. Furthermore, voter i supports $\mathbf{q}(\alpha^m)$ against $\mathbf{q}$ if

$$K(\alpha^i) \lesseqgtr \frac{J(\mathbf{q}(\alpha^m)) - J(\mathbf{q})}{H(\mathbf{q}) - H(\mathbf{q}(\alpha^m))} \quad \text{as} \quad H(\mathbf{q}) \gtreqless H(\mathbf{q}(\alpha^m)).$$

As $K(\alpha^i)$ is monotonic in α^i, the first condition implies that the second is fulfilled for at least half the voters. The policy vector $\mathbf{q}(\alpha^m)$ thus collects at least half the votes against any alternative policy.

Intuitively, the intermediate preference property allows us to project the conflict in a multidimensional policy space into a unidimensional parameter space, where we can apply a separation argument as before. Essentially, this can occur only when there is a single source of disagreement among different individuals.

In a general theoretical perspective, these restrictions on preferences may appear very stringent. As we discuss below, this is indeed the message from social choice theory and spatial voting theory. But both of these theories start their analysis by directly formulating the voters' preferences in some general outcome space. Applied analyses of economic policymaking instead generally derive agents' preferences over policy from assumptions about the economic environment. That is, they make assumptions about the usual primitives in economic analysis: agents' utility functions, technologies, and endowments and the available policy instruments. The intermediate-preference condition then turns out to be fulfilled in some nontrivial examples. In this applied perspective, the necessary assumptions may not appear considerably more restrictive than the assumptions in, say, macroeconomics, public finance, or contract theory.[4] Interestingly, in their historical analysis of congressional votes in the United States, Poole and Rosenthal (1991) indeed found that the voting pattern of U.S. congressmen can largely be aligned along a single dimension of disagreement that can be interpreted as left to right in the traditional ideological sense.

We now discuss a few examples.

Example 2. Endowment heterogeneity and taxation.   Suppose the basic heterogeneity among individuals is related to the endowments that govern their individual market supply

---

4. Caplin and Nalebuff (1988, 1991) further discuss restrictions on voters' preferences and provide rather general conditions under which the mean- (as opposed to median-) voter preferred outcome is unbeatable under a qualified majority rule (a 64%-majority rule).

of some tax base, as in example 1. Provided that their utility functions are the same, we can then allow government policy to be multidimensional. Individual policy preferences are still monotonic in endowments, as the policy preferences given by (2.7), and therefore satisfy the necessary monotonicity condition. In chapter 12 we discuss an example of this kind. Individual heterogeneity is one-dimensional, as in example 1, and voters choose the structure of taxation by setting distinct tax rates on labor and capital. In that chapter, government spending is held fixed such that the policy problem remains one-dimensional. But it would be straightforward to add endogenous government spending. Since preferences are intermediate, a median-voter equilibrium would continue to exist, with the equilibrium level of spending at the level preferred by the median voter.

A related example is contained in problem 3 of this chapter, which deals with redistributive taxation financed by labor and consumption taxes.

Example 3. Preference heterogeneity and public consumption. Suppose all individuals have the same exogenous income $y^i = y$ and are subject to the same income tax τ. They are thus subject to the same budget constraint

$$c = y(1 - \tau).$$

Government revenue per capita, τy, is spent on two types of public consumption, in per capita amounts q_1 and q_2, to satisfy the government budget constraint

$$q_1 + q_2 \leq \tau y.$$

Agents have heterogeneous preferences for these publicly provided goods, however, summarized in the following utility function for voter i:

$$w^i = U(c) + \alpha^i G(q_1) + (1 - \alpha^i) F(q_2),$$

where the weight α^i is distributed in the population on the interval $[0, 1]$.

In this setting it is easy to derive the policy preferences of agent i over the two-dimensional policy $\mathbf{q} \equiv (q_1, q_2)$, treating τ as a residual. These preferences are

$$W(\mathbf{q}; \alpha^i) = U(y - q_1 - q_2) + F(q_2) + \alpha^i (G(q_1) - F(q_2)).$$

These policy preferences clearly satisfy the intermediate-preference property. Problem 4 of this chapter deals further with the model formulated here. Tabellini and Alesina (1990) introduced this kind of model in the context of analyzing the politics of strategic debt issue in a dynamic setting. Many others have since used it. We will return to it in chapter 13.

Example 4. Risk heterogeneity and social insurance. Suppose all agents have the same gross income when working and the same preferences for private consumption $U(c)$. Some individuals are unemployed. An individual's employment probability depends on the aggregate state of the economy, s, as well as on the individual risk associated with his occupation, sector, or level of education. Specifically, a share α_s of the population has a job with income y_s in aggregate state s, $s = 1, \ldots, S$. The remaining share $(1 - \alpha_s)$ is unemployed in state s. State s has the probability π_s of being realized. The employment probability of agent i in state s is $\alpha_s + \alpha^i$ where α^i is a state-independent parameter distributed in the population with mean 0. No private insurance exists, but the government runs an unemployment insurance scheme that pays unemployed workers a (possibly state-dependent) lump sum transfer q_s. These transfers are financed with taxes on employed workers according to the budget constraints

$$\tau_s y_s = \frac{(1 - \alpha_s)}{\alpha_s} q_s.$$

Treating the state-contingent vector of replacement rates $\mathbf{q} \equiv \{q_s\}$ as the policy instruments, we can express the ex ante policy preferences of individual i by his expected utility (subject to the government budget constraints):

$$W(\mathbf{q}; \alpha, \alpha^i) = \sum_s \pi_s [\alpha_s U(y_s(1 - \tau_s)) + (1 - \alpha_s)U(q_s)]$$

$$+ \alpha^i \left[\sum_s \pi_s [U(y_s(1 - \tau_s)) - U(q_s)] \right],$$

where $\alpha \equiv \{a_s\}$. These policy preferences are monotonic in the single idiosyncratic parameter α^i and thus satisfy the intermediate-preference property. Persson and Tabellini (1996a) introduced this kind of model in the context of analyzing the politics of risk sharing in a federation. Similar models of unemployment insurance will be discussed in chapters 6 and 8.

2.3   Restricting Institutions

We have seen that meaningful restrictions on preferences can be formulated that guarantee the existence of a unique equilibrium under pure majority rule as we have defined it in A1–A3. If the conditions imposed by these restrictions are not met, a Condorcet winner generally does not exist. In that event, a number of problems arise under pure majority rule: an open agenda may lead to infinite voting cycles, incentives for agenda manipulation arise, and agents have strong incentives to vote strategically, rather than sincerely. We now turn to a discussion of these issues. Problem 1 of this chapter illustrates similar issues.

2.3.1   Nonexistence of a Condorcet Winner and Its Implications

In the case of a genuine multidimensional policy conflict, the conditions for existence of a Condorcet winner indeed become very strong. This has been forcefully demonstrated in the context of the multidimensional spatial voting model, which starts out from an a priori formulation of agents' preferences. In the notation above, these preferences have the general form $W(\mathbf{q} - \boldsymbol{\alpha}^i)$, where $\mathbf{q}$ is a policy vector and $\boldsymbol{\alpha}^i$ a vector of the coordinates describing voter i's bliss point in this policy space. Also, W is assumed to be decreasing and concave—typically symmetric and often spherical—in the distance $\|\mathbf{q} - \boldsymbol{\alpha}^i\|$. Results due to Plott (1967), Davis, de Groot, and Hinich (1972), and others demonstrate that the condition required for a point $\mathbf{q}^*$ to be a Condorcet winner is very strong. In particular, a hyperplane cutting through $\mathbf{q}^*$ in any direction must divide the set of individual bliss points into two subsets with an equal number of voters. The condition boils down to the existence of a "median in all directions," allowing for a separation argument like those applied in the previous section. A priori, such extreme symmetry in the distribution of individual bliss points seems an utterly unlikely occurrence, even though the intermediate-preference property discussed above implies that the individual bliss points lie along a continuous and monotonic curve in the policy space.

Many economic policy problems do generate policy preferences of such form. Nonexistence of a majority winner is particularly likely for policies that can be targeted to individual groups of voters. Many types of redistributive programs obviously fall into this category. In discussing the consequences of nonexistence of a majority winner, we consider a very simple example of targeted redistribution, namely, the so-called pie-splitting problem.

Example 5. Pure redistribution.   Consider redistribution of a fixed amount among three (groups of) voters. Voter i, $i = 1, 2, 3$, thus has preferences

$$W(\mathbf{q}) = U(q^i),$$

where U is a common concave utility function and q^i is a nonnegative transfer out of a fixed budget normalized to unity:

$$\sum_{i=1}^{3} q^i = 1.$$

By this budget constraint, the policy problem is two-dimensional. The three voters' policy preferences can thus easily be illustrated in a diagram drawn in (q^1, q^2) space with q^1 on the horizontal axis and q^2 on the vertical axis, as in figure 2.1.

In the figure, voter 1's most preferred point is $(1, 0)$, where he gets the whole available pie, whereas the most preferred points of voters 2 and 3 are $(0, 1)$ and $(0, 0)$, respectively. Furthermore, we can draw the indifference curves of voter 1 as straight vertical lines, those of voter 2 as straight horizontal lines, and those of voter 3 as straight lines with a slope of -1.

To illustrate how the open-agenda process, defined in A3, may lead to cycling, consider a simple case with only three exogenously given policy vectors, indexed by $\mathbf{q}_a$, $\mathbf{q}_b$, and $\mathbf{q}_c$

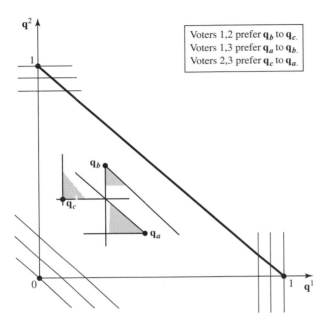

Voters 1,2 prefer $\mathbf{q}_b$ to $\mathbf{q}_c$.
Voters 1,3 prefer $\mathbf{q}_a$ to $\mathbf{q}_b$.
Voters 2,3 prefer $\mathbf{q}_c$ to $\mathbf{q}_a$.

Figure 2.1

in figure 2.1. Suppose a vote is first taken on $\mathbf{q}_b$ versus $\mathbf{q}_c$. Both voters 1 and 2 prefer $\mathbf{q}_b$, which lies on a higher indifference curve than $\mathbf{q}_c$ (they split the losses of 3). When $\mathbf{q}_b$ is pitched against $\mathbf{q}_a$ in the next round, voters 1 and 3 prefer $\mathbf{q}_a$. Yet when $\mathbf{q}_a$ is posed against $\mathbf{q}_c$, $\mathbf{q}_c$ collects a majority made up by voters 2 and 3. As $\mathbf{q}_c$ is then posed against $\mathbf{q}_b$, the same cycle starts again and can go on forever.

What if the agenda is restricted, so as to include voting only in a finite number of steps? Even though the restriction guarantees that an end point will be found, this does not, by itself, help us a great deal in making predictions about the policy outcome, for the set of possible outcomes is still very large. In a seminal paper, McKelvey (1976) has indeed shown that, with spatial (spherical) preferences, a sequence of pairwise votes connects any starting point with any possible outcome in the Pareto set. The latter is defined as the set of points at which no voter can be made better off without making another voter worse off; in the simple pure-redistribution example above, it is illustrated in figure 2.1 by the isosceles triangle connecting the bliss points of the three voters.

But if the agenda is restricted, these results clearly imply that whoever controls the agenda can use it to his own advantage. As an illustration, consider again the three alternatives

$(\mathbf{q}_a, \mathbf{q}_b, \mathbf{q}_c)$ in figure 2.1 and assume that only two rounds of pairwise voting can take place. Suppose that voter 1 sets the agenda. The optimal procedure from his point of view is to start the vote by pitching $\mathbf{q}_b$ versus $\mathbf{q}_c$. This selects $\mathbf{q}_b$, which is then bound to lose against $\mathbf{q}_a$, which is the alternative favored by voter 1. In the same vein, voter 2 (3) can implement his preferred alternative $\mathbf{q}_b$ ($\mathbf{q}_c$), by posing $\mathbf{q}_a$ against $\mathbf{q}_c$ ($\mathbf{q}_a$ against $\mathbf{q}_b$) in the first round. Restricted agendas thus open the door for strategic *agenda manipulation*. Notice, however, that it is the restricted-agenda assumption and not the nonexistence of a Condorcet winner that leads to the incentive for agenda manipulation. In other words, agenda setting may be valuable even if a Condorcet winner exists (we return to this point below).

So far in this chapter we have relied on assumption A2, that agents vote sincerely at every stage. The forces that render agenda manipulation profitable make that assumption questionable, however, as they also provide strong incentives for *strategic voting*. To see this, suppose that voter 1 sets the agenda, so as to achieve his preferred point $\mathbf{q}_a$ in the example of figure 2.1. Assume also that voters 1 and 3 continue to vote sincerely at both stages. Then voter 2 can improve his situation by voting strategically at stage 1, because voter 2 is pivotal at that stage. By voting for his nonpreferred alternative $\mathbf{q}_c$ at stage 1, voter 2 ensures that this alternative wins not only at stage 1, but also at stage 2 when posed against $\mathbf{q}_a$ (nobody can be better off by voting strategically at the last stage). Clearly, this outcome is better for voter 2, whose share of the pie is larger in $\mathbf{q}_c$ than in $\mathbf{q}_a$. Generally, foresight of the outcome at future stages of voting effectively makes the voters face more than two alternatives at the first stage.

Are the incentives for strategic voting an artifact of the special assumptions behind this simple example? Unfortunately not. On the contrary, they are inherent to almost any voting situation involving more than two alternatives. Indeed, fundamental results derived by Gibbard (1973) and Satterthwaite (1975) show that any democratic decision-making process, including majority rule, involving three or more alternatives is open to strategic preference manipulation. This means that sincere voting (A2) is not an attractive assumption if an open-agenda process (A3) does not imply convergence to a Condorcet winner.

2.3.2 Modeling Institutions of Policy Choice

By the mid- to late 1970s, theorists had clearly demonstrated that searching for a universally applicable theory of political equilibrium is a futile exercise. Furthermore, majority voting would generically lead to cycles, unless the voting agenda was restricted. Such restrictions, however, gave strong incentives to strategic manipulation, either of the agenda itself or of the preferences revealed in the voting process. The outlook of many researchers at the time was thus quite pessimistic: any positive theory of political choice—whether it was based on majority rule or not—seemingly had to rely on unattractive or arbitrary assumptions.

At the same time all the cycling and instability existing models suggested, however, did not seem to be a feature of democratic decision making in practice. A number of new ideas that were starting to make their way into political theory in the years around 1980, however, sowed seeds of a more optimistic view. These ideas appeared in the context of the *probabilistic voting* model associated with Hinich (1977), Coughlin and Nitzan (1981), and Ledyard (1981, 1984),[5] the *structure-induced equilibrium* model associated with Shepsle (1979) and Shepsle and Weingast (1981),[6] and the *agenda-setter* model associated with Romer and Rosenthal (1978, 1979).

These ideas stem from a common premise: policy choices are not made by the citizens themselves under direct democracy, but are delegated to elected representatives. Assumption A1 is thus relaxed, appealing to the organization of decision making in real-world democracies. The details of how policy is chosen impose additional structure on the political process that, in turn, can give rise to a well-defined equilibrium. Each of these approaches identifies a specific aspect of political institutions as a crucial determinant of policy. Probabilistic voting is a theory of electoral competition in which politicians offer policy platforms to the voters and specific assumptions are made about the voters' behavior. Structure-induced equilibrium and the agenda-setter model apply to collective decisions in smaller groups of political representatives, like a committee or a legislature, in which representatives have well-defined policy preferences and the institution imposes a particular procedure for decision making. Thus in these models the policy decision is the outcome of a game with a well-defined extensive form. In the following, we briefly introduce the main ideas behind each of these approaches.

Probabilistic Voting   The traditional starting point for analyzing electoral competition was the classical theory of Hotelling (1929) and Downs (1957). By the 1970s, formal results had verified the main insight of these authors. Suppose, as did Hotelling and Downs, that elections involve two identical politicians (or parties). The politicians are opportunistic in the sense of being purely office-motivated: they strive to maximize their vote share or, alternatively, the probability of winning. Moreover, these politicians can make binding commitments to policy platforms in the course of the electoral campaign. The outcome is a Condorcet winner, if such a policy exists. In the next chapter, we formally derive this result in the context of a specific policy example. But the intuition is very simple and closely related to the separation arguments in section 2.2. Faced with only two policy alternatives (the two electoral platforms), all citizens vote sincerely. Thus a policy platform coinciding with a Condorcet winner always captures at least half of the vote when it is up against

---

5. The probabilistic voting model in its later form was preceded by Hinich, Ledyard, and Ordeshook 1972.

6. The ideas behind structure-induced equilibrium had earlier appeared in Kramer 1972.

any other platform. Consequently, the situation in which both candidates select the policy preferred by the pivotal voter is the only one where no candidate (party) can discontinuously increase his probability of winning (its vote share). As the candidates are office-motivated, this is, by definition, a Nash equilibrium.

With multidimensional policy conflict, on the other hand, Downsian electoral competition games generally do not have any equilibria. This is a direct consequence of the cycling problems discussed above. If no policy dominates any other policy, one candidate can always find another policy that is preferable for a majority of the voters, given any policy platform proposed by the other candidate. The objective functions of the office-seeking candidates thus become highly discontinuous throughout the policy space.

Probabilistic voting models essentially smooth out these objectives by introducing uncertainty—from the candidates' viewpoint—about the mapping from policy to aggregate voting behavior. The argument comes in several guises, with different degrees of micropolitical foundations. Individual voters may abstain from voting if the proposed policies are too far away from their ideal points or if not too much is at stake. Or the candidates may perceive the probability that a particular voter (or group of voters) votes for a particular candidate as a continuous function, rather than a step function, of the distance between the two platforms. In either case, the expected number of votes becomes a smooth function of the policy platform, which guarantees existence of a Nash equilibrium under some regularity conditions on the underlying utility and distribution functions.

To illustrate these points more precisely, consider a policy choice like the one discussed in example 3. Thus two types of public consumption, q_1 and q_2, are financed by general taxation. As before, q_1 and q_2 are the policy variables with taxes residually determined. There are $\mathcal{I}$ voter types, $i = 1, \ldots, \mathcal{I}$ (with $\mathcal{I}$ a large number), who evaluate policy according to preferences $W(\mathbf{q}; \alpha^i)$. But now these preferences do not fulfill the monotonicity property imposed in example 3, meaning that an open-agenda process over pairs of policy vectors could give rise to cycling. Two parties, A and B, simultaneously announce their policy platforms ahead of the election, $\mathbf{q}_A$ and $\mathbf{q}_B$ respectively. The party winning the election implements his promised policy, and parties maximize the probability of winning.

Let π_P^i be the probability perceived by the candidates that voter i votes for party P, $P = A, B$, and suppose that these probabilities refer to independent events for different voters. Then the expected vote share of party P is

$$\pi_P = \frac{1}{\mathcal{I}} \sum_{i=1}^{\mathcal{I}} \pi_P^i. \tag{2.9}$$

Under Downsian electoral competition with two identical parties, π_P^i jumps discontinuously from 0 to 1 as voter i always votes with certainty for the party that promises the better policy.

Because of these discontinuous jumps, a Nash equilibrium in the electoral competition game may fail to exist. One way or the other, probabilistic voting models instead assume that $\pi_A^i = F^i(W(\mathbf{q}_A; \alpha^i), W(\mathbf{q}_B; \alpha^i))$, where $F^i(\cdot)$ is a smooth and continuous function, increasing in the first argument and decreasing in the second. This smoothness implies that a small unilateral deviation by one party does not lead to jumps in its expected vote share and thus gives rise to well-defined equilibria.

An interesting special case, which we use extensively throughout the book, restricts these probabilities to take the form $\pi_A^i = F^i(W(\mathbf{q}_A; \alpha^i) - W(\mathbf{q}_B; \alpha^i))$, where $F^i(\cdot)$ is a continuous and well-behaved cumulative distribution function (c.d.f.), associated with a probability distribution. Furthermore, suppose that parties maximize their expected vote share.[7] In this case, party A sets $\mathbf{q}_A$ to maximize:

$$\pi_A = \frac{1}{\mathcal{I}} \sum_{i=1}^{\mathcal{I}} F^i(W(\mathbf{q}_A; \alpha^i) - W(\mathbf{q}_B; \alpha^i)). \tag{2.10}$$

Clearly, party B faces a symmetric problem, and in a Nash equilibrium with simultaneous policy announcements both candidates announce the same equilibrium policies: $\mathbf{q}_A = \mathbf{q}_B$. Moreover, the first-order conditions for a maximum of (2.10), evaluated at the equilibrium policy $\mathbf{q}_A$, and taking $\mathbf{q}_B$ as given, can be written as

$$\sum_{i=1}^{\mathcal{I}} f^i(0) W_{q_{1A}}(\mathbf{q}_A; \alpha^i) = 0$$

$$\sum_{i=1}^{\mathcal{I}} f^i(0) W_{q_{2A}}(\mathbf{q}_A; \alpha^i) = 0.$$

In these expressions, $f^i(0)$ denotes the density corresponding to the c.d.f. $F^i(\cdot)$, evaluated at 0 (namely in equilibrium). Thus the equilibrium under this form of electoral competition implements the maximum of a particular weighted social welfare function, where voter i receives weight $f^i(0)$. Voters with higher $f^i(0)$ weigh more heavily, because in a neighborhood of the equilibrium they are more likely to reward policy favors with their vote. That is, more "responsive" voters, who have a higher density $f^i(0)$, receive a better treatment under electoral competition. Clearly, if all voters are equally responsive (if they all have the same value of $f^i(0)$), this form of electoral competition implements the utilitarian optimum.

---

7. When discussing probabilistic voting in subsequent chapters, we provide some microfoundations for the individual probabilities π_P^i. We also assume that parties maximize the probability of winning, that is, the probability that the vote share exceeds $\frac{1}{2}$, rather than maximize the vote share per se. In most cases the equilibrium is not sensitive to these slightly different assumptions, which are generally dictated by the models from which π_P^i is derived.

Alternative assumptions about how π_P^i depends on voters' welfare yield different specific results, though with a similar flavor.

The probabilistic voting model has become a useful tool for posing positive and normative questions in voting theory and applications. We rely on versions of this model in different chapters of the book and return to it already in chapter 3.

Structure-Induced Equilibrium   The next model of collective choice, structure-induced equilibrium, disregards elections. Instead it analyzes the decisions by a group of representatives, with given policy preferences, which is in charge of making policy decisions in a committee or a legislature. The political institution prescribes some procedure for reaching a consensus. Specifically, consider a situation in which the decision can be split in different stages, each stage being under the jurisdiction of a specific committee or being the outcome of a separate vote. The specific assumptions are most easily illustrated in the context of a concrete example. Reconsider therefore example 3, in which policy consists of two types of public consumption, q_1 and q_2, financed by general taxation. Policy choice is delegated to a legislature with three members i—we can interpret these as three parties, representing three groups of citizens—who evaluate policy according to preferences $W(\mathbf{q}; \alpha^i)$. These preferences do not, however, fulfill the monotonicity property imposed in example 3, so that an open-agenda process over pairs of policy vectors gives rise to cycling. Figure 2.2 illustrates examples of such preferences: the legislators' most preferred policies are given by the points $\mathbf{q}(\alpha^i)$, $i = 1, 2, 3$, with surrounding elliptic indifference contours.

Imagine that the decisions on each publicly provided good are made in an open-agenda process in which legislators vote separately and sequentially over each dimension. First decisions are made over, say, q_1, then over q_2 for a given q_1. All alternatives are compared pairwise in each dimension separately. This approximates the legislative practice of letting two different committees handle the two types of public consumption and only allowing the legislature to consider amendments under the jurisdiction of one committee at a time. A crucial assumption is that all legislators vote sincerely.

Consider the last stage, in which a vote is taken over q_2 for a given q_1. As figure 2.2 is drawn, voter 1 is the median voter. He is constrained to pick a point along the vertical line corresponding to the value of q_1 that was selected at the first stage. He thus selects the tangency point between the vertical line and his indifference curve. As we vary q_1, we thus trace out voter 1's "reaction function," the locus of points where the indifference curves of voter 1 have vertical slope. Consider now the first stage, at which a vote over q_1 is taken. Here, as figure 2.2 is drawn, the median voter is voter 3, who realizes that the final equilibrium will be a point on voter 1's reaction function. Voter 3 can choose which point by selecting a value of q_1. His best choice is obviously a point where voter 1's

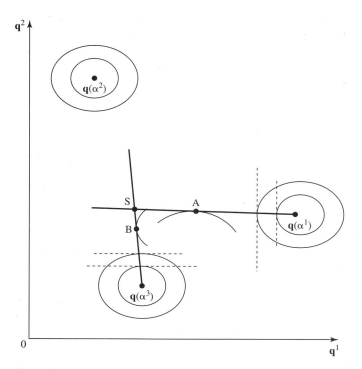

Figure 2.2

reaction function is just tangent to his own indifference curve, point *A* in figure 2.2. This simple outcome is valid if legislator preferences obey a "single-crossing condition in each direction," such that legislator 3 is always pivotal in the decision over q_1, whatever the level of q_2, and legislator 1 is always pivotal in the decision over q_2. If this regularity condition is not fulfilled, an equilibrium still exists, but the identity of the pivotal voter for each public good depends on the given supply of the other. Note that as we reverse the order of votes, the equilibrium changes to point *B*, where voter 3's reaction function is tangent to voter 1's indifference curve: point *B* in figure 2.2. Not surprisingly, the order of voting decisions matters for the final outcome. Problem 5 of this chapter includes a more detailed, algebraic treatment of the same example.

This is not exactly how Shepsle (1979) defined a structure-induced equilibrium: in his paper the equilibrium is the crossing point of these two reaction functions, point *S* in figure 2.2. The extensive form producing Shepsle's equilibrium can be thought of as a situation in which two votes are cast simultaneously, one over each dimension separately.

Shepsle's original argument also assumed that indifference curves were circular, in which case the order of votes does not matter; as the reaction functions are vertical or horizontal lines, points A, B, and S all coincide. In this instance, the equilibrium also becomes a median in two directions: it implements the pivotal voter's bliss point in each direction.

In many situations, however, decisions cannot be split finely enough to ensure existence of a Condorcet winner. For example, it would not be convincing to represent choices within a single transfer program by decisions over different dimensions, as these dimensions are then disbursements from the same program to different voters, in the same way as in the pie-splitting problem of example 5. The idea of sequential or separate decisions remains appealing and realistic, however, even if it does not always resolve existence problems. We use it in various parts of the book, with reference to specific budgetary procedures and together with other institutional assumptions. In particular, chapters 7 and 9 deal with implications of sequential budgeting, in which the size of the overall budget is determined before its allocation.

Agenda Setting   As indicated at the beginning of this subsection, agenda setting had a bad ring in the literature on political decision making; it was associated with agenda manipulation in situations of cycling, which in turn was associated with the failure to find a universally applicable method of aggregating individual preferences into political decisions. In many political decisions, however, specific politicians or bureaucrats do have a great deal of influence on the alternatives the decision makers face: they may not only have the power to propose, but also to prevent amendments from being made (gatekeeping power), such that a closed-agenda process is a better description of reality. Successful positive modeling of political decisions will then have to take these powers into account. The same argument applies, of course, irrespective of whether the policy issue at hand is one-dimensional and a Condorcet winner exists. Suppose it does. Then if the agenda setter's preferred policy does not coincide with the pivotal voter's, neither will the equilibrium policy. This is precisely the gist of the work by Romer and Rosenthal (1978, 1979). These authors also showed that an agenda-setting model empirically outperformed a median-voter model in explaining decisions on spending in Oregon school districts made by referenda.

As the discussion in section 3.1 suggests, however, assuming a closed agenda may also be a way to cut through the nonexistence problem in multidimensional policy examples. We now illustrate this possibility, and some additional implications of the agenda-setting model, in a slight modification of our earlier pure redistribution example.

Consider again the pie-splitting problem of example 5. The preferences of the three groups of voters are the same as in that example. But instead of voting on an exogenous set of alternatives, as before, we now let one of the groups $i = A$ (or a legislator representing that group) make a policy proposal, $\mathbf{q}_A = (q^1, q^2, q^3)$. For simplicity, we consider the simplest form of a closed agenda. There is thus only one round of voting, no amendments, and the (single) policy proposal pitched against a default policy: the status quo $\overline{\mathbf{q}} = (\overline{q}^1, \overline{q}^2, \overline{q}^3)$. If the proposal $\mathbf{q}_A$ collects a simple majority—the vote of two groups—it goes through, $\mathbf{q} = \mathbf{q}_A$; if not, the status quo is implemented, $\mathbf{q} = \overline{\mathbf{q}}$. Clearly, the proposer gets support from another group only if the latter is offered a share of the pie that exceeds its share in the status quo, such that $U(q_A^i) \geq U(\overline{q}^i)$ for at least one $i \neq A$.

The equilibrium outcome of this majoritarian "ultimatum game," when each of the groups has the power to propose, illustrates two important and general results. First, it illustrates the principle of *minimum winning coalitions,* which goes back to Riker (1962). When setting the agenda, each group seeks the support of only one other group: giving both the other groups at least their status quo allocations would be a waste of resources. Thus, the equilibrium allocation must always give zero to one player. Second, it shows that any agenda setter seeks majority support in the cheapest way, offering the status quo amount $\overline{q}_A^i$ (plus epsilon to break the tie) to the group with the worst status quo outcome. A weak bargaining position in this sense is thus beneficial, because it raises the likelihood of being included in the winning coalition and getting at least the status quo outcome. This contrasts with the properties of a regular two-person bargaining game, in which both players must agree and having more bargaining power is a good thing.

This kind of model has, in fact, been extended into a theory of noncooperative legislative bargaining games, in which different games in extensive form capture different rules for legislative decisions. A seminal paper is Baron and Ferejohn 1989, which extended the Stahl-Rubinstein noncooperative model of sequential two-person bargaining to majoritarian legislative bargaining with closed and open agendas. Baron and Ferejohn showed that equilibria always exist, even in infinitely repeated bargaining under open agendas, if one assumes that delay in coming to an agreement is costly. We will return to these ideas in chapter 5, and we will use legislative bargaining models in several chapters of the book.

The Role of Elections   The three models of politics we have just discussed (probabilistic voting, structure-induced equilibrium and agenda setting) all presuppose some form of representative democracy, where policy choices are delegated to political representatives. But they differ in one fundamental respect. Probabilistic voting is a model of electoral competition where two competing candidates commit to specific and detailed policy promises before the elections. It belongs to the world of preelection politics, to use the terminology coined in chapter 1. The last two models, on the other hand, describe policy formation within a legislature that is not bound by a precise electoral promise. They thus belong to the world of postelection politics. But as we will see in several chapters to follow, the more recent literature has added an electoral stage, at either the end or at the beginning of the policy formation stage, in which political representatives compete against an opponent. Elections thus play a role in both type of models, but the role is very different.

When political candidates can commit to a policy ahead of the elections, all the action with regard to policy choice takes place when the candidates locate themselves in the policy space. For this reason we refer to models of electoral competition as models of preelection politics. Theories of preelection politics are similar to models of location in economics (Hotelling 1929), or to models of final-offer arbitration, in which two parties in a dispute submit final offers to an arbitrator who, in turn, decides which offer wins (Brams and Merrill 1983, Wittman 1986). Here the voters are like the arbitrator and select among alternative policies. In this sense, elections truly aggregate the voters' policy preferences. As Riker (1982) has suggested, implicit in this role of elections is a populist view of democracies, namely the view that well-functioning democratic institutions really allow citizens to express their preferences among alternative policies.

In models of legislative bargaining, on the other hand, candidates cannot commit to policies in advance of the elections. In such models the voters do not select among alternative policies, but rather among alternative agents to be appointed and play the policy formation game. That is, elections are a way of monitoring an incumbent's behavior or to select the most appropriate representative, either in terms of talent or ideology. In this alternative perspective, nonexistence of a Condorcet winner is not such a dramatic problem: the rules and constraints on the policy formation game often give rise to a well-defined equilibrium, even if the voters' preferences over policies are not well behaved. In this view of politics, a political constitution is a bit like an incomplete contract. Political representatives are appointed not on the basis of their policy promises, but on how they will play or have played the policy formation game. Elections allow voters to assign or remove decision-making rights, and who gets elected may be important precisely because there is a fundamental incompleteness in the electoral mandate. As mentioned in chapter 1, we refer to this second strand of literature as postelection politics, because all the relevant policy action takes place once a candidate is in office, not before. As Riker (1982) points out, this line of research is more attuned to a liberal view of democracies, namely the view that the role of democratic institutions is to remove from office representatives who have not pursued the interests of their citizens. From the point of view of economic theory, theories of postelection politics borrow many tools and ideas from models of agency.

These radically different views on the role of elections have generated a tension in the literature, a tension that will be apparent and a theme of our discussion in several chapters of this book. It will be particularly evident in part 3 on comparative politics.

2.4 Discussion

What does the discussion in this chapter suggest for our main task, namely to build positive models of policymaking in representative democracies? Quite a few things, we believe. For one, we learn from the classical results in social choice and voting theory that we cannot hope for a general model of universal applicability. Thus, we have to judge on a case-by-case basis how to deal with specific policy applications.

We also get some guidance on how to make those judgments. One lesson is that what type of policy we want to investigate is important. For some applications, it may be a reasonable assumption that the essence of political disagreement runs in a single dimension. Such applications may include tax and spending policy with long-run consequences for the size of the public sector or aggregate demand management with short-run consequences for inflation and unemployment. In both cases, the major conflict is likely to be highly correlated with income in a single left-to-right dimension. If we are willing to make this simplification, we can generate policy preferences implying the existence of a Condorcet winner, using assumptions no more restrictive than those made in other applied work in macroeconomics, public finance, or contract theory. If, in addition, we are willing to assume that the policies are determined in Downsian electoral competition, we have a particularly simple equilibrium to analyze: the median-voter optimum.

But many, perhaps most, policies in public finance, regulation, or trade policy do not fall into this convenient class of general-interest politics. They are inherently multidimensional, because their benefits are targeted to specific, well-defined groups. In those instances of special-interest politics, we have seen that there are several ways of making predictions about the policy outcome. But we have also seen that precise predictions necessitate precise assumptions about the institutions in the policy process. Empirical observation, rather than analytical ease or theoretical principle, must then guide the modeling.

Specifically, analytical convenience makes it tempting to overuse the median-voter solution. Suppose we doubt that Downsian electoral competition successfully captures the political process governing the selection of a specific policy. Then a Condorcet winner may not be the right candidate for equilibrium policy, even if policy preferences are sufficiently well behaved to ensure its existence. The next three chapters will make this point more precisely. These chapters use a common policy example to illustrate different possibilities of modeling political equilibria in a representative democracy. Here the elected policymakers' decisions interject an important filter between voters' policy preferences and equilibrium policy. Therefore, we explore the policy outcomes under different assumptions about the objectives of these elected politicians, contrasting opportunistic and partisan objectives.

Finally, the importance of the policymaking institutions suggests an interesting topic of research. Different policymaking institutions aggregate conflicting policy preferences in different ways. Looking for systematic associations between policy outcomes and political institutions, then, constitutes a largely unexplored research program in comparative politics. We return to that theme later in the book, especially in part 3.

2.5 Notes on the Literature

A general overview of many theoretical results discussed in this chapter can be found in the survey by Inman (1987), which offers a nice perspective on central results in social choice from the perspective of political economy. Enelow and Hinich 1984 discusses the advances made in spatial voting theory, as does the more recent survey by Ordeshook (1997). Much of the material in the chapter is also covered in textbook form by Ordeshook (1986) and Mueller (1989).

References to the classical contributions discussed in the chapter are given in the text. For the specific contributions and approaches used as building blocks of analysis in future chapters, we give more detailed references in context.

2.6 Problems

1. Existence and nonexistence of a Condorcet winner under simple majority rule

Consider three voters indexed by $i \in \{1, 2, 3\}$, each characterized by an intrinsic parameter α^i, where $\alpha^1 < \alpha^2 < \alpha^3$. Agent i derives a utility $W(q_j; \alpha^i)$ over policy q_j. Three possible policies $q_j \in \{q_1, q_2, q_3\}$ can be implemented. A policy is selected by simple majority rule.

a. The preferences of agent $i \in \{1, 2, 3\}$ are such that

$$W(q_1; \alpha^1) > W(q_3; \alpha^1) > W(q_2; \alpha^1)$$

$$W(q_2; \alpha^2) > W(q_1; \alpha^2) > W(q_3; \alpha^2)$$

$$W(q_3; \alpha^3) > W(q_2; \alpha^3) > W(q_1; \alpha^3).$$

Moreover, the agenda is open and agents vote sincerely. Prove that no Condorcet winner exists under majority rule. Discuss.

b. Suppose that agents have the same preferences as in (a) but agent 1 is the agenda setter. He selects two rounds in which all agents vote sincerely. What is the optimal agenda from the perspective of agent 1? Suppose now that agent 1 sets the agenda and agents 2 and 3 vote sincerely. Can agent 3 improve his welfare by voting strategically? Discuss.

c. Suppose that the agents have the following preferences:

$$W(q_1; \alpha^1) > W(q_2; \alpha^1) > W(q_3; \alpha^1)$$

$$W(q_2; \alpha^2) > W(q_1; \alpha^2) > W(q_3; \alpha^2)$$

$$W(q_3; \alpha^3) > W(q_2; \alpha^3) > W(q_1; \alpha^3),$$

with $q_1 < q_2 < q_3$. Is there a Condorcet winner? Explain.

d. Suppose that the preferences of agent 2 are such that

$$W(q_2; \alpha^2) > W(q_1; \alpha^2) > W(q_3; \alpha^2),$$

with $q_1 < q_2 < q_3$. Construct the preferences (ordering) of agents 1 and 3 so that they verify the single-crossing property. Then show that the median voter is a Condorcet winner.

2. Simple majority rule and unidimensional public consumption

Consider a society inhabited by a continuum of citizens and normalize the size of the population to 1. Suppose that the preferences of agent i over a publicly provided good y and a privately provided good c^i are

$$w^i = c^i + \alpha^i V(y),$$

where $V(\cdot)$ is a concave, well-behaved function and α^i is an intrinsic parameter of agent i distributed according to $F(\cdot)$ with mean α. Assume, in addition, that all individuals have initial resources in private good $e^i = 1$ for all i. Suppose also that one unit of private good is required to produce one unit of public good. Last, suppose that to finance the production of the public good, the government raises a tax q on each individual so that agent i's budget constraint is $c^i \leq 1 - q$.

a. What is the (utilitarian) social optimum in this economy?

b. Compute each individual's policy preferences. What is the preferred policy $q(\alpha^i)$ of agent i?

c. Under majority rule, what is the selected policy? Compare this to the social optimum. When does the social optimum coincide with the equilibrium policy?

d. Suppose now that each agent's preferences are given by

$$w^i = c^i + (\alpha^i - \hat{\alpha})^2 V(y),$$

where $\hat{\alpha}$ is a given value of α^i. Again, compute the social optimum as well as the policy preferences of individuals. Do we reach the same conclusions as in question (c)?

3. Labor and consumption taxation

Consider an economy in which the preferences of individual i are quasi-linear, namely:

$$w^i = c^i + V(x^i),$$

where c^i represents the individual's consumption and x^i his leisure. Moreover, $V(\cdot)$ is increasing and concave in x^i. The private budget constraint of each agent is given by

$$(1 + q_C)c^i \leq (1 - q_L)l^i + f,$$

where q_L is the income tax rate, q_C the consumption tax rate, and f a fixed subsidy from the government. The real wage of each agent is exogenous and normalized to unity. Furthermore, each agent has a private productivity parameter α^i, so that agents have different amounts of effective time available. More precisely, they face the following time constraint:

$$1 + \alpha^i \geq x^i + l^i.$$

Assume that α^i is drawn from a distribution with mean α and median α^m.

a. Compute each individual's optimal labor supply. What effects does an increase in q_L (respectively, q_C) have on the individual labor supply? Discuss the result.

b. Write the government budget constraint and derive the level of the subsidy as a function of $\mathbf{q} = (q_L, q_C)$. Compute the policy preferences $W(\mathbf{q}; \alpha^i)$ of individual i.

c. Does a Condorcet winner exist in that case? If yes, who is the Condorcet winner?

d. Compute the utilitarian welfare and determine the socially optimal policy. What is the winning policy $\mathbf{q}$ when $\alpha^i = \alpha$ for all i? What happens if agents are heterogeneous?

4. Multidimensional public consumption in the presence of a Condorcet winner

Suppose that all individuals in the economy have the same exogenous income $y > 4$ and are subject to the same income tax τ. Government revenue per capita τy is spent on two types of publicly provided goods 1 and 2 in per capita amounts of q_1 and q_2. Individuals also consume a privately provided good, denoted by c. Agents have heterogeneous preferences for public goods and their utility function is summarized by

$$w^i = U(c) + \alpha^i G(q_1) + (1 - \alpha^i)F(q_2),$$

where α^i is an intrinsic parameter of agent i. The functions $U(\cdot)$, $G(\cdot)$, and $F(\cdot)$ are continuous, twice continuously differentiable, strictly increasing, and strictly concave.

a. Write each individual's budget constraint as well as that of the government. Derive the policy preferences of agent i and verify that they satisfy the intermediate-preference property. What does this imply? Determine the optimal quantity $q_1(q_2, \alpha^i)$ (respectively, $q_2(q_1, \alpha^i)$) from agent i's perspective for a given level q_2 (respectively, q_1). When q_2 (respectively, q_1) increases, what is the effect on the optimal provision of q_1 (respectively, q_2) for agent i? How does α^i affect these quantities?

b. To simplify the analysis, suppose that $U(x) = G(x) = F(x) = \ln(x)$. Compute agent i's bliss point $(q_1(\alpha^i), q_2(\alpha^i))$. Suppose the economy consists of three agents (or three groups of agents) $i = \{1, 2, 3\}$ with different intrinsic parameters. More precisely, $\alpha^1 = 0$, $\alpha^2 = \frac{1}{2}$, and $\alpha^3 = 1$. Determine the optimal provision of public goods for each agent. Which policy is implemented under majority rule?

c. Suppose now that the preferences of agent i are summarized by

$$w^i = U(c) + \alpha^i G(q_1) + (1 - \alpha^i) F(q_2) + h(\alpha^i) H(q_1, q_2),$$

where $U(x) = G(x) = F(x) = \ln(x)$ and $H(q_1, q_2) = \ln(q_1 q_2)$. Derive each individual's policy preferences. Discuss. Suppose that $h(\alpha^i) = (\alpha^i)^2$. Determine the optimal quantity $q_1(q_2, \alpha^i)$ (respectively, $q_2(q_1, \alpha^i)$) from agent i's perspective for a given level q_2 (respectively, q_1). When q_2 (respectively, q_1) increases, what is the effect on the optimal provision of q_1 (respectively, q_2) for agent i? Compute the equilibrium public consumptions. How does α^i affect these quantities?

d. Suppose that the economy consists of three agents $i = \{1, 2, 3\}$ for which $\alpha^1 = 0, \alpha^2 = \frac{1}{2}$, and $\alpha^3 = 1$. Determine the optimal provision of public goods for each agent. Is there a Condorcet winner?

e. Suppose now that voters' preferences are given by

$$w^i = U(c) + K(\alpha^i)[G(q_1) + F(q_2)],$$

with $U(x) = G(x) = F(x) = \ln(x)$. Compute public consumption levels in equilibrium. Suppose that $K(\alpha^i) = (\alpha^i - \frac{1}{2})^2$ and that the economy consists of agents with type $\alpha^1 = \frac{1}{4}$, $\alpha^2 = \frac{1}{3}$, and $\alpha^3 = 1$. Is there a Condorcet winner in this economy?

5. Structure-induced equilibrium and multidimensional public consumption

Consider the same model as in problem 4 but suppose now that the economy consists of three types of agents. The preferences w^i of type i are

$$w^1 = \ln(c) + \ln(q_1 + 1)$$

$$w^2 = \ln(c) + a \ln(q_2 + 1)$$

$$w^3 = \ln(c) + \ln(q_1 + 1) + b \ln(q_2 + 1).$$

a. Compute the bliss points of each type of agent. Is there a Condorcet winner if $y = 3$, $a = 3$, and $b = 1$?

b. Find the conditions under which a Condorcet winner does not exist. [Hint: It could be convenient to derive such conditions by first considering a vote over 1 versus 2 and by assuming that 1 wins in this round.] Verify that there is no Condorcet winner when $y = b = \frac{1}{a}$ with $y = \frac{11}{10}$.

c. Suppose that decisions related to the provision of public goods are made through an open-agenda process in which agents vote separately, sincerely, and sequentially over each good. Decisions are first made over q_1 and then over q_2. Describe the vote in the last stage (in which q_1 is taken as given). What is the selected quantity of q_2? Determine the policy selected at stage 1 anticipating the decision at stage 2. What happens if the agenda is reversed?

3 Electoral Competition

We now turn to a discussion of two-party electoral competition in representative democracy. The underlying policy question addressed in this chapter, as well as the remaining chapters of this part, is what determines the size of government spending. To make things as transparent as possible, we abstain from the difficulties caused by multidimensional policy conflict discussed in chapter 2. Instead, we deal with a very simple policy example, where conflict among the voters is unidimensional. The policy to be determined concerns the size of a program, supplying a publicly provided good, that benefits all the voters alike and is financed by proportional income taxes, income being the only dimension of heterogeneity among the voters. The same economic model is used in all the remaining chapters of part 1, with slight variations only.

Throughout the chapter we retain two key assumptions. First, political candidates are opportunistic. More precisely, their only motivation is to hold office. Candidates thus do not care what policy is implemented: they do not have partisan preferences, and they do not benefit directly from the policy because the rents from holding office are exogenously given and independent of policy. Alternative assumptions about candidate motivation are discussed in the next two chapters, in which we deal with agency problems and with partisan policy preferences, respectively. Second, throughout the chapter we assume that candidates commit to a well-defined policy ahead of the elections, sticking to the realm of preelection politics. Thus, electoral competition is viewed as a choice of location by two competing parties. The parties announce a policy platform, so as to maximize the probability of victory, and voters select the preferred policy. The policy announced by the winning candidate gets implemented.

This model of preelection politics with opportunistic politicians is widely used in the literature. It naturally directs the attention to the conflict among voters over alternative policies and to the question of which groups of voters are more influential. As we shall see, equilibrium policy here reflects features of the voters themselves, such as the distribution of their policy preferences, the ability of different groups to organize as a lobby, or the likelihood that different groups reward policy favors with a vote. Even under the maintained assumptions of this chapter, however, there is not a single model of electoral competition. On the contrary, depending on the specific assumptions about the likelihood that voters reward policy favors with a vote, different forces influence electoral competition and the resulting equilibrium policy.

In section 3.1, we formulate the underlying policy problem. Sections 3.2 and 3.3 discuss the simplest possible model of electoral competition, due to Downs's (1957) classical study, in which the competing parties are identical in all respects and voters care only about economic policy. Here, both parties converge to the median voter optimum. Section 3.4 illustrates the equilibrium under probabilistic voting, while section 3.5 adds lobbying. In these sections different political forces are at play and policy diverges from the median voter's bliss point.

3.1 A Simple Model of Public Finance

Consider a society inhabited by a large number (formally a continuum) of citizens, where we normalize the size (mass) of the population to unity. These citizens are of different types indexed by i. Each type i has the same basic and quasi-linear preferences over private consumption c and publicly provided goods g, which is given by

$$w^i = c^i + H(g), \tag{3.1}$$

where $H(\cdot)$ is a concave and increasing function. Implicit in (3.1) is also the (unrealistic) assumption that government spending cannot be targeted to specific groups but instead must be provided in the same, nonnegative, amount to everyone: $g^i = g \geq 0$. We can interpret g in different ways, as publicly provided private goods, or traditional public goods. In either case, we let g measure spending per capita. Nor can taxes be targeted, so government spending is financed by taxing the income of every individual at a common rate τ, bounded by $0 \leq \tau \leq 1$.

Income differs across individuals, however, implying that their consumption differs according to

$$c^i = (1 - \tau)y^i. \tag{3.2}$$

We assume that y^i is distributed in the population according to a cumulative distribution function (c.d.f.) $F(\cdot)$. The expected (average) value of a variable such as y^i is always denoted by a symbol without superscript, that is, $\mathsf{E}(y^i) = y$, where E denotes an expected value. Finally, the median value of y^i, labeled y^m, is implicitly defined by $F(y^m) = \frac{1}{2}$. We assume that $y^m \leq y$, so that the income distribution is skewed to the right, in accordance with evidence from virtually every country. The government budget constraint is then simply

$$\tau y = g.$$

Given these preliminaries, we can easily write down the policy preferences of citizen i as

$$W^i(g) = (y - g)\frac{y^i}{y} + H(g). \tag{3.3}$$

These preferences are concave in policy, implying that every citizen has a uniquely preferred policy. It is easy to see that this policy satisfies

$$g^i = H_g^{-1}(y^i/y). \tag{3.4}$$

Clearly, the policy conflict between different citizens is quite smooth in this model. This smoothness, of course, reflects the restrictive assumptions about the policy space, namely that neither government spending nor taxes can be targeted to specific voters or groups of voters and that politicians cannot appropriate tax revenues as rents for themselves. Policy preferences therefore become monotonic in the one parameter that distinguishes individuals, namely their relative income, y^i/y. Richer individuals want a smaller government because, with taxes proportional to income, they pay a larger share of the tax burden. By concavity of $H(\cdot)$, (3.4) implies that g^i is decreasing in y^i.

It is easy to see that these policy preferences fulfill the Gans-Smart single-crossing condition (2.4), introduced in chapter 2. Here, the corresponding condition is

If $g > g'$ and $y^{i\prime} < y^i$, or $g < g'$ and $y^{i\prime} > y^i$, then

$$W^i(g) \geq W^i(g') \Rightarrow W^{i\prime}(g) \geq W^{i\prime}(g'). \tag{3.5}$$

These properties of policy preferences considerably simplify the analysis to follow.

Let us also formulate a normative benchmark. As a basis for this benchmark, consider a utilitarian social welfare function that simply sums up (integrates over) the welfare of all individual citizens:

$$w = \int_i W^i(g)\, dF = W(g),$$

where the last term is just the utility of the average individual, namely the individual with average income. The second equality follows from the definition of $W^i(\cdot)$ and the fact that $\mathsf{E}(y^i) = y$. Even though a utilitarian objective is often quite restrictive, it is not very restrictive in conjunction with quasi-linear preferences, as these rule out meaningful distributional considerations anyway. According to the utilitarian objective, the socially optimal policy coincides with the policy desired by the average citizen:

$$g^* = H_g^{-1}(1).$$

Problem 2 of this chapter formulates an alternative simple model of public finance, in which agents are heterogenous in their preferences for public versus private goods, rather than in their income. Problems 2–5 deal with equilibria in this alternative model, under the same assumptions about the political environment as those we will make in sections 3.2–3.5.

3.2 Downsian Electoral Competition

Throughout the chapter, we maintain a number of assumptions about the nature of political competition and candidates that are akin to those in Downs's (1957) classical study. Like Downs, we postulate two candidates—or parties, as the two here boil down to the same thing—indexed by $P = A, B$. Each of these maximizes the expected value of some exogenous ego rents, R. These exogenous rents reflect the value attached to winning the elections and holding office, but they do not appear in the government budget. Candidate P thus sets his policy so as to maximize $p_P R$, where p_P is the *probability of winning* the election, given the other candidate's policy. If we use π_P to denote the *vote share* of candidate P, we can write $p_P = \text{Prob}\,[\pi_P \geq \frac{1}{2}]$.

The timing of events is as follows: (1) The two candidates, simultaneously and noncooperatively, announce their electoral platforms: g_A, g_B. (2) Elections are held, in which voters choose between the two candidates. (3) The elected candidate implements his announced policy platform. The candidates' commitments to their electoral platforms are thus assumed to be binding.

To see how the model works, we start with a very simple case. Assume that the income distribution is degenerate so that every citizen has the same income $y^i = y$. Voters thus face a very simple problem, and they just vote for the candidate whose platform gives them the highest utility. If indifferent, a voter tosses a coin to decide for whom to vote.[1] This implies the following probability of winning for candidate A:

$$p_A = \begin{cases} 0 & \text{if} \quad W(g_A) < W(g_B) \\ \frac{1}{2} & \text{if} \quad W(g_A) = W(g_B) \\ 1 & \text{if} \quad W(g_A) > W(g_B), \end{cases}$$

whereas p_B is just given by $1 - p_A$.

Suppose now that candidate A's announcement g_A is further away, utility-wise, from the unanimously preferred policy g^* than candidate B's announcement g_B. Obviously, A can then discontinuously increase his probability of winning by announcing a policy closer to g^*. As the same holds true for candidate B, there is a unique subgame-perfect equilibrium

$$g_A = g_B = g^*.$$

Both candidates thus converge to the socially optimal policy.

The normative implications are thus consistent with the claim made by the Chicago school: political competition indeed leads to an optimal outcome for society. The positive implications—thinking about variation in the size of government across countries or time—are also straightforward. Observed differences are entirely driven by voters' policy preferences. For example, trendwise growth in government could be consistent with Wagner's law if the marginal benefits of g are positively correlated with average income y (Wagner 1893). Similarly, it could be consistent with Baumol's disease if the relative cost of

---

1. We assume that everyone votes. Even so, individual voters may not vote according to their preferences, given that their votes will almost surely not affect the outcome, given how everyone else votes. Formally, we can eliminate such behavior by ruling out weakly dominated voting strategies, which guarantees sincere voting in two-candidate elections.

government versus private goods had an upward trend, because of an adverse productivity development due to the nature of government production (Baumol 1967). This could be formally shown by adding a parameter capturing the relative cost of public goods to the government budget constraint, as is done in the next chapter.

3.3   Median-Voter Equilibria

When voters disagree over the desired fiscal policy, the candidates must decide which voters to please, in order to enhance their chances of winning the election. To study this question, we assume that the income distribution is no longer degenerate and that the c.d.f. $F(\cdot)$ is indeed a continuous function. The equilibrium we will study in this setting is an application of the median-voter theorem, proposed by Black (1948) for voting in committees and applied to electoral competition by Downs (1957).

Voter i now votes for candidate A with certainty only if $W^i(g_A) > W^i(g_B)$. Under the other assumptions of the model, we have

$$p_A = \begin{cases} 0 & \text{if} \quad W^m(g_A) < W^m(g_B) \\ \frac{1}{2} & \text{if} \quad W^m(g_A) = W^m(g_B) \\ 1 & \text{if} \quad W^m(g_A) > W^m(g_B). \end{cases} \tag{3.6}$$

The pivotal role played by the voter with median income y^m is easy to establish. Recall from (3.4) that g^i is decreasing in y^i. This fact and the monotonicity of preferences (3.5) imply that whenever the median voter prefers one platform over the other, at least half of the electorate agrees. To see the logic behind this separation argument, suppose, for example, that y^m considers g_B too low relative to g_A. Then so does everyone with $y^i < y^m$, as they prefer an even larger government, $g^i > g^m$. More than half the electorate would thus vote for A. Given this, the only situation in which neither of the candidates can increase his probability of winning is when they have both converged to the policy preferred by the median voter: $g_A = g_B = g^m$. In the jargon of chapter 2, g^m is the unique Condorcet winner, that is, a policy capable of beating any alternative policy in a pairwise vote. Individuals with median income become pivotal, and both candidates converge to those individuals' bliss point.

The median-voter equilibrium suggests a new set of determinants to the size of the public sector. By (3.4), the first-order condition describing the equilibrium is

$$g^m = H_g^{-1}(y^m/y). \tag{3.7}$$

Thus as y^m drops relative to y, g^m rises: a relatively poorer median voter prefers a larger government. Thus (3.7) says that larger governments (a higher τ and g) are associated with a more skewed income distribution in the specific sense of a higher percentage gap between median and mean income. Furthermore, what matters for the political equilibrium is median income in the electorate, whereas, by the government budget constraint, average income refers to the population as a whole. An extension of the franchise, extending voting rights to poorer segments of the population, should therefore also raise the equilibrium size of government, since it widens the gap between the median voter's income and that of the average citizen. The normative properties are also simple to state. If the income distribution is symmetric, so that $y^m = y$, then electoral competition still implements a socially optimal allocation. But an income distribution skewed to the right implies overspending and overtaxation, at least relative to the utilitarian benchmark. The influential paper by Meltzer and Richard (1981) who, relied on earlier theoretical work by Romer (1975) and Roberts (1977), stressed similar implications. The inequality predictions, in particular, have been studied quite extensively, and we discuss this work in part 2. To summarize very briefly, however, it has been hard to find compelling empirical evidence supporting the predictions.

We rely on these kinds of median-voter equilibria in several parts of the book. Such equilibria are useful, for they are so simple to characterize; as a result, one can add much more structure to the model's economic side. We use them in chapter 6, especially, to discuss the determinants of pensions, unemployment insurance, and regional redistribution. In part 4 we analyze capital taxation and its implications for growth in a median-voter model. But as chapter 2 warned us, and as the following section illustrates, existence of a Condorcet winner does not mean this policy will be implemented.

3.4   Probabilistic Voting

Up to this point, voters have cared only about the economic policy platforms announced by the two candidates. But candidates, or parties, may also differ in some other dimension unrelated to this policy, g. We shall refer to this other dimension as "ideology," but it could also involve other attributes such as the personal characteristics of the party leadership. This ideological dimension is a permanent feature in that it cannot credibly be modified as part of the electoral platform.

Furthermore, we assume that voters differ in their evaluation of these features. One way to motivate this assumption is to think about a second policy dimension, orthogonal to fiscal policy, in which candidates cannot make credible commitments but set an optimal policy after the election according to their ideology. Voters' preferences over the alternative policy dimension imply derived preferences over the candidates themselves. Problem 1 of this chapter deals formally with this interpretation of the model.

In this setting, some groups of voters may become more attractive prey for office-seeking politicians, who are willing to modify policy in the direction of the favored groups. To illustrate this mechanism, we build on a version of the probabilistic voting model introduced in chapter 2, which Lindbeck and Weibull (1987) adapted to multidimensional redistribution problems.

To make the point in a transparent way, we now assume that the population consists of three distinct groups, $J = R, M, P$, representing the rich, the middle class, and the poor, respectively. Everyone in group J has the same income y^J, with the obvious ranking: $y^R > y^M > y^P$. The population share of group J is α^J, with $\sum_J \alpha^J = 1$. (Formally, $F(\cdot)$ is now a step function with $F(\cdot) = 0$, for $y^i < y^P$, $F(\cdot) = \alpha^P$, for $y^P \leq y^i < y^M$, and so on). Naturally, by definition of y, $\sum_J \alpha^J y^J = y$. At the time of the elections, voters base their voting decision both on the economic policy announcements and on the two candidates' ideologies. Specifically, voter i in group J prefers candidate A if

$$W^J(g_A) > W^J(g_B) + \sigma^{iJ} + \delta. \tag{3.8}$$

Here, σ^{iJ} is an individual-specific parameter that can take on negative as well as positive values. It measures voter i's individual ideological bias toward candidate B. A positive value of σ^{iJ} implies that voter i has a bias in favor of party B, whereas voters with $\sigma^{iJ} = 0$ are ideologically neutral, that is, they care only about economic policy. We assume that this parameter has group-specific uniform distributions on

$$\left[-\frac{1}{2\phi^J}, \frac{1}{2\phi^J} \right].$$

These distributions thus have density ϕ^J, and each group has members inherently biased toward both candidates. The parameter δ, which measures the average (relative) popularity of candidate B in the population as a whole, can also be positive or negative. Here, too, we assume a uniform distribution on

$$\left[-\frac{1}{2\psi}, \frac{1}{2\psi} \right].$$

Although the distributional assumptions regarding σ^{iJ} and δ are special, they facilitate a simple closed-form solution. We discuss below how to generalize these distributional assumptions.

The timing of events is as follows. (1) The two candidates, simultaneously and noncooperatively, announce their electoral platforms: g_A, g_B. At this stage, they know the voters' policy preferences. They also know the distributions for σ^{iJ} and δ, but not yet their realized values. (2) The actual value of δ is realized and all uncertainty is resolved. (3) Elections are held. (4) The elected candidate implements his announced policy platform.

To formally study the candidates' decisions at stage (2), let us identify the "swing voter" in group J, a voter whose ideological bias, given the candidates' platforms, makes him indifferent between the two parties:

$$\sigma^J = W^J(g_A) - W^J(g_B) - \delta. \tag{3.9}$$

All voters i in group J with $\sigma^{iJ} \leq \sigma^J$ prefer party A. Hence, given our distributional assumptions, candidate A's actual vote share is

$$\pi_A = \sum_J \alpha^J \phi^J \left(\sigma^J + \frac{1}{2\phi^J} \right).$$

Since σ^J depends on the realized value of δ, the vote share π_A is also a random variable. From the perspective of both candidates, the electoral outcome is thus a random event, related to the realization of δ.[2] Specifically, candidate A's probability of winning, given (3.9), becomes

$$p_A = \text{Prob}_\delta \left[\pi_A \geq \frac{1}{2} \right] = \frac{1}{2} + \frac{\psi}{\phi} \left[\sum_J \alpha^J \phi^J [W^J(g_A) - W^J(g_B)] \right], \tag{3.10}$$

where $\phi \equiv \sum_J \alpha^J \phi^J$ is the average density across groups. Obviously, candidate B wins with probability $1 - p_A$.[3]

This objective illustrates a general property of probabilistic voting models. As both individual utility and the distribution of ideological preferences are continuous functions, the probability of winning now becomes a smooth function of the distance between the two electoral platforms. In this sense, competition between the two candidates becomes less stiff than in the traditional model of the previous section. Hence, we should also expect equilibrium behavior to differ.

The unique equilibrium has both candidates converging to the same platform. Convergence follows from the two candidates' facing exactly the same optimization problem. To see this formally, notice that g_A and g_B enter the expression in (3.10) with opposite signs and that $p_A R = (1 - p_A)R$. Intuitively, the two candidates share the same concave preferences and the same technology for converting tax dollars into expected votes, so they end up finding the same policy announcements optimal.

In equilibrium, therefore, both candidates maximize a weighted social welfare function. The weights, $\phi^J \alpha^J$, correspond to group size, α^J, as in the utilitarian optimum, but also to

---

2. We assume that the distribution of δ is not too narrow, so that we can rule out corner solutions for σ^J.

3. To derive (3.10), note that

$$p_A = \text{Prob} \left[\sum_J \alpha^J \phi^J [W^J(g_A) - W^J(g_B)] \geq \delta \sum_J \alpha^J \phi^J \right].$$

By the distributional assumption on δ and by definition of ϕ, (3.10) follows.

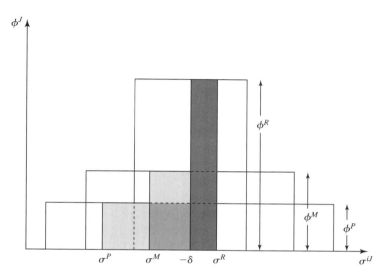

Figure 3.1

the group densities, ϕ^J, because these densities summarize how responsive are the voters in each group to economic policy, that is, how each group rewards policy with votes at the elections.

To illustrate the equilibrium, consider first figure 3.1, which depicts the distribution of σ^{iJ} in the three groups. All three distributions are symmetric around a mean of zero. The height of the distribution corresponds to the density ϕ^J and measures how many voters are gained in that group per marginal increase in economic welfare in the group.

As the figure is drawn, group R has the highest density and group P the lowest. In equilibrium, all candidates announce the same policy. Thus the equilibrium swing voter in each group is the individual with parameter $\sigma^J = -\delta$. Voters with σ^{iJ} to the left of $-\delta$ in each group vote for party A; the others vote for B.

Now consider a small unilateral deviation from the equilibrium policy by candidate A, promising a smaller government policy and lower taxes. The utility functions (3.3) of the three groups of voters are illustrated in figure 3.2, where g^* denotes the equilibrium policy.

A smaller government benefits group R, for whom equilibrium spending is too high, but hurts groups M and L, for whom the opposite is true. As a result of the deviation, party A thus gains votes in group R and loses votes in the other two groups. Going back to figure 3.1, the new swing voter in group R is individual σ^R, whereas the new swing voters in the other two groups correspond to the points σ^M and σ^L. Note that the horizontal distance between σ^J and $-\delta$ in each group is proportional to the utility gain or loss from

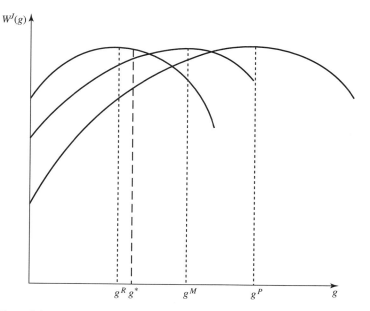

$W^J(g)$

g^R g^* g^M g^P g

Figure 3.2

the deviation. As the figure is drawn, the equilibrium is closest to the bliss point of group R, and the horizontal shift of the swing voter is accordingly smallest in that group, since at the margin the deviation affects him least. There are no incentives to deviate from the equilibrium when the shaded area to the right (the gain in votes) is equal to the shaded areas to the left (the loss in votes). Figure 3.2 illustrates the implication: equilibrium policy must be especially catered in favor of group R. As this group has many swing voters, it must have less-intense policy preferences, which implies an equilibrium policy relatively close to its bliss point. The opposite is true for group P.

To characterize the equilibrium algebraically, take the derivative of p_A with respect to g_A, using the definition of voter utility in (3.3). Setting the resulting expression equal to 0 and rearranging, we obtain

$$\sum_J \alpha^J \phi^J H_g(g) = \frac{1}{y} \sum_J \alpha^J \phi^J y^J.$$

Recalling the definition $\phi = \sum_J \alpha^J \phi^J$, we can write

$$g^S = H_g^{-1}(\tilde{y}/y), \tag{3.11}$$

where

$$\tilde{y} = \frac{\sum_J \alpha^J \phi^J y^J}{\phi}$$

and the S superscript stands for swing-voter equilibrium. This equilibrium can be socially optimal: if the density ϕ^J is the same in all groups $\phi^J = \phi$, we have $\tilde{y} = y$, and $g^S = g^*$. Both parties are trying to maximize their expected vote and are therefore appealing to the expected swing voters in each group. If the number of swing voters (slightly abusing the fact that within-group distributions are continuous) is the same, all groups get equal weight in the candidates' decision, which makes them maximize the average voter's utility. Generally, groups will differ, however, in how easily their votes can be swayed. Office-seeking candidates will therefore not give them equal weight. If ϕ^J is high, because the group is ideologically homogeneous, it has a large number of swing voters. In line with the discussion around figures 3.1 and 3.2, this makes the group attractive for the candidates, who thus tilt their policy in the direction desired by the group.

In drawing figures 3.1 and 3.2, we assumed $\phi^R > \phi > \phi^P$, so that the poor group had the least number of swing voters. In this case, obviously, $\tilde{y} > y$, implying a size of government that is below its benchmark: $g^S < g^*$. For given y, the bias is larger, the larger is the rich group (α^R higher)—as more votes can be gained—and the richer it is relative to the middle class ($y^R - y^M$ larger)—as the rich then have a higher stake in the policy. Furthermore, the bias is larger, the larger is the poor group relative to the middle class (lower ϕ given ϕ^R). We see that the conclusion runs exactly counter to the prediction of the median-voter model of the previous section, namely that more-skewed income distributions are associated with larger governments. The previous conclusion is salvaged only if we make the opposite assumption about ranking, namely $\phi^R < \phi < \phi^P$, so that the poor have the most political clout and $\tilde{y} < y$. In this event, more concentration of income at the top, or more poverty at the bottom, for a given y, indeed lowers $\tilde{y}$. This in turn leads to a larger government and a positive association between inequality and the size of government.

How does the equilibrium change for more general distributions of voters' ideological preferences, namely if the group distributions of the parameter σ^{iJ} are not uniform, but unimodal? Not much. The properties of the equilibrium are dictated by the group density of σ^{iJ} in a neighborhood of the equilibrium policy. But the interpretation remains the same: ideologically neutral groups are more responsive to policy (and hence care less about ideology) in a neighborhood of equilibrium; they are thus more likely to reward politicians with votes and get a policy closer to their bliss point. Naturally, the second-order conditions for an optimum impose additional restrictions on the distributional form, to guarantee existence of equilibrium. Problem 4 of this chapter deals formally with the extension to more general distributions in a similar model of probabilistic voting.

The general lesson from the probabilistic voting model is that ideological shifts in the population systematically alter the political power of different groups. Ideologically neutral groups with many mobile voters—those willing to swing their vote for small changes in economic policy—become an attractive target for office-seeking politicians. A seemingly small and trivial change in the underlying model of electoral competition (the competing parties are not identical but instead differ somewhat in voters' eyes) changes dramatically the implications for the equilibrium. Rather than trying to please the median individual, both parties now seek to please the more mobile voters. We know of no attempts in the literature to try to discriminate empirically between this model of electoral competition and the median-voter model. Direct tests of the probabilistic voting model would have to combine disaggregated historical electoral data, proxying for mobility in different voter groups, with data on economic policy.

We will use similar probabilistic voting models repeatedly in the following chapters. As discussed in chapter 2, these models have unique equilibria even when the policy conflict is multidimensional. As we have seen in (3.10), the voters' ideological preferences smooth the candidates' problems by eliminating sharp discontinuities in their probability of election, such as the one appearing in (3.6). We will use this property of the equilibrium with probabilistic voting in chapter 7, when dealing with special-interest politics, and in chapter 8, when contrasting alternative electoral rules. Probabilistic voting models are also relevant when politicians care about policy and not only about winning office. We thus use a probabilistic voting model in chapter 14, when studying public debt issued by partisan candidates. We also use such a model in chapter 4, where candidates care about economic policies not because of their ideology, but because they want to appropriate rents for themselves.

3.5   Lobbying

In the probabilistic voting model, groups derive their political power solely from their attributes as voters. But well-defined interest groups may also exert influence on the policy process through other forms of political action. Lobbying is a prime example. In this section, we extend the probabilistic voting model to encompass campaign contributions by interest groups, adapting a formulation suggested by Baron (1994).

Consider again the model in the previous section, but assume that all groups have the same density, $\phi^J = \phi$, making the members of each group, in their capacity as voters, equally attractive for office-seeking politicians. In the pure swing-voter model this assumption made the equilibrium policy socially optimal (recall (3.11)). Any departure from that benchmark will thus be due to lobbying activity.

We assume that groups may or may not be organized in a lobby; the indicator variable O^J takes a value of one if group J is indeed organized, zero otherwise. Organized groups have the capacity to contribute to the campaign of either of the two candidates: let C_P^J denote the contribution per member of group J to candidate P, constrained to be nonnegative. As we develop below, these contributions can be interpreted both as in cash and in kind. The total contributions collected by candidate P can thus be expressed as

$$C_P = \sum_J O^J \alpha^J C_P^J. \tag{3.12}$$

These contributions are given between stages (1) and (2) of the model, simultaneously by all lobbies, after the parties have announced their platforms, but before the elections and before δ is realized. We assume that candidates exploit these contributions in their campaign and that campaign spending affects their popularity. Specifically, the average relative popularity of party B, what we called δ in (3.8), now has two components:

$$\delta = \widetilde{\delta} + h(C_B - C_A). \tag{3.13}$$

In (3.13), $\widetilde{\delta}$ is again distributed uniformly with density ψ. According to the second term, a candidate who outspends the other becomes more popular, where the parameter h measures the effectiveness of campaign spending. This formulation is equivalent to assuming that some voters, but not others, are informed about the candidates' ideological attributes. But the present formulation is simple and serves our purpose.

The new formulation changes the definition of the swing voter in group J to

$$\sigma^J = W^J(g_A) - W^J(g_B) + h(C_A - C_B) - \widetilde{\delta}.$$

Following the same approach as in the last section and exploiting that $\phi^J = \phi$, we can then write candidate A's probability of election as

$$p_A = \frac{1}{2} + \psi \left[W(g_A) - W(g_B) + h(C_A - C_B) \right], \tag{3.14}$$

where $W(g_P) = \sum_J \alpha^J W^J(g_P)$ is the utilitarian social welfare function (recall that we are now assuming that all groups have the same density ϕ, so that in the probabilistic voting model they all receive the same weight). The last term reflects campaign spending's influence on the expected vote share.

Next, consider how lobbies choose their campaign contributions. If organized, group J chooses contributions with the objective of maximizing the expected utility its members derive from the election, minus the cost of contributions:

$$p_A W^J(g_A) + (1 - p_A) W^J(g_B) - \frac{1}{2} \left((C_A^J)^2 + (C_B^J)^2 \right). \tag{3.15}$$

The first two terms in the expression are obvious. The negative third term can be interpreted in two ways. If transfers are made in cash, different members of the group may differ in their willingness to give, which makes the costs convex. If transfers are made in kind—by working in the campaign—the increasing marginal cost may just reflect disutility of effort. Note that here, ideology plays no role in the lobby's objective function. Under our assumption that the lobby maximizes the average utility of its members, the opposite ideologies of its members exactly cancel out. Thus intrinsic party preferences matter when voting, but not in the lobbying decision (unless the interest group has an ideological bias in favor of one of the parties).

In view of (3.14) and of (3.15), group J's optimal contributions are easily derived:[4]

$$C_A^J = \text{Max } [0, \psi h(W^J(g_A) - W^J(g_B))]$$

$$C_B^J = -\text{Min } [0, \psi h(W^J(g_A) - W^J(g_B))].$$

$$(3.16)$$

Thus the group contributes only to the candidate whose platform gives the group the highest utility, and never to more than one.

We now return to the candidates and their optimal platform choice at stage (1). When making this choice, the candidates anticipate that organized groups will make contributions according to (3.16). But the symmetry of (3.16) preserves the symmetry of the two candidates' problems. Thus they once more converge on the same equilibrium policy. To characterize this policy, we substitute (3.16) into (3.14) and simplify. Candidate A, taking g_B as given, maximizes

$$\sum_J \alpha^J [\psi + O^J(\psi h)^2] W^J(g_A). \tag{3.17}$$

We immediately see that if all groups are organized ($O^J = 1$ for all J), or no groups are organized ($O^J = 0$ for all J), the equilibrium coincides with the utilitarian optimum. In these cases, we have returned to the previous probabilistic voting model, and optimality follows from our symmetry assumption $\phi^J = \phi$. It may appear surprising, at first sight, that the equilibrium is socially optimal when all groups are organized. The intuition is that the groups are all prepared to contribute in proportion to the marginal benefits and costs of g for their members. As a result, the candidates internalize all groups with the appropriate social weight, just paying attention to group size.

---

4. By (3.15) the first-order condition of the lobby J with respect to C_A^J is

$$\frac{\partial p_A}{\partial C_A^J}[W^J(g_A) - W^J(g_B)] - C^J \leq 0,$$

and by (3.14),

$$\frac{\partial p_A}{\partial C_A^J} = h\psi.$$

Repeating the same steps for C_B^J, we get (3.16).

Departures from the benchmark arise when only a subset of the groups is organized. To see this, take the first-order condition of (3.17) with respect to g_A. After some transformations we get:

$$g^L = H_g^{-1}(\hat{y}/y),$$

where the L superscript stands for lobbying equilibrium and where

$$\hat{y} = \frac{\sum_J \alpha^J [1 + O^J \psi h^2] y^J}{\sum_J \alpha^J [1 + O^J \psi h^2]}. \tag{3.18}$$

Thus, $\hat{y}$ is a weighted average of y^J, with weights reflecting whether or not the group is organized. As stated above, when all groups are organized (or no group is), the expression on the right-hand side of (3.18) reduces to y and the equilibrium is socially optimal: $g^L = g^*$. Otherwise, the organized groups receive greater weights and the equilibrium is tilted in their favor. Suppose for instance that only the richest group is organized. Then they receive greater weight in the computation of $\hat{y}$, so that $\hat{y} > y$: the size of government becomes smaller than the benchmark, $g^L < g^*$. Furthermore, spending is smaller the larger is group R's stake in the policy (the higher is y^R relative to y) and the more effective is campaign spending in swaying the vote (the higher is h). As in the probabilistic voting model, more income inequality can thus be associated with a smaller government.

Intuitively, the candidates seek only election victory, and the organized lobbies can help them achieve this goal by financing their campaigns. Both candidates thus bias their policy platforms in the direction desired by the lobbies. This illustrates a well-known point from the traditional public choice literature. Groups that have overcome the collective action problem and organized themselves have more influence on policy than nonorganized groups. This point goes back all the way to Olson (1965) and has been formalized in a growing literature on lobbying.

The public choice literature has also emphasized that groups with the largest stake in a particular policy are more likely to become organized. Applying the logic to this model, the rich or the poor would be more likely to form organized lobbies than the middle class. Strong stakes in policy are thus complementary: they make a group of citizens more likely to get organized and more willing to lobby hard once they are organized. Perhaps it is not so plausible, however, to think about lobby groups forming over general economic policies as the fiscal programs considered here. If organizations like trade unions or industrial associations already exist for other reasons, however, they are likely to use their political power to influence general economic policies. Strong organizations of this type can thus bias policy significantly to the left or to the right, even though neither the candidates themselves nor the general electorate has a corresponding bias. The specific predictions regarding the size of government from our simple model could be taken to the data.

More generally, many authors have suggested reasons why the size of government might be related to the number and orientation of interest groups. As discussed in the recent survey by Holsey and Borcherding (1997), however, empirical work has failed to find robust evidence of a tight link between interest group activity and the size of government.

The model also illustrates a more subtle point. In equilibrium no contributions are being paid, according to (3.16), as the candidates converge to the same policy. Obviously, this feature does not allow us to conclude that lobbying is unimportant for the policy outcome. The common argument that lobbying cannot be very important as observed contributions are so small relative to the policy benefits at stake (see Tullock 1988, for instance) should thus be treated with caution.[5]

We will use lobbying models in some of the coming chapters. They naturally belong in chapter 7 on special-interest politics—arising in areas such as trade policy, regulation, and regional transfers—where the formation of lobby groups are essential for the outcome. In chapter 7 we model additional functions of lobbying; apart from the election outcome, lobbies may attempt to influence either the design of policy proposals, or the voting pattern in the legislature. We also discuss lobbying behavior in chapter 14 on growth, where special interests associated with old technologies attempt to protect their rents by lobbying for policies discriminating against modern growth-promoting technologies.

3.6   Discussion

This chapter used a simple policy example to ask a fundamental question in political economics: how does electoral competition shape the economic policies proposed during an electoral campaign? As candidates seek to win the election, they design their campaign promises to win the support of a majority of voters. Hence the policy platforms reflect the features of the electorate and the environment in which electoral competition takes place. We end by summarizing the main lessons from the chapter and use them to look ahead.

All the models in this chapter imply that both candidates converge to the same policy platform. This result reflects the assumption that candidates do not care about the policy per se, an assumption that will not be preserved in the next two chapters, especially not in chapter 5, where candidates have partisan preferences.

When voters care only about economic policies, every voter is the same from the point of view of the competing candidates. What matters for them is just how many voters prefer the proposed policies over some alternatives, not how strong these preferences are. In the one-dimensional example we considered, the only equilibrium is then a median-voter

---

5. Note, however, that a less symmetric model resulting in policy divergence would imply positive equilibrium contributions, increasing in the distance between the policy platforms.

optimum, as this policy splits the electorate exactly in half. In this case, the equilibrium size of government reflects differences between median and average income.

Conclusions differ, however, as soon as we drop the assumption that voters care only about economic policies. If some voters are more likely to reward policy with a vote, these voters become more important than others in the candidates' eyes. They become more influential in the electoral campaign, and both candidates seek to please them, rather than the electorate at large. Intensity of preferences now matters for the equilibrium policy outcome, as voters trade off policy benefits against intrinsic party preferences. Electoral competition caters to all the voters, but with weights reflecting their relative responsiveness.

Voters' responsiveness to policy is not given, however. It reflects the voters' information and candidates' advertising. But money or direct work in the campaign can often buy these additional determinants of the election outcome. Campaign contributions matter because they allow politicians to increase their relative popularity in the electorate at large. Groups organized to provide such contributions become more influential in the electorate campaign and receive policy favors at the expense of the unorganized.

These insights will be exploited in several parts of the book. Part 2, in particular, focuses on the determinants of alternative redistributive policies, relying on median-voter models in chapter 6 and on probabilistic voting and lobbying models in chapter 7. In chapters 12 and 14 we draw out the implications of such redistributive programs for the structure of taxation and for economic growth. In these chapters we take the political institutions as given, pretty much as we have done in this chapter. But the standard model of electoral competition also allows us to ask questions of comparative politics: how does the electoral rule shape the equilibrium policies proposed in the course of the electoral campaign? We address this question in chapter 8, contrasting majoritarian and proportional elections.

3.7   Notes on the Literature

A penetrating survey of the theoretical literature on electoral competition can be found in Osborne 1995. The textbooks by Ordeshook (1986) and Mueller (1989) also cover most of the political modeling in this chapter. Holsey and Borcherding (1997) survey different (economic and political) explanations for the size of government and its growth over time.

Downs (1957) and Hotelling (1929) are the classical studies of two-party electoral competition with deterministic voting, as studied in sections 3.2 and 3.3. Bergstrom and Goodman (1973) pioneered the empirical application of the median-voter model to explain the supply of public goods. Romer (1975) and Roberts (1977) developed a theoretical median-voter model of redistributive taxation akin to the model in the chapter, a model that Meltzer and Richard (1981) extended and popularized.

Chapter 2 includes references to the early literature on electoral competition with probabilistic voting. Ledyard (1984) gives some micropolitical foundations for the probabilistic voting model in a spatial setting. He models the individual voter's decision whether to abstain or take the costly action of voting (for her favored candidate). Candidates are uncertain about the bliss points of individual citizens, and the expected vote changes smoothly with small changes in policy because the costs of voting are assumed to have a well-specified distribution in the electorate. In the model formulated in section 3.4, voters instead have preferences over some policy-independent (and nonpliable) attribute of the candidates, as also assumed by Enelow and Hinich (1982). The relative preferences for the candidates are distributed in the population, with a mean unknown to the candidates at the time they commit to their electoral platforms. This setting is adapted from Lindbeck and Weibull's (1987) model, which dealt with redistributive transfers to different groups of voters out of a given budget.

A rather different model of electoral competition, in which candidates commit to mixed strategies promising lotteries to voters, is due to Myerson (1993b). See also Aragones and Postlewaite 1999.

The classic studies of lobbying and influence activities by interest groups include Olson (1965) and Becker (1983). The specific extension of the probabilistic voting model to include lobbies follows Baron (1994) in letting campaign contributions influence the electoral outcome, given the candidates' platforms. Baron distinguishes between informed and uninformed voters, assuming that the latter can be influenced by campaign spending. The model in section 3.5 instead follows Bennedsen's (1998) formulation, which assumes that all voters can be influenced. Other functions and models of lobbying are discussed in chapter 7 on special-interest politics.

3.8 Problems

1. Noncredible commitments and probabilistic voting

Suppose that agents' preferences over policies (q_1, q_2) are given by

$$\ln(y - q_1 - q_2) + \alpha^i \ln(q_1) + (1 - \alpha^i) \ln(q_2),$$

with $y > 4$, $\alpha^i \in (0, 1)$, and $q_1 + q_2 < y$. The timing is as follows. First, two politicians $P = A, B$ select platforms (q_1^P, q_2^P). They can commit to implement policy q_1^P but not policy q_2^P. Second, the election is held. Last, the winner implements q_1^P and selects q_2^P according to his preferences, that is, he maximizes:

$$\max_{q_2} \left[\ln(y - q_1^P - q_2) + \alpha^P \ln(q_1^P) + (1 - \alpha^P) \ln(q_2) \right].$$

We assume that the intrinsic parameters of voters α^i are drawn from a common knowledge distribution $F(\cdot)$. At the date the platforms are offered, voters have beliefs about the politicians' preference parameters, α^P. They are represented by the probability distributions $F^P(\cdot)$.

a. Determine the policy q_2^P that the winner selects. Characterize the expected utility of voter i when politician P announces q_1^P. Show that the voters' preferences over politician P's policy depend on their beliefs.

b. Characterize the voter who is indifferent between voting for politician A and voting for politician B when q_1^A and q_1^B are announced. Characterize the vote share of politician A for all (q_1^A, q_1^B).

c. Suppose that agents have the same beliefs about politicians, that is, $F^A = F^B$. Which platforms guarantee half of the electorate for each politician? What happens if beliefs differ?

2. Downsian competition in a simple public-good model

Consider the economy described in problem 2 of chapter 2. More precisely, agent i's preferences over a publicly provided good y and a privately provided good c^i is expressed by

$$w^i = c^i + \alpha^i V(y),$$

where $V(\cdot)$ is a concave, well-behaved function and α^i is the intrinsic parameter of agent i that is drawn from distribution $F(\cdot)$ with mean α. Again, all individuals have initial resources only in the private good, $e^i = 1$ for all i, and one unit of private good is required to produce one unit of public good. To finance the public-good production, the government raises a tax q on each individual so that agent i's budget constraint is $c^i \leq 1 - q$.

a. Derive the policy preferences of each agent $W(q; \alpha^i)$ as well as the social optimum in this economy.

Suppose that two politicians $P = A, B$ select platforms q^A and q^B. Assume that each maximizes the expected value of some exogenous rent R. Call π_P the vote share for politician P; then P's probability of winning the election is $p_P = \text{Prob}\,(\pi_P \geq \frac{1}{2})$ and his expected utility is then $p_P R$. First, the two candidates announce their platforms simultaneously and noncooperatively. Then, elections are held. Last, the elected politician implements his announced policy.

b. Assume that $\alpha^i = \alpha$. Determine the candidates' probability of winning. What are the announced platforms and which one is implemented? Discuss.

c. Determine each candidate's probability of winning when agents are heterogeneous. What are the selected platforms in that case? Which one is implemented?

d. What are the model's economic predictions? Discuss.

3. A simple model of probabilistic voting

Consider the same model as in problem 2, but assume that three factors affect voter i's voting strategy: (1) the economic policy implemented q, (2) his individual ideological bias σ^i toward candidate B, and (3) the popularity δ of politician B. We assume that σ^i is uniformly distributed on $[-\frac{1}{2\phi}, \frac{1}{2\phi}]$. Moreover, δ is the same for all voters and is drawn from the uniform distribution on

$$\left[-\frac{1}{2\psi}, \frac{1}{2\psi}\right].$$

The distributions are common knowledge, but only agent i observes his own parameter σ^i. Then, i's preferences over the policy implemented by A are summarized by $W(q^A; \alpha^i)$, whereas the preferences over the policy implemented by politician B take the final form

$$W(q^B, \alpha^i) + \sigma^i + \delta.$$

The timing is as follows: first, each voter observes σ^i, and politicians simultaneously and noncooperatively announce platforms q^A and q^B. Second, δ is realized. Third, elections take place, and last, the announced policy is implemented.

a. Give an interpretation of σ^i. Characterize the agent who is indifferent between voting for politician A and voting for politician B for given policies q^A and q^B. Suppose that $\alpha^i = \alpha$. Deduce candidate A's vote share as well as his probability of winning.

b. Which platforms do the politicians select? Which one is implemented? Discuss.

c. Suppose that agents are heterogeneous. What does this imply for the equilibrium?

d. Discuss your results and compare them with the results obtained in problem 2.

4. Probabilistic voting in the presence of groups of voters

Consider a modified version of the previous model. More precisely, we assume that the population consists of three kinds of voters $J = \{R, M, P\}$ with intrinsic parameters α^J. The proportion of agents in group J is denoted by λ^J, and $\sum_{J=1}^{3} \lambda^J = 1$. Besides, $\sum_{J=1}^{3} \alpha^J \lambda^J = \alpha$. Once more, the voting strategy of voter i in group J is affected by (1) the economic policy that is implemented q, (2) his individual ideological bias σ^{iJ} toward candidate B, and (3) the popularity δ of politician B. We assume that σ^{iJ} is uniformly distributed on

$$\left[-\frac{1}{2\phi^J}, \frac{1}{2\phi^J}\right],$$

where ϕ^J is group specific, and that δ is drawn from the uniform distribution on

$$\left[-\frac{1}{2\psi}, \frac{1}{2\psi}\right].$$

As in the previous problem, the distributions are common knowledge, but only agent i observes his own parameter σ^i. The preferences of i over the policy implemented by A are summarized by $W(q_A, \alpha^J)$, whereas his preferences over the policy implemented by politician B are given by

$$W(q^B, \alpha^J) + \sigma^{iJ} + \delta.$$

The timing is the same as in problem 3.

a. Which voter is indifferent between voting for A and voting for B in each group? Deduce candidate A's vote share and compute his probability of winning for given platforms.

b. Characterize each politician's optimal platform. Is the selected policy the socially optimal one? Provide an economic intuition of the result.

c. Suppose now that σ^{iJ} is drawn from a general common-knowledge distribution $G^J(\cdot)$ with density $g^J(\cdot)$. Show that restricting oneself to a uniform distribution does not qualitatively affect the results.

d. Suppose that δ is drawn from the distribution $L(\cdot)$ with density $l(\cdot)$ and that σ^{iJ} remains uniformly distributed. Again, show that restricting oneself to a uniform distribution does not qualitatively affect the results.

5. Lobbying

Consider the same model as in problem 4 but now assume that each group can decide to contribute to the campaign of politician P. Let O^J be the indicator variable that takes the value of 1 if group J wants to finance a party and the value of 0 if group J does not contribute to any campaign. Suppose that the willingness to contribute is exogenous. Let C_P^J denote the contribution per member in group J to politician P. The total contribution of each member in group J is thus $C_A^J + C_B^J$. For any agent in group J, the cost of contributing to the campaign is $D(C_A^J + C_B^J) = \frac{1}{2}(C_A^J + C_B^J)^2$. Whenever a candidate receives a contribution, he spends the money and his popularity is affected. For simplicity, party B's popularity is given by

$$\delta = \tilde{\delta} + h \cdot (C_B - C_A),$$

where C_P represents the sum of the contributions received by party P, namely $C_P = \sum_J O^J \alpha^J C_P^J$, and h is a parameter measuring the campaign's effectiveness. Assume that $\tilde{\delta}$ is uniformly distributed with density on

$$\left[-\frac{1}{2\psi}, \frac{1}{2\psi} \right].$$

The timing is as follows. First, each voter observes σ^i and politicians announce their platforms. Second, groups fix their contributions simultaneously. Third, the popularity parameter is realized and the election takes place. Last, the winner's platform is implemented.

a. In each group, characterize the agent who is indifferent between voting for politician A and voting for politician B for given levels of contributions. Determine politician A's vote share as well as his probability of winning the election.

b. From an ex ante perspective, what is the objective function of each member in the group if the latter wants to finance politicians? Determine the optimal contribution per member in each group. Discuss.

c. Determine the platforms politicians select if all groups are willing to contribute (i.e., $O^J = 1$ for all J) or no group contributes (i.e., $O^J = 0$ for all J). What are the contributions in equilibrium? What happens if σ^i has the same distribution in all groups, namely $\phi^J = \phi$ for all J. Discuss.

d. Suppose now that some groups prefer not to finance politicians (i.e., there exists J such that $O^J = 0$). What are the politicians' platforms and which policy is finally implemented? Discuss. Which groups have the strongest incentives to become organized?

4 Agency

To what extent can political representatives exploit their political power to appropriate resources for themselves at the voters' expense? Can the voters discipline politicians just through the implicit incentives elections offer? And how does this depend on the economic and political environment? These are the questions addressed in this chapter.

The conflict of interest between voters and rent-seeking political representatives is an old theme of the public choice (Virginia) school and is perhaps most clearly spelled out in Brennan and Buchanan's (1980) model of the government as a malevolent revenue-maximizing Leviathan. According to the Chicago school, however, the forces of political competition can align politicians' and voters' interests, a point made most forcefully by Wittman (1989, 1995). This chapter picks up this theme by giving political candidates the ability and the incentives to extract rents, in the context of the public finance problem formulated in chapter 3. By a sequence of examples—different variations on this public finance problem—we show that elections generally serve to promote efficiency. But the extent to which rents are eliminated hinges on the assumptions about candidate attributes, enforceability, and information.

These agency issues are discussed in the mode of both preelection and postelection politics. We start in sections 4.1 and 4.2 with the model of electoral competition introduced in chapter 3, where candidates commit to policies ahead of the elections. A central question here is whether electoral competition induces the candidates to announce optimal policy platforms from the voters' viewpoint, or whether they instead announce policies with high taxes and low benefits, implying positive rents for themselves. The answer turns out to depend on the specific assumptions of how electoral competition takes place.

We drop the commitment assumption gradually in section 4.3, discussing the nonverifiability, nonobservability, and nonenforceability of electoral promises. The purpose is to gain some perspective on why it may be difficult for political candidates to commit themselves to a certain policy stance.

Sections 4.4 and 4.5 instead drop the commitment assumption completely, assuming that no electoral promises can be enforced. The political constitution is here viewed as an incomplete contract: politicians have complete discretion once in office, and all the voters can do is to oust them from office at the next elections. The central tension is still between policies that please the voters and rents appropriated by the politicians. But the role of elections is very different than in the first half of the chapter. We discuss two ways in which elections can discipline the incumbent. In the electoral accountability model of section 4.4, citizens vote retrospectively and deliberately punish bad behavior by removing misbehaving incumbents from office. In the career concern model of section 4.5, electoral incentives are more indirect. Economic performance signals the incumbent's competence, and voters reward competence with reappointment. This creates incentives to abstain from rent seeking, to appear more competent and increase the chances of reelection. Section 4.6 summarizes the main results and indicates some unresolved questions.

4.1 Efficient Electoral Competition

Since we want to focus on the agency problem, we add another possible use of tax revenues: government spending can also take the form of "rents" for politicians. Thus we write the government budget constraint as

$$\tau y = g + r, \tag{4.1}$$

where y is average income and r represents rents that benefit politicians but not the general citizen. As in chapter 3, however, r appears directly neither in the citizens' preferences nor in their budget constraint. We can conceptualize these rents in a variety of ways, from party finance to outright diversion of resources for private use in connection with the production of public goods. Whatever the interpretation, we assume that r is nonnegative and bounded: $0 \leq r \leq \bar{r}$. We start out by assuming that $\bar{r} = y$, that is, the only constraint on rents is the available tax base.

To give an incentive for rent seeking, we assume that the two political candidates value both the (exogenous) ego-rents, R, discussed in chapter 3 and the (endogenous) rents, r, introduced here. Thus, we write the objective function of candidate P as

$$\mathsf{E}(v_P) = p_P(R + \gamma r), \tag{4.2}$$

where E denotes the expectations operator, with expectations taken over the election outcome. The parameter γ measures the transaction costs associated with rent appropriation. We assume throughout that $0 \leq \gamma \leq 1$. The higher is γ, the lower are the transaction costs for rent appropriation. Transparency of the budget or administrative procedures may be important determinants of these transaction costs, but they are not part of the analysis, and hence γ is exogenously given. Otherwise, the economic model is the same as in chapter 3.

We start with the same political model as in section 3.3. That is, the income distribution $F(\cdot)$ is continuous; candidates have no ideological attributes, and are identical in all respects. The timing of events is as follows: (1) Platforms $\mathbf{q}_A = (g_A, r_A)$, $\mathbf{q}_B = (g_B, r_B)$ are announced. (2) Elections are held. (3) The winner's platform is implemented. It is most realistic to think about the candidates announcing a platform with a tax rate, as well as a level of government spending. Higher taxes than necessary then implies some rents lost in the process of public production. It is clearer analytically, however, to discuss the results in terms of g and r. Section 4.3 discusses more closely the assumption that candidates can commit to any platform.

How do voters evaluate the platforms? Using (4.1), we can now write the policy preferences of citizen i as

$$W^i(q) = (y - (g + r)) \frac{y^i}{y} + H(g).$$

Though defined over two dimensions, these preferences clearly satisfy the intermediate-preference property, definition 4 of chapter 2. All voters agree that rents are a waste, whereas the conflict over spending remains as before. Repeating the argument of optimal voting behavior in section 3.3 and appealing to the intermediate-preference property, we can write candidate A's probability of winning as

$$p_A = \begin{cases} 0 & \text{if} \quad W^m(\mathbf{q}_A) < W^m(\mathbf{q}_B) \\ \frac{1}{2} & \text{if} \quad W^m(\mathbf{q}_A) = W^m(\mathbf{q}_B) \\ 1 & \text{if} \quad W^m(\mathbf{q}_A) > W^m(\mathbf{q}_B). \end{cases}$$

That is to say, the voter with median income is still pivotal in the election.

Applying the same kind of separation argument as in section 3.3, we conclude that the unique equilibrium has both candidates announcing the median voter's preferred policy:

$$g_A = g_B = g^m = H_g^{-1}(y^m/y)$$
$$r_A = r_B = r^m = 0.$$

Why can the candidates not get away with a platform involving positive rents? Assume, to the contrary, that both have announced the pivotal voter's desired spending g^m and positive rents, $r' > 0$. But then any of the candidates can increase his probability of winning from $\frac{1}{2}$ to 1 by instead offering rents $r' - \varepsilon$ (and thus lower taxes) to the voters. Furthermore, this deviation is profitable, as long as the exogenous rents R are larger than $2\varepsilon - \gamma r'$. As ε could be made arbitrarily small, the argument is valid for any positive value of r'. Intuitively, there is a "Bertrand competition" for the exogenous rents R. This competition becomes so stiff that it drives the endogenous rents r to zero.

Here, the Chicago school claim is clearly correct, despite a conflict of interest among the voters over the size of government. The equilibrium is efficient from the voters' point of view (i.e., it entails no waste), because the prize for winning the elections keeps politicians honest. The positive implications for taxes and spending are identical to those derived and discussed in section 3.3.

4.2   Inefficient Electoral Competition

To see how positive equilibrium rents may remain in electoral competition, let us return to the probabilistic voting model of section 3.4. Our argument in this section is related to the recent work by Polo (1998) and by J. Svensson (1997).

We thus assume that the income distribution is discrete among three groups J. Candidates have ideological attributes in addition to their platforms and voters have preferences over these attributes. To highlight the implications for rents in the most transparent way, we assume the distribution of voters' ideological bias to be the same in all groups, making the number of swing voters identical: $\phi^J = \phi$ for all J.

In analogy with (3.10) and given $\phi^J = \phi$ for all J, we can derive candidate A's probability of winning as

$$p_A = \frac{1}{2} + \psi[W(g_A, r_A) - W(g_B, r_B)], \tag{4.3}$$

where $W = \sum_J \alpha^J W^J$. Thus, the group-specific parts of preferences over spending and taxes average out, as all groups are equally attractive targets for the candidates.

Faced with this election probability, candidate A sets policy to maximize expected rents in (4.2) and so does candidate B, with $p_B = (1 - p_A)$. By symmetry, both candidates face the same problem and choose the same platforms, in the same way as in section 3.3. But what platforms do they choose? Consider the first-order condition for g_A:

$$\frac{\partial[E(v_A)]}{\partial g_A} = (R + \gamma r_A)\frac{\partial p_A}{\partial g_A} = (R + \gamma r_A)\psi W_g(g_A, r_A) = 0.$$

As $W_{gr} = 0$, spending on public goods is socially optimal (i.e., it satisfies $W_g = 0$), whatever the level of r.

It is tempting to conjecture that optimality extends to rent extraction, but that conjecture turns out to be incorrect. To see why, note that by (4.3) candidate A's election probability is affected by a marginal increase in his rents—an increase in taxes with spending held constant—according to

$$\frac{\partial p_A}{\partial r_A} = \psi W_r = -\psi. \tag{4.4}$$

Although a platform with higher rents is attractive in itself, it also decreases the probability of election, creating a trade-off for the candidate. But unlike in the previous section, a marginal increase in rents does not imply discrete jumps in the probability of winning. Using (4.4), the first-order condition for r_A, evaluated at $q_A = q_B$, is

$$\frac{\partial[E(v_A)]}{\partial r_A} = (R + \gamma r_A)\frac{\partial p_A}{\partial r_A} + p_A\gamma = -(R + \gamma r_A)\psi + \frac{1}{2}\gamma \leq 0 \quad [r_A \geq 0],$$

where the second equality exploits the fact that $p_A = \frac{1}{2}$ in equilibrium. The second row states the complementary slackness condition for r. Thus equilibrium rents are

$$r = \max\left[0, \frac{1}{2\psi} - \frac{R}{\gamma}\right]. \tag{4.5}$$

Why are rents not always competed away, as in the median-voter model? Because the two candidates are no longer perfect substitutes for all voters, and hence the policy platforms do not entirely determine the electoral outcome. Swing voters in each group do indeed consider the candidates perfect substitutes and punish a rent-seeking candidate by immediately shifting their vote. But other voters do not, because of their ideological preferences. The uncertain outcome of relative popularity means that the identity of swing voters is not known. This creates electoral uncertainty, which weakens electoral competition, as candidate A's probability of winning falls only at the finite rate ψ for a marginal increase in rents. The lower is this rate—that is, the more uncertain is the election outcome (a lower ψ)—the larger is the scope for seeking rents, as stated in (4.5). Similarly, a lower exogenous value of holding office (a lower R) or lower transaction costs (a higher γ) promote high endogenous rents. As further discussed by Polo (1998) and in problem 1 of this chapter, the crux of generating positive rents is thus the uncertainty about the electoral outcome, as captured by the uncertainty about δ.

In this probabilistic voting model, equilibrium public goods are optimally provided. But equilibrium rents may be positive, implying that the voters pay more than the optimal amount of taxes. It is plausible to associate the rents with inefficiency in the production of public goods. In this interpretation, observed spending becomes higher than optimal. The model thus implies that, ceteris paribus, we should observe an association between rents cum high and inefficient government spending, on the one hand, and ideological dispersion or electoral instability, on the other. The empirical validity of this interesting prediction remains to be investigated. Alesina, Easterly, and Baqir (1997) provide some evidence of a positive correlation between the size of government and ethnic and linguistic fractionalization, however, which might be consistent with this theoretical model.

Of course, the whole argument in this section takes the political candidates' attributes as given. But with some entry barriers into politics, rents might not disappear even if candidate identity were to be endogenously determined. Moreover, if the distribution of relative popularity is not perfectly symmetric, as assumed here, policy convergence is lost, and the relatively more popular candidate can typically afford to grab bigger rents in equilibrium. Both results are discussed in Polo 1998. Moreover, problem 1 of this chapter deals formally with rents in lopsided elections.

4.3 Enforceability, Verifiability, and Observability

So far in this chapter, we have assumed that candidates can make binding commitments to electoral platforms. They have no discretion to seek rents after the election, even though they have strong incentives for this. In this section, we illustrate how postelection discretion may arise and its implications for policy. The discussion borrows some general insights and some terminology of modern contract theory (see in particular Hart 1995 and Tirole 1999).

Since voter and candidate heterogeneity are unrelated to the argument here, we assume that income distribution is degenerate, with $y^i = y$ for all i, and that the two candidates have no ideological attributes and are identical in all respects. To highlight the crucial role of information, however, we introduce a new variable: the cost of transforming private output into public goods. We denote this relative cost by θ and assume that it is a random variable. The government budget constraint can now be written as

$$\tau y = \theta g + r. \tag{4.6}$$

A higher value of θ means that public goods have become more costly. The new sequence of events is as follows: (1) Candidates announce their platforms. (2) Elections are held. (3) θ is realized. (4) The winner sets policy.

The cost of providing public goods is thus not fully known at the electoral stage. As an example, think about g as representing the provision of external or internal security to the citizens. In this case, the state of the international or national environment could easily shift so as to make it more or less costly to provide the same level of security. What the voters would like from each candidate is thus a *state-contingent* policy platform. This presents a problem in that it may be quite difficult to observe, verify, or even describe the state. Obviously, the efficient supply of public goods $g^*(\theta) \equiv H_g^{-1}(\theta)$ is decreasing in θ. We assume parameters are such that the associated level of efficient taxes

$$\tau^*(\theta) = \frac{\theta g^*(\theta)}{y}$$

is increasing in θ.[1] For simplicity, we start by assuming that θ can take on only two values, one low and one high, such that $\theta \in \{\underline{\theta}, \overline{\theta}\}$.

4.3.1 Enforceable and Verifiable Promises

Consider first the case in which an independent and benevolent judiciary is available. This third party can *enforce* promises made in the campaign after the elections. We thus assume that a politician who attempts to break his campaign promises can be stopped (by a large penalty), provided that the promises are (describable and) verifiable. To begin with, suppose that θ is indeed not only observable, but also verifiable. Then candidates are able to make binding commitments to state-contingent policy platforms $[g_P(\theta), r_P(\theta)]$. Candidates still maximize the objective in (4.2), augmented by the uncertainty over θ. Voters prefer the candidate whose platform gives them the highest expected utility $\mathsf{E}_\theta[W(g(\theta), r(\theta); \theta)]$, where E_θ denotes expectations taken over θ. Therefore, candidate A's probability of

---

1. This assumption requires the marginal utility of public goods, H_g, not to be too flat.

winning is

$$p_A = \begin{cases} 0 & \text{if} \quad \mathsf{E}_\theta[W(g_A(\theta), r_A(\theta); \theta)] < \mathsf{E}_\theta[W(g_B(\theta), r_B(\theta); \theta)] \\ \frac{1}{2} & \text{if} \quad \mathsf{E}_\theta[W(g_A(\theta), r_A(\theta); \theta)] = \mathsf{E}_\theta[W(g_B(\theta), r_B(\theta); \theta)] \\ 1 & \text{if} \quad \mathsf{E}_\theta[W(g_A(\theta), r_A(\theta); \theta)] > \mathsf{E}_\theta[W(g_A(\theta), r_B(\theta); \theta)]. \end{cases} \quad (4.7)$$

Given this probability and $p_B = 1 - p_A$, the two candidates face the same sharp incentives as in section 3.2. That is, whoever moves closer to the state-contingent policy the voters desire discontinuously increases his probability of winning. The outcome must thus be optimal with

$$g_A(\theta) = g_B(\theta) = g^*(\theta)$$
$$r_A(\theta) = r_B(\theta) = 0.$$

In this case, each candidate is thus able to offer the voters a "complete enforceable contract." The competition between the candidates over the exogenous awards from winning makes them both offer the best contract in the set of possible contracts. The combination of enforceability, verifiability, and electoral competition is thus sufficient to ensure implementation of the efficient state-contingent policy.

4.3.2 Enforceable Nonverifiable Promises

Suppose, as in the previous subsection, that the judiciary can enforce electoral promises after the election. But now the state θ, even though observable to the voters and the judiciary, is *nonverifiable*. Obviously, this makes it impossible to enforce state-contingent platforms. As a result, verifiable platforms have to take the form of a non-state-contingent pair $[g_P, \tau_P]$ (it is more instructive, at this point, to consider announcements of taxes rather than rents). Voters still prefer the candidate promising them the highest expected utility, so p_A is given by (4.7) if we replace state-contingent platforms with simple platforms. But now the candidates' postelection incentives come into play. Suppose the elected candidate faces the state $\theta = \underline{\theta}$, in which public goods are cheap. He can always claim the contrary, that is, that they are expensive, $\theta = \overline{\theta}$. Moreover, the winner always has an incentive to misreport precisely in this way; as the expensive state is associated with higher taxes and lower spending, he can pocket the difference in the form of rents.

From this argument, it follows that the best the voters can hope for is an optimal policy in the expensive state. Competition between the candidates in credible policy promises indeed leads them to converge to platforms with precisely that property:

$$g_A = g_B = g^*(\overline{\theta})$$
$$\tau_A = \tau_B = \overline{\theta} g^*(\overline{\theta})/y.$$

Equilibrium policy thus eliminates rents in the expensive state, $r(\overline{\theta}) = 0$. If it did not, one of the candidates could raise his vote share for sure by raising the voters' expected welfare. Although the voters would like a higher level of spending and a lower level of taxes in the cheap state, the candidates cannot credibly make such a state-contingent promise. Promising higher constant spending than $g^*(\overline{\theta})$ or lower constant taxes than $\overline{\theta}g^*(\overline{\theta})/y$ is also not credible, as such a policy would not be affordable in the expensive state. It follows that taxes must remain high and spending low in the cheap state. The elected candidate captures the difference as rents for himself. Formally, by the government budget constraint, we have

$$r(\theta) = (\overline{\theta} - \theta)g^*(\overline{\theta}).$$

The normative implications are clear. When candidates can only enter into "incomplete contracts" with the voters, delegating decision making to elected representatives means giving up real decision-making power. The elected candidate exploits this power to claim equilibrium rents when circumstances so allow. A positive implication is that public activities, the costs of which are hard to verify or describe, leave more scope for rent seeking. If defense is such an activity, "peace dividends" may not take the form of lower spending but instead show up in maintained spending levels and more inefficiency. Clearly, the scope for rent seeking is larger for a larger range of uncertainty regarding θ. This suggests that countries with more volatile political environments should have higher and more wasteful spending, ceteris paribus. It also follows that rent-seeking politicians may have an incentive to make public activities nontransparent so as to increase the scope for diversion.

Methodologically, we learn that full commitment to electoral platforms is a very strong assumption, if the politicians' postelection incentives are not in line with their preelection promises. We will encounter a similar point in chapter 5 on partisan politicians. In chapter 3, this tension did not arise because candidates did not care about the policy being implemented.

4.3.3 Nonenforceable Promises

Up to this point in the section, we have assumed that any ex post verifiable promises by politicians can indeed be enforced. That is a strong assumption, particularly since elected politicians appoint members of the judiciary and are capable of altering the legal code, making enforcement harder. If no outside enforcement (or other checks and balances) is present, the equilibrium in this model is disastrous for the voters. Preelection policy promises have no credibility whatsoever, and any elected candidate follows a "Leviathan policy," in which voters are fully taxed and no public goods are delivered in both states of the world:

$$g(\theta) = 0, \quad \tau(\theta) = 1, \quad r(\theta) = y. \tag{4.8}$$

An obvious counterargument is that a politician who engaged in such diverse behavior would completely ruin his reputation and never be reelected. The same critique may be levied against the equilibrium under nonverifiability to the extent that voters observe θ—even though they cannot verify it—so that they realize what is going on. This counterargument certainly has some force, but note well what it implies: "never reelect" must mean that citizens vote not in a *forward-looking,* but in a *backward-looking* way. We have, of course, forced them to look forward by the timing assumed in the policy games, so far. An alternative modeling assumption, necessary to make sense of the reputational argument, would be to study repeated, perhaps infinitely repeated, elections. In the next section, we use an even simpler setting to illustrate how elections may enforce discipline on elected incumbents, even when politicians are unable to commit. But such discipline does indeed require backward-looking voting behavior.

4.4   Electoral Accountability

To illustrate the prospective role of elections as a disciplining device, we adapt our simple static policy example so as to illustrate the basic insight from fully intertemporal models of electoral accountability. These have their roots in the work by Barro (1973) and Ferejohn (1986).

4.4.1   Rents from Incumbent Power

We change the model's timing to focus on the behavior of elected incumbents with full discretion: implicitly we are assuming nonenforcement (or nonverifiability), along the lines of the last subsection. Specifically, we assume that (1) θ is realized and observed by everybody. We now allow for a continuous realization of θ. (2) Voters set a reservation utility for reelecting the incumbent (see below). (3) The incumbent policymaker freely sets policy, q_I. (4) Elections are held in which the voters choose between the incumbent and an opponent. The opponent running against the incumbent is identical in all respects from the viewpoint of the voters. Thus the only reason for not reappointing the incumbent is to punish him ex post, and since the opponent is identical it is indeed (weakly) optimal for the voters to carry out this punishment.

The different timing requires a reformulation of the incumbent's objective:

$$\mathsf{E}(v_I) = \gamma r + p_I R. \tag{4.9}$$

The new formulation reflects the incumbent policymaker's full discretion over current rents r. At stake in the election are future rents, R, which should now be interpreted as the expected present value of holding office from the next period and on. In a full intertemporal setting the model would thus partly or fully determine R: see problem 2 of this chapter for an example.[2]

We assume that the voters coordinate on the same retrospective voting strategy, punishing the incumbent for bad behavior and rewarding him for good behavior. This voting strategy boils down to setting the reelection probability p_I as follows:

$$p_I = \begin{cases} 1 & \text{if} \quad W(g(\theta), r(\theta)) \geq \varpi(\theta) \\ 0 & \text{otherwise,} \end{cases} \tag{4.10}$$

where the voters' reservation utility $\varpi(\theta)$ is conditioned on the realized (and observable) state.

This voting strategy creates a trade-off for the incumbent. When setting policy at stage (3), he really has two alternatives. One is to please the voters to earn reelection. In this case he maximizes his rents subject to the constraint of generating $p_I = 1$. Solving this problem, using the definition of $W(\cdot)$ and the government budget constraint (4.6), the optimally chosen rents become

$$r(\theta) = y - \varpi(\theta) + H(g^*(\theta)) - \theta g^*(\theta). \tag{4.11}$$

In other words, the incumbent satisfies the voters' demands by choosing state-contingent spending in an optimal way and by giving them exactly the utility they require to effect his reelection, namely $W(g(\theta), r(\theta)) = \varpi(\theta)$. He keeps any remaining tax revenue as rents for himself. The incumbent's second alternative is not to satisfy the voters, thus foregoing reelection. When deviating, the best policy is to follow the Leviathan-like policy in (4.8), earning current rents corresponding to $r = y$. The incumbent prefers pleasing the voters if

$$\gamma r(\theta) + R \geq \gamma y. \tag{4.12}$$

In other words, as long as he is better off with moderate current rents plus future exogenous rents earned through reelection, he does not exploit his discretion fully.

Obviously, the voters prefer that rents be as small as possible. Suppose they are able to coordinate not only on the same retrospective voting strategy, but also on the optimal

---

2. Ferejohn (1986) embeds a related one-period game in an infinite-horizon setting with exogenous future benefits from office, whereas Persson, Roland, and Tabellini (1997) make the future benefits from office R endogenous, as the expected present value of endogenous rents from office r in future periods.

strategy. Then the voters' best choice is to set $\varpi(\theta)$ so as to satisfy (4.12) with equality in all states of the world. This strategy implies rents given by

$$r(\theta) = \text{Max}\left[0, \ y - \frac{R}{\gamma}\right] \equiv r^*,$$

for all realizations of θ. Suppose that giving up r^* leaves enough revenue for the optimal supply of public goods in every state θ, specifically,

$$\theta g^*(\theta) \leq \frac{R}{\gamma}, \quad \text{for all } \theta. \tag{4.13}$$

To achieve this level of equilibrium rents, by (4.11) the voters' reservation utility must be

$$\varpi(\theta) = y - \theta g^*(\theta) + H(g^*(\theta)) - r^*. \tag{4.14}$$

Voters thus obtain the optimal level of public goods in every state. But they have to give up some rents to avoid triggering a short-run transgression on the part of the incumbent. Note that in this equilibrium, the voters' utility is state contingent, whereas equilibrium rents are the same irrespective of the state of the world.

What determines equilibrium rents? Some implications are similar to those in section 4.2. As in that case, higher intrinsic value of public office (higher R) or higher rent extraction costs (lower γ) keep equilibrium rents down. But in the present case rents are higher if the tax base is higher (y higher). This reflects the different source of rents in the current model, namely the incumbent's discretion to use his current powers to extract maximum rents from the voters. A larger available tax base makes this discretion more threatening, and the voters have to renounce larger rents.

4.4.2 Rents from Asymmetric Information

Suppose now that the voters do not observe the realization of θ at stage (1). In this case, the properties of equilibrium are reversed: equilibrium rents are state dependent, whereas voters' reservation utility is not. In the favorable (low θ) states, the elected incumbent can collect additional informational rents by delivering public goods efficiently but raising taxes and collecting high rents as if θ were high, when θ is in fact low. Since the voters do not observe θ, the best they can do is to choose a non-state-contingent cutoff level for their utility:

$$p_I = 1 \quad \text{iff} \quad w \geq \varpi.$$

Faced with such a cutoff rule, the incumbent chooses just to satisfy the voters in order to gain reelection, when this is cheap enough to do, namely when θ is low. But when θ is high, satisfying the voters becomes too expensive relative to exploiting his discretionary short-run power. Thus each level of ϖ implies a critical state θ^*, below which the incumbent just satisfies his reelection constraint with equality and uses his informational advantage to collect additional rents, and above which he accepts electoral defeat and uses his discretion to make a maximum diversion. In other words, policy is set such that

$$
w = \begin{cases} \varpi(\theta^*) & \text{for} \quad \theta \le \theta^* \\ 0 & \text{for} \quad \theta > \theta^*, \end{cases}
\tag{4.15}
$$

with $\varpi(\theta^*)$ defined as in (4.14).

What is the best voting rule for the voters? Given the one-to-one relation between ϖ and θ^*, we can treat the choice of ϖ as a choice of θ^*. By (4.15), voters' expected utility can be written as a function of θ^*, namely

$$
E(w) = \int_{\underline{\theta}}^{\theta^*} \varpi(\theta^*) \, dF(\theta) + \int_{\theta^*}^{\overline{\theta}} 0 \cdot dF(\theta) = F(\theta^*)\varpi(\theta^*),
$$

where F is the c.d.f. for θ. Voters thus face a trade-off. They can insist on a higher utility by raising their cutoff ϖ. But then they get their cutoff utility less often, as it becomes more tempting for the incumbent to disregard the reelection constraint. Formally

$$
\frac{d\theta^*}{d\varpi} = \frac{1}{\varpi_\theta(\theta^*)} < 0,
$$

as the envelope theorem implies that

$$
\varpi_\theta(\theta^*) = -\frac{g^*(\theta^*)}{y} < 0.
$$

Requiring a higher cutoff level of utility implies a higher value of θ^* such that the incumbent will behave myopically more often. The optimal cutoff thus has to satisfy the first-order condition

$$
\frac{\varpi_\theta(\theta^*)}{\varpi(\theta^*)} = -\frac{f(\theta^*)}{F(\theta^*)},
$$

which uniquely pins down θ^*, if we assume that the "hazard rate" on the right-hand side is monotonically decreasing.

Clearly, the voters are worse off when θ is nonobservable than when it is merely nonverifiable. The supply of public goods is lower for high realizations of θ:

$$
g = \begin{cases} 0 < g^*(\theta) & \text{for} \quad \theta > \theta^* \\ g^*(\theta) & \text{for} \quad \theta \le \theta^*. \end{cases}
$$

Furthermore, we obtain equilibrium rents by inserting the constant $\varpi(\theta^*)$ in (4.11) and (4.14) and exploiting the definition of socially optimal taxes $\tau^*(\theta)$:

$$r(\theta) = \begin{cases} y > r^* & \text{for } \theta > \theta^* \\ r^* + (\tau^*(\theta^*) - \tau^*(\theta))y + H(g^*(\theta)) - H(g^*(\theta^*)) \geq r^* & \text{for } \theta \leq \theta^*. \end{cases} \quad (4.16)$$

Thus rents are higher under asymmetric information for all realizations of θ except θ^* (recall that $\tau^*(\cdot)$ is increasing in θ and $g^*(\cdot)$ decreasing). When public goods are cheap the incumbent satisfies the voters' demands in the cheapest possible way and pockets the remainder for himself.[3]

This model of elections and economic performance will be extended in two directions in part 3. In chapter 9 we add conflict between the voters by allowing the incumbent policymaker also to target redistributive transfers to specific voters or groups of voters. In this case, the equilibria discussed above break down and the incumbent can appropriate more rents. Voters become engaged in a Bertrand competition over the allocation of the transfers and thus bid their reservation utilities down, though not all the way down to zero. In chapters 9 and 10 we also add conflict between several politicians who share office and bargain among each other over policy, as in a legislature. Under appropriate institutions, the resulting checks and balances allow the voters to reduce both types of rents discussed in this sections.

4.5   Career Concerns

So far in the chapter, we have discussed two roles of elections: to select among alternative economic policies (sections 4.1 and 4.2) and to hold incumbents accountable ex post for bad behavior (section 4.4). In this section we discuss a third role of elections, namely to select the most competent or talented politician. When elections have this role, politicians have an additional incentive to perform well before the elections: incumbents refrain from rent seeking because they want to appear talented to the voters. Thus elections continue to create incentives for good behavior. But now voters look back at economic performance not because they want to punish rent extraction per se, but because past

---

3. The result above relies on voters' formulating their reelection rule in terms of *utility*. As voters are assumed to observe g and τ, even though they do not observe θ, they can in fact do better by also conditioning their reelection on policy. In this case, the incumbent would optimally deliver a policy with public goods and taxes both constant at the level associated with the cutoff state $g(\theta) = g^*(\theta^*)$, $\tau(\theta) = \tau^*(\theta^*) = \frac{\theta g^*(\theta^*)}{y}$ for $\theta \leq \theta^*$. In this case, rents would be lower than in (4.16), $r(\theta) = r^* + (\theta^* - \theta)g^*(\theta^*) \geq r^*$, but still higher than in the case where θ is observable.

performance might reliably signal future competence. The agency model we exploit was originally formulated by Holmström (1982) to describe how *career concerns* shape the incentives of managers inside an organization. We show how to adapt this model to a political setup.

This role of elections suggests an important difference between policy choices made shortly before elections and policy choices made early on in the legislature. When elections are imminent, the incentives to appear competent and to perform well are stronger. This leads to a theory of electoral cycles, as in the pioneering work of Rogoff and Sibert (1988) and Rogoff (1990). In preelectoral periods, incumbents perform better by abstaining from rent extraction or attempt to signal their competence through specific policy decisions. This kind of preelectoral strategic behavior may enhance or reduce the voters' welfare: voters benefit from smaller rent extraction, but the policy distortions introduced if policies are signals of competence may harm them.

4.5.1   A Simplified Two-Period Model

Consider a two-period version of the same model as before but with the following simplifications. Taxes are fixed at $\bar{\tau}$ and the government budget must be balanced in both periods. Preferences of the voters in period $t = 1, 2$ are

$$w_t = y(1 - \bar{\tau}) + \alpha g_t,$$

where $\alpha \geq 1$ is an exogenous parameter and y denotes income. With taxes fixed, the voters' only concern is to have the highest possible quantity of public goods in each period. To simplify the analysis, the voters' marginal utility from public consumption is assumed constant, an assumption that makes voters risk-neutral with regard to the kind of uncertainty discussed here.

Politicians' only choice in this model is whether to use the given tax revenues to provide public goods, pleasing the voters, or to appropriate rents for themselves. The government budget constraint is

$$g_t = \eta(\bar{\tau} y - r_t), \tag{4.17}$$

where η is a variable reflecting the politician's *competence* in providing the public good. A higher value of η corresponds to a more competent politician, as the same resources yield a higher utility flow to the voters. Thus η is formally identical to $\frac{1}{\theta}$ in the previous section, except for the interpretation. There θ referred to exogenous events affecting the relative cost of public goods. Here η is instead a feature of the particular politician in office. We assume that competence is a permanent feature: a politician with competence η in period 1 retains that level of competence in period 2 as well. Finally, we let η be a random variable with uniform distribution over

$$\left[1 - \frac{1}{2\xi}, 1 + \frac{1}{2\xi}\right].$$

Thus, its expected value is 1, and its density is ξ. The range of this distribution is such that, irrespective of the realization of η, a nontrivial choice between rents and the public good is always possible. If a politician with competence η is removed from office, a new politician is appointed, whose competence is drawn at random from the same distribution.

As before rents are constrained to be nonnegative. But we now assume that their upper bound is binding at a level below the available tax revenue $r_t \leq \bar{r} < \bar{\tau} y$. As we shall see, this assumption gives the voters a motive to maintain competent incumbents in office. The objective of the period 1 incumbent politician is

$$v_I = r_1 + p_I \beta(R + r_2),\tag{4.18}$$

where $0 < \beta < 1$ is a discount factor and p_I is the probability that the incumbent is reelected. The quantity r_t denotes rents grabbed in period t, and R denotes the exogenous rents from winning the elections. In terms of the previous notation, we thus simplify by setting $\gamma = 1$.[4]

Policy commitments are not possible ahead of the elections. Specifically, the timing of events is as follows: (1) An incumbent politician is in office in period 1 and chooses rents for that period, r_1, without knowing his own competence η. (2) The value of η is realized and public-good provision g_1 is residually determined so as to satisfy (4.17). Voters observe their own utility but neither η nor r_1. (3) Elections are held. If the incumbent wins, his competence remains η. If he loses, an opponent is appointed with competence drawn at random from the same distribution. (4) Period 2 rents r_2 are set, and public goods are residually determined, again so as to satisfy (4.17).

Under this timing, period 2 politicians have no incentive to behave well: they always appropriate maximum rents, $r_2 = \bar{r}$, implying public spending at $g_2 = \eta(\bar{\tau} y - \bar{r})$. Voters are clearly better off with more a competent (high η) politician, as this gives them higher period 2 utility. They thus use the elections to reappoint competent politicians and oust incompetent ones, taking into account their observed utility in period 1 and knowing that the opponent's expected value at the elections is $E(\eta) = 1$. We now describe how this occurs and how it shapes politicians' incentives in period 1. As in earlier sections, each incumbent politician perceives a trade-off between current rents and the probability of winning the elections, but the economic mechanism implicit in this trade-off is different.

---

4. It may be argued that a politician's competence in providing benefits for the voters is (positively) correlated with his competence in extracting rents for himself. The model could capture this possibility, by reintroducing a random γ, correlated with η.

Equilibrium Behavior   How is the incumbent's probability of victory at the elections affected by period 1 actions? To answer, we need to describe optimal voting behavior. Consider the voters' information at the time of the elections. They know that the incumbent maximizes (4.18). Let $\tilde{r}_1$ denote the solution to the incumbent's optimization problem in period 1 (yet to be derived). Note that $\tilde{r}_1$ does not depend on η, since competence is yet unknown to the politician. At the time of the elections, voters know g_1 and $\bar{\tau}$ and can compute $\tilde{r}_1$. Hence, by (4.17), the voters can form an estimate of incumbent competence, say $\tilde{\eta}$, as

$$\tilde{\eta} = \frac{g_1}{\bar{\tau} y - \tilde{r}_1}. \tag{4.19}$$

The voters' behavior is then simple to describe: the incumbent is reappointed only if his estimated competence exceeds his opponent's expected competence:

$$\tilde{p}_I = \begin{cases} 1 & \text{iff } \tilde{\eta} \geq \mathsf{E}(\eta) = 1 \\ 0 & \text{otherwise.} \end{cases}$$

We can now compute the probability of winning the elections, as perceived by the incumbent in period 1, when choosing rents. By assumption, he does not yet know his own competence. His probability of reelection p_I is therefore given by $\text{Prob}[\tilde{p}_I = 1] = \text{Prob}[\tilde{\eta} \geq 1]$. The incumbent sets r_1, knowing that g_1 is residually determined from the government budget constraint:

$$g_1 = \eta(\bar{\tau} y - r_1). \tag{4.20}$$

Combining (4.20) and (4.19), the event $\tilde{\eta} \geq 1$ is thus equivalent to the event

$$\eta \geq \frac{\bar{\tau} y - \tilde{r}_1}{\bar{\tau} y - r_1}. \tag{4.21}$$

From the point of view of the incumbent politician, therefore, the probability of winning the elections, p_I, is the probability that (4.21) is satisfied. Under our assumption that the distribution of η is uniform, this probability can be written as

$$p_I = \frac{1}{2} + \xi \left[1 - \frac{\bar{\tau} y - \tilde{r}_1}{\bar{\tau} y - r_1} \right] \tag{4.22}$$

The incumbent thus maximizes (4.18) subject to (4.22) by choice of r_1. The resulting first-order condition is

$$1 - \frac{\xi(\bar{\tau} y - \tilde{r}_1)}{(\bar{\tau} y - r_1)^2} \beta(R + \bar{r}) = 0. \tag{4.23}$$

In equilibrium, politicians' optimal choice must be consistent with the voters' conjectures about those choices: $r_1 = \tilde{r}_1$. Thus, solving (4.23) for r_1, we obtain equilibrium rents in the first period:

$$r_1 = \bar{\tau} y - \xi \beta (R + \bar{r}). \tag{4.24}$$

Given that $r_1 = \tilde{r}_1$, it follows from (4.22) that in equilibrium, the probability of winning is $p_I = \frac{1}{2}$. This is consistent with our assumption that the incumbent does not know his own competence when setting period 1 policy.

We may also note a similarity between the present accountability mechanism and that in the previous section. As there, voters assess their own welfare in the period just before the elections and reappoint an incumbent who delivers sufficiently high welfare. By inserting (4.24) in the government budget constraint, the voters realize that in equilibrium, $g_1 = G(\eta) \equiv \xi \beta (R + \bar{r}) \eta$. Thus they reappoint the incumbent if $g_1 \geq \xi \beta (R + \bar{r})$ and oust him from office otherwise. Equivalently, we can express the voting rule in terms of the voters' reservation utility in period 1, just as in (4.10):

$$\tilde{p}_I = \begin{cases} 1 & \text{iff } w_1 = y(1 - \bar{\tau}) + \alpha G(\eta) \geq \varpi \\ 0 & \text{otherwise,} \end{cases}$$

where now $\varpi = y(1 - \bar{\tau}) + \alpha \xi \beta (R + \bar{r})$. But here this behavior by the voters does not reflect a deliberate attempt to punish an incumbent who cheated them. Rather, it reflects their inference about the incumbent's competence and their forward-looking behavior, taking into account the implications for next-period welfare. Nevertheless, this voting rule disciplines incumbent politicians to some extent. And as shown in (4.24), equilibrium rents are lower the narrower is the range of uncertainty (the higher is the density ξ) and the larger is the value of winning the elections (as captured by the term $\beta (R + \bar{r})$).

So far we have made the strong assumption that the incumbent politician does not know his own competence when setting policy in period 1. What happens when the incumbent learns his competence before setting policy in period 1, but the timing is otherwise the same? Under such asymmetric information, performance can still reveal the incumbent's competence, but things become more complicated. Voters really have to deal with an adverse selection problem, in which policy can be used as a deliberate signal of competence. Problem 4 of this chapter deals with this case, which was first studied by Rogoff and Sibert (1988) in the context of political business cycles in monetary policy. We turn to that specific topic in chapter 16 but hint at the general idea of electoral cycles in the next subsection.

4.5.2 Electoral Cycles

The model described above suggests that the incentives for an incumbent to appear competent (and hence to perform well) are stronger just ahead of the elections. It can thus easily be extended to a model of electoral business cycles. We briefly discuss such an extension in this subsection.

Here the horizon is infinite, and elections are held at the end of every *other* period. The policy instruments are as in the previous subsection: there is no debt, and taxes are fixed at $\bar{\tau}$, such that (4.17) still gives the government budget constraint. But now η_t is a moving average of shocks to competence in the current and immediately preceding period:

$$\eta_t = \mu_t + \mu_{t-1}, \tag{4.25}$$

where μ_t continues to be distributed as in the previous subsection, with mean 1 and density ξ, and it is serially uncorrelated. Thus competence changes over time, but slowly. If a policymaker was competent yesterday, he retains some of his competence today, though some may depend on new factors. This assumption is plausible, in that circumstances change over time and a policymaker who was competent in some tasks need not remain so when the tasks change.

As in the previous subsections, we assume that policy decisions in each period t are made before knowing the realization of μ_t. The realization of μ_{t-1} is known to everyone (policymaker and voters) in period t. As above, information is thus symmetric between the voters and the incumbent. This is equivalent to assuming that the initial value μ_0 is known and that g_{t-1} is publicly observed in period t, because then the realization of μ_{t-1} can be inferred from the government budget constraint and knowledge of equilibrium rents.

Under these assumptions, the equilibrium is straightforward. In off-election periods, the incumbent faces no incentive to behave well, and rents are maximal: $r_t = \bar{r}$. Even though his performance in the current period t reveals the incumbent's μ_t, the voters do not care about it, as elections take place only in period $t + 1$. At that point, voters will look ahead at period $t + 2$. By (4.25), $E(\eta_{t+2} \mid g_{t+1}) = 1 + \mu_{t+1}$. Hence knowledge of μ_t is irrelevant for the svoters.

In on-election periods, on the other hand, things are different. When period $t + 1$ comes, policy choices indeed reveal the realized value of μ_{t+1}, as shown by $E(\eta_{t+2} \mid g_{t+1}) = 1 + \mu_{t+1}$. Policy choices thus determine the election outcome. Hence, during on-election periods, policy choices are shaped by exactly the same incentives as in the previous subsection, and equilibrium rents are given by (4.24). Thus the model predicts that performance improves just before the elections: wasteful spending decreases and the quality of public consumption improves. Moreover, competent incumbents who are able to please the voters are reappointed, whereas incompetent ones are ousted from office. In this simple model, the incumbent's incentive to appear competent induces better policy performance. Thus the voters are better off during on-election periods, or to put it in terms of institution design, the voters are better off if elections are held every period.

The incentive to appear competent, however, could very well induce policy distortions that reduce the voters' welfare. To see how this could happen, let's rewrite the government budget constraint as

$$g_t = \eta_t(\bar{\tau} y + s_t),$$

where now there are no endogenous rents r, and the new variable s_t denotes "seignorage," or more generally a hidden and distorting tax the voters observe and pay only after the elections. Politicians maximize the voters' welfare but also care about the probability of winning, because they value the exogenous rents from office, R.[5] They set s_t at the start of the period, knowing μ_{t-1}, and then μ_t is realized. Writing down these assumptions explicitly and solving for the equilibrium yields the result that the equilibrium policy is optimal for the voters during off-election periods but not just ahead of the elections. Problem 3 of this chapter deals explicitly with this extension, but it is worth stating the intuition for the results. During on-election periods the incumbent still wants to appear competent. To do so, he must increase public consumption, but now this implies increasing seignorage above the socially optimal level.

The two versions of electoral cycles thus have different implications for the voters. With endogenous rents, the incumbent trades off decreased rents for himself against a higher probability of winning the next election. Elections are thus good for the voters. With seignorage, the incumbent trades off additional policy distortions for the voters (about whom he cares) against a higher probability of winning. In this sense, elections reduce the voters' welfare. Yet elections still serve a useful purpose: namely, to select the best candidate for office. Hence it does not immediately follow that election dates ought to be very far apart, despite the induced policy distortions.

We will encounter the career concern model in different parts of the book, building on the basic ideas developed in this section. In chapter 9, we use it to discuss alternative electoral systems, contrasting local and national elections, and majoritarian and proportional elections. As already mentioned, we also use it in chapter 16 to analyze an electoral cycle that induces policy distortions with regard to monetary policy.

4.6 Discussion

In this chapter, we laid out a new set of tools for modeling political equilibria. Substantively, however, the chapter revolved around a fundamental question in political theory: to

---

5. When politicians also care about the voters' welfare, besides their own rents, we can relax the assumption that $\bar{\tau}$ is exogenously fixed. We made this assumption in the previous subsection because the equilibrium value of τ is indeterminate unless it is exogenously fixed. But with politicians who also care about the voters, a well-defined optimality condition pins down the value of τ.

what extent can elections solve the agency problem between the citizens and their elected representatives? We hinted at some prospective answers in very different models of politics.

In the preelection model of politics studied in sections 4.1 and 4.2, the answer depends on whether the voters perceive the two competing candidates as good substitutes. In the Downsian model with identical candidates, endogenous rents from office are entirely dissipated. When instead intrinsic differences remain between the candidates, so that economic policy is not the only determinant of elections, rents remain in equilibrium. We use this model again in chapter 8, when we ask how serious the agency problem is under different electoral rules. In the two postelection models of politics studied in sections 4.4 and 4.5, elections also discipline the politicians and limit rent extraction but through an entirely different mechanism, namely by making reappointment conditional on good economic performance. This kind of retrospective voting punishes the incumbent—directly or indirectly—for his bad behavior but still leaves him with positive rents. We use similar postelection models of politics extensively in chapters 9 and 10 to address a number of questions in comparative politics, including how different electoral rules and different political regimes handle the agency problem.

All these models capture important aspects of reality, but they are not without problems. The preelection model of politics stretches things too far by assuming credible commitments to policy platforms in the electoral campaign. As we have seen in section 4.3, this assumption—if taken literally—requires unrealistic assumptions about enforcement and information. Still, the promises in the electoral campaign are not irrelevant, perhaps because of reputational concerns.

The electoral accountability model (of section 4.4) does away with the commitment assumption. But voters are ex post indifferent between reappointing or not reappointing a misbehaving incumbent. This makes the equilibrium fragile by opening the door for multiple equilibria. Furthermore, the voting rule breaks down if the incumbent and his opponent differ in some important respect, say because they have different competence, different seniority, or different ideologies. Again, reputational concerns on the part of voters might restore these equilibria: they may realize that ex post deviation from ex ante optimal voting rules would destroy the incumbent's future incentives, or the voting rule may be interpreted as a sociological norm of behavior, which is logically consistent and self-enforcing. But reliance on such reputational arguments makes the multiple equilibrium problem even worse, particularly when the principals are a large number of uncoordinated voters.

The career concern model (of section 4.5) does not suffer from this fragility but has other deficiencies. With conflicts of interest among the voters themselves, having a competent government may be a small concern for individual voters or groups, whose primary concern is to make sure that policy is set according to their own interests, rather than to those of some other group of voters. Indirect electoral rewards based on estimates of competence may therefore be implausible in situations involving the most acute conflict of interest among the voters. It is perhaps no coincidence that this career concern model of politics has been fruitfully applied to monetary policy or to macroeconomic policy, in which the presumption of a low-dimensional conflict among voters might be most appropriate.

From a strict realism point of view, electoral promises are not binding, and policy is formed once in office. But equally clearly, what happens in the course of the electoral campaign has some relevance for the election outcome as well as for subsequent policy choices. The chapter thus points to a very interesting question, namely how to combine models of pre- and postelection politics. Austen-Smith and Banks (1989) have made an interesting attempt at progress on this difficult question, considering a two-period model of moral hazard. Even though information is symmetric, equilibria exist where the voters' strategy of reelecting the incumbent depends on the observed policy outcome relative to the platform upon which the incumbent was initially elected. This "reputational" mechanism disciplines the incumbent and creates an incumbency effect despite all politicians being identical. With asymmetric information, announcements could also play a role in information transmission, as in the standard models of regulatory agencies, starting with Baron and Myerson (1982) and Sappington (1982). Harrington (1993) indeed studies a model in which there is no agency problem but voters are asymmetrically informed about politicians' intended policies. This model has equilibria in which politicians find it optimal to reveal information truthfully to voters about their type (intended policies), as this enhances their chances of reelection. Moreover, if elected, politicians stick to their electoral campaign promises. We shall return to the difficult question of how to bridge pre- and postelection models of politics, particularly in the concluding chapter of the book.

4.7   Notes on the Literature

Brennan and Buchanan (1980) formulate the hypothesis of a Leviathan government attempting to maximize revenue for its own private agenda. A similar idea lies behind Niskanen's (1971) model of a budget-maximizing bureau, although the bureau interacts with the government rather than the voters. Breton (1974) assumes that the party holding government acts as monopolist but is constrained by the prospective entry of the opposition. Stigler (1972) and Becker (1983) suggest the idea that political competition may bring about optimal outcomes for the voters, even though these authors do not propose this as a general theory of government. Wittman (1989, 1995), in particular, has pushed the idea of the generally efficiency-enhancing effects of political competition. In a series of interesting papers, Grossman (1991, 1994, 1999) and Grossman and Kim (1996a, 1996b) focus on the agency problem in nondemocratic societies (or more generally, those in which agency is controlled through means other than elections). Laffont (1999) provides an extensive analysis of political incentive problems in regulation from the perspective of principal-agent theory. Shleifer and Vishny (1999) discuss corruption in a variety of public policy settings.

Our model of rent extraction, electoral competition, and probabilistic voting in section 4.2 is closely related to that in Polo 1998, which builds further on ideas in Grillo and Polo 1993. J. Svensson (1997) also studies a probabilistic voting model with forward-looking voters, in which electoral competition may discipline rent seeking. But in his model the rents are sought by bureaucrats who may or may not get bailed out by the politicians elected by the voters.

The discussion about commitment in section 4.3 borrows general ideas and some terminology from the theory of incomplete contracts. This theory is summarized in Hart 1995 and discussed by Tirole (1999).

The electoral accountability model of section 4.4 goes back to Barro (1973). Ferejohn (1986) extended it and studied subgame-perfect equilibria, rather than Nash equilibria. Ferejohn's infinite-horizon, incomplete-information model has exogenous rents from office and the incumbent politician minimizing effort. Persson, Roland, and Tabellini (1997) adapt that model to outright rent extraction. As discussed in the text, Austen-Smith and Banks (1989) study electoral accountability in a setting where voters adopt retrospective voting strategies that are conditioned on the difference between the incumbent's performance and his initial policy platform. Banks and Sundaram (1993) study a setting where the voters trying to hold a politician accountable face not only moral hazard, but also adverse selection problems. Banks and Sundaram (1996) add term limits and allow for more general voting strategies.

The career concern model of section 4.5 draws on Holmström 1982. Dewatripont, Jewitt, and Tirole (1999a, 1999b) discuss and extend the literature on agency and career concerns, with particular attention to alternative assumptions on information. Their approach is promising and has not been applied to politics, to our knowledge. Note, however, that the career concern model applied to a firm or an organization typically assumes that managers maximize the expected value of their competence (corresponding to $\tilde{\eta}$ in the model of section 4.5). Assuming, as we have done, that an incumbent politician maximizes his probability of reelection (and thus the probability that $\tilde{\eta}$ is above a certain threshold) is quite different, and hence the results do not immediately generalize.

A large theoretical and empirical literature on electoral or political business cycles goes back to Nordhaus 1975 and Lindbeck 1976. The first paper to study electoral cycles with rational voters and office-motivated politicians was by Rogoff and Sibert (1988), who studied a model of adverse selection with exogenous rents in which politicians care about both winning and voters' welfare. Chapter 16 further reviews the literature on electoral cycles in monetary policy.

4.8 Problems

1. Political rents in lopsided elections

This question deals with issues analyzed in Polo 1998. There are two political candidates (A and B) each proposing a level of taxes τ and a level of spending on public goods g. The public good g is financed through proportional income taxes. The candidates can, however, also use public funds for private consumption. The amount diverted to private consumption is denoted r. A continuum of citizens of measure one, indexed by i, all have the same income 1. The government's budget constraint is thus $\tau = g + r$. The citizens' preferences over private consumption, c, and a public good, g, are described by

$$u^i = c^i + H(g),$$

$c^i = (1 - \tau)$. Citizen i will vote for candidate A if

$$(1 - g_A - r_A) + H(g_A) > (1 - g_B - r_B) + H(g_B) + \sigma^i + \delta.$$

Parameters σ^i and δ describe the individual's preference in favor of party B and are distributed uniformly on

$$\left[-\frac{1}{2\phi}, \frac{1}{2\phi} \right]$$

and

$$\left[-\frac{1}{2\varphi}, \frac{1}{2\varphi} \right],$$

respectively. Political candidates care only about their private consumption, r, and their utilities are r if they win the election and zero otherwise.

a. First, consider the case in which the candidates know that the value of δ is zero. Solve for the equilibrium levels of taxes and rents.

b. Now consider the case in which the candidates know that the value of δ is greater than zero. Solve for the equilibrium levels of taxes and rents.

c. Now consider the case in which the candidates do not know the value of δ, but they know that its expected value is zero. Solve for the equilibrium levels of taxes and rents.

d. Finally, consider the case in which the candidates do not know the value of δ, and δ is uniformly distributed on

$$\left[\alpha - \frac{1}{2\varphi}, \alpha + \frac{1}{2\varphi} \right],$$

that is, one candidate may have a competitive advantage. Solve for the equilibrium levels of taxes and rents as well as the equilibrium probabilities of winning the election. Are expected rents higher in this equilibrium than in the equilibrium without advantages for either candidate? It is not necessary to specify the conditions for existence of equilibrium.

2. Rents with endogenous value of being in office

Consider the model in section 4.4. An incumbent politician proposes a level of spending on public goods, g, and a level of private rents for himself, r. The public good g is financed through proportional income taxes. A continuum of citizens of measure one, indexed by i, all have the same income y. The government's budget constraint is $\tau y = \theta g + r$, where θ is a parameter measuring the cost of providing public goods. Citizen i's preferences over private consumption c^i and a public good g are described by

$$u^i = c^i + H(g),$$

where $c^i = y(1 - \tau)$. The incumbent's utility consists only of consumption of the rents, $u = \gamma r$. The following game is repeated an infinite number of periods. (1) θ_t is realized and observed by everybody. (2) Voters set a reservation utility for reelecting the incumbent. (3) The incumbent sets the policy variables, r_t and g_t. (4) Elections are held in which the voters choose between the incumbent and an opponent with the same characteristics as the incumbent. A politician maximizes

$$\sum_{t=0}^{\infty} \beta^t p_t \gamma r_t,$$

where β^t is the subjective discount factor and p_t is the probability of the incumbent's being in office at period t. Assume that a politician who is voted out of office cannot be reelected.

The incumbent at period 0 maximizes

$$\gamma r_0 + \beta p_1 R_{I,1},$$

where $R_{I,1}$ is the value of being an incumbent in period 1. The voters coordinate on the same retrospective voting strategy, voting for the incumbent if their utility is higher than or equal to $\varpi_t(\theta_t)$.

a. Solve for the optimal voting strategy $\varpi_t(\theta_t)$.

b. Suppose that term limits are imposed that do not allow the incumbent to stay in office more than three periods. How will this affect the voters' ability to discipline the incumbent?

c. Now suppose that there are two parties to which the candidates may belong. As before, the politician may stay in office for a maximum of three terms. Assume that the voters use the rule to vote for a candidate belonging to the same party as the incumbent if and only if rents are below some specific level. Suppose further that a new party candidate may bribe the incumbent not to keep rents too high in his third term. What is the new equilibrium level of rents?

3. Electoral cycles with seignorage

Assume the following model of electoral cycles with seignorage. Let us write the government budget constraint as

$$g_t = \eta_t(\bar{\tau} y + s_t),$$

where $\bar{\tau}$ denotes fixed taxes, η_t denotes the incumbent's competency level, there are no endogenous rents r, and the variable s_t denotes "seignorage" or, more generally, a hidden and distorting tax observed and paid by the voters only after the elections. Therefore, voters' welfare is

$$w_t = y - \bar{\tau} - s_t - V(s_t) + \alpha g_t,$$

where $V(\cdot)$ is a convex function capturing the distortions of seignorage. As is common in these models, the politician's competency, η_t, is determined by

$$\eta_t = \mu_t + \mu_{t-1},$$

where μ_t is uniformly distributed with mean 1 and density ξ and is serially uncorrelated. Politicians maximize voters' welfare and reelection rents according to

$$E(w_t \mid \mu_{t-1}) + p_t R,$$

where p_t is the probability of reelection.

The stage game at time t is given by: The politician chooses s_t, given μ_{t-1} and without observing μ_t. Nature determines μ_t. Voters observe g_t only. If t is an on-election period voters reelect the incumbent politician or elect a new contender, drawn from the same distribution. If t is an off-election period, we move to the election period. The stage game is infinitely repeated.

a. Show that in off-election periods, the incumbent sets s_t optimally.

b. Find the equilibrium seignorage in on-election periods. Show that they are larger than off-election seignorage (the social optimum level).

c. Perform comparative statics with respect to the effects of the exogenous spoils of office R, the sensitivity of reelection probability ξ, and the total taxes available $\bar{\tau}$.

4. Equilibrium selection in the adverse selection model

Assume the following two-period model with adverse selection. In this model a politician knows his competence level when deciding on the rents he extracts. Specifically, suppose taxes are fixed at $\bar{\tau}$. Voters' preferences in period $t = 1, 2$ are

$$w_t = y(1 - \bar{\tau}) + \alpha g_t,$$

where $\alpha \geq 1$ is an exogenous parameter and $y = 1$ denotes income. Politicians' only choice is whether to use the given tax revenues to provide public goods, thus pleasing the voters, or to appropriate rents for themselves. The government budget constraint must be balanced in each period and is given by

$$g_t = \eta(\bar{\tau} y - r_t),$$

where η is a variable reflecting the politician's competence in providing the public good. The variable η can take on one of two values, $\frac{1}{\theta}$ and $\frac{1}{\lambda \theta}$, with equal probability, where $\lambda < 1$. A politician with competence η in period 1 also retains that level of competence in period 2. If the politician is not reelected, a contender is chosen with competence η^c, with $\frac{1}{\theta} < \eta^c < \frac{1}{\lambda \theta}$. Rents are constrained to be nonnegative. Assume the upper bound of rents to be binding at a level below the available tax revenue $r_t \leq \bar{r} < \bar{\tau} y$. The objective of the period 1 incumbent politician is

$$r_1 + p_I \beta (r_2 + R),$$

where $0 < \beta < 1$ is a discount factor and p_I is the probability that the incumbent is reelected. The quantity r_t denotes rents grabbed in period t, and R denotes the exogenous rents from winning the elections.

Policy commitments are not possible ahead of the elections. Specifically, the timing of events is as follows: (1) An incumbent politician is in office in period 1 and chooses rents for that period, r_1, knowing his own competence η. (2) The value of the public good provision g_1 is residually determined. Voters observe their own utility, but neither η nor r_1. (3) Elections are held. If the incumbent wins, his competence remains η. If he loses, an opponent is appointed with competence η^c. (4) Period 2 rents, r_2, are set, and the game ends.

a. Assume that if the politician's strategies do not reveal his level of competency, voters are not willing to reelect him. Show that pooling equilibria exist but do not survive the elimination of weakly dominated actions refinement.

b. Assume now that even if the politician's strategies do not reveal his level of competency, voters are nonetheless willing to reelect him. Show that pooling equilibria exist and survive the intuitive criterion.

5. Challenger selection procedure

In the same model as in problem 4, now assume that at the election stage a contender is drawn with competency η^c from a distribution of levels of competency $\frac{1}{\theta} - \varepsilon$ and $\frac{1}{\lambda\theta} + \varepsilon$ with equal probability (ε small). Observing η^c, voters then compare the contender's competency to the incumbent's expected competency and choose the candidate with the higher competency level. In case of a tie, the new candidate is chosen. The prior belief about the contender is that he has the levels of competency $\frac{1}{\theta}$ and $\frac{1}{\lambda\theta}$ with equal probability.

a. Write the expression for the incumbent's probability of winning.

b. Find a separating equilibrium in this model.

c. Show that pooling equilibria exist, but that they do not survive the intuitive criterion.

5 Partisan Politicians

In the previous two chapters, we have assumed that political candidates are motivated by the exogenous rents of public office and by the endogenous rents they may be able to extract by holding office. We have seen that, notwithstanding these motivations, the forces of political competition can still drive the candidates toward a policy that is beneficial for broad segments of the electorate. But an important tradition in the existing literature assumes that policy outcomes *directly* motivate political candidates or parties. This chapter uses again the basic public finance model of chapter 3 to illustrate different possible ways of modeling policy choice and the size of government with such *partisan* politicians.

In the next section, we show that, under the assumptions of full commitment ahead of the elections and voters caring only about the economic policies, the equilibrium continues to coincide with the median-voter optimum. Thus in this limiting case, the political candidates' true motivation is irrelevant, and all the results discussed in section 3.3 continue to hold.

Once we enter into postelection politics, however, by our dropping the commitment assumption, the candidates' ideological preferences drive the equilibrium. In section 5.2, we take the candidates' ideological position as fixed and assume that policy is set once the elected candidate is in office. Now the median voter continues to determine the election outcome. But equilibrium policy is at the winning candidate's bliss point, and the two candidates choose divergent policies if they have different partisan preferences.

This naturally leads to the following question: from where do these candidate preferences derive? We address this question in section 5.3, summarizing the main insights of the so-called "citizen-candidate" model. In that model different citizens simultaneously choose whether to run for office, trading off the cost of the electoral race against the benefit of implementing their desired policy if elected. Several equilibria turn out to exist, some with policy divergence, some in which the median voter runs uncontested.

Finally, in section 5.4, we consider a richer model of policy formation in which several politicians with different partisan preferences share office and bargain over policy. The model thus picks up the ideas about agenda setting and legislative bargaining introduced in chapter 2. It highlights different prospective determinants of equilibrium policy, such as the nature of the status quo policy or the strength of the power to propose.

5.1 Policy Convergence

Consider our basic model of public finance, in which income is continuously distributed in the population. Since rents are not central to the analysis, we restrict endogenous as well as exogenous rents to zero, $r = R = 0$, throughout the chapter. Thus the candidates' only motivation to win the election is to implement their desired policy. Selfish motivations could be added, but these would not yield additional or surprising insights beyond those already discussed in previous chapters. Moreover, since the relative cost of public goods does not play any role, we again set $\theta = 1$ throughout the chapter to simplify the notation. Thus the government budget constraint is once more given by

$$\tau y = g.$$

A simple way to represent the behavior of candidates directly motivated by the policy outcome is to associate each candidate with the policy preferences of a voter with a specific income level y^i, namely $W^i(g)$. The candidate then becomes a "citizen-candidate," to use the recent language introduced by Besley and Coate (1997).

We start by assuming two exogenously given political candidates, $P = L, R$. Candidate P's income level is y^P, and we assume $y^L < y^m < y^R$. Because the model naturally orders voters along a left-to-right scale, we may loosely interpret the two candidates as representing two political parties with different ideological positions, one left-wing and one right-wing, hence the notation.

In this section, we assume the following timing: (1) Each candidate announces a policy platform g_P. (2) Elections are held. (3) The winning candidate's platform is implemented. Thus the model coincides with the model of section 3.3, except for the candidates' objectives. In particular, binding commitments to policy are feasible. Wittman (1977) and Calvert (1985) first presented the ideas behind this model.

Because voters are in the same situation as in the model with office-motivated candidates, their optimal voting behavior is exactly the same. Adapting the earlier notation, we can thus reproduce (3.6) as

$$p_L = \begin{cases} 0 & \text{if} \quad W^m(g_L) < W^m(g_R) \\ \frac{1}{2} & \text{if} \quad W^m(g_L) = W^m(g_R) \\ 1 & \text{if} \quad W^m(g_L) > W^m(g_R). \end{cases} \tag{5.1}$$

When setting policy, candidate L sets g_L to maximize his expected utility:

$$\mathsf{E}[W^L(g)] = p_L W^L(g_L) + (1 - p_L)W^L(g_R), \tag{5.2}$$

given candidate R's platform g_R. Candidate R solves a symmetric problem.

Both "centrifugal" and "centripetal" political forces influence the candidates' policy choices here. Consider the incentives of the left-wing candidate, given a policy announcement $g_R < g^m$ by the right-wing candidate. On the one hand, he can raise the utility—conditional on winning—by increasing g_L toward his own bliss point

$$g^L \equiv H_g^{-1}\left(\frac{y^L}{y}\right):$$

this is the centrifugal force. On the other hand, he can increase his chances of winning by decreasing g_L toward the median voter's preferred policy: this is the centripetal force. As is evident from (5.1) and (5.2), given $g_R < g^m$, the optimal strategy for L is to decrease g_L just enough from his bliss point to raise p_L to unity but not any further. Because the same forces operate on candidate R, however, the only possible equilibrium point is that both candidates announce the median voter's preferred policy:

$$g_L = g^m = g_R.$$

Thus, the centripetal forces dominate, and we get full policy convergence, exactly as in the model of section 3.3 with office-seeking candidates and as in the model of section 4.1 with rent-seeking candidates.

Clearly, this strong result follows, since the voters care only about the candidates' policy announcements. One way to get policy divergence in equilibrium is to introduce a second dimension, making the candidates imperfect substitutes, as in the probabilistic voting model we have studied in sections 3.4 and 4.2. Because candidates lose voters at a finite rate when moving in the direction of their bliss points, the centrifugal political force manifests itself in equilibrium. Problem 1 of this chapter deals formally with this case. The result is analogous to the results in chapter 4, in which the probabilistic voting model permitted positive equilibrium rents, whereas the median-voter model did not. Probabilistic voting models with partisan candidates appear later in the book, for instance, in our discussion in chapter 14 about the politics of public debt.

But the fundamental reason why voters care only about candidates' policy announcements is our assumption that the candidates can make binding commitments to their electoral platforms. The next section relaxes this assumption, introducing a model of postelection politics with partisan politicians.

5.2 Policy Divergence

Fragility arises in the equilibrium discussed in the last section because the winning candidate sets a policy, after the election, that is off his bliss point—and potentially far off, if the distance $g_P - g^m$ is large. The problem is analogous to the tension arising in chapter 4, when a rent-seeking candidate had promised not to divert any rents from the voters. It is therefore natural to study the model with outcome-motivated candidates under the alternative assumption that binding commitments are not feasible. As in section 4.3, we could appeal to difficulties in verifying and enforcing contingent policies to give some underpinnings to the no-commitment assumption. But we shall not pursue that here. In any event, the model without commitment is essentially that suggested by Alesina (1988) in an article where he also criticized the political science literature with outcome-motivated candidates.

Consider the same setting as in section 5.1, except that the candidates now have discretion to alter their preelectoral announcements at stage (3) of the game. This has far-reaching consequences. Suppose candidate L has won the election. At that point, he has an incentive to set a policy g_L that maximizes his objective function (5.2), given that $p_L = 1$. The solution is obvious: candidate L just implements his bliss point, setting

$$g_L = g^L \equiv H_g^{-1}\left(\frac{y^L}{y}\right).$$

If candidate R wins, he acts in the same way. After the election, only the centrifugal political force is left to operate.

Clearly, no other announcements than the bliss points of candidates L and R have any credibility at stage (1). By the monotonicity of voters' policy preferences in y^i, the median voter is still pivotal. Therefore, the candidate whose bliss point appeals most to the median voter wins the election at stage (2). Thus candidate L wins if

$$W^m(g^L) > W^m(g^R),$$

whereas candidate R wins if the inequality goes the other way.

It is easy to see why this kind of model has become popular. An equilibrium, as simple as it is, reflects the interplay between the policy preferences of the electorate and the candidates. The model thus becomes a tool for meaningfully introducing partisan policy preferences into the analysis. It allows us to interpret shifts in power as reflecting shifting positions either of candidates/parties or of the electorate. In the context of the above model, right-wing and left-wing governments can hold office. The positive implication is thus that the size of government systematically correlates with its identity: right-wing governments choose lower spending and taxes than do left-wing governments. The pioneering study by Cameron (1978) as well as the more recent work by Blais, Blake, and Dion (1993) found cross-country evidence in line with this prediction. But the partisan effect is relatively small. Moreover, as the latter paper describes, other cross-country studies have failed to find a partisan effect on spending or taxes.

We will use simple partisan models of this sort at some points in the book, particularly in the discussion about the politics of monetary policy in chapter 16, but also when discussing public debt issue (chapter 13) and economic growth (chapter 14). Yet some questions appear immediately. One concerns the normative implications. Because candidates and pivotal voters have concave utility over g, they all have long-run preferences for a stable policy in the middle rather than a policy that shifts back and forth as governments change. In a setting with repeated elections, parties could coordinate on a self-enforcing cooperative equilibrium with middle-ground policies, or voters could enforce such an equilibrium by requiring middle-ground policies as a condition for reelecting a particular policymaker. Models with these features can be developed, as indeed, Alesina (1988) and Dixit, Grossman, and Gul (1999) in particular have done.

Another question concerns our assumption that the set of candidates is exogenous. A plausible conjecture is that if the candidates were endogenous, the centripetal political forces would tend to pull candidate identities and equilibrium policies toward the middle of the political spectrum. The next section speaks to precisely this issue.

5.3 Endogenous Candidates

If we take the notion of citizen-candidates seriously, we can render the set of electoral candidates endogenous in a natural way simply by introducing an entry stage in the policy game studied in the previous section at which any citizen can enter the electoral race if the benefits of entry exceed the costs. Recent work by Besley and Coate (1997) and by Osborne and Slivinsky (1996) takes just this approach to representative democracy. This section illustrates that approach in the context of our simple policy example.

Consider the following timing. (1) Any citizen, of any income type, in the population can enter as a political candidate at a (consumption) cost of ε. (2) An election is held among those candidates running. Each citizen chooses the candidate for whom to vote by maximizing his expected utility, given how every other citizen votes. The candidate who gets a plurality of the vote wins, with any ties resolved by the toss of a coin. (3) The elected candidate selects a policy g_P; if nobody runs, a default policy $\overline{g}$ is implemented.

From the discussion in the last section, we know how to characterize the outcome at stages (2) and (3). As there is no policy commitment, an elected citizen with income y^P simply sets policy so as to maximize his utility, which gives stage (3) outcome

$$g^P \equiv H_g^{-1}\left(\frac{y^P}{y}\right).$$

Voters at stage (2) realize that this will take place. Their monotonic preferences over policy thus induce monotonic preferences over candidates. In one- or two-candidate elections, the candidate who appeals most to the median voter is thus the winner. If there are more than two candidates, the median voter may no longer be pivotal, as citizens are assumed to vote strategically—they condition their own vote on the voting by others—in line with Besley and Coate (1997).[1]

---

1. Osborne and Slivinsky (1996), in contrast, assume that citizens vote sincerely.

A prospective candidate foresees this outcome when deciding whether to enter at stage (1). He enters the race only if running gives a higher expected utility, net of entry costs, than not running, given other citizens' entry decisions.

This model has more than one equilibrium, and we start by describing the simplest of these equilibria. Suppose a median candidate m with income y^m were to win the election. We know he would choose to set policy g^m. As that policy is a Condorcet winner, the median candidate would beat any other individual with different income (and thus a different preferred policy) in a pairwise vote. If m has decided to run, no other income type would ever find it worthwhile to incur the entry cost involved in inducing a two-candidate election. As the other type would be sure to lose without affecting the policy outcome, the only possible result would be for him to lose the cost of running. Furthermore, since there are no benefits from holding office per se, no second candidate with income y^m has an incentive to run, as he too would only incur the entry cost without influencing policy. Whenever m runs in equilibrium, he must thus run as an uncontested candidate (or in an election with more than two candidates). The condition for an equilibrium to exist where only the median voter is a candidate is

$$W^m(g^m) - W^m(\overline{g}) \geq \varepsilon. \tag{5.3}$$

The utility gain to m from choosing his preferred policy rather than the default policy must outweigh the entry cost, a condition that is obviously fulfilled if the default policy $\overline{g}$ is far enough away from g^m or if the running cost is small enough. Problem 2 of this chapter includes an alternative example of a citizen-candidate model and a treatment of its equilibria. As illustrated in that problem, there are other one-candidate equilibria with candidates close to the median running uncontested.

This equilibrium thus confirms the conjecture at the end of last section. Centripetal political forces may pull an endogenous candidate toward the middle. Indeed, the predicted policy outcome coincides with the standard median-voter equilibrium.

Candidates do occasionally run uncontested in majoritarian electoral systems. In congressional and gubernatorial elections in southern U.S. states, for example, Democratic candidates have sometimes run uncontested, but such examples are certainly not very common. The model also allows for equilibria with two candidates: R and L, say. In such equilibria a candidate with income y^R must find it worthwhile to run, given that another candidate with income y^L is running, and vice versa. This requires that the possible influence on policy outweighs the entry cost, as in the single-candidate equilibrium above. It also requires that each candidate stand some chance of winning. In our model, in which the voters' preferences for candidates are monotonic, this means that voters with median income must be indifferent between R and L. In this event, the two candidates have the same chance of winning.

The discussion suggests the following sufficient conditions for a two-candidate equilibrium:

$$W^m(g^R) = W^m(g^L)$$

$$\frac{1}{2}[W^R(g^R) - W^R(g^L)] \geq \varepsilon \tag{5.4}$$

$$\frac{1}{2}[W^L(g^L) - W^L(g^R)] \geq \varepsilon,$$

where a candidate of type y^P is associated with policy: $g^P \equiv H_g^{-1}(y^P/y)$. By inspection of (5.4), it is easy to see that we have a multiplicity of two-candidate equilibria. The first condition requires that the median voter get the same utility from the policies of R and L. This is satisfied for many different pairs of candidates with incomes on opposite sides of y^m, because W^m has a single peak at g^m and the function relating g^P to y^P is monotonic. The remaining two conditions require that each candidate in such a pair have an incentive to enter. This is also fulfilled for many pairs, provided that the other candidate's policy preferences are different enough. That is, if only $y^R - y^L$ is large enough, a fifty-fifty chance of winning generates an expected utility gain sufficiently large to outweigh the cost of running.

Why is a third candidate, with income between y^L and y^R, not entering the race? In each of these equilibria, a right-wing candidate with $y^R > y^m$ balances a left-wing candidate with $y^L < y^m$ at the same utility distance from the median voter's preferred policy. All voters with endowments $y^i < y^m$ vote for candidate L, whereas all voters with $y^i > y^m$ vote for R. These voting strategies and our assumption that citizens vote strategically keep a third intermediate candidate from entering. Suppose a candidate with median income y^m would enter. This candidate might capture the votes of other individuals with income at y^m (who are indifferent between y^L and y^R), but he would capture no other votes. Individuals with income $y^m + \alpha$ (α being a small positive number), for instance, would not vote for the middle candidate, given that all other voters stick to their equilibrium voting strategies. For by switching his vote from candidate R to the new entrant, the $y^m + \alpha$ citizen would give candidate L the upper hand in the election,[2] and that would yield a lower expected utility than a fifty-fifty chance of getting the policy associated with candidate R. Thus the entering candidate would need the coordinated support of a large coalition of voters. A new political party might provide such a coalition, but the model as it stands has no role for parties, in this sense. (See also problem 2 of this chapter.)

---

2. If citizens instead voted sincerely, as in Osborne and Slivinsky 1996, this argument would no longer apply. In that case, only the entry cost would keep a third intermediate candidate from entering, which would eliminate the most extreme equilibria. See also problem 2 of this chapter.

Generally, however, there are also equilibria with three (or more) citizen candidates running. We shall not deal with these kinds of equilibria in the present model, but problem 4 of this chapter includes an example in which candidates enter the race to influence the election outcome despite having no chance of winning.

Interestingly, the model demonstrates how centrifugal political forces may also provoke entry. Thus, two-candidate equilibria do not necessarily imply convergence to a policy in the middle of the political spectrum. Moreover, policy outcomes are systematically related to the type of government, exactly as in the last section.

We will appeal to citizen-candidate models with entry at various points in the book, for example, when discussing strategic delegation through elections in chapters 7 and 12. Problem 3 of this chapter anticipates this discussion, demonstrating how one can embed a simple model of lobbying into a citizen-candidate model.

An attractive aspect of citizen-candidate models is that they offer a general equilibrium approach to politico-economic modeling; assumptions are made only about primitives such as individuals' preferences, endowments, and technologies (and about the electoral system). The results thus lend themselves to a clean welfare analysis of political equilibria. Furthermore, citizen-candidate models can handle multidimensional policy problems or unidimensional problems with nonmonotonic policy preferences, as equilibria exist under very general conditions, including those in which no Condorcet winner exists. Problem 4 of this chapter shows an example.

The approach taken in this section is not, however, without weaknesses. Multiple equilibria make it difficult to generate sharp testable hypotheses. Moreover, even though the main focus is on the entry stage in the political arena, the lack of preexisting electoral candidates makes it hard to discuss political parties' role in elections. The lack of political parties was also mentioned in the above discussion about two-candidate equilibria. Some interesting recent papers make progress in this direction, however. Morelli (1998) tries to combine a model of legislative bargaining with endogenous party formation in a citizen-candidate model. His paper studies how citizen-candidates form parties ahead of elections, when voters also take into account the postelection legislative bargaining between the parties. Rivière (1999) and Kalandrakis (1999) also focus on party formation in citizen-candidate models.

5.4 Legislative Bargaining

So far, all our models of policy choice have assumed that a single candidate or party wins the election and has complete control over the policymaking process. This assumption ignores much of the postelection bargaining over economic policy that goes on in actual political systems. In parliamentary regimes, this bargaining takes place in government formation, as well as in preparations of and decisions on the budget, particularly if no single party holds a majority of the seats in the assembly. But postelection bargaining also takes place in congressional regimes among party groups and presidents, or among members of different committees. In this last section, we completely abstract from elections and look instead at majority decisions in the legislature, given policy proposals made by specific politicians. In the process, we return to the Romer and Rosenthal (1978) approach to agenda setting and the Baron and Ferejohn (1989) approach to legislative bargaining introduced in chapter 2.

Assume that three partisan politicians of income type J have been elected. These incumbents constitute the legislature. We label them L, M, and R. Politician J has income y^J, with $y^L < y^M < y^R$. The politicians' policy preferences are thus given by $W^J(g)$, with associated bliss points

$$g^J = H_g^{-1}\left(\frac{y^J}{y}\right),$$

such that $g^L > g^M > g^R$. It is reasonable to interpret these politicians as associated with three political parties ordered on a left-to-right scale. Indeed, each of these parties could be a perfect delegate for a particular income group, if we assumed a three-group income distribution, as we did in chapters 3 and 4.

5.4.1 One-Round Bargaining

We first consider the simplest possible closed-rule bargaining over policy, as in chapter 2. The sequence of events is as follows: (1) One of the three parties is appointed agenda setter, labeled a. (2) The agenda-setting party a makes a policy proposal, g_a. (3) The legislature votes on the proposal; if at least two parties are in favor, $g = g_a$, otherwise a default policy, $g = \overline{g}$, is implemented.

Think about these events as a government formation phase. The default policy $\overline{g}$ will be a key determinant of the equilibrium. We can think of $\overline{g}$ as determined in the constitution, which prescribes what happens after a failure to form a government. One drastic possibility would be that "the government closes down," so that $\overline{g} = 0$. Another is that "previous programs stay in place," so that $\overline{g} > 0$. More reasonable is perhaps that "bargaining continues." We consider such a continuation below.

The outcome of this game depends on which party has the right to make the proposal. First assume that, at stage (1), the centrist party gets to make the proposal: $a = M$. Then the result is simple, namely party M proposes its own preferred policy at stage (2), which is accepted at stage (3): $g = g_M = g^M$. This is, of course, nothing but an application of the median-voter theorem. Policy g^M is a Condorcet winner in the legislature, so at least one other party prefers g^M to $\overline{g}$. Generally, at stage (3) a party always votes yes to a proposal that gives a payoff at least as high as the default outcome.

Now assume instead that one of the extreme parties gets to make the proposal, say the left-wing party: $a = L$ (the result is completely analogous if $a = R$). Observe first that L actively seeks the support only of party M. Seeking support from other parties involves departing further from party L's bliss point, and two votes are enough to implement policy. It follows that party L seeks only a minimum winning coalition with the centrist party, the party with a bliss point closest to its own. To characterize the solution, define $\widetilde{g}^M$, the default equivalent policy for M, as the policy leaving M indifferent between $\widetilde{g}^M$ and the status quo:

$$W^M(\widetilde{g}^M) = W^M(\overline{g}). \tag{5.5}$$

The equilibrium proposal is then

$$g_L = \begin{cases} g^L & \text{if} \quad g^L \leq \overline{g} \\ \overline{g} & \text{if} \quad g^M \leq \overline{g} < g^L \\ \text{Min}(\widetilde{g}^M, g^L) & \text{if} \quad \overline{g} < g^M. \end{cases} \tag{5.6}$$

Why this outcome? First of all, L would never push the size of government above its own bliss point, for which it gets (unanimous) support when $g^L \leq \overline{g}$. This explains the first row in (5.6). When seeking support from M, L is never obliged to bring g below g^M. If $g^M \leq \overline{g} < g^L$, M finds it optimal to vote no to any $g > \overline{g}$, and thus L optimally proposes $\overline{g}$. This explains the second row. Finally, if $\overline{g} < g^M$, L proposes the default equivalent policy with $g = \widetilde{g}^M > g^M$ (or he proposes g^L if $g^L \leq \widetilde{g}^M$). Thus, the left-wing party performs better, the worse is the "outside option" for the centrist party. If $\overline{g} = 0$, for instance, not making an agreement and closing down the government really hurts, and M is willing to go along with a higher value of g.

5.4.2 Two-Round Bargaining

Suppose now that the bargaining starts in exactly the same way. But defeat of the proposal at stage (3) no longer triggers the default policy $\overline{g}$. Instead the game continues as follows: (4) A party other than the first-round proposer (now called a_1), is picked to make a second proposal, $J = a_2 \neq a_1$. (5) Party a_2 makes the new proposal g_2. (6) The legislature votes; if at least two parties are in favor, $g = g_2$; if not, $\overline{g}$ is implemented.

Clearly, proposals and votes from the first round are bygone, if the second round is reached. Thus the second-round outcome is identical to the single-round equilibrium above. Assume that delay to the second round is potentially costly to the parties, such that second-round outcomes are discounted by $\beta \leq 1$.

Assume that the centrist party gets to make the proposal in the first round, $a_1 = M$. Then the result is simple: the centrist party proposes its bliss point, $g_1 = g^M$, and one of the other parties accepts, because the expected discounted value of the second-round outcome must be worse for at least one of the other parties. That is, it must be the case that

$$\beta \mathsf{E}_{g_2}[W^J(g_2)] \leq W^J(g^m)$$

for at least one $J \neq M$. One of the other two (risk-averse) parties must necessarily be worse off with a delayed (and potentially uncertain) policy than with a certain middle-ground policy without delay. Party M thus seeks support for its most preferred policy from the party with lowest expected utility.

What if instead the left-wing party makes the first proposal, $a_1 = L$? Let the centrist party ($M = a_2$) become the second-round proposer with probability p and let the right-wing party propose ($R = a_2$) with probability $(1 - p)$. We can then define the continuation value for M by

$$V^M(\beta, p, g_R) = \beta[p W^M(g^m) + (1 - p) W^M(g_R)],$$

where g_R, the future equilibrium proposal by party R, is determined as in (5.6). Note that $V^M(\cdot)$ is increasing in all its arguments. Clearly, party L has to give M a first-round utility corresponding to $V^M(\beta, p, g_R)$, rather than $W^M(\overline{g})$ as in the single-round game. Various possibilities exist. If $\beta = 1$ and either $p = 1$ or $g_R = g^M$, M can insist on its bliss point, so $g_L = g^M$. Generally, however, g_L goes up as any of β, p, g_R go down. If delay is more costly (β lower), M has a lower probability of setting the agenda himself in the next round (p lower), or if the right-wing party has more bargaining power in the second round (g_R lower), M's continuation value falls, and the left-wing party can increase the size of government toward its bliss point g^L. It is clearly never optimal for party L to make an unacceptable proposal.

What are the lessons from the simple models in this section? We learn, as in earlier sections, that the mere existence of a Condorcet winner is not sufficient to ensure its implementation. Nevertheless, the strategic location of party M makes it a very strong player. As a result, this party is part of every coalition, and its preferences carry a lot of weight in the solution. Two related points were also encountered already in chapter 2. The model illustrates how the power to propose gives the agenda setter the power to push the size of government in its preferred direction—note the result when party L is the agenda setter. This power is governed by the status quo. The model also shows the force of minimum winning coalitions under majority decision making, a point to which we will return at several points in the book. Finally, the model illustrates how the rules for continuation after a rejected proposal influence the incentives in the first round. Problem 5 of this chapter provides a further illustration of the last point. There a committee makes a proposal to the legislature, but rejection of the committee's proposal leads to a new proposal by the majority leader of the legislature.

The particular result on the advantage of a strategic location, however, hinges crucially on the policy space's being unidimensional. Recall the simple redistributive pie-splitting game of example 5 in chapter 2. In that case, there was no natural central location, which made the competition to get into the winning policy coalition much stiffer, something that helped increase the proposer's power. Instead, the player with the worst status quo position had an advantage and was part of every coalition. The Baron-Ferejohn (1989) legislative bargaining model has often been brought to bear on such multidimensional policy problems of a pure redistributive nature. Problem 6 of this chapter offers an introduction to this model.

5.5 Discussion

In this chapter, we have introduced a number of models with partisan politicians. In pre-election politics, we have seen that the policymaker's objective is unimportant (at least in the simple models of two-party competition we have considered in this part of the book). In the context of postelection politics, however, partisan policy preferences make a crucial difference. We have then assumed that policy is either unilaterally set by a single politician (party), as in sections 5.2–5.3, or determined by several politicians (parties) in postelection bargaining, as in section 5.4.

Models with a single partisan policymaker are easy to deal with. They play a special role in parts 4 and 5 on dynamic politics and monetary policy. When policymakers are partisan and electoral promises are not binding, the identity of the appointed policymaker(s) matters a great deal. This has two implications. First, rational voters can exploit the option of strategic delegation: appointing a policymaker with preferences different from their own enables this policymaker to better cope with incentive constraints arising at the policy-making stage. A celebrated example of strategic delegation arises in monetary policy. As discussed extensively in chapter 17, citizens may find it optimal to delegate monetary policy to an independent and conservative central banker to enhance credibility of a low-inflation outcome. The same idea comes up in chapter 12 in the context of capital taxation, in which electing a candidate richer than yourself may curtail the incentives to overtax capital ex post and thus lend credibility to an optimal tax policy. In settings with tax competition (chapter 12) or monetary policy coordination (chapter 18), it may be efficient to appoint a policymaker who can help achieve a favorable outcome in the Nash equilibrium of a subsequent policy game.

A second implication is that electoral uncertainty generates additional incentive constraints on economic policy. Partisan governments, aware of the possibility that governments with different partisan preferences may replace them in the future, have incentives to manipulate state variables such as public debt or public investment strategically to influence the future policy choices. This idea plays a prominent role in chapter 13 on public debt issue and also comes up in chapter 14 in studying the implications of political instability for economic growth.

Models with many postelection policymakers are more intricate than winner-takes-all models, but such legislative bargaining models are used as the central analytical tool in several parts of the book. As discussed in chapter 2, the agenda-setting cum legislative bargaining approach is attractive in that it easily produces equilibria when policy conflict is multidimensional and other approaches fail. Another attractive feature is that this approach offers a way of modeling different constitutional rules in a precise way. It therefore becomes useful when asking questions of comparative politics. Yet the simple version of the model we have studied in section 5.4 raises obvious questions. From where do the legislator preferences derive? More generally, how do the rules for legislative decision making interact with other types of political activity, such as elections and lobbying? We will repeatedly return to these questions in the subsequent parts of the book, particularly in chapter 7, dealing with special-interest politics, and in Part 3, addressing questions of comparative politics.

5.6 Notes on the Literature

Wittman (1977, 1983), Calvert (1985), and Roemer (1994, 1997) all studied electoral competition between candidates with partisan preferences who can commit to electoral platforms. Roemer's (1997) paper also includes a probabilistic voting model in which candidates are uncertain about the median voters' bliss point, which produces policy divergence. Lindbeck and Weibull (1993) derive related results, using a model like that in chapters 3 and 4, in which the voters have preferences over a second dimension of the candidates, in which commitments are infeasible.

The divergence result of section 5.2 when candidates cannot commit is due to Alesina (1988). Alesina also shows that reputational mechanisms may stabilize policy between the divergent bliss points of two partisan candidates in a setting of repeated electoral interactions. Dixit, Grossman, and Gul (1999) derive results on sustainable policy compromise in a fully dynamic game. The simple model of postelection policy choices by single partisan candidates with exogenous policy preferences has been a popular tool in many theoretical studies, particularly by macroeconomists. We give references to these applications in parts 4 and 5.

Besley and Coate (1997) and Osborne and Slivinsky (1996) independently proposed the citizen-candidate model discussed in section 5.3. Besley and Coate (1998a) also show how to use the citizen-candidate model for stringent welfare evaluation of political equilibria.

More references to its applications are given in later chapters. The aforementioned survey by Osborne (1995) carefully discusses many of the theoretical issues in sections 5.1 through 5.3.

As mentioned in chapter 2, the agenda-setting model in section 5.4 is due to Romer and Rosenthal (1978, 1979). This model was developed to deal with a number of issues, including the effects of different proposal, amendment, veto, and gatekeeping powers in political systems. Rosenthal (1990) surveys its further developments and applications. Baron and Ferejohn (1989) developed the so-called legislative bargaining model, which can be seen as a generalization of the Stahl-Rubinstein model of noncooperative two-person bargaining and decisions by unanimity to multiagent noncooperative bargaining and decision by majority under different rules for proposals and amendments. The model has since become one of the workhorse models in the rational choice approach to U.S. congressional politics. We give references to its many applications in subsequent chapters.

5.7 Problems

1. Probabilistic voting with outcome-seeking politicians

Assume that the indirect utility function of tax policy is described by

$$w^i = -(\tau - \tau^i)^2.$$

There are two political parties, one with the preferred tax rate zero, the other with preferred tax rate one. The parties can commit to a party platform that will be implemented should the party win the election. The political parties are uncertain about the most preferred tax rate τ^m of the median voter and assign a uniform probability distribution between $(\frac{1}{2} - a)$ and $(\frac{1}{2} + a)$ to τ^m. The parameter a lies in the interval $(0, 1)$. The parties are exclusively policy motivated. Let τ_0 and τ_1 be the policies proposed by parties 0 and 1, respectively.

a. Show that the parties will never choose their bliss points and will never converge completely.

b. Solve for the equilibrium policy, given that it is symmetric, that is, $\tau_0 = 1 - \tau_1$. Discuss how the equilibrium policies depend on the level of uncertainty, as described by a.

c. Show that the equilibrium must be of the form $\tau_0 = 1 - \tau_1$.

2. The citizen-candidate model

Consider a society inhabited by a continuum of citizens with incomes uniformly distributed between zero and two. Each citizen i has preferences over private consumption c

and a publicly provided private good g that are given by

$$w^i = \sqrt{c^i} + \sqrt{g}.$$

The public good g is financed through a proportional income tax τ, and the government budget constraint is $\tau y = g$, where y is the average income. Private consumption is $c^i = (1 - \tau)y^i$.

Consider the following timing: (1) Any citizen may enter as a political candidate at a cost ε. (2) An election is held among the candidates; the candidate who gets plurality wins the election, and a tie is resolved by the toss of a coin. (3) The winning candidate selects a tax rate; if there are no candidates, then a default tax rate $\bar{\tau}$ is implemented.

a. What policy would be implemented by a winning candidate with income y_i?

b. Suppose that $\varepsilon = \sqrt{2} - \sqrt{\frac{3}{4}} - \sqrt{\frac{1}{4}}$. In what region must the status quo policy, $\bar{\tau}$, lie in order for the equilibrium to exist where only the citizen with median income is a candidate? Are there other one-candidate equilibria?

c. Characterize the two-candidate equilibria.

d. Describe what would happen in a two-candidate equilibrium if the median candidate were to enter. How would the set of possible equilibria change if voters voted sincerely, that is, voted for the candidate giving them the highest utility.

3. Lobbying in a representative democracy

This problem is based on Besley and Coate 1997, 1999. Consider a model with N citizens, $i \in \{1, \ldots, N\}$, who derive a utility from consuming a private and a public good. Each citizen is endowed with $y^i = 1$ units of private good. The public good can be produced at any level g. One unit of private good is required to produce one unit of public good. Let c^i be the quantity of private good consumed by agent i, his utility being

$$w^i = c^i + \theta^i \ln(g),$$

where θ^i represents the preference of agent i for the public good. Assume that $\theta^i \in \{\theta^1, \ldots, \theta^T\}$, where $\theta^{k+1} = \theta^k + 1$ for all $k \in \{1, \ldots, (T - 1)\}$. Let η^k be the number of citizens with type θ^k. Naturally, $\sum_{k=1}^{T} \eta^k = N$. There exists a median type denoted by θ^m. The timing of the game is as follows. First, each citizen decides whether to become a candidate and pays a cost δ if he does. Second, the voting stage takes place, and at most one candidate is elected. Denote the elected candidate by e. Assume that citizens vote sincerely and abstain when indifferent. Moreover, when n candidates receive the same vote share, each is elected with probability $\frac{1}{n}$. If nobody is elected, the game ends. Last, there exists a single lobby of type $\theta^l > \theta^m$ composed by $n^l \leq \eta^l$ citizens. The lobby maximizes the sum of its members' utilities and chooses a contribution to e of $B_{le}(g) \geq 0$. Then e chooses the amount of public good to produce, financed through a per-citizen tax $t = \frac{g}{N}$.

a. Determine the policy preferences of citizens as well as the optimal provision of public good for each agent of type θ^i, denoted by $\hat{g}(\theta^i)$.

b. Consider the last stage of the game. Characterize the lobby's optimization problem. Determine the provision of the public good $g^*(\theta^e, \theta^l)$ as well as the lobby's contribution when the elected citizen is of type $\theta^e \neq \theta^l$ and $\theta^e = \theta^l$. Compare $g^*(\theta^e, \theta^l)$ with $\hat{g}(\theta^e)$. What is the utility of citizen e and what are the utilities of all citizens $j \neq e$. Discuss.

c. Show that an ordinary citizen is indifferent between electing a member of the lobby and electing a citizen of the same type as the lobby members. Demonstrate that for each citizen j, there exists a unique type $\theta^*(\theta^j)$ that he prefers as candidate. Verify that both ordinary citizens and lobby group members have single-peaked preferences over candidates.

d. Consider an equilibrium with identical candidates. Demonstrate that if δ (the cost of candidacy) is sufficiently small, $\theta^*(\theta^m)$ has an interest in becoming a candidate against any other candidates of types θ^l and $\theta^k \neq \{\theta^l, \theta^*(\theta^m)\}$. What is the maximum number $s^{\max}$ of candidates of type $\theta^*(\theta^m)$? Show that when

$$\delta \in \left(0, \frac{B_{l\theta^*(\theta^m)}}{2}\right),$$

then $s^{\max} > 0$ and the equilibrium exists.

e. Consider a vote over q versus r with $\theta^q < \theta^r < \theta^l$. Moreover, suppose that the median group divides the electorate exactly into two (i.e., $\sum_{k=1}^{m-1} \eta^k = \sum_{k=m+1}^{T} \eta^k$) and that citizens in the median group are indifferent between $g^*(\theta^q, \theta^l)$ and $g^*(\theta^r, \theta^l)$. Assume as well that $g^*(\theta^q, \theta^l) \neq \hat{g}(\theta^r)$. Show that the number of citizens preferring r to q is equal to the number of citizens preferring q to r. Demonstrate that any entrant s will lose the election if $\eta^m < \frac{N}{3} - 1$. Last, prove that both r and q have an interest in becoming candidates when δ is sufficiently small.

4. Equilibria when the single-crossing condition is violated

This problem is based on Besley and Coate 1997. Each citizen i has preferences over private consumption c and a publicly provided private good g that are given by $c + H(g)$. Assume that the individuals have themselves provided the service g to a certain level g_i and that the utility from the government-provided good is described by $H(g) = \frac{3}{2}\sqrt{g - g_i}$. There are five groups, with $g_i = \{0, 0.4, 0.5, 0.7, 1\}$, and these groups have sizes $\{35, 10, 20, 20, 10\}$, respectively. The public good g is financed through a proportional income tax τ, and the government budget constraint is $\tau y = g$, where y is the average income. Private consumption is $c^i = (1 - \tau)y^i$. All groups have the same income of 1.

Consider the following timing: (1) Any citizen may enter as a political candidate at the cost $\varepsilon = 1$. (2) An election is held among the candidates; a candidate getting plurality wins the election, and a tie is resolved by the toss of a coin. (3) The winning candidate selects a tax rate; if there are no candidates, a default tax rate $\bar{\tau}$ is implemented.

a. Show that this utility function does not satisfy the Gans-Smart condition.

b. What policy would a winning candidate from each group advocate, and how would members of the different groups rank the policies put forward by the candidates?

c. What would be the equilibrium outcomes in pairwise elections between the bliss points?

d. Show that there exists a three-candidate equilibrium where three citizens, with $g_i = 1$, $g_j = 0.4$, and $g_k = 0$, are candidates. Discuss the reasons why the different candidates stay in the race and why the policy that would lose in a pairwise election against either of the other alternatives nevertheless wins the three-candidate election.

5. The agenda-setting model

A committee proposes a level of spending, g, of a government-provided good. If the proposition passes a vote in the legislature, g will be the policy enacted, otherwise a status quo policy $\bar{g}$ will be implemented. The preferences for spending are described by $w(g; \alpha^i) = -|g - \alpha^i|$. The preference parameters are α^c and α^m for the members of the committee and the median voter in the legislature respectively, where $\alpha^m < \alpha^c$.

a. Plot how the proposed policy g changes with the position of the status quo policy $\bar{g}$.

b. Assume that if the proposed policy g does not gain a majority in the legislature, then the leader of the majority party, with the preference parameter $\alpha^l < \alpha^m$, will make a new proposal. If this amended proposal does not gain a majority, then the status quo policy $\bar{g}$ will be implemented. Plot how the equilibrium policy will depend on the status quo policy.

c. The status quo policy is often determined endogenously. A typical status quo policy for the budget of the subsequent year is the budget of the current year. Consider again the setup in question (a), in which the status quo policy is implemented if the policy proposed by the committee fails to gather a majority in the legislature. Suppose that the present budget is $1 million. Suppose further that the legislature becomes more favorable to spending on this issue as time passes, perhaps because of an increasing tax base. The legislature serves for four years, and the preference parameter of the median voter in the legislature is $2 million,

$3 million, $3.5 million, and $4 million in each of the four years, respectively. Assume that the voters in the legislature are myopic: they treat each vote as a one-shot game. Neither the members of the committee nor the legislature discount the future. Can the committee improve its situation by not maximizing the budget each year separately? What is the best strategy for the committee over the four years?

d. Now assume that the voters are not myopic and, for simplicity, limit the game to the first two years. Do the committee members gain or lose when voters are myopic?

6. Political rents with endogenous value of being in office

This question is based on Baron and Ferejohn 1989. Consider a legislature with n members who may divide rents of size r among themselves. The members derive utility solely from the consumption value of the rents $w^i(r) = r$. A member of the legislative body has proposed an allocation of r, and the legislature votes on the proposition. If the proposition is not passed, then a new member is given the right to propose an allocation of r. The discount rate is $\beta \in [0, 1]$. This member is randomly chosen, and the chance of any one member's being selected to make the proposal is $\frac{1}{n}$. This proposal is voted on, and if it does not pass, then all rents are dissipated.

a. What allocation will the first proposition imply? Discuss the proposed allocation: Is it concentrated or dispersed? How does the advantage of the member making the first proposition relate to the size of the legislature? Will all propositions receive support in the legislature?

b. Now suppose that the stage game in which a member is randomly chosen to make a new proposal is instead repeated an infinite number of times. Restrict the attention to equilibria in which the continuation values for each structurally identical subgame are the same. In these equilibria, the proposed division of r will be the same at any stage of the game. Show that the allocation proposed in (a) is an equilibrium in the infinitely repeated game.

II REDISTRIBUTIVE POLITICS

Having devoted part 1 of the book largely to methodology, we now turn to substantive policy issues. The two chapters in this part deal with different forms of redistribution. Redistributive policies have become a predominant phenomenon in modern democracies. Transfers and subsidies have been the most rapidly growing component of government spending in the postwar period. Two studies involving a group of seventeen industrialized democracies, for instance, found that transfers and subsidies were almost nonexistent in those countries a century ago. Subsequent growth in these countries has been particularly rapid in the postwar period: the average transfer subsidy share of GDP stood at about 8% around 1960 but grew to about 23% by around 1990. Not only is this growth of welfare state programs spectacular, so is the cross-country variation: the 1990 GDP share in Japan was below 10%, whereas the Netherlands spent close to 40% of GDP on these items.[1] Moreover, redistribution also takes a variety of forms, not only outright cash payments. Some redistribution is made in kind, by more or less targeted government consumption and investment programs. Yet other forms of redistribution are indirect. Prominent examples are tariffs, which alter factor rewards, and various forms of regulation, which alter market conditions so as to create rents for specific groups.

Redistribution quickly takes us right into the heartland of politics. To keep the beginning simple, we relegate the dynamics of policy determination to part 4 and limit ourselves to once-and-for-all policy choices in simple and basically static economic environments.

It is useful to distinguish between two different kinds of redistribution. Some redistributive programs are general, handing out general transfers to all members of some broad socioeconomic group, such as the old, the sick, or the unemployed. Other programs are instead targeted, taking the form of selective subsidies to more-narrow groups of beneficiaries. These different forms of redistribution are likely to have differing political determinants. Broad redistributive programs potentially benefiting a large number of voters are likely to reflect the wishes of the majority, or at least of a large number of influential voters. Hence their political determinants can be fruitfully analyzed in the models of electoral competition introduced in chapter 3. Small and narrowly targeted redistributive programs, on the other hand, impose small costs on the majority of citizens, but the stakes may be huge for the few beneficiaries. The political process is likely to reflect this strong asymmetry in the intensity of preferences. Whereas voters at large can afford to take lightly the existence of such targeted programs, the beneficiaries have strong incentives to be politically active. The size and form of narrowly targeted redistribution is therefore likely to reflect institutional features, such as a group's ability to be organized as a lobby or the identity of influential office holders, rather than the distribution of voters' preferences at large.

---

1. The data are taken from Tanzi and Davoodi 1997 and Tanzi and Schuknecht 1995.

Chapter 6 is devoted to the analysis of equilibrium policies in broad redistributive programs. Relying on the discussion in chapter 2, we assume that policy conflict can plausibly be reduced to a single dimension, so that we stay in the domain of general-interest politics. We also assume that Downsian electoral competition resolves this policy conflict. We thus analyze median-voter equilibria of the type introduced in chapter 3. This allows us to keep the political side of the analysis very simple and add more economic detail. We then study how the distribution of voters' preferences determines the size and structure of different transfer programs. Specifically, we deal with general transfers financed by distortionary taxation, pension programs, unemployment insurance, and regional transfer schemes. In each case, the main contribution of the analysis is to highlight how the specific economic policy instrument determines the voters' preferences.

Chapter 7 moves into multidimensional policy conflict and special-interest politics. The collective choice problem involves selecting a vector of local, group-specific, public goods financed out of a common pool of tax revenue. Each group would like a lot of spending on the public good from which it benefits, because its cost is shared among all groups. Here, we adopt a strategy opposite to that in chapter 6. We keep the economic side constant and very simple throughout the chapter. Instead—and again returning to a theme discussed in chapter 2—we vary the assumptions about the institutional details of policymaking, studying how these institutions aggregate the policy preferences of different interest groups. In this way, we illustrate a number of alternative approaches, extending the modeling introduced in part 1. Each approach highlights a different aspect of the political process, suggesting different determinants of which interest groups emerge as winners or losers. Specifically, we study legislative bargaining, lobbying, and electoral competition, as well as the possible interactions between these forms of political activity.

6 General-Interest Politics

This chapter deals with some prominent welfare state programs that transfer cash directly to broad socioeconomic groups. We mainly address a positive question: How do voters' preferences shape such programs? As in chapters 3–5, we also discuss some normative properties of equilibrium policies.

The political analysis in this chapter relies exclusively on simple median-voter equilibria. Such equilibria have been a popular approach among economists. One explanation for this popularity is undoubtedly ease of analysis: median-voter equilibria are the solution to a modified optimal taxation problem, with a very special social welfare function in which only the utility of the median individual carries positive weight. The simple political setting enables the researcher to study richer policy problems and more complex economic environments. In part 1, we warned against the temptation of analytical convenience, but in the case of broad redistributive programs, it may not be a bad first approximation to describe the central source of disagreement among the voters as aligned on a single dimension, making the median-voter equilibrium a natural solution concept.

If this approximation is valid, median-voter equilibria identify a basic political force shaping economic policy. Virtually everyone dislikes equilibrium policy, but half the electorate wants to move policy in one direction, and the other half wants to move it in the opposite direction. This fundamental balance of political forces does not reflect political institutions, which may in themselves be endogenous to the political process. In this sense, a median-voter optimum resembles a Walrasian equilibrium: once we have reached an equilibrium, fundamental forces tend to keep policy in place. In part 1 we discussed how such an equilibrium may come about in representative democracy. Electoral competition between two office-seeking candidates, who care only about winning the election and can make binding electoral promises, drives both candidates to this equilibrium policy (see chapter 3). In this Downsian representation of the political process, the two candidates thus become the analog of the Walrasian auctioneer. The same solution might also be obtained with rent-seeking or outcome-seeking candidates, but this requires strong assumptions about their commitment capacity (see chapters 4 and 5).

We start in section 6.1 by studying general tax-financed transfers that redistribute from *rich to poor* voters. Here heterogeneity is one-dimensional, and voters' preferences over a distortionary income tax are monotonically related to their idiosyncratic productivity. The main result is that the size of redistributive programs increases with a specific measure of pretax income inequality.

Section 6.2 turns to pension programs, which add another source of policy conflict, namely the conflict between *young and old*. Policy is still one-dimensional, but heterogeneity becomes two-dimensional: voters' preferences over the generosity of the pension system are systematically related to their age as well as their income. A coalition of poor and elderly voters supports large public pensions, exceeding the social optimum, since future generations of taxpayers cannot participate in the voting.

Section 6.3 studies how *regional conflict* shapes redistributive policies. The framework is similar to that of section 6.1. But as in section 6.2, we add a second source of heterogeneity: individuals belong to two different regions that have different average incomes. We study how redistributive policies interact with the decision to integrate or separate the two regions when there are efficiency gains from integration. On the one hand, redistribution changes the incentives to integrate, weakening them for rich regions and strengthening them for poor ones. On the other hand, the threat of regional secession can limit the scope of equilibrium redistribution in an integrated nation.

Finally, section 6.4 is devoted to unemployment insurance and other labor market programs. Here, the conflict is between *employed and unemployed* individuals. Thus, agents' employment status or the risk of becoming unemployed shape the preferences over the generosity of unemployment insurance and the structure of other labor market programs. The powerful majority of "insiders" with stable jobs support an overregulated labor market and underprovision of unemployment insurance.

6.1   General Transfers

How do voters evaluate redistributive programs? And how much income is redistributed through such programs? Can fundamental political forces account for the observed growth of social transfers over time as well as the large observed cross-country differences in the size of these transfers? These questions motivate the literature surveyed in this section.

6.1.1   A Simple Model of Redistribution

As explained in chapter 2, Romer (1975) and Roberts (1977) originally proposed the standard model of redistributive taxation, and Meltzer and Richard (1981) extended and popularized it. We already encountered this model in example 3 of chapter 2. Because we will use this model as a stepping stone for our analysis in sections 6.2 and 6.3, it is worthwhile to restate the model here.

Consider a static economy producing a single commodity. There is a continuum of individuals, differing in one dimension only. As economic agents, they work and consume. As voters, they evaluate a simple redistributive program that pays a lump sum to each individual, financed by a proportional income tax.

To avoid unnecessary complications, we have reformulated the standard model slightly, assuming quasi-linear preferences and a somewhat different representation of heterogeneity.

The preferences of the ith individual are

$$w^i = c^i + V(x^i),$$

where c and x denote consumption and leisure, respectively, and $V(\cdot)$ is a well-behaved concave utility function. The private budget constraint is

$$c^i \leq (1 - \tau)l^i + f,$$

where τ is the income tax rate, l^i individual labor supply, and f a lump sum transfer. The real wage is unity. Quasi-linear preferences imply that consumption absorbs all income effects, which simplifies the analysis of tax distortions and the voting equilibrium.

To model income differences, we assume that individual productivity differs and that productivity, in turn, is equivalent to having more "effective time" available. That is, individuals are also subject to a "time constraint":

$$1 + e^i \geq x^i + l^i, \tag{6.1}$$

where e^i captures individual productivity. More-productive individuals have a larger effective time endowment, e^i.[1] We assume that e^i is distributed in the population according to a known distribution function $F(\cdot)$ with mean e and median $e^m < e$.

Solving the consumer problem is straightforward and leads to the following expression for optimal labor supply:

$$l^i = L(\tau) + (e^i - e), \tag{6.2}$$

where $L(\tau) \equiv 1 + e - V_x^{-1}(1 - \tau)$ is decreasing in τ by concavity of $V(\cdot)$.[2] Thus as expected, a higher tax rate distorts the labor-leisure choice and induces the consumer to work less. By our assumption that $F(\cdot)$ is skewed, the distribution of income is skewed to the right, in conformity with available data in all countries. Also note that because of our simplifying assumption, the tax has the same distorting effect on all individuals' labor-leisure choices, irrespective of their productivity e^i.

We follow the notational convention introduced in part 1 and write average variables without a superscript. Thus l denotes average labor supply. Since the average of e^i is e, we

---

1. The original model assumes that individuals have different productivities only when working, whereas we are implicitly assuming that more-talented individuals are more productive at generating income as well as at enjoying their leisure time. As the next footnote shows, however, quasi-linear preferences imply that all individuals find it optimal to consume the same amount of leisure, whereas more-talented individuals have more income and more consumption.

2. Maximize individual i's utility subject to the budget and time constraints. The first-order condition implies $1 - \tau = V_x(1 + e^i - l^i)$, where a subscript denotes a derivative. Take the inverse of $V_x(\cdot)$ and simplify to get the expression for l^i in the text. Note that $L_\tau = 1/V_{xx}(x^i) < 0$.

have $l = L(\tau)$. The government budget constraint can therefore be written

$$f \le \tau l \equiv \tau L(\tau). \tag{6.3}$$

Policy is set as in the median-voter model of chapter 3. Two political candidates who care only about winning the election thus compete for office, committing themselves to electoral platforms formulated over the tax rate. Whoever wins the election enacts his preannounced policy.

6.1.2   Equilibrium Redistribution

Consider the voters' preferences over policy. Define the indirect utility function of individual i, over τ, as

$$W^i(\tau) \equiv \widehat{c}^i + V(\widehat{x}^i) \equiv (1 - \tau)(L(\tau) + (e^i - e)) + \tau L(\tau) + V(1 - L(\tau) + e), \tag{6.4}$$

where a $\widehat{}$ refers to the private equilibrium choices and the right-most expression is derived from the private budget and time constraints and the government budget constraint.

Let τ^i be the tax rate preferred by the ith individual, with τ^i implicitly defined by the first-order condition $W^i_\tau(\tau^i) = 0$. We differentiate the right-most expression in (6.4), noting that we can set the sum of the terms in $\frac{d\widehat{l}^i}{d\tau}$ equal to zero by the envelope theorem. We then obtain:[3]

$$W^i_\tau(\tau) = -(e^i - e) + \tau L_\tau(\tau) = 0. \tag{6.5}$$

Consider the two terms in this condition. The first one represents the marginal benefit of a higher tax rate cum redistribution. It is positive for a voter poorer than the average $(e^i - e < 0)$ and negative for a voter richer than the average $(e^i - e > 0)$. The second term is the marginal cost of higher distorting taxes in the form of a smaller tax base; this term is always negative, as $L_\tau < 0$. Thus each voter trades off the marginal redistributive benefit (or cost) of taxation against its deadweight loss. Equation (6.5) implicitly defines the tax rate voter i prefers:

$$\tau^i = \frac{e^i - e}{L_\tau(\tau^i)}. \tag{6.6}$$

As $L_\tau < 0$, (6.6) implies that a poor voter $(e^i < e)$ prefers a positive tax rate, which is larger the poorer he is (the larger is $(e^i - e)$ in absolute value), whereas a rich voter $(e^i > e)$ prefers an income subsidy $(\tau < 0)$ financed by a lump sum tax.

Individual preferences are thus monotonic in e^i. Formally, (6.4) satisfies the single-crossing condition (2.4) defined in chapter 2, ensuring the existence of a Condorcet winning

---

3. Throughout the chapter we always assume that the second order conditions of the optimal taxation problems are satisfied. Here this amounts to imposing some restrictions on $L_{\tau\tau}$, and hence on the third derivative of V.

tax rate. As in chapter 3, there is thus only one political equilibrium: both candidates commit to τ^m, the policy preferred by the median voter. If either of the candidates were to announce a different value τ', the other candidate could ensure victory by announcing a policy in the interval (τ', τ^m). Hence the equilibrium tax rate, τ^m, coincides with the policy the median voter prefers:

$$\tau^m = \frac{e^m - e}{L_\tau(\tau^m)}. \tag{6.7}$$

Without repeating the argument, we shall assume that all the political equilibria in this chapter are the outcome of this simple form of Downsian electoral competition.

6.1.3   Implications and Evidence

The model thus predicts that the size of general redistributive programs reflects the preferences of the middle classes (the likely median voters) and is determined by their relative position on the income scale. By (6.7), taxes are higher the greater is the distance between median and mean income, a specific measure of income inequality. This qualification is important. To see this, consider two shifts in the income distribution in the direction of more inequality as measured by another common inequality measure: the Gini coefficient. If the middle classes become relatively better off, because of more extreme poverty in a pocket of the population, equilibrium redistribution becomes smaller. If the middle classes instead become relatively worse off, with the majority of income more concentrated at the top, equilibrium redistribution becomes larger. Thus the model predicts a precise link between skewedness of income distribution and the generosity of general redistribution schemes. Concentration of income at the top makes redistribution more attractive for the median voter and hence implies a high equilibrium tax rate. But more-extreme poverty has the opposite effect, because it reduces the benefit of redistribution for the median voter. The model also predicts that the larger are the deadweight costs of taxation, as captured by the absolute value of L_τ, the smaller is equilibrium redistribution. Note, however, that the model really says nothing about selective or targeted transfer schemes, such as welfare payments.

Can this simple model explain secular growth in the size of redistributive programs and observed cross-country differences? Two features of the theory can possibly account for the early growth of redistribution. First, the extension of suffrage to poorer voters early in this century certainly reduced the median voter's relative income in Western democracies. Second, again at the beginning of this century, economic progress and institutional change very likely reduced the transaction costs of collecting taxes, particularly income taxes, and hence the distortions associated with taxation. In the United States, for instance, income taxes became constitutional only in 1913. But what about the period after the late 1960s? Electoral laws did not change, and no major improvements in tax collection technologies occurred, yet government transfers continued to increase as a fraction of national income. Problem 1 of this chapter illustrates some of the above comparative statics results formally.

Lindert (1994, 1996) systematically investigates these questions in a panel of OECD countries, in the periods 1880–1930 and 1962–1981, respectively. Running panel regressions that also control for average income, demographic structure of the population, and other variables, he obtains conflicting results. On the one hand, voter turnout and redistributive transfers are positively related.[4] As voter participation is positively correlated with relative income, this supports the theory developed above. Moreover, high concentration of income (measured as the income share of the top quintile on the income scale relative to that of the middle quintile) is indeed positively related to redistributive transfers, as the theory predicts. And even though the evidence is weaker, poverty (the income share of the bottom quintile relative to that of the middle quintile) is negatively related to government transfers, which the theory also predicts. Income distribution can account for a large fraction of the observed cross-country differences in spending: the lower spending in the United States, in particular, could be attributed to lower voter turnout among poorer voters and to more-extreme poverty, which raises the median voter's relative position. On the other hand, when the share of the middle quintile, which should be a good proxy for the relative position of the median voter, replaces these measures of income distribution, this share always turns out to be statistically insignificant.

The model we have discussed is static. Part 4 discusses dynamic extensions in more detail. Let us simply mention here that Alesina and Rodrik (1994), Persson and Tabellini (1994b), and many others have analyzed simple dynamic versions, in which higher redistributive income taxation hurts the incentives to invest in physical or human capital and therefore economic growth. Greater wealth inequality (in the sense of lower median relative to mean wealth) should thus be associated with higher taxation and slower growth. Alesina and Rodrik as well as Persson and Tabellini find robust evidence in historical and cross-country data that more income inequality is indeed associated with slower growth, but this is only indirect evidence, and the link between inequality and growth might be due to other economic or political mechanisms. Perotti (1996) obtains negative results when trying to relate various measures of income distribution to government transfers in similar broad cross-country data. Data problems are, however, likely to be paramount in such broad data sets. The evidence from U.S. states, whose inequality data are more comparable, seems mixed.[5]

Krusell and Rios-Rull (1999) focus on sequential voting decisions in a full-fledged dynamic economy. They calibrate a version of a neoclassical growth model with heterogeneity in wealth and labor income in which the same income tax applies to both labor and capital

4. See, for instance, Shields and Goidel 1997.
5. See Partridge 1997 and Panizza 1998.

income. They formulate the model so that heterogeneity affects only political decisions, whereas only average magnitudes matter for the economic equilibrium. A median-voter result applies, similar to that illustrated above. But the median voter in their model faces a more demanding problem: tax rates are chosen sequentially over time, and the decision in each period is made in full anticipation of how current policy influences the political equilibrium in the next period through its effect on the relevant state variables. Krusell and Rios-Rull numerically compute the political equilibrium and calibrate the model's steady state to data for the U.S. economy. Both steady-state tax rates and transfers are remarkably close to recent U.S. data. Interestingly, the model's dynamics plays an important role: with fixed capital and variable labor supply (a static version of the model), the same numerical calibration implies excessively high tax and transfer rates. Thus the investment elasticity to the tax rate is important for quantitative success. Their paper, however, attempts to explain neither the secular rise of taxes and transfers nor the observed cross-country differences.

Overall, the empirical results described above are somewhat disappointing. As mentioned in the introduction to this chapter, the secular increase in government transfers and the cross-country differences are huge, even if we restrict the sample to the last thirty years. A closer look at the timing of policy changes reveals a further weakness. In most countries, transfers rose most quickly during the 1960s and 1970s, when income inequality was generally on the decline; during the 1980s and 1990s, in contrast, inequality instead turned upward, whereas redistributive transfers rose less quickly.

One reason why the theory may fail to account for the increase in government transfers in the last thirty years is that the data on transfers do not fit the theory very well. Pensions and health-related transfers are the most rapidly growing components of government transfers. Because these systematically benefit older individuals, the simple median-voter model above needs to be modified to allow for heterogeneity in age, as is done in the next section. Regional transfers are important in many countries, particularly those in which average income is very different across regions; such transfers are the topic of section 6.3. Yet other transfers belong to social insurance, such as transfers to the unemployed. This kind of spending also differs a great deal across countries. Section 6.4 investigates the determinants of unemployment insurance, which also differs from simple redistribution between rich and poor voters in several ways. Finally, some transfers are very clearly targeted to more narrow groups. Such policies, and the associated special-interest politics, are the topic of chapter 7.

6.2 Pensions

Why have pension expenditures risen so rapidly in all countries in the postwar period, and with so little political opposition? What political forces stand in the way of pension reforms in most industrial countries? And how can a reform package be designed so as to be politically feasible? These are the questions motivating this section. We build on the simple median-voter model of section 6.1 but add age as a second dimension of heterogeneity. Pay-as-you-go public pension schemes redistribute *across* generations by definition, and redistribution *within* generations is also a realistic feature of most pension systems. Social security contributions tend to be proportional to income, whereas benefits are often regressive.[6] This two-way redistribution plays a key role in the political equilibrium, as voters' coalitions form along two dimensions: age and income. The two-dimensional coalition formation complicates the analysis somewhat. But it is useful to spell out the details, as they show how one may compute median-voter equilibria with multidimensional heterogeneity, as long as the policy itself is one-dimensional. Details not found in the text are discussed in problem 2 of this chapter.

6.2.1   A Simple Model of Pensions

Consider an overlapping-generations economy in which each generation lives for three periods and the population grows at a constant rate (three-period lives make coalition formation more interesting than two-period lives). There is no altruism across generations. Individuals work in the first two periods of life and retire in the last. They can invest their savings in a worldwide capital market at a given rate of return. Within each generation, labor income is heterogeneous. As in the previous section, some individuals have more effective time to allocate between labor and leisure; we assume these productivity differences to be permanent throughout life. A proportional income tax levied on working generations pays for retirees' pensions, which consist of the same nonnegative lump sum payment for every old individual. Thus the pension system redistributes both across and within generations. For simplicity, we treat the pension system in isolation from other parts of the budget; thus taxes are collected only to finance pensions to the old under a balanced budget, whereas working generations receive no transfers.

When young, individual i maximizes the following utility function:

$$w^{iY} = U(c^{iY}) + \frac{1}{(1+\upsilon)}U(c^{iM}) + \frac{1}{(1+\upsilon)^2}c^{iO} + V(x^{iY}) + \frac{1}{(1+\upsilon)}V(x^{iM}), \qquad (6.8)$$

where υ denotes the subjective discount rate; the notation otherwise coincides with that of the previous section, except that the upper-case superscripts denote the period of life (Y for young, M for middle-aged, O for old). Linearity of consumption when old implies that all c^{iO} absorbs all income effects. The intertemporal budget constraint of a young

---

6. For the United States, see for instance the computations by Boskin et al. (1987) and Galasso (1998).

generation is

$$c^{iY} + \frac{c^{iM}}{1+\rho} + \frac{c^{iO}}{(1+\rho)^2} = l^{iY}(1-\tau) + \frac{l^{iM}(1-\tau)}{1+\rho} + \frac{f}{(1+\rho)^2}, \tag{6.9}$$

where ρ denotes the given world real interest rate and f the pension received when old. By assumption, the same tax rate τ is paid in both working periods (see further below). Finally, we assume that $\upsilon = \rho$. When choosing between labor and leisure, individuals face the time constraint (6.1) in each period, as in the previous section, which means that (6.2) still gives labor supply when individuals are young and (planned) labor supply when they are middle-aged. Consumption when individuals are young and (planned consumption) when they are middle-aged is given by $c = U_c^{-1}(1)$, with income effects completely absorbed by old-age consumption.

A middle-aged individual behaves in a similar fashion. He maximizes $(1+\upsilon)w^{iY}$, except that all variables from young age are now given. As there is perfect foresight, his decisions accord with the plans made at young age. An old individual, finally, just consumes his pension plus his assets (minus his liabilities).

Let n be the exogenous rate of population growth. Then the government budget constraint can be written in per-retiree form:

$$f = \tau l^M(1+n) + \tau l^Y(1+n)^2 = \tau L(\tau)(1+n)(2+n). \tag{6.10}$$

(As before, variables without an i superscript denote averages.) For each old individual, there are $(1+n)$ middle-aged and $(1+n)^2$ young individuals; the right-most expression follows from (6.2) with some rewriting. This constraint (6.10) is typical of a balanced pay-as-you-go pension system, in which the working generations' contributions finance the pensions of the currently old.

As real interest rates and real wages are both given in our simple perfect foresight model, the pension system has three effects only: it redistributes across generations, it redistributes within generations, and the taxes needed to finance it distort labor-leisure choices. In a richer model the pension system would have general equilibrium effects via endogenous factor prices and would provide social insurance in the wake of individual income uncertainty.

Voters' Preferences How do different individuals evaluate the generosity of the pension system? Let us start with the simplest case of complete commitment. Individuals are thus assumed to vote over τ (or, equivalently, over f). Once a policy is approved, it remains forever (or, equivalently, for three periods, so that all generations who voted for it have died).

All old voters clearly want the revenue-maximizing tax rate, as they internalize only benefits and no costs of higher taxes. Young and middle-aged individuals, however, base their policy preferences on both income and age. Generally, poorer and older individuals prefer higher public pensions, as they benefit more from either intragenerational or intergenerational redistribution.

Specifically, consider a young voter of type i. Let $W^{iY}(\tau)$ be his indirect utility function/policy preferences, defined by his optimal consumption and labor supply choices and the government budget constraint. By the envelope theorem, a marginal change in τ affects his welfare according to

$$
\begin{aligned}
W_\tau^{iY}(\tau) &= -\left[\widehat{l}^{iY} + \frac{\widehat{l}^{iM}}{1+\rho}\right] + \frac{1}{(1+\rho)^2} \cdot \frac{df}{d\tau} \\
&= -\frac{(2+\rho)}{(1+\rho)}[L(\tau) + e^i - e] + \frac{(1+n)(2+n)}{(1+\rho)^2}[\tau L_\tau(\tau) + L(\tau)],
\end{aligned}
\tag{6.11}
$$

where a $\widehat{}$ denotes a privately optimal choice, as in the previous section, and where the right-most expression follows from (6.2), (6.10), and some manipulations. The expressions in (6.11) are easily interpreted: increasing τ entails a benefit when old (the last term) and a cost in the first two periods of life due to higher taxes (the first term). The benefit is the same for all young voters. But the cost of higher taxes is higher for the richer among the young (i.e., for those with a higher e^i). The policy preferences are thus monotonic in e^i. Moreover, higher population growth n makes public pensions more attractive, because the same tax rate now gives a higher pension. A higher real interest rate ρ would have the opposite effect, reducing the present value of net benefits from the pension system.

Consider the special, "golden-rule" case of $\rho = n$. Setting (6.11) equal to zero, we get a condition identical to (6.5), that is, the condition for the optimal tax rate in the previous section's static model. When $\rho = n$, the average young individual (with $e^{iY} = e^i = e$) gains nothing from the social security system. But since taxes are distorting, he prefers $\tau = 0$. The social security system becomes attractive for the average young only if $\rho < n$. Young voters poorer than average ($e^i < e$), on the other hand, prefer $\tau > 0$ even if $\rho = n$, as they stand to gain from the *intra*generational redistribution, just as in the simple model.

Finally, consider a middle-aged voter of type i. By the same logic, a marginal change in τ affects his welfare according to

$$
\begin{aligned}
W_\tau^{iM}(\tau) &= -\widehat{l}^{iM} + \frac{1}{1+\rho} \cdot \frac{df}{d\tau} \\
&= -[L(\tau) + e^i - e] + \frac{(1+n)(2+n)}{(1+\rho)}[\tau L_\tau(\tau) + L(\tau)].
\end{aligned}
\tag{6.12}
$$

Comparing this expression with (6.11), we see that preferences are still monotonic in e^i. But the marginal benefit of pensions is now higher because it is closer in time, and the marginal cost is lower because taxes are now paid for one period only. Thus a voter with the same relative income position $e^{iY} = e^{iM} = e^i$ prefers a higher tax rate when middle-aged than when young. In particular, the average $(e^{iM} = e)$ middle-aged voter would prefer $\tau > 0$, even if $\rho = n$, though he would stop short of full revenue maximization.

By (6.11) and (6.12), we can identify a pair of young and middle-aged individuals who always vote alike. Setting the right-most expressions in each of these conditions equal to zero, subtracting one from the other, and simplifying, we get

$$e^{iM} = e^{iY} + \frac{(1+n)(2+n)}{2+\rho}[L(\tau) + \tau L_\tau(\tau)]. \tag{6.13}$$

For any young voter of type e^{iY}, there is thus always a middle-aged voter of type e^{iM} with identical policy preferences. This middle-aged voter is richer than his young counterpart; by (6.13), $e^{iM} > e^{iY}$. The intuition was given above; older voters favor social security more just as do poorer voters. Hence, for a young individual to prefer the same taxes as a middle-aged individual, he must have a lower income to compensate for his lower age.

The policy preferences of the population can thus be succinctly summarized. Preferences are monotonic in income and age, older and poorer voters always preferring a higher value of τ.

6.2.2 Equilibrium Pensions

We are now ready to characterize the political equilibrium.[7] Policy preferences are single peaked, and a median-voter solution exists. But who is the pivotal voter? To determine the pivotal voter's identity, we exploit the monotonicity of individual preferences in income and age. Clearly, all old individuals prefer the revenue-maximizing tax rate. Conversely, all young individuals richer than the average prefer tax rates at zero. Other voters prefer an interior solution, depending on their age and their endowments. Unless n takes on an extreme value, making the old or the poor young a majority, the equilibrium is an interior solution. In particular, the median voter corresponds to a pair of voters: a poor young and a richer middle-aged voter who both prefer the same tax rate. Let e^{*m} be the middle-aged median voter (yet to be identified)—that is, not the individual with the median endowment—and τ^{*m} his preferred policy. The relation between e^{*m} and τ^{*m} is obtained by setting the right-most expression in (6.12) equal to zero and solving for $e^i = e^{*m}$:

$$e^{*m} = e + \frac{(1+n)(2+n)}{1+\rho}[\tau^{*m}L_\tau(\tau^{*m}) + L(\tau^{*m})] - L(\tau^{*m}). \tag{6.14}$$

As before, let e^i be distributed in the population, with c.d.f. $F(\cdot)$. In equilibrium, the number of voters in favor of $\tau > \tau^{*m}$ equals the number of voters in favor of $\tau < \tau^{*m}$.

---

7. We consider only interior equilibria, such that $0 < \tau < \arg \max_\tau \tau L(\tau)$.

Furthermore, by (6.13) we can identify the young voter who prefers $\tau = \tau^{*m}$. The requirement of an equilibrium can thus be formulated as

$$1 + (1+n)F(e^{*m}) + (1+n)^2 F\left(e^{*m} - \frac{(1+n)(2+n)}{2+\rho}[L(\tau^{*m}) + \tau^{*m}L_\tau(\tau^{*m})]\right)$$

$$= \frac{1 + (1+n) + (1+n)^2}{2}. \tag{6.15}$$

The left-hand side of (6.15) represents the size of the coalition of those voters in favor of taxes higher than τ^{*m}, namely all of the old and a fraction of the middle-aged and the young, respectively. In equilibrium, this coalition must make up exactly half the electorate, the measure of which is given by the expression on the right-hand side. We can also consider (6.15) an illustration of our previous claim: a coalition of elderly and poor voters supports high pensions, as those two groups stand to benefit from the inter- or intragenerational redistribution.

To obtain the equilibrium policy τ^{*m}, we combine (6.14) and (6.15):

$$(1+n)F\left(e + \frac{(1+n)(2+n)}{1+\rho}[\tau^{*m}L_\tau(\tau^{*m}) + L(\tau^{*m})] - L(\tau^{*m})\right)$$

$$+ (1+n)^2 F\left(e + \frac{(1+n)(2+n)}{(1+\rho)(2+\rho)}[\tau^{*m}L_\tau(\tau^{*m}) + L(\tau^{*m})] - L(\tau^{*m})\right)$$

$$= \frac{(1+n) + (1+n)^2 - 1}{2}. \tag{6.16}$$

As F is a monotonic function, (6.16) implicitly defines a unique equilibrium tax rate, τ^m, that is a decreasing function of ρ. A higher ρ has two effects. First, it reduces the present discounted value of future pensions. Second, it reduces average labor supply (the function $L(\tau)$ is now a decreasing function of ρ). Both effects reinforce each other, making young and middle-aged voters less favorable to public pensions. A higher population growth rate n, in contrast, has ambiguous effects on τ^m. On the one hand, a higher n increases the weight of the young and reduces the weight of the old, thus shifting the median-voter identity toward someone less favorable to pensions. On the other hand, a higher n makes pensions more attractive for all young and middle-aged voters. Either effect might prevail, depending on functional forms. Finally, the shape of the income distribution, as described by $F(\cdot)$, also affects equilibrium policy. But then, not only median income matters, as the decisive voters are not median-income recipients. In general, however, greater income inequality is likely to make the decisive voters more willing to exploit the pension system for intragenerational redistribution and increase the system's equilibrium generosity.

It is useful to consider the special case where $\rho = n$. Here it can be shown that τ^m is greater than the equilibrium tax rate of the static redistributive model in the previous section. In fact, the two tax rates would coincide if only the young individuals were eligible to vote. As noted above, if $\rho = n$ the young do not benefit from the intergenerational redistribution, and only the intragenerational motives for redistribution would shape their votes. But the old and middle-aged do benefit from intergenerational redistribution, even if $\rho = n$. Their votes thus raise the equilibrium generosity of the pension system beyond the preference of the median young.

Suppose we let the normative benchmark be a utilitarian optimum defined as the maximum of the discounted sum of the welfare of all currently alive and future generations. By the quasi linearity of preferences, this translates into a discounted sum of the welfare of the average individual in each generation. It is easy to see that the utilitarian optimum has $f = 0$.[8] Relative to this benchmark, the political equilibrium we have studied entails too much redistribution, both across and within generations. First, it redistributes to poor individuals at the expense of rich. As in the previous section, this is a consequence of majority rule and of the distribution of income being skewed to the right. Second, the equilibrium redistributes to the currently old and middle-aged voters at the expense of future generations. This new feature is a consequence of the fact that the generations yet unborn (obviously) do not participate in the vote that determines their future taxes. Powerful political forces thus support the introduction of a pay-as-you-go social security system that is excessive relative to the social optimum.

One of the political distortions keeping public pensions too high is that even though the system very much affects future generations, they do not vote on it. This suggests a simple constitutional remedy, namely to allow only the young generation to vote on social security. Under our assumptions, this would implement the social optimum, as the young are the only living generation correctly internalizing the entire tax burden of public pensions. This constitutional constraint is hard to enforce, however, as a majority of voters would always be willing to repeal it. Moreover, the political equilibrium described above hinges on the assumption of commitment; once voted upon, the policy remains for as long as all generations participating in the vote are alive. Below, we discuss how to relax this assumption.

6.2.3 Evidence and Extensions

We have just illustrated how political forces may bring about and shape a pension system of the kind observed in many Western democracies. Does the evidence support some of the model's specific predictions? Few empirical studies have been conducted in this area.

---

8. Other reasons, such as social insurance, may render socially optimal pensions positive. As these are not included in our simple model with risk neutrality, the argument should be interpreted as deviations from some benchmark, whatever the level of pensions in that benchmark.

The population's demographic composition is clearly an important determinant of the size of pensions. Lindert (1996), Perotti (1996), and Tabellini (1990a) all find that, in panels of industrial countries and in cross-sectional correlations of larger country groups, pension expenditures as a fraction of GDP are larger the greater is the proportion of elderly in the population. This finding does not, however, discriminate well against other possible models of equilibrium pensions. A social planner, for example, would also spend more on pensions with a larger number of elderly people. The model really predicts that pensions *per retiree* will be higher, the higher the weight on old voters (a lower n in the model), as this shifts the median-voter equilibrium toward a more generous pension system.[9] Furthermore, population growth is, in reality, not constant over time. To be faithful to the theory, one should also look at the effect of changes in expected future population trends (this is the second and opposite effect of n on the political equilibrium above), but no empirical study of which we know incorporates these features, nor has anyone, to our knowledge, studied the effect of the real interest rate, ρ.

The model also predicts that pensions will increase with appropriate measures of income inequality. The evidence supports this only very weakly. Lindert (1996) and Perotti (1996) find no significant effect of income distribution variables on pensions. Tabellini (1990a) finds a positive correlation between a Gini index of inequality and pensions in a large sample of countries, controlling for age and initial income, but measures of inequality are bound to be highly imperfect for such a large sample of countries. Measuring income distribution in accordance with the model is even more tricky; as noted above, the decisive voter's relative income depends on age and does not coincide with median income.

The simple model studied in this section can be generalized in many directions. If we add capital accumulation to the model, the social security system generates general equilibrium effects, at least in a closed economy. Expanding the program reduces private savings, raises the real interest rate, and lowers the real wage. This benefits rich savers and hurts borrowers, thus adding another dimension to the political determinants of the equilibrium. As Cooley and Soares (1999) show, these general equilibrium effects can sometimes play a dominant role in determining the preferences over the pension system.

With individual income uncertainty, the pension system also has social insurance benefits. Conesa and Krueger (1999) incorporate both general equilibrium and social insurance effects in their analysis of the political support for pension reform. They study a rich model with heterogeneity in three dimensions: age, assets, and income. Conesa and Krueger use numerical methods to study the economy's dynamic transitional adjustment

---

9. In a cross-sectional study of social spending in Swedish municipalities, Strömberg (1996) explicitly tested—and found support for—a political model based on the age of the median voter against a social-planner alternative.

over time to a new long-run equilibrium in the face of different types of pension reform. Their results clearly illustrate how hard it is to muster majority support among the present voters for reforms of the pension system, even though the reforms entail significant long-run benefits.

The assumption of commitment can also be modified without altering the nature of the results. Suppose that the effect of majority decisions lasts only one period, rather than forever, as assumed above. Thus every other period, voters get to decide on social security contributions today and tomorrow. In the absence of reputational effects, all young voters would now vote against any positive contributions, since the current vote does not affect the pension they will receive two periods ahead. The old and a fraction of the middle-aged individuals, on the other hand, continue to support the social security system. Unless the young outnumber them, the same factors as above, namely ρ, n, and the function $F(\cdot)$, will shape the equilibrium policy, even though the precise characterization will differ and the system will be less generous. Indeed, such a model of limited commitment might be a good vehicle for studying the evolution of social security over time in the face of changing population trends. The ongoing and predicted aging of the population experienced in most Western democracies would introduce interesting dynamics in the public support for the pension system. Studying these dynamics might provide a deeper understanding of the forces behind the political struggle over pension reform.

Absent any commitment, the simple model of this section could not sustain positive pensions, except through reputational forces. All taxpayers would oppose the system, as their pensions would be independent of the current vote. Presumably, two generations of taxpayers would also outnumber the old generation. Absence of any commitment is, however, as unrealistic as full commitment. Abolishing the pension system from one day to another would not only meet political resistance that our simple median-voter model does not fully capture but would be ruled out as unconstitutional in many countries. Moreover, reputational mechanisms could link the voting outcomes across periods, and in this case equilibria with social security could be sustained even without commitment.[10]

Altruism across generations is another mechanism that may help sustain equilibria with positive social security in the absence of commitment. Tabellini (1991, 1990a) shows that even if altruism is so weak that it will not support private inter vivos transfers, it can nevertheless affect political behavior. Poor young and middle-aged individuals could be

---

10. Reputational equilibria in overlapping-generations (OLG) models may be quite different from those in the usual applications of the folk theorem in that they may require generational chains of punishments or rewards. In a simple two-period OLG model, for example, sustaining a reward from the current young to the current old requires that the current young expect that their hypothetical deviation from the equilibrium would lead to future punishment from the next (yet unborn) generation.

induced to vote in favor of the social security system, since the (lump sum) benefit to their parents or grandparents outweighs the cost of the (comparatively) small taxes they must pay. With a larger number of poor voters than rich, this might be sufficient to support public pensions.

An important assumption in our model is the restriction to just one policy instrument: a lump sum transfer when old, financed by a wage tax. Yet as Mulligan and Sala-i-Martin (1999a) emphasize, a variety of policy dimensions characterize social security systems, and a good theory ought to be able to explain most of them. In this vein, Galasso and Conde Ruiz (1999) consider an overlapping-generations model combining the two redistributive policy tools discussed in this and the previous sections: a purely intragenerational scheme of redistribution like that of section 6.1 and the pension scheme of this section, which redistributes both within and across generations. In their model preferences are no longer single peaked, and hence they study a structure-induced equilibrium like that of section 2.2. They find that both tools are used in equilibrium, but consistent with the evidence, the intragenerational scheme turns out to be much smaller than the existing pension system, because the old constitute a large and homogenous coalition that supports pensions but not other forms of redistribution. This intuition may also help explain why pensions are financed out of wages, with no explicit or implicit taxes on accumulated wealth (pension benefits are almost never conditional on individual wealth holdings): taxing wealth would break the homogeneity of the old generation vis-à-vis the policy and reduce the size of the coalition in favor of larger pensions.

Another important policy dimension is the age of retirement. Why is retirement compulsory in virtually all public pension systems? And what determines retirement age? As suggested by Mulligan and Sala-i-Martin (1999b), compulsory retirement is likely to increase the elderly's political influence: lacking other sources of income makes the economic interest of the old more homogeneous and increases their stakes. This by itself is likely to increase their political influence. A similar effect would arise in the models of probabilistic voting or lobbying introduced in chapter 3. Problem 3 at the end of this chapter deals formally with pensions in the probabilistic voting model. Mulligan and Sala-i-Martin (1999b) also focus on yet another aspect: retirement frees up leisure time that can be devoted to lobbying and other political activities.

6.3   Regional Transfers

Income inequalities often reflect regional (as opposed to individual) features. Regions are rich or poor because of their endowments of natural resources, their sectorial or occupational composition, their cultural and sociological attributes, or just historical accident. Programs redistributing income across individuals also redistribute income among regions. But regional conflicts sometimes lead to more drastic political consequences than orderly majority decisions on taxes. In particular, acute regional conflict can lead to secession. Redistributive gains, in contrast, may induce poor regions to seek political integration with richer regions. But secession or integration also entails other considerations relating to economies of scale in public-good provision, heterogeneity in tastes, and political and cultural values. Recent developments in Europe and elsewhere in the world provide an obvious motivation to study these issues.

In this section we therefore address the following questions. Which regions or groups of voters are more likely to integrate politically? And which are more likely to favor secession? How does the threat of secession modify the size of redistributive programs? How does political integration affect the size of these programs? We pose these questions in a simple extension of the model from section 6.1 suggested by Bolton and Roland (1997) and Persson and Tabellini (1994d). Redistribution is individually based, and there are no intergovernmental transfers. But since average income differs across regions, a policy that redistributes from rich to poor individuals also redistributes across regions, and regions, unlike individuals, have the option to opt out of a redistributive program or join it through integration. We study how the voters' policy choices within broad redistributive programs interact with their decisions to secede or integrate in political equilibrium.

6.3.1 A Simple Model of Regional Redistribution

Consider again our basic model of redistribution from rich to poor individuals in section 6.1, but now let the population be spread over two regions, $J = R, P$. These regions are identical in all respects, except in the distribution of individual endowments, e^i, and in population size. Let N^J be the population of region J, and total population $N = N^R + N^P$. Average and median endowments in region J are denoted e^J and e^{mJ}, respectively. Region R has a higher average endowment, specifically: $e^R \geq 0 \geq e^P$. We normalize such that the nationwide average endowment is zero: $(N^R e^R + N^P e^P)/N = 0$. As before, the nationwide median endowment is below the average: $e^m < 0$.

We need some motive for the two regions to form a single jurisdiction. A natural assumption is that public revenue can also be allocated to the consumption of a national public good, g, which yields the same per capita utility $H(g)$ to every citizen in every region. The public good is nonrival and excludable across, but not within, regions. Enjoying the utility from this public good requires the two regions to be politically united. If they are separate, the public good must be provided separately in each region, foregoing the economies of scale associated with common provision. Examples of these types of public goods are national defense, the administration of justice, and the enforcement of law and order. The government budget constraint, if the regions remain united, is $Nf + g = N(\tau L(\tau))$, or:

$$f + \frac{g}{N} = \tau L(\tau). \tag{6.17}$$

The notation is the same as in section 6.1. Thus, f is a lump sum transfer to every individual, τ is a proportional income tax rate, and $L(\tau)$ is average labor supply derived from agents' optimizing economic choices.

Under separation, each region J faces the same budget constraint, except that averages refer to regional averages, and N is replaced by regional population N^J:

$$f^J + \frac{g^J}{N^J} = \tau^J L^J(\tau^J) = \tau^J(L(\tau^J) + e^J).$$

Throughout the section, we assume that equilibrium redistributive transfers are positive $(f > 0)$, with or without separation. Under this assumption, there is no conflict between citizens over the amount of public goods to provide, and the equilibria with or without separation are straightforward extensions of the results derived in section 6.1. Under national policy, we can write the policy preferences of agent i in any region as

$$W^i(\tau, g) = (1 - \tau)(L(\tau) + e^i) + \tau L(\tau) + V(1 - L(\tau)) + H(g) - \frac{g}{N}. \tag{6.18}$$

Suppose that the two regions indeed remain united. As in section 6.1 (with $e = 0$), the pivotal voter with median endowment prefers the tax rate $\hat{\tau}^U = e^m / L_\tau(\tau^m)$. Moreover, all voters agree that the public good should be provided in the quantity

$$\hat{g}^U = H_g^{-1}\left(\frac{1}{N}\right). \tag{6.19}$$

Intuitively, the opportunity cost of providing one more unit of the public good is a reduction of lump sum transfers for all voters. Since the marginal utility of income is 1, the opportunity cost for every voter is $\frac{1}{N}$. Equating this to the marginal benefit of the public good, H_g, yields (6.19), which coincides with the standard Samuelsonian efficiency condition for a pure public good. (Even though each voter internalizes only $\frac{1}{N}$ of the marginal benefits, he also internalizes only $\frac{1}{N}$ of the marginal social cost, so that a single voter faces the right social trade-off.)

Next, suppose that the regions are separated. We must then modify the policy preferences of citizen i in region J to

$$W^{iJ}(\tau, g) = (1 - \tau)(L^J(\tau) + e^{iJ} - e^J) + \tau L^J(\tau) + V(1 - L(\tau)) + H(g) - \frac{g^J}{N^J}. \tag{6.20}$$

Voters within each region agree that the optimal amount of the public good in region J is $\hat{g}^J = H_g^{-1}(1/N^J)$, for $J = R, P$. As in section 6.1, the tax rate preferred by the regional median voter is a function of the difference between median and average endowments within each region, given by

$$\widehat{\tau}^J = \frac{(e^{mJ} - e^J)}{L_\tau(\widehat{\tau}^J)}. \tag{6.21}$$

The lump sum transfer is residually determined from the relevant government budget constraint, given the equilibrium values $\widehat{\tau}^J$ and $\widehat{g}^J$.

6.3.2   Integration or Not?

We now ask which of these equilibria is preferred by a majority of voters within each region. This is the appropriate question when analyzing the determinants of political integration, that is, when two separate regions consider whether to become politically united. Formally, suppose that in the game's first stage, voters in both regions must vote yes or no to a proposal of integration in separate regional referenda. If a majority votes yes in both regions, nationwide policy is subsequently set in national electoral competition, producing policy $(\widehat{\tau}^U, \widehat{g}^U)$. If a majority votes no in at least one region at the first stage, regionwide policy is subsequently set in regional electoral competition, producing regional policies $(\widehat{\tau}^J, \widehat{g}^J)$, $J = R, P$. As discussed further below, a decision about separation may require a more complex procedure than a majority vote in each region. Moreover, in the presence of a credible threat to secede, equilibrium national policy may be adapted to avoid disruptive separation.

As preferences are single peaked and monotonic in endowments, the preferences of the regional median voters—given the perfectly foreseen policy consequences in each case—are decisive for the outcome of each regional referendum. Let $[W^{mJ}(\widehat{\tau}^J) + H(\widehat{g}^J) - \frac{\widehat{g}^J}{N^J}]$ be the equilibrium indirect utility of the median voter in region J if the regions are separated, given the regional equilibrium tax rate $\widehat{\tau}^J$ and public good $\widehat{g}^J$. The term

$$W^{mJ}(\tau) \equiv (1 - \tau)(L(\tau) + e^{mJ}) + V(1 - L(\tau)) + \tau(L(\tau) + e^J) \tag{6.22}$$

refers to the indirect utility from private consumption and leisure and is defined in consistency with (6.20). Given (6.22) and the definitions in (6.18)–(6.20), the equilibrium indirect utility of the median voter in region J, if the two regions are united, is

$$\left[W^{mJ}(\widehat{\tau}^U) - \widehat{\tau}^U e^J + H(\widehat{g}^U) - \frac{\widehat{g}^U}{N} \right],$$

where $\widehat{\tau}^U$ is the equilibrium national tax rate (such that $f > 0$) and $\widehat{g}^U$ is optimal public-good provision. From the regional median voter's point of view, integration evidently matters for three reasons: the equilibrium tax rate is different; the lump sum transfer he receives is different, as both the tax rate and the tax base differ; and the quantity and cost of the public good are different.

Exploiting the above expressions, we can express the net gain from integration for the median voter in region J as

$$\Delta^J \equiv W^{mJ}(\widehat{\tau}^U) - \widehat{\tau}^U e^J + H(\widehat{g}^U) - \frac{g^U}{N} - \left[W^{mJ}(\widehat{\tau}^J) + H(\widehat{g}^J) - \frac{\widehat{g}^J}{N^J} \right]$$

$$= [W^{mJ}(\widehat{\tau}^U) - W^{mJ}(\widehat{\tau}^J)] - \widehat{\tau}^U e^J + \Gamma^J, \tag{6.23}$$

where Γ^J is defined by $\Gamma^J = (H(\widehat{g}^U) - \widehat{g}^U/N) - (H(\widehat{g}^J) - \widehat{g}^J/N^J)$. If Δ^J is positive (negative), a majority of voters in region J find integration superior (inferior) to separation. The expression in the second line of (6.23) identifies three effects of integration. The first term, within square brackets, is a purely political "autonomy loss." If the relative incomes of the regional and national median voters do not coincide—that is, if $(e^{mJ} \neq e^m)$—integration changes the identity of the decisive voter and thus the equilibrium tax rate (i.e., $\widehat{\tau}^J \neq \widehat{\tau}^U$). This can never improve the welfare for the regional median (as $W^{mJ}(\widehat{\tau}^J)$ constitutes a maximum), so the autonomy loss must be nonpositive. The second term, $-\widehat{\tau}^U e^J$, is a "tax base effect" due to differences in average per capita income between regions. The tax base effect from integration is negative (positive) for the median in the rich (poor) region, as $e^R > 0$ ($e^P < 0$). The last term, Γ^J, is a measure of the "efficiency gain" of integration due to the economies of scale in public-good provision. We know that $\Gamma^J > 0$ by a simple revealed-preference argument: $\widehat{g}^U$ is chosen rather than $\widehat{g}^J$ under integration, even though the per capita cost of choosing $\widehat{g}^J$ would be lower because of the larger population.

Consider first the special case $e^J = 0$, that is, average income in region J is identical to the national average. This means that the tax base effect is zero and that (6.23) reduces to $\Delta^J = [W^{mJ}(\widehat{\tau}^U) - W^{mJ}(\widehat{\tau}^J)] + \Gamma^J$. Integration could still be suboptimal for a majority in region J if the regional distribution of relative income differs enough from the nationwide distribution. In that case, the autonomy loss may be large enough to compensate for the efficiency gain. Next, suppose that $\widehat{\tau}^J = \widehat{\tau}^U$, because $e^{mJ} - e^J = e^m$. Then (6.23) reduces to $\Delta^J = -\widehat{\tau}^U e^J + \Gamma^J$. Clearly, the poor region always gains from integration, whereas the rich region could lose if it is so rich that the negative tax base effect more than offsets the efficiency gain. Not surprisingly, the poor region is thus more likely to prefer integration. It is entirely possible, however, for the rich region to favor integration and the poor region to oppose it, if, for example, e^R is small and $e^{mR} \simeq e^m$ (that is, the rich region is not very rich and its income distribution is similar to that of the integrated nation, whereas the income distribution in the poor region is very different from that of the integrated nation, so that the autonomy loss in taxation is very costly for the poor region). Finally, note that the efficiency gain, Γ^J, is always larger for a smaller region (that is the smaller is N^J relative to N), as the economies of scale are then more important. Summarizing, poorer and smaller regions, as well as regions with a relative income distribution more similar to that of the rest of the nation, have larger gains from integration.

Integration could be efficient for reasons besides the economies of scale in public-good provision. In particular, the parameter Γ^J could also reflect lower trade and transaction costs under political integration. This observation suggests that as economic integration increases throughout the world, secession becomes a more likely outcome. That is, international economic integration could lead to political disintegration, because it reduces the cost of political separation. The idea of a "Europe of regions" is a natural implication of this line of thought. Alesina, Spolaore, and Wacziarg (1997) document the effect of trade openness on country size and note that in the fifty years after World War II, a period of great trade liberalization, the number of countries in the world more than doubled.

But efficiency is not a sufficient condition for integration to occur. If the decision whether to integrate is made democratically under majority rule, efficiency-enhancing political integration might be foregone for fear of its redistributive consequences. Alesina and Spolaore (1997) analyze a related setup but focus on heterogeneity in preferences rather than heterogeneity in income. They conclude that democracy can lead to an inefficiently large number of nations or, equivalently, can limit the size of democratic countries to one that is inefficiently small.

Finally, what effect does integration have on the size of government? It is easy to see that even though g^U is larger than g^J, the implied tax burden is smaller, as

$$\frac{g^U}{N} < \frac{g^J}{N^J}.$$

The effect of integration on the size of f can go either way, depending on whether integration increases or reduces the distance between median and mean income. But Persson and Tabellini (1994d) show that in other aspects than average income, with enough symmetry, integration is likely to *reduce* the equilibrium size of redistributive programs.[11] Both forces thus push in the same direction: political integration is likely to create smaller governments. Alesina and Wacziarg (1998) provide empirical evidence supporting this proposition. Controlling for a number of other variables, they show that larger countries tend to have smaller governments. This effect is particularly robust for government consumption, on which the

---

11. Suppose that the two regions are of equal size and the distribution is the same within each region, so that $e^{mR} - e^R = e^{mP} - e^P < 0$. Then by (1.21), they also have the same tax rate if separated, $\hat{\tau}^J$. To compare $\hat{\tau}^J$ and $\hat{\tau}^U$ we need to compare the median income of the integrated nation, e^m, with the average of the regional medians, $(e^{mR} + e^{mP})/2$. If $e^m > (e^{mR} + e^{mP})/2$, then integration reduces the distance between median and mean income (recall that, by assumption, $e^m < 0$ and $(e^R + e^P)/2 = 0$), and the size of government shrinks; the opposite happens if inequality goes the other way. It turns out that if the regional distributions are skewed to the right, then $e^m > (e^{mR} + e^{mP})/2$ is more likely (Persson and Tabellini 1994c provides a sufficient condition).

economies of scale are likely to have the strongest effect. The effect of country size on government transfers is more fragile, however, and disappears when controlling for openness to international trade.[12]

In chapter 7 we discuss the effect of centralization on equilibrium spending on *local,* rather than national, public goods. There we show that, contrary to the results of this section, centralization of policy can very well lead to larger equilibrium spending.

6.3.3 The Threat of Secession

The analysis in the previous subsection really assumes that integration is an irreversible decision. If that is not the case, policymaking in a unified state may anticipate that policies that appear too extreme may cause some region to secede. We therefore pose the following question. How does the threat of secession influence redistributive policies, if two regions are already politically integrated? The answer depends on aspects of the constitution, such as the procedure for seceding and for setting national policy. In this subsection, we assume that secession is constitutionally feasible if approved by a majority of the citizens in *either* of the two regions, and we continue to assume that redistributive policies are the result of electoral competition between two office-motivated politicians. Specifically, consider the following three-stage game: (1) A tax rate and a level of public goods (τ^U, g^U) are set in (Downsian) electoral competition at the nationwide level. (2) Voters in each region make a decision, by referendum, on whether or not to secede. (3) If a majority of voters in one region approves it, secession takes place, and both regions reset their policies in connection with new regional elections.

From the previous analysis, we already know the outcome at stage (3) to be $\widehat{\tau}^J$ and $\widehat{g}^J$. At stage (2), voters will reject secession if neither regional median voter gains from it. Given that equilibrium policy at stage (1) will always produce the efficient level of public goods $\widehat{g}^U$, the condition for no secession is that the nationwide tax rate belongs to the set

$$NS \equiv \{\tau \mid \Delta^J(\tau) \equiv [W^{mJ}(\tau) - W^{mJ}(\widehat{\tau}^J)] - \tau e^J + \Gamma^J \geq 0, J = R, P\}, \tag{6.24}$$

where $\Delta^J(\tau)$ is defined exactly as in (6.23), but for an arbitrary nationwide tax rate. (We have also not made explicit this set's dependency on the model parameters (such as N^J, e^J, etc.)).

If the no-secession set is empty, that is, if no tax rate exists to fit the specifications of (6.24), secession is the only feasible outcome: no tax rate can induce both regions to stay

---

12. Rodrik (1998) and Cameron (1978) emphasize the positive correlation between openness and the size of government, explaining that more-open economies are more exposed to exogenous shocks and thus prefer higher social insurance.

united. As noted in the previous subsection, an empty NS is more likely if the efficiency costs of breaking apart are small (Γ^J is small for J), or if the two regions are very different either in average income or in regional income distribution.

If NS is nonempty, on the other hand, secession never occurs in equilibrium, and the equilibrium tax rate belongs to NS, because by definition of NS, both regional median voters are worse off with secession than with integration and $\tau \in NS$. Hence, a majority of the voters in the united nation are also worse off with secession than with integration and $\tau \in NS$. Anticipating the secession outcome, a majority of voters prefers $\tau \in NS$ to any alternative $\tau' \notin NS$ at stage (1). Hence the equilibrium belongs to NS, and secession does not take place.

Identifying the equilibrium tax rate in this setting is not straightforward, however. Because of the possibility of secession, some individuals may find it optimal to vote strategically at stage (1). The argument is similar to the one made in chapter 2. By voting for an extreme alternative, these voters may help trigger secession and an eventual policy outcome that is preferable to them against a moderate stage (1) alternative. In view of this, the pivotal voter need not have median endowment e^m. In general, the equilibrium tax rate could be anywhere in NS, but it is more likely to be at the boundary of NS if the average income in the two regions differs a great deal. In this case, voters in the rich region can credibly threaten to secede if the tax rate is too high. To avoid this outcome, the optimal tax rate for whoever is the pivotal voter at stage (1), $\hat{\tau}^U$, leaves the rich region just barely indifferent between secession and integration: $\Delta^R(\hat{\tau}^U) = 0$. Buchanan and Faith (1987) studied this case, in which the threat of secession limits the extent of politically feasible redistribution.

But the opposite situation is also possible: a majority of the voters in the poor region want high tax rates and can make a credible threat to secede. To prevent this, the nationwide policy could involve a higher tax rate than is otherwise optimal for the national pivotal voter, taking the equilibrium to the opposite boundary of NS, where the poor region is just barely indifferent to secession: $\Delta^P(\hat{\tau}^U) = 0$. A higher tax rate is more likely if the costs of breakup are small, for instance, because both regions can exploit the economies of scale on their own, and income inequality in the poor region is much greater than in the whole nation, so that the poor region values autonomy highly, because its preferred tax rate is much higher than that imposed with integration. In this case, the threat of secession does not constrain redistribution but instead enhances the political power of the region preferring high taxes or, more generally, enhances the power of the poor voters.

To summarize: if the national policy is set in nationwide electoral competition, the threat of secession can influence the equilibrium policy in either direction: secession can impose either a ceiling or a floor on equilibrium tax rates. But in general, rich and large regions are more likely to secede, and a rich region's secession threat is likely to impose a ceiling on the equilibrium tax rate.

From a normative point of view, we can view the right of secession as a constitutional protection of regional minorities from extreme policies imposed by the overall majority. Of course, other constitutional provisions serve a similar purpose, such as the requirement of a qualified majority for certain decisions, or overrepresentation of small regions by senate-like arrangements.

A central assumption in this chapter has been that policies in a united nation cannot directly target inhabitants of different regions. Clearly, many programs in existing democracies violate this assumption, however, and the next chapter deals with the determinants of government programs with group-specific benefits and dispersed costs. Targeted regional policies are one of the prime examples of such programs.

6.4 Unemployment Insurance

So far in this chapter we have assumed that voters know their relative income with certainty when formulating their policy preferences. An important role of some redistributive transfer programs, however, is to provide insurance against income risks, as in the case of unemployment insurance or public health insurance.[13] Voters evaluate such programs on the basis of their relative risk as well as their relative income. In labor markets, government regulation, such as hiring and firing rules, also affects the distribution of risk among individuals. This section analyzes the political determinants of unemployment insurance as well as labor market regulations.

A central determinant of labor market programs, emphasized by Wright (1986) and Saint-Paul (1993, 1996), is the likely conflict of interest between employed and unemployed voters or, more generally, between *insiders* (those with a well-paid and protected job) and *outsiders* (the unemployed and workers in secondary markets). To keep things simple, we abstract from idiosyncratic unemployment risk, even though risk differences are realistic and could be added along the lines of example 4 in chapter 2 (see also section 8.5). The remaining conflict of interest then becomes very stark: the risk of future unemployment is lower for currently employed workers/voters, who therefore want less unemployment insurance than the unemployed. Currently employed voters instead find it more expedient to protect

---

13. We rarely observe private unemployment insurance. But we do not discuss the underlying informational problems, which presumably provide a rationale for government insurance. It is not straightforward, however, to provide such a rationale. Under moral hazard, a government facing the same information constraints as private agents would generally be unable to outperform the market. Under adverse selection, there is more scope for outperforming the market, as the government might rely on compulsion.

themselves against unemployment risk through tight firing restrictions, even though such restrictions would increase unemployment and unemployment duration. As employed voters constitute a majority, political equilibria generally exhibit underprovision of unemployment insurance and overly restrictive labor market regulations. Closing the section, we discuss how labor market reforms may become politically feasible.

6.4.1 A Simple Model of Unemployment Insurance

All individuals are alike, apart from their employment status, and they maximize expected discounted lifetime utility of consumption over an infinite horizon:

$$W^J = U(c_0^J) + \mathsf{E}_0 \sum_{t=1}^{\infty} \beta^t U(c_t^J), \quad I, J \in \{E, U\},$$

where E_0 is the expectations operator conditional on information available at time 0, t the time period, β a discount factor ($\beta = \frac{1}{1+\upsilon}$ in the notation of section 6.2), and $U(\cdot)$ a well-behaved concave utility function. Individuals are either employed or unemployed, and the E and U superscripts denote these two states. Labor supply is exogenous and set equal to one. For simplicity, we also assume that there are no credit markets (see further below). Hence unemployment insurance entails no distortions, and consumption equals current income. If employed, individuals thus consume their real wage, normalized to unity, less taxes, $c_t^E = 1 - \tau_t$. If unemployed, they consume their unemployment benefit, $c_t^U = f_t$.

Individual employment status follows an exogenous first-order Markov process. In each period, a currently employed individual becomes unemployed with probability φ (for firing rate), whereas a currently unemployed individual becomes employed with probability ϑ (for hiring rate). We assume that these transition probabilities remain constant over time, irrespective of an individual's employment history, and are the same across individuals. Moreover, we assume that the flows in and out of unemployment are independent of the generosity of unemployment insurance. Under these assumptions, the aggregate rate of unemployment u_t follows the first-order difference equation

$$u_t = \varphi(1 - u_{t-1}) + (1 - \vartheta)u_{t-1}. \tag{6.25}$$

In each period, unemployment consists of the previously employed who were laid off (the first term) plus the previously unemployed who did not find a job (the second term). We assume that the root of this difference equation is stable ($\varphi + \vartheta < 1$), which implies monotonic convergence of u_t to a stationary constant unemployment rate. Solving (6.25) for $u_t = u_{t-1} = u$ yields

$$u = \frac{\varphi}{\varphi + \vartheta}. \tag{6.26}$$

We assume that $\vartheta > \varphi$, so that u is less than 50%. In the following, we focus on policymaking when the economy has already converged to a stationary state.

As in the previous sections, we treat this government transfer program in isolation from other policies. The government budget constraint implies that unemployment subsidies must be financed through taxes on currently working individuals:

$$uf_t = \tau_t(1 - u).$$

Using (6.26), the government budget constraint can be written as

$$f_t = \tau_t \frac{\vartheta}{\varphi}. \tag{6.27}$$

Voters' Preferences Assume initially that unemployment insurance is chosen today (at $t = 0$), given that u is already at its steady-state value, and remains in place for ever: that is, $\tau_t = \tau$, and $f_t = f$ for all t. How do voters evaluate such a program? To answer this question, consider the value functions of employed and unemployed voters, respectively. Making use of the previous expressions for c^E and c^U and treating τ as the policy instrument, these can be written as

$$W^E = U(1 - \tau) + \beta[(1 - \varphi)W^E + \varphi W^U]$$

$$W^U = U\left(\tau \frac{\vartheta}{\varphi}\right) + \beta[\vartheta W^E + (1 - \vartheta)W^U]. \tag{6.28}$$

The solution yields the state utilities as a function of the policy τ:

$$W^E = \frac{\beta \varphi U\left(\tau \frac{\vartheta}{\varphi}\right) + (1 - \beta(1 - \vartheta))U(1 - \tau)}{(1 - \beta)(1 - \beta(1 - \vartheta - \varphi))}$$

$$W^U = \frac{(1 - \beta(1 - \varphi))U\left(\tau \frac{\vartheta}{\varphi}\right) + \beta \vartheta U(1 - \tau)}{(1 - \beta)(1 - \beta(1 - \vartheta - \varphi))}. \tag{6.29}$$

Taking the derivative of these expressions with regard to the policy τ and setting it equal to zero, we find the insurance policy desired by employed and unemployed individuals, respectively:

$$\frac{U_c(c^E)}{U_c(c^U)} = \frac{\beta \vartheta}{1 - \beta(1 - \vartheta)} \leq 1$$

$$\frac{U_c(c^E)}{U_c(c^U)} = \frac{1 - \beta(1 - \varphi)}{\beta \varphi} \geq 1, \tag{6.30}$$

where the inequalities follow from $\beta \leq 1$. Evidently, the currently employed prefer incomplete insurance $(c^E \geq c^U)$, whereas the currently unemployed prefer overinsurance

$(c^U \geq c^E)$. Even though both sets of voters face a probability of changing status in the future, accounting for this is not enough to compensate for the fact that current unemployment insurance redistributes from employed to unemployed voters. By contrast, a utilitarian social planner—equivalently, an individual maximizing his expected utility behind a veil of ignorance over his current employment status—would always prefer full insurance, $c^E = c^U$. This is intuitive, as there is neither aggregate risk nor individual incentive problems due to information or distorting taxation. Adding such inefficiencies would lower the desired insurance levels discussed above but would not eliminate the conflict between employed and unemployed individuals.

Note that the qualitative results do not hinge on the absence of credit markets. With perfect credit markets and no aggregate risk, individuals would be able to fully insure their unemployment risk. Yet some individuals would still want to use public unemployment insurance to redistribute in their favor. In particular, unemployed voters or, more generally, voters whose risk of being unemployed is higher than average would want public unemployment insurance, since it would redistribute toward them in expected value (discussed by Wright (1986) and Persson and Tabellini (1996a)). If private insurance markets were absent but individuals could still save, they would have an incentive to self-insure. As a result, the tax cost of financing the program would weigh more heavily in their preferences and they would prefer less unemployment insurance in the labor market (discussed by Hassler and Rodriguez Mora (1999)).

6.4.2 Equilibrium Unemployment Insurance

With two types of voters only, the political equilibrium is simply the policy preferred by the largest group, namely those currently employed.[14] To get explicit results, let the utility function be isoelastic, $U(c) \equiv c^{1-\gamma}/(1-\gamma)$, with γ denoting the coefficient of relative risk aversion. The first expression in (6.30) and the definitions of c^E and c^U imply that the equilibrium tax rate τ^E satisfies

$$\frac{\tau^E \vartheta}{(1-\tau^E)\varphi} = \left[\frac{\beta \vartheta}{1-\beta(1-\vartheta)} \right]^{1/\gamma}. \tag{6.31}$$

From the government budget constraint (6.27), we can easily derive the corresponding equilibrium unemployment benefit, f^E, desired by the employed.

---

14. The equilibrium generalizes to the case (discussed in example 4 of chapter 2) of idiosyncratic unemployment risk, in which the latter is modeled as idiosyncratic hiring and firing parameters ϑ^i and φ^i. The political equilibrium would still be a median-voter equilibrium even with such two-dimensional heterogeneity. As in the case of pensions, the decisive voters would be a pair, namely an employed high-risk type, and an unemployed low-risk type, with different values for ϑ^i and φ^i.

How do changes in the model's parameters affect equilibrium policy? Applying the implicit function theorem to (6.27) and (6.31), we get

$$\frac{\partial \tau^E}{\partial \varphi} > 0, \quad \frac{\partial f^E}{\partial \varphi} < 0; \quad \frac{\partial \tau^E}{\partial \vartheta} \lesseqgtr 0, \quad \frac{\partial f^E}{\partial \vartheta} > 0$$

$$\frac{\partial \tau^E}{\partial \beta} > 0, \quad \frac{\partial f^E}{\partial \beta} > 0; \quad \frac{\partial \tau^E}{\partial \gamma} > 0, \quad \frac{\partial f^E}{\partial \gamma} > 0. \tag{6.32}$$

A higher firing rate φ reduces the equilibrium unemployment benefit but raises the equilibrium tax. Intuitively, with a higher firing rate, employed voters still want to retain the same marginal rate of substitution between consumption if employed or unemployed, as is evident from (6.30). But that rate has become more expensive, as equilibrium unemployment is higher, as is evident from (6.26). The optimal solution is to adjust both margins, raising the tax rate but reducing the unemployment benefit. Conversely, if the hiring rate ϑ is higher, the probability of staying unemployed is smaller, and the decisive voter is willing to accept a higher marginal rate of substitution of consumption if employed versus unemployed. In this sense, less insurance is needed. But insurance is now cheaper to buy, as unemployment falls with a higher ϑ. Hence the unemployment benefit rises and the tax rate falls only if the individual is sufficiently risk averse (more precisely, if $\gamma > 1$).[15] A higher discount factor or a higher rate of risk aversion, finally, would imply a more generous program, as the future risk of unemployment now carries more weight in the decision.

Evidence and Extensions   From a positive point of view, it is interesting to note that the equilibrium unemployment benefit, f, is negatively related to unemployment: parameter changes that increase unemployment also reduce the unemployment benefit, because the decisive voter reacts to changes in the cost of providing unemployment insurance.[16] The model also makes unambiguous predictions regarding the effect of the general turnover in the labor market on the generosity of equilibrium unemployment insurance. To see this, consider a fall in both ϑ and φ such that the ratio $\frac{\vartheta}{\varphi}$ and hence, aggregate unemployment u, stay constant. It is easily shown that both τ and f decrease for such an increase in turnover. (Problem 4 of this chapter deals formally with this experiment.) It is unclear whether these two predictions are consistent with the development over time of unemployment insurance

15. Note that these are pure comparative statics experiments. Specifically, they assume that a parameter difference has fully manifested itself in a different steady-state unemployment rate before the choice of unemployment insurance takes place.

16. These comparative statics results would be less clear-cut with individual specific hiring and firing rates. In that case, parameter changes would alter the median voter's identity and as unemployment increases, the median voter would be more likely to be unemployed. This would tend to move the size of equilibrium unemployment insurance (also as measured by benefits) in the same direction as the rate of unemployment.

in European countries, where indeed unemployment has generally increased and turnover in the labor market has generally decreased over the last two decades. It is quite clear, however, that the model's predictions for Europe versus the United States are counterfactual: Europe has both higher unemployment and lower turnover than the United States, at least in recent times, but higher unemployment benefits.

Such counterfactual cross-sectional predictions motivate Hassler and Rodriguez Mora (1999) to study the role of self-insurance. They show that once self-insurance is allowed, higher turnover does indeed make the employed prefer less generous unemployment insurance: when turnover is high, private savings become a close substitute for unemployment insurance, making the latter less valuable. Hassler and Rodriguez Mora also discuss the difficulty of sustaining positive unemployment insurance if there is no commitment to policy in future periods; this point is closely related to our discussion about the sustainability of the pension system in section 6.2.

Our simple model of endogenous policy focuses on the link from unemployment and its determinants to unemployment benefits. Much of the traditional literature on exogenous policy discusses the link in the opposite direction: that is, generous unemployment benefits may generate higher unemployment, either by pushing up equilibrium wages or by pushing down equilibrium search effort.[17] In an interesting recent paper, Hassler et al. (1998) try to incorporate links in both directions in a model with labor market search and endogenous policy. They show that there may very well be multiple equilibria: one with high unemployment and generous benefits and another with low unemployment and less generous benefits. This could contribute to explaining why European and U.S. (more generally Anglo-Saxon) labor markets differ so much.[18] Problem 5 of this chapter provides an example of how this section's simple model can be amended to generate multiple equilibria.

6.4.3   Equilibrium Labor Market Regulations

Unemployment insurance is not the only policy over which the preferences of the employed and the unemployed clash. Labor markets in many industrial countries, particularly in Europe, are heavily regulated. Firing thus becomes restricted or costly for firms, not by contract, but by law. Labor regulations can be seen as an indirect form of redistribution. Specifically, they protect those currently employed but harm the unemployed, since they discourage new hires and thus increase the duration of unemployment. We now investigate the political determinants of these regulations, largely following Saint-Paul (1996).

---

17. Nickell and Layard (1999) survey the relevant literature.

18. Cohen (1999) argues that in terms of welfare differences between employed and unemployed workers, the European and U.S. models are similar: the higher replacement rate offered to European unemployed workers compensates for the welfare loss due to their lower exit rate from the unemployment status.

Consider the same economy as above but without public unemployment insurance: the unemployed earn a given subsistence wage, and consumption of the employed is exogenously given.[19] To model firing regulations, redefine the probability of becoming unemployed, φ, as

$$\varphi = \chi + q,$$

where q is voluntary quits, and χ is firing (layoffs) by the firms. We treat q as an exogenous parameter but χ as a policy variable capturing the influence on firings of specific labor market legislation. The more difficult it is to legally fire a worker, the lower is χ, and hence the lower is φ. We can thus interpret χ as a measure of labor market flexibility: a higher χ amounts to more flexibility. As discussed by Saint-Paul (1996), who uses earlier results by Pissarides (1990), firing restrictions also make firms less willing to post vacancies. Thus firing restrictions reduce the hiring rate ϑ. Specifically, suppose—as does Saint-Paul (1996)—that the hiring rate is a given concave function of the firing rules:

$$\vartheta = H(\chi), \quad \text{such that} \quad H_\chi > 0, \quad H_{\chi\chi} < 0. \tag{6.33}$$

That is, more-flexible labor markets allow firms to increase firing (χ increases) but also tend to increase hiring, though at a decreasing rate. Firms are thus assumed to be more willing to hire workers if they know it is easier to lay them off during bad times. This means that increasing labor market flexibility involves a trade-off between firing and hiring rates. This trade-off is more favorable when labor markets are very rigid, that is, when χ is low, for the hiring rate increases more, in this case, as a result of increased flexibility.

This formulation implies that labor market flexibility generally has an ambiguous effect on steady-state unemployment, depending on the value of χ. In fact, by (6.26)

$$\frac{\partial u}{\partial \chi} = \frac{H(\chi) - (\chi + q)H_\chi(\chi)}{(\varphi + \vartheta)^2} \lessgtr 0. \tag{6.34}$$

By concavity of $H(\chi)$, this derivative is more likely to be negative for low values of χ. That is, additional labor market flexibility is more likely to reduce unemployment when labor markets are very rigid, because of the greater marginal effect on hiring noted above. We make this explicit by assuming that $u(\chi)$, that is, unemployment as a function of labor market flexibility for given q, has a unique minimum $u(\widetilde{\chi})$ at a specific level of labor flexibility $\widetilde{\chi}$.

---

19. This rules out general equilibrium effects of changes in the unemployment rate operating through the government budget constraint. Such effects would make the voting problem dynamic, as voters would have to consider the dynamic adjustment to the steady state: recall that by (1.25), unemployment gradually adjusts to the steady state. Although these dynamic effects would be unlikely to overturn the conclusions of this subsection, they would complicate the analysis considerably.

This simple model is obviously a shortcut, in that it does not treat firm behavior explicitly, squeezing what is essentially a dynamic problem into a static reduced-form hiring function. The ambiguous effect of firing protection on unemployment due to the opposite reaction of the firing and hiring rate is also a well-known property of more-sophisticated theoretical models of unemployment (see, for instance, Mortensen and Pissarides 1998 for a survey of the theoretical literature on the natural rate). Indeed, this ambiguous effect is often the basis for arguments that easier firing rules would not necessarily help reduce the high European unemployment (see, for instance, Blanchard 1998).

Without further excuses, we now turn to the political equilibrium. Clearly, employed and unemployed voters disagree over firing flexibility: the currently employed insiders want to protect their jobs, and thus dislike flexibility, whereas the unemployed outsiders welcome flexibility, as it raises the hiring rate. The unemployed constitute a minority, however, and equilibrium policy is thus chosen so as to please the employed voters.

Formally, the equilibrium policy is the value of χ that maximizes the employed voters' expected lifetime utility. As in the previous subsection, the maximand is given by W^E in (6.28), except that φ is now replaced by $\chi + q$ everywhere. The first-order condition for χ is obtained by taking the partial derivative of W^E with respect to χ, given (6.33), and setting it equal to zero. After some rewriting, we can express the equilibrium condition as

$$H(\chi) - (\chi + q)H_\chi(\chi) = -(1 - \beta)/\beta. \tag{6.35}$$

The right-hand side of (6.35) is strictly negative, as must be the left-hand side. But then it also follows from (6.34) that, in equilibrium, $\frac{\partial u}{\partial \chi} < 0$. That is, equilibrium unemployment is above its minimum, defined by $u(\widetilde{\chi})$, and additional labor market flexibility would reduce it. To protect their jobs, the majority of employed voters restrict firing to the extent that unemployment increases. This also entails costs for the insiders, however. Should they become unemployed in the future, they will have to wait longer for a job. At some point, these costs of unemployment become high enough to outweigh the benefits to insiders of tighter labor market restrictions.[20]

This result, that high equilibrium unemployment is also caused by overly tight firing rules, contrasts with the previously quoted argument, namely that increasing labor market flexibility would not necessarily reduce European unemployment. Such an argument is based on an incomplete theory, however, as it views the level of existing regulations as random. But policy choices are certainly not random: existing labor market regulations largely reflect the preferences of the majority of "insiders." If so, their predicted effect on unemployment

---

20. Endogenous income taxes or unemployment subsidies would carry a further cost of higher unemployment: providing unemployment insurance becomes more expensive, as taxes must increase, or equivalently, lower unemployment benefits can be financed out of given tax revenues.

is clear: looser firing rules, if politically feasible, would reduce unemployment. The view that existing policy choices are not random, but systematically related to the political and economic environment, also has important implications for how to approach the unemployment effects of alternative labor market policies and institutions in empirical work. These implications have been neglected so far in the existing empirical literature on the economic causes of unemployment.

Extensions   Are there policy reforms which retain job security for insiders and at the same time, reduce unemployment? If so, they would clearly be politically feasible, for they would receive the support of both employed and unemployed voters. Higher public employment could be one solution. Marginal employment subsidies or other devices to stimulate labor demand among private firms would be another. In both cases, however, some taxpayers would have to foot the bill. It would also be more difficult to fully analyze the equilibrium provision of alternative public policies. One way would be to combine this model with the one studied in section 6.1, in which there is income heterogeneity among employed workers but workers do not share the tax burden evenly.

Saint-Paul (1996) discusses other paths to reform. One is labor market segmentation. Suppose the law provided two kinds of firing restrictions: tighter ones for old jobs, but looser restrictions (or no restrictions at all) for new jobs. Such a two-tier system would protect insiders' job security, while at the same time reducing unemployment. Thus it would be an improvement for all voters and would receive political support. In the long run, a problem might emerge, however. As more and more workers would become employed on more-flexible contracts, insiders might become a political minority in the sense that their labor market protection could be scrapped and their rents eroded. Expectations of this long-run outcome could reduce insiders' support for a two-tier labor market. Saint-Paul (1996) shows a possible solution to this dilemma. Less-protected jobs should remain so only temporarily. That is, the law should specify a conversion clause: after a certain time, new jobs should either become regular and enjoy the full benefits of tight firing rules or be scrapped. Such a reform would still reduce unemployment without adverse long-run political consequences.

Research on these issues is still scarce. High equilibrium unemployment has become a pervasive and persistent phenomenon in Europe in the last two decades. At a general level, the discussion above suggests that this phenomenon reflects similar political forces from country to country, namely the political preferences of the majority, consisting of the insiders in the labor market. But there is also a very interesting variation across countries with regard to the extent of the unemployment problem and the timing and type of policy reforms adopted. Some countries, notably Spain, that introduced tight labor market restrictions at an early stage experienced very high unemployment and have only lately introduced reforms in the direction of a two-tier system.[21] In the U.K., labor markets were instead deregulated in more conventional ways in the 1980s, through various reforms diminishing the influence of unions. Countries like Sweden introduced legislation providing higher job security in the early 1970s but avoided high unemployment—for some time, at least—by expanding public employment. Understanding such differences in policy reform is an important topic for future research.

Another interesting question is why different countries resort to different combinations of firing protection and unemployment insurance to protect the insiders against the risk of becoming unemployed. Buti, Pench, and Sestito (1998) point out that cross-country data show a negative relationship between these two policies: countries such as Italy in which firing is very difficult also tend to have very small unemployment insurance programs, and vice versa. In the previous subsection, we discussed some comparative statics results relating equilibrium unemployment insurance to exogenous hiring and firing rates. But what makes countries choose different combinations of these instruments? One possible answer is related to the insiders' political influence: firing protections are of more benefit to the currently employed, whereas unemployment insurance is of more benefit to the currently unemployed. Thus the combination of these two tools that is chosen probably reflects the insiders' relative political influence. But to address this issue more thoroughly, we must go beyond the simple median-voter model discussed so far and investigate other sources of political influence. Labor unions in many countries are very well organized and well connected with political parties on the left. Moreover, their political activities go well beyond their members' voting behavior. Such activities take us far from the median-voter model used throughout this chapter and into the realm of probabilistic voting or lobbying models introduced in chapter 3. These other models of policy choice are illustrated in chapter 7 with reference to a general problem of special-interest politics. Problem 6 of this chapter considers probabilistic voting in a version of the unemployment insurance model of this section.

6.5 Discussion

The redistributive programs discussed in this chapter make up the core of the modern welfare state: pensions, unemployment insurance, assistance to the poor, labor market regulations. For simplicity, each of these programs has been considered in isolation and reduced to a single policy dimension. The main contribution of the analysis has been to identify the conflict

---

21. Differences in wages, rather than in job security, have characterized recent U.S. movement toward two-tier labor contracts. This difference may relate to the oft-noted difference in wage flexibility on the two sides of the Atlantic. (We owe this observation to Alan Auerbach.)

of interest among different citizens over these redistributive programs within a simple but coherent economic model. Because each program redistributes along a specific dimension (or set of dimensions), such as income, age, or risk, conflict is related to different dimensions of heterogeneity. The general lesson suggested by this chapter is that the equilibrium policy for each of these programs reflects the distribution of these individual features over the voting population. Thus the distribution of income, the age profile of the population, the concentration of risks, and the size of each jurisdiction determine the equilibrium size of these redistribution programs.

Clearly, these economic models are simple abstractions of a much more complex reality. We should offer no apology for that: the role of any theory is to simplify and make some crucial abstractions. But have we made the right simplifications? And how sensitive are the results to our modeling assumptions?

With regard to economics, we have chosen economic models with a very simplistic view of the social functions the modern welfare state performs. Except for unemployment insurance, a benevolent social planner in these models would choose to have none of these redistributive programs (the utilitarian optimum corresponds to a policy of $\tau = 0$ in the models of sections 6.1–6.3). And even section 6.4, which reveals the optimal policy to be full unemployment insurance, really offers no discussion of the role of public versus private insurance. We don't feel too bad about these simplifications, however. There is already a large body of literature on the roles of many of these programs from a Pigovian perspective.[22] Our goal is not to add another review of that literature but rather to identify forces that may bring about deviations from socially optimal policies.

We have also made several political assumptions. On the one hand, we have considered one policy choice at a time. On the other hand, we have assumed all voters to be equally influential (aside from constraints on suffrage). These assumptions, reflected in the median-voter result, clearly determine the properties of the resulting equilibrium. Dropping them would lead to a different aggregation of individual preferences, with some voters being more influential than others. Nevertheless, many of the insights gained in this chapter are likely to survive in more general or different models of electoral competition. In particular, our political assumptions do not drive the nature of economic conflicts, and it would be straightforward to replace the median-voter equilibrium with models of probabilistic voting or lobbying. The equilibrium would then implement a modified social planner's optimum in which all voters are weighted, though some more than others. (See problem 3 of this chapter.) These alternative models of political equilibrium would also enable one to relax the assumption of a single policy instrument. The different dimensions of the welfare state

---

22. Atkinson (1999) takes such a perspective in his interesting recent discussion of the literature on the welfare state.

could then be studied in the same economic and political framework. Such an exercise would be worthwhile, for it would provide interesting empirical predictions about the composition of the welfare state and not just the size of the different welfare programs.

A more bothersome feature of the analysis is the unimportance of the status quo. In these models of electoral competition, and in particular in the median-voter model, history plays no role. Reversing a preexisting policy is the same thing as expanding a program that already exists or initiating a new program. Similarly, the distinction between discretionary spending and entitlements cannot be easily addressed in these political models, except through the strong assumption of commitment to an irreversible policy decision (or no commitment at all). This reflects the simplistic view of political institutions implicit in these models of electoral competition. The next chapter will move one step toward a more satisfactory analytical treatment of institutions, but the reader will have to await part 3 for a more complete and satisfactory picture.

6.6   Notes on the Literature

The model in section 6.1 is based on Romer 1975, Roberts 1977, and Meltzer and Richard 1981. It is straightforward to replace transfers with public consumption as in chapters 3–5, or to incorporate public consumption as an additional policy instrument, provided the benefits of public consumption are not concentrated in particular income groups. Meltzer and Richard (1985) show that the same incentives to redistribute in cash then arise with respect to redistribution in kind. Cukierman and Meltzer (1991) replace the proportional income tax with a three-parameter tax schedule. Under plausible conditions on skewness of income distribution and labor supply elasticity, a median-voter equilibrium exists, and the decisive voter chooses marginal progressivity. Peltzman 1980 is an influential early contribution based on a very different political model and reaching very different conclusions.

A large empirical literature on the determinants of the size of redistributive programs is surveyed in Mueller 1989. An early and influential empirical paper is Cameron 1978. The prediction that higher income inequality among voters leads to increased government redistribution has received particular attention in empirical studies. Lindert (1994, 1996) examines a panel of Organization for Economic Cooperation and Development countries with mixed results. The analysis of U.S. time series data supports the theory in Meltzer and Richard 1983, as does the different approach, based on calibration, of Krusell and Rios-Rull (1999). Husted and Kenny (1997) show that the expansion of voting franchise correlates positively with the size of redistributive programs in U.S. states and local governments. Mueller and Stratmann (1999) study empirically the effects of voters' participation in a broad sample of countries. Empirical research has also investigated the idea that the expansion of redistributive programs can be attributed to a reduction in the administrative costs of tax collection and the deadweight costs of taxation. The works of Becker (1985), North (1985), Kau and Rubin (1981), and more recently, Becker and Mulligan (1998), provide empirical support for this idea. A number of papers have studied the political determinants of tax structures; see in particular Hettich and Winer 1988, 1997, and Volkerink and de Haan 1999. Chapter 14 discusses the recent literature studying the links between redistributive policies, income inequality, and growth.

The theory of voting over pensions has followed different approaches. Browning (1975) and Boadway and Wildasin (1989a, 1989b) have studied the determinants of social security in voting models with commitment in which all voters have the same income and differ only in age. Cukierman and Meltzer (1989) consider public debt (equivalent to social security in their model) in an overlapping-generations economy with income heterogeneity, weak altruism within the family, and policy commitments. Tabellini (1990a) formulates a median-voter model with income heterogeneity and weak altruism within the family, but no commitment (i.e., in each period, voters choose a tax rate with lump sum transfers to the currently old). The model of section 6.1, in which voters differ in age and income but there is commitment and no altruism, combines features of all these approaches. These results are perhaps closest to those of Cukierman and Meltzer 1989, though that paper focuses on general equilibrium effects on the real interest rate and neglects tax distortions. General equilibrium effects and their effect on voters' preferences have also been studied by Cooley and Soares (1999). Conesa and Krueger (1999) include not only general equilibrium effects but also social insurance benefits of the pension system in their analysis. Verbon (1988) provides a general survey of the positive political theories of social security, whereas Feldstein (1998) and Siebert (1998) discuss the recent reform experiences of various developing and industrial countries.

A number of recent papers have examined the link between pensions and other policy tools. Besides the papers by Galasso and Conde Ruiz (1999) and Mulligan and Sala-i-Martin (1999b) mentioned in section 6.2, Lambertini and Azariadis (1998) have studied an overlapping-generations model with capital in which policy consists of pensions to the elderly and welfare payments to the poor. Policy is set through legislative bargaining, as in part 1. Higher income inequality can lead to the formation of a coalition like the one discussed in section 6.2—namely of old voters and poor young voters—which implies higher equilibrium transfers of both types. Boldrin and Montes Alonso (1998) have studied the joint determination of pensions and public education, arguing that both policy tools must be studied together to obtain a complete characterization of intergenerational redistribution.

The idea that in the absence of policy commitment, reputational equilibria can sustain social security systems was pursued by Kotlikoff, Persson, and Svensson (1988) and more recently by Boldrin and Rustichini (1996), Cooley and Soares (1999), and Azariadis and Galasso (1997). Shepsle (1999) considers reputational equilibria in overlapping generations of finite agents in an abstract setting. The idea that altruism within the family also induces voters to support intergenerational redistribution is investigated by Tabellini (1990a, 1991).

Some papers have studied the political determinants of intergenerational transfers in settings different from voting. Grossman and Helpman (1998) consider a model in which members of different generations lobby the government, as in chapter 7. Earlier papers relying on the idea that the ability of different generations to influence the political process affects the size and viability of social security include Patton 1978, Stuart and Hansson 1989, and Loewy 1988. In Mulligan and Sala-i-Martin 1999b, net intergenerational transfers are determined by a "political pressure" function (Becker 1983), which in turn is defined over the time each generation devotes to political activities—or, equivalently, to leisure time.

Lindert (1994, 1996) has investigated, with negative results, the validity of the empirical prediction that more inequality leads to more spending on social security, whereas Tabellini (1990a) obtained more encouraging results on the same issue. Looking at data of Swedish municipalities, Strömberg (1996) finds support for the prediction that the composition of social spending is systematically related to the age of the median voter.

Several recent surveys on local public finance and fiscal federalism also focus on political economics. See, in particular, Inman and Rubinfeld 1997 and Inman 1987, as well as the early work by Oates (1972). One of the first papers to study the economic determinants of the size of nations was Friedman 1977, which modeled the government as a tax-maximizing Leviathan. Our model of integration in section 6.4 draws on Persson and Tabellini 1994d and Bolton and Roland 1997. The political choice of whether to integrate was also studied by Alesina and Spolaore (1997), Casella and Feinstein (1990), and Casella (1992), who focus on heterogeneity of preferences rather than income.

The choice whether to integrate politically is similar to the constitutional choice of instrument assignment to a vertical hierarchy of governments, which political economists have also studied. With a theoretical perspective, Besley and Coate (1998a) discuss how equilibrium policies and the choice between centralization and decentralization hinge on economic factors (such as the strength of externalities) and political factors (such as the structure of decision making in the legislature). Crémer and Palfrey (1996a, 1996b), Lockwood (1997), and Myers and Sengupta (1997) also analyze the voters' choice over the degree of centralization, contrasting alternative constitutional procedures. Empirical studies of the determinants of centralization include Oates 1972 and Panizza 1999 with regard to a sample of countries and Wallis and Oates 1988 with regard to U.S. states.

Buchanan and Faith (1987) and Bolton and Roland (1997), among others, have studied the question of how the threat of secession modifies equilibrium redistribution. Olofsgård (1999) extends this work to allow for mobility across borders. Alesina, Spolaore, and Wacziarg (1997) discuss the evidence relating the size of government to country size. Persson and Tabellini (1996b) study the determinants of risk sharing and redistribution among regions when the threat of secession (or opting out of the risk-sharing contract) determines regional bargaining power. Bordignon and Brusco (1999) ask why most political constitutions do not explicitly allow for secession, emphasizing contractual incompleteness and the distinction between ex ante and ex post optimality.

Finally, a huge literature discusses how exogenous economic policy affects unemployment. For recent surveys see Bertola 1999, Nickell and Layard 1999, and Mortensen and Pissarides 1998. Research on what mechanisms determine the economic policies that have an impact on the labor market, however, is much more scant. The model of voting over unemployment insurance in section 6.4 draws on Wright 1986. One can extend the model, allowing for individual-specific unemployment risk, as in Persson and Tabellini 1996a. The model can also be extended to allow self-insurance through borrowing and lending, as in Hassler and Rodriguez Mora 1999, or to allow feedback effects from unemployment insurance to equilibrium unemployment, as in Hassler et al. 1998. Saint-Paul (1993, 1996, 1999) has studied the political conflict between insiders and outsiders and politics of labor market regulations, and he also discusses the political feasibility of alternative reforms.

6.7 Problems

1. The Meltzer-Richard model

Consider an economy in which a proportional tax on labor income is used to finance lump sum transfers to the citizens. Individual i's preferences over consumption, c, and leisure, x, are described by

$$w^i = c^i - a(b - x^i)^2.$$

The private budget constraint is $c^i = (1 - \tau)l^i + f$, and the government budget constraint is $f = \tau l$. The individual is also subject to a time constraint $1 + e^i = l^i + x^i$. The individual productivity parameters e^i are distributed by a density function linearly decreasing from 2 at $e^i = 0$ to 0 at $e^i = 1$.

a. Compute each individual's labor supply as well as the total labor supply, given the tax rate. Compute the equilibrium tax level.

b. Assume that only citizens with incomes above 0.05 are allowed to vote, which excludes approximately 10% of the lowest-income earners from the electorate. Compute the new equilibrium tax rate.

c. Now suppose that 10% of the citizens of each income level were to retire and thus be moved to productivity $e^i = 0$. Compute the new equilibrium tax rate.

d. Finally, assume that tax collection is costly, and that of any unit of taxes collected, a fraction $1 - \theta$ would be used to pay for the administration of tax collection. Compute the new equilibrium tax rate.

2. Pensions

Consider the model of section 6.2. There are three generations: young, middle-aged, and old. The population grows at rate n. The government finances a pension scheme with lump sum transfers f to the old generation with a proportional tax, τ, on labor. The government budget constraint is

$$f = \tau l^{iY}(1 + n)^2 + \tau l^{iM}(1 + n).$$

The subjective discount rate β equals the real interest rate ρ, and all individuals may save assets at the real interest rate. A young individual i's lifetime utility from the pension scheme is

$$w^{iY} = U(c^{iY}) + \frac{1}{1 + \beta}U(c^{iM}) + \frac{1}{(1 + \beta)^2}c^{iO} + V(x^{iY}) + \frac{1}{1 + \beta}V(x^{iM}),$$

and a young individual's intertemporal budget constraint is

$$c^{iY} + \frac{c^{iM}}{1 + \beta} + \frac{c^{iO}}{(1 + \beta)^2} = l^{iY}(1 - \tau) + \frac{l^{iM}(1 - \tau)}{1 + \beta} + \frac{f}{(1 + \beta)^2}.$$

a. Solve for the individual's optimal consumption path and labor supply.

b. What is the total present value of the pension scheme to a young person of productivity e^i? What is the pension scheme's net value to a young person of average productivity? How much larger is the net present value of an individual of productivity $e^m < e$ relative to that of an individual of average productivity? Describe how these two values relate to redistribution between and within generations. Write down the equation describing the tax rate preferred by a young individual with productivity e^i and relate the terms in this expression to the above discussion.

c. Suppose that productivity is higher for middle-aged individuals than for young individuals. In particular, a young individual with productivity e^{iY} will achieve productivity

$$e^{iM} = e^{iY} + \frac{(1 + n)(2 + n)}{2 + \beta}[L(\tau^i) + \tau L(\tau^i)]$$

when middle aged (τ^i is the tax rate preferred by the individual with productivity e^{iY}).

Therefore, the share of young voters with productivity lower than e^{iY} equals the share of young voters with productivity lower than

$$e^{iY} + \frac{(1+n)(2+n)}{2+\beta}[L(\tau) + \tau L(\tau)].$$

The distribution of productivities is $F(e^{iY})$ for the young.

Show how the share of young and middle-aged voters who support higher taxes in equilibrium depends on n. Discuss how large a share of the young and middle-aged voters will support higher taxes in equilibrium when $n = 0$ and when n becomes very large.

d. Suppose that voting rights are extended to a generation of very young individuals who have no labor income and receive no pension transfers. These individuals will be young in the next period and know what their productivity parameters will be. Find the tax rate that an individual with productivity e^{iY} in this group would prefer. Describe how the productivity of the new median voter will differ from the productivity of the median voter before the extension of voting rights. Discuss the equilibrium tax rate.

e. Suppose that voting rights are curtailed to exclude people with very low incomes. The people excluded from the franchise exist in equal proportion among the young, middle-aged, and old. Describe how the equilibrium tax rate would change. Discuss the relation to within- and between-generations redistribution.

3. Pensions and probabilistic voting

Consider again the setup of section 6.2. There are three generations: young, middle-aged, and old. The population grows at rate n. The government finances a pension scheme with lump sum transfers f to the old generation with a proportional tax on labor, τ. The government budget constraint is

$$f = \sum_{iY} \tau l^{iY}(1+n)^2 + \sum_{iM} \tau l^{iM}(1+n).$$

The subjective discount rate, β, equals the real interest rate ρ, and all individuals may save assets at the real interest rate. The lifetime utility of a pension scheme to a young individual is

$$w^{iY} = U(c^{iY}) + \frac{1}{1+\beta}U(c^{iM}) + \frac{1}{(1+\beta)^2}c^{iO} + V(x^{iY}) + \frac{1}{1+\beta}V(x^{iM}),$$

and a young individual's intertemporal budget constraint is

$$c^{iY} + \frac{c^{iM}}{1+\rho} + \frac{c^{iO}}{(1+\rho)^2} = l^{iY}(1-\tau) + \frac{l^{iM}(1-\tau)}{1+\rho} + \frac{f}{(1+\rho)^2}.$$

There are two political candidates, A and B, who try to maximize votes by choosing an election platform consisting of a tax to finance the pension scheme. Individual i receives utility σ^i from other policies if candidate B is elected. The preference parameter, σ^i, is uniformly and symmetrically distributed around zero with densities f^Y, f^M, and f^O, for the young, middle-aged, and old, respectively. The individuals choose labor and their consumption path given the tax rate. $W^{iY}(\tau)$ denotes a young individual's utility of tax rate, given optimal savings and labor decisions.

a. Suppose that there is a vote on the pension system in every period and that there is no commitment. Write the equation determining the equilibrium level of pensions. Compare this with the equilibrium level of pensions in the median-voter model.

b. Suppose that there is commitment, so that an enacted pension scheme will remain in place forever. Write the equation determining the equilibrium tax rate.

4. Unemployment insurance

Consider the model of section 6.4.1. Individuals maximize lifetime utility of consumption over an infinite horizon:

$$V^J = \mathsf{E}_0 \left[\sum_{t=0}^{\infty} \beta^t U\left(c_t^I\right) \mid I = J \text{ at } t = 0 \right], \quad I, J \in \{E, U\},$$

where β is a subjective discount factor, and the E and U superscripts denote the state of being employed or unemployed, respectively. If employed, individuals consume their real wage, net of taxes, $l(1 - \tau)$. In each period, a currently employed individual becomes unemployed with probability φ, whereas a currently unemployed individual becomes employed with probability ϑ.

a. Assume that $U(c) = \ln(c)$. Compute the equilibrium tax and benefit size.

b. Discuss how the tax rate and the unemployment benefit depend on firing rates and hiring rates.

c. Show that an increase in both firing and hiring rates, keeping unemployment constant, will increase the unemployment benefit. Discuss the results.

5. Unemployment insurance with multiple equilibria

This problem is based on Hassler and Rodriguez Mora 1999. Unemployment insurance may be more valuable when the expected unemployment spells are long. Individuals may, for example, have precautionary savings that are depleted if the spells are long. To model this idea in an analytically simple fashion, assume that a fired worker receives a severance payment of s/d per period, where d is the average duration of the unemployment spell. With long unemployment spells, this payment per period thus becomes smaller. Given the hiring rate ϑ, the expected duration of the unemployment spell is $\frac{1}{\vartheta}$. Use the model specified in the previous problem, but include this feature.

a. Compute the equilibrium tax and show that it is decreasing in the hiring rate, and decreasing in the firing rate.

b. Assume that the unemployment rate is $u = 0.06$, that the discount factor is $\beta = \frac{4}{5}$ and that the severance payment is $s = \frac{4}{5}$. By plotting the unemployment benefit as a function of the firing rate, show that an increase in both firing and hiring rates, keeping unemployment constant, may decrease the unemployment benefit. Discuss the results.

c. Now suppose that the firing rate is constant at $\varphi = 0.05$, whereas unemployment may vary. Show that the unemployment benefit is lower when the hiring rate is high and unemployment is low.

d. It has been argued that higher unemployment benefits will make unemployed workers more reluctant to accept job offers. Assume, for this reason, that higher unemployment benefits make hiring more difficult, so that hiring is decreasing in the level of benefits. More precisely, assume that

$$\vartheta = \frac{1}{15f}.$$

Show that there are two equilibria: one where unemployment is high, the unemployment benefit is high, and duration is long, and another where unemployment is low, unemployment benefits are low, and duration is long. Explain the equilibria.

7 Special-Interest Politics

Many economic policy decisions create concentrated benefits for a few well-defined groups, with the cost diffused in society at large. This occurs not only in public finance, but also in trade policy and regulation. Whenever economic policy benefits narrowly defined special interests, the political incentives to influence the design of such policies are much stronger for the beneficiaries than for the majority bearing the cost. A classical example of this systematic bias is agricultural policy. Virtually all democracies provide generous support for their farmers through trade policies, direct subsidies, and various other programs. Several explanations have been suggested for this phenomenon. Many of these stress that farmers have more homogenous economic interests than other groups and therefore find it easier to get organized. Others emphasize that farmers are less ideologically biased than other groups and therefore become a natural target for politicians who vie for electoral support. Some also point out that farmers are concentrated in rural electoral districts, which are often overrepresented in legislatures, or that legislators representing rural interests often hold important positions as ministers or chairmen of congressional committees.

The public choice literature has emphasized one of these mechanisms in particular. Because of their higher stakes, beneficiaries of various programs are more likely to get politically organized. They can thus influence political outcomes, whereas the interests of the unorganized general public are neglected. This idea dates back to the work of Schattschneider (1935), Tullock (1959), Olson (1965), Weingast, Shepsle, and Johnsen (1981), Becker (1983, 1985) and several others. Mueller 1989 and 1997 include excellent surveys of the earlier literature. More recent contributions have focused on structural models of the political process, trying to identify specific features of the political system that confer power on some groups rather than others or that entail systematic biases in aggregate spending. In this part, we survey some of these recent contributions.

As discussed in part 1, multidimensional policies mean that we must specify the institutional details of the policy process to predict which groups will be most powerful in the struggle for benefits. Different branches of political economics have taken this route in recent years, specifying the policymaking process as an extensive form game and assuming rational individual behavior. Some of the empirical implications are not very different from those of earlier public choice literature. The older approach often lacked micropolitical foundations, however, relying instead on nonderived influence functions, political support functions, or vote functions. Contributors to the more recent literature have tried to fill this gap by being more explicit on the institutional assumptions and more uncompromising on the requirements of individual rationality.

To illustrate the effects of the different political determinants of policy, we stick to the same economic example throughout the chapter.[1] This example is simple; yet, it highlights

---

1. The treatment in this chapter extends a survey along similar lines in Persson 1998.

the more general phenomenon of concentrated benefits and dispersed costs in a transparent way. Thus we study a society in which the government uses a common pool of tax revenues to finance an array of publicly provided goods, the benefits of which are completely concentrated in well-defined groups. Two underlying questions motivate the analysis. The first and most important concerns the allocation among groups: which groups are politically powerful, and how is this related to political institutions? The other concerns aggregate outcomes: what effect do alternative institutions have on the overall size of government?

In section 7.1, we formulate the basic model and derive some benchmark allocations. In the subsequent sections, we apply three different state-of-the-art models to our policy example. Each of these sections studies a specific feature of the political process in detail.

In section 7.2, we work with a legislative bargaining model, developed by researchers in U.S. congressional politics, to study decision-making rules and budgetary procedures. As mentioned already in chapters 2 and 5, political power here reflects the assignment of agenda-setting or amendment rights and the sequencing of decisions. Institutions centralizing decision-making power by conferring strong proposal rights and limiting amendments induce a small size of government but distort the allocation of benefits in favor of whoever holds such powers.

In section 7.3, we use a model of lobbying as common agency, developed by researchers in trade policy, to study the influence activities of organized interest groups. As mentioned in chapter 3, lobbying models direct attention to campaign contributions and the organizational pattern of interest groups. Groups organized as a lobby influence final allocations disproportionately, which generally makes them suboptimal. If taxpayers are less politically organized than the beneficiaries of the spending programs, because they have smaller stakes individually, a large government emerges.

In section 7.4, we move to a model of electoral competition, developed by public economists, to study the electoral platforms chosen by two vote-maximizing parties. This is a version of the probabilistic voting model introduced in chapter 3, in which voters trade off their predetermined ideological party preferences against economic policy platforms. Political power here reflects the distribution of voters' ideological preferences across groups; more-powerful groups include a large number of swing voters who are mobile across parties because they do not care about ideology. To win the elections, both parties direct economic benefits toward these nonideological voters.

Although these approaches yield useful insights, each still gives only a partial answer to the question of which groups are the most powerful. A formal integration of the different approaches is only beginning to take shape. Section 7.5 discusses some existing results. We start by studying the interaction between elections and lobbying, along the lines introduced in chapter 3: office-seeking politicians use lobbying revenues to influence voters. Next, we illustrate the interaction between legislative bargaining and elections: voters in each of multiple voting districts elect outcome-motivated politicians as their representatives in a subsequent legislative bargaining game. Strategic delegation is a feature of the equilibrium. Finally, we study the interaction between legislation and lobbying: different lobbies seek to influence finance-motivated politicians involved in legislative bargaining to confer benefits on their groups. These interactions yield surprising results that sometimes modify the insights obtained from partial models in important ways.[2]

Overall, the results in this chapter move us far away from simple median-voter outcomes. Politics is much more than simple vote counting. To understand the political determinants of policy, we must pay attention to many fine details of the political process, and thus we move closer to the world of postelection politics introduced in part 1. But the research surveyed here is mainly theoretical. For us to gain a more complete understanding of the relative importance of each of these details, the research needs to become better integrated with empirical work.

7.1   A Model of Local Public Goods

Consider a society with J distinct groups of identical individuals. Group $J = 1, \ldots, J$ has size (mass) N^J, $\sum_J N^J = N$, where N is the size of the entire population. Individuals in group J have the quasi-linear preferences

$$w^J = c^J + H(g^J), \tag{7.1}$$

where c^J denotes the consumption of private goods (the same for every group member) and g^J is the per capita supply of a publicly provided good. The increasing and concave function $H(\cdot)$, with $H(0) = 0$, is thus defined over a good that benefits group J only and must be publicly provided in an equal amount per capita (we could easily add some externalities onto other groups, at the cost of additional algebraic complexity). Individual income is equal in all groups: $y^J = y$. A unit of income (private consumption) can be costlessly converted into one unit of any of the J publicly provided goods, and taxation is lump sum. This model can

---

2. An important omission from our discussion of special-interest politics is an examination of bureaucratic behavior and its interaction with other parts of the political process. Economists have recently built structural models of the interaction between interest groups and the bureaucracy to study regulatory capture (Laffont and Tirole 1993) and political scientists have studied the legislature's control of bureaucracy (McCubbins, Noll, and Weingast 1987).

be interpreted in a number of ways: groups can be defined by their preferences, occupation, age or other personal attributes, or geographical location.

7.1.1   A Normative Benchmark

As a normative benchmark, consider the utilitarian optimum, obtained by maximizing the Benthamite welfare function, $\sum_J \frac{N^J}{N} w^J$, subject to the resource constraint $\sum_J N^J (g^J + c^J) = Ny$. The resulting benchmark allocation is pretty obvious, namely to set the vector $\mathbf{g} \equiv (g^J)$ such that the average marginal benefit in each group equals the marginal social cost of unity:

$$H_g(g^*) - 1 = 0. \tag{7.2}$$

For future reference, we denote aggregate spending associated with this allocation as $G^* = Ng^*$.

This allocation could easily be implemented if group-specific lump sum taxes, τ^J, financed each of the group-specific goods, so that: $c^J = y - \tau^J = y - g^J$. If full decentralization of spending and financing to each group were feasible, this would be the optimal institutional arrangement. Policymakers' incentives would not be distorted, and the socially optimal policy would emerge as an equilibrium. In the real world, however, it is often impossible to design a tax system so that the taxpayers' financing of a group-specific good precisely coincides with the beneficiaries. For instance, these beneficiaries may be identified by their personal attributes or occupation and not by residence, or else their individual characteristics may be unobservable, as in the case of preferences.

Our goal in this part is to explore the incentive problems arising under centralized financing and how different political institutions change these incentives and the resulting allocations. We therefore retain the stark but simplifying assumption that all publicly provided goods are financed out of a common pool of tax revenues, with equal contributions from each group. The policy instruments are always the same—the vector $\mathbf{g} \equiv (g^J)$ of publicly provided group-specific goods and a common lump sum tax, τ—and they are always subject to the same government budget constraint: $N\tau = \sum_J N^J g^J \equiv G$, where G, as above, denotes aggregate expenditures.

In this setup, individuals have distorted incentives, and there is sharp disagreement over policy, because the groups share the cost of financing the public good. Hence beneficiaries of a particular public good would like to overspend on that good, since they share the cost of providing this good with others. Conversely, every group wishes to reduce spending on public goods of which they are not the beneficiaries, since they internalize no benefit from them but must nonetheless share the cost of providing them.

Adding externalities, so that the local public good g^J also affects the utility of groups other than J, adds other considerations (these are discussed by Besley and Coate 1998a), but the incentive problems discussed in this chapter remain. Even if full decentralization were feasible, it would not deliver the social optimum, as the externalities would not be internalized. And under full centralization, the incentive problems due to cost sharing would still be relevant as long as different groups preferred different combinations of public goods. For simplicity, we thus neglect externalities.

7.1.2   The Basic Common-Pool Problem

To illustrate the incentive problems that arise from centralized financing, we start with a simple decision-making procedure. Each group decides freely on the supply of each public good, whereas the tax rate is residually determined. Individual utility in group J can then be written as

$$W^J(\mathbf{g}) = y - \tau + H(g^J) = y - \sum_I g^I \frac{N^I}{N} + H(g^J). \tag{7.3}$$

An equilibrium is a vector $\mathbf{g}^D$ (the D superscript for *decentralized* spending), such that each group J maximizes $W^J(\mathbf{g})$ with respect to g^J, taking equilibrium expenditures by all other groups as given. It is straightforward to verify that equilibrium spending here satisfies

$$H_g(g^{J,D}) - 1 = \frac{N^J}{N} - 1. \tag{7.4}$$

Since the right-hand side of (7.4) is negative, all groups overspend compared to the social optimum defined by (7.2): $g^{J,D} > g^*$ for all J. Furthermore, smaller groups overspend to a larger extent. This is the familiar "common-pool" problem: each group fully internalizes the benefit of its own public good, but (as financing is shared) it internalizes only the fraction N^J/N of the social marginal cost of higher taxes. The problem here lies in the collective choice procedure, in which the tax rate is residually determined once all spending decisions have been made in a decentralized fashion. Concentration of benefits and dispersion of costs lead to excessive spending when such spending is residually financed out of a common pool of tax revenue.

Even though the nature of the problem is evident, the remedy of full decentralization of financing may be difficult to enforce. As mentioned above, it may be hard to adapt the system of financing to the relevant group structure. Common-pool problems thus arise in many situations. For instance, they can be due to lack of information, so that some spending decisions must be decentralized to local governments, government agencies, or public enterprises, whereas financing remains centralized. Moreover, the incentive problem does not disappear even under fully centralized decisions on spending, as each group still seeks to influence the central government to satisfy its own interests. Concentration of benefits and dispersion of costs imply that with centralized spending, each group retains a political incentive to demand overprovision of goods to its own group and underprovision to the other groups so as to avoid paying high taxes. Which groups will be most politically powerful in taking advantage of this opportunity depends both on group attributes and on political and budgetary institutions. The remaining sections discuss how the different groups' policy preferences are aggregated to an equilibrium policy in alternative institutional settings.

7.2 Legislative Bargaining

A large empirical literature has studied how budgetary institutions correlate with fiscal outcomes. Most of this literature focuses on intertemporal fiscal policy choices, however. As we will further discuss in chapter 13, cross-sectional comparisons suggest that specific procedures are associated with smaller budget deficits. In particular, centralization of budgetary power to the prime minister or the finance minister, two-stage budgeting with prior setting of deficit targets, restrictions on amendments of spending proposals, and constitutional limits on deficit spending seem to promote more fiscal discipline.[3] Less attention has been devoted to the implications for the size of government of alternative budgetary procedures, with a few exceptions noted below. This is an unfortunate oversight, as one of the underlying problems that "stricter" budgetary procedures are supposed to solve, namely the common-pool problem, also distorts the level of spending.

As noted in the previous section, the common-pool problem stems from excessive decentralization of spending: each group is the arbiter of spending on its own local public good. In this section, we analyze a centralized procedure: the policy vector $(\mathbf{g}, \tau)$ is now assumed to entail spending on geographical districts. To be implemented, a policy must be approved by a majority of districts, according to specific procedural rules. If there is no agreement, a default outcome, the status quo, kicks in. This section's model purports to describe decision making in a legislature, and its rules capture stylized features of the budget process. We pick up the legislative bargaining approach introduced in chapters 2 and 5. As mentioned before, this approach follows the work by Baron and Ferejohn (1989), whose legislative bargaining framework has become a workhorse model for analyses of the U.S. Congress and other legislatures. We ask how bargaining power is determined inside the legislature and how alternative procedures shape aggregate spending.[4]

---

3. In the United States, a procedure similar to giving such power to the Treasury is to require all spending proposals to be channeled through one committee; see Cogan 1994.

4. Baron (1993) has applied the legislative bargaining model to a similar policy problem.

7.2.1 A Simple Legislative Bargaining Model

In the model of this section, groups are distinguished by their geographical location. Each location is represented by one member of the legislature who is an outcome-motivated perfect delegate of her constituency, in that her preferences are of the same form as in (7.3). The number of districts and representatives $\mathcal{J}$ is now assumed to be odd, with $\mathcal{J} \geq 3$. These assumptions fit well the system of representation in the U.S. Congress, with plurality elections in multiple single-member districts. Interpretations more fitting to parliamentary systems with proportional representation are also possible but less straightforward.

The budget process in a legislative session consists of the following sequence of events: (1) One of the representatives, $J = a$, is chosen to be the agenda setter. (2) Representative a makes a policy proposal, **g**. (3) The legislature votes on the proposal. If a simple majority approves the proposal—that is, at least $\frac{\mathcal{J}-1}{2}$ other legislators vote in favor—then **g** is implemented (a always votes for her own proposal). If not, a status quo outcome, $\bar{\mathbf{g}} = (\bar{g}^J) : \bar{\tau} = \sum \frac{N^J}{N} \bar{g}^J$, is implemented.

In the jargon of the legislative bargaining literature, we are thus considering a *closed rule*—that is, proposals cannot be amended—with only one round of proposals. Amendments and multiple rounds, with proposal rights alternating between legislators, are discussed below.[5]

7.2.2 Political Equilibrium

Consider first the choices by legislators $J \neq a$ at the voting stage (3). Clearly, any legislator will approve only proposals **g** that, from her own point of view, are not worse than the status quo (we assume that indifferent legislators always vote yes to a proposal). From (7.3) and the definition of $\bar{\mathbf{g}}$, legislator $J \neq a$ votes in favor of **g** if

$$W^J(\mathbf{g}) - W^J(\bar{\mathbf{g}}) = H(g^J) - H(\bar{g}^J) - \sum_I \frac{N^I}{N}(g^I - \bar{g}^I) \geq 0. \tag{7.5}$$

Consider next the proposal stage (2). Here the agenda setter maximizes her own payoff, given by (7.3), subject to the government budget constraint, the "incentive compatibility constraints" (7.5) holding for a majority coalition $\mathcal{M}$, including at least $\frac{\mathcal{J}-1}{2}$ other legislators, and the nonnegativity constraints $g^J \geq 0$ for all J. Eliminating the multipliers from the Kuhn-Tucker conditions to this problem and manipulating the solution, we

---

5. We do not model the criteria for selecting the agenda setter. A large political science literature on congressional politics has addressed this question. Not many papers have tried to model this formally, however. Two important papers are Austen-Smith and Banks 1988 and McKelvey and Riezman 1991, which relate agenda-setting power to electoral outcomes and seniority, respectively (see also problem 4 of this chapter and the discussion at the end of section 7.2.2).

can write the following conditions describing the equilibrium proposal, denoted with a ^{B} superscript:[6]

$$H_g(g^{J,B}) = \frac{N^J}{N} \frac{1}{1 - \sum_{I \in \mathcal{M}} \frac{N^I}{N} \frac{1}{H_g(g^{I,B})}}, \quad J = a$$

$$g^{J,B} = 0, \quad J \notin \mathcal{M}$$

$$H(g^{J,B}) - H(\overline{g}^J) = \sum_{I \in \mathcal{M}} \frac{N^I}{N}(g^{I,B} - \overline{g}^I), \quad J \neq a, J \in \mathcal{M} \tag{7.6}$$

$$|\mathcal{M}| = \frac{\mathcal{J} - 1}{2}.$$

To understand this equilibrium, consider a's incentives. To get support from other legislators, a must spend costly tax revenue in their districts. We can consider a's problem in two stages. In the first stage, she minimizes the tax rate τ necessary for obtaining support for every value of g^a, implying an increasing function $T(g^a)$. The cost minimization stage basically involves minimizing the term $\sum_{I \in \mathcal{M}} \frac{N^I}{N} \frac{1}{H_g(g^I)}$ in the denominator of the right-hand side of the first equation in (7.6). Given this "cost function," she then simply maximizes $H(g^a) + y - T(g^a)$ in the second stage with respect to g^a. This has several consequences, some of which were present already in the simpler settings of example 5 in chapter 2 and of section 5.4.

1. A version of Riker's (1962) so-called size principle will hold: a chooses a minimum winning coalition, $\mathcal{M}$, composed of $\frac{\mathcal{J}-1}{2}$ other legislators. All districts outside the winning coalition get no spending at all, even though they bear the cost of taxes.

2. For the members of $\mathcal{M}$, a spends only as much as necessary to get their vote (i.e., to satisfy (7.5) with equality), leaving them as well off as with the default policy.

3. The minimum winning coalition is composed of those legislators whose support is cheapest to obtain. These are the legislators with the lowest default payoffs, $\overline{g}^J$, and

---

6. The first-order conditions for this problem imply

$$H_g(g^a) - \frac{N^a}{N} - \frac{N^a}{N} \sum_{J \in \mathcal{M}} \mu^J = 0$$

$$-\frac{N^J}{N} + \mu^J H_g(g^J) - \frac{N^J}{N} \sum_{I \in \mathcal{M}} \mu^I = 0 \quad \text{for} \quad J \in \mathcal{M},$$

where μ^J is the Lagrange multiplier associated with the incentive constraint (2.5). These conditions imply that

$$\mu^J = \frac{H_g(g^a)N^J}{H_g(g^J)N^a}.$$

representing the smallest districts, that is, those with the smallest N^J. A weak status quo position may thus be to the advantage of a legislator and her district, contrary to what happens in two-player Nash bargaining. Even though a district with a weak position gets less public goods when its legislator is part of $\mathcal{M}$, the chance of being part of the majority is higher the weaker its position. In a richer model, in which legislators also differ in the relative weight attached to private versus public consumption, the majority would include the legislators who care *more* about public consumption, since their vote is cheaper to buy; this point is again discussed in section 7.5. District size matters because the status quo payoffs are defined in terms of per capita public goods. Hence smaller districts are cheaper to please, and they are thus more likely to be included in the majority (recall that each legislator has one vote irrespective of district size).

4. The resulting allocation is asymmetric and socially suboptimal, given the utilitarian benchmark. Districts not in $\mathcal{M}$ certainly get less (namely zero) spending than in the utilitarian optimum. Whether the members of the majority get more or less depends on parameters and on the shape of $H(\cdot)$. As long as the majority districts' default allocations $\overline{g}^J$ are not too high, however, they will typically get less than the optimum: $g^{J,B} < g^*$ for $J \neq a$, $J \in \mathcal{M}$. Under these circumstances, district a certainly gets more: $g^{a,B} > g^*$. To show this formally, rewrite the first equation of (7.6) as:

$$H_g(g^{a,B}) - 1 = -\frac{\lambda_{\mathcal{N}} + \sum_{I \in \mathcal{M}} \frac{N^I}{N}\left(1 - \frac{1}{H_g(g^{I,B})}\right)}{1 - \sum_{I \in \mathcal{M}} \frac{N^I}{N} \frac{1}{H_g(g^{I,B})}},$$

where the left-hand side is the expression defining the utilitarian optimum. Thus the right-hand side measures the deviation from the normative benchmark. Note that the first term in the numerator, $\lambda_{\mathcal{N}} \equiv \sum_{I \notin \mathcal{M}} \frac{N^I}{N}$, is the population share of the districts not belonging to the majority. As the second term in the numerator is also positive, given $H_g(g^{J,B}) - 1 > 0$ for $J \in \mathcal{M}$, overprovision to district a follows. Furthermore, the overprovision to a is larger, the smaller is the majority's population share (the larger is $\lambda_{\mathcal{N}}$), as this reduces the cost of expanding g^a while compensating the legislators in the majority. The asymmetry also depends on the default positions; the lower is the average value of $\overline{g}^J$, the more powerful is the agenda setter. Since $\overline{g}^J$ refers to the status quo if the new legislation is voted down, this suggests that we should observe more asymmetric benefits for certain types of government programs. Specifically, infrastructure projects—for which the natural status quo is no projects—should be more asymmetrically distributed across groups than entitlement programs—for which the natural status quo is the existing policy (and of which the beneficiaries are probably also more evenly distributed across voting districts).

5. Finally, whether the model predicts aggregate overspending depends on parameters and on the concavity of $H(\cdot)$, and there is no presumption that the bias goes either way.[7] But this model contains two useful lessons for the design of budgetary procedures. First, aggregate spending is more likely to be low, the smaller are the default outcomes in $\bar{\mathbf{g}}$. If the status quo entails little spending, as with zero-base budgeting, one legislator's strong agenda-setting powers discipline all the others (though this also leaves more room for the agenda setter to spend more for himself). Second, suppose that different legislators differ in their valuation of public versus private spending and that agenda-setting power is given to a legislator who spends little for his constituency or—thinking of bargaining within government—to a minister without portfolio, such as the finance or Treasury minister. Then the agenda setter does not expand his preferred public good, and concentration of proposal power delivers small aggregate spending.

The political science literature has discussed other reasons for conferring strong agenda-setting powers on some legislators besides control of aggregate spending. All legislatures necessarily display some division of labor across issues, because of the need to split the workload as well as the varying background of legislators. Giving control over certain issues to some individuals provides incentives for them to invest in issue-specific competence and information gathering. In the U.S. Congress, for instance, this specialization and control is manifested in powerful standing committees with considerable agenda-setting powers over the issues under their jurisdiction.[8] Parliamentary systems also have standing committees, although in such systems the ministries have many of the corresponding agenda-setting tasks. The model thus captures something important: real-world legislatures are organized in a way that makes some representatives more powerful than others over certain issues, a power that influences the allocation of spending.

7.2.3   Extensions

The procedures adopted in real-world legislatures modify and dilute power associated with proposal rights in several ways. One mechanism by which this occurs is the amendment right of other legislators; another is separation of proposal powers: different legislators have

---

7. The flatter is H_g, the more likely is overspending. Consider the special case in which $\mathcal{J} = 3$, such that the majority $\mathcal{M}$ consists of a single legislator m. Furthermore, assume that $\bar{g}^J = 0$ and $H(g^J) = \alpha[\ln(g^J)]$. We then get $g^a = 3\alpha - e$, $g^m = e$, and thus $G = 3\alpha = G^*$. Thus the allocation of spending is distorted with $g^a > g^m$, if $\alpha > \frac{2e}{3}$, and $g^m > g^*$, if $\alpha < e$ (where e is the base of the natural logarithm), but the aggregate level of spending coincides with the utilitarian optimum.

8. An informational view on legislative organization, including the rationale for vesting agenda-setting powers with legislators and committees, has been emphasized in the political science literature; see in particular Krehbiel 1991.

agenda-setting rights over different policy dimensions. We briefly discuss each of these in turn.

Amendment Rights   Instead of the closed rule analyzed earlier, assume now an open rule, according to which some other legislator can amend the initial proposal. It is common practice to pitch an offered amendment against the initial proposal in a vote, and then either to allow a new round of amendments to the winning proposal or pitch the winning proposal against a default policy. Including such amendment rights in the model above diminishes the gains that a could expect from equilibrium policy. Because the amendment right allows the amender to tilt the proposal in her own favor, albeit at the cost of legislative delay, any initial proposal must make a majority of the legislators better off, not relative to the default outcome, but relative to their continuation value from further bargaining. The simple bargaining game of section 5.4 introduced such continuation values. Baron and Ferejohn 1989 and Baron 1993 demonstrate that equilibrium policy generally entails more equally distributed benefits under open rule than under closed rule. Although the precise results depend on the details of the amendment procedure, equilibria may, in some cases, come close to implementing the efficient solution. These models have an infinite horizon, however, and to simplify, the size of government is exogenously given. Problems 1 and 2 of this chapter illustrate different examples of legislative bargaining under an open rule with an infinite horizon. Problem 2 in particular allows for an endogenous budget.

A related model is due to Lockwood (1998), who adapts previous results by McKelvey (1986) and Ferejohn, Fiorina, and McKelvey (1987) to a setting similar to ours. The legislature must choose how many projects of a given size to activate. Different projects benefit different legislators and can impose externalities on other districts. Financing is shared among all districts. Legislative rules are as follows. First, each legislator makes a proposal. These proposals are then randomly ordered into an agenda and are voted on sequentially. Finally, the winning proposal is voted on against the status quo. This procedure ensures that an equilibrium exists and is unique, even if there is no Condorcet winner. If externalities are weak or negative, only a bare majority of the projects are funded; these are the projects with the lowest cost. If externalities are strongly positive, on the other hand, a larger number of projects are funded. Moreover, which projects are funded reflects the costs and the externalities, but not the intensity of preferences of individual legislators with regard to their favorite projects. Thus this procedure does not guarantee an egalitarian outcome, but it reduces the importance of particularistic political preferences.

Separation of Budgetary Powers   Many existing legislatures split the budgetary procedures into two stages: first, aggregate spending is determined, to be followed by allocative decisions. It is often argued that this two-stage budgeting insulates the decision on aggregate spending from the special-interest politics that disrupts incentives and that this leads to better aggregate decisions.[9] The intuitive reasoning is that two-stage budgeting makes it possible to confer agenda-setting powers over different decisions to different legislators. This dilutes the agenda setter's power without reintroducing a common-pool problem. We now investigate whether this is true in our simple model.

For simplicity, assume that $\mathcal{J} = 3$ and that all groups are of equal size, for simplicity normalized to unity. Thus, $N^J = 1$ and $N = 3$. Suppose that the budgetary procedure involves two stages. In the first stage the legislature decides on overall spending G, or, equivalently, on the common tax rate $\tau = \frac{G}{3}$. This decision is taken by a single majority under a closed rule, after a proposal by agenda-setting legislator a_τ. A defeated proposal results in default aggregate spending, $\overline{G}$. In the second stage, a different agenda setter, $a_g \neq a_\tau$, makes an allocation proposal, subject to $\sum_J g^J = G$, with G given from the first stage. If this proposal is defeated, the first-stage budget is split according to a simple sharing rule $\overline{g}^J = \frac{1}{3}G$, in which the assumption of equal sharing is made for simplicity. The status quo for aggregate spending in the second stage is the equilibrium outcome from the first stage.

The second-stage equilibrium is simple. To get the necessary majority, agenda setter a_g must propose to spend enough in one of the other districts, say m_g, to just exceed the status quo outcome: $g^{m_g} = \frac{1}{3}G$. He spends nothing in the minority district, n_g, and allocates the remaining budget to his own district: $g^{a_g} = \frac{2}{3}G$. Because the total budget and the tax rate are already fixed, taxes do not enter the allocation decision. The allocation distortion remains, but we are now mostly interested in the level of spending.

The first-stage outcome depends on who makes the proposal and whether the composition of the second-stage majority is known. Suppose first that the first-stage proposal is made by somebody who knows that she is a member of the second-stage majority. Thus we have $a_\tau = m_g \neq a_g$. The optimal level of G for the first-stage proposer then solves $\max[H(g^{m_g}) - \frac{1}{3}G] = \max[H(\frac{1}{3}G) - \frac{1}{3}G]$, and satisfies

$$G^{m_g} = 3H_g^{-1}(1).$$

Thus, G^{m_g} coincides with our benchmark optimum G^*. The intuition is simple: at the first stage, m_g internalizes the full benefits of aggregate spending to her own district, and these are equal to a third of the social benefits. Because she also internalizes a third of the social costs (her district's share of the tax bill), she faces the right marginal incentives when it comes to aggregate spending.[10] If the future majority composition is indeed known, G^* always collects a majority against $\overline{G}$. Interestingly, if $G^* > \overline{G}$, a_g supports G^* because she wants

---

9. See, for instance, von Hagen 1998 and Kontopoulos and Perotti 1997, 1999.

10. Naturally, the allocative distortion remains, and thus nothing ensures that G^* is still socially optimal, given that allocative distortion.

as high a revenue as possible to allocate at the second stage. A stable majority thus suggests the two parts of the budget. If the status quo instead involves aggregate "overspending" $G^* < \overline{G}$, a_τ instead gets the support of n_g, the minority legislator at the next stage, who has an obvious incentive to keep aggregate spending and taxes down.

In parliamentary systems, there is indeed a presumption that majorities are predictable; this is discussed in more detail in part 3 on comparative politics. But without further institutional detail, nothing in the model pins down the second-stage majority. Therefore, consider an alternative case in which $a_\tau \neq a_g$, but a_τ is part of the future majority with only 50% probability. In this case, the optimal level of G, from the point of view of a_τ, solves $\max[\frac{1}{2}H(\frac{1}{3}G) - \frac{1}{3}G]$, namely

$$G^n = 3H_g^{-1}(2).$$

Clearly, $G^n < G^{m_g} = G^*$. When the first-stage proposer is not certain of being a "residual claimant" on the second-stage budget, she has a stronger interest in keeping down the size of the budget. We will repeatedly encounter a similar point in part 3, in which we deal at length with institutional design questions. The desirability of such separation of powers in the political system is perhaps not obvious in the present setting, but separation of powers can unambiguously play to the voters' advantage, once we introduce agency problems.

We conclude this section with a general remark. Most of the work in the legislative bargaining literature is quite partial in that it takes the legislature's preferences as given. Where do legislators' outcome-oriented preferences come from? As discussed in chapters 3 and 4, motives different from those of the voters, such as a desire to raise funds, to get reelected, or to use political power for their own private agenda, may influence legislators' behavior, creating an agency problem vis-à-vis the voters. If lobbies and voters understand these motives and how the legislative process works, do they not adapt their behavior to influence the policy outcome? To answer such questions, we must obviously leave partial models behind and study interactions among different aspects in the political process. Having dealt with partial models of lobbying and voting, we turn to such interactions in section 7.5. Part 3 deals further with agency issues—as formally introduced in chapter 4— and their dependence on the political institutions.

7.3 Lobbying

Our next model of policymaking focuses on the influence or lobbying activities of interest groups. Policy decisions are assumed to be centralized in the hands of a semibenevolent government, but the government can be influenced by organized interest groups. How does this influence activity modify the allocation and level of government spending? Which groups are likely to be favored? Recent rational choice–oriented analyses have focused either on the incentives for lobbies to gather information and provide it to the policymakers or on their influence-seeking activities. In the latter tradition, Grossman and Helpman (1994, 1995) and several others have adapted the common-agency model of Bernheim and Whinston (1986) to something of a workhorse model of lobbying, which has been used for studying trade policy, commodity taxation, and other policies. Here, we follow Persson (1998) in applying the common-agency model to study group-specific government spending.[11]

This model of lobbying differs in two respects from the one introduced in chapter 3. On the one hand, there are no elections. The lobbies attempt to influence policy formulation directly, rather than the election outcome given some policy proposals, as in chapter 3. On the other hand, we assume that lobbies can commit to provide contributions (or "bribes") contingent on future policies before the government has made any policy choice. Because of this timing and the assumptions about the government motivation, the present model of lobbying is more of a "black box." As shown in section 7.5, however, both models of lobbying lead to essentially the same results.

7.3.1   A Simple Lobbying Model

As Olson (1965) noted long ago, influence activities entail a free-rider problem: all members of a group benefit, irrespective of whether they contribute to the lobbying. Some groups successfully overcome this free-rider problem, others do not. We follow the literature by not modeling how this takes place and just assume that a subset $\mathcal{L}$ of groups are organized to influence public-goods allocation in their favor. Thus we study a policy game with two stages: (1) Every lobby J noncooperatively and simultaneously presents its common agent, "the government," with a per capita contribution schedule $C^J(\mathbf{g})$, giving a binding promise of payment, conditional on the chosen policy. The lobby's objective is to maximize its members' net welfare, namely $N^J(W^J(\mathbf{g}) - C^J(\mathbf{g}))$, where $W^J(\mathbf{g})$ denotes the welfare from the economic policies, as defined in (7.3). (2) The government sets $\mathbf{g}$ so as to maximize a weighted sum of social welfare and contributions:

$$W(\mathbf{g}) = \eta \sum_J N^J W^J(\mathbf{g}) + (1 - \eta) \sum_{J \in \mathcal{L}} N^J C^J(\mathbf{g}), \tag{7.7}$$

where η, $0 \leq \eta \leq 1$, is a measure of the government's benevolence.

An equilibrium of the game is a subgame-perfect Nash equilibrium in the contribution schedules and the chosen policy vector. For simplicity, we shall confine ourselves to

---

11. Persson and Tabellini (1994d) study local public-goods provision in a common-agency model but impose unappealing restrictions on the strategies used by interest groups.

equilibria in (globally) truthful contribution schedules, namely those satisfying

$$C^J(\mathbf{g}) = \max[W^J(\mathbf{g}) - b^J, 0],\qquad(7.8)$$

where b^J is a constant the lobby sets optimally.[12]

7.3.2 Political Equilibrium

To derive an equilibrium in truthful strategies, we can exploit the fact that allocations in such equilibria must be jointly Pareto optimal for the government and all the lobbies. The equilibrium vector $\mathbf{g}$ therefore maximizes the sum of the net welfare of the organized lobbies $\sum_{J \in \mathcal{L}} N^J(W^J(\mathbf{g}) - C^J(\mathbf{g}))$ and the government objective $W(\mathbf{g})$, component by component. Using the definitions above, it is thus as if the equilibrium policy maximizes the weighted sum

$$\eta \sum_{J \notin \mathcal{L}} N^J W^J(\mathbf{g}) + \sum_{J \in \mathcal{L}} N^J W^J(\mathbf{g}),\qquad(7.9)$$

where aggregate welfare for the nonorganized groups is defined in the same way as in (7.3) (see problem 3 of this chapter for an explicit derivation of this result). In other words, the equilibrium coincides with the solution to a planning problem in which the nonorganized groups are underweighted relative to the organized groups to an extent that depends on the government's benevolence. The first-order conditions to (7.9) define the equilibrium allocation, denoted with an L superscript:

$$H_g(g^{J,L}) - 1 = -(1 - \lambda_{\mathcal{L}})(1 - \eta) \leq 0, \quad J \in \mathcal{L}$$

$$H_g(g^{J,L}) - 1 = \lambda_{\mathcal{L}}(1 - \eta)/\eta \geq 0, \quad J \notin \mathcal{L},\qquad(7.10)$$

where

$$0 \leq \lambda_{\mathcal{L}} = \sum_{J \in \mathcal{L}} \frac{N^J}{N} \leq 1$$

is the share of the population organized in a lobby. The left-hand side of (7.10) is the expression defining the utilitarian optimum, so the right-hand side measures the deviation

---

12. A globally truthful contribution schedule has the property that

$$\frac{\partial C^J(\mathbf{g})}{\partial g^I} = \frac{\partial W^J(\mathbf{g})}{\partial g^I}$$

for any I and everywhere. That is, the slope of the contribution schedule in any direction is equal to the true marginal benefit of the policy in that direction for lobby J. The literature has typically dealt with *locally* truthful strategies, in which this property holds only at the equilibrium point. See Grossman and Helpman 1994 and Dixit, Grossman, and Helpman 1997 as well as problem 3 of this chapter for further details and for a thorough discussion of the restriction to truthful strategies in common-agency games.

from the optimum benchmark. Several results are apparent, some of which were anticipated already in the lobbying model of chapter 3.

1. As is evident from (7.10), the equilibrium can be socially optimal: $\mathbf{g}^L = \mathbf{g}^*$. Unsurprisingly, this happens when $\eta = 1$, so that the government is completely benevolent and does not value contributions at all, or when $\lambda_{\mathcal{L}} = 0$, with no contributing groups to worry about. But it also happens when $\lambda_{\mathcal{L}} = 1$, when everyone belongs to a lobby. Stated otherwise, suboptimal policies are enacted only because of incomplete participation in lobbying. The reason is that each group has a strong incentive to lobby not only for large g^J, for itself, but also for low provision to other groups, to pay lower taxes. When all groups are organized, they offset each other's influence. Since they reveal their marginal preferences to the government by their truthful contributions, the policy decision correctly internalizes the true marginal social cost.

2. Public consumption is generally misallocated, however: organized groups get more and unorganized groups less than the optimal amount. Intuitively, the amount of overprovision to the organized lobbying groups is larger if the government values contributions more (η is smaller) and hence pays more attention to the preferences the lobbies have expressed. If $\eta \to 0$, the government cares only about contributions, and provision to the unorganized groups also goes to zero. The amount of overprovision is also larger, the lower is the share of the organized groups (the lower is $\lambda_{\mathcal{L}}$), because the lobbies—and indirectly the government—then internalize a smaller share of the social marginal costs. Note, however, that only the combined size of the organized lobbies influences the outcome; large and small organized groups obtain as much support per capita. Clearly, our implicit assumption that all members of each group belong to the lobby is driving this result.

3. There is no presumption of aggregate overprovision. Although there is certainly overprovision to organized groups, there is underprovision to nonorganized ones. Not only do the preferences of the nonorganized receive a smaller weight in the policy decision, but the tax burden of provision to nonorganized groups is internalized by organized groups, which communicate this to the government. In a richer model, with individual heterogeneity over the preferences for private versus public consumption, lobbies might plausibly consist of individuals with a high preference for the public good, who have a higher stake on the policy outcome and hence are more likely to overcome the free-rider problem of getting organized. The intuition as to why consumers are underrepresented in lobbying is familiar from games over trade policy. In this event, it is easily shown that lobbying results in aggregate overspending compared to the normative benchmark.

We can easily adapt this model to include also the choice over a global public good that benefits all groups in the same way. In this case, it is easily shown that lobbying does not distort the provision of this public good. Intuitively, lobbying induces the government to underweigh the welfare of unorganized individuals, but the national public good affects these individuals just like anyone else, both as taxpayers and as beneficiaries. With enough symmetry, neglecting their welfare does not distort the policy choice. The general lesson is that lobbying distorts policy that has a different impact on different groups, as in our case of local public goods.

The common-agency model of lobbying elegantly and simply aggregates the influence activities of many interest groups into a policy decision. It also sheds light on how the pattern of organization across groups shapes the policy outcome. The model leaves some crucial issues aside, however. The major problem is that we lack a precise model of the process whereby some groups get politically organized and others not. This is a difficult question to which there is still no satisfactory answer. The asymmetries driving the misallocation of public goods must thus be assumed or defended on empirical grounds rather than explained. An interesting conjecture is that groups are organized and solve their free-rider problem also thanks to government policy. Just as public policy confers monopoly privileges on some economic actors, it can also preserve and promote organized groups, from whom politicians then draw political or economic benefits. A prime example of this idea are the laws regulating trade union activities and representation in many industrial countries. Such legislation can help trade unions organize political activities, which in turn helps left-wing parties gather support at the time of elections.[13]

A second issue is that the "government" and the process of policy choice is still a black box. If the lobbying model captures what takes place between elections, what exactly does the objective function in (7.7) capture? And how can lobbies commit to a contingent contribution schedule before policy is set? It is really impossible to answer these questions without a structural model of policy choice. In the last section of the chapter, we follow the approach of chapter 3, embedding a lobbying model into the electoral framework suggested in the next section (see also Grossman and Helpman 1996). We then show that the parameter η can be interpreted as reflecting more-structural assumptions. In the last section, we also open the black box in another way, namely by combining lobbying and legislative bargaining.

7.4   Electoral Competition

We have seen how interest groups' ability to organize into lobbies and be represented by powerful legislators gives them an edge in the struggle for policy benefits. Some groups, however, may also have particular attributes, in their role as voters, that make them an

---

13. Mulligan and Sala-i-Martin (1999b) provide a formal example of this idea with regard to early retirement legislation, which they argue has the effect of freeing up more time for political activities by the elderly.

attractive target for office-motivated politicians. Our last partial model of centralized policymaking and special-interest politics therefore focuses on electoral competition. In this model, there is no lobbying, no legislative bargaining, and no separation of decisions on spending and taxes. Instead, we adapt the probabilistic voting model introduced in chapter 3 to our policy problem with group-specific public consumption out of an endogenous pool of tax revenue. Here we draw on the modeling of Lindbeck and Weibull (1987) and Dixit and Londregan (1996). Two competing candidates who maximize their probability of winning the election thus make policy decisions. They make binding promises of policy favors to interest groups ahead of the elections. When announcing policy favors, the candidates take into account which groups are more likely to be swayed. The question we ask is which groups have the greatest influence on electoral promises.

7.4.1 A Simple Model of Electoral Competition

Consider the model of section 7.1, but add two office-motivated political parties, $P = A$, B. Before the election, both parties noncooperatively commit themselves to specific policy platforms, $\mathbf{g}_A$ and $\mathbf{g}_B$. Parties also differ in another dimension, unrelated to the announced economic policies. As before, we refer to this dimension as "ideology," although it could also involve other features, such as the personal characteristics of the party's leadership. This ideological dimension is a permanent attribute of each party in the sense that it cannot be changed at will during the electoral campaign.

As in chapter 3, voters' preferences reflect this ideological difference among parties: each voter has an "ideological bias" for or against party B. Specifically, member i of group J has the extended utility function

$$w^{iJ} = \kappa^J W^J(\mathbf{g}) + (\sigma^{iJ} + \delta) D_B, \tag{7.11}$$

where D_B takes a value of unity if party B wins the election and zero otherwise. Further, σ^{iJ} is an individual-specific parameter, κ^J is a group-specific parameter, and δ is a random variable capturing the party preferences of the whole population. Thus two features distinguish individuals: the group to which they belong, indexed by J, and their individual party bias, σ^{iJ}. Individuals with $\sigma^{iJ} > 0$ (< 0) have a bias in favor of (against) party B, which is stronger the greater is σ^{iJ} (in absolute value). Individual party bias is distributed within each group according to a uniform distribution on the interval

$$\left[-\frac{1}{2\phi^J}, \frac{1}{2\phi^J} \right].$$

That is, the distribution of σ^{iJ} for all i belonging to group J has density ϕ^J. Thus each group has members inherently biased toward both parties and on average neutral, but the distribution of party bias differs across groups. Moreover, groups also differ in the strength of their ideological motives; the larger is the parameter κ^J, the more all the individuals in J care about economic well-being relative to ideology. Finally, the random variable δ captures party B's average popularity in the population as a whole. We assume that δ has a uniform distribution on $[-\frac{1}{2\psi}, \frac{1}{2\psi}]$. The realization of δ is unknown to the parties when announcing their policy platforms, so that the election outcome is uncertain from their point of view.

Equations (7.3) and (7.11) imply that voters in group J supporting party A all have $\sigma^{iJ} < \kappa^J[W^J(\mathbf{g}_A) - W^J(\mathbf{g}_B)] - \delta$. Let us identify the swing voters in group J as the voter who, given the parties' platforms, is indifferent between the two parties. We denote swing voters' party bias as $\sigma^J(\mathbf{g}_A, \mathbf{g}_B, \delta)$, defined by

$$\sigma^J(\mathbf{g}_A, \mathbf{g}_B, \delta) \equiv \kappa^J[W^J(\mathbf{g}_A) - W^J(\mathbf{g}_B)] - \delta. \tag{7.12}$$

Swing voters toss a coin when deciding how to vote.

7.4.2   Political Equilibrium

The two parties simultaneously and noncooperatively choose their platforms so as to maximize the probability of winning the election.[14] To specify the party objectives, first note that the distributional assumptions allow us to write party A's vote share as

$$\pi_A = \sum_J \frac{N^J}{N} \phi^J \left[\sigma^J(\mathbf{g}_A, \mathbf{g}_B, \delta) + \frac{1}{2\phi^J} \right].$$

As in chapter 3, by definition of σ^J in (7.12) and the assumption that δ is uniformly distributed with density ψ, party A's probability of winning can be written as

$$p_A = \text{Prob}\left[\pi_A \geq \frac{1}{2}\right] = \frac{1}{2} + \frac{\psi}{\phi}\left[\sum_J \frac{N^J}{N}\phi^J \kappa^J[W^J(\mathbf{g}_A) - W^J(\mathbf{g}_B)]\right], \tag{7.13}$$

where $\phi \equiv \sum \frac{N^j}{N}\phi^J$ is the average density of party bias across groups. Party A sets its platform so as to maximize this expression, subject to the budget constraint. As in chapter 3, we get a convergence result. Party B's probability of winning is given by $1 - p_A$, but $\mathbf{g}_B$ affects p_A in the same way as it does $\mathbf{g}_A$, although with the opposite sign. Because the two parties face the same budget constraint, they effectively face the same decision problem. Specifically, this optimization problem does not include any party-specific variables. Furthermore, the problem is concave by our distributional assumptions and the concavity of $W^J(\cdot)$. It should thus come as no surprise that a Nash equilibrium involves identical policy platforms,

---

14. The Nash equilibrium obtained if parties maximize their vote share is identical (see Lindbeck and Weibull 1987 and Dixit and Londregan 1996). In this case, the random variable δ can be omitted from the model.

$\mathbf{g}_B = \mathbf{g}_A$. By (7.12), this implies $\sigma^J(\mathbf{g}_A, \mathbf{g}_B, \delta) = -\delta$. Because the expected value of δ is zero, each party is doing its best to capture the votes of the ideologically neutral swing voters in each group, namely those with $\sigma^i = 0$.

In view of this, the first-order conditions determining the allocation of equilibrium spending across groups can be written as

$$\frac{N^J}{N} \frac{\phi^J}{\phi} \kappa^J H_g(g^J) - \frac{N^J}{N} \sum_I \frac{N^I}{N} \frac{\phi^I}{\phi} \kappa^I = 0. \tag{7.14}$$

The equilibrium thus entails a generalized Hotelling-type result. Despite the multidimensional policy space, the two parties converge on the same platforms. The intuition for this is simple: the parties compete for the same voters and are thus both trying to buy the electoral support from the same marginal voters in each group. Furthermore, they have the same technology for converting money into expected votes. As a result, the distribution of voters' preferences alone decides the unique equilibrium election outcome.

To characterize equilibrium spending, $\mathbf{g}^E$, it is useful to rewrite (7.14) as

$$H_g(g^{J,E}) - 1 = \frac{\sum_I \frac{N^I}{N} \phi^I \kappa^I - \phi^J \kappa^J}{\phi^J \kappa^J}. \tag{7.15}$$

As in the previous two sections, the expression on the right-hand side of the equation determines deviations from the utilitarian optimum. A number of insights emerge.

1. As in chapter 3, electoral competition implements the utilitarian optimum, $\mathbf{g}^E = \mathbf{g}^*$, in a politically homogenous society (that is, a society in which the ideological bias is the same across groups, such that the densities ϕ^J and the parameters κ^J coincide for all J). This is intuitive: because both parties try to buy expected votes by influencing the voters' marginal utility, they have marginal incentives identical to those emanating from a utilitarian objective, if each group is identical as concerns how easily its vote can be swayed. This result is well-known from the literature on probabilistic voting in a spatial setting; it was first demonstrated by Coughlin and Nitzan (1981).

2. As in chapter 3, the term $\phi^J \kappa^J$ conveniently summarizes the political clout of a specific group J. If this term is higher than the weighted average of all groups, the right-hand side of (7.15) is negative, implying $g^{J,E} > g^*$. The term ϕ^J measures the density of ideologically neutral voters, that is, of voters who care only about economic policies. These are the most mobile voters, and both parties want to please them. The greater is the density of these swing voters within group J, the greater is the expenditure directed toward this group. The parameter κ^J, in contrast, reflects to what extent voters in group J care about economic well-being as opposed to ideology. Groups that care less about ideology (i.e., groups with a greater κ^J) are favored, since their voters are more mobile. If these features characterize middle-class voters particularly well, the model thus confirms what Stigler (1970) minted

as "director's law," namely that redistributive policies generally favor the middle class. Inversely, groups caring a great deal about ideology and groups with few swing voters lose out, because buying a large number of expected votes in those groups is too expensive.[15]

3. Group size plays no role in determining political clout. On the one hand, a large group has many voters and is therefore an attractive target for vote buying. On the other hand, it is more expensive to pay for the votes of a large group. As the expression in (7.15) shows, these two effects cancel each other out. Note, however, that we have assumed that parties maximize their probability of winning taken over the whole population. Thus we can consider this an implicit assumption of an electoral system with strict proportional representation. Chapter 8 considers alternative electoral rules in a similar model.

4. Total spending has no first-order bias relative to the utilitarian optimum. As (7.15) shows, some groups get more and others get less. The effect on total spending depends in a complicated way on the interplay between political clout, relative group size, and the concavity of the $H(\cdot)$ function. Intuitively, spending is entirely "supply determined" by the two political parties. The presence of a latent common-pool problem with incentives to expand spending at the group level does not influence the outcome, since each party, in its attempt to buy votes from all groups, properly internalizes the aggregate budget constraint.

The analysis can be extended and modified in a number of directions. In papers by Lindbeck and Weibull (1987) and Dixit and Londregan (1996), direct income transfers support each group's private consumption. Poorer groups systematically obtain more support, ceteris paribus, since their marginal utility of income is higher (as it would be for a benevolent planner). The same would apply here with a concave utility of private consumption; common taxes would hurt poor voters necessitating compensation with greater public consumption. Strömberg (1998b) lets groups differ in their turnout rates, denoted as t^J. The political clout of group J in the model above becomes $t^J \phi^J \kappa^J$. Groups with higher turnout rates would thus get more support. The transaction costs in buying votes may also differ systematically across groups. If these costs or the uncertainties in vote buying are lower among the groups belonging to the party's core supporters (because transfers can be more precisely targeted), this may become a counterweight to a strong party bias and rationalize so-called machine politics, in which parties give more favors to their traditional support groups, as discussed in the model by Cox and McCubbins (1986). Dixit and Londregan (1998a) study a more general model in which parties and voters also have

---

15. A more general formulation of the model would have the idiosyncratic parameters σ^{iJ} distributed according to general group-specific c.d.f. $S^J(\cdot)$ with different means. In this case, the relevant density would be $\phi^J(0)$ and groups with an ideological bias (a mean far from 0) would lose out, as they would have few ideologically neutral voters.

some ideological concerns about income distribution, which allows them to derive endogenously the result that groups composed of middle-class voters are likely to have the most electoral clout.

The model in this section certainly highlights important aspects of how parties may favor special interests in their election campaigns, but it also leaves out important aspects of policy making. For one, there is no interest group activity; each group is just a target for the politicians, and their members just cast their vote like everybody else. And as discussed in chapters 3 and 4, the assumption of binding electoral promises is dubious; in the running of business, the incumbent government and its administration make many policy decisions between elections. Part 3 discusses at length how electoral competition is played out, through retrospective voting in this case.

7.5   Interactions

So far this chapter has studied three different models of special-interest politics, each focusing on a separate aspect of political activity. Real-world politics, however, involves a great deal of interaction between these separate aspects. If lobbies or voters understand how decisions are made in the legislature, they will adapt their lobbying behavior or their candidate preferences accordingly. And if electoral platforms systematically favor certain organized groups, those groups will also adapt their campaign contributions accordingly. In the absence of a grand unified theory of special-interest politics—a structural model simultaneously encompassing legislation, lobbying, and elections—we devote the remainder of the chapter to the analysis of three pairwise forms of interaction.

7.5.1   Lobbying and Elections

The previous model of lobbying is most straightforwardly interpreted as a model of bribes to the government. In practice, however, most lobbying takes the form of campaign contributions, either in cash or in kind, through actions affecting the electoral outcome. To illustrate how electorally motivated lobbying may influence policy, we now combine the lobbying and voting models from this chapter. The resulting model in the present multidimensional problem is the same as the model used in the one-dimensional problem of section 3.5, with the central conclusion that the insights gained in that section survive and carry over to this more general model. Both the lobbying activity and the voters' attributes influence equilibrium policy: organized groups and groups with more swing voters are overrepresented in the political process. Moreover, additional insights are gained about how the lobbies' effectiveness and the size of equilibrium contributions are determined. The analysis is a variant on that in Bennedsen 1998, which in turn extends and simplifies earlier work by Baron (1994) and Grossman and Helpman (1996).[16]

We thus combine the models of sections 7.3 and 7.4 but make some simplifications. Two vote-maximizing parties, B and A, set policy platforms $\mathbf{g}_B$ and $\mathbf{g}_A$, respectively, in advance of the elections. As before, these parties differ in some ideological dimensions. We now assume that all groups are of equal size normalized to unity, such that $\frac{N^J}{N} = \frac{1}{\mathcal{J}}$, and place the same weight on economic outcomes versus ideology, also normalized to unity, $\kappa^J = 1$. Voters in group J still have preferences

$$w^{iJ} = W^J(\mathbf{g}) + (\sigma^{iJ} + \delta)D^B, \tag{7.16}$$

but now δ is given by

$$\delta = \widetilde{\delta} + h(C_B - C_A).$$

Thus, party B's average popularity has two components. The term $\widetilde{\delta}$ is a random variable, as previously, uniformly distributed on $[-\frac{1}{2\psi}, \frac{1}{2\psi}]$. But the total campaign contributions received by parties B and A, C_B and C_A, respectively, also now influence the two parties' overall relative popularity. Specifically, voters are biased in favor of the party receiving more contributions, with $h > 0$ being a parameter capturing the sensitivity to the difference in campaign spending.[17] This has more than one interpretation: C_B might measure advertising expenditures or media exposure of party B's leaders, but it might also refer to support actions in favor of party B's candidate or against her electoral opponent.[18] As in section 7.4, σ^{iJ} is distributed according to group-specific distributions uniform on

$$\left[-\frac{1}{2\phi^J}, \frac{1}{2\phi^J} \right]$$

with density ϕ^J.

By the same logic as previously, the indifferent voter in group J is an individual with preference parameter

$$\sigma^J \equiv W^J(\mathbf{g}_A) - W^J(\mathbf{g}_B) + h(C_A - C_B) - \widetilde{\delta}. \tag{7.17}$$

16. Riezman and Wilson (1997) study restrictions on contributions in a setting where competing political candidates instead "sell" policies to different interest groups.

17. Allowing h to differ across groups or individuals does not matter for the results, since only the average value of h (across groups and individuals) enters the equilibrium expressions. Note that $h > 1$ is allowed.

18. Grossman and Helpman (1996) suggest a slightly different interpretation that leads to a similar formulation. Some voters are fully informed and uninfluenced by campaign contributions. Other voters are uninformed about economic policy platforms and respond exclusively to campaign contributions. The overall effectiveness of campaign contributions in swaying voters is then related to the frequency of uninformed voters in the population.

Thus campaign spending affects the identity of this swing voter. All voters in group J with $\sigma^{iJ} > \sigma^J$ prefer party B; all those with $\sigma^{iJ} < \sigma^J$ prefer A. Following the same approach as in section 7.4, we can derive the probability of winning for party A as

$$p_A = \frac{1}{2} + \psi \left[\frac{1}{\mathcal{J}} \left[\sum_J \frac{\phi^J}{\phi} (W^J(\mathbf{g}_A) - W^J(\mathbf{g}_B)) \right] + h(C_A - C_B) \right]. \qquad (7.18)$$

A subset $\mathcal{L}$ of the groups is organized into lobbies. As in section 7.3, $\lambda_{\mathcal{L}}$ denotes the fraction of the population organized. Lobby J maximizes the expected utility derived from economic policy, net of the per capita cost of its contributions, namely

$$p_A W^J(\mathbf{g}_A) + (1 - p_A) W^J(\mathbf{g}_B) - (C^J)^2/2, \qquad (7.19)$$

where $C^J = C_B^J + C_A^J$ is the per member campaign contribution by lobby J to both parties, and C_B^J and C_A^J are constrained to be nonnegative. As each group has a share $1/\mathcal{J}$ of the population, the total contributions received by party P are

$$C_P = \frac{1}{\mathcal{J}} \sum_{J \in \mathcal{L}} C_P^J.$$

Unlike in section 7.3, the cost of lobbying is taken to be a convex function of C^J, the last term in (7.19).[19] As mentioned in chapter 3, this could reflect increasing marginal costs of enticing potential contributors with different willingness to give, in which case the lobby would naturally start by tapping those members of the group from whom collecting is easiest. Alternatively, if C represents contributions in kind, such as work in the campaign, the convexity may represent increasing disutility of effort.

The timing of events is as follows: (1) Both parties simultaneously announce policy platforms. (2) Having observed these announcements, all lobbies simultaneously set their campaign contributions. (3) Elections are held. Stages (1) and (2) are thus reversed relative to section 7.3, in which the lobbies instead moved first by setting contingent contribution schedules. The present timing assumption considerably simplifies the analysis and may also be more plausible. It portrays lobbying as an activity attempting to influence the electoral process, given the promises made by the parties. Note, however, that lobbying still influences policy formation, since parties anticipate how the lobbies will adapt their contributions to the parties' policy promises. Intuitively, each party wants to win the election, and one way of winning is to announce a platform appealing to the lobbies and let the lobbies help garner electoral support by raising money or working for the party.[20]

---

19. With linear cost functions for C^J, the lobbies' reaction functions would not be continuous in the policy platforms in this setup.

20. Grossman and Helpman (1996) instead consider a setup in which the lobbies move first, and they derive rather similar results.

We are now ready to characterize the equilibrium. The electoral outcome at stage (3) has already been discussed. Consider the optimization problem the lobbies face at stage (2) for given policy platforms announced at stage (1). Maximization of (7.19) with respect to C_A^J and C_B^J, subject to (7.18), yields:[21]

$$C_A^J = \text{Max}\left[0, \frac{h\psi}{\mathcal{J}}(W^J(\mathbf{g}_A) - W^J(\mathbf{g}_B))\right]$$

$$C_B^J = -\text{Min}\left[0, \frac{h\psi}{\mathcal{J}}(W^J(\mathbf{g}_A) - W^J(\mathbf{g}_B))\right]. \tag{7.20}$$

By (7.20), each lobby campaigns only in favor of a single party and does not campaign at all if the two parties announce identical platforms. This feature of the model is quite sensible—the lobbies want to influence the voters, not the parties—and it is consistent with some available evidence suggesting that lobbies seldom spend for both candidates in elections.[22] Summing this expression across all lobbies in $\mathcal{L}$, we get

$$C_A - C_B = \frac{h\psi}{\mathcal{J}^2}\sum_{J\in\mathcal{L}}[W^J(\mathbf{g}_A) - W^J(\mathbf{g}_B)]. \tag{7.21}$$

That is, campaign spending goes to the party that, on average, is more successful in pleasing the lobbies.

Let us now turn to the party optimization problem. Here maximizing the vote share and the probability of winning amount to the same thing. By (7.18), (7.19), and (7.21), party A's objective function can then be written as

$$\max \frac{\psi}{\mathcal{J}}\left[\sum_{J}\frac{\phi^J}{\phi}[W^J(\mathbf{g}_A) - W^J(\mathbf{g}_B)] + \gamma\sum_{J\in\mathcal{L}}[W^J(\mathbf{g}_A) - W^J(\mathbf{g}_B)]\right], \tag{7.22}$$

where $\gamma = \psi h^2/\mathcal{J} > 0$ is an extra weight on the lobbies' utility related to how effectively campaign spending influences the voters: the more influential it is, the greater is the weight on the lobbies' utilities. Note the similarity to the assumed reduced-form objective of the government in the common-agency model in section 7.3; in that case, the organized lobbies also get an additional weight in the policymaker's objective. Thus, γ in the present model closely corresponds to $(1 - \eta)$ in section 7.3.

---

21. To derive (7.20), note that by (7.18) we have:

$$\frac{\partial p^R}{\partial C_R^J} = \frac{h\psi}{\mathcal{J}} = -\frac{\partial p^L}{\partial C_L^J};$$

also recall that contributions are nonnegative.

22. For U.S. evidence on this point, see Poole and Romer 1985.

By the same logic, party B solves an identical problem. Hence, as in section 7.4, both parties announce the same policies, $\mathbf{g}_A = \mathbf{g}_B$, which then implies that equilibrium campaign spending is zero: see (7.21).[23] This does not mean that the presence of the lobbies is irrelevant; on the contrary: out of equilibrium, they do spend on the party that pleases them most, and this induces both parties to tilt public policy in their favor. Specifically, taking the first-order conditions of problem (7.22) and rewriting them, we can define the equilibrium allocation by the following expressions:

$$
\begin{aligned}
H_g(g^J) - 1 &= \frac{\phi}{\phi^J + \gamma\phi}\left[1 - \frac{\phi^J}{\phi} - \gamma(1 - \lambda_{\mathcal{L}})\right] \quad \text{if } J \in \mathcal{L} \\
H_g(g^J) - 1 &= \frac{\phi}{\phi^J}\left[1 - \frac{\phi^J}{\phi} + \gamma\lambda_{\mathcal{L}}\right] \quad \text{if } J \notin \mathcal{L}.
\end{aligned}
\tag{7.23}
$$

That is, g^J is overprovided, relative to the social optimum, if there are many swing voters in J (ϕ^J is larger than ϕ, the average of the other groups), precisely as in section 7.4. If group J is organized as a lobby, there is also overprovision, and the lobbying effect is stronger the higher is γ, that is, the more effective are campaign contributions in influencing the voters. Also, a smaller fraction of lobbies among the groups, a smaller $\lambda_{\mathcal{L}}$, increases the amount of overprovision for the lobbies but decreases the amount of underprovision for the unorganized groups, as in section 7.3. Thus, the lobbying and probabilistic voting models naturally complement each other, and the more general formulation preserves the insights gained when each is considered in isolation.

The model can easily be generalized to introduce other attributes of the voters. As noted above, Grossman and Helpman (1996) and Baron (1994) distinguish between informed and uninformed voters. The former are fully informed and completely unaffected by campaign contributions, like the voters in section 7.4. The uninformed, on the other hand, are completely unaffected by economic policies, and their preferences respond only to campaign spending by the parties: namely, their preferences are simply given by the contributions term $h(C_A - C_B)$. Let groups also differ in their share of informed and uninformed voters, besides the density ϕ^J, and let α^J denote the share of informed voters in group J. Then repeating the same steps as above, it can be shown that parameter α^J influences the allocation in the same way as ϕ^J in expression (7.23). That is, the parties treat groups with a larger share of informed voters better, since those voters are more responsive to economic policies. Stated otherwise, voters' responsiveness, one of the key determinants of the equilibrium allocation in the voting model, can reflect either a small weight given to ideology within the group (or small electoral turnout), or equivalently, a small share of uninformed voters.

---

23. Grossman and Helpman (1996), with their different timing assumption, get a different result: in their model, party platforms do not converge, and equilibrium contributions are positive.

This discussion naturally suggests two questions: How do voters obtain their information? And why are some voters informed whereas others are not? An obvious answer to the first question is that voters obtain their information from the media. Strömberg (1998a) sets up a formal model of politics and the media to address the second question. He shows that the interaction between electoral competition (modeled as in section 7.4) and competition between profit-maximizing media provides an answer to the second question. Optimal behavior by the media tends to bias the information, and hence also the policy outcome, toward groups that are attractive to advertisers.

To summarize, the model in this subsection provides a richer set of determinants of success in special-interest politics compared to the partial models in sections 7.3 and 7.4. There are no surprises, however, and the results combine our earlier findings. As we shall see in the next two subsections, however, this is not always the outcome of interactions between two different types of political activity.

7.5.2   Elections and Legislative Bargaining

To study the interaction between elections and legislation, we add an election stage at the beginning of the legislative bargaining game discussed above. In district-wide elections, forward-looking voters appoint a representative for the coming legislative session, which, as we shall see, gives rise to strategic delegation. To make that point, we now assume that candidates for office are outcome-motivated. As in chapter 5, they care about the policy enacted once in office, and different candidates have different views on what is the optimal policy. The modeling here follows the recent study by Chari, Jones, and Marimon (1997) quite closely.

Consider a four-stage game in which the last three stages are identical to the game in section 7.2. In the first stage, every district simultaneously elects a representative by plurality rule. We assume that in each district, voters can choose among candidates with heterogeneous preferences for private versus public consumption. Specifically, a candidate of type α for district J has preferences

$$W^{J,\alpha} = c^J + \alpha H(g^J). \tag{7.24}$$

That is, candidates with high values of α care a great deal about publicly provided goods. Candidates are outcome-motivated in the sense that once elected, they act so as to maximize (7.24), and their type (ideology) is not an object of choice for the candidate himself. Candidates are thus characterized by their utility function (7.24), or more compactly, by their preference parameter α.

For simplicity, we also make the following symmetry assumptions: (1) In all districts, there is a continuum of candidates from which to choose, with values of α in the same range

$[\alpha^L, \alpha^U]$ for all districts. (2) We continue to assume that voters are all identical within each district and have preferences as in (7.24), but with $\alpha = 1$. Adding voter heterogeneity, with voter preferences distributed over the same range $[\alpha^L, \alpha^U]$ as candidates, would not change the results. (3) All districts have the same size, namely $\frac{N^J}{N} = \frac{1}{J}$ for all J. (4) The default allocation is symmetric, namely $\overline{g}^J = 0$ for all J, implying $\overline{\tau} = 0$. (5) Every representative has the same probability, $\frac{1}{J}$, of being chosen as the agenda setter.

Once more, we look for a subgame-perfect Nash equilibrium. Consider first the legislative bargaining stages. By (3), (4), and the results in section 7.2, it is easily shown that the chosen agenda setter will pick the $\frac{J-1}{2}$ representatives with the highest values of α as members of the majority coalition, $\mathcal{M}$. These representatives are easiest to please, because they value public consumption a lot and the status quo has $\overline{g}^J = 0$ (i.e., their incentive constraints (7.5) are the easiest to relax). At the elections stage, voters realize this. Recall that voters in district J get compensated with some public goods for the taxes they pay only if the candidate they elect is part of the majority, whereas they get no compensation if the candidate they elect finds himself in the opposition. Hence all districts have an incentive to elect a candidate with a value of α higher than that of the candidates the other districts elect, since that would with certainty make him part of the majority. This pushes all districts into a corner: under a mild condition on preferences, all districts elect the most spendthrift candidate, type α^U, in equilibrium. With this constellation of representatives, the voters in each district have a fifty-fifty chance of being included in the winning coalition. If any district appointed a smaller spender—a candidate with a lower α—this chance would drop to zero, thus bringing about a discontinuous expected welfare loss.[24]

Thus we have an instance of strategic delegation: voters in each district elect a big spender, because unless they act in this way, they are left in the opposition. Clearly, this voting equilibrium makes the allocation more biased toward overspending on the part of the agenda setter, since she also has a high α, on top of her better bargaining power, and diminishes the differences between districts inside and outside the majority.

---

24. Some conditions are needed to ensure that this is an equilibrium, since by electing a spendthrift candidate, the voters might also incur a cost: in the event that he is appointed agenda setter, a spendthrift ends up spending more than is optimal for the voters who elect him. This (expected) cost thus needs to be sufficiently smaller than the potential benefit, due to a discretely higher probability of his being included in the majority, to make it worthwhile to vote for him. With a large enough number of districts, the probability of his becoming agenda setter is sufficiently small, and this condition is satisfied.

   The model could be extended to an entry stage in which candidates sort themselves out as in the citizen-candidate model of chapter 5. Suppose that voters too are heterogeneous and have the same preferences as the candidates (7.24). Applying proposition 2 (and corollary 1) in Besley and Coate 1997, this equilibrium would, in fact, be sustainable in an extended citizen-candidate model with an initial entry stage, in which every voter in each district could enter as a candidate, at a cost. The candidate with α^U optimally running and winning as an (unopposed) candidate in each district would be an equilibrium, if the entry cost was low enough and the default outcome bad enough (g^J valuable enough). See Coate 1997 for a full-fledged analysis of legislative bargaining and elections in a citizen-candidate model.

As Chari, Jones, and Marimon (1997) point out, this equilibrium is broadly consistent with opinions often expressed by U.S. voters, who typically are quite disconcerted with the composition and actions of Congress as a whole but, at the same time, are pleased with their own representative; the strong incumbency advantage of legislators serving in congressional elections also bears testimony of this. In the equilibrium studied, voters in any district J would indeed have a higher expected utility if all other districts had representatives with $\alpha < \alpha^U$ but the voters in J could maintain the identity of their own representative.

The model is obviously very stylized, but it still teaches us a lesson: it is important to look beyond the apparent bargaining powers that different legislators derive from a particular set of legislative rules, as these powers are endogenously modified in the interaction with their principals, the voters. Introducing elections thus pushes the legislative bargaining solution toward a more extreme outcome rather than toward a more balanced one, as might have been the first guess. The same point will reappear, even more forcefully, in the next subsection.

Nevertheless, the model neglects important aspects of the interactions between elections and legislative bargaining. Specifically, there is no connection between the election outcome and the proposal rights in the legislature. In reality, the party affiliation and seniority of legislators determines the allocation of these proposal rights, which can be revised by each elected Congress.

In a remarkable paper, McKelvey and Riezman (1991) study these aspects in a dynamic game involving infinitely repeated elections in multiple districts in which each newly elected Congress can set its own seniority rules before engaging in legislative bargaining over a fixed budget. McKelvey and Riezman show that seniority rights in agenda setting and a strong electoral incumbency advantage of senior legislators jointly emerge as a stationary equilibrium outcome. Interestingly, the endogenous seniority rights apply only to the initial proposal. If proposal rights in multiround bargaining were to be given in the order of decreasing seniority, senior legislators would be at a disadvantage in the legislative bargaining. Because they would have higher continuation values in each legislative session, it would be more expensive to bring them into the majority, in the same way that the vote of low-α legislators is more expensive in model of this subsection.

Another important and related contribution is by Austen-Smith and Banks (1988), who discuss how government formation, in a parliament with three parties, affects an election in which voters anticipate the outcome of the government formation game. Problem 4 of this chapter summarizes some of the points in that paper.

7.5.3   Lobbying and Legislative Bargaining

We now set voters aside and consider how influence activities by interest groups interact with legislative bargaining. Research on this topic is still very scant. One antecedent is

Snyder 1991, which studies how lobbies interact with legislators in the context of a spatial voting model. A central insight from the paper is that lobbies will focus their contributions on the "marginal" legislators, those who are close to indifferent between a policy proposal (favorable to the lobbies) and the status quo.[25] Our analysis in this subsection draws on Helpman and Persson 1998.

With a structural model of government decision making in place of a single policymaker, we must now take a stance on who lobbies whom. We restrict each interest group to making contributions only to a single congressman, "their own." This kind of fixed association is arbitrary but has some empirical support: campaign contributions in the United States tend to go to representatives from the same district as the donor or to a member of the committee holding jurisdiction of regulation or grants applying to the donor group. There is much less systematic information about political contributions in Europe, but in some countries there are very tight relations between interest groups, like trade unions and agricultural lobbies, and specific political parties.

Legislators still play the same legislative bargaining game as in section 7.2. We retain the symmetry assumptions (3) and (4) of the previous subsection. In addition, we also abstract from asymmetries in the organization across groups and assume that all groups are organized in lobbies: $|\mathcal{L}| = \mathcal{J}$, in the notation of section 7.3. The policy game is as in section 7.2 but with an additional contributions stage. The timing is as follows. (1) Nature selects a legislator, $J = a$, to be the agenda setter. (2) Contribution schedules are simultaneously announced by the lobbies and observed by all legislators.[26] (3) Finally, the agenda setter formulates a take-it-or-leave-it proposal, and the legislature votes on this. If the proposal is defeated, the default policy is as in the previous subsection: $\bar{\mathbf{g}} = \mathbf{0}$, $\bar{\tau} = 0$. We assume that legislators care only about the contributions they receive.[27]

Group J presents its congressional representative with a truthful contribution schedule, which offers

$$C^J(\mathbf{g}) = \begin{cases} \max\left[W^J(\mathbf{g}) - b^J, 0\right] & \text{if } J \text{ supports } \mathbf{g} \\ 0 & \text{otherwise,} \end{cases} \tag{7.25}$$

where the zero contribution if legislator J does not support a policy $\mathbf{g}$ can be shown to be

---

25. Another antecedent is Groseclose and Snyder 1996, which studies a game where two lobbies buy votes from legislators about to decide on a public project. Interestingly, Groseclose and Snyder show that when votes are bought sequentially, the prediction of a minimum winning coalition may fail.

26. With the opposite timing (contributions made first), it would be natural to assume that contributions were made contingent on the legislator's status (agenda setter, or not). The results would be identical to the case considered in the text.

27. Problem 5 of this chapter discusses alternative assumptions about the rules of legislative bargaining and about the candidates' motivations.

an optimal strategy.[28] As in section 7.3, we can think of b^J as the reservation utilities of group J. Representatives maximize the value of their contributions and hence want these reservation values to be as low as possible. And as in section 7.3, interest groups maximize their utility net of their contributions. Thus they want the reservation utilities in (7.25) to be as high as possible.

Consider first the agenda setter's problem for given contribution schedules. She wants to maximize

$$C^a(\mathbf{g}) = \text{Max}\,[W^a(\mathbf{g}) - b^a, 0] = \text{Max}\left[H(g^a) + y - \frac{1}{\mathcal{J}}\left(\sum_I g^I\right) - b^a, 0\right], \qquad (7.26)$$

subject to the incentive compatibility constraints that legislators in $\mathcal{M}$ be better off than with the default outcome:

$$W^J(\mathbf{g}) - b^J = H(g^J) + y - \frac{1}{\mathcal{J}}\left(\sum_I g^I\right) - b^J \geq 0 \quad \text{for} \quad J \in \mathcal{M} \qquad (7.27)$$

(recall that contributions are 0, if the proposal is voted down). Again, a finds it optimal to collect a minimum winning coalition, that is, to include only $\frac{\mathcal{J}-1}{2}$ additional members in $\mathcal{M}$. It is easily shown that Max $[W^a(\mathbf{g})]$ is decreasing in all b^J, $J \in \mathcal{M}$. The agenda setter wants to satisfy (7.27) with equality for all members of the majority, because this maximizes her own district's utility and hence the contribution to herself. Thus she picks the representatives with the lowest values of b^J as her coalition partners, setting $g^J = 0$ for everyone else, as in section 7.2.

Now let us return to the contribution stage and consider the optimal contributions for group J, $J \neq a$. Clearly, group J is better off if its representative is included in the majority, as long as that gives the group at least a tiny piece of public goods.[29] This sets up a fierce Bertrand competition among the interest groups. Because $\mathcal{M}$ includes only legislators with the lowest reservation utilities, the only equilibrium has every group J setting its reservation utility at the lowest possible level, namely

$$b^J = y - \frac{1}{\mathcal{J}}\left(\sum_{I \in \mathcal{M}} g^I\right).$$

Returning to the agenda setter's problem in (7.26)–(7.27), we then find that the optimal

---

28. Helpman and Persson (1998) show that equilibrium contributions indeed pay zero in the event that a legislator does not support a proposal. They also relax the assumption that legislators care only about money and show that the qualitative results are not affected, if legislators also care about the welfare of their district.

29. If the representative is not included in the majority, group J's utility is $W^J(\mathbf{g}\,|\,J \notin \mathcal{M}) = y - \frac{1}{\mathcal{J}}\left(\sum_{I \in \mathcal{M}} g^I\right)$, whereas the utility if she is included is $W^J(\mathbf{g}\,|\,J \in \mathcal{M}) = H(g^J) + y - \frac{1}{\mathcal{J}}\left(\sum_{I \in \mathcal{M}} g^I\right)$.

solution satisfies

$$H_g(g^a) = \frac{1}{\mathcal{J}}$$

$$g^J = 0, \quad \text{all } J \neq a. \tag{7.28}$$

Group a implements this choice at the lowest cost, namely zero, by setting its reservation utility $b^a = H(g^a) + y - \frac{g^a}{\mathcal{J}}$.

A useful way of thinking about this equilibrium is to rely on the same intuition as in the previous subsection. Each interest group badly wants to avoid having its representative be left in the minority, so that it only pays taxes but receives no public good. To avoid this outcome, each group reduces its reservation utility to make the vote of its representative cheaper to buy. Because all interest groups have the same objective, this competition drives equilibrium public goods down to zero for every district. Obviously, the agenda setter's district is the beneficiary. The logic is similar to that in Dixit, Grossman, and Helpman 1997, which studies a general common-agency model and shows that competition between the interest groups allows the single government to implement its preferred solution. Here, however, the benefit goes to one powerful district, not to a semibenevolent government.

Note that also in this case, politicians collect no contributions in equilibrium. Clearly, this does not provide a safe ground for concluding that influence activities are unimportant, as some commentators like Tullock (1988) have suggested. Note also that in equilibrium every legislator is willing to vote for the proposal (at least they have no incentive to vote against it). Thus despite the force of minimum winning coalitions outside of equilibrium, the equilibrium majority is more than minimal. The model is thus consistent with a stylized fact underlying the literature on "universalism" in the U.S. Congress, namely that distributive bills often pass with broad majorities. But the universalism literature has weak micropolitical underpinnings (it is hard to model as the outcome of an extensive form game), and universalism is often accounted for by referring to a "norm of deference" ("you scratch my back and I scratch yours"). In our setting we could imagine a sequence of legislative sessions in which different representatives (approximating different committees) take turns as agenda setters. The outcome after these sessions would coincide with a universalist allocation, like the one in Weingast, Shepsle, and Johnsen 1981.

Note also that the results obtained in this section are not a convex combination of the results in the partial models studied above. Specifically, the distribution of benefits is more skewed than in the legislative bargaining model of section 7.2, even though the lobbying model of section 7.3 predicted a very even distribution of benefits (with all groups organized and symmetric, as we have assumed in this section, the common-agency model predicts equal b^J for all J).

These results illustrate, with additional force, the general point made in the previous subsection: optimal private behavior alters the bargaining powers inherent in legislative procedures. Here it amplifies the misallocation of public goods by a legislature in which agenda-setting powers are conferred upon individual members or committees. Naturally, the simple structure of this game gives rise to an extreme outcome. Real-world legislatures have introduced various safeguards against such extreme outcomes. Section 7.2 discussed some of these safeguards, and part 3 will discuss others. We thus want to give more emphasis to the general logic than to specific results.

7.6   Discussion

This chapter studied a multidimensional policy problem. When redistribution can be narrowly targeted toward specific groups, economic policy confers concentrated benefits to a few, with the costs dispersed among many. We asked what determines the allocation of benefits among groups and the overall size of such redistributive programs. Our answers have emphasized a variety of political mechanisms, each focusing on a particular aspect of policy formation. Legislative bargaining models focus on the institutional position of the representatives of different groups and on the specific legislative procedures involved. Lobbying models stress different groups' ability to solve a free-rider problem and organize as an active pressure group. Electoral competition models draw the attention to the ideological attitudes of a group's members and their responsiveness to policy favors.

Each of these models, although identifying specific determinants of the policy choices, also raises new questions. The model of legislative bargaining entails a detailed set of assumptions about the rules for approving legislation. The detail is crucial, and changing the extensive form of the game can lead to radically different results. Think for instance about the role of the status quo payoffs. If unanimity is required, as in two-person Nash bargaining, increasing a player's status quo payoff increases his bargaining power. But in the majoritarian legislative bargaining of section 7.2, the opposite happens: a player with a higher status quo payoff is more likely to be left out of the winning coalition and has no bargaining power at all. Similar remarks apply to the distinction between open and closed rules, to the procedure for selecting the agenda setter, to the sequencing of decisions when more than one policy dimension is involved, and so on. A countless variety of possible detailed assumptions can be made about the extensive form of these games. Which assumptions are more reasonable and appropriate given the policy issues or the countries involved? How can we avoid the risk of arbitrary or convenient assumptions with little counterpart in real-world legislatures? These are still open questions, and to be more confident in this approach we need careful empirical and applied research. In this regard, Peltzman (1992), Levitt and Poterba (1994), and Lowry, Alt, and Ferree (1998) offer interesting empirical results with reference to U.S. states.

Similarly, the models of lobbying and probabilistic voting raise other long-standing questions: what determines a group's ability to be organized and politically active? And what is the source of the voters' ideological preferences? An interesting idea is that politicians themselves try to foster and nurture these ideological preferences even when they contradict the voters' true economic interests, and likewise, that politicians use public policy to solve the free-rider problems of pressure groups in order to keep them politically active. Ideology can thus create a sense of party loyalty, and similarly, pressure groups help politicians to garner electoral support or even obtain economic benefits for themselves. Further exploring these issues, trying to make the voters' ideological preferences endogenous and studying the role of public policy in creating and preserving pressure groups seems a very fruitful, though difficult, area of research.

Which of the various approaches illustrated in this chapter is more appropriate, and under what circumstances? To some extent, the answer will have to await further empirical research assessing their relative ability to explain specific applied policies. Each approach identifies only a particular aspect of the political process, however, and it could be highly misleading to consider each of them in isolation. An important lesson of section 7.5 is precisely that integrating these partial political models leads to new and surprising results. The integration attempted in this chapter is incomplete, however. On the one hand, we have jumped back and forth relying on different assumptions about the politicians' motivation, the timing of events, and the forms of political participation. On the other hand, we have completely neglected the agency problem that is at the core of any political delegation. Part 3 tries to remedy these limitations: it formulates a more complete model of the political process that focuses explicitly on agency and relies as much as possible on a common set of assumptions.

7.7   Notes on the Literature

The model formulated in section 7.1 draws on Persson and Tabellini 1994d, whereas much of this chapter follows the survey by Persson (1998). Similar models have been extensively used to discuss incentive problems in local public finance and to contrast alternative budgetary procedures. In particular, Besley and Coate (1998a), Lockwood (1998), and Daveri (1998) consider a similar setup but assume that local public goods impose externalities on other groups. They contrast decentralized and centralized arrangements, pointing to a trade-off between two opposite incentive problems. Centralization makes it more likely that spillover effects are internalized, but cost sharing generates the incentive problems discussed throughout this chapter. Full decentralization, on the other hand, prevents the externalities from being internalized. The preferred institutional arrangement thus depends on which of these incentive problems is worse.

When there is a vertical hierarchy of decision makers, as with federal and local governments, the principal's lack of commitment may impose a "soft budget constraint" on the agent. Like common-pool problems, soft-budget-constraint problems may lead to overspending. Dewatripont and Maskin 1995 is the classical reference on soft budget constraints in a principal-agent setup. Qian and Roland (1998) and Bordignon, Manasse, and Tabellini (1997) have studied versions of this problem in local public finance. Maskin and Xu (1999) survey the literature on the soft budget constraint, with special emphasis on transitional economics.

The formal literature on extensive form games of collective choice dates back to the pioneering work of Shepsle (1979) on structure-induced equilibria and of Romer and Rosenthal (1979) on agenda-setting powers. Models of legislative bargaining were first formulated by Baron and Ferejohn (1989) and Epple and Riordan (1987) in an infinite-horizon pie-splitting problem and applied to the provision of local public goods by Baron (1991, 1993). A different extensive form game, allowing for amendments in a particular way, was studied by McKelvey (1986) and Ferejohn, Fiorina, and McKelvey (1987); its applications to public finance are yet to be explored: the only paper so far is a recent one by Lockwood (1998). Shepsle 1989, Baron 1994, Myerson 1995, and Moser 1997 are good surveys of the formal theories of legislative politics.

Sequential budgeting has been studied in various settings. Von Hagen (1998) discusses it in a comprehensive analysis of budgetary procedures. Persson, Roland, and Tabellini (1997) assess the benefits of two-stage budgeting coupled with strong agenda-setting powers in a model of agency. Their point is dealt with again in part 3. Ferejohn and Krehbiel (1987) analyze a median-voter model with sequential voting in different dimensions and argue that two-stage budgeting may fail to deliver the alleged benefits, but their setup does not entail a common-pool problem.

A large empirical literature compares alternative budgetary institutions across political systems, from European countries (von Hagen 1992, von Hagen and Harden 1994), to those in Latin America (Alesina, Hommes, et al. 1996, Inter-American Development Bank 1997), to those of U.S. states (Alesina and Bayoumi 1996, Poterba 1994, Bohn and Inman 1996). This literature indicates that specific procedures are associated with smaller budget deficits. The correlation of alternative budgetary institutions with the size or composition of spending has been little discussed, except by Kontopoulos and Perotti (1997, 1999). See also the contributions in Poterba and von Hagen 1999.

Austen-Smith (1997) and Rodrik (1995) give a recent survey of the literature on lobbying, whereas Mueller (1989) surveys the older literature. An influential branch of the literature, not discussed here, approaches lobbying as the strategic transmission of asymmetrically held information; see Potters and van Winden 1992 and Austen-Smith and Wright 1992. Grossman and Helpman (1994) were the first to use Bernheim and Whinston's (1986) common-agency approach to model lobbying in the case of trade policy. Earlier contributions on lobbying include Denzau and Munger 1986, Magee, Brock, and Young 1989, and Rasmusen 1993.

Dixit (1996b) applies the common-agency approach to commodity taxation, showing why the well-known Diamond-Mirrlees production efficiency prescription would almost surely be violated in political equilibrium. Aidt (1998) adopts the common-agency approach in analyzing environmental taxes, and Rama and Tabellini (1998) analyze lobbying by trade unions and firms over both trade policy and a minimum wage policy. Lobbying in a model with politicians and bureaucrats is analyzed by Mazza and van Winden (1995). Dixit, Grossman, and Helpman 1997 contains a general discussion of the common-agency approach with applications to public finance. Boylan (1995) points to the similarities between this approach and the literature on auctions.

The amount of empirical literature on lobbying is still relatively small, though there is a much larger literature on campaign contributions in the United States (see Bronars and Lott 1995 and the survey in Mueller 1989, chap. 11). Liebert (1995) discusses lobbying in European parliamentary democracies. Recent empirical analyses include Goldbe and Maggi 1997, on campaign contributions and trade protection in the United States, and Alt et al. (1999), on lobbying for government subsidies by Norwegian firms. An interesting experimental study of lobbying is described by Potters and van Winden (1992).

As mentioned in chapter 2, the probabilistic voting approach was developed in the spatial voting model to guarantee the existence of equilibrium in situations, such as a multidimensional policy space, in which a Condorcet winner fails to exist; see Coughlin 1992 for an overview of probabilistic voting and Osborne (1995) for an overview of spatial voting theory. Lindbeck and Weibull (1987) adapted this framework to redistribution among multiple interest groups, and Dixit and Londregan (1996) extended their approach. These papers, and the other papers mentioned in the text, identify a priori the set of interest groups and the group affiliation of each voter. A general treatment of redistribution among ex ante identical voters resulting from electoral competition between political candidates—without additional attributes—can be found in Myerson 1993b, who derives an equilibrium in which each candidate selects a randomized redistribution strategy.

Strömberg (1998a) develops a model of parallel competition between political candidates and between profit-maximizing media. Strömberg (1998b) successfully applies this kind of model empirically to explain how New Deal spending was allocated across U.S. counties depending on the availability of radio receivers.

Our model of the interaction between elections and lobbying in section 7.5.1 draws on Baron 1994, Grossman and Helpman 1996, and Bennedsen 1998. Besley and Coate (1999) study lobbying and elections in a citizen-candidate model; Riezman and Wilson (1997) study legal redistributions or contributions in a setting in which policymakers compete for the support of different lobbies. An early contribution on the interaction between lobbying and elections is Austen-Smith 1987.

The interaction between elections and legislative behavior is naturally of first-order importance in political economics. Little formal work combines extensive form legislative games with elections and rational voters, which might be due to the difficulty of these issues. Austen-Smith and Banks (1988) and Baron (1993) are among the few that have studied the interaction between voting and government formation in a three-party setting. McKelvey and Riezman (1991) study the interactions between voting and legislative bargaining and show how a seniority system may emerge endogenously in a sequence of congressional elections. Section 7.5.2 draws on Chari, Jones, and Marimon 1997. Coate (1997) demonstrates that the strategic delegation equilibrium considered by Chari, Jones, and Marimon is consistent with endogenous entry in a citizen-candidate model.

Work on the interdependencies between lobbying and legislation, assuming rational behavior of interest groups and legislators, is even more scarce. Denzau and Munger (1986) study a reduced-form model in which interest groups give contributions to legislators who choose effort on different legislative activities so as to maximize expected votes. Snyder (1991) analyzes lobbies' contributions to a set of legislators who have different ideal points in a spatial voting model. Groseclose and Snyder (1996) study a game in which two lobbies buy votes from legislators who will make a decision on a public project. Section 7.5.3 draws on Helpman and Persson 1998.

7.8   Problems

1. Legislative bargaining with amendment rights

This problem is based on Baron and Ferejohn 1989. Consider a legislature with three members who must divide rents of size 1 among themselves. The consumption value of the rents to legislator i is $w^i(r) = r$. The rents are divided according to the following procedure. A member of the legislature is randomly selected to propose a division of rents. If a majority of the members in the legislature do not accept the proposition, then another member is randomly selected to make a new proposition. Each time a new proposition is made, the payoffs are discounted by a factor δ. The game continues until a proposition is accepted.

a. Compute the equilibrium with stationary (that is history-independent) strategies in this game.

b. Now consider what happens when amendments are allowed. First, one member of the legislative body has been selected to be the agenda setter and to propose an allocation of rents, r_1, that will be named the proposition on the floor. Then another member is randomly selected among the legislators other than the agenda setter. This other member can let the legislative body vote on implementing r_1. He may also propose an amended allocation r_2. In this case, there is a vote between r_1 and r_2. The winner becomes the proposition on the floor. Then a new member is randomly chosen. This other member can let the legislative body vote on implementing the proposition on the floor. He may also propose an amended allocation, r_3. In this case, there is a vote between the proposition on the floor and r_3. The winner becomes the proposition on the floor. The process continues until an allocation is implemented. The members are assumed to have a common discount factor $\delta \in [0, 1]$. Every time the allocation is amended, the value of the payoffs is discounted by δ.

Consider stationary equilibria of the following form: the member proposing the allocation keeps a share y of the budget to himself and gives $1 - y$ to one other member and nothing to the remaining member. If a member is indifferent between a bill and an amendment, he will vote for the amendment. Compute the optimal stationary strategy y for the member proposing an allocation.

c. Now consider stationary equilibria of the following form: the member proposing the allocation keeps a share y of the budget to himself and gives $\frac{1-y}{2}$ to each of the two remaining members. Compute the optimal strategy y.

d. Discuss when it is optimal for the agenda setter to offer positive rents to only one other member (a minimum winning coalition, as in question (b)) and when it is optimal to offer rents to all members of the legislature (universalism, as in question (c)). Discuss how allowing amendments affects the agenda-setting power.

e. Suppose that there was a prior stage in which the legislative body chose by majority decision whether to use an open or a closed rule. Assume that it is known who would be the first agenda setter and who would be included in prospective coalitions. Which rule would prevail?

2. Budgetary powers and amendments rights in legislatures

Suppose that individuals receive utility from private consumption, c, and consumption of a publicly provided private good, g, described by the utility function $v = u(c) + g$. The public good is financed through a proportional income tax τ. There are three groups, each of size 1, and all individuals receive income 1. The budget constraint is thus $3\tau = g_1 + g_2 + g_3 = G$.

a. What is the socially optimal level of taxes?

b. Suppose now that a representative from one of the groups chooses taxes in the first stage. In the next stage, a representative from another group proposes an allocation of G. It is not known whether the agent setting taxes will receive positive allocation from this proposal. If the proposed allocation is not accepted, then one of the two other groups is randomly chosen to have its representative propose a new allocation. The discount rate is δ. Compute the level of taxes and the allocation of G. Are taxes too high or too low in equilibrium?

c. Now suppose that G is allocated using a rule with amendment rights, as described in question (b) of problem 1. Furthermore, assume that the discount rate is higher than 0.73, so that only one group other than the agenda setter receives publicly provided services. It is not known whether the agent setting taxes will be included in the winning coalition. Compute the level of taxes and the allocation of G. Are taxes too high or too low in equilibrium?

d. Now suppose that G is allocated using a rule with amendment rights but that the discount rate is smaller than 0.73, so that there is a universalistic equilibrium where all groups receive publicly provided services. Compute the level of taxes and the allocation of G. Are taxes too high or too low in equilibrium?

e. Finally, assume that a_τ (the first-stage proposer) is elected by the members of all groups and thus cares about all groups. For example, imagine a president being elected in national election, and state representatives deciding over the state allocation of G. What level of taxes would be chosen under each rule?

3. Truthful strategies in the lobbying model

Consider the simple lobbying model of section 7.3.1. A subset L of groups are organized in lobbies. Each lobby j simultaneously and noncooperatively presents a contribution schedule, $C_j(\mathbf{g})$, to the incumbent. Each of the lobbies maximizes the net welfare of its members: $N_j(W_j(\mathbf{g}) - C_j(\mathbf{g}))$. The incumbent sets $\mathbf{g}$ to maximize the weighted sum of social welfare and contributions:

$$W(g) = \eta \sum_j N_j W_j(\mathbf{g}) + (1 - \eta) \sum_{j \in L} N_j C_j(\mathbf{g}),$$

where $\eta \in [0, 1]$.

a. Explain why an equilibrium must be jointly Pareto optimal for the government and the lobbies.

b. Now suppose that the lobbies set differentiable contribution schemes. Show that the truthful strategy

$$C_j(\mathbf{g}) = \max [W_j(\mathbf{g}) - b_j, 0]$$

satisfies the condition for an optimal strategy.

4. Coalition formation in a three-party legislature

This question is based on Austen-Smith and Banks 1988. Suppose that three parties in a parliament are indexed L, M, R, corresponding to "leftist," "middle," and "rightist," respectively. The parties set a policy $y \in [0, 1]$ and divide the exogenous rents of being in office, that is, they select a vector $\mathbf{r} = (r_L, r_M, r_R)$, subject to $r_L + r_M + r_R \leq \bar{r}$. The parties have preferences over the policy described by utility function $u_k = r_k - (x_k - y)^2$, $k \in \{L, M, R\}$, where $x_L = 0$, $x_M = \frac{1}{2}$, and $x_R = 1$.

Prior to the parliamentary session, an election has been held, giving the parties vote shares $w_L > w_M > w_R$. As is often the case in practice, the largest party may propose a policy and an allocation of rents that is implemented if it receives support from a government coalition in the parliament. If the suggested policy is not accepted, then the second-largest party is asked to try to form a coalition. If the policy is again not accepted, then the smallest party is asked to form a coalition. If this fails, then all parties receive a payoff of 0.

a. Describe the equilibrium proposals. Explain why a large leftist party may wish to form a coalition with a small rightist party (or vice versa).

b. Now suppose that $w_L > w_R > w_M$. Compute the equilibrium outcome. Assume that M attempts to form a coalition with R in the last period (M is indifferent between coalition partners). Compute the party members' equilibrium utilities.

c. Assume that the members of the electorate have bliss points x_L, x_M, or x_R. Further, assume that there are more voters with bliss points x_L than with bliss points x_M and one more voter with bliss point x_M than with bliss point x_R. Could there be an equilibrium in which all voters vote for the party whose policy platform they most prefer?

d. An argument for having a proportional electoral system with more than two parties is that the legislature's composition, and therefore policy, in such a system better represents the voters' preferences than the first-past-the-post system with only two parties. Discuss this argument in the light of the answers to questions (a) through (c).

Remark.   The analysis in this problem could be expanded, first by finding strategies that are optimal for the voters, given the mapping from electoral outcomes to policy outcomes in the legislature, and second by finding the three parties' optimal policy platforms, given the voters' strategies and the policy outcomes these induce. Austen-Smith and Banks 1988 gives an example of this type of full equilibrium.

5. Legislative bargaining and lobbying

Consider the following game of lobbying and legislative bargaining, which is a slight modification of that presented in section 7.5.3. A legislature has three members, who allocate a fixed set of public expenditures, G, to three electoral districts. The policy vector is thus $\mathbf{g} = (g_1, g_2, g_3)$, and $g_1 + g_2 + g_3 = G$. In each representative's electoral district, there is a lobby group lobbying this representative exclusively. The lobby group in district i has utility $g_i - C_i$, where C_i is the contribution paid to the representative. The legislators care only about the contributions they get from the lobbies.

Each legislative session takes the following form. First, Nature randomly selects an agenda setter. Then the lobby groups present their representative with a truthful contribution schedule: $C_i(\mathbf{g}) = \max[g_i - b_i, 0]$. These schedules are simultaneously announced and observed by all legislators. Finally, the agenda setter formulates a take-it-or-leave-it offer, and the legislature votes on this proposal. If the proposal is not accepted, then a new legislative session begins in which Nature randomly draws another agenda setter. For each legislative session, the payoffs are discounted by the discount factor δ.

a. Compute the policies, contributions, and payoffs in the stationary equilibrium.

b. Suppose that the legislators also care about the amount of public spending that benefits their electoral district. Compute the stationary equilibrium in the game as above, but assume that the legislators also care about public spending in their district and have the utilities $u_i = g_i + \eta C_i$.

c. Suppose the game is changed so that the legislature may amend the agenda setter's proposal. The legislative game is the same as in question (b) of problem 1, but now the lobby groups may set truthful contribution schedules during each session. More precisely, each legislative session now takes the following form. First, Nature randomly selects an agenda setter. Then the lobby groups present their representative with a truthful contribution schedule: $C^J(\mathbf{g}) = \max[g_i - b^J, 0]$. These schedules are simultaneously announced and observed by all legislators. The agenda setter proposes an allocation $\mathbf{g}_1$. Finally, Nature selects another member of the legislature, who can either let the legislative body vote on implementing $\mathbf{g}_1$ or make a new amended proposition $\mathbf{g}_2$, in which case there is a vote on whether to keep $\mathbf{g}_1$ or to accept the amended proposition $\mathbf{g}_2$. For each amendment, the payoffs are discounted by the discount factor δ.

Consider stationary equilibria of the following form: the member proposing the allocation keeps g_a to himself and gives $g_p = G - g_a$ to one other member and nothing to the remaining member. If a member is indifferent between a bill and an amendment, he will vote for the amendment. Compute the optimal stationary strategy, g_a, for the member proposing an allocation.

d. Now consider stationary equilibria of the following form: the member proposing the allocation keeps a share g_a of the budget to himself and gives $\frac{1-g_a}{2}$ to each of the two remaining members. Compute the optimal strategy g_a. Discuss when it is optimal for the agenda setter to offer positive rents to only one other member (a minimum winning coalition) and when it is optimal to offer rents to all members of the legislature (universalism). Discuss how allowing amendments and lobbying affects the agenda-setting power.

III COMPARATIVE POLITICS

In this part of the book, we adopt a comparative politics approach to public finance. That is, we seek to explain variety in fiscal policy as the result of different political institutions. We study two fundamental features of political institutions, namely the electoral rule and the regime type, asking how each influences policy formation and government incentives. Our analysis of electoral rules focuses on the contrast between majoritarian and proportional elections, but we also discuss national versus local elections. When discussing regime types, our main emphasis is on the contrast between presidential and parliamentary regimes.

The voluminous literature on the size of government has neglected the specific question of how the political constitution influences fiscal policy. Political scientists have put much effort into comparing political systems, and comparative politics is indeed a well-established subfield of political science. A large body of theoretical, empirical, and descriptive research concentrates precisely on electoral rules and regime types. This work is typically confined, however, to the analysis of political phenomena, such as how the electoral rule affects the number of parties, or how the regime type affects the frequency of political crises or protests by the citizens.[1] Economists have studied the effect of some constitutional features on single policy programs, most notably budgetary arrangements and federal institutions. But only very recently has work begun to appear linking broad fiscal policy choices to fundamental constitutional features, such as the electoral rule and the regime type. In this part of the book, we try to exemplify how economists may pursue an approach of comparative politics, drawing on a small emerging literature.[2]

Throughout most of this part, we rely on a very simple economic model. Elected politicians can tax the voters and choose how to allocate the revenue among three alternative uses: to rents benefiting themselves, to a public good benefiting all voters, or to redistributive transfers benefiting a more narrow group of voters. We use this model to contrast alternative constitutional features, investigating how they affect equilibrium policy. Some of the questions we ask were already posed in parts 1 and 2. What determines the size of government spending, or the amount of wasteful spending and rents appropriated by politicians? But these earlier analyses were typically cast in the context of a single policy program. Here, we instead emphasize the positive question of how the overall size and composition of public spending are determined.

---

1. Recent classics on comparative politics include Bingham Powell 1982, Lijphart 1984, Taagepera and Shugart 1989, Shugart and Carey 1992, and Cox 1997. Myerson 1999 also discusses this literature.

2. Von Hagen and Harden (1996), Alesina and Perotti (1995b), and Inter-American Development Bank (1997) contrast alternative budgetary institutions, but their main focus is on budget deficits, not on the size or composition of spending. Roubini and Sachs (1989) and Grilli, Masciandaro, and Tabellini (1991) discuss electoral rules and party structures of OECD countries, but again with regard to public debt accumulation. There is also a literature on fiscal federalism and the size of government, which is surveyed in Inman and Rubinfeld 1997. Finally, a small but interesting literature discusses how direct democracy shapes government size (see, for instance, Pommerehne and Frey 1978).

Politicians are assumed in this part to be opportunistic and rent-seeking, rather than partisan. This assumption is natural, given our purpose. If we want to analyze how different political institutions handle the agency problem between voters and their representatives, we had better give politicians a rent-seeking motive. We deal with both preelection and postelection models of politics in this part, for political institutions are likely to affect the policy incentives for candidates in electoral campaigns as well as the policy incentives for incumbents engaged in legislative bargaining.

Chapter 8 starts off the analysis in the mode of preelection politics. We study the standard model of two-candidate electoral competition with opportunistic politicians, as introduced in chapter 4. Because politicians can make binding commitments to policy platforms, elections perform the role of directly choosing among policies. Forward-looking voters choose the policy platform most favorable to them. In this setting, we ask how the electoral rule influences policy choices, contrasting "majoritarian" and "proportional" elections. The central difference is that majoritarian elections make politicians concentrate their competition for votes on certain "marginal" electoral districts, which typically harbor more-mobile voters, whom electoral promises can more easily sway. Hence electoral competition is stiffer under majoritarian elections, as politicians try to please swing voters just in the marginal districts rather than swing voters in the population as a whole. This leads to an increase in targeted redistribution at the expense of public-good provision or broad social insurance programs benefiting a large majority of voters. Stiffer competition also means smaller rents for politicians.

In chapter 9, we turn our attention to postelection politics. In the chapter's model, incumbent politicians set policy once they are in office. Elections therefore serve the role of assigning (or reassigning) decision-making authority. The political constitution is thus viewed as an "incomplete contract," specifying how to appoint incumbents and which incumbents have the right to propose, veto, or amend policy, and in which dimensions. In the context of the career concern model from chapter 4, voters reappoint only those incumbents with a high enough revealed competency. The incentives for good performance vary with the electoral rule, however. As a consequence, we should expect to see systematic differences in the electoral cycle under majoritarian and proportional elections. In the context of the political accountability model from chapter 4, voters reappoint only those incumbents with a good enough performance. In this setting, majoritarian elections as in chapter 8 imply more narrowly targeted redistribution than proportional elections, but the conclusions for equilibrium rents are reversed. The political accountability model is also appropriate for investigating the effects of separation of powers in the allocation of agenda-setting and veto rights. Here we simplify by ruling out redistribution among voters. The main result is that, if coupled with appropriate checks and balances, separation of powers increases the accountability of politicians to their voters and reduces equilibrium rents.

Chapter 10 focuses on postelection politics in different political regimes. Here we return the layer of sharp conflict among voters by allowing for targeted redistribution. As in the last part of chapter 9, interests also clash among elected incumbents who have to choose policy in legislative bargaining. The rules that govern that bargaining are precisely what distinguishes a political regime. In this multiprincipal, multiagent setting, we investigate two basic regimes. A presidential regime entails institutions with stronger separation of powers, whereas a parliamentary regime has institutions that more easily produce "legislative cohesion," namely, stable legislative majorities. A presidential regime therefore turns out to have stiffer competition among different voters as well as among different politicians. Politicians compete more fiercely among themselves because they are held directly and separately accountable by the voters. Compared to the situation in a parliamentary regime, this limits the scope of collusion. Because coalitions among politicians are more unstable, voters end up competing more fiercely for redistributive transfers. These features of presidential regimes imply that they spend less on every budget item than parliamentary regimes, with drastic consequences for the predicted size of government.

8 Electoral Rules and Electoral Competition

Our exploration of comparative politics begins in the world of preelection politics. In our discussion, electoral competition takes place between two opportunistic and rent-seeking candidates. In the electoral campaign these candidates make binding promises of how much they will tax voters and how they will spend the revenue. They can choose to please all voters, promising to levy low taxes or to supply a public good benefiting everyone. They can please some voters but not others, targeting redistribution to some specific groups. Or they can please no one and appropriate rents for themselves. How do politicians, competing to win the election choose among these alternatives? And—most importantly—how does the electoral rule shape their choices? These are the questions addressed in this chapter.

We can draw extensively on the models and results of several earlier chapters. As in chapter 7, we use a model with probabilistic voting to handle electoral equilibrium in cases where policy is inherently multidimensional. As in chapter 4, we allow for endogenous rents in addition to the traditional assumption of pure office motivation. The chapter focuses on the electoral rule, however, drawing on very recent work by Persson and Tabellini (1999b) and Lizzeri and Persico (1998).

In particular, we contrast multiple-district and single-district elections. Throughout the chapter, we shall loosely refer to single-district elections as proportional and to multiple-district elections as majoritarian. This is different from the more precise labeling in the literature on comparative politics in political science. There proportionality refers to another concept, namely to the electoral formula deciding on how votes translate to seats in individual electoral districts, more-proportional systems having a ratio of seat shares to vote shares closer to 1 for every party, compared to majoritarian systems. Given our perspective of policy selection from the viewpoint of society as a whole, however, we think it makes sense to refer to larger districts as being associated with more proportionality. Clearly, proportional representation requires that each district have more than one member. Empirically, one also finds a strong correlation between district magnitude and the electoral formula: one common form of elections combines single-member districts with plurality rule, whereas countries with proportional representation usually have relatively large districts. The reader is free, however, to disagree with our labeling, which actually conflates two different concepts. Naturally, electoral systems differ in many other respects: some have two (or more) tiers of electoral districts, some set minimum thresholds to obtain representation, and so forth.[1] Unfortunately, the simple model of two-party electoral competition that we will use in the chapter cannot capture these aspects well.

---

1. See Taagepera and Shugart 1989, Lijphart 1994, and Cox 1997 for extensive and illuminating treatments of the different dimensions of electoral systems as well as an account of the variation in real-world electoral systems across time and countries.

Under all electoral rules, the political equilibrium of this model implies that public goods are underprovided relative to the social optimum, that politicians earn positive rents, and that influential voters benefit from targeted redistribution. The electoral rule does make an important difference, however. Majoritarian elections induce politicians to pay most attention to voters in marginal electoral districts. Compared to proportional elections, this induces less public-good provision (since the benefits of the public good for voters in the other districts are disregarded) but more concentrated redistribution targeted toward the marginal districts. At the same time, however, majoritarian elections also reduce rents for politicians. Because voters in the marginal districts are more mobile, electoral competition is stiffer, and voters punish politicians more severely for wasteful spending. Thus from a positive point of view, the theory has clear predictions for how the electoral rule affects the composition of spending. The normative implications are ambiguous, however, as proportional elections induce more public-good provision but also more rents for politicians.

Clearly in this model we can capture only a few possible effects of different electoral rules. In particular, we hold the party structure fixed, ignoring convincing theoretical arguments (as in Cox 1987a, 1990a, 1990b and Myerson 1999) and pervasive empirical evidence (as in Lijphart 1994 and Taagepera and Shugart 1989) for a larger number of parties under proportional elections. Our excuse is pragmatic: we simply do not know how to analyze multidimensional policy consequences of electoral competition in a multiparty setting.

In the next two sections, we formulate the basic model and discuss the political trade-offs it entails. In sections 8.3 and 8.4, we study the equilibrium under proportional (single-district) and majoritarian (multidistrict) elections, respectively. Section 8.5 compares equilibria under proportional and majoritarian elections in a different economic model with local public goods and broad redistributive programs. This comparison provides an additional perspective on our basic comparative politics question, that is, which kind of policies we should expect which kind of electoral rules to favor.

8.1 The Economic Model

Consider a society with three distinct groups of voters, denoted $J = 1, 2, 3$. Each group has a continuum of voters with unit mass. Preferences over government policy are identical for every member of group J and given by the quasi-linear utility function

$$w^J = c^J + H(g) = 1 - \tau + f^J + H(g). \tag{8.1}$$

Here, c^J is the private consumption of the average individual in group J, τ is a common tax rate, f^J is a transfer targeted to individuals in group J, and g is the supply of a (Samuelsonian) public good, evaluated by the concave and monotonically increasing function $H(g)$. Thus we assume that income gross of taxes is equal to 1 for all individuals, that taxes are nondistorting, and that the tax rate is the same for every group.

The public policy vector $\mathbf{q}$ is defined by

$$\mathbf{q} = [\tau, g, r, \{f^J\}] \geq 0,$$

where all components are constrained to be nonnegative. Any feasible policy must satisfy the government balanced budget constraint

$$3\tau = \sum_J f^J + g + r. \tag{8.2}$$

The component r reflects (endogenous) rents to politicians and is a deliberate object of choice. As discussed in chapter 4, we can think of r as an outright diversion of resources, such as corruption or party financing, or more generally, as an allocation of resources benefiting the politicians' private agenda but appearing as an inefficiency for the voters. From the voters' viewpoint, these rents thus constitute a pure waste. As in chapter 4, rent extraction is associated with some transaction costs $(1 - \gamma)$, such that only γr benefits the politicians.

To make the public finance problem more interesting, we could extend the model with economic behavior affected by the policy, say, a labor supply choice distorted by taxation. Below we comment on how our results would change in this richer formulation. But even the simple model at hand entails a very rich micropolitical problem. It involves three conflicts of interest: that between different voters (over the allocation of redistributive transfers, $\{f^J\}$), that between voters and politicians (over the size of rents, r), and that between different politicians (over the distribution of these rents among themselves). As we shall see in this chapter (and the next), different electoral rules alter the intensity of and the interaction between these conflicts, basically by inducing more or less competition between politicians or voters.

The socially optimal policy here entails $r^* = 0$ and g^* such that $H_g(g^*) = \frac{1}{3}$. Redistributive transfers are indeterminate, because of our assumptions that taxes are lump sum and the marginal utility of consumption is constant. But with identical voters, concavity of the utility of private consumption would imply equal transfers f^{J*} to all J in the social optimum (see problem 1 of this chapter). Moreover, a tiny amount of tax distortion would imply no transfers whatsoever: $f^{J*} = 0$ for all J.

8.2 The Politics of Electoral Competition

Before the elections, two parties or candidates (A and B) commit to policy platforms, $\mathbf{q}_A$ and $\mathbf{q}_B$. They act simultaneously and do not cooperate. The winning party's platform is implemented. As we emphasize below, the precise conditions for winning depend on the electoral rule. Both parties are rent-seeking. Thus as in chapter 4, when announcing its policy platform, party P maximizes the expected value of rents, namely

$$E(v_P) = p_P \cdot (R + \gamma r), \tag{8.3}$$

where R denotes the (exogenous) ego rents associated with winning the elections, and p_P denotes the (endogenous) probability that P wins the right to set policy, given $\mathbf{q}_A$ and $\mathbf{q}_B$.

We assume probabilistic voting. Thus as in earlier chapters, the election outcome is uncertain when platforms are chosen, and different voters evaluate the ideological or personal attributes of these parties in different ways. Specifically, let $W^J(\mathbf{q})$ denote the preferences of voters in group J over government policy. That is, $W^J(\mathbf{q})$ is the indirect utility obtained by substitution of (8.2) into (8.1). Then voter i in group J votes for party A if

$$W^J(\mathbf{q}_A) > W^J(\mathbf{q}_B) + (\delta + \sigma^{iJ}), \tag{8.4}$$

where the term $(\delta + \sigma^{iJ}) \lesseqgtr 0$ reflects voter i's ideological preference for party B. This term includes two components; δ is common to all voters, and σ^{iJ} is idiosyncratic.

As before, the random variable δ reflects the general popularity of party B and is uniformly distributed on $[-\frac{1}{2\psi}, \frac{1}{2\psi}]$. Thus the density of this distribution is given by ψ and the expected value of δ is zero. Since δ is realized between the announcement of the party platforms and the election, the parties announce their platforms under uncertainty about the election outcome.

The distribution of individual ideology σ^{iJ} differs across groups J, and it is uniform on

$$\left[-\frac{1}{2\phi^J} + \overline{\sigma}^J, \frac{1}{2\phi^J} + \overline{\sigma}^J \right], \quad J = 1, 2, 3.$$

Thus two parameters, $\overline{\sigma}^J$ and ϕ^J, fully characterize this distribution, and groups differ over both. In other words, groups differ in their average ideology, captured by the group-specific means $\overline{\sigma}^J$. But they also differ in their ideological homogeneity, a higher density ϕ^J being associated with a narrower distribution of σ^{iJ}. We make specific assumptions about differences in these distributions. Suppose we label the three groups according to their average ideology $\overline{\sigma}^J$: $\overline{\sigma}^1 < \overline{\sigma}^2 < \overline{\sigma}^3$. Then we assume that group 2 also has the highest density: $\phi^2 > \phi^1, \phi^3$. This is the substantial assumption. For convenience, we also assume that $\overline{\sigma}^2 = 0$ and that $\overline{\sigma}^1\phi^1 + \overline{\sigma}^3\phi^3 = 0$.[2]

Figure 8.1, in which we have drawn the distributions for σ^{iJ} in the three groups, illustrates these assumptions. Each of the three groups has an ideologically neutral voter with $\sigma^{iJ} = 0$,

---

2. We assume that the parties know these group-specific distributions when they announce their policy and that the electoral uncertainty derives entirely from uncertainty about the common component, δ. Alternatively, we could have generated electoral uncertainty by assuming the group means $\overline{\sigma}^i$ to be random.

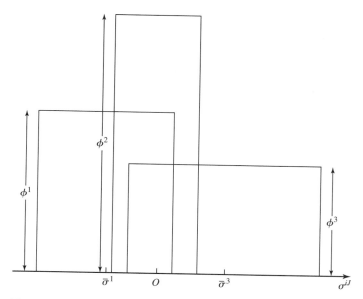

Figure 8.1

and the farther to the right we go in the figure, the more likely we are to find a voter voting for party B. As the figure illustrates, our assumptions imply that the group which on average is ideologically neutral also has the largest number of ideologically neutral voters.[3] (We sometimes find it more convenient to talk about the number of voters instead of the density, even though we are formally assuming that the distributions are continuous.) It is natural to think of this group as consisting of middle-class voters.

Recalling our discussion in chapter 4, we can use this figure to illustrate how the parties evaluate the announcement of different policies. Suppose party A contemplates a deviation from a common policy announcement, $\mathbf{q}_A = \mathbf{q}_B$. Such a deviation alters the number of votes party A can expect by changing the identity of the swing voters. For example, a lower tax rate τ or more public goods g benefit voters in all groups symmetrically. Taken separately, such measures thus push the identity of the swing voter in all groups to the right by the same distance, say to σ', and party A can expect to capture the voters between 0 and σ' in all groups (as the expected value of δ is equal to zero). Similarly, more transfers to group 1, financed by fewer transfers to group 3, shift the swing voter in group 1 to the right and the

---

3. With more general distributions, this association between the group's average ideological position and the number of ideologically neutral voters would be a natural property of all unimodal distributions.

swing voter in group 3 to the left by the same distance (recall that we assume the groups to be of the same size). This redistribution implies a net gain in votes, as there are more swing voters in group 1 than in group 3, that is, $\phi^1 > \phi^3$. Finally, higher rents r mean losing votes in all three groups and a lower probability of winning. As the announced policies must respect the budget constraint, the two parties effectively trade off votes for votes, or rents for votes, when designing their platforms.

As a final preliminary, we define $\pi_{A,J}$, that is, the vote share of party A in group J. Given our assumptions about the group-specific distributions, $\pi_{A,J}$ can be expressed as

$$\pi_{A,J} = \phi^J [W^J(\mathbf{q}_A) - W^J(\mathbf{q}_B) - \delta - \overline{\sigma}^J] + \frac{1}{2}, \qquad (8.5)$$

where the expression within square brackets is a formal definition of the swing voter in group J. Clearly, party B's vote share in group J is given by $1 - \pi_{A,J}$. From both candidates' point of view, $\pi_{A,J}$ is a random variable, since it is a transformation of the random variable δ capturing party B's average popularity.

8.3   Single-District (Proportional) Elections

Consider first the equilibrium policy under an electoral rule in which it is equally important to win votes in all groups. Specifically, we study a very stylized case in which (as in the Netherlands or Israel) there is only one voting district, comprising all voters in the population. We assume that there is perfect proportional representation, in the sense that the parties obtain a seat share in perfect proportion to their vote share in the entire population. We then add the specific winning rule that the party obtaining more than 50% of the seats earns the right to set policy according to its electoral platform. Under this electoral rule, p_A is clearly given by

$$p_A = \text{Prob}\left[\frac{1}{3} \sum_J \pi_{A,J} \geq \frac{1}{2} \right], \qquad (8.6)$$

where the probability refers to the random variable δ. By (8.5) and our previous assumption that δ has a uniform distribution, we have

$$p_A = \frac{\psi}{3\phi} \sum_J [\phi^J (W^J(\mathbf{q}_A) - W^J(\mathbf{q}_B))] + \frac{1}{2}, \qquad (8.7)$$

where $\phi \equiv \sum_J \phi^J / 3$ is the average density across groups. By symmetry, party B's probability of winning is $(1 - p_A)$.

Given our distributional assumptions and the concavity of $H(g)$, a unique equilibrium exists, in which both A and B choose the same policy. Formally, they face the same maximization problems, since $p_B = (1 - p_A)$ and since $\mathbf{q}_A$ and $\mathbf{q}_B$ enter (8.7) symmetrically but with opposite signs. To characterize the equilibrium policy, we maximize party A's objective function (8.3) with regard to $\mathbf{q}_A$, taking $\mathbf{q}_B$ as given. Exploiting (8.1), (8.2), and (8.7), and evaluating the resulting first-order conditions at the point $\mathbf{q}_A = \mathbf{q}_B$, we obtain the conditions that must hold at an equilibrium.

The equilibrium involves positive redistribution to group 2 only; that is, $f^2 > 0$, and $f^1 = f^3 = 0$. This stark result follows from there being more swing voters in group 2, by our assumption that $\phi^2 > \phi^1, \phi^3$, and from the marginal utility of private consumption being constant. Thus both parties target their redistribution programs toward the middle class, since this group contains the most-responsive voters.

The equilibrium supply of public goods follows from the optimal trade-off between g and f^2. The corresponding condition is

$$\phi^2 \cdot 1 = \sum_J \phi^J \cdot H_g(g), \tag{8.8}$$

where 1 refers to the marginal utility of private consumption and superscripts refer to groups. Intuitively, cutting the supply of the public good to all voters by one unit can yield an additional unit of redistribution for the middle-class group. This means an expected gain of votes proportional to $\phi^2 \cdot 1$ in group 2 (captured by the left-hand side) but an expected loss of votes in every group J proportional to $\phi^J \cdot H_g(g)$ (the right-hand side). It is optimal for the two parties to equate the marginal gain of votes to the marginal loss of votes. Recalling our definition of $\phi \equiv \sum_J \phi^J / 3$, (8.8) can be rewritten as

$$H_g(g) = \frac{\phi^2}{3\phi} > 1/3.$$

Thus compared to the socially optimal policy, the public good is underprovided in political equilibrium: $g < g^*$. Politically, targeting transfers to the mobile middle-class voters pays more than trying to please all voters with public goods.

A similar trade-off between τ and f^2 pins down the optimal tax rate. Raising the tax rate by one third for all voters can also yield an additional unit of redistribution to the middle-class group. This leads to the complementary slackness condition:

$$\phi^2 \cdot 1 \geqslant \sum_J \phi^J \cdot \frac{1}{3} = \phi \qquad [\tau \leqslant 1].$$

Here the gain of votes in group 2 always exceeds the loss, as $\phi^2 = \max_J [\phi^J]$. Since taxes are not distortionary, the optimum is a corner solution with $\tau = 1$.

Clearly, the more responsive is the middle-class group (the higher is ϕ^2), the higher is the opportunity cost of public goods. Thus the two parties find it optimal to announce a lower supply of public goods and to increase transfers to this powerful group. We therefore have a comparative statics result that will prove useful when comparing electoral rules: the larger is the density of ideologically neutral middle-class voters (the higher is ϕ^2), the smaller is equilibrium public-good provision, and the larger are the transfers to middle-class voters. With distortionary taxes and an interior solution for τ, the equilibrium tax rate also increases in ϕ.

Finally, the optimal rents implied by the two candidates' platforms are obtained as in chapter 4. Consider the trade-off between r and f^2. The complementary slackness condition corresponding to this margin is

$$p\gamma \leqslant -[R + \gamma r] \cdot \frac{\partial p}{\partial r} = [R + \gamma r] \cdot \frac{\phi^2 \psi}{3\phi} \qquad [r \geqslant 0]. \tag{8.9}$$

The left-most expression reflects the marginal benefits of additional rents, whereas the remaining expressions reflect the inframarginal rents times the greater probability of losing the election. As is evident from the condition, equilibrium rents r might well be positive. Because p is equal to $\frac{1}{2}$ in equilibrium, this is more likely when R (the exogenous rents) are low. As in chapter 4, electoral competition does not eliminate rent seeking. The parties perceive electoral uncertainty because they are not perfect substitutes in the eyes of any voters except for swing voters. This implies that $\frac{\partial p}{\partial r}$ is negative but finite. The more imperfect substitutes are the two parties, the larger are equilibrium rents. Hence we have a second comparative statics result: a larger number of ideologically neutral (swing) voters (a higher ϕ^2) reduces equilibrium rents in an interior optimum. Finally, rents are larger the higher is the variance in electoral outcomes (the lower is ψ). Higher variance implies that the expected vote share is not very sensitive to policy; given this, candidates find it optimal to take a greater risk by insisting on larger rents.

8.4   Multiple-District (Majoritarian) Elections

What if elections are instead conducted under plurality (first-past-the-post) rule in multiple one-seat electoral districts? Specifically, assume that there are three electoral districts, each with one seat. We then add the following winning rule: earning the right to set policy requires winning at least two seats out of three. This setting can be interpreted as a parliamentary election in which two competing parties field candidates in all three districts running on the same platform. The party winning in a majority of the districts has a majority in the assembly and can thus implement its preannounced policy. Alternatively, the setting can be interpreted as a presidential election (as in the United States), where (because of the structure of the electoral college) a candidate, again, needs only a majority of the votes in a majority of the districts, rather than in a majority of the population, to be elected president.

We start with a simplifying assumption: the three electoral districts coincide with the three groups in the population. Later we show that all comparative politics results generalize if groups and districts do not completely overlap. In the present setting, existence of equilibrium is not guaranteed without further assumptions. Essentially, we must assume that the ideological bias toward party A in group 1 and toward party B in group 3 are large enough; that is, the group-specific means $\overline{\sigma}^1$ and $\overline{\sigma}^3$ are sufficiently distant from zero. The conditions for the existence of equilibrium are included as (part of) problem 2 of this chapter. When these conditions are fulfilled, we have an equilibrium in which A and B announce equal policies and the entire competition takes place in the "marginal district" made up of the middle-class (group 2) voters. Party A wins district 1 with large enough a probability and loses district 3 with large enough a probability so that neither party finds it optimal to seek voters outside the marginal district; recall that only two districts are required for winning the election.

In the present model, the electoral uncertainty derives from an aggregate popularity shock. In its equilibrium, district 2 is the pivotal voting district with probability 1, whereas districts 1 and 3 both are pivotal with probability 0. In a more general setting in which we also added (independent) shocks to the group-specific means $\overline{\sigma}^J$, we would instead have a probability of district 2 being pivotal lower than unity but higher than the positive probabilities of districts 1 and 3 being pivotal. This would lead to the same kind of qualitative comparative politics results and ensure existence of an equilibrium without too stringent assumptions.[4]

Under our assumptions, the relevant expression for party A's probability of winning the election is just the probability that party A wins district 2. By the same argument as in the previous section, this can be written as

$$p_A = \text{Prob}\left[\pi_{A,2} \geq \frac{1}{2}\right] = \psi \cdot [W^2(\mathbf{q}_A) - W^2(\mathbf{q}_B)] + \frac{1}{2}. \tag{8.10}$$

Compared to (8.6), the expression in (8.10) thus depends only on what takes place in the marginal district. We may now follow the same steps as in the previous section to characterize the policies in a convergent electoral equilibrium. Obviously, only the middle class—the sole group in the marginal district—gets the entire transfer budget. Furthermore, it is optimal for both candidates to propose more redistribution than under proportional elections. Intuitively, such redistribution has the same benefit to the parties as under proportional elections, namely

---

4. Strömberg (1999) shows formally how to derive equilibria for this more general case in a probabilistic voting model similar to the one of this chapter but applied to purely redistributive policy within the U.S. electoral college.

the marginal votes gained from the middle-class voters, but the costs are smaller, as the parties do not now internalize the votes lost in the nonmarginal districts. As a result, it is still optimal to set the tax rate at its maximum: $\tau = 1$. With distortionary taxes, however, the lower costs of taxation would have led to a higher tax rate.

The sharper incentives to redistribute also shape the optimal supply of public goods, because the optimal trade-off between f^2 and g now fulfills

$$\phi^2 = \phi^2 \cdot H_g(g). \tag{8.11}$$

By (8.11), $H_g(g) = 1$, whereas by (8.8), $H_g(g) < 1$ under proportional elections. Clearly, the supply of public goods is smaller under majoritarian elections.

Finally, equilibrium rents are also smaller. To see this, note that the complementary slackness condition for f^2 versus r now becomes

$$p\gamma \leqslant -[R + \gamma r] \cdot \frac{\partial p}{\partial r} = [R + \gamma r] \cdot \psi \qquad [r \gtrless 0]. \tag{8.12}$$

The condition is identical to (8.9), except that ψ replaces $\frac{\phi^2 \psi}{3\phi}$ in the expression for $-\frac{\partial p}{\partial r}$. Since $\phi^2 < 3\phi = \sum \phi^J$, higher rents make the candidates lose votes at a higher rate in majoritarian elections. Intuitively, the electoral competition is stiffer, because it is now focused on the district with the most responsive voters. Since the election outcome is more sensitive to policy, the two parties become more disciplined and forego some prospective (endogenous) rents.

Qualitatively, nothing happens to these comparative politics results if we relax the extreme assumption about a perfect overlap between groups and districts, provided that the middle-class group 2 is a *dominant group* in one of the districts.[5] Let the population share of group J in district k be denoted by $n^{J,k}$. Then group 2 is a dominant group in one of the districts if $n^{2,k} > \frac{1}{3}$ and $n^{1,k}, n^{3,k} < \frac{1}{3}$ in some k. If the middle class dominates district 2, in this sense, electoral competition will take place only in district 2. Furthermore, district 2 is an asymmetric replica of the whole population, in which group 2 receives more weight. As illustrated in figure 8.2, this asymmetry has the same effect as a higher relative density $\frac{\phi^2}{3\phi}$ of group 2 under proportional elections, the result of which was discussed in the previous section: more redistribution toward group 2, less public goods, and less rents. Problem 4 of this chapter deals with the formal derivation of this result.

This chapter's central comparative politics results can be succinctly summarized as follows. Majoritarian elections concentrate electoral competition in some key marginal districts, resulting in increased targeted redistribution towards a narrower constituency. This

---

5. The conditions for the existence of equilibrium become stricter, however, as we relax the assumption of perfect overlap.

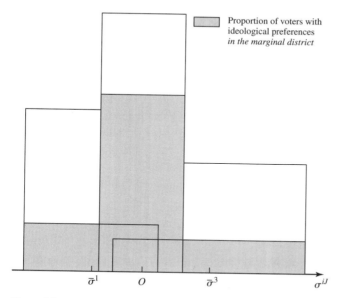

Figure 8.2

is associated with a smaller supply of public goods, as the benefits of the public good for voters in the other (nonmarginal) districts are disregarded. It is also plausible to assume, as we have done, that voters in these marginal districts are more mobile, in the sense of being more responsive to economic benefits. This makes electoral competition stiffer and reduces equilibrium rents. Extending the model with distortionary taxes, we also get the prediction that majoritarian elections should be associated with larger governments. Problem 3 of this chapter formulates the model including distortionary taxes.

8.5   Broad versus Targeted Redistribution

The theoretical concepts of spending in the previous model, public goods versus targeted redistribution, do not perfectly match with the available empirical measures of spending. For instance, transportation, health, and other classes of public spending on goods and services combine general public goods with local public goods and redistribution in kind; they may also entail some inefficiency (corresponding to r in the model). Furthermore, as we stressed in chapter 6, redistributive transfers are often designed to favor broad groups of citizens, such as the elderly or the unemployed, which are generally spread out over the electoral districts. The general results suggested by the model are that majoritarian elections induce politicians to target resources to specific groups in specific districts, reducing nontargeted spending that benefits the population at large. In many cases, narrow interests can be targeted by increasing local public-good provision and reducing general transfers. That is, the theory generates predictions for nontargeted versus targeted spending, rather than for public goods versus redistribution as such. We now illustrate this point by contrasting majoritarian and proportional elections in a different economic model that has both local public consumption, as in chapter 7, and broad redistribution, as in chapter 6. Its main result is that majoritarian elections induce more spending on local public goods and less spending on redistributive transfers than proportional elections.

Again, there are three regions, $J = 1, 2, 3$. The economic model is different, however. Like the model in section 6.4, it has employed and unemployed individuals. Employed individuals consume $c = y(1 - \tau)$, where y is income and τ a nondistorting tax. Unemployed individuals receive an unemployment subsidy, f. Individuals are risk averse and evaluate private consumption with a concave utility function $U(\cdot)$. Let us also assume that individuals differ in the probability of being employed, as in example 4 of chapter 2. Let n^k denote the probability that an individual of type k is employed. The average value of n^k in the population is n, which also denotes the fraction of employed individuals. There are K different types, $k = 1, 2, \ldots, K$, and each type forms a continuum. Individuals also draw utility from local public consumption, and g^J denotes local public consumption per capita in region J. At present, suppose that the utility from local public consumption is linear (below, we discuss the implications of relaxing this assumption). Thus an individual of type k residing in region J has preferences:

$$w^{kJ} = n^k U(c) + (1 - n^k) U(f) + g^J.$$

For simplicity, we abstract from rents r. Summing over risk types k, the government budget constraint can be written as

$$n y \tau = (1 - n) f + \frac{1}{3} \sum_J g^J.$$

As before, individuals trade off economic benefits and ideology when deciding how to vote. Let $W^{kJ}(q)$ be the indirect utility function of a voter of type k in region J as a function of the policy vector $\mathbf{q} = [\tau, f, \{g^J\}]$. Then the swing voter of type k in region J is defined as usual, namely as a voter with an ideological bias given by

$$\sigma^{kJ} = W^{kJ}(\mathbf{q}_A) - W^{kJ}(\mathbf{q}_B) - \delta.$$

Finally, suppose that the distribution of individual ideological preferences is uniform and specific to each region cum risk type, with density ϕ^{kJ} for type k in region J. As before, different regions also differ in the mean of the distribution, and these means are sufficiently different that the conditions for existence of a political equilibrium under majoritarian elections are satisfied (see problem 2 of this chapter). Under majoritarian elections, regions and voting districts coincide. Region 2 is the middle district, with zero mean and the highest density.

In this setup, we can easily describe the difference between political equilibria under proportional and majoritarian elections. Repeating the steps of the previous sections, proportional equilibria solve the problem of maximizing $\sum_k \sum_J \alpha^{kJ} \phi^{kJ} W^{kJ}$, where α^{kJ} is the share in the population as a whole made up of region J individuals of type k. Majoritarian equilibria instead solve the problem of maximizing $\sum_k \alpha^{k2} \phi^{k2} W^{k2}$. That is, as already discussed in the previous section, majoritarian elections concentrate the electoral competition in the middle region/voting district.

To illustrate these different equilibria, make the simplifying assumption that all types have the same distribution of ideological preferences: $\phi^{kJ} = \phi^J$ for all k. That is, only individuals from different regions/districts differ systematically in their distribution of ideological preferences. Furthermore, assume that $\alpha^{kJ} = \frac{1}{K}$ for all pairs (k, J) (recall that the population of each region has mass 1 and that there are K types). Under these simplifying assumptions, it is easily shown that both electoral systems imply full unemployment insurance: $c = f$. Intuitively, the political equilibrium sets f and τ in both cases so as to maximize the utility of the average voter, which calls for full insurance.

The two electoral systems differ with regard to local public-good provision, however. Given the linearity of preferences, both electoral systems have only $g^2 > 0$, with $g^J = 0$ for $J \neq 2$. Under majoritarian elections, optimal public-good provision (the derivative of the objective function with respect to g^2) satisfies the following condition:

$$\frac{1}{3} U_f(f) \phi^2 = \phi^2. \tag{8.13}$$

The right-hand side of (8.13) captures the marginal political benefit of more public consumption for region/district 2: the marginal economic benefit of g^2 is unity, and ϕ^2 gives the marginal number of swing voters in district 2. The left-hand side captures the marginal political cost: as all districts pay for the public good, district 2 bears only one-third of the cost, and the opportunity cost of less resources is less unemployment benefits for all K consumer types in district 2, each type having $\frac{1}{K}$ members.

Repeating the same steps under proportional elections, we instead get the following optimality condition:

$$\frac{1}{3} U_f(f) \sum_I \phi^I = \phi^2. \tag{8.14}$$

The marginal political benefit of public consumption in region 2 is still given by ϕ^2, but the expression differs from (8.13) on the left-hand side. The costs of less unemployment insurance in all other regions are now internalized, such that the cost for any single district, namely $\frac{1}{3} U_f(f)$, is multiplied by the term $\sum_I \phi^I$. It follows immediately from (8.13) and (8.14) that unemployment insurance is more generous under proportional elections. Moreover, since $c = y(1 - \tau) = f$, taxes must be lower under proportional elections. Because proportional elections induce lower taxes and more unemployment insurance, they must also be associated with less total public consumption. The results are thus analogous to those in the previous section: compared to proportional elections, majoritarian elections entail more targeted spending (local public consumption), less nontargeted spending (unemployment insurance), and a larger size of government (higher taxes).

8.6 Discussion

How general are these results? First, do the results in section 8.5 generalize if we assume concave preferences for local public consumption, as in chapter 7? Some of the results become ambiguous. Concave preferences for g^J introduce an additional difference between policy under the two electoral rules. Under proportional elections, all groups J receive some local public consumption. Under majoritarian elections, only group 2 receive a positive amount (as the other groups/districts have zero weight in the politicians' objective function). It thus becomes ambiguous which electoral rule implies higher overall public consumption. Even though citizens in the marginal district experience higher public consumption under majoritarian elections than under proportional elections, this may be offset by the lower spending on other groups. Problem 5 of this chapter provides a formal discussion of these points in an example with concave preferences for private and public consumption.

A potential fragility of some theoretical results to the specification of preferences arises also in the model of sections 8.1–8.4, in which we postulated linear preferences for private consumption. Concave preferences might lead to some ambiguities in the comparison of electoral systems. Therefore, the general and robust insight is that by concentrating competition in the marginal districts, majoritarian elections lead to more narrowly targeted redistribution in those districts. Whether this is accompanied by lower spending on nontargeted items and higher overall spending may depend on the model.[6]

As stated earlier in the chapter, we have not taken into account that different electoral rules may generate differences in the number of parties. A possible counterargument to our results is that allowing for a larger number of parties under proportional elections could allow parties that are more narrowly specialized to cater more effectively to the preferences

---

6. Problem 1 of this chapter considers proportional elections with concave preferences for private and public goods.

of narrower interest groups. This is a possibility, but it is hard to develop this idea into a specific hypothesis without the aid of a formal model. Unfortunately, multiparty competition in a multidimensional policy context goes beyond the current state of the art in the explicit modeling of political equilibria.

Myerson (1993a) studies voters' ability to control corruption in electoral competition under different electoral rules, assuming that some political parties are (exogenously) corrupt, whereas others are not. In that case, proportional elections are better for the voters than majoritarian elections, because they allow voters not to vote for corrupt parties without compromising their partisan preferences.

What about the empirical evidence? It is so far very scant but still indicates some systematic differences for different electoral rules. Motivated by the model in sections 8.1–8.4, Persson and Tabellini (1999) consider a sample of more than fifty democracies around 1990. Controlling for other economic and social variables, they find that spending on public goods (such as education, order and safety, transportation, or health) as a percentage of GDP is indeed lower in countries with majoritarian elections (countries with plurality rule in single-member districts). The empirical results are fragile, however, as the specification of the model and the sample of countries affects them. Persson and Tabellini (1999b) also find weak evidence of larger total government expenditures in countries with majoritarian elections.

Preliminary results in the same cross section of countries, again controlling for economic and social variables, also suggest that governments in majoritarian countries spend more (as a fraction of GDP) on government consumption and less on transfers, compared to those in proportional countries. This is in line with the model of section 8.5, as many redistributive transfers are related to broad welfare and pension programs and hence cannot easily be targeted to specific districts. Government consumption, on the other hand, reflects public employment and purchases of goods and services from the private sector. This kind of spending may allow politicians more discretion in targeting the benefits to certain electoral districts.

Milesi-Ferretti, Perotti, and Rostagno (1999) study a panel data set for government spending in the OECD countries from the 1960s onward. They relate the size and composition of government spending to different measures of the degree of proportionality, obtaining results that are broadly consistent with the predictions in this chapter. Thus they find that transfer payments by general government—measured both as a share of government expenditures and as a share of GDP—are strongly positively related to the degree of proportionality. The share of total expenditure in GDP is also positively related to the same measures.

In the paper mentioned at the end of chapter 7, Baqir (1999) studies the effect of different electoral arrangements in U.S. cities and finds a negative result: the size of city government is not significantly affected if city council members are elected in different districts (ward systems) rather than in the whole city (at-large systems).

More empirical work is certainly needed on these important issues. More theoretical work on how the electoral rule shapes the incentives or electoral competition would also be welcome. It is reassuring, however, that Lizzeri and Persico (1998) arrive at the same conclusions as this chapter on the trade-off between redistribution and public goods, relying on a different model (an extension of Myerson 1993b) of preelection politics than the probabilistic voting model employed in this chapter. As we shall see in the next chapter, the electoral rule may also shape the postelection policy choices.

8.7   Notes on the Literature

Research on the questions addressed in this chapter is still in its infancy. The modeling in sections 8.1–8.4 draws on Persson and Tabellini (1999b). Lizzeri and Persico (1998) ask a very similar question in a different model of electoral competition, namely that of Myerson (1993a). They obtain a very similar result: that majoritarian electoral competition discourages public-good provision in favor of targeted redistribution. With regard to rents and wasteful spending, our model draws on Polo (1998) and J. Svensson (1997), as well as other works already mentioned in chapter 4.

Empirical work on the effects of the electoral rule on the composition and size of public spending can be found in Persson and Tabellini 1999b, which relies on recent cross-sectional data (five-year averages) for 54 countries. Milesi-Ferretti, Perotti, and Rostagno (1999) use panel data from 1960 for twenty OECD countries. Whereas the former study mostly employs dummy variables to characterize the electoral rule, the latter uses alternative continuous measures of the degree of proportionality. Baqir (1999) deals with the determinants of the size of U.S. city governments, including the rules for electing members to city councils.

Political scientists have studied electoral rules extensively. Some classics are Bingham Powell 1982, Lijphart 1984, Taagepera and Shugart 1989, and Cox 1997. Their analysis has been confined, however, to political phenomena and to the party structure. Myerson (1995) surveys some of this literature. A much emphasized result is that proportional elections tend to increase the number of parties represented in the legislature. Naturally, this can also profoundly affect policy formation. Roubini and Sachs (1989), Grilli, Masciandaro, and Tabellini (1991), Edwards and Tabellini (1994), Alesina and Perotti (1995b), and Hallerberg and von Hagen (1999) discuss this point informally with regard to budget deficits, pointing out how proportional elections are associated with coalition governments in the data, and these governments, in turn, with debt accumulation.

Cox (1987a, 1990a, 1990b) characterizes equilibria in the one-dimensional spatial model under a variety of electoral rules. Rivière (1998) contrasts electoral systems with more than two parties. Morelli (1999) takes an important step toward making the party structure endogenous under different electoral rules. Rigorous theoretical studies of multidimensional policy formation with an endogenous party structure under alternative electoral rules have not yet been attempted, as the problem is very difficult.

8.8   Problems

1. Proportional elections and concave utility

Consider a society with three distinct groups of voters, denoted $J = 1, 2, 3$. Each group has a continuum of voters with unit mass. Preferences over government policy are identical for every member of group J and given by the utility function

$$W^J = u(c^J) + H(g) = u(1 - \tau + f^J) + H(g).$$

Here, c^J is the private consumption of the average individual in group J, τ is a common tax rate, f^J is a transfer targeted to individuals in group J, and g is the supply of a (Samuelsonian) public good, evaluated by the concave and monotonically increasing function $H(g)$. Assume $u(\cdot)$ also to be concave.

The public policy vector $\mathbf{q}$ is defined by

$$\mathbf{q} = [\tau, g, r, \{f^J\}] \geq 0,$$

where all components are constrained to be nonnegative. Any feasible policy must satisfy the government balanced budget constraint

$$3\tau = \sum_J f^J + g + r.$$

The component r reflects (endogenous) rents to politicians and is a deliberate object of choice. Rent extraction is associated with some transaction costs $(1 - \gamma)$, such that only γr benefit the politician.

Consider proportional elections:

Before the elections, two parties or candidates (A and B) commit to policy platforms $\mathbf{q}_A$ and $\mathbf{q}_B$. They act simultaneously and do not cooperate. The winning party's platform is implemented. Party P maximizes the expected value of rents, namely

$$E(v_P) = p_P \cdot (R + \gamma r),$$

where R denotes the (exogenous) ego rents associated with winning the elections, and p_P denotes the (endogenous) probability that P wins the right to set policy, given $\mathbf{q}_A$ and $\mathbf{q}_B$.

Assume probabilistic voting. Thus the election outcome is uncertain when platforms are chosen, and different voters evaluate these candidates' ideological or personal attributes in different ways. Specifically, let $W^J(\mathbf{q})$ denote the preferences of voters in group J over government policy. Then voter i in group J votes for party A if

$$W^J(\mathbf{q}_A) > W^J(\mathbf{q}_B) + (\delta + \sigma^{iJ}),$$

where the term $(\delta + \sigma^{iJ}) \lesseqqgtr 0$ reflects voter i's ideological preference for party B. δ is common to all voters and σ^{iJ} is idiosyncratic. δ is uniformly distributed on $[-\frac{1}{2\psi}, \frac{1}{2\psi}]$. σ^{iJ} differs across groups J and is uniform on

$$\left[-\frac{1}{2\phi^J} + \bar\sigma^J, \frac{1}{2\phi^J} + \bar\sigma^J\right], \quad J = 1, 2, 3.$$

Assume further that $\bar\sigma^1 < \bar\sigma^2 < \bar\sigma^3$, $\phi^2 > \phi^1$, and $\bar\sigma^1\phi^1 + \bar\sigma^3\phi^3 = 0$.

a. Compute the social planner's policy choice.

b. How do transfers in the proportional election model compare with the social optimum?

c. Write down the condition for the choice of rents, r, in equilibrium.

d. How does the provision of the public good differ from that of the model with linear utility of voters?

2. Existence of majoritarian equilibria

For the same model as in problem 1, now assume multiple-district (majoritarian) elections: Assume that the three groups of voters, $j = 1, 2, 3$, correspond to three electoral districts, each with one seat. Earning the right to set policy now requires winning at least two seats out of three. Assume further that voters' utility for consumption is linear ($u(c) = c$).

Let g^* be the solution to

$$H_g(g^*) = 1.$$

a. Show that the level of transfer provided to group 2 voters in an equilibrium in which both parties compete only for district two is given by

$$f^{2*} = 3 - g^* - \frac{1}{2\psi} + \frac{R}{\gamma}.$$

b. Show that such an equilibrium exists if and only if

$$\bar\sigma^3 \geq 3 - g^* - \frac{1}{2\psi} + \frac{R}{\gamma} \quad \text{and} \quad \bar\sigma^1 \leq -\left(3 - g^* - \frac{1}{2\psi} + \frac{R}{\gamma}\right).$$

3. Distortionary taxes and electoral competition

Examine the two models, those of proportional and majoritarian elections (problems 1 and 2), with distortionary taxes: Voters must now choose e (effort). The amount of effort chosen determines the amount of income earned according to the production function $y = e$. Effort is a costly activity with a cost function $c(e) = \frac{e^2}{2}$. The tax rate is proportional, so that a voter with income y pays τy. Assume further that utility for consumption of voters is linear ($u(c) = c$).

a. Characterize the voters' choice of effort, their income, and the resulting government revenue as functions of the tax rate τ.

b. Show that taxes in the majoritarian model are higher and public-good provision lower than in the proportional model.

4. Districts and voter groups that do not coincide

In the same model as in problem 3, assume that districts and groups do not overlap and that $n^{2,district\,2} > \frac{1}{3}$ and $n^{1,district\,2} < \frac{1}{3}$, $n^{3,district\,2} < \frac{1}{3}$, where $n^{j,district\,i}$ denotes the share of voters of group j in district i. Assume that parameters are such that an equilibrium exists in which parties compete on district 2 alone.

a. Show that the majoritarian equilibrium corresponds to a proportional equilibrium with different weights for the groups. Compute these weights.

b. Compare the majoritarian model and the proportional model in terms of the weights given to the different groups.

5. Broad versus targeted policy and a concave utility for local public goods

Consider the following modification of the model in problems 1–4. Once more, there are three regions, $J = 1, 2, 3$. The economic model is different, however. Voters are employed or unemployed. Employed individuals consume $c = y(1 - \tau)$, where y is income and τ a nondistorting tax. Unemployed individuals receive an unemployment subsidy, f. Individuals are risk-averse and evaluate private consumption with a concave utility function $U(\cdot)$. Let us also assume that individuals differ in the probability of being employed. Let n^k denote the probability that an individual of type k is employed. The average value of n^k in the population is n, which also denotes the fraction of employed individuals. There are K different types, $k = 1, 2, \ldots, K$, and each type forms a continuum. Individuals also draw utility from local public consumption, and g^J denotes local public consumption per capita in region J. Suppose that the utility from the local public consumption is linear. Thus an individual of type k residing in region J has preferences

$$w^{kJ} = n^k U(c) + (1 - n^k) U(f) + H(g^J),$$

where $H(g^j)$ is a concave utility function for the local good. Summing over risk types k, the government budget constraint can be written as

$$ny\tau = (1 - n)f + \frac{1}{3} \sum_J g^J.$$

Individuals trade off economic benefits and ideology when deciding how to vote. Let $W^{kJ}(q)$ be the indirect utility function of the type k voter in region J as a function of the policy vector $\mathbf{q} = [\tau, f, \{g^I\}]$. Then the swing voter of type k in region J is defined as usual, namely as a voter with an ideological bias given by

$$\sigma^{kJ} = W^{kJ}(\mathbf{q}_A) - W^{kJ}(\mathbf{q}_B) - \delta.$$

Finally, suppose that the distribution of individual ideological preferences is uniform and specific to each region cum risk type, with density ϕ^{kJ} for type k in region J. Different regions also differ in the mean of the distribution, and these means are sufficiently different that the conditions for the existence of a political equilibrium under majoritarian elections are satisfied (see problem 2). Under majoritarian elections, regions and voting districts coincide. Region 2 is the middle district, with mean 0 and the highest density. Compare proportional and majoritarian elections in this model. Assume $\phi^{k,j} = \phi^j$.

a. Show that group 2 enjoys more public-good provision under majoritarian elections than under proportional elections.

b. Assume that $U(c) = \ln c$ and $H(g) = \ln g$. Show that the amount of total spending on public goods and the amount of spending on unemployment insurance are equal in the two election models.

9 Institutions and Accountability

The previous chapter assumed that politicians' promises can somehow be enforced. We now drop the commitment assumption and turn to the realm of postelection politics. Elections no longer select among alternative policies. Policies are now chosen once in office, and elections enable the voters to select the most competent candidate or to oust badly performing candidates. Throughout the chapter, our emphasis remains on comparative politics. We touch upon several issues, within two models introduced in chapter 4, the career concern model and the accountability model. In the first part of the chapter, we discuss how the details of the electoral rule affect the agency problem. Elections are not the only means of disciplining politicians, however. Even if electoral promises cannot be enforced, a politician is not free to do anything he wants once in office. Thus in the second part of the chapter, we discuss how separation of powers increases political accountability.

We start with the career concern model, in section 9.1, contrasting local and national elections as well as majoritarian and proportional elections. Here, we pick up an idea first formalized by Seabright (1996), although in a different model. With centralized policymaking and national elections, the electoral outcome reflects the politicians' competence in performing multiple tasks. As a result, a national politician has weaker incentives to perform well: he will be removed from office only if he disappoints the voters in a majority of localities. With decentralized policymaking and separate elections in each locality, politicians are instead elected on the basis of their local instead of their average competence and face stronger incentives to please their local constituency. For this reason we should expect greater efficiency and accountability in a decentralized arrangement. But centralization also has a benefit. As the value of office is higher at nationwide elections than at local elections, centralization may increase accountability, because politicians care more about winning. The overall effect can go either way, depending on which force is the stronger.

We show that when all policy tasks are performed centrally, majoritarian and proportional elections yield similar policy differences as do local and national elections. Majoritarian elections are similar to local elections, in that a single incumbent runs for office in each district, and the voters can judge him on the basis of his own performance. Under proportional elections, on the other hand, several incumbents typically run for office simultaneously, and citizens vote for a list, not for an individual candidate. The link between individual performance and reappointment is weaker in proportional elections, since it depends on the candidate's position on the party list and on the performance of the other candidates on the list. This dilutes incumbent incentives to perform well and increases agency rents.

In section 9.2, we return to the same feature of electoral rule as in chapter 8, namely the number of electoral districts. We extend the accountability model of chapter 4 to allow for conflict among voters over the allocation of redistributive transfers. A single politician in office unilaterally decides on policy. To win reappointment, he needs to please only a minimum winning coalition of voters. As suggested by Ferejohn (1986) in a different economic model, redistributive conflict among the voters helps the incumbent. Because voters compete to be included in that minimum winning coalition, the incumbent can get away with higher rents. We show that the electoral rule changes the equilibrium by affecting the size of the required minimum winning coalition. With majoritarian (multiple-district) elections, the incumbent needs to please only roughly one-fourth of the voters (half the voters in half the districts), whereas he needs to please one-half of the voters under proportional (single-district) elections. Competition among voters is stiffer under majoritarian elections, which implies a lower amount of public goods and higher agency rents. The results for public goods and targeted redistribution (but not for rents) and their logic are reminiscent of those in chapter 8 for electoral competition.

Finally, section 9.3 deals with separation of powers among different office holders as a means of reducing wasteful spending (corruption). All democratic constitutions incorporate various checks and balances to prevent policy mistakes or outright abuse. The underlying idea that constitutional checks and balances can prevent the abuse of political powers goes back at least to Montesqieu and Locke and was particularly emphasized in the federalist debate preceding the adoption of the U.S. Constitution. In our model, policy decisions are once more made by politicians in office. The constitution splits decision-making power between the holders of two different offices: one has the power of initiative, the other has a veto right. This creates checks and balances, that is, conflicts of interest between the politicians. To focus on the conflict among politicians, we return to the simple accountability model of chapter 4 without redistributive transfers. Drawing on Persson, Roland, and Tabellini 1997, we illustrate two results. First, separation of powers increases the transparency of policy decisions, by facilitating the transmission of information from government officials to voters. Appropriate separation of powers concentrates the informational rents in a single office and compels the other office to share the information without making it a residual claimant on the informational rents, thus aligning its interests with those of the voters. Second, appropriate checks and balances in the budgetary process further reduce equilibrium rents by giving sharp agenda-setting rights to different politicians over different policy dimensions but giving other politicians a veto right. Decisions are made sequentially, first over the budget size, then over its allocation. This separation reduces wasteful spending: the politician controlling the size of the budget is not a residual claimant on rents. Both results thus illustrate how the right constitutional design may help align the interests of opportunistic politicians with those of the voters.

9.1 Electoral Rules and Career Concerns

We adapt the career concern model of section 4.5 to allow for several localities. There are two periods, no redistributive transfers among voters, and local—rather than national—

public goods. Tax revenue is fixed at $\bar{\tau}$, and the government budget must be balanced in both periods. There are three localities, indexed by J, which may or may not coincide with voting districts, depending on the electoral rule. Each locality has a population of identical voters, the size of which is normalized to unity. Localities differ among one another only in that each enjoys utility from a different local public good, g^J. As in section 4.5, the voters' preferences in locality J and period t are:[1]

$$w_t^J = y - \bar{\tau} + \alpha g_t^J,$$

where $\alpha \geq 1$ is an exogenous parameter and y denotes income.

Politicians choose how to allocate tax revenues between public goods and rents for themselves. A separate government budget constraint applies in each locality and in each period, irrespective of the degree of centralization or of the form of the electoral system:

$$g_t^J = \eta^J \left(\bar{\tau} - r_t^J \right). \tag{9.1}$$

As in chapter 4, η^J denotes the competence of the politician in charge of providing the public good, and r_t^J denotes rents in locality J. Rents are constrained to be nonnegative and have an exogenous upper bound $\bar{r}$: $0 \leq r_t^J \leq \bar{r}$. Rent extraction is thus associated with specific local public goods, in the sense that politicians cannot reshuffle tax revenues across localities. Thereby, we abstract from the kind of special-interest politics already discussed in chapter 7.

As in chapter 4, competence is a random variable, uniformly and independently distributed in each locality, with an expected value of 1 and with density ξ in all localities. Politicians are rent-seeking, and their utility function is reproduced here for convenience:

$$\mathsf{E}[v] = r_1 + p_I \delta (R + r_2), \tag{9.2}$$

where p_I is the probability that the incumbent is reappointed. The exact meaning of endogenous and exogenous rents depends on the institutional arrangement. With decentralization, r_t is given by r_t^J, rents in locality J, whereas in a centralized setup, r_t is the sum of rents in all localities: $r_t = \sum_J r_t^J$.

Finally, as in chapter 4, no policy commitments can be made ahead of the elections. Specifically, the timing of events in this section is as follows: (1) An incumbent politician is in office in period 1 and chooses rents for that period, r_1^J, without knowing his own competence η^J. (2) The value of η^J is realized and public-good provision g_1^J is residually determined, so as to satisfy (9.1). Voters observe their own utility but do not directly observe η^J or r_1^J. (3) Elections are held. If the incumbent wins, his competence in locality J remains

---

1. In chapter 4, $\bar{\tau}$ denoted a tax rate. To keep the model in this section similar to that of the other sections in this chapter, $\bar{\tau}$ here instead denotes per capita tax revenue collected from locality J.

η^J. If he loses, his opponent's competence in locality J is drawn at random from the same distribution. (4) Period 2 rents r_2^J are set, and public goods are residually determined to satisfy the government budget constraint (9.1).

Clearly, politicians have no incentive to behave well in period 2. Thus irrespective of the degree of centralization, all politicians always appropriate maximum rents, $r_2^J = \bar{r}$, implying $g_2^J = \eta^J(\bar{\tau} - \bar{r})$, in all J. The voters are thus better off with more-competent politicians and use elections to remove incompetent incumbents. How efficiently elections can be used for this purpose depends on the electoral rules. We start our examination of this topic by contrasting local and national elections.

9.1.1 Local versus National Elections

With decentralized policymaking and local elections, voters in each locality make a decision whether to reappoint an incumbent based on his performance in that particular locality. Since each locality acts independently of the others and nothing links their election outcomes, the equilibrium under local elections is identical to that discussed in chapter 4. Hence the incumbent in locality J is reappointed if $\tilde{\eta}^J \geq 1$, where $\tilde{\eta}^J$ is his competence as inferred by the voters after observing g_1^J. Using the derivation in section 4.5, the probability of winning the local election as perceived by incumbent J can be expressed as

$$p_J = \text{Prob}\,[\tilde{\eta}^J \geq 1] = \frac{1}{2} + \xi\left[1 - \frac{\bar{\tau} - \tilde{r}_1^J}{\bar{\tau} - r_1^J}\right]. \tag{9.3}$$

Here, $\tilde{r}_1^J$ denotes period 1 rents anticipated by the voters, and r_1^J denotes equilibrium rents appropriated by the incumbent. Equilibrium rents are obtained as follows. First, maximize (9.2) by choice of r_1^J, subject to $r_1 = r_1^J$ and $p_I = p_J$ in (9.2) to (9.3) and taking $\tilde{r}_1^J$ as given. This produces the following first-order condition:

$$1 - \frac{\xi\left(\bar{\tau} - \tilde{r}_1^J\right)}{\left(\bar{\tau} - r_1^J\right)^2}(\delta R + \bar{r}) = 0. \tag{9.4}$$

Next, impose the equilibrium condition $\tilde{r}_1^J = r_1^J$ and simplify. This gives the same expression for equilibrium rents as in chapter 4, namely

$$r_1^J = \bar{\tau} - \xi\delta(R + \bar{r}) \quad \text{for all } J. \tag{9.5}$$

What if, instead of being decentralized, policy is set by a single central policymaker performing multiple tasks but elected in a single nationwide election? Except for these differences, the model remains the same. In particular, a separate government budget constraint still applies in each locality, and the amount of local public goods provided reflects the national policymaker's competence in that particular task, η^J, $J = 1, 2, 3$. Thus a national policymaker has a locality-specific talent, reflecting his ability to provide a public good at a low cost in that particular locality. Keeping the model identical in these respects helps in identifying the specific role of going from central to local policymaking cum elections.

Again, we start from period 2. As before, period 2 rents are maximal: $r_2^J = \bar{r}$ for all J. Now, however, winning the election enables the incumbent to appropriate rents in all localities, rather than only in one. Using $r_t = \sum_J r_t^J$, the value of winning the elections entering in the incumbent objective function (9.2) is $\delta(R + 3\bar{r})$ (recall that there are three localities). The value of winning is thus larger than in the decentralized arrangement. We assume the ego rents of holding office to be the same in the two arrangements. Naturally, these could also be larger in national elections (see below).

Next, turn to period 1. Because there are no externalities and competence is uncorrelated across localities, voting behavior in each locality is identical to that described in section 4.5. The probability p_J that the incumbent policymaker wins the support of voters in locality J continues to be defined by (9.3). The probability of winning the national elections no longer coincides with p_J, however. Here the national incumbent wins if he gets the support of at least two localities out of three. Since the random variables η^J are independently distributed, the probability of victory for the incumbent, p, is now given by[2]

$$p = p_1 p_2 + p_1 p_3 + p_3 p_2 - 2 p_1 p_2 p_3. \tag{9.6}$$

We are then able to formulate the optimization problem faced by a national incumbent in period 1. He maximizes

$$\mathsf{E}(v) = \sum_{J=1}^{3} r_1^J + p\delta(R + 3\bar{r}),$$

by choice of r_1^J, $J = 1, 2, 3$, subject to (9.6) and (9.3). Taking the first-order conditions of this problem with respect to, say, r_1^J and using (9.3), we get

$$1 - \frac{\xi\delta(R + 3\bar{r})(\bar{\tau} - \tilde{r}_1^J)}{(\bar{\tau} - r_1^J)^2}(p_I + p_K - 2p_I p_K) = 0, \qquad J \neq K \neq I. \tag{9.7}$$

The condition looks very similar to (9.4), but it has two noticeable differences. On the one hand, the value of winning is higher. On the other hand, the second term is multiplied by the expression $(p_I + p_K - 2p_I p_K)$, namely by the probability that locality J is pivotal in

---

2. This has been obtained as follows: the event that the incumbent wins in all three localities has the probability $p_1 p_2 p_3$. The event of winning in localities I and J but not in K has the probability: $p_I p_J (1 - p_K)$. Summing all these probabilities and simplifying yields (9.6).

winning the national elections.[3] As before, in equilibrium the voters' conjectures must be correct, $\tilde{r}_1^J = r_1^J$, and $p_J = \frac{1}{2}$ in all localities J. Solving (9.7) for equilibrium rents in locality J thus yields

$$r_1^J = \bar{\tau} - \xi\delta(R + 3\bar{r})/2. \tag{9.8}$$

Comparing this expression with (9.5), we detect two differences, each going in a direction opposite the other. The value of winning is higher, because future endogenous rents are multiplied by three, reflecting the fact that the winner now sets policy throughout the nation and thus grabs more rents if reappointed. But the probability of winning is now less sensitive to performance (it is divided by two). Satisfactory performance in locality J matters for electoral victory only if that locality is pivotal in the national election, which occurs only with probability $\frac{1}{2}$. Despite the greater value of office, national elections could thus reduce politicians' overall accountability to the voters, because they weaken the link between good performance and reappointment.[4]

Another difference between local and national elections is not captured by (9.8). With local elections, incompetent incumbents are always ousted from office. With national elections, on the other hand, an incumbent who is incompetent only in one locality can remain in office by winning in (the other) two localities out of three. Since competency governs period 2 public-good provision, this reduces the efficiency of national elections, irrespective of what happens to period 1 equilibrium rents.

9.1.2 Majoritarian versus Proportional Elections

We can use the same model to analyze a central difference between majoritarian and proportional elections. If we reinterpret localities as electoral districts, what we called local elections could also capture the functioning of a majoritarian electoral system at the national level, in which each district elects a single candidate. That is, majoritarian elections allow voters to condition their vote on the performance of the specific incumbent in their district and remove an incompetent incumbent from office. With proportional elections, on the other hand, several candidates are elected in the same district and voters often vote

---

3. The probability that district J is pivotal is given by the probability that the incumbent wins two districts including J, plus the probability that the opponent wins two districts including J, namely

$$p_I p_J(1 - p_K) + p_J p_K(1 - p_I) + p_I(1 - p_J)(1 - p_K) + p_K(1 - p_I)(1 - p_J).$$

Simplifying this expression gives $(p_I + p_K - 2p_I p_K)$.

4. We postulated that the ego rents from office, R, are the same in local and national elections. If they are higher in national elections, equilibrium rents could still be ambiguous, as long as these ego rents do not increase in proportion to the number of localities.

for a list rather than for a specific candidate. Proportional elections may thus not give voters the option of removing a specific incumbent. Voters can reduce the probability that a specific incumbent is reappointed by voting for the opposition party, but the outcome depends on the overall vote share of the list, including the specific incumbent and his order on that list. The incumbent's incentives to perform become weaker, because his reelection depends not only on his own performance, but also on the performance of the other candidates on the list. Like national elections, proportional elections may thus raise equilibrium rents.

To see this point more clearly, continue to assume that there are three localities indexed by $J = 1, 2, 3$. Suppose that policymaking is centralized, but with three incumbents. Each incumbent has the specific task of providing a public good in a specific locality. A reelected incumbent gets to perform the same task in period 2. All incumbents act simultaneously.

Under majoritarian elections, each candidate behaves as in section 4.5. Equilibrium rents in each locality are thus given by (9.5), and total rents $r = \sum_J r^J$ under majoritarian elections are given by

$$r = 3\bar{\tau} - 3\xi\delta(R + \bar{r}).$$
(9.9)

Next, consider proportional elections. All three incumbents run for office in a single district encompassing all three localities. Suppose that all three incumbents belong to the same party. Moreover, the order of each candidate in the party list coincides with the number of his locality. Voters can vote either for the incumbent party's list or for a list presented by a single opposition party. The number of reelected incumbents is strictly proportional to the incumbent party's vote share.[5] All candidates in the opposition have an expected competence of 1. In this setup, voters' optimal behavior is simple to describe. Voters in locality J vote for the incumbent party's list in period 2 if the incumbent setting policy in J performed well in period 1, in the sense that his inferred competence $\tilde{\eta}^J$ satisfies $\tilde{\eta}^J \geq 1$, precisely as in section 4.5. Otherwise, they vote for the opposition.[6]

How do the incumbents behave in period 1? Let an individual incumbent's perceived probability of pleasing his voters, $p_J \equiv \text{Prob}\,[\tilde{\eta}^J \geq 1]$, be defined as in (9.3), and let $\hat{p}_J$ be the perceived probability of reappointment, which depends on the order of J in the list of his party's candidates. Given the convention that the order in the list coincides with the

5. In this simple two-period model, in which all politicians act in the same way in period 2, it does not matter what we assume about the links between the electoral result and the allocation of policymaking tasks in period 2. In a multiperiod model, we would have to be more specific on this point.

6. This voting behavior remains optimal for voters in district J even under this modified electoral system. They are not certain of removing their specific incumbent by voting against his list—or, conversely, that he will be reappointed if they vote for his list. But the probability of removal changes in the desired direction depending on the vote, which is sufficient for optimality.

value of J, we can write $\hat{p}_J$ as

$$\hat{p}_1 = p_1 [(1 - p_2)(1 - p_3)] + [p_2 p_3 + p_3(1 - p_2) + p_2(1 - p_3)] = p_1 \frac{1}{4} + \frac{3}{4}$$

$$\hat{p}_2 = p_2 [p_1(1 - p_3) + p_3(1 - p_1)] + p_1 p_3 = p_2 \frac{1}{2} + \frac{1}{4} \qquad (9.10)$$

$$\hat{p}_3 = p_3 p_1 p_2 = p_3 \frac{1}{4}.$$

The last equality of each expression follows from the fact that in equilibrium each incumbent has a 50 percent chance of pleasing his voters, so that $p_I = \frac{1}{2}$. Consider the incumbent $J = 1$, that is, the candidate at the top of the list. With probability $\frac{1}{4}$, his own performance will determine his own reelection (if the other two incumbents turn out to be incompetent). With probability $\frac{3}{4}$, however, he is reappointed irrespective of his own performance (it is enough that at least one of the incumbents in the list turns out to be competent). Conversely, the incumbent at the bottom of the list, $J = 3$, has the lowest probability of reappointment. The probability of his performance's determining his fate is, once more, only $\frac{1}{4}$, for he is elected only if both other incumbents are competent. Thus both the first and the last incumbent on the list face very weak incentives to perform. Their performance is unlikely to be pivotal for their own reelection, since one of them is often reappointed, whereas the other is rarely reappointed notwithstanding their actions. Interestingly, candidate $J = 2$ has stronger incentives, but the probability of his efforts' being pivotal is still only $\frac{1}{2}$ and thus lower than under majoritarian elections.

On the basis of (9.10), we can repeat the previous steps, computing equilibrium rents in period 1 for each of these candidates. Defining total rents as $r_1 = \sum_J r_1^J$, it is easily shown that

$$r = 3\bar{\tau} - \xi\delta(R + \bar{r}). \qquad (9.11)$$

Comparing (9.9) and (9.11), we note that equilibrium rents are clearly higher under proportional elections. Incentives are weaker, as in the case of national elections. When voters vote for a list, rather than for a candidate, satisfactory individual performance is not certain to guarantee an incumbent's reappointment. Hence the incentives to grab rents and rely on good luck for reappointment are much stronger, and the average performance is more disappointing. As in the case of national elections, there is a second source of inefficiency: voters cannot always remove an incompetent incumbent, and thus the average competence of politicians in office is lower than with majoritarian elections.

This difference between electoral systems suggests an interesting and testable prediction. Suppose we were to embed the two electoral rules above in a model of electoral cycles, such as the model discussed in chapter 4. Because majoritarian elections provide incumbents with stronger incentives to perform, the difference in equilibrium rents between preelection periods and off-election periods should be starker under majoritarian than under proportional elections. We would thus predict electoral business cycles to be stronger under majoritarian elections. As already discussed in chapter 4, this has ambiguous implications for efficiency, since electoral cycles to signal competence can take the form of distorted policy choices and not just of lower agency rents.

9.1.3 Discussion

How seriously can we take the implications following from such a simplistic model of policy choice as that presented in this section? Some of the model's limitations are evident from the start: each incumbent can allocate a budget only of a given size, and there is no room for reallocating resources or rents across localities. Moreover, the model presumes that voters care only about local and individual-specific performance: there are no national issues and no conflict among the voters. Relaxing these assumptions or introducing externalities between the districts would be interesting extensions of the analysis. Politicians would then end up dealing with multiple tasks. As suggested by Dixit (1997) in his extension of Holmström and Milgrom's (1988) analysis, different policy or administrative tasks may be complements or substitutes in effort choice, which gives the organization of public administration a nontrivial role in sharpening or weakening incentives. In a similar vein, the sharper or weaker incentives associated with different electoral rules may be more or less desirable in different environments. See problem 1 of this chapter for an extension of the above model to include externalities.

Under the assumptions of the model in this section, only competence and rents affect performance. In reality, performance also reflects other factors, such as sheer luck or temporary events. Furthermore, η^J is specific to the activity in locality J. Suppose that a common shock, say, ε, also affected the performance in every locality according to

$$g_t^J = (\eta^J + \varepsilon_t)(\bar{\tau} - r_t^J).$$

In this setting, voters would not be able to infer a politician's competence perfectly from his performance. One way of improving the voters' information would be to compare performance across localities. By observing g_1^J for different J, voters would also obtain some information about ε_1, which would make their conditional probability distribution tighter for the event that $\eta^J \geq 1$. A decentralized setting would thus create room for yardstick competition, in which voters would benefit from comparing different policymakers' performance. Problem 2 of this chapter illustrates the forces of yardstick competition in a simple example. Besley and Case (1995a) consider a theoretical framework along similar lines, though with adverse selection (politicians know their own type). They also provide supporting empirical evidence for the model from the U.S. states. Under centralization rather than decentralization, voters would instead benefit by comparing a single policymaker's performance on a multitude of tasks.

Obviously, the model in this section abstracts from many important differences across electoral systems, including differences in the observed number of parties (see the discussion in the previous chapter). Even within the limitations of our model, the difference between proportional and majoritarian elections would disappear if the order in the list was made conditional on individual performance, with the better candidates appearing at the top. A "party leader" who wanted to maximize the vote share might have good reasons for doing exactly this, so as to make the list more appealing to voters at large. This would weaken the difference between proportional and majoritarian elections, even though the party leader's private objectives might introduce a different kind of agency problem. A serious study of these questions requires a model of the party's internal organization, however. The recent paper by Carillo and Mariotti (1999) provides an interesting perspective on candidate selection. They consider the selection of a single candidate in the electoral campaign by opportunistic, purely office-seeking parties. In their model, the parties' optimal appointment decisions run afoul of the electorate's preferences, in that incompetent incumbents—whom the electorate would have liked to be replaced—are too often kept.

Despite these qualifications, however, we think that the model draws attention to a simple but important point. When citizens vote on a list, rather than on an individual candidate, the incentives for good individual performance may be diluted, and elections become a less powerful tool for disciplining politicians.

9.2 Electoral Rules and Accountability

We now turn from the career concern model to the accountability model of elections. In this section, we extend the model of section 4.4 to allow for redistributive transfers among voters. We deal here with only a single incumbent—consider a president or a majority parliamentary government—but section 9.3 and the next chapter study policy choice in legislative bargaining among multiple incumbents. As we shall see, the electoral rule is once more vital for the outcome, albeit for very different reasons than in section 9.1.

There are N groups of voters indexed by J, and the size of each group is normalized to unity (the distinction between individual voters and groups is of no importance here). Voters in group J have preferences

$$w^J = c^J + H(g) = y - \tau + f^J + H(g).$$

The model and the notation follows chapter 8, with g denoting a general public good benefiting all voters and f^J denoting nonnegative lump sum transfers to members of group J. An exogenous state of nature, θ, captures the cost of converting private goods into public. Thus the government budget constraint is

$$\theta g = N\tau - r - f,\tag{9.12}$$

with $f = \sum_J f^J$. As before, we restrict all policy instruments to be nonnegative and assume that appropriating rents entails some transaction costs $(1 - \gamma)$. Thus the incumbent maximizes

$$\mathsf{E}(v_I) = \gamma r + p_I R,\tag{9.13}$$

where R, the exogenous rents from office, can be interpreted as the expected present value of holding office from the next period onward.

The timing of events is as in chapter 4: (1) The state of nature θ is realized and observed by everyone. (2) All voters simultaneously choose a retrospective voting rule. (3) The incumbent chooses policy—$\{f^J\}$, g, τ, and r—which is fully observed by voters. (4) Elections are held. At the electoral stage, the voters perceive no difference between the incumbent and the opponent in terms of ideology or competence: the two candidates are identical in the voters' eyes, except for their past histories.

Clearly, the optimal policy for voters in this setting, if we could abstract from informational or agency problems, would be always to set $r = 0$ and to have public goods fulfill the Samuelson criterion:

$$N H_g(g) = \theta.\tag{9.14}$$

As in chapter 4, this condition defines g as an increasing function $G(\theta)$. The socially optimal value of $\{f^J\}$ is indeterminate here, but with a tiny amount of tax distortion, $f^J = 0$ for all J. Hence, the corresponding optimal tax rate is $\tau = T(\theta) = \theta G(\theta)/N$. But this policy cannot be enforced under the assumed timing. In chapter 4, we showed that even though the equilibrium policy entailed optimal public-good provision, taxes were higher than optimal, as the incumbent earned positive rents.

Our first question is whether the equilibrium discussed in chapter 4 can still be enforced in this richer setting, with a conflict among voters over redistributive transfers. To review the results in chapter 4, neglect the transfers $\{f^J\}$ for the time being. Voters then condition reelection on aggregate performance only, through a voting rule in the class

$$p^I = \begin{cases} 1 & \text{iff} \quad W(\theta) \equiv y - \tau + H(g) \geq \varpi(\theta) \\ 0 & \text{otherwise.} \end{cases}\tag{9.15}$$

As shown in section 4.4, the optimal voting rule in this class leaves the incumbent indifferent between two strategies: pleasing the voters with a policy satisfying the top row in (9.15) and being rewarded with reelection, with a total payoff of $v = \gamma r + R$, or foregoing reelection, myopically maximizing rents as a Leviathan policymaker, setting $\tau = y$ and $g = 0$, and collecting the maximal rent $v^d = \gamma N y$. The indifference condition can then be stated as

$$r^* = \max\left[0, Ny - \frac{R}{\gamma}\right].\tag{9.16}$$

This expression defines the minimum level of rents that voters must tolerate in the equilibrium of this game, under the restriction that redistributive transfers among the voters themselves are ruled out. Suppose that foregoing r^* leaves sufficient revenue for optimal public-goods provision in every state θ, specifically

$$\theta G(\theta) \leq \frac{R}{\gamma} \quad \text{for all } \theta.\tag{9.17}$$

Then it is optimal for the voters to require not only minimum rents but also the optimal level of public goods. In other words, the voters should optimally set their reservation utility at

$$\varpi(\theta) = y - r^* - \frac{\theta G(\theta)}{N} + H(G(\theta)).\tag{9.18}$$

We now ask whether this remains an equilibrium when policy tools also include redistributive transfers, contrasting single and multidistrict elections.

9.2.1 Single-District Elections

Let us begin with proportional elections. Here the incumbent runs for office in a single district against an identical opponent. If the incumbent can also redistribute resources among voters, the above equilibrium breaks down, since the incumbent needs to please only a minimum winning coalition—that is, a bare majority of the voters—to win reelection (say $\frac{N}{2}$ voters, to keep the notation simple). Hence, if faced with a voting rule like (9.18), he can increase rents for himself by setting taxes at a maximum, $\tau = y$, reducing g somewhat, and offsetting all this by means of positive transfers f^J to $\frac{N}{2}$ voters to keep a majority satisfied. Since taxes fall on everyone whereas transfers are given to only half the voters, and since by (9.14) the public good has a relatively small marginal utility, he has the room to do this and strictly increase rents for himself. But then some voters are hurt and do not reach their required reservation utility. Anticipating this outcome, voters left out of the winning coalition bid down their reservation utility just below (9.18), so as to be included in the minimum winning coalition. Hence this cannot be an equilibrium.

In this richer setting, an equilibrium must satisfy an additional optimality condition. Let $\varpi^J(\theta)$ be the reservation utility group J chooses. Then in equilibrium, $\varpi^J(\theta)$ must be a best response to $\varpi^I(\theta)$, for all $I \neq J$, taking into account what happens in the subsequent stages of the game. Thus we are implicitly saying that voters within the group cooperate, by setting the same voting rule, but play Nash against all other groups. When this requirement is added, the equilibrium must have the following properties. First, voters must not be so demanding that the incumbent prefers to forego reappointment. Second, the equilibrium policy must be optimal for the incumbent, given that he needs to please only a majority of the voters to win reelection. Third, no group of voters can benefit from a unilateral change in its reservation utility, given what the other groups are asking.

Consider the first two properties. A policy vector satisfying these two properties can be computed as the solution of the problem of maximizing rents for the incumbent, subject to the government budget constraint (9.12), to the usual nonnegativity constraints and the upper bound on taxes ($\tau \leq y$), and to the constraint that $\frac{N}{2}$ voters receive their reservation utility, namely

$$y - \tau + f^J + H(g) \geq \varpi^J(\theta), \tag{9.19}$$

for some given $\varpi^J(\theta)$. The third property implies that all voters must receive the same reservation utility. Hence in equilibrium, $f^J = 0$ for all J. Combining these requirements, we obtain the result that the equilibrium policy satisfies:[7]

$$\begin{aligned}
\tau &= y \\
N H_g(g) &= 2\theta \\
r &= Ny - \theta g.
\end{aligned} \tag{9.20}$$

Contrasting (9.20) with (9.14), (9.16), and (9.12), we immediately see that the presence of conflict among the voters makes them worse off compared to the equilibrium without any transfers. Note also that the incentive constraint is satisfied in equilibrium. The incumbent can now exploit the voters' conflict to his own benefit. As noted by Ferejohn (1986) in a related model, this reflects the contractual incompleteness at the core of this setting. The opponent cannot promise that he will not play the disruptive game of pitting the groups of voters against each other, which leaves the voters at the incumbent's mercy. Ferejohn's model has no public good, only transfers and effort—the equivalent of (negative) rents—and equilibrium effort ends up being minimal. Here instead, there is an indivisible public good that puts an upper bound on the equilibrium rents. The indivisibility of the public good allows voters to set their reservation utility contingent on a measure of aggregate performance. Even though they do not act cooperatively, the public good provides an implicit coordination

---

7. This equilibrium is computed as follows: maximize rents by choice of τ, g, $\{f^J\}$, subject to the constraints mentioned in the text and for given reservation utilities $\varpi^J(\theta)$. This immediately gives the first two equations in (9.20). Then add the requirement that in equilibrium, $\varpi^J(\theta)$ is the same for all voters. This implies $f^J = 0$, and hence the last equation in (9.20).

mechanism that helps the voters stop fighting each other and discipline the incumbent. Problem 3 of this chapter investigates the importance of coordination among the voters.

Note that in equilibrium we observe no redistributive transfers. But the mere possibility of resorting to this policy tool profoundly affects equilibrium policy. This insight reminds us of the equilibria with lobbying and electoral competition discussed in chapters 3 and 7, in which no campaign contributions are observed in equilibrium, but the mere possibility of using them exerts a strong political influence.

9.2.2 Multiple-District Elections

In this model as well, the details of the electoral rule are important for the equilibrium. As in chapter 8, consider majoritarian elections that take place in multiple districts according to plurality rule. The single incumbent in office now runs for reelection in $M < N$ electoral districts. To win reappointment, he now needs only half the votes in half the districts. Districts are identical, and in each district there are $\frac{N}{M}$ (groups of) voters. The equilibrium can be computed as in section 9.2.1, with one difference: to be reappointed, the incumbent needs to please $\frac{1}{2}\frac{N}{M}$ voters in $\frac{M}{2}$ districts. That is, he only needs to please $\frac{N}{4}$ voters. This means that in computing the equilibrium, the incentive constraint (9.19) must now be satisfied for only $\frac{N}{4}$ voters, rather than for $\frac{N}{2}$ voters. By the same derivation as in section 9.2.1, we can compute the equilibrium under majoritarian electoral rule. The expressions turn out to be identical to the expressions in (9.20), except for the equilibrium condition for the public good, which can now be written as

$$NH_g(g) = 4\theta. \tag{9.21}$$

Public-good provision thus turns out to be even lower than with single-district elections. Furthermore, as $r = \tau - g = y - g$, rents turn out to be even higher.

To understand the intuition, consider an electoral reform from proportional to majoritarian elections. The reform allows the incumbent to make a profitable deviation from the previous equilibrium. By decreasing the supply of public goods from the point defined by $NH_g(g) = 2\theta$ and raising the redistributive transfers for a quarter of the electorate, he can maintain a winning majority and still earn more rents. The operation reduces utility by $\frac{2\theta}{N}\Delta g$ for all voters but releases $\theta\Delta g$ units of revenue. Compensating $\frac{N}{4}$ of the voters for the utility loss thus costs $\frac{2\theta}{N}\Delta g\frac{N}{4} = \frac{\theta\Delta g}{2}$, which leaves $\frac{\theta\Delta g}{2}$ for additional rents. A deviation of this sort ceases to be profitable when public-goods provision has reached the point given by (9.21).

Under majoritarian elections, competition among voters for inclusion in the winning coalition is even stiffer than under proportional elections, because the size of the minimum winning coalition has shrunk by half. The incumbent then takes advantage of this by pitting voters one against the other to a greater extent. In equilibrium, the benefits of the public good are thus internalized for a smaller group of voters.

9.2.3 Discussion

Despite the very different models, we obtain a result similar to that in chapter 8. In both cases, going from single to multiple districts—from what we labeled proportional to majoritarian elections—induces politicians to target equilibrium redistribution toward a more narrow group of voters. As a result, public-good provision, or more generally provision of nontargeted policies, is always more generous under proportional elections.

Note, however, that agency rents change in opposite directions in the two political models. In the preelection politics model of chapter 8, multiple-district elections have smaller equilibrium rents than single-district elections. This is because majoritarian elections make electoral competition stiffer between politicians. In the postelection politics of this section, multiple districts are instead associated with larger rents for the incumbent. Here majoritarian elections make competition stiffer among voters over the policy favors handed out by elected incumbents. Some but not all comparative politics results on the policy consequences of different electoral rules thus appear robust.

9.3 Separation of Powers

To some degree, all democratic constitutions in the Western world incorporate the principle of separation of powers. To study the role of this institution, we extend the model to include two political offices, the holders of which are both subject to reelection. We can consider these offices in various ways: as two legislative chambers, or as the executive and the legislative branch of government. In line with the latter interpretation, we label them the executive, X, and the legislature, L. To focus the analysis on the conflict among politicians, we remove the conflict among voters, constraining $f^J = 0$ for all J. Thus the voters are unanimous, as in the model of section 4.4. As compared to the model in section 9.2, we are now studying a setting with multiple agents rather than multiple principals. Here the distinction between single- and multiple-district elections becomes irrelevant. The next chapter considers a general multiprincipal-multiagent model with no restrictions on policy instruments and with conflicts among voters as well as among politicians.

The general structure of the model in this section is the same as in the previous section, except that the voters now choose retrospective voting strategies for X and L separately. The two office holders split total rents from office, $r_L + r_X = r$, and a specific policy decision must be made with regard to the allocation. Each incumbent office holder has an objective like (9.13):

$$\mathsf{E}(v_I) = \gamma r_I + p_I R_I,$$

where $I = X, L$. As in chapter 4, we distinguish the case in which the voters can observe the cost of public goods from the one in which they cannot. As we shall see, checks and balances can diminish rents in both cases. We start by assuming that θ is observable, whereas the next subsection discusses the case of an unobservable θ.

9.3.1   Checks and Balances

Consider a constitutional arrangement that, like the one in section 7.2, imposes sequential decision making and separates proposal powers sharply over two policy dimensions. Specifically, consider the following game. (1) θ is realized and observed by everyone. (2) The voters choose a retrospective voting rule. (3) The incumbent X proposes a tax rate τ. (4) If the incumbent L approves, then τ is implemented; otherwise a default tax rate $\tau = \bar{\tau} > 0$ is implemented. (5) The incumbent L proposes public-goods spending cum a rent allocation $[g, r_L, r_X]$ subject to the tax rate from the prior stage: $g + r = N\tau$. (6) If X approves the proposal by L, it passes; if X vetoes, a default allocation $g = \tau - \bar{r}_L - \bar{r}_X \geq 0$, $r_L = \bar{r}_L$, $r_X = \bar{r}_X$, is implemented. (7) Voters observe g and τ. (8) Elections are held in which each incumbent runs against an opponent identical to himself.[8]

Sticking to the main interpretation, this arrangement thus implies a specific separation of the political powers between the president and Congress in a presidential democracy. It could also be interpreted, however, as a separation of powers between the members of different standing committees in a congressional setting (or perhaps between different ministries in a parliamentary setting). In any event, it strengthens the voters' ability to impose accountability on politicians and to limit equilibrium rents. If the two incumbents have sufficiently strong reelection incentives (in a sense specified below), the voters can actually achieve the socially optimal solution, with $r = r_L = r_X = 0$, $g = G(\theta)$, and $\tau = T(\theta) = \frac{\theta G(\theta)}{N}$.

To see why the first best is achievable, first assume that voters have indeed adopted a demanding voting rule conditioning the reelection of both incumbents, $I = X, L$, on receiving the first-best utility:[9]

$$p_I = \begin{cases} 1 & \text{iff} \quad W(\theta) \geq y - \dfrac{\theta G(\theta)}{N} + H(G(\theta)) \\ 0 & \text{otherwise.} \end{cases}$$

Then consider the incentives for the two office holders at the expenditure decision stages

---

8. Note that the rents in the second-stage default, $\bar{r}_X$ and $\bar{r}_L$, are fixed numbers and do not depend on the first-stage decision. This is essential for the results stated below. As discussed later, separation of powers is helpful only under appropriate budgetary procedures, and our formulation of the default outcome is an essential part of these procedures.

9. This kind of voting rule implies that one would always observe the executive and the legislature being thrown out of office together, violating the experience in many presidential democracies. Although the best outcome for voters is unique in utility, many different voting strategies can nevertheless support it, including those that would condition reelection on policy choices rather than utilities, which might well imply less-than-perfect correlation between the electoral fate of the two offices (outside of equilibrium).

(5)–(6). Their only chance of getting reelected is if taxes have been set at the right level, $\tau = T(\theta) = \theta G(\theta)/N$, at the taxation stages (3)–(4). If this is the case, L can either propose $r = 0$, $g = G(\theta)$, satisfying the voters, or else divert everything, setting $r = NT(\theta) = \theta G(\theta)$. The former choice gives L the payoff R_L and X the payoff R_X. Full diversion requires giving X at least $\gamma \bar{r}_X$—since X knows she will not be reelected, she requires at least the default payoff to persuade her not to veto a diversive proposal—making the net payoff of L equal $\gamma(\theta G(\theta) - \bar{r}_X)$. Clearly, L prefers pleasing the voters if

$$\theta G(\theta) \leq \frac{R_L}{\gamma} + \bar{r}_X. \tag{9.22}$$

Does X have the appropriate incentives to propose the right level of taxes at stages (3)–(4)? If she proposes $\tau = T(\theta) = \theta G(\theta)$ and (9.22) holds, L will please the voters and X gets R_X. If she sets any other tax rate, L (who then cannot please the voters) proposes a maximal diversion and, according to the argument above, X nets $\gamma \bar{r}_X$. Thus it is better for X to go along with the voters if

$$\bar{r}_X \leq \frac{R_X}{\gamma}. \tag{9.23}$$

Finally, it is always better for L to accept a proposal of the right level of taxes, unless the default level of taxes is too high.[10]

If the value of office is high enough, in the sense that both (9.22) and (9.23) hold, the voters may thus credibly insist on the politicians' delivering the unconstrained optimum. Adding these two conditions and comparing the result to (9.17), we note that a sufficient condition for full optimality is that the total value of office under separation of powers is at least as large as that without it: $R_L + R_X \geq R$. The agency problem of the previous section is thus completely eliminated, in the sense that equilibrium rents fall from r^* to ϕ.

Why does separation of powers strengthen accountability in this drastic way? The key is to deprive L, who controls the allocation of rents, of proposal power over the size of the budget. The agent with proposal rights over taxes, X, is not a residual claimant on tax revenue, as L captures any additional rents created by higher taxes. This removes the conflict of interest between X and the voters. X can earn reelection only by setting taxes at the level the voters desire. A single office holder, on the other hand, is always a full residual claimant on tax revenues; she can therefore threaten the voters with maximal diversion ($r = N\tau = Ny$). To avoid this, the voters must leave her some rents.

Note that separation of proposal powers by itself is not enough for reducing rents, however. It must be accompanied by appropriate checks and balances, also involving the allocation

---

10. After a veto, leading to the tax rate $\bar{\tau}$, L would always make a diversive proposal at the next stage, giving her a payoff of $\gamma(N\bar{\tau} - \bar{r}_X)$. Thus a sufficient condition for L not to veto is that $\bar{\tau} \leq T(\theta)$ for all θ, given that the incentive compatibility condition above holds.

of amendment and veto rights. In this model, X has only veto rights and is therefore nailed to its status quo payoff by the take-it-or-leave-it proposal made by L in the last stage. This creates a strong conflict of interest between X and L that the voters can exploit. A more open bargaining procedure with amendment rights for X would make X a residual claimant on taxes and align the politicians' interest against that of the voters, eliminating the benefit of separation of powers. Problem 4 of this chapter deals with this point.

In fact, separation of powers could even be detrimental for the voters, if it created a common-pool problem among the two expected officials. This would happen if veto rights were removed such that X and L could unilaterally determine how much to divert for themselves, r_X and r_L, with taxes or public consumption residually determined. In this case, equilibrium rents would be even higher than with a single policymaker. Problem 5 of this chapter and Persson, Roland, and Tabellini 1997 illustrate this result. The results of this subsection thus reinforce the general message anticipated in chapter 7 about the importance of appropriate budgetary procedures and the virtues of sequential budgeting.

9.3.2   Revelation of Information

Suppose now that in contrast to section 9.3.1, the voters cannot observe θ. To focus on the possible information revelation role of separation of powers, we abstract from the possible gains of separating the proposal powers across different offices. The main advantage of having two offices, rather than one, is then to allow the voters to extract information from the office with the lowest stake in any informational rents created by withholding information.

We illustrate this point in a very simple and stark example. Once more, consider two incumbents, executive X and legislature L, with the same objectives as in section 9.3.1. These incumbents interact with the voters as follows. (1) θ is realized; X and L observe it, but the voters do not. (2) Voters adopt retrospective voting strategies. (3) X is required to announce a state of the world, θ_X. (4) L proposes a policy (g, τ, r_X, r_L). (5) X may veto the proposal or not; if she vetoes, a default allocation $(\bar{g}, \bar{\tau}, \bar{r}_X, \bar{r}_L)$ is implemented. (6) Voters observe g, τ, and θ_X. (7) Elections are held in which each incumbent runs against an opponent identical to herself.

The legislature thus has the full proposal powers over policy. Although the executive has a veto power over the whole policy proposal, she is also required to make a report to the voters—a required "state of the union address." The arrangement thus shares certain features with the rules in the U.S. Constitution. It allows for equilibria in which the informational rents are completely eliminated. To see how this can happen, assume that the voters adopt the following voting rule, for $I = X, L$:

$$p_I = \begin{cases} 1 & \text{iff} \quad w = y - \tau + H(g) \geq \varpi_L(\theta_X) \\ 0 & \text{otherwise.} \end{cases}$$

In this voting rule, $\varpi_L(\theta_X)$ is defined in fashion analogous to that in (9.18), namely

$$\varpi_L(\theta_X) = \frac{R_L}{\gamma N} - \frac{\theta_X G(\theta_X)}{N} + H(G(\theta_X)),$$

but evaluated at the value of θ announced by X, rather than at the true state. Clearly, if the executive makes a truthful announcement, $\theta_X = \theta$, and the legislature pleases the voters, the allocation has optimal public-goods provision $g = G(\theta)$ and minimal non-state-dependent rents $r(\theta) = r^* = Ny - \frac{R_L}{\gamma} - \bar{r}_X$.

Assume that X has indeed announced the true state of θ. If L pleases the voters, total available rents are equal to r^*. Provided that (9.22) holds, L can set $r_X = 0$ and, take all the rents herself ($r_L = r^*$), netting $\gamma r^* + R_L$. Alternatively, she can use her powers to propose a maximum diversion, getting X to agree by promising her $\bar{r}_X$, thus netting $\gamma(Ny - \bar{r}_X)$. By the definition of r^*, L indeed prefers to please the voters.

Will X announce the truth? There are certainly equilibria in which she does. As in the previous subsection, X is not a residual claimant on additional rents. By overreporting θ, she does create prospective informational rents for L, but her own payoff does not depend on her report, meaning that X is indifferent between lying or not. Perhaps we might reasonably assume that X prefers to tell the truth. But the model as it stands also has equilibria in which X pleases L by fulfilling her desire for higher rents rather than pleasing voters by realizing their desire for higher utility. To better discriminate between the possible outcomes, we could extend the model to allow for collusion between different politicians and/or cooperation between politicians and voters. Both of these are possible outcomes in either a repeated-game setting or a setting with political parties.

As in the previous subsection, a key feature of the separation of powers arrangement is the maximal bargaining power of L in the decision-making process, which creates a conflict of interest between the two political office holders. The weaker office holder's interests thus become (at least weakly) aligned with the voters' interests, which facilitates the voters' task of holding the more powerful office holder accountable.

9.3.3 Discussion

The general conclusion emerging from this section is thus that political accountability is more easily achieved if the governing constitution unambiguously allocates certain control rights to separate political offices. To put it differently, accountability can work well only if it is clear who is responsible for an observed abuse of power.

The benefits of separation of powers are lost, however, if the two offices can collude against the voters. For example, the truth-telling equilibria we have just discussed would cease to exist if the two office holders could make a binding agreement in which the legislature compensates the executive making the announcement of θ with a sweet budget proposal for not telling the truth. With such collusion we would, essentially, return to the situation with one political body. Such a binding agreement would be hard to make, however: once the executive had made the false announcement, the legislature would gain from deviating and holding the executive down to its minimum payoff. Repeated interactions between the executive and the legislature would, however, invite self-enforcing collusion sustained by reputational forces. Investigating what kind of constitutional rules would make such collusion more difficult in a richer framework of asymmetric information is an interesting issue for further work. Term limits for at least one of the bodies—although they would be terrible in a repeated version of the model studied here—might serve that purpose.[11] In a different context, Laffont and Martimort (1999) argue that separation of powers between different regulatory agencies may limit the collusion between these agencies and the firms they regulate.

The model of this section can be thought of as a model of a presidential regime, in the sense that the voters elect the executive and the legislature separately. But we have also assumed a particular distribution of proposal and veto powers over legislation. As Shugart and Carey (1992) discuss, existing presidential regimes are far from homogenous when it comes to these properties. More theoretical work is thus needed to capture the finer details of existing presidential regimes. The next chapter offers some extensions.

New issues also arise in a parliamentary regime, in which the executive is only indirectly accountable to the voters through the legislature. Persson, Roland, and Tabellini (1997) show that gains from separation of powers still exist in parliamentary regimes. Interestingly, however, these gains require one of the constitutional features observed in almost every parliamentary regime. To prevent collusion between the legislature and the executive over appointment decisions, the executive should lose power after a parliamentary election in the absence of the approval of the newly elected legislature. But existing parliamentary regimes, like presidential regimes, are not homogenous. Some have upper houses with considerable veto rights, which clearly entail aspects of separation of powers. Again, more work is needed to enable us to understand the consequences of these features.

In the last section, we have also deliberately simplified the voters' task of holding their political agents accountable by assuming that policy cannot redistribute between voters. In the next chapter, we relax this assumption by studying policy choices in a genuine multiprincipal-multiagent setting and concentrate on the differences between the legislative institutions in presidential and parliamentary regimes. As we shall see, the two regimes imply stark and systematic policy differences.

---

11. In a study of fiscal policies of governors in U.S. states, however, Besley and Case (1995b) find that governors systematically pursue less prudent policies in periods and states in which they are facing a binding term limit.

9.4   Notes on the Literature

References to the Holmström (1982) model providing the analytical underpinnings to the model in section 9.1 can be found in chapter 4. The distinction between local and national elections made in that section is due to Seabright (1996), who formulates it in a version of Ferejohn 1986 with an exogenous voting rule. The model of majoritarian and proportional elections in section 9.1.2 is new. Besley and Case (1995a) discuss a simple example of yardstick competition and adverse selection; they also provide supporting empirical evidence from the U.S. states. Holmström and Milgrom (1988) formulate a simple model with multiple principals and multiple tasks for the common agent, and Dixit (1997) generalizes this model. Carillo and Mariotti (1999) study the optimal choices of incumbent identity by vote-maximizing parties involved in electoral competition.

There are, of course, many other aspects of electoral rule than those studied in this chapter. As an example, Pande (1999) studies a theoretical model of postelection politics with ideological (outcome-seeking) politicians in which political parties may face a binding constraint to field a minimum share of candidates belonging to a particular minority. She uses exogenous variation in Indian electoral laws to test some of the predictions of the model with the main empirical finding that increased minoritarian representation has indeed increased policies targeted to the corresponding minorities. Mudambi, Navarra, and Nicosia (1996) and Mudambi, Navarra, and Sobbrio (1998) study empirically the consequences of an electoral reform that changed the electoral rule from proportional to semimajoritarian in some Italian municipal elections.

As discussed in chapter 4, electoral accountability in a principal-agent framework was first discussed by Barro (1973), then by Ferejohn (1986) and others. Besley and Case (1995b) study a model of electoral accountability in which the incumbent may be subject to a term limit. They estimate the behavior of governors in U.S. states and find that those governors running up against a term limit are indeed associated with systematically less prudent fiscal policies. To the best of our knowledge, the model of section 9.2 has not previously been dealt with in the literature . It starts from the insight in section 4 of Ferejohn 1986. Ferejohn's model (which has costs of effort rather than benefits of rents) has only redistribution, however, and no general public good.

Section 9.3 draws on Persson, Roland, and Tabellini 1997, which emphasizes the benefits of separation of powers. In the earlier literature, Brennan and Hamlin (1994) had found that separation of powers was associated with costs rather than benefits. Separation of powers has also been discussed by Laffont and Martimort (1999) with regard to regulation by supervisory agencies. Shugart and Carey (1992) discuss how actual presidential regimes differ, with an emphasis on their separation-of-powers properties. Tsebelis (1995) discusses formally how to model political systems from the viewpoint of the number of players who can impose a veto on legislative proposals.

Laffont (1999) provides an excellent survey of the recent literature on collusion with politically motivated agencies, whereas Tirole (1994) discusses collusion and organizations more generally. Hart (1995) and Tirole (1999) survey the large literature on incomplete contracts. Aghion and Bolton (1998) also discuss how to view constitutions as examples of incomplete contracts. Bennedsen (1999) studies how private versus public ownership of enterprises affects public policy and resource allocation as interest groups endogenously adapt their behavior to the different control rights in the two regimes.

9.5 Problems

1. Local versus national elections and externalities among local public goods

Consider the following model with multiple localities and externalities among local public goods. There are two periods, no redistributive transfers among voters, and local—rather than national—public goods. Tax revenue is fixed at $\bar{\tau}$, and the government budget must be balanced in both periods. There are three localities, indexed by J, which may or may not coincide with voting districts, depending on the electoral rule. Each locality has a population of voters identical within the locality; the size of this population is normalized to unity. The localities differ only in that each enjoys utility from a different local public good, g^J. Voters' preferences in locality J and period t are

$$w_t^j = y - \bar{\tau} + \alpha g_t^j + \beta \left(g_t^i + g_t^k \right),$$

where $\alpha > \beta$ and $\alpha > 1$ as before. Assume that voters in each district can observe the public goods in all the other districts.

Politicians choose for themselves how to allocate tax revenues between public goods and rents. A separate government budget constraint applies in each locality and in each period, irrespective of the degree of centralization or the form of electoral system:

$$g_t^J = \eta^J \left(\bar{\tau} - r_t^J \right),$$

where, η^J denotes the competence of the politician in charge of providing the public good and r_t^J denotes rents in locality J. Rents are constrained to be nonnegative and have an exogenous upper bound $\bar{r}$: $0 \le r_t^J \le \bar{r}$. Competence is a random variable, uniformly and independently distributed in each locality, with an expected value of 1 and with density ξ in all localities. Politicians' preferences are given by

$$E[v] = r_1 + p_I \delta (R + r_2),$$

where p_I is the probability that the incumbent is reappointed. The exact meaning of endogenous and exogenous rents depends on the institutional arrangement. With decentralization, r_t is given by r_t^J, rents in locality J, whereas in a centralized setup, r_t is the sum of rents in all localities, $r_t = \sum_J r_t^J$.

The timing of events is as follows: (1) An incumbent politician is in office in period 1 and chooses rents for that period, r_1^J, without knowing his own competence η^J. (2) The value of η^J is realized, and public-good provision g_1^J is residually determined. Voters observe their own utility but do not directly observe η^J or r_1^J. (3) Elections are held. If the incumbent wins, his competence in locality J remains η^J. If he loses, his opponent's competence in locality J is drawn at random from the same distribution. (4) Period 2 rents r_2^J are set, and public goods are residually determined.

In a regime of national elections, one policymaker runs for office in the three regions and wins if he gets more than half the votes of the whole population. Under local elections, three different elections are held in three different localities. A candidate who gets more than half the shares in a certain locality wins the election for that locality.

a. Solve the equilibrium for national and local elections. Determine the expression for the probability that the incumbent is reelected in the national-elections model.

b. Show that when $\alpha > \beta$, reelecting the incumbent in the national election is not socially optimal (when a social planner is constrained to choose only one policymaker for the three districts).

c. Show that when $\alpha = \beta$, reelecting the incumbent in the national election is socially optimal. Is this reelection rule better than that in the local elections?

2. Yardstick competition

Assume the same framework as in problem 1, without externalities and with two localities. Then group j voters' preferences are given by

$$w_t^j = y - \bar{\tau} + \alpha g_t^j,$$

where $\alpha > 1$. Now let $g_2^j = (\eta^j + \varepsilon)(\bar{\tau} - \bar{r})$, where η^j and ε are distributed normally, with $\mu_\eta = 1$ and $\mu_\varepsilon = 0$ as means and σ_η and σ_ε as standard deviations, respectively. Assume elections are held locally.

a. Show that voters' optimal voting rule should depend both on the level of public goods in their own district and on the level of public goods in the other district.

b. Show that the voting rule for voters in district j has the property that the incumbent's reelection probability is increasing in district j's public-good provision and decreasing in district i's public-good provision.

c. Show that for a high variance of ε, voters rely less on district's j's public good.

3. Groups with coordinated voting

There are N voters. Voter j has preferences

$$w^J = c^J + H(g) = y - \tau + f^J + H(g),$$

with g denoting a general public good benefiting all voters and f^J denoting nonnegative lump sum transfers to voter j. An exogenous state of nature, θ, captures the cost of converting private goods into public. Thus the government budget constraint is

$$\theta g = N\tau - r - f,$$

with $f = \sum_J f^J$. We restrict all policy instruments to be nonnegative and assume that appropriating rents entails some transaction costs $(1 - \gamma)$. Thus the incumbent maximizes

$$E(v_I) = \gamma r + p_I R,$$

where R is the exogenous rents from office.

The timing of events is as follows: (1) The state of nature θ is realized and observed by everyone. (2) All voters simultaneously choose a retrospective voting rule. (3) The incumbent chooses policy—$\{f^J\}$, g, τ and r—which is fully observed by voters. (4) Elections are held.

Assume that M voters are organized so that they coordinate their votes to maximize the sum of utilities in the group.

a. Assume $M > \frac{n}{2}$. Characterize the ensuing equilibrium.

b. Assume $M < \frac{n}{2}$. Characterize the ensuing equilibrium.

c. Compare the results in questions (a) and (b) and discuss the relation between group size and political power.

4. Checks and balances with bilateral bargaining

Consider the following model of separation of powers. There are two political offices, the holders of which are both subject to reelection. We label them the executive, X, and the legislature, L. The voters now choose retrospective voting strategies for X and L separately. Total rents from office are split between the two office holders, $r_L + r_X = r$, and a specific policy decision must be made with regard to the allocation. Each incumbent office holder has an objective of the form

$$E(v_I) = \gamma r_I + p_I R_I,$$

where $I = X, L$. As before, the policy choice is limited by a budget constraint

$$\theta g = N\tau - r,$$

where θ is observable to voters.

The structure of the game is as follows: (1) θ is realized and observed by everyone. (2) The voters choose a retrospective voting rule. (3) Incumbent X proposes a tax rate, τ, and public spending, g. (4) The allocation of rents, $\{r_X, r_L\}$, is then decided upon through bargaining between the two politicians. Specifically, assume that the rents available to the politicians, after τ and g have been set, are divided between the politicians, with a share α of total rents going to X. (5) Voters observe g and τ. (6) Elections are held in which each incumbent runs against an opponent identical to himself.

a. What is the minimum utility that X can always guarantee himself?

b. Can voters guarantee optimal public-good provision? If yes, characterize such an equilibrium. If no, why not?

c. What are the total rents the politicians appropriate?

5. Separation of powers and the common-pool problem

As suggested in the text, consider the case in which separation of powers creates a common-pool problem. In the framework of problem 4, suppose that first X chooses $r_X (r_X \leq Ny)$, and then L chooses r_L (such that $r_L \leq Ny - r_L$). Given these two values, taxes and public goods are chosen (namely maximizing voters' utility subject to the constraint of providing politicians with the rents chosen). Suppose that $R_X > R_L$.

a. Can voters enforce the optimal outcome of $r_X = r_L = 0$ and $g = G(\theta)$? If yes, under what conditions? If no, why not?

b. Suppose both politicians get rents in equilibrium. Characterize such an equilibrium and specify the conditions for the public good to be set at the optimal level.

c. Compare the total rents of politicians in this model and in the model with a single politician.

10 Political Regimes

In this chapter, we continue our investigation of policy selection in different political systems. As in chapter 9, we assume that binding electoral promises are not enforceable, such that elected politicians have the discretion to choose policy. In this chapter, however, we allow for redistribution among voters, while assuming that several politicians decide on policy in legislative bargaining. Thus we study policy choice in a genuine multiprincipal-multiagent setting. This means that we have conflicts of interest running in three dimensions: between voters and politicians at large, over the aggregate rents; among voters, over the distribution of income; and among politicians, over the distribution of rents. We ask primarily two questions. How do the equilibrium size of overall spending, the provision of public goods to voters, and the rents to politicians interact with equilibrium redistribution across different groups of voters? And how do the control rights laid down by different constitutions shape equilibrium policy in this richer setting?

Why would the three conflicts of interest be resolved differently under different constitutions? As stressed before, in a setting of postelection politics, the political constitution is like an incomplete contract. The constitution allocates the decision-making authority to specific groups or individuals: who has the right to make policy proposals and who can approve, amend, or veto them. It also specifies how these groups or individuals can maintain these rights. Because of the conflicting interests in our policy problem, the outcome hinges on how and by whom these authorities are exercised. We illustrate this general point by contrasting two main types of democracies: presidential-congressional versus parliamentary regimes. We concentrate on two important features of these regimes, namely their rules for allocation and maintenance of the proposal powers for economic policy.

A presidential-congressional regime of the U.S. type has more-dispersed proposal powers than a parliamentary regime of the European type. This may concern the relation between legislature and executive, as alluded to in the previous chapter. Even more importantly, however, proposal powers over legislation typically reside with powerful congressional committees, and different committees hold power over different policy dimensions. In a parliamentary regime, on the other hand, the proposal powers over legislation are more concentrated. These powers are typically associated with ministerial portfolios, and the policy initiative thus belongs to the government coalition. In both regimes, electoral outcomes and seniority determine which politicians end up with these proposal powers after an election.

To maintain these proposal powers throughout the election period, the members of government in a parliamentary regime need the legislature's continuous confidence. Moreover, government crises can erupt during the election period due to the rights of initiating votes of confidence or nonconfidence, of dissolving the government, or of calling early elections. Since partners in a government coalition risk losing valuable agenda-setting powers after a crisis, the coalition has strong incentives to form a stable legislative majority that does not shift from issue to issue. In a presidential regime, the allocation of proposal powers instead takes place once and for all in an election period. Once this has occurred, no stable congressional majority is needed to support the executive, as the latter is directly elected for an entire election period and cannot be voted down by Congress. The incentives for maintaining a stable majority in Congress are therefore small, and legislative majorities often change from issue to issue. To use a term from modern political science, parliamentary regimes have more *legislative cohesion*. Note that this argument goes beyond party discipline: cohesion between parties supporting coalition governments is typically much higher than cohesion within parties in the U.S. Congress.[1]

The latter difference between the two types of regimes has only recently been formally modeled. Huber (1996) showed how the power to associate a vote on a bill with a vote of confidence modifies the bargaining power of the coalition partners, who fear the negative consequences of a government crisis. The pioneering work of Diermeier and Feddersen (1998) showed, more generally, how disciplined voting by the members supporting a governing coalition arises when it is costly for a majority coalition to break up, since it loses valuable agenda-setting powers associated with participation in the coalition. The extent to which a political regime displays such legislative cohesion thus largely depends on the rights laid down by the constitution concerning the formation and dissolution of governments.

In this chapter we study how separation of powers and institutions producing more or less legislative cohesion affect policy choices. The modeling of the former draws on the last section of the previous chapter and thus on Persson, Roland, and Tabellini 1997. The modeling of the latter draws on the insights of Diermeier and Feddersen 1998. We present a simplified treatment of the analysis in Persson, Roland, and Tabellini 1998a, which studies infinitely repeated policy choices in different political regimes. Our results suggest that the two political regimes are associated with very different policy outcomes. Separation of powers in the presidential-congressional regime produces a smaller government with less waste and less redistribution but also inefficiently low spending on public goods. Intuitively, separation of powers enables the voters to discipline the politicians, and this reduces waste and moderates the tax burden. The sharp conflict of interest among politicians, however, prevents them from internalizing all benefits of public-good provision. Legislative cohesion in the parliamentary regime, on the other hand, leads to a larger government, with more taxation and more waste, but also more spending on public goods and redistribution benefiting

---

1. Naturally, not all parliamentary regimes exhibit the same degree of legislative cohesion, since rules for government breakup and formation differ across countries (see Huber 1996 and Baron 1998). Similarly, not all presidential regimes entail the same separation of powers: in the French fifth republic, agenda-setting powers rest within the government, which is, in turn, accountable to the legislature; in many Latin American countries, the legislatures have much weaker powers relative to the president than in the United States. See also Lijphart 1992 and Shugart and Carey 1992 for further discussion of these issues.

a broader group of voters. Intuitively, there is now further scope for collusion among politicians, which increases waste and taxation. But policy aims at pleasing a majority group of voters, which increases public-good provision, calls for a more equal redistribution, and makes the majority support a high level of taxation.

Even though we do not stress the normative questions, our results point to a trade-off in institution design. A well-functioning presidential-congressional regime performs better in terms of accountability, because it can cope well with the agency problem between voters and politicians, but a parliamentary regime is better in terms of global public-good provision, since it solves the conflict among groups of voters more effectively.

In section 10.1, we reintroduce the notation and the basic policy problem. We also study the political equilibrium in a simple legislature that has neither separation of powers nor the institutions producing legislative cohesion. This setting allows us to discuss some of the building blocks of the analysis in detail. After these preliminaries, we present the main comparative politics results for a presidential-congressional regime (section 10.2) and for a parliamentary regime (section 10.3).

10.1   Policy Choices in a Simple Legislature

The economy in this section is identical to that in the full-fledged public finance model of chapters 8 and 9. Thus there are three groups of voters, $J = 1, 2, 3$, all of size (mass) unity. Groups coincide with electoral districts, each represented by a single legislator, $l = 1, 2, 3$. Thus we assume majoritarian elections throughout the chapter. Voters in district J have preferences

$$w^J = c^J + H(g) = y - \tau + f^J + H(g), \tag{10.1}$$

where the notation is the same as in the previous chapters. Even though voters care only about their net taxes (transfers), $\tau - f^J$, it is still important to distinguish between τ and f^J, as the control rights over taxes and transfers are allocated to different politicians. As before, g denotes a general public good benefiting all voters. We assume $\theta = 1$ throughout.

We continue to assume that politicians can appropriate rents and must choose how these should be allocated through a legislative decision. Denoting by r_l the rents captured by legislator l, we write the government budget constraint as

$$3\tau = g + \sum_J f^J + \sum_l r_l = g + f + r, \tag{10.2}$$

where f denotes aggregate transfers. Items in the government budget constraint must all be nonnegative. As in earlier chapters, $\mathbf{q}$ denotes the full policy vector.

Clearly, the social optimum for any symmetric (and strictly concave) social welfare function defined over the utility of voters, but not incorporating the rents to politicians, is to eliminate rents, setting $r_l = r = 0$, and to provide public goods in accordance with the Samuelson rule, $3H_g(g^*) = 1$. Net taxes $\tau - f^J$ should be equal across groups, implying $f^J = \frac{f}{3}$, even though optimal gross transfers are indeterminate. With a tiny bit of tax distortions, however, $f = 0$ becomes optimal.

Policy choice is delegated to politicians, not to a benevolent social planner, however. As before, we assume that legislators maximize the sum of endogenous and (future) exogenous rents in office

$$v_l = \gamma r_l + p_l R,$$

where p_l is the probability that legislator l is reappointed. For simplicity, the exogenous rents from office, R, are assumed to be equal for all incumbent lawmakers. Voters hold the incumbent lawmakers separately accountable through the adoption of retrospective voting strategies. The incumbent legislator runs against an identical opponent in elections held in each district after policy choices have been made. Problem 3 of this chapter shows that R can be interpreted as the equilibrium continuation value of being in office next period, given that all rents are endogenous.

We start by discussing a very simple and unrealistic assignment of control rights labeled a "simple legislature." The incumbent legislators decide on public policy in a very simple legislative bargaining game embedded in the sequence of events illustrated in figure 10.1, that is to say: (1) Nature randomly selects an agenda setter a among the three legislators. (2) Voters formulate their reelection strategies, setting p_l contingent on the welfare level they have experienced. This strategy becomes publicly known. (3) Legislator a proposes the entire policy vector $\mathbf{q}$. (4) The legislature votes on the proposal. If a majority (at least two legislators) supports the proposal, it is implemented. If not, a default policy $\overline{\mathbf{q}}$ is implemented, with $\tau = r_l = \overline{r} > 0$ and $g = f^J = 0$. (5) Voters observe the outcome of the legislative decision and all elements in the policy vector. Elections are held.

As in chapter 9, we restrict our attention to equilibria in which voters from the same constituency coordinate their strategies, but voters across constituencies do not cooperate. Thus voters in each district adopt simple retrospective voting rules, conditional on their representative's being the agenda setter or not. Formally, they set

$$p_l = \begin{cases} 1 & \text{iff} \quad W^J(\mathbf{q}) \geq \varpi^J, \quad J = l \\ 0 & \text{otherwise.} \end{cases} \tag{10.3}$$

As before, we assume that voters in all regions simultaneously set their reservation utilities ϖ^J in a utility-maximizing fashion. Although cooperating within districts, voters thus play

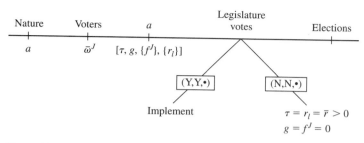

Figure 10.1

Nash against all other districts; see the definition of equilibrium below. The vector of these reservation utilities, ϖ, is thus known to politicians when the policy proposal is made. Legislators therefore have an incentive to act in the interest of their constituencies.[2]

Our assumption about the point at which voters formulate their strategies deserves some discussion. The timing presented above means that the voters form their expectations and make their demands on politicians once they know their representative's institutional role at the beginning of the policy formation process. That is, voters want to hold their representative accountable for her deeds in the course of the legislative process. Allowing voters to reoptimize their demands just before the election date would not change the results: as discussed below, the voting rule is ex post optimal for the voters, since the incumbent and the opponent are identical. Under a different timing, however, there would be many other equilibria besides the one discussed here. Thus our timing assumption really amounts to a selection criterion: among the possible equilibria emerging if voters do not commit to a voting rule, we select the only one surviving under the timing spelled out above. If, however, legislators and candidates were inherently different in their competence or other features, as in the career concern model or the probabilistic voting model of chapters 8 and 9, the timing assumption would be more critical, since the equilibrium voting rule would no longer be ex post optimal.[3]

An equilibrium of this game has to satisfy three conditions (the L superscript stands for the simple legislature). First, for any given vector of reservation utilities ϖ, at least one legislator $l \neq a$ must weakly prefer policy $\mathbf{q}^L(\varpi)$ to the default policy $\bar{\mathbf{q}}$. Second, for any given ϖ, the agenda-setting legislator a must prefer $\mathbf{q}^L(\varpi)$ to any other policy that can

---

2. Allowing voters to condition their reelection rules directly on the policy instruments or on the vote of the politicians would not change any of the results.

3. Banks and Sundaram (1993, 1996) formulate retrospective voting models with heterogeneity among candidate types together with asymmetric information over types.

obtain a majority in the legislature. Third, the reservation utilities ϖ^J are optimal for the voters in each district J, taking as given the reservation utilities in other districts and taking into account that policies in the current period are set according to $\mathbf{q}^L(\varpi)$.

A unique subgame-perfect equilibrium satisfies these three conditions. Its properties can be summarized as follows:

$$r^L = 3y - \frac{R}{\gamma} - \bar{r}$$

$$\tau^L = y$$

$$g^L = H_g^{-1}(1)$$

$$f^{aL} = \frac{R}{\gamma} + \bar{r} - g^L > 0, \qquad f^{JL} = 0 \quad \text{for} \quad J \neq a$$

$$\varpi^{aL} = H(g^L) + f^{aL}, \qquad \varpi^{JL} = H(g^L) \quad \text{for} \quad J \neq a.$$

All politicians are reelected.

Thus in equilibrium, taxes are maximal, public goods are underprovided relative to the social optimum, some redistribution goes to a minority of voters, and the legislators appropriate positive rents from office. To understand how the model works, it is useful to prove these features in steps.

We first show that only the district of the omnipotent legislator making the policy proposal may obtain positive transfers. That is, $f^J = 0$, for districts $J = m, n \neq a$. The key to this result is that any equilibrium entails a minimum winning coalition. As in chapter 7, the equilibrium proposal needs approval by only one other legislator besides the agenda setter. To get the support of the third legislator, the agenda setter would have to spend resources either on her or on her district, but these resources are better used to increase r_a. Hence if legislator n, say, is excluded from the winning coalition, then $r_n = f^n = 0$.

By the same logic, the legislator included in the winning coalition together with the agenda setter is the one whose vote is the cheapest to buy. As all legislators have the same default payoffs, which district is cheapest to buy depends only on the reservation utilities, ϖ^n and ϖ^m, the voters demand. Realizing this, the voters in districts m and n have an incentive to underbid each other up to the point where $f^m = f^n = 0$, that is, up to the point where $\varpi^m = \varpi^n = y - \tau + H(g)$. As in the previous chapter, the voters become engaged in a Bertrand competition game for the redistributive favors of the agenda-setting incumbent. The voters outside district a do not directly interact with the incumbent in charge of the policy proposal. Instead, they attempt to make their own legislator an attractive coalition member by bidding down their reservation utilities like the lobbies in section 7.5. But the utility of voters in district m is still discontinuous in the reservation value ϖ^m, at the point where $\varpi^m = \varpi^n$, unless $f^m = 0$. The same argument holds for voters in n. Hence the only equilibrium must be at the corner where $f^m = f^n = 0$.

Next, we show that in equilibrium, $r \geq 3 - \frac{R}{\gamma} - \bar{r}$, and all legislators are reappointed. Consider the agenda setter's optimal behavior, and let m be the other legislator supporting her proposal. Then if a seeks reappointment, she will never offer m more than max $[0, r_m]$, with r_m satisfying

$$\gamma r_m + R = \gamma \bar{r}.$$

The value of r_m in this equation would leave m indifferent between voting yes and being reappointed or voting no, getting the default payoff $\gamma \bar{r}$, and losing the election. To simplify the analysis, we assume that the parameters are such that $\bar{r} \leq R/\gamma$, such that the nonnegativity constraint on r^m is always binding. (With the opposite assumption, a would need to compensate m with positive transfers, but the qualitative results to be derived below would still hold, even though the algebra would differ slightly.) Suppose instead that a does not seek reappointment and makes a proposal that would lead to a loss of office for all legislators under the given voting rules. In this case, she must offer at least $\bar{r}$ to m to win approval for her proposal. Since she does not care about pleasing her voters, the agenda setter can appropriate all available resources, setting $g = f = 0$ and $\tau = 1$. Thus a will seek reappointment if and only if

$$\gamma r_a + R \geq \gamma (3y - \bar{r}).$$

The left-hand side of this inequality denotes the agenda setter's overall utility if she makes a proposal consistent with reappointment under the given voting rule. The right-hand side is her maximal payoff, given that she does not seek reappointment and must pay $\bar{r}$ to m.

It follows that legislators a and m will implement a policy leading to their reappointment if and only if:

$$r = r_a \geq 3y - \frac{R}{\gamma} - \bar{r}. \tag{10.4}$$

The optimal voting rule can never be more demanding than (10.4): if the legislators were induced to forego reappointment, they would appropriate all resources and leave the voters with low utility. Hence the optimal voting rule must satisfy (10.4), and both the agenda setter and the legislator supporting the proposal are reelected. The reservation utility of voters in districts m and n is the same, as both districts receive zero transfers. Because these voters pay the same τ and enjoy the same level of g, legislator n will also be reelected.

Note that (10.4) is an incentive compatibility condition on the overall diversion of resources. Note also that legislator a is the "residual claimant" on resources for given reelection strategies. It is thus optimal for her not only to minimize the payment to legislator m, but also to satisfy the reelection constraints of voters in districts a and m with equality, appropriating any remaining resources for herself. If it is consistent with her own reelection, she would thus like to set $\tau = 1$.

We can now complete the characterization of the equilibrium. Consider legislator a. We know that $f^a = f$, by the previous argument. The policy maximizing the utility of voters in district a is therefore the solution to

$$\max [f + y - \tau + H(g)],$$

subject to the government budget constraint (10.2) and the incentive constraint on legislators a and m (10.4). Combining the two constraints, we get

$$3(\tau - y) + \frac{R}{\gamma} + \bar{r} \geq f + g.$$

The solution to the optimization problem implies: $\tau = y$, $g = \min [H_g^{-1}(1), \frac{R}{\gamma} + \bar{r}]$, $f = \frac{R}{\gamma} + \bar{r} - g$, $r = 3y - \frac{R}{\gamma} - \bar{r}$. If we make an assumption like (9.17), we can ignore possible corner solutions for g. Then this is precisely the equilibrium policy $\mathbf{q}^L$ described above.

We know that all legislators are reappointed in equilibrium. Inserting the equilibrium policies in the voters' utility functions yields the equilibrium reservation utilities. Because voters choose their reelection strategies simultaneously, no voter has any incentive to change her vote if she considers herself pivotal, given the optimal behavior by other voters and legislators.[4]

The outcome is obviously related to the equilibrium in section 9.2. As in that case, voters compete across but not within districts. This competitive situation is detrimental to voters outside district $J = a$. Voters of the non-agenda-setting regions cannot discipline their representatives to ask for more equitable redistribution, since they compete with each other to be included in the majority. But unlike in chapter 9, the incumbent agenda setter can earn reelection only from the voters in her own district because of the electoral rule. Therefore, the voters in the agenda setter's region can still discipline the agenda setter and keep rents to a minimum. As in the accountability model of chapter 4, they achieve this by adopting a reelection rule that keeps legislator a indifferent between diverting as much as possible today but losing office and diverting a small amount today but holding on to office and continuing to reap rents in the future. Because $f > 0$, voters in region a obtain net redistribution to their district at the expense of voters in other districts. They therefore prefer their representative to set taxes at their maximum: $\tau = 1$. This results in an underprovision of public goods, since the agenda setter effectively sets policy so as to maximize the utility of

---

4. As remarked above, the voting rule is ex post (weakly) optimal, since the incumbent and the opponent are identical in each district. Hence even without the assumption that voters are committed to their voting rule, the equilibrium would still be sequentially rational (though many other equilibria would also exist).

voters in district a only. She therefore trades off redistribution to region a and public-goods provision one for one—and hence sets $H_g(g) = 1$.

Note also that the interests of voters in district a and their legislator are aligned in some dimensions but not in others. Both want maximal taxes, but the voters and the legislator each want to keep the revenue to themselves, voters wishing to expand f^a and the legislator wishing to expand r_a. Holding their legislator accountable for performance, the voters can limit the waste as long as they respect the incentive constraint (10.4).

This simple model illustrates a form of legislation that Jefferson called "elective despotism" in his *Notes on North Virginia* (cited by Madison in Federalist Paper XLVIII, p. 310):

All the powers of government, legislative, executive, and judiciary, result to the legislative body. The concentrating these in the same hands is precisely the definition of despotic government. It will be no alleviation that these powers will be exercised by a plurality of hands, and not by a single one. One hundred and seventy-three despots would surely be as oppressive as one. . . . An elective despotism is not what we fought for.

In summary, this simple legislative model displays three political failures, each associated with a departure from the socially optimal policy: some spending is wasteful ($r^L > 0$); public goods are underprovided ($g^L < H_g^{-1}(\frac{1}{3})$); and a politically powerful minority receives any equilibrium redistribution ($f^{aL} > 0$). We now ask what form these three political failures take under alternative—and more realistic—political constitutions.

10.2 Presidential-Congressional Regimes

We first depart in this section from the simple legislature in section 10.1 by introducing separation of proposal powers along the same lines as in chapter 9. As discussed in the introduction to this chapter, this is motivated by the features of a presidential-congressional system like that of the United States, which has considerable separation of powers: different congressional committees hold proposal powers over legislation in different policy dimensions, and the president has veto power. To capture these features, we study a two-stage budget procedure in which the proposal powers on taxes and the allocation of spending are allocated to two different legislators. We thus abstract from the president and his veto powers, but these could be introduced without changing the thrust of the main results; see for instance problems 2 and 6 of this chapter. We could split the proposal power further over spending, giving each of the three legislators some agenda-setting privileges, but once more this would not affect the main results.

The congressional policy game has the following timing, illustrated in figure 10.2. (1) Two different agenda-setters, a_τ and a_g, the "finance committee" and the "expenditure committee," respectively, are appointed among the three legislators. (2) Voters set the

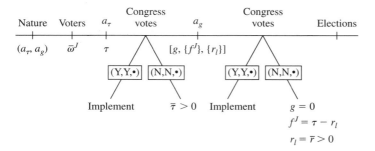

Figure 10.2

cutoff utilities ϖ^J in their reelection rules optimally, conditional on the status of their legislator. (3) a_τ proposes a tax rate, τ. (4) Congress votes: if it is approved by a majority, the tax proposal becomes law; if not, the default tax rate is $\bar{\tau} > 0$. (5) a_g proposes g, $\{f^J\}$ and $\{r_l\}$ subject to $3\tau \geq g + f + r$. (6) Congress votes: if the proposal is rejected by a majority, the default allocation is $g = 0$, $f^J \equiv \tau - r_l \geq 0$, $r_l = \bar{r}$.[5] (7) Voters observe everything and elections are held. As in chapter 9, there are thus two agenda setters, but now policies do not need unanimous approval, just a simple majority in Congress. Policy decisions are made sequentially, first on the overall size of government and then on the allocation of spending. Not only are proposals sequential, but so are congressional votes. Specifically, the outcome of congressional votes over tax revenues constrains spending proposals in the second stage.

To understand the features of equilibrium allocations, we can appeal to several results in the previous section and in previous chapters. At the last stage, the expenditure committee a_g needs the support of just one legislator besides herself in order to prevail. Hence she seeks a minimum winning coalition and the support of the legislator who is cheapest to buy, in the sense of demanding the least for her constituency. Thus voters in districts $J \neq a_g$ once more become engaged in a Bertrand competition for the spoils allocated by a_g. Given that they pay taxes anyway, they are better off getting some transfers, however small, rather than nothing. Hence in order not to be excluded from the majority coalition, they reduce their reservation utilities until their demand for redistribution is driven to zero. Any equilibrium thus has $f^J = 0$, if $J \neq a_g$.

This leaves a_g free to please her voters, for all redistributive transfers go to her district ($f^J = f$ if $J = a_g$). As in the simple legislature, the public good is traded off against redistribution, one for one. This leads to severe underprovision of the public good, since

---

5. We must thus assume that $\bar{\tau} \geq \bar{r}$.

only one-third of the social benefits are internalized. Specifically, in equilibrium:[6]

$$g^C = \widehat{g} \equiv H_g^{-1}(1).$$

What about equilibrium rents? As in the simple legislature, the maximum threat legislator a_g can impose on the voters is to go for the maximum diversion, $r = 3\tau$. Having bought the vote of one additional lawmaker, she is then left with a payoff of $\gamma(3\tau - \bar{r})$. Alternatively, she can satisfy the voters. Given the earlier assumption that $\gamma \bar{r} \leq R$ and given that her proposal is consistent with the cutoff utilities demanded by the voters in the other districts, a_g is not obliged to give anything to legislator m. Thus pleasing the voters gives her the net payoff of $\gamma r + R$. The incentive constraint on the minimum rents in stage (5) thus becomes

$$r \geq \max\left[3\tau - \frac{R}{\gamma} - \bar{r}, 0 \right]. \tag{10.5}$$

What are the incentives of the taxation committee a_τ and the voters in the corresponding district at the taxation stage (3)? Because voters in district a_τ receive no transfers, they would like τ to be as low as possible, consistent with $\widehat{g}$ being financed. The best possible outcome for voters in district a_τ is therefore associated with a minimal tax rate, $\tau = \widehat{g}/3$, implying $r = f = 0$. As $\widehat{g} < \frac{R}{\gamma}$, this is consistent with incentive compatibility as defined in (10.5). Thus it is optimal for a_g to go along with $r = 0$. The interests of voters in district a_τ are well aligned with those of legislator a_τ, for she is not a residual claimant on taxes, the sole residual claimants on additional revenue being legislator a_g or her voters. Assuming, as above, that $R > \gamma \bar{r}$, it is optimal for a_τ to go along with the minimal tax rate, which is the only way she can earn reelection by her voters and a payoff of R. Proposing a higher tax rate at stage (3) does create room for rents. But legislator a_g will never offer a_τ more than the minimum payoff of $\gamma \bar{r}$ at stage (5), even if she exploits the opportunity to capture higher rents at stage (5). Finally, given the minimal tax rate voters in a_τ required the voters in district a_g are better off accepting no transfers than making an incompatible demand on their legislator that would trigger a deviation, leading to maximal rents.[7]

It follows that we have an equilibrium with $r = f = 0$ and $\tau = \widehat{g}/3$. This equilibrium is supported by voting rules with cutoff utilities

$$\varpi^J = y + H(\widehat{g}) - \frac{\widehat{g}}{3}$$

for all voters.

---

6. In deriving this expression, we have to assume that the nonnegativity constraint on f^{a_g} is not binding. It can be shown that this requires $\widehat{g} = H_g^{-1}(1) \leq \frac{R}{\gamma} + \bar{r}$, an assumption that is implied by a condition like (9.17), already imposed above.

7. We assume that g is valuable enough that the voters prefer not to make incompatible demands, as this would trigger a deviation, with $g = f = 0$ and positive τ (financing positive rents to a_g and at least one more legislator).

There are other equilibria, however. Any tax rate $\tau \leq \frac{1}{3}[\frac{R}{\gamma} + \bar{r}]$ is compatible with zero rents, according to the incentive constraint (10.5). The best possible outcome for voters in district a_g would be the highest of these tax rates, $\tau = \frac{1}{3}[\frac{R}{\gamma} + \bar{r}]$, with the additional tax revenue being used for redistribution for themselves: $f = \frac{R}{\gamma} + \bar{r} - \hat{g}$. (Above this level, a_g would capture additional resources in the form of rents.) As the reservation utilities are set simultaneously, this outcome, too, is an equilibrium in the Nash game between the voters. Thus it is better for the voters in a_τ to acquiesce to higher demands by the voters in a_g than to trigger a Leviathan-like deviation. Exactly where taxes and transfers end up depends on the strategies chosen by voters in districts a_τ and a_g. Indeed, there is a continuum of equilibria associated with tax rates in the interval

$$\tau \in \left[\frac{\hat{g}}{3}, \frac{1}{3}\left(\frac{R}{\gamma} + \bar{r} \right) \right]$$

and with transfers to the powerful district in the interval

$$f^{a_g} \in \left[0, \frac{R}{\gamma} + \bar{r} - \hat{g} \right].$$

In summary, the presidential-congressional regime addresses two of the political distortions in the simple legislature of the previous section. Thus, rents and taxes are minimized: $r^C = 0 < r^L$, $\tau^C \leq \frac{1}{3}[\frac{R}{\gamma} + \bar{r}] < \tau^L$. This follows from voters' exploiting the separation of powers property of the congressional institution and from our assumption about the default outcome.[8] Public goods are, however, still severely underprovided, $g^C = H_g^{-1}(1) = g^L$, because of the strong agenda-setting powers of a minority over the allocation of spending, leading to competition over transfers. Voters in the district that controls the politician enjoying those powers prefer to direct the available resources toward themselves rather than sharing them with everyone through more public-good provision. Anticipating this minoritarian orientation of redistributive transfers, voters in the district in charge of taxation try to keep tax revenues to a minimum. Transfers to the minority are bounded above by transfers in the simple legislature $f^C \leq \frac{R}{\gamma} + \bar{r} - g^C = f^L$.

10.3 Parliamentary Regimes

In this section, we modify the simple legislature of section 10.1 in a different direction than we did in section 10.2. As discussed in the introduction to this chapter, parliamentary systems

---

8. If the default outcome $\bar{r}$ at the expenditure stage is positively related to τ decided upon in the taxation stage, it becomes harder to discipline the politicians, and the equilibrium has $r > 0$ (see Persson, Roland, and Tabellini 1998a).

lack a pronounced separation of powers. Instead, they have institutions producing legislative cohesion—the predisposition for majority coalitions to stick together. Disagreement within the majority in the legislature is a serious business that can lead to a government crisis. As a result, bargaining power is more evenly shared within the majority coalition, making the parliamentary regime less competitive for voters than the presidential-congressional regime. As we saw in the last section, in the latter regime, the formation of different coalitions at different points in time was the core of the Bertrand competition result, in which the legislator of the spending proposal could pit one group of voters against another. As we shall see, this difference in the cohesiveness and stability of coalitions in the two regimes is both good and bad for the voters in the parliamentary regime. It is good because it increases the equilibrium provision of public goods. It is bad because it weakens the separation of powers and increases politicians' equilibrium rents.

We continue to assume that two different legislators control the proposals on taxes and expenditures, respectively. No vote is taken, however, until both proposals have been made. It is therefore appropriate to identify these legislators with cabinet ministers and the proposal phase with the budget preparation inside the government. Both government coalition partners have veto power over the budget, and a veto triggers a government crisis. This assumption approximates having a vote of confidence attached to the government budget proposal. Obviously, this creates a strong incentive not to break up the coalition.

The new timing is illustrated in figure 10.3: (1) Two incumbent legislators (a_g, a_τ) are appointed to act as expenditure and finance ministers, respectively. (2) Voters set their reservation utilities conditional on their legislator's status. (3) The finance minister, a_τ, proposes a tax rate τ. (4) The expenditure minister, a_g, proposes expenditures $(g, \{f^J\}, \{r_l\})$, subject to the budget constraint and the proposed tax rate. (5) Either member of the government can veto the proposal. If neither of them does, the proposal passes, and elections are held. (5') If at least one of them vetoes, the government breaks down, and a default policy is imple-

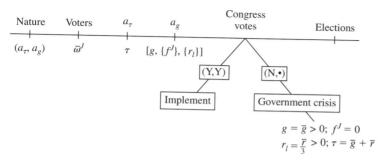

Figure 10.3

mented with $\overline{g} = \widehat{g}$ (and $\widehat{g}$ defined as above), $f = 0$, $\overline{r} = 3y - (\frac{R}{\gamma} + \overline{r})$, $r_l = \frac{\overline{r}}{3}$, $\tau = \overline{g} + \overline{r}$, and reelection guaranteed for each legislator.

The default policy and outcome in (5′) may appear strange at first sight. Its payoffs are designed to match the expected payoffs for both voters and politicians after a government crisis in a more complex setting in which a government crisis leads to a new subgame. In this subgame, a "caretaker government"—a single legislator—is picked at random, voters reformulate their reelection rules, the caretaker legislator makes the entire budget proposal, and this proposal is approved or not by the legislature (see Persson, Roland, and Tabellini 1998a and problem 4 of this chapter).[9] Refraining from explicitly studying this subgame is, of course, a shortcut. Our assumption captures the essential feature, however, namely that the two government partners and their voters recognize that they have valuable agenda-setting powers inside the government and that a breakup is costly, in that these agenda-setting powers are reshuffled among all three legislators after a crisis.

We now discuss the properties of equilibrium. Problem 5 of this chapter asks for a more detailed derivation. In this parliamentary regime, the coalition partners share bargaining power more equally than in the simple legislature and the presidential-congressional regime, because of the ability of each coalition member to veto the joint budget proposal at stage (5). The equilibrium allocation must split welfare more equally among voters backing the majority coalition, as well as among their politicians, than that in the presidential-congressional regime.

In particular, equilibrium rents are almost as high as in the simple legislature and clearly higher than in the presidential-congressional regime. As both government members have bargaining power against each other, they become joint residual claimants on rents. They therefore have a joint incentive to collude against the voters. If the government moves as a unified actor, it can impose the same maximum threat on the voters as in section 10.1, namely to set $\tau = y$ and $f = g = 0$, foregoing reelection. To prevent this, voters must leave some rents to the governing coalition, at least to satisfy the joint incentive constraint $r \geq 3y - 2R/\gamma$. Clearly, in equilibrium, the incentive constraint always binds, and equilibrium rents are

$$r^P = 3y - 2R/\gamma.$$

This expression is similar to that for the equilibrium rents in section 10.1, except that in this case, the rents from office refer to the two legislators in the coalition rather than a single politician. As $\overline{r} < R/\gamma$ by assumption, we have $r^P \leq r^L = 3y - R/\gamma - \overline{r}$. Aggregate rents

---

9. A richer model along the lines of Diermeier and Feddersen 1998 or Baron 1998 would have a new process of government formation following a crisis.

are then split among legislators according to their bargaining power, which here reflects their veto rights.[10]

That the government coalition is preassigned also makes the regime less competitive for the voters in the two districts backing the government, as long as the coalition sticks together. Bilateral monopoly thus replaces Bertrand competition in the redistribution game between these voters, implying that the equilibrium allocation of redistributive transfers and public goods must be jointly optimal for voters in the majority coalition, subject to the incentive constraint on rents. As a consequence, redistribution typically favors the majority, and the benefits of the public goods for the majority are internalized. To see this formally, maximize the utility of voters in, say, district a_g, for a given utility level of voters in district a_τ. The solution satisfies

$$f^{JP} \geq 0, \qquad J = a_\tau, a_g$$
$$\frac{1}{2} \leq H_g(g^P) < 1, \tag{10.6}$$

with $H_g(g^P) = \frac{1}{2}$ if $f^{JP} > 0$ for both $J = a_\tau, a_g$.

The equilibrium allocation is not unique, however. Since voters set their reservation utilities simultaneously, welfare can be split among them in many different ways. All equilibria satisfy (10.6), hence in all these equilibria, public-good provision is larger than in the presidential system, and in most of them, redistributive transfers benefit a majority of voters.

Finally, voters in the majority now benefit from higher taxes at the expense of the minority. Both legislators in the coalition are also pleased to go along with high taxes, as their rents are maximized when $\tau = y$. Thus in equilibrium, a_τ proposes $\tau^P = y$, and a_g is pleased to accept it; voters in their districts are pleased as well.[11]

In summary, the parliamentary regime addresses the political distortions encountered in the simple legislature in a different way than the presidential-congressional regime. Rents are unambiguously higher than in the presidential-congressional regime, as their mutual veto rights give all members of the government coalition some bargaining power. Because they are joint residual claimants of higher taxes, voters can no longer exploit the conflict of

---

10. In particular, the finance minister will veto any proposal r_{a_τ} that does not give her at least as much as after a government crisis, namely $r'/3$. Note that politicians are reelected in equilibrium as well as after the crisis.

11. The parliamentary equilibrium is supported by the voting strategies

$$\varpi^{a_g} = f^{a_g} + H(g^P)$$
$$\varpi^{a_\tau} = 2\frac{R}{\gamma} - f^{a_g} - g^P + H(g^P).$$

Clearly, as f^{a_g} varies, so does the equilibrium utility of the two groups of voters, reflecting the multiplicity of equilibria. See also problem 5 of this chapter.

interests between the legislators to their own benefit, except that they can appeal to reelection for both members of the coalition. Thus we have $r^C < r^P \leq r^L$. Voters in the districts behind a stable government majority are also pleased to support higher taxes, because the members of this majority obtain redistributive benefits by jointly exploiting the remaining minority. As a result, we have $\tau^C < \tau^P = \tau^L$. The majoritarian redistribution makes it less costly to provide public goods than in the other regimes, however, thus making underprovision less severe: $g^L = g^C < g^P$.

These comparative politics results emerge from the interaction between the political regime and voters' endogenous behavior. In the same way, organized interest groups will adapt their behavior to the political regime. Helpman and Persson (1998), as well as Bennedsen and Feldmann (1999), contrast lobbies' behavior in parliamentary and presidential-congressional regimes. Their results indicate that the same kind of forces drive the results when lobbies, rather than voters, attempt to influence the policy outcomes in the two regimes.

10.4 Discussion

From a positive point of view, the analysis in this chapter implies that parliamentary regimes lead to a larger size of government compared to presidential-congressional regimes, with effective separation of powers and weaker incentives for legislative cohesion. Persson and Tabellini (1999b) find strong empirical support for this prediction in a sample of more than fifty democracies in developed and developing countries. Controlling for per capita income, the degree of openness of the economy, and the age, race, and language composition of the population, as well as other socioeconomic variables, public spending is lower by about 10% of GDP in presidential-congressional regimes compared to parliamentary regimes. Naturally, the theoretical models are very stylized, and it is a hard task to match the extensive forms of these games with observable institutional features. But the observed difference in spending between presidential-congressional and parliamentary regimes is so large that the empirical result is likely to be robust to small errors in classifying regime types.

Another clear prediction of this chapter's analysis is that parliamentary regimes should provide more public goods. More generally, the prediction, as in chapter 8, concerns broadly oriented spending programs versus narrowly targeted programs. Persson and Tabellini (1999b) also test this prediction. As in the case of the electoral rule, discussed in section 8.5, the results are not very strong. Regressing the share of public-goods spending in GDP, dummies for presidential democracies do come out with the expected negative sign, but the results are generally not statistically significant. When the two features of the political systems are combined, however, significant statistical results do appear. Countries with parliamentary regimes *and* proportional electoral rules do indeed spend more on public goods than other countries. These preliminary findings are suggestive, but more work is clearly needed.

From a normative point of view, the analysis in this chapter suggests a trade-off in institution design. In both political regimes, equilibrium policy differs from the social optimum: the institutional features generating legislative cohesion also increase the rents to politicians, whereas separation of proposal powers induces legislative competition, and this, in turn, leads to more severe underprovision of public goods. Which distortion is worse depends on circumstances. The parliamentary regime appears better for voters if the underprovision problem is great (because public goods are very valuable), whereas the presidential regime dominates if the political agency problem is highly relevant (because politicians face small transaction costs in rent extraction or the punishment from losing the next election is small—for instance, because of barriers to entry in the political arena).

More generally, the material in this part of the book suggests a number of interesting questions on how different constitutions shape equilibrium spending and taxation. Problems 1, 2, and 6 of this chapter suggest some variations on this theme. A possible counterargument against such a research program in positive public finance is that it might involve a great deal of arbitrariness: "the possible assignments of control rights are infinite, and you can prove anything with extensive form game theory." Although this may be a valid criticism of certain theories of industrial organization, we do not find it too damaging here, because constitutional rules are very well established, both legally and historically. Different democracies display rich variation in how they carry out elections and allocate political control. A wealth of historical, descriptive, and legal studies document these differences. In other words, the rules—for proposing, amending, or vetoing policy proposals, for forming or dissolving governments, or for electing political representatives—that define a particular extensive form game need not be arbitrary. They can be given a solid empirical foundation, as attempted in the promising work of Diermeier and Merlo (1999).

Political scientists have done a great deal of analytical work, theoretical as well as empirical, on comparative politics. But that work is typically confined to consequences or correlations within the domain of the political system: certain electoral systems are found to be associated with a larger or smaller number of "effective parties," presidential systems are found to be more politically unstable than parliamentary systems, certain rules for dissolving governments may be more prone to generate minority governments, and so on. As already mentioned, there is also some work on economic policy: for example, on the correlation between different budget processes, different electoral systems, and the propensity to run budget deficits. What is lacking is a systematic investigation of how commonly adopted constitutional arrangements shape fiscal policy choices. The need for this kind of investigation sets a very interesting agenda for future research. Aside from the very broad comparisons posed in this part, this agenda includes a number of more specific questions. Does the recently adopted presidential line item veto in the United States decrease or increase the equilibrium policy favors granted to special interests? (Problem 6 suggests a tentative answer to this question.) What kind of electoral reform could address the lack of political accountability that seems evident in countries like Japan, Italy, and Belgium? Over what policy issues are referenda more likely to be desirable, and when might they be counterproductive? And so on.

Suppose we find mappings, by theoretical and empirical work, between political institutions and policy choices. What do we make of such results? Can we use them to make normative recommendations for institutional reform? Perhaps yes, perhaps no. One view is that recommendations would be futile, because constitutions, like policy choices, are endogenous and not subject to easy manipulation. In other branches of economics, like contract theory, information economics, and corporate governance, the working assumption is often that observed institutions are efficient. Some researchers have also taken this view of political institutions.

We are sympathetic to the general idea of efficiency-oriented reform but skeptical about its being used as an overall approach for understanding existing political institutions. Constitutional reforms are rare, because of their large transaction costs. Unanticipated historical events may require new institutions, no matter how well-meaning were the constitutional framers. There is also a second argument. In some rare circumstances—like those of the U.S. Constitutional Convention—constitutional reform may have taken place under a veil of ignorance about the future beneficiaries of certain rules. Reform is more often marginal, however, and reformers are seldom disinterested framers internalizing the average citizen's desires. More commonly, reformers tend to be active politicians understanding the conflicts of interests and participating in the political process after reform has taken place. In terms of our simple example in the previous section, suppose the agency problem dominates the underprovision of public goods from the point of view of the voters' welfare. Then a constitutional assembly representing the voters at large would prefer a congressional system to limit political rents. But a constitutional choice made by politicians expecting to be elected as representatives might instead prefer the parliamentary system. Thus the agency problem reappears at the level of constitutional choice.

10.5 Notes on the Literature

A very large empirical literature by political scientists compares different types of political regimes. Some recent classics include Bingham Powell 1982, Lijphart 1984, Taagepera and Shugart 1989, Shugart and Carey 1992, and Cox 1997. Myerson (1995) surveys some of this literature. Laver and Shepsle (1990, 1996) and Schofield (1993) have studied cabinet formation in a spatial setting and with no economic policy analysis. Tsebelis (1995) compares the role of veto rights in alternative political systems.

The comparison between parliamentary and presidential-congressional systems in this section draws on Persson, Roland, and Tabellini 1998a, 1998b, and Diermeier and Feddersen 1998. Breton 1991 also compares some features of parliamentary and congressional systems. Empirical evidence on the size of government and amount of public goods in presidential and parliamentary regimes, as well as on majoritarian versus proportional electoral systems, is discussed in Persson and Tabellini 1999b.

Huber (1996) studies the role of the motion of confidence in parliamentary systems. Baron (1998), Baron and Diermeier (1999), and Diermeier and Merlo (1998) discuss how legislative cohesion, government crises, and government formation depend on the rules for government breakup in parliamentary regimes, whereas Diermeier and Merlo (1999) study empirically which bargaining procedures are consistent with the data from twelve democracies. Stenmark (1999) studies the size and composition of government spending in legislative bargaining involving single-party majority, single-party minority, and coalition governments; this sheds light on the consequences of different electoral rules, because the type of government is systematically related to the number of parties.

The idea that economic institutions can be studied within the framework of contract theory, as optimal contractual arrangements, has been debated at length among economists, also contrasting complete and incomplete contracts. Coase (1960), Williamson (1985), Hart (1995), Tirole (1999), and Laffont (1999) express different views on this issue. Some researchers have also taken the view that political institutions can be studied as efficient arrangements. Wittman (1989, 1995) very explicitly applies this to the political system as a whole, whereas Krehbiel (1987, 1991) and Gilligan and Krehbiel (1989) take a similar approach in their information-based theory of the organization of Congress. The idea that political institutions largely reflect the self-interest of politicians working within the system underlies another approach in the literature that is common among rational choice–oriented political scientists. These insights go back a long time but are clearly exposed by Mayhew (1974), Fiorina (1977), and Weingast and Marshall (1988).

10.6 Problems

1. A model with a prime minister

Assume the following model of policy choice. There are three groups of voters, $J = 1, 2, 3$, all of size (mass) unity. Groups coincide with electoral districts, each represented by a single legislator, $l=1, 2, 3$. Moreover, a prime minister, P, heads the government. Voters in district

J have preferences

$$w^J = c^J + H(g) = y - \tau + f^J + H(g),$$

where τ denotes taxes, f^J denotes transfers to group j, and g denotes a general public good benefiting all voters.

Politicians can appropriate rents and must choose through a legislative decision how these should be allocated. Denoting by r_i the rents captured by legislator i or the prime minister, we write the government budget constraint as

$$3\tau = g + \sum_J f^J + \sum_l r_l + r_P = g + f + r,$$

where f denotes aggregate transfers. Items in the government budget constraint must all be nonnegative, and $\mathbf{q}$ denotes the full policy vector.

The prime minister, P, proposes a policy vector, $\mathbf{q}$, and his proposal is subject to a vote in the legislature. The prime minister remains in office only if his proposal is accepted in parliament. Legislators' districts hold them accountable. The timing of the game is as follows:

(1) Voters formulate their reelection strategies, setting p_l contingent on the welfare level they have experienced. This strategy becomes publicly known. (2) The prime minister proposes the entire policy vector $\mathbf{q}$. (3) The legislature votes on the proposal. If a majority (at least two legislators) supports the proposal, it is implemented, and the prime minister remains in office. If not, the prime minister loses office and a default policy $\overline{\mathbf{q}}$ is implemented, with $\tau = r_l = \overline{r} > 0$ and $g = f^J = 0$. (4) Voters observe the outcome of the legislative decision and all elements in the policy vector. Elections are held. What will the level of public-goods provision be in this regime? Who will end up with positive rents, and who with transfers?

2. Adding a president

Now consider a presidential-congressional model. The framework is the same as in problem 1, but now, we have a president, P, instead of a prime minister. The congressional policy game has the following timing. (1) Two different agenda setters, a_τ and a_g, the "finance committee" and the "expenditure committee," respectively, are appointed among the three legislators. (2) Voters set the cutoff utilities ϖ^J in their reelection rules optimally, conditional on their legislator's status. (3) a_τ proposes a tax rate, τ. (4) Congress votes on the tax proposal; if it is approved by a majority, the tax proposal becomes law; if it is not, the default tax rate is $\overline{\tau} > 0$. (5) a_g proposes g, $\{f^J\}_{j=1,2,3}$, and $\{r_i\}_{i=1,2,3,P}$, subject to $3\tau \geq g + f + r$. (6) Congress votes on the allocation proposal: if the proposal is rejected by a majority, the default allocation is $g = 0$, $f^J \equiv \tau - r_l \geq 0$, $r_l = \overline{r}$. (7) The president decides whether to veto the decision of the Congress. If he does, the default allocation is implemented. (8) Voters observe everything and elections are held. The president is elected in national elections, and the legislators contest in their districts. Assume R to be large.

a. Construct an equilibrium in which public goods are provided at a level $H_g(g^*) = 1$.

b. Show that there are an infinite number of equilibria with $H_g(g^*) = 1$ and positive transfers for the district of a_g.

c. Compare the results of the model with a president and the model without one. Why does the addition of the president not change the equilibria?

3. Infinitely repeated presidential-congressional regime

In the framework of problems 1 and 2, now assume that there is no president. Consider an infinitely repeated game in which the following is played at each period: (1) Two different agenda setters, a_τ and a_g, the "finance committee" and the "expenditure committee," respectively, are appointed among the three legislators. (2) Voters set the cutoff utilities ϖ^J in their reelection rules optimally, conditional on their legislator's status. (3) a_τ proposes a tax rate, τ. (4) Congress votes on the tax proposal: if it is approved by a majority, the tax proposal becomes law; if not, the default tax rate is $\bar{\tau} > 0$. (5) a_g proposes g, $\{f^J\}$, and $\{r_l\}$ subject to $3\tau \geq g + f + r$. (6) Congress votes on the allocation proposal: if it is rejected by a majority, the default allocation is $g = 0$, $f^J \equiv \tau - r_l \geq 0$, $r_l = \bar{r}$. (7) Voters observe everything, and elections are held.

Assume there are no exogenous rents but there is an endogenously determined continuation value for reelection. Suppose that at the beginning of each period, each legislator is chosen with equal probability for each position a_g, a_τ, and $j \neq a_g, a_\tau$.

a. Construct a stationary equilibrium for this model in which $H_g(g^*) = 1$.

b. Compute the continuation value for staying in office, the rents gained by the politicians, and reservation utilities for voters.

4. The "caretaker government" subgame

In this problem, we consider a continuation game following the breakdown of a parliamentary coalition. In the same framework as that of the last three problems, assume that a "caretaker government"—a single legislator—is picked at random after the breakdown, voters reformulate their reelection rules, the caretaker legislator makes the entire budget proposal, and this proposal is approved or not by the legislature. Assume that if the coalition breaks down after this subgame, the defaults are given by $r_j = \bar{r}$ to all legislators and $g = 0$, $f = 0$, and $\tau = 0$. Solve the subgame and compute the expected payoffs for entering into this subgame.

5. Calculating the equilibria in the parliamentary regime

Using the results of problem 4, calculate the equilibria of the full model of parliamentary regimes (as in the text): (1) Two incumbent legislators (a_g, a_T) are appointed to act as expenditure and finance ministers, respectively. (2) Voters set their reservation utilities conditional on their legislator's status. (3) The finance minister, a_τ, proposes a tax rate τ. (4) The expenditure minister proposes expenditures $(g, \{f^J\}, \{r_l\})$ subject to the budget constraint and the proposed tax rate. (5) Either member of the government can veto the proposal. If neither does, the proposal passes and elections are held. (5′) If at least one of them vetoes, the government breaks down, and a default policy is implemented with payoffs as in problem 4. Under what conditions does an equilibrium with public good provided at a level of $H_g^{-1}(\frac{1}{2})$ exist?

6. Presidential line-item veto

Consider a presidential-congressional model with line-item veto. The framework is the same as in problem 1 only now we have a president, P, instead of a prime minister. The congressional policy game has the following timing: (1) An agenda-setter, a_g is appointed among the three legislators. (2) Voters set the cut-off utilities ϖ^J in their reelection in both congressional and presidential elections, conditional on the status of their legislator. (3) a_g proposes a tax rate, τ, g, $\{f^J\}_{j=1,2,3}$, and $\{r_i\}_{i=1,2,3,P}$ subject to $3\tau \geq g + f + r$. (4) Congress votes: if rejected by a majority, the default allocation is $\bar{\tau} > 0$, $g = 0$, $f^J \equiv \tau - r_l \geq 0$, $r_l = \bar{r}$. (5) The president decides whether to veto the whole public goods program, g, or any of the specific cash transfers, f^J. If he vetoes, he may take the resources saved as private rents, r_p, or to lower taxes. (6) Voters observe everything and elections are held. The president is held accountable in national elections and the legislators in their districts.

It is assumed that the benefits from the public goods program are such that $H(g) - H(0) \geq \frac{2}{3}g$. Starting with the veto stage (5), the president may default and use all available resources for private rents. In order to avoid this, he must at least be given rents satisfying

$$\gamma r + R \geq \gamma\left(g + \sum_J f^J\right).$$

We will first assume that the rents R are large enough so that this is always satisfied.

a. Show that the president will not veto the public goods program.

b. Show that at the veto stage, the president will veto the transfer to the group that would receive the largest cash transfers under the allocation of the legislative game.

c. Show that the president must return all the funds saved from cancelling the transfer program to the tax payers.

d. Compute the equilibrium allocation of rents, public goods provision, transfers, and taxes in the legislative game and discuss the results.

IV DYNAMIC POLITICS

So far we have analyzed once-and-for-all policy decisions and their determinants. We are now ready to take another step by studying sequential collective policy decisions. Thus we will consider environments in which policy decisions are made at different points in time and agents in the private sector also face an intertemporal optimization problem. Methodologically, this introduces novel and important features into the analysis. Expectations of future economic policies—by the private sector and by current policymakers—become an essential part of the analysis. This gives rise to a new incentive constraint on policy formation referring to the credibility of policy. In a dynamic environment, state variables reflect earlier private decisions and collective policy decisions. These state variables also play an important role in the analysis, opening the door for multiple equilibria and strategic behavior by policymakers at different points in time.

We focus on two sets of policy problems. One involves the taxation of capital and other determinants of private savings and investment. The other involves the accumulation of public debt or public capital. These dynamic problems have particular economic relevance, because these policies influence economic growth. The influence is either direct or, most often, indirect, working via the incentives for private investment and innovation. For both sets of policy problems, it is difficult to account for observed policy regularities with the theory of optimal taxation or, more generally, any theory assuming a benevolent government facing no incentive constraint.

For instance, the basic principles of optimal taxation suggest that labor should be taxed much more heavily than capital, as the latter tax base is more elastic, particularly in the long run. The models of Chamley (1986) and Lucas (1990) prescribe a tax rate on capital income that starts out high but rapidly converges to zero as the economy approaches its steady state. Yet tax rates on capital vary considerably across countries and fluctuate over time, with an upward trend until the late 1980s. In many countries, estimates of effective tax rates on capital are typically as high as, and often higher than, tax rates on consumption or labor.

Similarly, Barro's (1979) tax-smoothing model of deficits might successfully explain wartime deficits, but it cannot explain the persistent accumulation of debt occurring in many industrial countries since the 1970s, nor the endemic deficits observed in some developing countries, notably in Latin America. Under similar circumstances, some countries have built up massive debts, whereas others have not.

Moreover, as discussed throughout this part, data on policies, investment, and political institutions suggest that social, political, and institutional factors play an important role in shaping fiscal policy.

We devote this part to possible explanations of such phenomena as well as to studying the political determinants of economic growth. As already mentioned, we extend the theory formulated in parts 1 and 2 to allow for sequential decisions at different points in time.

Chapter 11 presents a methodological discussion of the new issues arising in dynamic policy problems, both in the abstract and in some simple examples.

Chapter 12 deals with capital taxation. We start by discussing the well-known capital levy problem, which is perhaps the clearest example of how incentive constraints might lead to credibility problems in policy. We then introduce other incentive constraints associated with politics and elections and with tax competition when capital is internationally mobile.

Chapter 13 surveys alternative models of public debt accumulation. Here we show how interest groups' or politicians' optimal behavior might explain policy myopia leading to debt accumulation or delays in the stabilization of an unsustainable deficit. We also illustrate how incumbent policymakers might want to use debt as a strategic tool to influence future policy choices. This idea has many applications that go beyond public debt: for instance, with regard to privatization, institution design, or public investment.

Finally, in chapter 14 we briefly discuss the literature on politics and economic growth. Drawing on ideas from this and other parts, we discuss how growth is affected by the general- and special-interest politics addressed in part 2 and also by the political instability and policy myopia studied in chapter 13.

We keep the economic model as simple as possible throughout this part. Except for an example in chapter 11, we always rely on a simple two-period economic model that is kept very similar across chapters. The simplifying assumption of a two-period horizon is needed to obtain closed-form analytical solutions. Most results are likely to generalize to an infinite horizon, but we would typically need to solve the model numerically rather than analytically. Politics is analyzed with many of the tools introduced in part 1 and used in part 2: models of pre- and postelection politics and models with opportunistic and partisan politicians. Throughout this part, however, we neglect the agency problem that took center stage in part 3. As a result, the delegation games are much simpler but less rich in institutional detail. This reflects the original contributions underlying these chapters, many of which were written in the late 1980s or early 1990s and therefore could not take into account the recent progress in understanding the policy consequences of different political institutions.

11 Dynamic Policy Problems

In an intertemporal setting, the consequences of any given economic policy depend crucially on the expectations of future policy held by the private sector. Likewise, expected future policies also influence current policy decisions. Modeling expectation formation correctly is far from easy, however. When private agents and policymakers are rational and act purposefully, we need to study a dynamic game. Expectations in such a game are based on the equilibrium outcome of the game's determining future policies, notwithstanding the structure of that game. Furthermore, actual policies are formulated sequentially, period after period, taking this expectations formation mechanism into account but taking as given the history of past decisions—as summarized by the relevant state variables. Hence expectations must be solved jointly with the equilibrium policy.

Since the seminal work by Kydland and Prescott (1977) and by Calvo (1978), it has been understood that sequential decision making gives rise to important incentive constraints on policy formation. In a dynamic setting, policymakers generally lose control of private-sector expectations. In the absence of a strong commitment technology, private agents expect policymakers to make optimal choices at future dates: they expect future policy to be ex post optimal. When there are relevant externalities or, more generally, when policymakers lack some policy instruments (for instance, nondistorting taxes), ex post optimality can be very different from ex ante optimality. An ex ante optimal policy rule is the best one at the starting date of the dynamic policy game. Such a policy takes into account all intertemporal effects of economic policies, including those on, say, private capital accumulation decisions. An ex post optimal policy rule, in contrast, describes the policies appearing optimal from the perspective of any later date, with all previous private decisions, such as capital accumulation decisions, taken as given. Because rational private agents expect policies to be ex post optimal, even a benevolent social planner may be forced to enact ex ante suboptimal economic policies. To use a catchier phrase, such suboptimality reflects a lack of *credibility*, for only ex post optimal policies can be credible and thus will be anticipated by rational individuals.

Ex post optimality is relevant not only for normative policy evaluation but also from a positive point of view. To understand the determinants of economic policy, we must realize that policymakers are engaged in a dynamic game. Their current decisions thus reflect contemporaneous incentive constraints but may also be motivated by the desire to relax future incentive constraints. Adding politics further enriches the dynamic policy game, since equilibrium policy no longer reflects the wishes of a single decision maker. Politicians, voters, and organized lobbies interact contemporaneously and over time; moreover, their identity may change, because elections or other economic and political events may change the set of players over time. Despite the many possible facets of this dynamic economic and political interaction, a common method can be used to study these problems. The goal of this chapter is to illustrate this method. To highlight the new aspects of the analysis, we abstract from politics. Throughout the chapter, we thus describe the private sector through a representative consumer and the government through a benevolent social planner.

We start in section 11.1 with a general discussion of how to solve dynamic policy games in an infinite-horizon economy. We provide a precise definition of the appropriate equilibrium concepts in a general dynamic setting with sequential policy choice; thus we contrast two solution concepts that apply under different assumptions about the rules of the game. One is the equilibrium with policy commitments; here, a policy rule is chosen once and for all at the start of the game. The other is the equilibrium without such commitments (the literature also calls it "equilibrium under discretion"); here, policy is chosen sequentially, and in every period the government reoptimizes. We draw in our analysis on the work by Krusell, Quadrini, and Rios-Rull (1997).

Section 11.2 illustrates these concepts through three simple examples. Since we want to solve the examples analytically, the economic environment we use is simpler than that in section 11.1: either we study a two-period economy, or we rely on other simplifying assumptions. These three examples illustrate the root of the credibility problem in dynamic taxation, the prospective welfare losses caused by the credibility problem, and the possibility of manipulating state variables to relax incentive constraints in later periods.

11.1   Analyzing Dynamic Policy Games

This section illustrates the concepts of equilibrium used throughout this part of the book. Since we want these concepts to be fairly general but nonetheless defined with some precision, we need a rather high level of abstraction and a complex notation. Parts of this section may therefore appear somewhat pedantic. Understanding all the implications of these concepts is not easy, however, and it has taken the existing literature quite some time to clarify these issues.

The first subsection lays out the notation and defines the economic equilibrium for an exogenously given policy rule. The next subsection discusses two concepts of equilibrium in which the policy rule is made endogenous. Different equilibrium concepts correspond to different rules for policy choice. Thus which equilibrium concept is more appropriate in a particular instance depends on the institutional process governing policy formation.

11.1.1   Economic Equilibrium

Consider an infinite-horizon dynamic economy in discrete time, with a representative consumer small enough (of measure zero) to take aggregate (average) variables as given. Let q_t be a policy variable chosen by the government in period t, such as a tax rate. Let u_t^i be an individual choice variable chosen at date t, such as individual consumption or labor supply, and let s_t^i be a state variable predetermined at date t but chosen by our atomistic individual in the previous period, including the holdings of variables such as wealth, capital stock, or public debt. Finally, let s_t be a corresponding average (aggregate) state variable, also predetermined at time t. All these variables can also be vectors. Even though we abstract from individual heterogeneity, we thus rely on the same notation as in previous parts, letting superscripted and nonsuperscripted variables denote individual and average outcomes, respectively.

Consumer preferences are represented by the objective function

$$\sum_{t=0}^{\infty} \beta^t R\left(u_t^i, s_t\right),$$ (11.1)

where β is a discount factor and $R(\cdot)$ is a concave utility function. The consumer is subject to a dynamic constraint (typically a budget constraint or a resource constraint) that we write as

$$s_{t+1}^i = S\left(u_t^i, s_t^i, s_t, q_t\right).$$ (11.2)

Two points in this formulation are worth noting. First, we distinguish between the choice of the state variable made by the individual consumer, s^i, and the corresponding economy-wide average, s. Even in our representative consumer economy, this distinction is essential, for in most examples of this part the economic equilibrium is not a Pareto optimum. In our formulation, the average state variable enters the consumer's preferences and dynamic constraint; this could capture externalities or general equilibrium prices, for instance. We could also have included the average control variable u_t, corresponding to u_t^i, without changing the essence of the argument. Second, we assume that policies chosen at time t have an immediate economic effect via the consumer's dynamic constraint. We could also have assumed, without changing the essence of the argument, that policies have a direct effect via the consumer's preferences or that they are implemented with some delay.

The solution to the representative consumer's intertemporal optimization problem depends on his expectations of policies and average states in all future periods. Hence we can express his optimization problem recursively only once we have formulated a policy rule and a recursive law of motion for the average state variable.

Specifically, suppose that policy is set according to

$$q_t = \Psi(s_t),$$ (11.3)

a state-contingent, time-invariant policy rule that is constrained to feasible policies, that is, to those policies satisfying the relevant constraints, such as the government budget constraint.

Suppose also that given the function $\Psi(\cdot)$, the law of motion of the average state variable can be expressed recursively as

$$s_{t+1} = G(s_t; \Psi). \tag{11.4}$$

Note that the function $G(\cdot)$ depends on the policy rule $\Psi(\cdot)$. This captures two things. First, the direct mapping from s_t to q_t and on to s_{t+1}^i via (11.2). Second, the equilibrium law of motion of the average state must be consistent with the consumer's optimal intertemporal choices, which in turn depend on the policy rule through expectations of future policy. In other words, the rational expectations of future policy change with the policy rule, which changes optimal private behavior and thus the law of motion of the economy. At this point, this formulation is a bit vacuous, as we have not precisely defined the state variable s_t. Most applications seek a formulation over a minimal state space, however.

On the basis of this notation, we can express the consumer optimum as the solution of the following dynamic programming problem:

$$W\left(s_t^i, s_t; \Psi\right) = \max_{u_t^i} \left[R\left(u_t^i, s_t\right) + \beta W\left(s_{t+1}^i, s_{t+1}; \Psi\right) \right], \tag{11.5}$$

subject to (11.2), (11.3) and (11.4). To emphasize the policy rule's importance for characterizing the economic equilibrium, in (11.5) we made explicit the dependency of the value function $W(\cdot)$ on Ψ. This reflects two features. The policy rule Ψ has been used to substitute for and eliminate q, such that the value function is defined over the average state s but not over the policy instrument q. Also, the law of motion of the state, $G(\cdot)$, depends on Ψ. Naturally, W also reflects the law of motion of the average state, G, but since this mapping is not our central concern, we leave it implicit.

The solution to this problem yields a law of motion for s^i that we can express as

$$s_{t+1}^i = G^i\left(s_t^i, s_t; \Psi\right). \tag{11.6}$$

For a given policy rule Ψ, the law of motion of the average state variable (11.4) and the individual solution (11.6) must be consistent with one another in equilibrium. The consumer problem also yields a solution for the choice variable u_t^i as a function of the individual and aggregate state, which is also part of the equilibrium. To simplify the notation, we leave this solution implicit in our formal definition:

DEFINITION 5   An **economic equilibrium under a policy rule** Ψ is a law of motion for the average state variable, $G(\cdot; \Psi)$, a law of motion for the individual consumer state variable, $G^i(\cdot; \Psi)$, and a value function $W(\cdot; \Psi)$ such that

1. The function $G^i(\cdot; \Psi)$ is optimal for the consumer and the function $W(\cdot; \Psi)$ solves his dynamic programming problem, given the policy rule Ψ and the function $G(\cdot; \Psi)$.

2. The consumer choices are consistent with the average law of motion: $G^i(s^i_t, s_t, ; \Psi) = G(s_t; \Psi)$ for any $s^i_t = s_t$ and for any Ψ.

Note that the policy rule is an integral part of the definition of an economic equilibrium. Without a policy rule, we cannot pin down expectations and thus cannot define the law of motion of the economy. This explains why it is difficult to make policy endogenous in a dynamic economy: we must solve jointly for the economic equilibrium and that of the policy formation game.

11.1.2 Equilibrium Policy Rules

We now turn to a characterization of equilibrium policy rules. Throughout this subsection, we assume that the government is benevolent and maximizes the consumer's objective function (11.1). Even so, a conflict of interest generally remains between the government and the representative consumer, for the government, unlike the consumer, takes into account the effect of its choices on aggregate economic behavior. With externalities or tax distortions, the allocation the government prefers would thus not be implemented in an economic equilibrium. This conflict of interest is one of the important underlying causes of the incentive constraints we are about to discuss.

Ex Ante Optimal Policy We start with a normative benchmark, namely the best possible policy rule Ψ from the point of view of the benevolent government. Suppose that the government chooses the policy rule Ψ once and for all. The government thus makes an irreversible commitment to Ψ but nevertheless takes into account how this affects expectations from date t onward and, through expectations, the law of motion of the economy in (11.4). Then we have

DEFINITION 6 An **equilibrium under commitment** is a policy rule Ψ, a law of motion for the average state variable $G(\cdot; \Psi)$, a law of motion for the individual consumer state variable $G^i(\cdot; \Psi)$, and a value function $W(\cdot; \Psi)$ such that

1. $G(\cdot; \Psi)$, $G^i(\cdot; \Psi)$, and $W(\cdot; \Psi)$ constitute an economic equilibrium under Ψ.

2. Ψ is optimal for the government, taking into account how Ψ affects the economic equilibrium.

Such a policy rule is often called the "ex ante optimal policy rule" to reflect the commitment assumption. It is fulfilled by a function Ψ maximizing the left-hand side of (11.5). Solutions to dynamic policy problems, such as those in Calvo 1978 or Chamley 1986, are examples of ex ante optimal policies conforming to this definition.

A qualification is, however, appropriate at this point. The basic policy problem for a benevolent government under commitment is to choose a sequence of policies $\mathbf{q} \equiv \{q_t\}_{t=0}^{\infty}$

so as to maximize (11.1), subject to an initial condition, and the equilibrium response of private choices u_t^i and $s_t^i = s_t$ to $\mathbf{q}$ at all t. Expressing the solution, say $\mathbf{q}^*$, to this problem in the form of a time-invariant policy rule may require the introduction of fictional state variables.[1] Alternatively, $\mathbf{q}^*$ may have to be expressed as a time-dependent rule $\Psi_t(s_t)$ (which would also require a slight reformulation of definitions 5 and 6). Whether $\mathbf{q}^*$ can be expressed as a time-invariant policy rule is non-essential for the following argument regarding equilibrium policy rules without commitment.

Example 2 of this chapter illustrates an equilibrium with commitment with a time-varying policy rule. Part 5 provides various examples of time-invariant equilibrium policy rules. Problem 5 in chapter 15 gives an example of a dynamic policy problem, where the equilibrium policy rules in the presence and absence of commitment fit nicely with the formalization in this section.

Equilibria without Commitment   Irreversible policy commitments are typically not enforceable. We have already discussed some problems with the commitment assumption in parts 1 and 3. There the problem concerned politicians' ability to commit before an election to a policy to be carried out after the election. Here the fact that policies are carried out sequentially over time adds another layer of complications, in that most policy decisions can be reversed or modified at later points in time under normal legislative procedures. The literature often refers to regimes of sequential policy choice as discretion to reflect the margins for reoptimization. In a regime without commitment, even a benevolent government with preferences as given in (11.1) will generally be unable to implement an ex ante optimal policy. Whereas such a policy is optimal from the vantage point of the starting date, it is not from the vantage point of later dates. This is the well-known "time-inconsistency problem" of optimal policy discovered by Kydland and Prescott (1977) and Calvo (1978). An ex ante optimal but time-inconsistent policy is not credible in the eyes of private agents, because the government has an incentive to deviate from it. If policy is chosen sequentially over time, the equilibrium policy rule must satisfy an additional incentive constraint ruling out policy surprises.

More precisely, consider the same dynamic economy, but suppose now that in each period t, the government can reoptimize and freely choose a policy $\tilde{q}_t$, possibly different from that prescribed by the policy rule Ψ. In equilibrium, the government must have no incentive to deviate from the proposed policy rule, given the equilibrium continuation values of this dynamic game—that is, given that the private sector uses the proposed policy rule to form expectations about future policies.

---

1. Chang (1998) discusses how to formulate and derive equilibria in infinite-horizon policy games. Building on Kydland and Prescott 1980, he shows how to formulate the policymaker's problem in Calvo 1978 as a recursive dynamic programming problem, both in the presence and absence of commitment.

To formalize this condition, consider a one-period deviation $\tilde{q}_t$ from a given policy rule Ψ in period t. From period $t+1$ onward, however, policy is expected to revert to Ψ. Let the modified law of motion of the average state variable, given the deviation $\tilde{q}_t$ and the expected future behavior according to the rule Ψ, be

$$s_{t+1} = \tilde{G}(s_t, \tilde{q}_t; \Psi). \tag{11.7}$$

The effects of this one-period deviation on private behavior can therefore be obtained by solving a modified dynamic programming problem, namely

$$\widetilde{W}\left(s_t^i, s_t, \tilde{q}_t; \Psi\right) = \max_{u_t^i} \left[R\left(u_t^i, s_t\right) + \beta W\left(s_{t+1}^i, s_{t+1}; \Psi\right)\right], \tag{11.8}$$

subject to (11.2), (11.7), and to (11.3) from $t+1$ onward. Notice that the value function W on the right-hand side is still as defined in (11.5). The modified value function $\widetilde{W}$ thus summarizes the effects on the individual consumer's welfare of the one-period deviation, $\tilde{q}_t$, given the modified laws of motion of the average state, and given that expectations are consistent with the proposed policy rule Ψ from the next period on and hence with the value function W. The solution of this modified dynamic programming problem gives a new law of motion for the individual consumer state variable:

$$s_{t+1}^i = \widetilde{G}^i\left(s_t^i, s_t, \tilde{q}_t; \Psi\right). \tag{11.9}$$

In the economic equilibrium corresponding to the one-period policy deviation, the function $\widetilde{G}^i(\cdot)$ must be consistent with the average law of motion $\tilde{G}(\cdot)$ in (11.7). More precisely:

DEFINITION 7   An **economic equilibrium after a one-period deviation $\tilde{q}_t$ from the policy rule** Ψ is a law of motion for the average state variable, $\tilde{G}(\cdot; \Psi)$, a law of motion for the individual consumer state variable, $\widetilde{G}^i(\cdot; \Psi)$, a modified value function $\widetilde{W}(\cdot; \Psi)$, and a set of functions $G(\cdot; \Psi)$, $G^i(\cdot; \Psi)$, and $W(\cdot; \Psi)$, such that

1. The functions $G(\cdot; \Psi)$, $G^i(\cdot; \Psi)$, and $W(\cdot; \Psi)$ constitute an economic equilibrium under the policy rule Ψ according to definition 5.

2. The function $\widetilde{G}^i(\cdot; \Psi)$ is optimal for the consumer, and the function $\widetilde{W}(\cdot; \Psi)$ solves his modified dynamic programming problem in (11.8), given the deviation $\tilde{q}_t$, the policy rule Ψ, the function $\tilde{G}(\cdot; \Psi)$, and the value function $W(\cdot; \Psi)$.

3. Consumer choices are consistent with the average law of motion: $\widetilde{G}^i(s_t^i, s_t, \tilde{q}_t; \Psi) = \tilde{G}(s_t, \tilde{q}_t; \Psi)$ for any $s_t^i = s_t$, $\tilde{q}_t$, and Ψ.

If the government chooses its policies sequentially, period after period, then the equilibrium policy rule must be self-enforcing in the sense that the government has no incentive to deviate from the rule. That is, in every period and from every state of the economy, the equilibrium policy rule must prescribe a policy choice that is optimal for the government, given that the private sector expects the policy rule to be followed in all subsequent periods and states. This requirement basically coincides with the condition for Markov-perfect equilibrium in game theory—see Fudenberg and Tirole 1993, chap. 13, for an example—except that here, policy is conditional only on the aggregate state and not each individual state.[2] More precisely:

DEFINITION 8   An **equilibrium without commitment** is a policy rule Ψ, a law of motion for the average state variable $G(\cdot; \Psi)$, a law of motion for the individual consumer state variable $G^i(\cdot; \Psi)$, a value function $W(\cdot; \Psi)$, and a set of functions $\tilde{G}(\cdot; \Psi)$, $\tilde{G}^i(\cdot; \Psi)$, and $\tilde{W}(\cdot; \Psi)$ such that

1. $G(\cdot; \Psi)$, $G^i(\cdot; \Psi)$ and $W(\cdot; \Psi)$ constitute an economic equilibrium under Ψ according to Definition 5.

2. $\tilde{G}(\cdot; \Psi)$, $\tilde{G}^i(\cdot; \Psi)$ and $\tilde{W}(\cdot; \Psi)$ constitute an economic equilibrium after a one-period deviation from Ψ according to Definition 7.

3. The government has no incentive to deviate from Ψ in any period and for any state variable, taking into account the economic equilibrium after a one-period deviation:

$$\Psi(s_t) = \underset{\tilde{q}_t}{\text{Arg max}}\ \tilde{W}\left(s_t^i, s_t, \tilde{q}_t; \Psi\right) \quad \text{for all} \quad s_t \quad \text{and for} \quad s_t^i = s_t. \tag{11.10}$$

Typically, the ex ante optimal policy under commitment differs from the equilibrium policy without commitment: this is the time-inconsistency problem. A policy rule relates future expected policy to the future expected state. Furthermore, current private choices are related to future expected policy. Once the future state has been realized, however, the link to private choices via expectations formation is gone. If the ex ante optimal policy is the basis for private expectations, it may thus be optimal for the government to deviate from it temporarily. In the equilibrium without commitment, however, such deviations are ruled out. Because the equilibrium must be self-enforcing, we must impose an additional incentive constraint, namely equation (11.10). Under this constraint, the government chooses not to deviate from the equilibrium rule. If the incentive constraint binds, however, then there must be an overall loss of welfare; because the government's choice set is more narrow, it must be worse off. The equilibrium policy rule under discretion thus leaves the government worse off compared to the ex ante optimum. That is, commitment is valuable because it enables the government to relax an incentive constraint. In more practical terms,

---

2. The distinction is similar to that between subgame perfection and sequential rationality in an anonymous game (see Chari and Kehoe 1990 for a discussion of these concepts).

the benefit of commitment is enhanced credibility and ability to influence private-sector expectations.

11.1.3 Discussion

From a positive point of view, imposing the incentive constraint (11.10) modifies equilibrium policy rules in two important ways. First, equilibrium policy rules become more myopic, in the sense that they tend to ignore the long-run effects of economic policy on private behavior. Such long-run effects operate through expectation formation, but the incentive constraint forces the government to ignore some of them. Examples of myopic policies that will be studied in this and later parts include suboptimally high taxation of wealth, suboptimal public debt issue, and suboptimally high inflation. Second, the government may want to manipulate state variables to try to relax this constraint (11.10) in later periods. For instance, by choosing the denomination or the maturity of public debt, the government may make it more or less difficult to renege on its obligations in later periods, affecting policy credibility and equilibrium interest rates.

As the formalism above indicates, it is quite hard to compute and characterize equilibrium policy rules without commitment. On the one hand, the economic equilibrium and the policy rule are jointly determined. On the other hand, to impose the incentive constraint we must consider economic equilibria after hypothetical deviations from the rule. Except in very simple examples, one cannot compute analytical solutions in an infinite-horizon economy. Instead, researchers have tried to compute such equilibria numerically. Computation exploits the recursive formulation and the fixed-point condition implicit in the incentive constraint (11.10). That is, the equilibrium policy rule Ψ obtained by maximizing the modified value function $\widetilde{W}$ should be consistent with the rule entering into $\widetilde{W}$ and into W. To verify that, we must compute both an equilibrium under the policy rule Ψ and an equilibrium under an arbitrary deviation $\tilde{q}$ as well. For an illuminating exposition of how to go about this procedure, see Krusell, Quadrini, and Rios-Rull 1997. To avoid numerical computation, however, we will largely rely on very simple examples with a finite horizon, where the solution can be computed analytically, starting from the last period and moving backward.

The analysis in this section can be extended to more-general settings. At a conceptual level, it is relatively straightforward to add heterogeneity among consumers or to change the government objective function. The distinction between equilibria with and without commitment concerns the sequence of events, not the contents of the government objective function. This distinction and the corresponding definitions would carry over (with some adaptations) to political settings like those discussed in previous parts, in which the policy rule solves the optimization problem of a median voter or of a partisan politician or maximizes a weighted social welfare function, as in the equilibria with probabilistic voting. The specific difficulties of finding an equilibrium multiply quickly, however, because the state space easily becomes very complicated in dynamic economies with individual heterogeneity. Krusell, Quadrini, and Rios-Rull (1997) discuss in detail how to compute a median-voter equilibrium with growth and capital taxation.

It is also possible to enrich the mechanism of expectations formation to allow for reputational effects. But this too leads to considerable complexity. The incentive constraint (11.10) in the equilibrium without commitment requires the equilibrium policy rule to be self-enforcing in each period and from every state, and the policy rule is postulated to depend only on the current state, $\Psi(s_t)$. If the state vector included not only current variables, but also longer histories including past policy choices, we would be violating the spirit of the Markov assumption. This would open the door for reputational equilibria, though, in which the incentive constraint could be relaxed if the private sector punishes unexpected deviations from the equilibrium policy rule by reverting to unfavorable expectations about future policies. We will discuss such reputational equilibria in chapter 12 on capital taxation and in chapter 15 on monetary policy.

Finally, the incentive constraint (11.10) relates to the strategic interaction between the government and the private sector in connection with expectations formation or, more generally, with policy credibility. Chapter 13 on public debt issue and chapter 14 on growth also discuss another set of incentive constraints, these concerning the strategic interaction between different policymakers choosing policy at different points in time. Such political incentive constraints reflect specific features of political processes and institutions that are best discussed in the context of a particular economic and political model.

11.2   Examples

In the remainder of this chapter, we illustrate by simple examples some of the concepts introduced so far. Problems 1 through 5 of this chapter provide further illustrations.

11.2.1   Example 1: Public Debt Repayment

We start with an example adapted from Persson and Tabellini 1990, section 6.4, illustrating the tension between ex ante and ex post optimality. Relative to the treatment in section 11.1, we simplify by assuming a finite rather than an infinite horizon. Consider a two-period representative-consumer economy without capital, $t = 1, 2$. Policy is set by a benevolent social planner who maximizes the representative individual's utility, namely

$$w^i = c_1^i + c_2^i + V\left(x_1^i\right) + V\left(x_2^i\right) + (1+\alpha)g_1 + (1-\alpha)g_2, \tag{11.11}$$

where the notation is as in earlier chapters, with c_t and g_t denoting private and public consumption, respectively. The parameter $\alpha > 0$ implies that public consumption is more valuable in the first than in the second period; for simplicity, the marginal utility of private and public consumption is constant. $V(.)$ is a well-behaved concave utility function. Leisure and labor, x_t and l_t, must sum to unity in each period t. Taxes are distorting, and the consumer budget constraints are

$$c_1^i + b^i = (1 - \tau_1)l_1^i$$
$$c_2^i = (1 - \tau_2)l_2^i + (1 - \theta)\rho b^i, \tag{11.12}$$

where τ_t is a labor tax rate, ρ the gross interest rate, b^i the individual holding of public debt—which is the only available form of savings—and θ a tax on savings.

Solving the consumer problem leads to labor supply functions $L(\tau_t)$ identical to those in chapter 6. The private state variable b^i depends on the policy rule determining the future tax rate on wealth. Denote the tax rate the consumer expects in period 1 by θ^e. By the absence of discounting and the linearities in the utility function, an interior equilibrium for the private state variable b^i requires $\rho = 1/(1 - \theta^e)$. That is, individual debt holdings satisfy

$$b^i = 0 \quad \text{if} \quad \rho(1 - \theta^e) < 1$$
$$b^i \in \left[0, (1 - \tau_1)l_1^i\right] \quad \text{iff} \quad \rho(1 - \theta^e) = 1. \tag{11.13}$$

Finally, the government budget constraints are

$$g_1 = \tau_1 l_1 + b$$
$$\rho(1 - \theta)b + g_2 = \tau_2 l_2. \tag{11.14}$$

Thus there are two policy vectors, one for each period, namely $\mathbf{q}_1 = (g_1, \tau_1, b)$ and $\mathbf{q}_2 = (g_2, \tau_2, \theta)$. No state variables exist in period 1, and the only relevant aggregate state variable in period 2 is the outstanding debt b. In equilibrium, $b^i = b$, and the equilibrium law of motion of this aggregate state variable must be consistent with the individual optimality condition, equation (11.13).

Ex Ante Optimal Policies   Suppose policy decisions on $\mathbf{q}_1$ and $\mathbf{q}_2$ are made once and for all at the start of period 1. What is the optimal tax and spending policy? To answer this question we now describe the equilibrium under commitment, as defined in section 11.1. We denote policy outcomes in this equilibrium by a superscript C (for "commitment").

Under this timing, any policy rule $\mathbf{q}_2 = \mathbf{\Psi}^C(b)$ is immediately incorporated into private-sector expectations. Hence $\theta^e = \theta$ for any value of b, and wealth taxes are reflected one for one into higher interest rates on public debt. Thus the government's choice of θ is irrelevant for private choices (as long as $\theta < 1$). For simplicity, we simply set $\theta^C(b) = 0$. Moreover, since $\alpha > 0$ and the marginal utility of public consumption is constant, it is optimal to spend only in period 1. Hence $g_2^C(b) = 0$. The government then distributes taxes over the two available tax bases, l_1 and l_2, so as to minimize tax distortions. With identical labor supply elasticities in each period, Ramsey's principle of optimal taxation implies $\tau_2^C(b) = \tau_1^C$. A condition equating the marginal utility of private and public consumption, also taking into account tax distortions, then pins down these common tax rates:

$$1 + \alpha = 1/(1 + \epsilon_L(\tau_t C)), \qquad t = 1, 2, \tag{11.15}$$

where $\epsilon_L(\tau) \equiv \tau L_\tau / L < 0$ is the elasticity of labor supply.[3] Thus optimal public consumption in period 1 amounts to $g_1^C = 2\tau_1^C L(\tau_1^C)$, and public debt is used to distribute tax distortions over both periods and implement the optimal tax rule: $b_C = \frac{1}{2} g_1^C$. With this, we have fully characterized the equilibrium under commitment.

Equilibrium without Commitment   Suppose instead that policy choices are made sequentially, period by period. Thus at the start of period 1 the government chooses the vector of policies $\mathbf{q}_1$, then at the start of period 2, it chooses $\mathbf{q}_2$. Having observed economic policies for that period, the private consumer makes his decisions. The government is benevolent and maximizes the representative consumer's welfare. Since binding policy promises across periods are not possible, this setting corresponds to the equilibrium without commitment defined in the previous section; we denote this equilibrium by a ^{D} superscript (for discretion).

Here we must impose an incentive constraint, the analogue of (11.10). In a two-period setting, this incentive constraint is easy to impose: equilibrium policy must be optimal ex post from the vantage point of every period to which it refers. Thus to compute the equilibrium, we start from the last-period policy rule, $\mathbf{q}_2 = \mathbf{\Psi}^D(b)$.

Consider the government optimization problem in period 2. The resource constraint implies that $c_2^i = L(\tau_2) - g_2$.[4] Inserting this into (11.11) and simplifying, we can write the government optimization problem in period 2 as

$$\max_{\tau_2, g_2, \theta} [(L(\tau_2) - g_2) + V(1 - L(\tau_2)) + (1 - \alpha)g_2],$$

subject to the ex post government budget constraint, namely $\rho(1 - \theta)b + g_2 = \tau_2 L(\tau_2)$, the

---

3. Inserting the government budget constraint into the consumer utility function, taking the first-order condition with respect to τ_t, and invoking the envelope theorem, we get

$$-L(\tau_t) + (1 + \alpha)(L(\tau_t) + \tau_t L_\tau(\tau_t)) = 0,$$

from which (11.15) follows.

4. By Walras's law, in this one-good economy, the private and government budget constraints imply the resource constraint. Note that $L(\tau_2)$ is still the relevant labor supply function, even under this timing. As discussed in problem 2 of this chapter, this is not a general property. In this example, it is implied by our assumption of linear preferences for c_2.

second equation in (11.14). Clearly, if $b > 0$, the optimal policy entails $\theta^D(b) = 1$: since labor taxes are distorting, the ex post optimal policy in period 2 must always be to renege on any outstanding debt. Moreover, as under commitment, it remains optimal to set $g_2^D(b) = 0$ (since $\alpha > 0$ and labor taxes are distorting). Together, this implies that period 2 labor is not taxed at all: $\tau_2^D(b) = 0$.

Anticipating this outcome in period 1, private agents correctly expect $\theta^e = \theta^D(b) = 1$ for any positive b. Hence nobody is willing to buy any debt from the government. In the equilibrium with discretion, the ex post optimality constraint prevents the government from issuing any debt at all, so that $b^D = 0$. The government thus faces two separate budget constraints, one for each period. Equation (11.15) still gives the equilibrium tax rate in period 1. Thus $\tau_1^D = \tau_1^C$. Since $\tau_2^D(b) = 0$, however, we now have $g_1^D = \tau_1^C L(\tau_1^C) = \frac{1}{2} g_1^C$. Equilibrium public consumption is half its value in the equilibrium with commitment, since the government loses the proceeds of taxation in period 2.

Thus lack of commitment results in a loss of welfare. The government cannot credibly promise to repay its debts and underprovides valuable public consumption because it cannot spread the costs of taxation optimally over time. Naturally, this simple model abstracts from other costs of reneging on public debt, such as disruption to financial markets, arbitrary redistribution, or loss of reputation in other government contracts with the private sector, that mitigate the incentives to renege on public debt and thus contribute to relaxing this particular incentive constraint. We will return to this point in chapter 12.

The ideas illustrated in this simple example easily generalize to other forms of taxation of wealth, such as capital taxes or inflation. The tax on any asset suffers from a fundamental credibility problem—the so-called capital levy problem. Ex ante—before the asset is accumulated—the supply of the tax base is elastic with respect to the tax rate. But ex post—once the asset has been accumulated—the supply of the tax base becomes completely inelastic. This drastic change in elasticity causes the credibility problem, by creating incentives for policy surprises in the form of capital levies. Chapter 12 deals at length with such credibility problems, their consequences, and their prospective resolution in the classical setting of capital taxation. The next example illustrates the capital levy problem in yet another incarnation, namely the choice of an optimal inflation tax in an infinite-horizon economy.

11.2.2   Example 2: Inflation and Labor Taxation

Consider an economy populated by identical representative consumers, each of whom has an infinite-horizon discounted present-value objective like (11.1). In each period, consumers derive utility from the consumption of a single good, c, and of leisure, x, and from real balances at the end of the period, m. Specifically, their per-period utility function (the equivalent of $R(.)$ in the previous section) is of the familiar quasi-linear form:

$$w_t^i = c_t^i + V\left(x_t^i\right) + U\left(m_t^i\right). \tag{11.16}$$

There is no capital or debt, so savings can only take the form of real balances. The period t time and budget constraints are

$$l_t^i + x_t^i = 1 \tag{11.17}$$
$$m_t^i = (1 - \pi_t)m_{t-1}^i + (1 - \tau_t)l_t^i - c_t^i.$$

Thus, as in the previous example, the consumer splits his time between leisure and work and faces a distortionary labor tax. The inflation tax, measured as $\pi_t = \frac{P_t - P_{t-1}}{P_t}$, dilutes last period's real balances in value. The government controls the price level, and hence inflation, in each period, through its control of the nominal money stock.[5] Notice that $\pi_t \leq 1$ and thus, naturally, has the same dimension as the labor tax rate. Policy choices are made by a benevolent government. The government uses tax receipts and the proceeds from seignorage to finance an exogenous and constant revenue requirement, g:

$$g = \tau_t l_t + \pi_t m_{t-1} + m_t - m_{t-1}. \tag{11.18}$$

This example can be rewritten in the notation introduced in section 11.1. The current control for the consumer, $\mathbf{u}_t^i$, can be identified with the vector (c_t^i, x_t^i, l_t^i). The individual state variable, corresponding to s_t^i, is m_{t-1}^i. The second equation in (11.17) gives its law of motion (the analogue of (11.2)). The relevant aggregate state variable at t is thus m_{t-1}. We can identify the policy vector $\mathbf{q}_t$ with (τ_t, π_t).

Note that, in contrast to the situation in section 11.1, only the policy instruments, and not the aggregate state, enter the individual consumer optimization problem directly. In this simple problem it is easier to solve for the consumer optimum without resorting to the dynamic programming formulation of section 11.1. Inserting (11.17) into (11.16), the consumer maximizes the following intertemporal objective function:

$$\max \sum_{t=0}^{\infty} \beta^t \left[(1 - \pi_t)m_{t-1}^i + (1 - \tau_t)l_t^i - m_t^i + V\left(1 - l_t^i\right) + U\left(m_t^i\right)\right]. \tag{11.19}$$

He chooses a sequence of $\{m_t^i, l_t^i\}$, taking as given initial money balances m_{-1}^i and the sequence of all current and future policy vectors $\{\mathbf{q}_t\}$, or equivalently, taking as given the policy rule and the law of motion of the aggregate state variable.

---

5. If M_t is the nominal money stock and P_t the price level, equilibrium requires

$$P_t = \frac{M_t}{m_t}.$$

Solving this consumer intertemporal optimization problem yields the following interior solution:

$$l_t^i = L(\tau_t)$$
$$m_t^i = M\left(\pi_{t+1}^e\right), \tag{11.20}$$

where $L(\tau_t) \equiv 1 - V_x^{-1}(1 - \tau_t)$ is the labor supply function familiar from previous chapters and example 1, and the function $M(\pi_{t+1}^e) \equiv U_m^{-1}(1 - \beta(1 - \pi_{t+1}^e))$ is the consumer's demand for real balances as a function of the nominal interest rate. As in the previous example, the superscript e denotes the private sector's expectations. The solution to the consumer problem is thus very simple. By the linearity in the utility function, current consumer choices do not depend directly on current state variables, but only on current policy and expected policy in the next period.

In equilibrium, $m_t^i = m_t$. Hence the second equation in (11.20) and the policy rule pinning down inflation expectations, π_{t+1}^e, jointly define the equilibrium law of motion of the aggregate state, m_t, the analogue of the function $G(\cdot; \Psi)$ in section 11.1. Note that the equilibrium law of motion of the aggregate state only reflects the dynamics implicit in the policy rule. If the policy rule prescribes a constant inflation rate, then the economy converges immediately to the steady state. This feature of the solution simplifies the analysis considerably and makes it possible to characterize analytically the equilibria with and without commitment.

Note also that expected inflation, like the labor tax, distorts economic choices. The first-best allocation in this economy (without any alternative assets) has real balances at the point at which their marginal utility, $U_m(m_t)$, equals the marginal cost of holding them, given by the subjective real interest rate factor $(1 - \beta)$. This is consistent with the private optimum condition $U_m(m_t) = (1 - \beta(1 - \pi_{t+1}^e))$ only if $\pi_{t+1}^e = 0$. Finally, as in the previous example, private behavior depends on the expected tax rate on savings (here expected inflation, π_{t+1}^e), not on actual inflation. This is the source of the capital levy problem, which is present also in this example.

Equilibrium under Commitment   We start by studying the equilibrium under commitment. For simplicity, we characterize the optimal policy rule only in the steady state. That is, we compute a stationary equilibrium in which the private sector is in the steady state given the policy rule, and the policy rule is (ex ante) optimal and prescribes stationary values for the policy instruments.

Consider the optimization problem of a benevolent government. It maximizes (11.19) by choosing the whole sequence of (π_t, τ_t), for $t = 0, 1, 2, \ldots, \infty$, subject to (11.20), to $\pi_{t+1}^e = \pi_{t+1}$ and to the government budget constraint (11.18) for all $t \geq 0$ and for a given value of initial money balances, m_{-1}. We omit writing down the first-order condition for

$t = 0$, since it has a special form and we seek to characterize the stationary equilibrium only.[6] Exploiting the envelope theorem, the first-order conditions of the government optimization problem for all subsequent dates $t \geq 1$ can be written as

$$-L(\tau_t) + \lambda_t [L(\tau_t) + \tau_t L_\tau(\tau_t)] = 0 \tag{11.21}$$
$$-M(\pi_t) + \lambda_t [M(\pi_t) + \pi_t M_\pi(\pi_t) - M_\pi(\pi_t)] + \lambda_{t-1} M(\pi_t)/\beta = 0,$$

where λ_t is the multiplier associated with the government budget constraint in period t.[7] Even though real money demand entails no gradual adjustment—see (11.20)—the optimal policy rule does; it is of the form $\mathbf{q}_t = \mathbf{\Psi}(m_{t-1}, \mathbf{q}_{t-1})$.[8] The reason for this difference is that the government problem, unlike the private problem, includes the government budget constraint, which is a dynamic equation. Hence the adjustment to the steady state under the ex ante optimal policy occurs gradually over time.

Consider the implications of (11.21) in a stationary equilibrium. Setting $\lambda_t = \lambda_{t-1} = \lambda$, we obtain

$$\frac{L(\tau)}{L(\tau) + \tau L_\tau(\tau)} = \frac{\beta M(\pi)}{\beta M(\pi) + (1 - \beta + \beta\pi)M_\pi(\pi)} = \lambda. \tag{11.22}$$

This is the Ramsey rule familiar from optimal taxation: the marginal cost of public funds must be equal across tax bases. As in example 1, these conditions can be given an intuitive interpretation in terms of the elasticities of the tax bases. Let us denote the optimal tax rates that solve these conditions and the government budget constraint by (τ^C, π^C). Notice that the solution always entails a positive labor tax rate, $\tau^C > 0$. Whether or not $\pi^C > 0$ is ambiguous and depends on the properties of the utility function.[9] Equation (11.22) also implies that $\lambda^C > 1$: the marginal cost of public funds is thus higher than the marginal utility of private consumption (unity), reflecting the distortions of economic activity imposed by taxation.

Equilibrium without Commitment   Next, consider the more realistic setting in which policy decisions are made sequentially over time, once in each period. In any period t the

6. Because of the particular solution for the first period, the optimal policy rule under commitment can thus not easily be written in time-invariant form. The same is true for other dynamic optimal tax problems.

7. It is easier to solve the government optimization problem under commitment by means of optimal control than by dynamic programming. The Hamiltonian of the dynamic policy problem is

$$\sum_{t=0}^{\infty} \beta^t [(1 - \pi_t)m_{t-1} + (1 - \tau_t)l_t - m_t + V(1 - l_t) + U(m_t) + \lambda_t(\tau_t l_t + \pi_t m_{t-1} + m_t - m_{t-1} - g)].$$

8. This is still consistent with the general policy rule in section 11.1, given by (11.3), as the state variable s_t could be expanded to include q_{t-1}.

9. This follows from the fact that even at $\pi = 0$, the term in the middle of (11.22) is larger than unity. Hence the left-hand side of (11.22) must also be greater than unity, which implies $\tau > 0$ (as $L_\tau < 0$).

government chooses (π_t, τ_t) so as to maximize (11.19), subject to (11.20) and the sequence of government budget constraints in (11.18). In this maximization the government takes as given initial money balances, m_{t-1}, as well as future policy and future expectations consistent with the equilibrium policy rule and $\pi_{t+i}^e = \pi_{t+i}$ in all future periods. In period t, however, π_t^e is taken as given, and nothing constrains π_t to equal π_t^e. Letting λ_t again denote the multiplier on the period t government budget constraint, the conditions for an optimum can be written

$$-L(\tau_t) + \lambda_t(L(\tau_t) + \tau_t L(\tau_t)) = 0$$

$$-m_{t-1}(1 - \lambda_t) \gtreqless 0 \quad [\pi_t \lessgtr 1].$$

The first condition is the same as in the equilibrium under commitment, (11.21). The second, the complementary slackness condition, reflects the government's temptation to deviate from the policy rule. As outstanding money balances, m_{t-1}, are taken as given, but period t labor supply is not, it is ex post optimal to tax money as much as possible, so as to minimize tax distortions on the current labor-leisure choice. If outstanding money is great enough to finance all of g at $\pi \leq 1$, the government can set $\tau_t = 0$, that is, all the current distortions are eliminated, and $\lambda_t = 1$. Formally, the ex post optimal policy satisfies

$$\widetilde{\pi}(m_{t-1}) = \min\left[\frac{g}{m_{t-1}}, 1\right]$$

$$\widetilde{\tau}(m_{t-1})L(\widetilde{\tau}(m_{t-1})) = g - \widetilde{\pi}(m_{t-1})m_{t-1},$$

$$(11.23)$$

where the second line simply follows from the government budget constraint. For this to be an equilibrium without commitment, we need an additional condition: m_{t-1} must be consistent with the representative consumer's optimal choice in the previous period, when the resulting inflation tax is correctly anticipated, that is, when $m_{t-1} = M(\widetilde{\pi}(m_{t-1}))$.

As already noted, private behavior is independent of current state variables. Hence after only one period, the economy converges to a stationary equilibrium—where the representative consumer accumulates money, correctly anticipating the equilibrium policy rule in (11.23). The equilibrium policy rule has no serial correlation here, in contrast to the equilibrium with commitments. Let us assume that $U_m(g) > 1$, or equivalently that $M(1) > g$. Under that assumption, the equilibrium has $\pi^D < 1$, $\tau^D = 0$, and $\pi^D M(\pi^D) = g$, where the ^{D} superscript denotes an equilibrium under discretion. Thus the private sector correctly anticipates that the inflation tax collects all government revenue. Real balances are still valuable enough in the current period, however, that the resulting tax base satisfies the revenue requirement at less than a confiscatory tax rate.[10]

---

10. As discussed at length in chapter 12, this is not the only equilibrium without commitment. When policy is set under discretion, multiplicity of equilibria tends to be the norm.

In this equilibrium, the government—and thus the representative consumer—is worse off than in the equilibrium with commitment. Optimal policy under commitment smooths the necessary distortions by taxing both labor supply and real balances in each period. But the equilibrium without commitment has an unbalanced tax structure, imposing all the tax distortions on one of these margins only: $\pi^C < \pi^D$, and $0 = \tau^D < \tau^C$. As discussed in section 11.1, the additional constraint of ex post optimality implies a welfare cost. This is just another instance of the capital levy problem illustrated in the previous example.

Credibility problems in dynamic taxation are not uniquely tied to capital levy situations, however. On the contrary, such problems are the norm rather than the exception whenever the government cannot enter into binding commitments. Consider, for instance, an economy where the government could tax only labor and where taxation of debt or any other asset (including the human capital component of labor remuneration) was completely ruled out. As discussed in Persson and Tabellini 1990, chap. 8, the ex ante optimum under commitment is generally not credible under discretion in this kind of economy either. Intuitively, the ex post elasticity of period t labor supply at date t is generally different from the ex ante elasticity of period t labor supply at date $j < t$. One reason for this difference is that the possibility of forward intertemporal substitution disappears as j approaches t; another is that the consumer accumulates wealth, which may alter the response of labor supply to taxes. As long as the ex ante and ex post elasticities differ, even though the latter are nonzero, the tension between ex ante and ex post optimality remains. Problem 2 of this chapter further illustrates this point.

11.2.3 Example 3: Public Debt Management

This example illustrates how manipulation of state variables may allow the government to relax the incentive constraint of ex post optimality. Consider the same kind of two-period economy as in example 1. Assume, however, that the representative consumer derives utility from holding real money balances, in addition to his consumption of goods and leisure, in the same way as in example 2. Thus his utility function can be written

$$u^i = w^i + U\left(m_1^i\right) + U\left(m_2^i\right), \tag{11.24}$$

where w^i was defined in (11.11). The government controls the same variables as in example 1 as well as the price level in each period through its control of the nominal money stock. Let us first assume that the entire government debt is indexed to the price level and that, contrary to example 1, debt cannot be repudiated or taxed in any way (other than possibly through inflation, see further below). We can then write the private budget constraints in real terms as

$$c_1^i + b^i + m_1^i = l_1^i(1 - \tau_1)$$
$$c_2^i + m_2^i = l_2^i(1 - \tau_2) + \rho b^i + m_1^i(1 - \pi),$$

where

$$\pi = \frac{P_2 - P_1}{P_2}$$

measures the inflation tax as in example 2. Notice that there are no money balances outstanding at the outset, so there is no initial capital levy problem. As in example 1, any interior solution for b^i (and c^i) requires that $\rho = 1$. We impose this equilibrium condition below.

The solution to this problem implies the same labor supply functions $l_t^i = L(\tau_t)$ as before. Real second-period money holdings are constant and given by $m_2^i = U_m^{-1}(1)$, whereas first-period money demand is given by

$$m_1^i = M(\pi^e) \equiv U_m^{-1}(1 - \pi^e),$$

a continuously declining function of the expected inflation rate.

The government budget constraints in the two periods (using $\rho = 1$) are

$$g_1 = \tau_1 l_1 + m_1 + b$$
$$g_2 + b + m_1 = m_2 + \tau_2 l_2 + \pi m_1. \tag{11.25}$$

The fact that the consumer is willing to hold money balances gives the government some seignorage revenue. Part of this, namely m_2, takes the form of a lump sum tax. But the inflation tax on first-period money holdings is proportional to the inflation rate realized (through monetary policy) in period 2 and, as in the previous example, distorts consumer choices. The policy vectors are thus the same as in example 1, $\mathbf{q}_1 = (g_1, \tau_1, b)$ and $\mathbf{q}_2 = (g_2, \tau_2, \pi)$, except that π replaces θ. The relevant state variables in period 2 are now (b, m_1).

Commitment or Not First, let a benevolent government choose policy under commitment. As in example 1, $\alpha > 0$ makes it optimal to spend in period 1 only, implying $g_2^C(b, m_1) = 0$. Ex ante optimal Ramsey financing now spreads the distortions equally across the three sources of financing:

$$\epsilon_L(\tau_1^C) = \epsilon_L(\tau_2^C) = \epsilon_M(\pi^C),$$

where $\epsilon_M(\pi) = \pi M_\pi / M < 0$ is the elasticity of the base for the inflation tax. Equation (11.15) still gives the optimal level of the labor tax rates. These conditions imply that the optimal inflation tax is state independent, $\pi^C(b, m_1) = \pi^C$. Optimal first-period spending g_1^C and debt b^C, finally, follow from the budget constraints in (11.25).

Now consider instead the equilibrium without commitment, starting with the ex post incentives. Once period 2 is reached, it is still optimal for the government to abstain from spending, setting $g_2^D(b, m_1) = 0$. As in example 1, the government has strong incentives to tax outstanding assets to reduce the distortionary second-period labor tax. Although the government now cannot tax debt by assumption, it can use the surprise inflation tax, diluting the real value of outstanding nominal money. By an argument analogous to that in example 2, it will choose to raise π toward its maximal value of unity, as long as the implied value for $\tau_2 L(\tau_2)$ on the right-hand side of the second equation in (11.25) is positive. The ex post optimal inflation tax can thus be written as the following incentive constraint:

$$\pi^D(b, m_1) = \min\left[1, 1 + \frac{b - m_2}{m_1}\right].$$

The only credible inflation rates are thus very high. The ex post optimal value $\tau^D(b, m_1)$ is then determined from the period 2 budget constraint in (11.25). As in examples 1 and 2, the incentive constraint tied to $q_2^D(b, m_1)$ drives the equilibrium policy away from the ex ante optimum. To fully characterize the equilibrium solution involves studying the government's period 1 incentives, given this constraint. As this is somewhat complicated, however, we stop at this point, turning instead to the possible relaxation of the incentive constraint.

A Richer Debt Structure   Suppose now that the government has access to two types of instruments. Some of its debt is indexed to the period 2 price level, exactly as above. This debt is denoted by b^I and carries a gross real return of ρ^I. Some of its debt (or assets), however, is nominally denominated. We denote the real value of this debt by b^N and its real return by $\rho^N(1 - \pi)$, where ρ^N is the nominal return. The private budget constraints can then be written

$$c_1^i + b^{iI} + b^{iN} + m_1^i = l_1^i(1 - \tau_1)$$
$$c_2^i + m_2^i = l_2^i(1 - \tau_2) + \rho^I b^{iI} + (\rho^N b^N + m_1^i)(1 - \pi).$$

Clearly, for both types of debt to be held, they must have the same expected real return. This, in turn, requires

$$\rho^I = 1 = \rho^N(1 - \pi^e).$$

As in the case of expected repudiation in example 1, for the consumer to be indifferent between nominal or real financial instruments, the nominal rate of return for private agents needs to compensate on a one-for-one basis for expected inflation.

When the government has access to commitment, ex ante expected inflation and the level of inflation actually chosen are identical. This makes the two forms of debt perfect substitutes, and optimal policy remains the same as before.

Absent commitment, on the other hand, the two forms of debt are different in that the real value of b^I is independent of realized inflation, whereas b^N is not. To see why this is important, write the government's ex post budget constraint in period 2 as

$$g_2 + (b^I + \rho^N b^N) + m_1 = m_2 + \tau_2 l_2 + \pi(m_1 + \rho^N b^N).$$

The ex post base for surprise inflation is now the total nominal position of the government vis-à-vis the private sector, namely $(m_1 + \rho^N b^N)$, which permits a government that carefully manages its debt issue in period 1 to relax the incentive constraint and implement the ex ante optimal solution. Suppose that the government in period 1 issues debt so as to set

$$b^I + b^N = b^C$$

$$\rho^N b^N = -M(\pi^C). \tag{11.26}$$

In other words, the government issues the same amount of total debt as in the commitment optimum, but it chooses the composition in such a way that the total nominal position against the private sector is zero. Given that the private sector holds the same amount of money as in the commitment optimum, this means holding nominal bonds as a claim on the private sector. Such a debt structure clearly nullifies the ex post incentives to engage in surprise inflation, as the ex post tax base is zero. Yet it preserves the money stock as the base for the expected inflation tax (the return on the government's nominal assets compensates for expected inflation, since $\rho^N = 1/(1 - \pi^e)$), whereas the consumer gets no corresponding compensation on his holdings of nominal money). Issuing debt according to (11.26) in period 1, the government thus relaxes the ex post incentive constraint completely. The ex ante optimal policy can and will be implemented without any commitment.

A version of the above result was first derived by Persson, Persson, and Svensson (1987). Similar results apply to home-currency- and foreign-currency-denominated debt. As the example shows, balancing nominal claims and liabilities may allow the government to sustain the ex ante Ramsey solution, even without commitment. But nominally denominated liabilities can also offer valuable insurance against unanticipated fluctuations in government spending, if the government does not have access to contingent debt. Calvo and Guidotti (1990) and Bohn (1990) study the choice between nominal and indexed debt as a trade-off between credibility and flexibility.

This is an example of a more general mechanism whereby a rich enough debt structure may allow a benevolent government to relax future incentive constraints tied to the ex post temptation to renege on desirable policies. Lucas and Stokey (1983) were the first to derive such a result, showing that the ex ante optimal policy rule for labor taxation can be implemented with a sufficiently rich maturity structure of public debt (and contingency structure, in the case of uncertainty), even if labor taxes are chosen sequentially with no commitment. The result can be interpreted by analogy with the Modigliani-Miller irrelevance theorem in corporate finance, which, according to the literature in that field, breaks down in the presence of incentive problems in the firm, say in the form of conflicting interests between a firm's owners and managers. The capital structure indeed becomes a strategic tool for dealing with such incentive problems (see Hart 1995, for instance). Under commitment, the government capital structure is unimportant here as well. But absent commitment, the

Modigliani-Miller theorem breaks down because of the incentive problems associated with the requirement of ex post optimality. As a result, the government capital structure once more becomes nonneutral, even if a Modigliani-Miller theorem about the irrelevance of the government financial structure applies in the absence of these incentive constraints. Problem 3 of this chapter illustrates these ideas in a simple example.

Of course, all these results are conditional on government debt being honored despite the incentives to renege on it ex post that we identified in example 1. As mentioned above, we will return to this issue in chapters 12 and 13.

11.3 Discussion

The main idea stressed in this chapter is that credibility problems are inherent in dynamic policy choice. Lack of credibility is a binding incentive constraint on policy formation when two conditions are met. The first condition is that irreversible policy commitments are not possible, that is, policy is chosen sequentially over time. In a dynamic environment, this means that some policies are chosen after the private sector has made some irreversible decisions, such as accumulating an asset or signing a contract. These private decisions are therefore made on the basis of expectations of future policies. This is why expectations matter.

But lack of binding commitments is not enough to create a credibility problem. We also need a second condition: there must be a conflict of interest between the policymaker and the private sector. Such a conflict implies that the policymaker has an incentive to undertake policy surprises. In equilibrium, with rational agents and full information, an incentive constraint rules out policy surprises: equilibrium policy must be ex post optimal, given private expectations. All the examples of this chapter assumed a benevolent government. Conflict between the government and the private sector was due to a lack of policy instruments: the government could raise revenue only through distorting taxes. There are many other possible sources of such conflict, however, arising from externalities, or redistributive goals, or even the agency problems discussed in part 3.

A credibility problem has several consequences. First of all, the incentive constraint forces the government to take private expectations as given, and policy becomes suboptimally myopic, whatever the government objective. Hence there is value in certain institutions enabling the government to enter into binding commitments or, as a second best, reducing the flexibility with which policy makers can reverse a previously announced course of action. Examples of such institutions include trust funds to repay government debt, exchange rate agreements that constrain monetary policy, and provisions for delegating policy choice to an independent agency with a clear and focused mandate. We discuss various aspects of these institutional features with reference to monetary policy in part 5.

A second important consequence of lack of credibility is that it may interact with other incentive constraints originating from the political system or from other aspects of the policy environment. Such interaction affects positive and normative consequences of these other incentive constraints in important ways. The next chapter will discuss a few examples of this phenomenon, but the general lesson is that in a dynamic environment, it might be wrong to study these other incentive constraints in isolation, abstracting from lack of credibility.

A final consequence of lack of credibility is that, earlier policy decisions typically affect the incentive constraint, which opens up new intertemporal effects of economic policy. If the current government controls certain state variables entering into future policy problems, it can influence future policy by affecting future incentive constraints. We used this idea in example 3 with regard to public debt management to show how the government can sometimes tie its own hands at a future date to escape current credibility problems, but a moment's reflection reveals that a similar mechanism could be used when current and future governments do not share the same policy preferences. The ability to affect future policy incentives could then help the current government impose its preferred policy on a future government with different preferences. We discuss this possibility further in chapters 13 and 14, in which incumbent governments use state variables, such as public debt or public capital, to influence future governments with different policy preferences.

We close the chapter with a caveat. Private expectations have played a critical role throughout this chapter. We have stressed rationality and equilibrium behavior. At the same time, however, we relied on very simple mechanisms of expectations formation, ruling out learning or repeated interaction between the government and private agents. This is significant, because repeated interaction creates strong incentives for the government to maintain a reputation. As stressed by a large literature, reputational forces can replace institutional commitments and thus relax the incentive constraints discussed in this chapter.

11.4   Notes on the Literature

The distinction between rules and discretion in economic policy dates back to the seminal work of Kydland and Prescott (1977) and Calvo (1978). Since then, a very large literature has discussed these ideas, both from a methodological point of view and with regard to specific applications. Our discussion of dynamic incentive constraints in section 11.1 largely follows Krusell, Quadrini, and Rios-Rull 1997, which also allows for consumer heterogeneity and nonbenevolent policymakers. Chang (1998) discusses related issues and gives a more general condition, characterizing the time-consistent policies. He shows how to find the equilibria in a recursive fashion, both with and without commitment, in the context of the model in Calvo 1978. Obstfeld (1997a) provides an insightful analysis of time-consistent equilibria in a dynamic model of seignorage. An earlier recursive formulation in a simpler linear quadratic model is due to Cohen and Michel (1988). Reputation and history-dependent policy rules in a dynamic framework are studied by Chari and Kehoe (1990, 1993); see also chapter 12. Persson and Tabellini 1990 surveys the early literature on reputation and monetary policy; see also chapter 15.

A large literature deals with public debt repayment and wealth taxation, much of which is surveyed in chapter 12 with reference to capital taxation. Eaton and Fernandez (1995) survey the related literature on sovereign debt.

The seminal paper by Lucas and Stokey (1983) studies the credibility of optimal tax structures in a general intertemporal context without capital and also discusses optimal debt management as an incentive device. Subsequently, Persson and Svensson (1984) and Rogers (1986, 1987) reinterpret and clarify some of the general issues concerning the credibility of optimal intertemporal taxation. Chari, Christiano, and Kehoe (1992) and Persson and Svensson (1986) also generalize and interpret the debt management implications of the Lucas and Stokey paper. Persson, Persson, and Svensson (1987) extend the Lucas and Stokey result to a monetary economy, including the result in example 3. Persson, Persson, and Svensson (1996) also show that the temptation to generate surprise inflation may be much stronger than the theoretical literature suggests, once the full set of nominal rigidities in public expenditure and tax programs are taken into account. Missale and Blanchard (1994) study how the maturity structure required to make a low-inflation policy incentive compatible varies with the level of debt. Bohn (1990) and Calvo and Guidotti (1990) study the credibility-flexibility trade-off in formulating the optimal composition of public debt among indexed and nonindexed securities.

11.5   Problems

1. Debt structure, labor taxation, and money

This problem is adapted from section 7.2 in Persson and Tabellini 1990. Consider the following two-period model. At date 1, the agent's initial assets are 0. The agent consumes an amount c_1 of private good, he supplies labor l_1, and he can invest in bonds d_1 or hold money balances m_1. We assume the real wage to be unity. Moreover, the return from bonds is $R = 1$. Money balances pay a zero nominal wage of return and depreciate. The per-unit depreciation in the real value of money is $\pi = \frac{p_2 - p_1}{p_2}$, where p_t is the market price at date t. Finally, government consumes an exogenous per capita amount g and taxes labor income. We call τ_1 the tax rate. In period 2, the agent's consumption level is c_2, his labor supply is l_2, and his demand for money balances is m_2. Labor is also taxed in period 2, and the tax rate is τ_2. Then the government finances g by raising taxes in periods 1 and 2. We assume that one unit of labor is necessary to produce one unit of good; then the resource constraints in periods 1 and 2 are $c_1 + g = l_1$ and $c_2 = l_2$, respectively. The individual's preferences are summarized by

$$w = c_1 + c_2 - V(l_1) - V(l_2) + U(m_1) + U(m_2),$$

where $V(\cdot)$ is increasing and convex and $U(\cdot)$ is increasing and concave.

a. Determine the agent's intertemporal budget constraint. Determine the agent's supply-of-labor and demand-for-money functions.

b. Determine the government's budget constraint as well as its optimization program when it is committing to future policy rules at the beginning of date 1. What is the optimal policy?

c. Suppose now that the government cannot commit. Determine the implemented policy. Compare your result with that of question (b).

2. Credibility problems in labor taxation when government consumption is endogenous

This problem is based on section 8.2 in Persson and Tabellini 1990. Consider the following two-period model. In each period $t = 1, 2$, the representative consumer has preferences over private consumption c_t and leisure x_t. His labor supply is denoted by l_t and satisfies the time constraint $x_t + l_t = 1$. Assume that the real wage is 1. The government consumes, only in period 2, a quantity g_2. The agent's utility is

$$w = F(c_1, l_1, c_2, l_2) + H(g_2),$$

where $F(\cdot)$ is decreasing (respectively, increasing) and concave with respect to labor (respectively, consumption) at each period and $H(\cdot)$ is increasing and concave. Labor is taxed in each period, and the tax rate is denoted by τ_t. In addition, the representative agent's initial wealth is b_1. Finally, the consumer can invest in foreign assets and government bonds in the first period, which both pay 0 return. Denote by d_1 the chosen level of investment. Government choices are made by a benevolent social planner who determines g_2 and uses the tax receipts to finance it.

a. Suppose that the government can commit. Determine the agent's intertemporal budget constraint. What is his optimization program? Write his ex ante indirect utility function, which we will denote by $W(\tau_1, \tau_2; b_1)$. Determine the government's intertemporal budget constraint and write its optimization program. Determine the optimal fiscal policy.

b. Suppose now that the government cannot commit. What is the agent's wealth b_2 at the beginning of period 2? Write the budget constraint of the representative agent in period 2 and characterize his ex post indirect utility $\widetilde{W}(\tau_2; b_2)$. Determine the government budget constraint. What is the second-period optimal fiscal policy?

c. When does the equilibrium under no commitment coincide with the equilibrium under commitment? What happens if $F(c_1, l_1, c_2, l_2) = U(c_1) - V(l_1) + c_2 - V(l_2)$? Do we have the same result when $F(c_1, l_1, c_2, l_2) = c_1 - V(l_1) + U(c_2) - V(l_2)$? Why or why not?

3. Debt structure and labor taxation

This problem is inspired by section 8.3 in Persson and Tabellini 1990. Consider a three-period model in which the representative agent has preferences over his private consumption levels c_t, his labor supply l_t, and the government consumption levels g_t for all $t = 1, 2, 3$. The real wage is 1. In the first period, there is no production, so $l_1 = 0$. The representative agent has an initial endowment b_1 that can be spent on his private consumption c_1 and government consumption g_1. In other words, $b_1 \geq c_1 + g_1$. Government consumption is financed through borrowing, which is repaid at dates 2 and 3. In the second and third periods, the government does not consume, so $g_t = 0$ for all $t = 2, 3$. Then the endogenous resources l_t are used only to produce, that is, $l_t = c_t$ for $t = 2, 3$. The government repays the debt by raising taxes. Let τ_2 and τ_3 be the tax rates in periods 2 and 3. The utility of the representative agent is given by

$$w = c_1 + U(c_2) - V(l_2) + U(c_3) - V(l_3),$$

where $V(\cdot)$ is increasing and convex in labor supply and $U(\cdot)$ is increasing and concave in consumption. Let d^s (respectively, d^l) be the debt issued by the government in period 1 and maturing in period 2 (respectively, in period 3). We will refer to these as short-term and long-term debt, respectively. Denote by r_t the interest rate between periods t and $t + 1$. Naturally, given the three-period model, there are only two subsequent interest rates, r_1 and r_2.

a. Determine the representative agent's overall intertemporal budget constraint. What is his maximization program? Determine his optimal choice.

b. Suppose that the government can commit to a tax policy in period 1. Determine its budget constraint at the beginning of period 1. Write its optimization program and derive the ex ante optimal tax policy.

c. Suppose now that the government cannot commit. What is the government budget constraint in period 2? Determine its optimization program and characterize the optimal policy from the perspective of period 2.

d. What are the sources of the differences between the optimal tax policy under commitment and that under no commitment, respectively? What happens if $d^s > d^l$ and if $d^s < d^l$? In which case does the optimal tax policy under commitment coincide with the optimal tax policy under no commitment? Discuss.

4. Capital taxation and inflation surprise

This problem is related to the analysis of chapter 6 in Persson and Tabellini 1990. Consider an economy in which the representative agent has preferences over private consumption c_t and labor l_t, where $t = 1, 2$. At date $t = 1$, the agent's initial capital endowment is b_1 and he does not work, so $l_1 = 0$. He can save part of his endowment but cannot borrow. Then if his savings are denoted by s_1, we impose $s_1 \geq 0$. At date $t = 2$, the agent works and consumes. The real wage is unity. In addition, the gross return associated with the first-period savings is R. Labor and capital are taxed at rates τ and θ, respectively. The government consumes an exogenous per capita amount g_2 at date 2 that is financed through taxes. The individual's preferences are summarized by

$$w = U(c_1) + c_2 - V(l_2),$$

where $U(\cdot)$ is increasing and concave and $V(\cdot)$ is increasing and convex. In addition, we assume that $U_{ccc}(\cdot) \geq 0$.

a. Would the analysis be modified if g_2 were endogenous and included in the agent's preferences? Determine the agent's intertemporal constraint. Suppose that the government can commit. What are the agent's labor supply and savings level? How do they vary with the level of taxes?

b. Determine the budget constraint as well as the government's optimization program when it commits to future policy rules at the beginning of date 1. What is the optimal policy? [Hint: It may be convenient to write the government's program in terms of labor and consumption, rather than in terms of taxes.]

c. Suppose now that the government cannot commit. What does this imply? Again, determine the implemented policy and discuss.

Now consider the same model as before, but suppose that s_1 is constrained to be 0. Savings can take only the form of money holdings that pay a zero nominal rate of return. Let p_t be the market price at date t; then the real return is

$$-\pi = -\frac{p_2 - p_1}{p_2},$$

that is, the opposite of the inflation rate. In other words, money holdings depreciate, and the per-unit depreciation is π. Let m_t be the demand of money at date $t = 1, 2$. The individual's preferences are now

$$w = U(c_1) + c_2 - V(l_2) + H(m_2),$$

where $H(\cdot)$ is increasing and concave. The government finances g_2 by raising taxes on labor and by printing money. Let M_2 be the nominal quantity of money in the economy; the equilibrium in the money market at date 2 is $M_2 = p_2 m_2$.

d. Determine the agent's supply-of-labor and demand-for-money functions. What is the optimal policy decided by a government that can commit at the beginning of period 1? Compare your results with the results obtained in the first part of the problem.

e. Suppose now that the government cannot commit. What are its ex post incentives? Discuss.

5. Labor and capital taxation when agents are heterogeneous

This problem is based on section 7.3 in Persson and Tabellini 1990. Consider a model with two types of agents. Agents of the first type live for two periods. At date 1, their initial endowment in capital is b_1. They consume an amount c_1 of private goods and invest an amount k. The return from capital is $R(1 - \theta)$, where θ is a capital tax. In the second period, they consume $kR(1 - \theta)$. We denote the second period consumption by c_2^1. The utility of the representative agent of the first type is

$$w^1 = c_1 + U(c_2^1),$$

where $U(\cdot)$ is increasing and concave. Agents of type 2 live only in period 2. They have no endowment and get income only from labor. The real wage is unity. Their labor supply is denoted by l_2. They consume their labor income net of taxes, τ. Their consumption is denoted by c_2^2. The representative agent in this group has the following utility function:

$$w^2 = c_2^2 - V(l_2),$$

where $V(\cdot)$ is increasing and concave. The government maximizes $\phi w^1 + w^2$, where ϕ represents the weight assigned to the first group. Moreover, it collects taxes to finance an exogenous per capita amount of expenditures g_2 at date 2.

a. Determine the budget constraint of the representative agent in each group. What is the private optimal behavior for a given announced policy (τ, θ)?

b. Determine the optimal policy when the government can commit.

c. Suppose now that the government cannot commit. Which policy is implemented in that case?

12 Capital Taxation

Our main goal in this chapter is to address a positive question. How is the tax structure of a country determined? In particular, what determines how the tax burden is split between labor and capital? According to the basic principles of optimal taxation, the tax structure depends on the elasticity of alternative tax bases. More-inelastic tax bases should carry a higher tax rate, since they react less to tax distortions. With competitive-factor markets, this implies that labor should be taxed much more than capital: capital is a much more elastic tax base, particularly in the long run. Indeed, many proponents argue that the optimal steady-state tax rate on capital income is zero.[1] Yet as we already remarked in the introduction to this part, observed effective tax rates on capital are positive and often high. In a sample of fourteen OECD countries, the average effective tax rates on capital and labor were about the same (about 38%) over the period 1991–1995. These measured tax rates vary considerably across countries and over time. A number of countries, such as the United Kingdom and the United States, actually have higher effective tax rates on capital than on labor, even though their labor markets are fairly competitive.[2] Thus the positive question motivating much of this chapter can be reformulated. Why are tax rates on capital income so much higher than what is seemingly efficient? To answer this specific question, we consider the effects of imposing a number of incentive constraints on the choice of tax policy.

First, we discuss an incentive constraint due to lack of credibility. This is the celebrated capital levy problem (Fischer 1980), very similar to that already discussed in chapter 11. As the elasticity of capital already accumulated is zero, promises of a low tax rate on capital are not credible and, in equilibrium, capital is taxed much more heavily than what is ex ante optimal for the representative voter.

A second simple reason for inefficiently high taxes on capital is redistribution. This result emerges immediately once we generalize the simple model to add heterogeneity in the functional distribution of income. Capital income is more concentrated than labor income. Hence a majority of the voters gain from shifting a larger share of the tax burden to capital, despite the efficiency losses. Politics may also provide a partial remedy to the lack of credibility, since the voters take into account politicians' varying degrees of susceptibility to the capital levy problem. As plausible as it may be, however, the idea that redistributive goals can account for the observed tax structure remains to be tested empirically. Some features of cross-country data seem to contradict it. Estimated effective tax rates on capital are higher in the United States than in many European countries, despite the generally

---

1. This result is originally due to Chamley 1986; see also Lucas 1990. But with unionized labor markets, a labor tax can be as distorting as or even more distorting than a capital tax; see, for instance, Daveri and Tabellini 1997.

2. The source is Daveri and Tabellini 1997, which in turn extends a methodology formulated by Mendoza, Razin, and Tesar 1994 exploiting information on tax income and aggregate tax bases. Effective tax rates on capital from detailed studies of the tax code using the methodology originally developed by Jorgenson, such as King and Fullerton 1984, often give a rather different picture than the "macro" methodology of Mendoza et al.

larger size of redistributive transfers, the more-organized labor movements, and (for some countries) the higher concentration of capital income in Europe.

There is another incentive constraint, however, pushing in the opposite direction that might explain the puzzling difference in capital tax rates between the United States and Europe. When capital is free to move across jurisdictions, it chooses the location with higher returns and hence, ceteris paribus, lower tax rates. In some circumstances, such *tax competition* creates incentives to reduce tax rates on capital. Tax competition may be particularly fierce among European countries, at least with regard to some forms of capital income, because of the close integration of European capital markets. In this chapter, we also discuss the interaction between the three incentive constraints associated with tax competition, the capital levy problem, and politics.

The chapter also has a methodological goal: to further explore *strategic political delegation,* a phenomenon already encountered in chapter 7. In a setup where dynamic incentive constraints play a key role, strategic delegation is particularly relevant. Policy choices are largely made after elections, possibly much later. At the time of the elections, voters realize that the policymaker will choose future policy in an environment where he will face a different set of incentive constraints. To cope with these forthcoming incentive constraints, they find it optimal to elect someone with preferences different from their own. Thus strategic delegation allows voters to circumvent the capital levy problem or to exploit the strategic interaction with another government to their advantage.

The outline of the chapter is as follows. Section 12.1 lays out the basic economic model. Section 12.2 then discusses lack of credibility and its implications in a representative-consumer setting. Section 12.3 picks up the political conflict between labor and capital, and there we also discuss strategic delegation to solve the capital levy problem, as well as the entry of candidates in a political equilibrium (the citizen-candidate model introduced in chapter 5). Finally, section 12.4 deals with tax competition and its interaction with credibility and politics.

12.1 A Simple Model of Dynamic Taxation

Consider a two-period model of a closed economy, $t = 1, 2$. The economy produces a single storable commodity. A representative consumer has preferences defined over consumption in both periods, c_t^i, and leisure in the second period, x^i, represented by

$$w^i = U\left(c_1^i\right) + c_2^i + V(x^i). \tag{12.1}$$

In the first period, the consumer either consumes his exogenous and untaxed endowment, e, or invests a nonnegative amount in a linear storage technology with unitary gross returns.

In the second period, he devotes his unitary time endowment to labor, l^i, or leisure time, x^i, and consumes his entire income and wealth after having paid taxes. His budget constraints are

$$c_1^i + k^i = 1$$
$$c_2^i = (1 - \tau_K)k^i + (1 - \tau_L)l^i, \tag{12.2}$$

where k^i denotes (nonnegative) investment in the storage technology, τ_K and τ_L are the capital and labor income tax rates, respectively, and the real wage is unity.

How does the private sector respond to the tax rates? Its first-order conditions are

$$U_c(1 - k^i) \geq 1 - \tau_K$$
$$V_x(1 - l^i) = 1 - \tau_L, \tag{12.3}$$

where the equality in the first condition applies at an interior optimum with positive investment. We assume throughout that $U_c(1) < 1$, implying that at $\tau_K = 0$ the consumer is at an interior optimum with $k > 0$. Each tax rate thus drives a wedge between the relevant marginal rates of transformation and substitution. Inverting these two expressions, we obtain the private-sector savings function max $[0, K(\tau_K)]$, where $K(\tau_K) \equiv 1 - U_c^{-1}(1 - \tau_K)$, and the labor supply function $L(\tau_L) \equiv 1 - V_x^{-1}(1 - \tau_L)$. The partial derivatives K_τ and L_τ are both negative. By the utility function's separability and quasi linearity, each tax base depends on its own tax rate only. As in chapter 11, we define the elasticities of these two tax bases with respect to their own tax rate, as $\epsilon_K(\tau_K) = \tau_K K_\tau / K$, $\epsilon_L(\tau_L) = \tau_L L_\tau / L < 0$, respectively.

Finally, the government must finance a given amount of second period per capita public consumption, G. Thus the government budget constraint is

$$G = \tau_L l + \tau_K k. \tag{12.4}$$

Taxes are paid only in the second period, and lump sum (i.e., nondistorting) taxes are not available. We follow the public finance tradition of treating the set of available Ramsey taxes as exogenous; ultimately, the nonavailability of (personalized) lump sum taxes must be due to some heterogeneity that the government can observe only imperfectly.

12.2 Credibility

What is the optimal tax structure in the economy described in section 12.1? And what is the equilibrium tax structure if the government lacks credibility? We address both questions in turn. As already discussed in chapter 11, sequential (or discretionary) decision making and a lack of policy instruments imply that the government loses control of private-sector expectations. The economy gets trapped in a third-best equilibrium in which the government relies excessively on a highly distorting policy instrument. Sections 12.2.1 and 12.2.2, contrasting the equilibrium with and without commitment, discuss these issues. Section 12.2.3 treats another consequence of lack of credibility: the possibility of multiple equilibria and confidence crises, features that are often observed in countries with high public debts. Finally, reputation can mitigate the adverse effects of the ex post incentive constraint, and institutions can be designed to relax it; section 12.2.4 briefly discusses these remedies.

12.2.1   The Ex Ante Optimal Policy

To derive a normative benchmark, we assume that at the start of period 1, before any private decision is made, the government commits to a tax structure $\tau = (\tau_K, \tau_L)$ for period 2. The private sector observes the decision which cannot be changed. There is no uncertainty, and period 2 public consumption, G, is fixed and known already in period 1.

The optimal tax structure maximizes consumer welfare, subject to the private-sector (12.2) and government (12.4) budget constraints and the private-sector first-order conditions (12.3). Specifically, as in previous chapters, we can write the consumer indirect utility function as a function of both tax rates:

$$W(\tau) = U(1 - K(\tau_K)) + V(1 - L(\tau_L)) + (1 - \tau_L)L(\tau_L) + (1 - \tau_K)K(\tau_K). \qquad (12.5)$$

The ex ante optimal policy maximizes (12.5) by choice of τ_K and τ_L, subject to the government budget constraint (12.4). This problem boils down to minimizing the deadweight loss of the two tax rates, illustrated in figure 12.1 by the two shaded triangles.[3] Because quasi-linear preferences and constant factor prices are assumed, this problem is particularly simple. Specifically, neither of the curves displaying the marginal rate of transformation of first-period goods and leisure for second-period goods (the horizontal lines at unity in each graph), nor the curves displaying the corresponding marginal rates of substitution (the downward-sloping marginal utility schedules in each graph) shift because of changes in the tax rates.

---

3. To construct the figure, substitute the government budget constraint into (2.5) and add and subtract expressions in first-best savings and labor supply $K(0)$ and $L(0)$ to get

$$W(\tau) = [U(1 - K(0)) + V(1 - L(0)) + L(0) + K(0) - G]$$
$$-[U(1 - K(0)) - U(1 - K(\tau_K)) - (K(\tau_K) - K(0))]$$
$$-[V(1 - L(0)) - V(1 - V(\tau_L)) - (L(\tau_L) - L(0))].$$

The first line on the right-hand side of this expression corresponds to the first-best allocation, whereas the two next lines correspond to the triangles in figure 12.1.

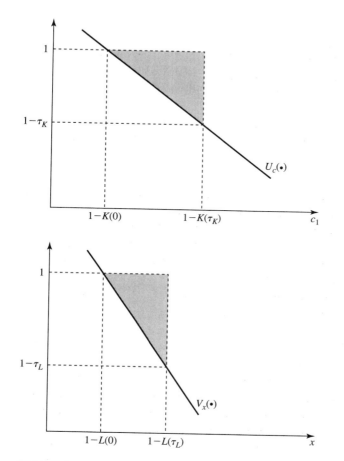

Figure 12.1

Solving this optimization problem yields the following version of the Ramsey rule:[4]

$$\epsilon_K(\tau_K) = \epsilon_L(\tau_L). \tag{12.6}$$

Equation (12.6) implicitly defines the ex ante optimal tax structure. This optimal tax

---

4. By the envelope theorem, the first-order conditions for the government optimal taxation problem are

$$-L + \lambda(L + \tau_L L_\tau) = -K + \lambda(K + \tau_K K_\tau) = 0,$$

where λ is the Lagrange multiplier on the government budget constraint. By our previous definition of elasticity, equation (12.6) follows.

structure, which we call τ^*, equates the marginal distortions on the last dollar raised by each of the two tax rates. What are the general properties of the prescribed policy? Recall that each elasticity is strictly increasing in absolute value in its own tax rate and is zero if $\tau = 0$. Then, the following results hold. First, optimal tax rates are higher on the more inelastic tax base. Second, it is always optimal to tax both bases, as long as both elasticities are finite and strictly positive. Finally, both tax rates move in the same direction if the revenue requirements change; higher public consumption drives up both tax rates in proportion to their elasticities. It is empirically plausible that labor supply is much more inelastic than investment, particularly in the long run. Then (12.6) says that the optimal tax rate on labor is indeed much higher than that on capital. Because taxes are distorting, the economy reaches a second-best, not a first-best, allocation.

12.2.2   Equilibrium without Commitment

Now suppose that the policy decision is made at the start of period 2, after period 1 investment decisions have been made, rather than at the start of period 1 as in the last subsection. This timing is much more plausible, as a sovereign country can change its tax structure at any time under a normal legislative procedure. Under this timing, however, not every tax structure promised in period 1 is credible. A credible tax structure must be optimal ex post, from the vantage point of period 2. More precisely, as explained in chapter 11, a credible equilibrium tax structure satisfies three requirements. (1) Individual economic decisions are optimal, given the expected policies and the decisions of all other individuals in the economy. (2) The tax structure is ex post optimal, given outstanding aggregate capital and individual equilibrium responses to the tax structure after a policy deviation. (3) Individual expectations are fulfilled and markets clear in every period. Let us consider each of these requirements.

(1) The functions K and L and the corresponding elasticities still summarize optimal individual behavior. But the investment function and the corresponding elasticity are now defined over the expected, not the actual, capital tax rate, as the tax structure is decided in period 2, after the investment decision. Thus $k^i = K(\tau_K^e)$ and $\epsilon_K(\tau_K^e)$. We call this elasticity the *ex ante elasticity of investment,* since it is defined over τ_K^e rather than τ_K.

(2) The Ramsey rule (12.6) also continues to describe the ex post optimal tax structure but with one important proviso. The investment elasticity that enters is now the ex post elasticity, that is, the elasticity with respect to the actual tax rate τ_K, since that is what the government is choosing. By the argument at point (1), this ex post elasticity is zero: k^i depends on τ_K^e, not on τ_K. Condition (12.6) then implies that for any given capital stock k the ex post optimal capital tax rate, τ_K, must satisfy the policy rule

$$\tau_K(G, k) = \min\left[1, \frac{G}{k}\right]. \tag{12.7}$$

The optimal labor tax rate τ_L follows from the government budget constraint. In particular, $\tau_L = 0$ if $\tau_K = G/k < 1$. This result is intuitive and similar to that already discussed in example 2 of chapter 11. When tax policy is chosen, the supply of capital is completely inelastic at k, whereas the supply of labor continues to have a positive elasticity, because the private sector chooses it after observing tax policy. Hence the government finds it ex post optimal to set the capital tax rate either as high as possible, at its maximum of 1, or as high as necessary to finance all of public consumption with capital taxes, driving labor taxes to 0.

(3) Rational individuals correctly anticipate government policy. Hence $\tau_K^e = \tau_K(G, k)$ and $k^i = K(\tau_K(G, k))$. Combining this last result with (12.7) and the consistency requirement $k^i = k$, we define the equilibrium tax rate by

$$\tau_K = \min\left[1, \frac{G}{K(\tau_K)}\right].$$

We illustrate the possible equilibria in figure 12.2. The solid curve is the ex ante revenue function for different values of τ_K. Tax revenues first grow with the tax rate, but at a decreasing rate, since the tax base shrinks as τ_K rises. Once we reach the top of the Laffer curve, where $\epsilon_K = 1$, tax revenue begins to shrink, as the reduction in the tax base more than offsets the higher tax rate.[5]

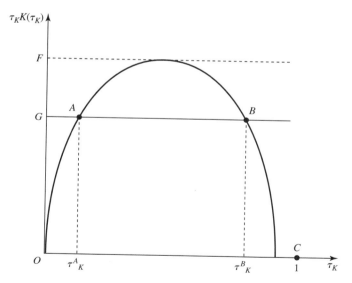

Figure 12.2

---

5. The Laffer curve is unimodal, as drawn in figure 12.2, only under a restriction on the third derivative of $U(\cdot)$. If the curve has several peaks, the multiplicity problem discussed below may be even more severe.

If G is sufficiently high (higher than point F), only one equilibrium exists, where $\tau_K(G, k) = 1$ and $k = 0$ (point C in the diagram). Irrespective of private expectations, the government fully expropriates any outstanding capital stock. Anticipating this, nobody invests. It is easily verified that all three requirements for an equilibrium are fulfilled. Private individuals optimize and have correct expectations about policy. Moreover, the government also optimizes, for even with no capital outstanding, $\tau_K = 1$ is (weakly) optimal, as confirmed by (12.7). This equilibrium is disastrous: there is a prohibitive tax on capital, but still a large tax on labor that is the only available tax base. Yet the government can do nothing to change the outcome. No promise to tax capital at a rate lower than 1 would be credible, for it would be ex post optimal for the government to fully expropriate any piece of outstanding capital, however tiny. This means that no single individual has a unilateral incentive to deviate from his zero-savings plan.

If G is below point F in figure 12.2, this disastrous outcome exists together with two other equilibria. Suppose that government spending corresponds to the horizontal line at G in figure 12.2. Then points A and B are also equilibrium outcomes. At point A, every consumer expects $\tau_K^e = \tau_K^A$ and invests $K(\tau_K^A)$. Hence the government can just finance G by setting τ_K exactly at τ_K^A while keeping the labor tax equal to 0. Thus the government is at an ex post optimum. The same argument establishes that point B is also an equilibrium.

These equilibria are clearly Pareto ranked: A is better than B, which is better than C. They are all worse than the ex ante optimal tax structure, since they tax capital too heavily and labor too lightly (except at point C, where both bases are taxed too heavily). If the government is unable to commit, the economy is trapped in a third-best (or worse) allocation.

As we have already shown in chapter 11, very similar results apply to the taxation of other forms of wealth, in particular to public debt and real money balances. The logic is always the same. Once an investment decision has been made, the tax base is fixed, and it becomes ex post optimal to tax it as much as needed or as much as possible. Moreover, credibility problems are not confined to wealth taxes but are generic in a dynamic economy with sequential policy decisions.

12.2.3   Multiple Equilibria and Confidence Crises

The multiplicity of equilibria when policy is chosen sequentially reflects an indeterminacy in the economy and helps explain the occurrence of the sudden speculative attacks or capital flights that have plagued many economies. Absent a commitment technology, private expectations drive policy rather than the other way around. Equilibria under discretion thus become intrinsically fragile, because investors face a difficult coordination problem. The ex post optimal policy depends on aggregate investment, but aggregate investment depends on the simultaneous decisions of many independent individuals, which in turn are driven by expectations about policy. Thus there is a strategic complementarity. A single investor expecting nobody else to invest also finds it optimal not to invest: he realizes that aggregate capital will be small, and hence full expropriation is inevitable. Thus individual expectations are self-fulfilling and, as they are not nailed down by any economic fundamentals, can fluctuate widely. The resulting policy uncertainty is yet another drawback of an environment with sequential policy choice.

These problems arise in many policy decisions. Consider public debt repayment in a two-period economy, and suppose that in the second period debt can be partially defaulted or taxed away at a cost proportional to the size of the default. Calvo (1988) shows that we then get multiple equilibria. In a good equilibrium, every investor expects the debt to be fully repaid and demands a low interest rate. To avoid the cost of default, the government indeed services the outstanding debt. In a bad equilibrium, every investor expects partial default and demands a higher interest rate. The cost of servicing this debt is now higher, and with distorting taxes the government prefers a partial default; hence default expectations are self-fulfilling. The equilibrium with default is Pareto inferior, as the net amount serviced is the same, but default costs are borne. Problem 1 of this chapter treats this kind of equilibrium further.

Another example, studied by Velasco (1994) and Giavazzi and Pagano (1990), concerns exchange rate crises in a high public debt economy. By assumption, the cost of outright default is prohibitive, but the outstanding debt could be inflated away. In a good equilibrium, investors expect the exchange rate peg to be viable, and the domestic interest rate equals the foreign interest rate; at this low interest rate, it is optimal to service the outstanding public debt through tax revenue alone. In a bad equilibrium, investors expect the peg to collapse. They demand a higher interest rate, which raises the cost of servicing the debt through tax revenue; at the higher interest rate, it becomes optimal to fulfill the expectations, the peg is abandoned, and debt is partially monetized through higher inflation.[6]

Related coordination problems arise in sequential (as opposed to simultaneous) investment decisions. Alesina, Prati, and Tabellini (1990) and Cole and Kehoe (1996a, 1996b) study an infinite-horizon economy with a large public debt. As in Calvo 1988, default is costly, but the cost is assumed to be lump sum. In the good equilibrium, debt is rolled over forever at low interest rates, and distorting taxes are raised to pay interest on the debt. The bad equilibrium has a "debt run," since nobody wants to buy the outstanding debt for fear that—in the following period—investors will refuse to roll it over. Faced with such a

---

6. A high cost of servicing the debt is not the only reason an exchange rate peg may not be credible. In a related argument, Bensaid and Jeanne (1997) show that multiple equilibria can arise if raising the interest rate to defend an exchange rate peg proves too costly for the government because of its repercussions for unemployment.

situation, it is indeed ex post optimal for the government to default on the debt, rather than repaying it all at once. The investors' fears are indeed both rational and self-fulfilling.

12.2.4 Enforcement of Better Outcomes

Even though the previous treatment illustrates that credibility problems may cause very high equilibrium tax rates, we rarely observe confiscatory taxes on wealth. The literature indeed suggests a number of possible mechanisms that may limit the consequences of a prospective credibility problem.

One possibility is that the government has access not to full but to partial commitment. Klein and Rios-Rull (1999) study optimal capital and labor taxation in the standard infinite-horizon neoclassical growth model. They assume that the government can commit to capital tax rates one period in advance, which may be a plausible assumption, given the lags of making and implementing fiscal policy decisions. They numerically compute Markov-perfect equilibria under this assumption and compare them to the Ramsey policies under full commitment. Interestingly, when the period between policy decisions is two years, the equilibrium has average tax rates on capital around 50% and labor tax rates around 20%, which is not too far from recent U.S. experience.

The literature has also appealed to the well-known idea that repeated interaction creates incentives to maintain a reputation, which may mitigate the capital levy problem. Suppose that future expected capital tax rates depend on the current tax structure. Even though the government takes existing capital as given, it still perceives future investment as responding to current tax rates through expected future tax rates, which discourages overtaxation. Let us briefly illustrate this kind of reputation mechanism in an infinitely repeated version of this simple two-period model, following the approach in Chari and Kehoe 1990.

Formally, consider an infinite sequence of stage games, $s = 1, \ldots, \infty$, each identical to the game under discretion in section 12.2.2. For analytical simplicity, though the assumption is an awkward one, we assume that aggregate capital at stage s, k^s, completely depreciates before stage $s + 1$ begins, so that this becomes a repeated, rather than a dynamic, game. (As explained in chapter 11, the interaction of intrinsic dynamics and history-dependent strategies is generally too complex to allow analytical results.)

As before, the government is benevolent. It has the intertemporal objective

$$\sum_{s=1}^{\infty} \beta^{(s-1)} w^{i,s},$$

where β is a discount factor and $w^{i,s}$ is the representative consumer's welfare at stage s. By the previous results, $w^{i,s} = W(\tau^s)$, where τ^s is the tax policy at stage s and $W(\cdot)$ is the function defined in (12.5).

Suppose private agents form expectations about future tax policy on the basis of past tax policy. Moreover, suppose that all agents coordinate their expectations (denoted by an e superscript) according to the following rule:

$$\tau^{1,e} = \tau^*$$

$$\tau^{s,e} = \begin{cases} \tau^* & \text{iff } \tau^j = \tau^* \quad \text{for all } j < s \\ \tau^E & \text{otherwise} \end{cases} \quad \text{for } s \geq 2, \tag{12.8}$$

where τ^* is the Ramsey tax policy in section 12.2.1 and $\tau^E = (1, \tau_L^E)$ is the full expropriation equilibrium outcome in section 12.2.2. Thus the public starts out in good faith. But whenever the government deviates from the Ramsey policy, the public expects it to pursue a short-run opportunistic policy at all stages in the future.

We now ask whether the Ramsey policy is sustainable under discretion. Following this policy yields the outcome $w^{i,s} = W(\tau^*)$ in every period. What is the optimal deviation from this policy? First of all, if a deviation is ever profitable, it is most profitable in stage 1. Denote by τ^D the best policy under a deviation, given that the public expects τ^* and accordingly saves $k^i = K(\tau_K^*)$. Clearly we have $\tau^D = [\tau_K^D, \tau_L^D]$, where $\tau_K^D = \min[1, G/K(\tau_K^*)] > \tau_K^*$ and $\tau_L^D < \tau_L^*$ solves $\tau_L^D L(\tau_L^D) = \max[0, G - K(\tau_K^*)]$. By taxing outstanding capital at a confiscatory rate and lowering the distortionary labor tax, the government achieves the welfare level $\tilde{W}(\tau^D, \tau^*) > W(\tau^*)$, where $\tilde{W}$ denotes welfare after a deviation from the expected tax structure τ^*. The one-time gain of $\tilde{W}(\tau^D, \tau^*) - W(\tau^*)$ is depicted graphically by the dark gray area in figure 12.3, which is constructed along the same lines as figure 12.1.

On the other hand, the government must bear the punishment of the expected confiscatory policy at all future stages. Because τ^E is an equilibrium of the stage game under discretion, the government indeed finds it optimal to comply with the expectation of this policy at stages $s = 2, \ldots, \infty$. At each of these stages, the government thus faces the loss $W(\tau^*) - W(\tau^E)$, is illustrated by the light gray areas in figure 12.3.

Sustainability of τ^* thus boils down to the condition

$$\tilde{W}(\tau^D, \tau^*) - W(\tau^*) \leq \frac{\beta}{1 - \beta}(W(\tau^*) - W(\tau^E)).$$

This condition is clearly satisfied for a relatively farsighted government with a high enough value of β.[7]

---

7. Reversion to the expected tax structure τ^E is the worst possible punishment for the government and, at the same time, it is also a (Nash) equilibrium of the "one-shot" (single-stage) game. In other models, the worst possible punishment is not a Nash equilibrium of the "one-shot" game. The reputational equilibrium then needs to satisfy an additional incentive constraint to make sure that the government finds it ex post optimal to bear the punishment, fulfilling the private-sector expectations; see Persson and Tabellini 1990, chap. 3, for a more extensive discussion.

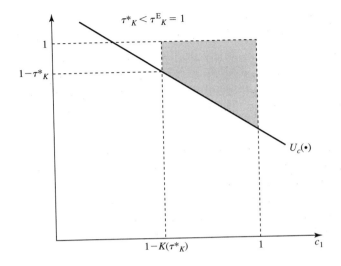

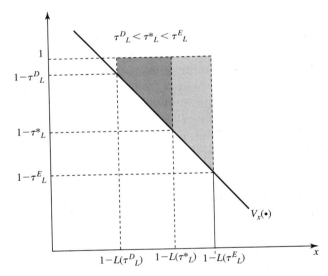

Figure 12.3

Kotlikoff, Persson, and Svensson (1988) show that a related enforcement mechanism may be available in an overlapping-generations economy. A misbehaving government is then not deterred by investors' expectations, but by the threat that future generations of taxpayers will withdraw their intergenerational transfers to a generation breaking "the social contract" by overtaxing capital. Problem 2 of this chapter deals with this case.

The possibility of such reputational mechanisms is, of course, no more—and no less—than an application of the Folk theorem of repeated games. As is well known, multiplicity of equilibria is a generic property of infinitely repeated games, and reputational equilibria are contained in a strict subset of these. Making the assumption that the public manages to coordinate on the expectational mechanism underlying the trigger strategy in (12.8) or some other trigger strategy obviously requires a leap of faith.

When we consider default on public debt, however, reputational equilibria encounter additional difficulties. Suppose that savers punish a defaulting government by refusing to buy public debt in the future. The government's punishment thus consists of its being unable to smooth tax distortions over time in the face of fluctuating public spending or tax bases. Is this sufficiently strong to deter default? Bulow and Rogoff (1989) argue that it is not. Suppose that a defaulting government can never borrow again but can nevertheless still invest budget surpluses in assets earning the market rate of return (for instance, by accumulating reserves of a foreign asset). Then a simple arbitrage argument implies that the government is always better off defaulting rather than repaying its debt.[8] Thus simple reputation models cannot explain public debt repayment. There must be other reasons why benevolent governments honor their debts: either reputational spillovers across policy instruments or other costs incurred after a default, such as distress in the banking system, arbitrary redistributions, or sanctions credibly enforced by the international community.

In the next two sections we discuss other realistic features, related to politics and capital mobility, that mitigate the capital levy problem. This requires some extensions of our simple model.

12.3   Politics

In this section, we reintroduce politics into the picture by adding a redistributive conflict between labor and capital and studying its interaction with the credibility problem. Since capital income is more concentrated than labor income, a majority of voters gain from shifting a large share of the tax burden to capital, despite the efficiency losses. We also study

---

8. Bulow and Rogoff (1989) develop their argument in the case of sovereign loans that finance consumption or investment, with no tax distortions, for arbitrary concave utility and production function, but their result generalizes to a model with tax distortions.

strategic delegation to mitigate the credibility problem in capital taxation. At the time of the elections, voters realize that the policymaker will choose policy in an environment where he faces a different set of constraints. To cope with these forthcoming incentive constraints, they find it optimal to elect a citizen-candidate with preferences different from their own. As suggested by Persson and Tabellini (1994c), strategic delegation allows voters to circumvent the capital levy problem: the elected policymaker has stronger ex post incentives to protect accumulated capital than the majority itself. We extend the model further and ask whether the suggested equilibrium is in fact consistent with optimal entry into the political process. Here we return to Besley and Coate's (1997) model of representative democracy introduced in chapter 5.

12.3.1 Capital versus Labor

To deal with capital formation and credibility problems in a simple way, we extend the simple model of section 12.1 to allow for individual endowment heterogeneity, along the same lines as in chapter 6. Specifically, in period 1, individual i faces the budget constraint

$$c_1^i + k^i = 1 - e^i,$$

whereas in period 2 his time constraint is given by

$$1 + e^i = l^i + x^i.$$

Thus to avoid two-dimensional individual differences, we make the simplifying (but counterfactual) assumption that type i's endowments of initial wealth $1 - e^i$ and of effective time $1 + e^i$ are perfectly negatively correlated. The idiosyncratic parameter e^i thus captures the relative importance of labor and capital in an individual's income. Apart from this, the model is identical to that in section 12.1.

Solving the utility maximization problem for given tax rates, we get the labor and capital supply functions, which, by the quasi-linear preferences, depend only on the "own tax rate":

$$l^i = L(\tau_L) + e^i \tag{12.9}$$

$$k^i = K(\tau_K) - e^i. \tag{12.10}$$

As in chapter 6, we assume that e^i is distributed with a c.d.f. $F(\cdot)$. For simplicity, we set the mean to zero: $e = 0$. We also assume that $U_c(1) < 1$, so that positive investment takes place if $\tau_K = 0$. Since asset income is more concentrated in the population than labor income, it is now natural to assume that the median value of e^i, defined by $F(e^m) = \frac{1}{2}$, is positive. Finally, we also assume that $\max[\tau_L L(\tau_L)] > G > 1$: the labor tax base is large enough to finance the whole of G, but the capital tax is never sufficient for this purpose. This assumption, which could be relaxed somewhat, rules out the multiple equilibria discussed above.

12.3.2   Equilibrium Taxation with Office-Seeking Candidates

In this subsection, we study equilibrium tax policy in preelection politics. We use the traditional assumption of Downsian electoral competition, in which two office-seeking candidates run against each other in a plurality election. Each candidate makes a binding commitment to an electoral platform, namely a vector of tax rates $\tau = (\tau_L, \tau_K)$. In equilibrium, both candidates announce the same policy platform, namely that platform preferred by the median voter at the time of elections. The voters' preferences hinge crucially on the timing of elections.

Ex Ante Elections   We start by assuming full commitment. Thus the sequence of events is as follows. (1) Elections take place at the beginning of period 1. (2) Private agents choose the amount to save in period 1. (3) The winning candidate's platform is enacted without further reoptimization. (4) Labor supply decisions are made. (A different sequence of events, with ex post elections, is discussed below.)

To characterize the voters' policy preferences, let $W^i(\tau)$ be individual i's indirect utility function:

$$W^i(\tau) = W(\tau) + (\tau_K - \tau_L)e^i,$$

where the function $W(\tau)$ is as defined in (12.5). Note that $W^i(\tau)$ is linear in the idiosyncratic parameter e^i and that substituting the government budget constraint into this expression does not destroy monotonicity. As in parts 1 and 2, this ensures existence of a well-defined Condorcet winner, namely the policy preferred by the median voter with endowment e^m.

Maximizing this function with regard to tax policy, subject to the government budget constraint and the supply functions defined above, we can rewrite the first-order conditions to get a modified Ramsey rule from voter i's point of view:

$$\frac{K\left(\tau_K^i\right) - e^i}{K\left(\tau_K^i\right)}\left[1 + \epsilon_L\left(\tau_L^i\right)\right] = \frac{L\left(\tau_L^i\right) + e^i}{L\left(\tau_L^i\right)}\left[1 + \epsilon_K\left(\tau_K^i\right)\right]. \tag{12.11}$$

Together with the government budget constraint (12.4), this condition defines the tax policy preferred by voter i, τ^i.

Consider first the policy preferred by the individual with average relative income from labor and capital, $e^i = e = 0$. In this case, (12.11) reduces to (12.6). Intuitively, the average individual does not care about redistribution, only about efficiency: thus his favored tax policy simply minimizes the deadweight loss associated with taxation. We continue to refer to this Ramsey policy as τ^*. Because of the quasi-linear preferences, this is also the utilitarian optimum.

When $e^i \neq 0$, redistributive preferences modify this pure efficiency condition predictably and monotonically. That is, individuals with more labor than capital income ($e^i > 0$) prefer the tax rate on capital to be higher and the rate on labor income to be lower, the more so the higher is e^i. An individual with $e^i < 0$ prefers the opposite structure (recall that elasticities are defined to be negative):

$$
\begin{aligned}
\tau_K^i &\lesseqqgtr \tau_K^* \\
&\qquad\qquad \text{as} \quad e^i \lesseqqgtr 0. \\
\tau_L^i &\gtreqqless \tau_L^*
\end{aligned}
\tag{12.12}
$$

What does the median voter prefer? As $e^m > 0$, the implied equilibrium tax policy τ^m taxes capital at a higher rate and labor at a lower rate than our normative benchmark policy τ^*. In this sense, capital is thus overtaxed, because of the skewed distribution of wealth, which implies that the pivotal voter relies relatively more on labor income than capital income.

Why does the fact that policy is enacted after the savings decision not give rise to a credibility problem? We have ruled this out by assuming commitment to electoral platforms. If candidates are truly office-seeking, there is no tension between their promise and ex post preferences. Thus with Downsian candidates, the timing of the elections and the voters' preferences at that point, rather than the candidates' preferences, can produce a credibility problem.

Ex Post Elections   Suppose then that we reverse the timing as follows: (1) Savings decisions are made. (2) Elections are held at the end of period 1. (3) Policy is enacted. (4) Labor supply is chosen. Political choices are thus made under discretion, as defined in the previous section. Now we need to consider the voters' ex post policy preferences.

To describe these preferences, notice that when elections are held the elasticity of capital with regard to the actual tax rate is zero: $\epsilon_K(\tau_K) = 0$. The capital stock depends on the expected tax rate; once the capital is in place, changing τ_K does not further reduce it. With this in mind, consider the average voter, with $e^i = 0$. This voter has no stake in redistribution and cares only about efficiency. He would like to tax capital as highly as possible (the inelastic factor) so as to reduce the distorting tax on labor (the elastic factor). Thus his ex post optimal policy is $\tau_K = 1$, for any aggregate capital stock inherited from the past.[9] For a "laborer," with $e^i > 0$, the redistributive motive reinforces these incentives for ex post expropriation. Because $e^m > 0$, a majority of voters clearly want to set $\tau_K = 1$ for any outstanding capital stock.

It follows that this is the tax policy both candidates announce in their electoral platforms. Because this is perfectly foreseen when the savings decision is made, nobody saves anything. In equilibrium, $k = 0$, and the government's entire revenue must be raised by taxing labor alone: $\tau_L L(\tau_L) = G$. This is the capital levy problem discussed in the previous section. Even

---

9. Recall our previous assumption that the capital tax base cannot be large enough to finance the whole of G.

though our simple two-period framework does not lend itself to a precise discussion of the timing of elections, it is still reasonable to interpret the capital levy problem as resulting from short political horizons imposed by frequently held elections. Renström (1997) and Klein and Rios-Rull (1999) demonstrate how the intervals of policy choice affect the equilibrium capital tax rate in general infinite horizon models.

We now show that under different assumptions about politicians' motivations, representative democracy can restore ex ante optimality, or at least move the equilibrium tax structure in the right direction.

12.3.3 Equilibrium Taxation with Citizen-Candidates

Downsian electoral competition entails two crucial assumptions about the political process. First, candidates are opportunistic: they care only about winning the election per se. Second, they can make binding promises ahead of the elections. Both assumptions, and particularly the second, are questionable. As we have discussed in several parts of the book, it is hard to justify the assumption of binding electoral promises: policy decisions are made once the candidate is in office, unconstrained by promises made during the electoral campaign. Moreover, politicians often have their own political agenda, their ideology or view of the world, that motivates their policy decisions once in office. In this subsection, we consider a different model of postelection politics based on alternative assumptions. Politicians are partisan "citizen-candidates." That is, each candidate for political office is just an ordinary individual in society who, like everybody else, is solely motivated by her utility function. Moreover, tax policy is chosen after the election, once the winning candidate is in office. As discussed in chapter 5, this means that preelection announcements by political candidates are never credible. Voters are forward-looking and select among candidates on the basis of their partisan preferences, correctly predicting that an elected candidate will simply set the ex post optimal policy.

We first follow Persson and Tabellini (1994c) by showing that this kind of environment naturally invites the voters to resolve credibility problems in capital taxation via strategic delegation. We then discuss another important aspect of the political process to which this approach naturally directs our attention: the entry stage on the political arena. Applying Besley and Coate's (1997) model, which was introduced in section 5.3, we show that such strategic delegation is indeed an equilibrium—though not the only one—in a game with endogenous and costly entry by citizen-candidates.

Preferences over Candidates   Assume that the prospective policymaker is one of the individuals in the model, uniquely identified by his endowment e^P, where P stands for policymaker. The timing of elections is also crucial in this setting. Here we assume that elections are held at the start of period 1 and that everyone observes the election outcome before they make the savings decision.[10] Policy, however, is set at the end of period 1, after the elections and after capital has been accumulated.

Once in office, an elected policymaker maximizes his ex post utility. He then takes into account that capital is already in place and $\epsilon_K(\tau_K) = 0$. As discussed in the previous subsection, any elected policymaker with $e^P \geq 0$ finds it optimal to set $\tau_K = 1$ for all k. A policymaker with $e^P < 0$, however, behaves differently. He still perceives $\epsilon_K(\tau_K) = 0$, which pushes him toward setting a high τ_K. But the redistributive motive pulls him back in the opposite direction. As can be verified from (12.11), he is always at an interior optimum. Furthermore, his preferences for τ_K can be obtained from this expression by setting $\epsilon_K(\tau_K) = 0$. We denote this interior optimum capital tax rate as a function of e^P and k by $T(e^P, k)$, implicitly defined by (12.11) with $\epsilon_K(\tau_K) = 0$ and by the government budget constraint (12.4). It is easy to show that this function has partials $T_e, T_k > 0$. Intuitively, the higher is the average tax base k, the greater is the efficiency gain from taxing it; conversely, the smaller is e^P algebraically, the greater is capital income relative to labor income for policymaker P, and hence, the lower is his desired capital tax rate.

We can summarize the above discussion as follows. Policymaker P, if elected and given outstanding capital k, enacts tax rates defined by

$$\tau_K^P = \begin{cases} 1 & \text{for} \quad e^P \geq 0 \\ T(e^P, k) & \text{for} \quad e^P < 0 \end{cases}$$

$$\tau_L^P L(\tau_L^P) = \begin{cases} G - K(1) & \text{for} \quad e^P \geq 0 \\ G - T(e^P, k)k & \text{for} \quad e^P < 0. \end{cases} \tag{12.13}$$

Consider now the election stage. Given the assumed timing, voters have well defined ex ante preferences over tax rates, defined by (12.11) and (12.4). Voters are rational and forward-looking. Hence they realize that once in office, a policymaker will behave according to (12.13). Thus the voters' ex ante policy preferences map into well-defined preferences over candidates' types. As before, let $\tau^i = (\tau_K^i, \tau_L^i)$ be the ex ante optimal tax structure, defined by (12.11) and (12.4). Let e^{iP} be the type of policymaker who finds it ex post optimal to implement this tax structure. Knowing τ_K^i, we can implicitly find e^{iP} from the expressions

$$\tau_K^i = T\left(e^{iP}, K\left(\tau_K^i\right)\right) \tag{12.14}$$

$$\tau_L^i L(\tau_L^i) = G - \tau_K^i K\left(\tau_K^i\right).$$

10. If elections were held ex post, after the capital accumulation decision, nothing essential would change relative to the Downsian equilibrium. This case is thus ignored.

Policymaker e^{iP} is thus voter i's preferred candidate. Intuitively, voters and investors know and understand the behavioral equations defined in (12.13) at the time of elections. Once they have seen who wins the elections, investors correctly anticipate the forthcoming tax policy and invest accordingly. Voters also take this into account when they vote: they realize that electing a policymaker with a high value of e^P discourages investment through the expectation of high capital tax rates. Conversely, a policymaker with a low value of e^P is a credible signal that τ_K will be kept low.[11]

Recall that $T(\cdot)$ is increasing in e^{iP} only for $e^{iP} < 0$, whereas the ex ante optimal tax rate on capital for voter i, τ_K^i, is increasing in e^i over the whole range of e^i. Several conclusions then follow from (12.14), (12.11), and (12.13). First, every voter prefers a policymaker with a greater share of capital income than herself—that is, $e^{iP} < e^i$. Indeed, every voter prefers a policymaker in the minority of the population, with $e^P \leq 0$. Right-wing candidates thus have a natural advantage in this setting. Their stake in redistributive tax policy makes them credible protectors of capital from overtaxation. Second, the induced preferences over policymaker types are themselves monotonic in voter type.

In other words, a long enough electoral horizon provides a motive for strategic delegation: to protect capital from expropriation, the majority elects a policymaker with higher capital income than average. Indeed, by the monotonicity established above, the policymaker, e^{mP}, preferred by the median voter, e^m, is the unique Condorcet winner in the population; that is, he is the only candidate who would win a pairwise contest against any other candidate. As discussed in chapter 5, however, we cannot jump to the conclusion that the election of e^{mP} and the ex post implementation of τ^m, that is, the median voter's ex ante optimal policy, is the equilibrium outcome. Why would e^{mP} find it optimal to run as a candidate? He would also rather have somebody else set policy, given the credibility problem. To know whether e^{mP}'s running and getting elected is an equilibrium, we really must study an explicit prior stage in which political candidates enter the competition.

Endogenous Entry of Candidates   Let us thus assume that an entry decision of prospective political candidates precedes the ex ante elections–cum–policy game. With this addition, the game has the following stages. (1) Any individual (of any type e^i) in the population can decide to run as a candidate, at the cost (in terms of second-period consumption) of ε. (2) An election is held among those running as candidates; whoever receives a plurality of the vote wins, and any tie is resolved by tossing a coin. (3) Individuals make their savings decisions. (4) The elected candidate chooses a tax policy τ; if no candidate has

---

11. Persson and Tabellini (1994c) discuss restrictions on $K(\cdot)$ that may be needed to ensure that the mapping from τ_K^i to e^{iP} indeed identifies a unique value of e^{iP}.

decided to run, a default policy $\bar{\tau}$ is implemented. (5) Individuals make their labor supply decision.

From the discussion above, we already know how to characterize the outcome from stages (3)–(5). At stage (2), each individual anticipates this outcome and votes for the candidate who gives her the highest expected utility, given the vote of other individuals. At stage (1), again anticipating the outcome at the following stages, an individual chooses to enter only if this gives her higher expected utility than not entering, given other individuals' entry decision.

We now follow section 5.3 in adapting the results in Besley and Coate 1997 to this model and characterizing some of its equilibria (we consider only one- and two-candidate equilibria).

We have already argued that the policymaker type e^{mP} preferred by the median voter e^m is the unique Condorcet winner among potential candidates. Thus e^{mP} is assured to win against any other candidate if she decides to run. But if she runs, no alternative single candidate $e^{P'}$ will ever find it worthwhile to incur the entry cost of running; this would in no way affect the policy outcome and hence not the utility of $e^{P'}$, who would thus only bear the cost of running and derive no benefit. This means that whenever e^{mP} runs in equilibrium, she must run as an uncontested candidate, or else there must be more than two candidates.

Let $\tau(e^P)$ be the tax structure that is ex post optimal for a candidate with endowment e^P, as defined implicitly by (12.14). Then the condition required for a single-candidate equilibrium to exist can be written as follows:

$$W^{mP}(\tau(e^{mP})) - W^{mP}(\bar{\tau}) \geq \varepsilon. \tag{12.15}$$

The condition says that e^{mP}'s utility gain, relative to the default policy, from running and choosing her ex post optimal policy must outweigh the cost of running. It is obviously fulfilled if the default policy $\bar{\tau}$ is sufficiently far from the equilibrium policy τ or if the running cost is small. In this equilibrium, the majority thus succeeds in completely resolving the credibility problem by strategic delegation to a right-wing policymaker who is sure to win the election and who has the correct ex post incentives to implement the policy τ^m that the majority prefers ex ante.

Single-candidate races are not very common, however. When do equilibria exist with two candidates, say e^R and e^L (with superscripts R and L denoting right-wing and left-wing, respectively, as in previous chapters)? Intuitively, a two-candidate equilibrium requires that e^R find it worthwhile to run, given that e^L is running, and vice versa. For each candidate this involves the same kind of calculation as for a single candidate, namely a trade-off between policy influence and entry costs. But a two-candidate equilibrium also requires that each candidate stand some chance of winning. With monotonic candidate preferences, the individual with median policy preferences e^m must thus be indifferent between the two candidates. In this event, the two candidates have the same chance of winning. Using the same notation as above, these conditions can formally be expressed as follows

$$W^m(\tau(e^R)) = W^m(\tau(e^L))$$

$$\frac{1}{2}[W^I(\tau(e^I)) - W^I(\tau(e^J))] > \varepsilon, \qquad I, J = R, L, \quad I \neq J. \tag{12.16}$$

Here two candidates on opposite sides of the median voter's preferred type e^{mP} are running against each other. Each enters to balance the other candidate, provided that their endowments are different enough (otherwise, a fifty-fifty chance of winning does not offset the cost of running). It follows that there may be many different two-candidate equilibria. In each of these, a right-wing candidate with $e^R < e^{mP}$ balances a left-wing candidate with $e^L > e^{mP}$ at the same utility distance from the median voter's preferred policy. All voters with endowments $e^i < e^m$ vote for e^R, whereas all voters with $e^i > e^m$ vote for e^L. As further discussed in chapter 5 and in Besley and Coate 1997, this prevents a third candidate from running.

Note that in a two-candidate equilibrium, voters succeed in delegating the credibility problem only in an expected sense; once elected, the two candidates will pursue different policies on opposite sides of the Ramsey policy. As discussed in chapter 5, the prediction that equilibrium policy in two-candidate elections does not converge to the median voter's preferred policy (if such a voter exists) stands in stark contrast to the prediction of the Downsian model.

12.4 Tax Competition

This section introduces a new incentive constraint emanating from spillover effects across international or regional boundaries. Rational governments have a temptation to exploit these spillovers for their own benefit or for the benefit of their own citizens. The literatures on international policy coordination and on local public finance have advocated cooperation among countries as a means of abstaining from this individualistic behavior. When countries or regions cooperate over capital taxes, welfare-maximizing governments set tax policy according to some version of a Ramsey rule. Without cooperation, on the other hand, governments have an incentive to keep taxes low, attempting to attract capital from the other jurisdiction to expand the domestic tax base. Because both governments do this, capital does not move in a (symmetric) Nash equilibrium. Capital tax rates are inefficiently low, however, which is the classic case for cooperation put forward by Gordon (1983) and many others.

The main point we want to stress in this section is that taking into account the incentives arising from the domestic policy process enriches the analysis of policy interactions. These domestic incentives can be tied either to credibility issues or to politics. Policy coordination need not always be welfare-improving, for it may exacerbate the effects of domestic incentive constraints on policy choice. At a general level, we identify a two-way interaction: the incentives in the domestic policy process spill over into the international arena, and international strategic considerations partly shape domestic policy. Unformalized research in political science, triggered by Putnam's (1989) influential article, has stressed this two-way interaction. In his critical discussion of the concrete attempts to coordinate macroeconomic policy in the 1980s, Feldstein (1988) raises similar issues.

We first adapt our simple model to include two jurisdictions between which capital, but not labor, can move freely. In section 12.4.2, we contrast the equilibrium with and without international cooperation, neglecting other incentive constraints: a benevolent government under commitment chooses policy maximizing national welfare. We abandon this assumption in the succeeding two subsections, asking whether the absence of cooperation exacerbates or weakens other domestic policy distortions. In section 12.4.3 we illustrate an idea originally due to Rogoff (1985b): cooperation may be counterproductive if it weakens government credibility. Here tax competition has the advantage of reducing the government temptation to overtax capital: when governments do not cooperate, investors can take their capital abroad. In section 12.4.4, we eliminate these credibility problems by assumption and instead study the interaction of domestic politics and tax competition. As in section 12.3, tax competition creates scope for strategic delegation: voters in both countries want to elect governments that are particularly apt to face the incentive constraint due to tax competition.

12.4.1   Capital Mobility

The model here is similar to that of section 12.1, except that there are two jurisdictions rather than just one. We refer to these as countries, although they could equally well be regions of the same country with independent tax authority. We start by assuming a representative consumer, adding individual heterogeneity later on. Throughout the section, variables referring to the foreign country are denoted with an asterisk. In the first period, capital can be invested in either country according to an identical investment technology. One unit invested today yields one unit tomorrow, gross of taxes. Foreign investment, however, carries some "mobility costs" meant to capture the extra transaction and information costs associated with foreign investment. For simplicity, investors bear these costs in the second period, when the fruits of investment mature. Capital invested at home is taxed at the domestic rate τ_K, whereas capital invested abroad is taxed at the foreign rate τ_K^*. Labor is, in contrast to

investment, completely fixed and cannot move across borders. Under these assumptions, we can write the representative consumer's budget constraints as

$$1 = c_1^i + k^i + f^i = c_1^i + s^i$$
$$c_2^i = (1 - \tau_K)k^i + (1 - \tau_K^*)f^i - M(f^i) + (1 - \tau_L)l^i \qquad (12.17)$$
$$= (1 - \tau_K)s^i + (\tau_K - \tau_K^*)f^i - M(f^i) + (1 - \tau_L)l^i,$$

where k and f denote domestic and foreign investment, $s \equiv k + f$ denotes savings, and M is a function capturing the mobility costs of foreign investment. We assume that $M(0) = 0$, $M_f > 0$ if $f > 0$, and $M_{ff} > 0$.

Finally, the government budget constraint in the second period is

$$G = \tau_K k + \tau_K f^* + \tau_L l = \tau_K (s - f + f^*) + \tau_L l, \qquad (12.18)$$

where G denotes exogenous public consumption. Equations (12.17) and (12.18) thus implicitly assume that capital is taxed according to the source principle, not the residence principle, and that the same tax rate applies irrespective of who owns the capital.[12]

By the private optimality conditions, savings are a function of the domestic tax rate in an interior optimum, $s^i = S(\tau_K) \equiv 1 - U_c^{-1}(1 - \tau_K)$, with $S_\tau < 0$. Moreover, investment abroad is given by the function $f^i = F(\tau_K, \tau_K^*) \equiv M_f^{-1}(\tau_K - \tau_K^*)$, with $F_\tau = -F_{\tau^*} > 0$. Thus a unilaterally higher capital tax rate at home (abroad) encourages (discourages) capital flight. Finally, domestic investment at home can be written as $k^i = K(\tau_K, \tau_K^*) = S(\tau_K) - F(\tau_K, \tau_K^*)$. A higher capital tax rate in the home country discourages home investment in two ways: it reduces savings and induces capital flight by home citizens. The foreign country is identical to the home country in all respects. In particular, $F_{\tau^*}^* = F_\tau$ and $F_\tau^* = F_{\tau^*}$. The labor supply function remains exactly as before.

12.4.2 Cooperation versus Noncooperation

Consider first the cooperative equilibrium, defined as the pair of policies maximizing worldwide welfare. The timing of events is as follows. (1) In period 1, governments choose tax policy. (2) Having observed the policy selection, consumers choose how much to save and where to invest. (3) In period 2, no new policy decision is made, and consumers choose how much to work and consume, given their period 1 choices. Thus we begin in the typical framework of normative optimal taxation theory, abstracting from politics and any credibility problem.

---

12. This assumption is appropriate in the case of industrial capital and foreign direct investments. Even in the case of financial capital, it may not be too far-fetched if there are problems with the enforcement of interfacial tax treaties.

To compute the optimal tax rates, we use the previous notation to write the home consumer indirect utility function as

$$W(\tau, \tau_K^*) \equiv U(1 - S(\tau_K)) + (1 - \tau_K)S(\tau_K) + (\tau_K - \tau_K^*)F(\tau_K, \tau_K^*)$$
$$- M(F(\tau_K, \tau_K^*)) + (1 - \tau_L)L(\tau_L) + V(1 - L(\tau_L)),$$

subject to the government budget constraint. The foreign consumer indirect utility function, $W^*(\tau^*, \tau_K)$, is analogously defined. Optimal tax rates are set at stage (1) to maximize $[W(\tau, \tau_K^*) + W^*(\tau^*, \tau_K)]$. Appealing to the envelope theorem, exploiting symmetry, and going through this optimal taxation exercise, one can pin down the equilibrium tax structure in the home country using the following version of Ramsey rule:[13]

$$\epsilon_S^C(\tau_K) = \epsilon_L(\tau_L). \tag{12.19}$$

Because a similar condition holds for the foreign country and because the two countries are identical, we have $\tau_K = \tau_K^*$.

The key determinant of the equilibrium tax rate on capital is thus the elasticity $\epsilon_S^C(\tau_K)$. In a cooperative equilibrium, this elasticity can be written as

$$\epsilon_S^C(\tau_K) = S_\tau(\tau_K)\tau_K / S(\tau_K). \tag{12.20}$$

Note that the elasticity $\epsilon_S^C(\tau_K)$ reflects only the savings elasticity, thus neglecting the investment elasticity due to the international movements of capital: when the two governments cooperate, they refrain from exploiting international capital mobility for their own benefit.

The outcome is different under noncooperative policymaking. Specifically, consider the Nash equilibrium, in which both governments at stage (1) maximize their own citizens' welfare, taking the tax rate in the other country as given. Thus the home government maximizes $W(\tau, \tau_K^*)$, defined above, given τ_K^*, and the foreign government behaves symmetrically. A condition identical to (12.19) defines the home government's reaction function, except that the following elasticity now replaces the elasticity $\epsilon_S^C(\tau_K)$ on the left-hand side:

$$\epsilon_S^N(\tau_K, \tau_K^*) = (S_\tau(\tau_K) + 2F_\tau^*(\tau_K, \tau_K^*))\tau_K / S(\tau_K). \tag{12.21}$$

---

13. Equation (12.19) is obtained as follows. By symmetry, the first-order conditions to the optimal taxation problem with respect to τ_K and τ_L simplify to

$$-S + F - F^* + (S - F + F^* + \tau_K S_\tau)\lambda = 0$$
$$-L + \lambda(L + \tau_L L) = 0,$$

where λ is the Lagrange multiplier of the government budget constraint. By symmetry and by the definitions of elasticities, (12.19) and (12.20) follow.

where the N superscript is a reminder that the elasticity is computed in the Nash equilibrium.[14]

Consider now a symmetric equilibrium with $\tau_K = \tau_K^*$. Contrasting (12.20) and (12.21) and recalling that $F_\tau^* < 0$, it follows immediately that $|\epsilon_S^C(\tau_K, \tau_K^*)| < |\epsilon_S^N(\tau_K)|$: the perceived elasticity of the capital tax base is lower (in absolute value) with than without cooperation. By (12.19), then, the equilibrium tax rate on capital is higher, and the equilibrium tax rate on labor is correspondingly lower, with than without cooperation. That is, tax competition induces both governments to rely more on labor taxes (the immobile factor) and less on capital taxes, compared to the ex ante optimum. The intuition is straightforward. In the absence of cooperation, both governments face an incentive to reduce capital taxes unilaterally to attract foreign capital and to keep domestic capital within their borders. This incentive is stronger the greater is international capital mobility (i.e., the more negative is F_τ^*). The immobile factor, namely labor, bears an additional tax burden.

Thus lack of cooperation reduces worldwide welfare. In the Nash equilibrium, no capital flows from either country. Tax competition does not pay: it simply distorts governments' incentives. In both countries, capital tax rates are too low and labor tax rates are too high, compared with the (second-best) optimal taxation rule. This distortion is greater (and so is the benefit from cooperation) the more mobile is capital. In the limit, if capital is perfectly mobile across countries (if $F_\tau = \infty$), the only Nash equilibrium has zero tax rates on capital, and both countries tax only labor.

12.4.3 Credibility and Cooperation

We now show that cooperation can nevertheless be counterproductive because of the interplay with another incentive constraint. Specifically, if governments lack credibility, the

---

14. Equation (12.21) is derived from the problem of maximizing the consumer indirect utility function subject to the government budget constraint and taking the foreign tax rate as given. The first-order condition for that problem with respect to τ_K turns out to be

$$-S + F - F^* + (S - F + F^* + \tau_K S_\tau - \tau_K F_\tau + \tau_K F_\tau^*)\lambda = 0.$$

Recall that by the private optimality conditions discussed in the previous subsection, $K_\tau = S_\tau - F_\tau$ and $-F_\tau = F_\tau^* < 0$. The first-order condition can thus be written

$$\lambda = \frac{1}{1 + \epsilon_S^N(\tau_K, \tau_K^*)},$$

where the elasticity of the capital tax base is written

$$\epsilon_S^N(\tau_K, \tau_K^*) = \frac{(S_\tau(\tau_K) + 2F_\tau^*(\tau_K, \tau_K^*))\tau_K}{S(\tau_K) + F^*(\tau_K, \tau_K^*) - F(\tau_K, \tau_K^*)}.$$

By symmetry, both governments choose the same equilibrium tax rate. Hence in equilibrium $F = F^* = 0$, and (12.21) follows.

important issue is whether cooperation between governments makes government policy more or less credible. Since the government maximizes social welfare, cooperation
can be undesirable for society as a whole as well as for the government engaging in
cooperation.

To illustrate this point, which is due to Rogoff (1985b) and Kehoe (1989), suppose that
we change the timing of events in the model of the previous section as follows. (1) In
period 1, individuals save (decide on s). (2) In period 2, the governments of both countries
choose tax policy. (3) Finally, individuals choose the location of their investment (decide
on k versus f), as well as how much to work and consume in period 2. Thus savings and
investment are temporally separated, or equivalently, capital can move across borders after
policy choices have been made.

This timing reintroduces the credibility problems studied in sections 12.2–12.3. The individuals' savings decision anticipates the forthcoming equilibrium tax policy. Governments
cannot credibly convince savers that taxes will be low, however, as they have ex post incentives to tax savings a lot when taxes are set. In this case, cooperation can make things
worse, because it effectively removes the only remaining check on high capital taxation,
namely international mobility.

To make the argument more precise, note that savings have an ex post elasticity of zero.
We can thus remove the term S_τ from the elasticities expressions (12.20) and (12.21). With
cooperation, the elasticity of the tax base becomes zero, $\epsilon_S^C(\tau_K) = 0$, creating the same
kind of capital levy problem as in section 12.2. In the Nash equilibrium, in contrast, the
elasticity $\epsilon_S^N(\tau_K, \tau_K^*)$ remains negative (though it is a larger number than in the previous
subsection, because in (12.21) both S_τ and $F_\tau^* < 0$). By (12.19) it follows that the equilibrium
tax rate on capital is higher, in both the noncooperative and the cooperative regime, when
credibility problems are present. But the cooperative equilibrium has a prohibitive tax rate,
whereas with no cooperation the capital tax rate is less than 1. Tax competition is still
operative, without cooperation so that capital taxes remain lower than with cooperation—
even though they are higher than in the Nash equilibrium of the previous subsection. In this
specific model the tax policy without cooperation is closer to the ex ante optimum. Thus tax
competition is socially desirable, as it gives some credibility to a policy of nonconfiscatory
capital taxes.

The general insight of this subsection is that policy coordination among governments
can be counterproductive when the international and the domestic incentive constraints pull
the equilibrium policy in opposite directions. Tax competition by itself pulls the tax rate
below the Ramsey optimum, but lack of credibility pulls it above. Hence the equilibrium
where both incentive constraints are binding may be superior to that where only one of
them is. The same idea will reappear in part 5, when we discuss international coordination
of monetary policy.

12.4.4   Domestic Politics

So far we have discussed whether there are prospective gains from international cooperation in fiscal policy. But assuming such gains make it worthwhile, how can cooperative outcomes be implemented? This question is very important, given that each country involved has incentives to deviate unilaterally from the cooperative equilibrium, unless there is some enforcement mechanism. We now show that domestic political institutions can go some way toward implementing the cooperative outcome, a result that is of interest because it demonstrates that better outcomes may be achievable without any need to enforce international agreements. As in section 12.3, strategic delegation is central to the argument. Here it reflects a different incentive constraint, though: not lack of credibility, but the strategic interaction between the home and foreign governments.

To make this point, we take up a theme that has also been studied in recent work in political science (Putnam 1989). When individual citizens are heterogeneous and governments are politically motivated, there are different domestic policymakers or political actors within each country. In a representative democracy, the relationship between voters and their governments is not fixed. If international policy spillovers are important enough, voters elect a government that is fit to play the international policy game. International policy spillovers thus have domestic political repercussions. Domestic politics also plays a role in the international policy equilibrium, however. In the specific model of this section, domestic politics mitigates the adverse consequences of tax competition and reduces the need for international policy coordination.

As in section 12.3, we add individually heterogenous labor and capital endowments to the model of the previous subsection. Specifically, the period 1 budget constraint of an individual of type i in the home country is

$$1 - e^i = c_1^i + k^i + f^i = c_1^i + s^i,$$

whereas his time constraint is given by

$$1 + e^i = l^i + x^i.$$

As before, the idiosyncratic parameter e^i is distributed with a c.d.f. $\mathfrak{F}(\cdot)$ with mean zero. To simplify, we assume that the distribution is symmetric, so that median and average endowments coincide. In this case, the median-voter optimum also maximizes a utilitarian social welfare function. Finally, we assume that $U_c(1) < 1$, such that if $\tau_K = 0$, some positive investment takes place. We consider only interior equilibria. For the rest of the assumptions, the model remains the same. In particular, the last expression in (12.17) still gives the period 2 budget constraint. To preserve symmetry, the distribution $\mathfrak{F}(\cdot)$ is the same in the two countries.

As in the previous section, solving the utility maximization problem for given tax rates, we get the labor and capital supply functions, which—by the quasi-linear preferences—depend only on the "own tax rate" and are linear in the idiosyncratic parameter e^i:

$$l^i = L(\tau_L) + e^i, \qquad s^i = S(\tau_K) - e^i \tag{12.22}$$

$$f^i = F(\tau_K, \tau_K^*), \qquad k^i = K(\tau_K, \tau_K^*) - e^i, \tag{12.23}$$

where the functions L, S, F, K are all defined as earlier in the chapter. Note that our specification of preferences with linear period 2 consumption and additively separable costs of capital mobility implies that all individuals invest the same amount abroad, irrespective of their endowments. Individual heterogeneity thus matters only for labor supply and home investment.

Politicians are outcome-motivated citizen-candidates who maximize the welfare function corresponding to their type, once in office. The sequence of events is as follows: (1) Elections are held simultaneously in both countries. (2) The elected governments simultaneously and noncooperatively choose tax policy once and for all at the start of period 1. (3) All private economic decisions are made, first for period 1 and then for period 2.

Thus we remove all credibility problems through our assumptions. But we also assume away any international institutions capable of enforcing international agreements. An equilibrium is defined by two conditions (in addition to individuals' optimal economic behavior). It must be a Nash equilibrium among the elected policymakers, who choose the optimal tax rate, given foreign policy. It must also be a political equilibrium. That is, the elected policymakers must be preferred to any other candidate by a majority of the voters in their own country, given the outcome of foreign elections and how the policymakers behave once in office. For simplicity, we disregard the entry stage in the political arena and consider only the political equilibrium with a single candidate, that preferred by the median voter in each country at the time of elections. An entry stage could be added along the same lines as in section 12.3, however.

This definition makes clear that a strategic motive partly drives elections. Policymakers behave as Nash players with respect to each other once in office. Voters do not take the foreign tax rate as given when comparing different candidates, but they do take the foreign electoral outcome as given. As shown below, this makes voters desire to elect a policymaker who does not share their own preferences, yielding a more favorable Nash equilibrium in the subsequent policy game.

Equilibrium of the Policy Game   Suppose that policymakers of type e^P and e^{P*} have been elected in the home and foreign country respectively. The Nash equilibrium among them is obtained exactly as in the previous subsection. A condition like (12.19), modified to take individual heterogeneity into account, therefore defines the home policymaker's optimal tax structure:

$$\frac{S\left(\tau_K^P\right) - e^P}{S\left(\tau_K^P\right)}\left[1 + \epsilon_L\left(\tau_L^P\right)\right] = \frac{L\left(\tau_L^P\right) + e^P}{L\left(\tau_L^P\right)}\left[1 + \epsilon_S^N\left(\tau_K^P, \tau_K^{*P*}\right)\right]. \tag{12.24}$$

A similar condition holds in the foreign country. The elasticity ϵ_S^N is still given by (12.21).

Equations (12.24) and (12.21), together with the budget constraint, implicitly define the home policymaker's reaction function, namely a function $\tau_K = T(e^P, \tau_K^*)$, and similarly for the foreign policymaker: $\tau_K^* = T(e^{P*}, \tau_K)$. The slope of this function (the derivative T_{τ^*}) has an ambiguous sign. As τ_K^* increases, capital flows into the home country, and the tax base for the home capital tax increases. This has two opposite effects. On the one hand, with a fixed revenue requirement, the government can afford to reduce tax rates on both capital and labor. On the other hand, the capital tax base becomes more inelastic, which induces the home government to raise τ_K and lower τ_L.[15] Thus as τ_K^* rises, τ_L unambiguously falls, but τ_K can go up or down, depending on which effect prevails. It is perhaps more plausible that τ_K and τ_K^* move in the same direction (i.e., that they are strategic complements); this in fact becomes more likely if government spending is also endogenous. Hence, let us assume that the reaction functions are upward sloping, $T_{\tau^*} > 0$, and similarly for the foreign country.[16] It can be shown (without further restrictions) that $T_{\tau^*} < 1$ and $T_{\tau}^* < 1$. Hence both reaction functions can be drawn as in figure 12.4. The position of these reaction functions depends on the government type, as captured by the parameters e^P and e^{P*}. We can also show that $T_e > 0$; that is, a higher value of e^P (say $e'^P > e^P$) shifts the domestic reaction function to the right, toward the dotted line in the figure. Quite intuitively, an elected policymaker at home with a higher e^P is willing to set higher capital taxes for any foreign tax rate, as he has a higher labor income relative to capital income. Since the foreign government's best response is then to raise τ_K^*, the equilibrium tax rates on capital in *both* countries go up as e^P rises. The same argument holds with respect to e^{P*}.

15. Formally, $\partial \epsilon_S^N (\tau_K, \tau_K^*)/\partial \tau_K^*$ this can be derived from the formula in note 14, under the assumption that the second derivatives of F (or equivalently the third derivative of the mobility cost function M) are negligible.

16. A set of sufficient conditions for this to be true in a neighborhood of $e^P = 0$ is that (1) the third derivatives of V and M are negligible, so that L_τ and F_τ are nearly constant, and that (2) the elasticity of savings is sufficiently higher in absolute value than the elasticity of labor supply; more precisely, that

$$\frac{-\epsilon_S^N}{\tau_K S} > \frac{-\epsilon_L}{\tau_L L}\frac{1 - \epsilon_L}{1 + \epsilon_L}$$

(recall that both elasticities are negative, by definition). These sufficient conditions can be derived formally by applying the implicit function theorem to the government budget constraint and the Ramsey rule for the home country. Identical conditions hold for the foreign country.

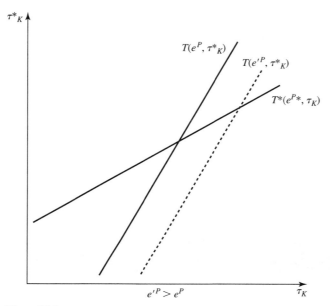

Figure 12.4

In summary, the equilibrium tax rate on capital in each country is an increasing function of the policymakers' labor to capital ratio e^P and e^{P*}. It is through this feature of the equilibrium that elections matter for the equilibrium outcome.

Political Equilibrium   With this result in mind, let us now turn to the election stage of the game. Because the voters' preferences are monotonic, the only Condorcet winner in each country is the candidate preferred by the median voter. Moreover, as in section 12.3, the median voter in each country prefers a candidate different than himself. Voters realize that tax competition in the subsequent stage of the game will force the elected governments to keep taxes on capital inefficiently low and taxes on labor inefficiently high. By electing a left-wing policymaker, who will be more willing to tax capital than labor once in office, the home median voter can induce the foreign policymaker to increase his equilibrium tax rate on capital, which has a positive spillover effect at home. The same argument applies in the foreign country. Hence in both countries, a candidate with a lower e^i than the median voter wins the election, and the resulting equilibrium policy entails correspondingly higher tax rates on capital.

To illustrate this point more formally, let us compute the capital tax rate τ_K that the home median voter would wish to see implemented at home. Under the assumed timing, the home median voter does not take the foreign rate τ_K^* as given. He instead realizes that the foreign reaction function, $\tau_K^* = T(e^P, \tau_K)$, with e^{P*} taken as given, determines the foreign tax rate. The home median voter therefore maximizes his own preferences, subject to the usual government budget constraint and the additional incentive constraint: $\tau_K^* = T(e^{P*}, \tau_K)$.

Recalling our assumption that the median voter coincides with the average individual (i.e., $e^m = 0$), the tax structure solving this optimization problem must satisfy the usual Ramsey rule but with a different elasticity of capital:

$$\epsilon_L(\tau_L) = \epsilon_S^{NR}(\tau_K, \tau_K^*).$$ (12.25)

The elasticity ϵ_S^{NR} is now given by the expression

$$\epsilon_S^{NR} = (S_\tau + 2F_{\tau_K}^*(1 - T_\tau))\tau_K/S.$$ (12.26)

Comparing this new elasticity with the corresponding expression in (12.21), we see that $\epsilon_S^{NR} > \epsilon_S^N$, since $1 > T_\tau > 0$. Hence at the election stage, the home median voter prefers a higher tax rate on capital than the one he himself would implement in a Nash equilibrium, though not as high as in the cooperative equilibrium. When voting, the median voter does not take the foreign tax structure as given; instead he takes the foreign policymaker and thus the foreign reaction function as given. He then realizes that the foreign policymaker reacts to a higher home capital tax rate τ_K (implemented by a more left-wing policymaker type) by raising τ_K^*. This reduces the perceived elasticity of the tax base, because it reduces the danger of capital flight following the election of a liberal government type. The median voter implements his preferred tax rate by electing a left-wing policymaker type, that is, someone with a higher labor to capital ratio than the average: $e^P > 0$.[17]

Persson and Tabellini (1992a) discuss the comparative statics of an increase in capital mobility in a similar model (think of the F function as more sensitive to the tax rate because of a lower marginal cost M_f of moving capital abroad). Problems 3 and 4 of this chapter deal formally with this model and comparative statics exercise. If policymaker types are held constant, higher mobility would produce a large drop in capital taxes due to stiffer tax competition. But in the model, the political equilibrium changes too. Specifically, the pivotal voter in each country reacts by electing an even more left-wing policymaker, and this dampens the effect of higher mobility on equilibrium tax policy. Persson and Tabellini wrote that paper in the early 1990s, in the face of the planned deregulation of intra-European capital markets in the single-market program. At that time all European Union countries except a few had center or right-wing government. Interestingly, at the time of writing this book, all EU countries except two have center or left-wing governments.

---

17. This can be verified by comparing equations (12.24) and (12.25), together with $\epsilon_S^{NR} > \epsilon_S^N$.

Two general lessons can be drawn from this example. First, political delegation may help relax the international incentive constraint, making tax competition less damaging and the benefits from policy coordination less stark. Second, domestic politics and international policy spillovers are closely intertwined. The tax competition externality favors left-wing candidates in the political race, because they yield a better international policy equilibrium.

Some of these results are not general, however, since they rely on strategic complementarity of the policy instruments. Under different assumptions, policy instruments could very well be strategic substitutes, so that the reaction functions would be negatively sloped. In this case, political delegation could make things worse, in that the political equilibrium would yield lower welfare than the simple Nash equilibrium. Vickers (1985) discusses some related examples with reference to managerial delegation by oligopolistic firms.

12.5   Discussion

This long chapter started with a positive question: How is the structure of taxation across labor and capital determined? In particular, why are observed taxes on capital so much higher than those prescribed by the efficiency principles of optimal taxation? To answer this question we emphasized the effects of three incentive constraints on policy formation: lack of credibility, redistributive politics, and international tax competition. Lack of credibility implies that policymakers pay insufficient attention to the distorting effects of taxes on capital, since such effects operate through expectations, not through actual policy choice. Thus lack of credibility tilts the tax structure toward excessively high capital taxation.

Redistributive politics as we have modeled it reinforces this effect. We assumed that the political conflict between capital and labor is one-dimensional. As in the general-interest politics of chapter 6, the political equilibrium then reflects the wishes of the majority of voters. Since capital income is much more concentrated than labor income, the majority benefits by overtaxing capital and undertaxing labor.

Whereas the effect of the first two incentive constraints is consistent with the stylized facts motivating the analysis, international tax competition pulls in the opposite direction. To attract foreign capital or prevent capital flight, governments are forced to tax labor more heavily than capital. This effect is stronger the greater is the asymmetry between the mobility of capital and the immobility of labor across tax jurisdictions.

Throughout the chapter we also emphasized the interactions between these three incentive constraints. One important lesson is that these interaction effects can reverse some normative implications. For instance, even though international coordination is desirable when tax competition is considered in isolation, the opposite may be true when it interacts with lack of credibility, because these two incentive constraints pull in opposite directions and tend to offset each other. Thus tax competition may restore credibility to a policy of low capital taxes. A second lesson is that the interactions also shape the political equilibrium. Right-wing candidates are favored when policy credibility is an issue, because they are less prone to overtax capital. On the other hand, international tax competition may favor left-wing candidates, because they are less likely to overtax labor and hence may be more fit to interact strategically with foreign governments. Through these channels, political delegation may mitigate the effects of the incentive constraints.

We have deliberately kept the model in this chapter very simple to derive analytical results and to preserve unity throughout the chapter. This has not been without costs, however. One the most restrictive economic assumptions we have made might be that of perfectly competitive labor markets. This assumption implies that, given plausible quantitative values for the elasticity of individual labor supply, it is efficient to impose most of the tax burden on labor, since this tax base is much more inelastic. Yet allowing for labor market imperfections could overturn this implication. Negotiating wages through bargaining could shift the burden of a labor tax onto the firm, with bigger distorting effects on both employment and investment. Clearly, decentralized and competitive labor markets are not the norm among industrial countries. Pissarides (1998) discusses the effects of labor taxation in a variety of theoretical models of wage formation, and Daveri and Tabellini (1997) provide empirical evidence of the large distorting effects of labor taxes in OECD countries (see also the survey in Nickell and Layard 1999). None of these papers, however, attempts to make the tax structure endogenous.

A second simplifying economic assumption we have made is that of a two-period horizon. Extending the model to an infinite horizon is not likely to change the theory's qualitative implications, though it would reinforce the inefficiency of capital taxes. The economic model would have much more credible quantitative implications with an infinite horizon, however, which could be taken to the data to assess the quantitative relevance and plausibility of some results. Klein and Rios-Rull 1999 is an interesting example of this kind of work.

We have also kept the political model very simple, through the assumption of one-dimensional heterogeneity among the voters, which enabled us to easily identify the economic conflicts over the policy. The mechanism for aggregating these conflicting interests could be made much more realistic, however, by exploiting the analytical tools elaborated in earlier chapters. Recall, for instance, the cautionary results regarding income distribution in sections 3.4 and 3.5. Applied here, we would say that high concentration of capital gives capital owners a high stake in low taxes. Suppose now that this group has a larger number of swing voters, because of weaker ideological attachments or higher turnout rates, or is better organized for lobbying than other groups. Then a probabilistic voting model—augmented by lobbying, or not—would predict that these higher stakes should result in low equilibrium tax rates on capital.

Rodriguez (1997) studies a model with exactly those features. Capitalists and workers pay the same income tax, but only capitalists are organized to pay campaign contributions to the government. In exchange, they obtain tax exemptions on capital income; as a result, higher stakes for capital owners lead to lower (effective) tax rates. Another interesting example of a different political model is that of Rodrik and van Ypersele (1999), who investigate capital market liberalizations in a setting with productivity shocks and endogenous returns to capital and labor. They argue that international coordination of capital taxes may be needed to compensate the losers (labor) for an efficiency-enhancing liberalization.

Finally, as in many other topics covered in the book, careful empirical work linked with the theory is badly needed and could have high payoffs.

12.6   Notes on the Literature

The capital levy problem has a long history in economics. Eichengreen (1990) provides a historical account. Fischer (1980) explained and formally analyzed (although with numerical solutions) the problem and its welfare consequences in a two-period problem of capital and labor taxation. Klein and Rios-Rull (1999) compute perfect Markov equilibria of capital and labor taxation under an assumption of partial commitment; see also section 11.4.

A large literature deals with speculative attacks and multiple equilibria. In this section, we have focused only on multiple equilibria that arise when policy is endogenous and there is a credibility problem. Many authors have studied confidence crises concerning public debt, in particular Calvo (1988), Alesina, Prati, and Tabellini (1990), Cole and Kehoe (1996a, 1996b), and Giavazzi and Pagano (1990). The literature has also extensively treated multiple equilibria with discretionary monetary policy, in particular works by Obstfeld (1997b), Bensaid and Jeanne (1997), Chari, Christiano, and Eichenbaum (1996), and Velasco (1994).

Kotlikoff, Persson, and Svensson (1988), Chari and Kehoe (1990), and more recently, Benhabib and Rustichini (1996) discuss reputation and capital taxation, whereas Grossman and van Huyck (1988) and Chari and Kehoe (1993) have applied reputation to a model of public debt repayment. The idea that reputation can fail in the case of sovereign debt repayment is due to Bulow and Rogoff (1989), whereas Chari and Kehoe (1993) show that enforcement problems on both sides of the market can restore a role for reputation. Cole and Kehoe (1994) discuss reputational spillovers across contracts. Political delegation and capital levies are modeled in Persson and Tabellini 1994b and discussed by North and Weingast (1989) in a fascinating historical context. Persson and Tabellini (1995) survey the literature on international tax competition and credibility.

The idea that strategic delegation allows the principal to cope with binding incentive constraints for the agent was first applied in industrial organization by Vickers (1985),

Fershtman and Judd (1987), and Fershtman, Judd, and Kalai (1991). The idea has found several other natural applications in political economics, with regard to credibility problems in monetary policy (Rogoff 1985a) and capital taxation (Persson and Tabellini 1994c), international policy coordination (Persson and Tabellini 1992a), hierarchical decision making by different levels of government inside a federation (Persson and Tabellini 1996a), bargaining inside a legislature (Chari, Jones, and Marimon 1997, Besley and Coate 1998a); see also section 7.7.

The literature dealing with international policy cooperation began with the insightful work of Hamada (1974, 1976). Although Hamada dealt with monetary policy in the pre–rational expectations tradition, he used modern game theory to illustrate how decentralized noncooperative policymaking would result in suboptimal outcomes. Optimal taxation when tax bases are internationally mobile has been extensively studied and is surveyed in Persson and Tabellini 1995. A general analysis can be found in Gordon 1983 and in Razin and Sadka 1991. Frenkel, Razin, and Sadka 1991 provide a comprehensive summary. Wilson (1987) adds endogenous wage rates to a model similar to that of section 12.4.

The idea that lack of credibility can make policy coordination counterproductive is due to Rogoff (1985b), who introduced it in the case of monetary policy. Van der Ploeg (1988) provided microfoundations for this analysis, whereas Jensen (1996) further extended it to include a monetary and fiscal policy authority in each country. Kehoe (1989) extended Rogoff's argument to a capital taxation model similar to the one presented here. Tax competition has also been studied with much more emphasis on institutional detail. See, for instance, Giovannini, Hubbard, and Slemrod 1993 and, with reference to European integration, Keen 1993 and Sørensen 1991. Political incentive constraints, just like lack of credibility, can also make international cooperation counterproductive. Tabellini (1990b) illustrates this result with regard to cooperation over the size of budget deficits, in a model similar to that in chapter 13; Vaubel (1985) discusses the problem more generally.

Putnam 1989 and the contributions in Evans, Jacobsen, and Putnam 1993 view international negotiations as a two-stage game between voters and politicians. The model and the results on strategic delegation in an international tax competition game draw on Persson and Tabellini 1992a.

12.7   Problems

1. Multiple equilibria and credibility in taxation problems

This problem is based on Calvo 1988. Consider the following two-period model. The economy is summarized by a representative agent with the initial endowment y. In period 1, he splits his endowment between government bonds b and capital investment k. The interest factors of bonds and capital are R_b and R, respectively. In period 2, the agent works and consumes. His labor supply and his consumption are denoted by l and c, respectively. Debt can be partially defaulted (repudiated), which means that the agent receives a return $(1 - \theta)R_b$ on each bond, where $\theta \in (0, 1)$ represents the proportion of bonds that are repudiated. Therefore, in a perfect-foresight equilibrium, the consumer is indifferent between the two assets if and only if

$$R = (1 - \theta)R_b.$$

In addition, the government bears a cost of defaulting on the debt: the per capita cost per unit of repudiated debt is $\alpha \in (0, 1)$. Government raises a tax τ on labor to finance debt repayment $(1 - \theta)bR_b$, the cost of repudiation $\alpha \theta b R_b$, and public expenditures g. We assume g to be exogenous. The representative agent has utility

$$w^i = c - V(l),$$

where $V(\cdot)$ is increasing and convex such that $\frac{V_l}{lV_{ll}} = \eta$ for all l.

a. Determine the agent's labor supply. Write the government's budget constraint as well as its optimization program under commitment. First, characterize the tax rate on labor by neglecting the constraint $\theta \in (0, 1)$, then compute the unconstrained total amount collected through taxation.

b. How does the government have to constrain the amount of collected taxes to satisfy $\theta \in (0, 1)$? Draw a graph of this amount as a function of R_b. How does the optimal repudiation share in period 2 vary with the interest rate R_b contracted in period 1? Discuss.

c. Suppose that the agent can exactly predict the repudiation share θ (then $R = (1 - \theta)R_b$ must hold). Derive the condition that must be satisfied by the budget constraint in equilibrium. Show that several equilibria exist, depending on R_b, and characterize these.

d. Rank the different equilibria and discuss your results.

2. Solving time-inconsistency problems through social contracts

This problem is an adaptation of Kotlikoff, Persson, and Svensson 1988. Consider the following overlapping-generations model. Each individual lives two periods. In period 1, the agent's work supply is l_1, he consumes a quantity c_1 and saves $s_1 \geq 0$ (borrowing is not allowed). The net rate of return to capital is R, and the wage rate is normalized to 1. In period 2, the agent's labor supply and consumption are l_2 and c_2, respectively. There are absolute taxes on labor in period 1 and 2 as well as on savings that are denoted by τ_1, τ_2 and θ, respectively. In other words, the net wage is $1 - \tau_t$ for each $t = \{1, 2\}$, and the total net return to capital is $(R - \theta)s_1$. A consumer has preferences described by

$$w^i = d(c_1 - \lambda l_1) + c_2 - \mu l_2,$$

where λ and μ are the constant marginal rates of substitution between leisure and consumption when the individual is young and old, respectively, and d is the gross rate of time preferences. We assume that $\lambda < 1$, $\mu < 1$, and $R > d$. Consumption and labor are constrained to be such that

$$0 \le \underline{c_1} \le c_1, \quad 0 \le \underline{c_2} \le c_2$$

$$l_1 \in [\underline{l_1}, \overline{l_1}], \quad \text{with } 0 \le \underline{l_1}$$

$$l_2 \in [\underline{l_2}, \overline{l_2}], \quad \text{with } 0 \le \underline{l_2},$$

where $\underline{c_1}, \underline{c_2}, \underline{l_1}, \overline{l_1}, \underline{l_2}$ and $\overline{l_2}$ are exogenously given.

a. Determine each agent's savings and labor decisions. Discuss.

b. Assume now that each generation is represented by a council that supplies a fixed amount of public good g to its generation when the generation is old. This expenditure is financed by taxing the generation in both periods. Suppose that the council has access to lump sum taxes and imposes a second-period lump sum tax equal to g on the old and sets all other taxes equal to 0. Determine the labor and savings decisions in this case. What is the utility level for the generation? We call this equilibrium the "first best."

c. Suppose now that the council cannot resort to lump sum taxes. Then it taxes labor in the first period and saves this amount at rate R. In the second period, it taxes its generation's savings as well as labor. Moreover, the council receives the return from its own period 1 savings and spends g.

We first assume that the council can commit. Determine the council's intertemporal budget constraint. Characterize the maximum nondistortionary taxes. What happens if these taxes are sufficient to finance g? Suppose instead that the taxes are not sufficient to finance g. Determine the deadweight losses caused by an increase in each tax. Assume that the deadweight loss from distorting τ_2 is smaller than other distortions. What does this imply? Suppose, in addition, that distortionary taxation of l_2 raises enough revenue to finance g. Determine the "second-best" optimum. What is the utility level in that case? Compare it with the first best.

d. Under which condition is the second-best optimum nonenforceable? Suppose that this condition holds. Determine the tax the council sets on capital when it cannot commit. What then are the taxes on labor, and what is the agent's equilibrium behavior? Compare the equilibrium utility with the first-best and second-best utilities. This equilibrium is referred to as the "third best."

e. Now assume that commitment is not possible. Suppose, however, that each young generation can set up a social contract with the following prescriptions: (1) Capital taxation above the maximum nondistortionary level is prohibited. (2) The council of the young contributes a transfer t to the council of the old, setting up the social contract costs ψ in terms of second-period utility (i.e., is discounted by 1 and not by d).

Consider any generation. What are the budget constraints of the council when setting up the contract and if the next generation fulfills this contract. Determine the equilibrium for this generation. Characterize the conditions under which the first generation wants to set up the social contract (when young) and fulfills it (when old). Consider now the next generation. As before, determine the equilibrium when the generation fulfills the contract. Characterize the conditions under which this second generation is willing to fulfill the contract rather than creating its own and pursuing the third-best optimum. Show that when all these conditions are satisfied, the contract yields a self-enforcing equilibrium.

3. Tax competition and international cooperation

Consider a two-period, two-country model in which countries are denoted by A and B. Both countries produce the same good and have access to the same technology. Consider country A, which is inhabited by individuals with preferences

$$w^i = U\left(c_1^i\right) + c_2^i,$$

where c_1^i and c_2^i denote consumption in the first and the second period, respectively. At the beginning of the first period, individual i receives an endowment $1 + e^i$ that he can invest in domestic investment d^i and foreign investment f^i. Assume that e^i is distributed on $(-1, 1)$ with zero mean and negative median e^{Am}. In the second period, individual i pays capital taxes in each country in which he has invested. We call θ^A the tax rate in country A and θ^B the tax rate in country B. He also receives a lump sum subsidy g from the government. The individual incurs mobility costs of investing in country B, denoted by $M(f^i) = (f^i)^2$. Government finances g through the revenue received from taxes on domestic and foreign investment. The model is the same for country B, the median agent of which is denoted by e^{Bm}.

a. Suppose that $e^i = e$ for all agents in both countries. Determine the representative agent's consumption and investment decisions. Suppose that both countries cooperate and maximize their joint welfare. On which pair of taxes do they agree? Suppose now that countries do not cooperate. What is the equilibrium in that case? Compare your results under cooperation and noncooperation and discuss.

b. Suppose now that agents are heterogeneous. The game is such that agents first select a policymaker under majority rule in each country. Then each policymaker chooses the tax rate in his country by maximizing his own utility function. Suppose that a policymaker of type e^A (respectively, e^B) is elected in country A (respectively, B). Characterize the pair of taxes in the two countries in equilibrium. How do they vary with the policymakers' endowments?

c. Show that the utility function of each agent in each country satisfies the intermediate-preference property. Is there a Condorcet winner in each economy? If so, who is the Condorcet winner? Characterize the endowment of the elected policymaker in each economy. Discuss your results.

d. Suppose again that $e^i = e$ and that citizens of both countries choose tax rates by majority rule under the constraint $\theta^A = \theta^B$. Moreover, citizens in each country are called to ratify this rate before making their savings decision. Determine the tax selected in the first vote. Do citizens in country A have an incentive to deviate and not ratify the vote? Explain briefly what is expected to happen when agents are heterogeneous.

4. The effects of capital mobility on taxation

This problem is inspired by Persson and Tabellini 1992a. Consider the same model as in problem 3, in which agents have heterogeneous endowments. Moreover, assume that the mobility costs incurred by an agent of country P when investing in country $Q \neq P$ is described by the function $M(f^i; \mu^Q)$, where $\mu^Q > 0$ represents the size of the mobility costs. For simplicity, we assume that $M(f^i, \mu^Q) = \mu^Q(f^i)^2$. As in question (b) of problem 3, individuals in each country select a policymaker, who then chooses the tax rate by maximizing his own utility.

a. Determine the consumption and investment decisions of agents in both countries. Let e^A (respectively, e^B) be the endowment of the elected policymaker in country A (respectively, B). Characterize the equilibrium when $\mu^A = \mu^B$ and when $\mu^A \neq \mu^B$.

b. Suppose that $\mu^A = \mu^B$. What effects does a decrease in the size of the mobility costs have? Characterize the endowment of the policymaker who is elected under majority rule. Determine the equilibrium when $e^{Am} = e^{Bm}$ and when $e^{Am} < e^{Bm}$.

c. Answer question (b) when $\mu^A \neq \mu^B$.

13 Public Debt

Debt accumulation varies greatly across time and countries. How can we explain this variation? Barro's (1979) tax-smoothing model of deficits can successfully explain wartime deficits but not the persistent accumulation of debt that has occurred in many industrial countries since the 1970s. Moreover, debt and deficits appear to be correlated with specific political and institutional features: debts have typically been accumulated by countries ruled by coalition governments and/or unstable governments. Budgetary procedures that confer veto rights or disperse political power among several decision makers are also correlated with debt accumulation. These facts suggest that political and institutional factors play an important role in shaping public debt policy. This chapter's goal is to survey the literature that can shed light on these issues.

In section 13.1 we formulate a simple two-period economic model that embeds features of the special-interest politics discussed in chapter 7. We then use this two-period model, with marginal amendments, throughout the chapter.

We begin with the idea that deficits arise in political systems with more-dispersed political powers, as in the case of coalition governments or powerful political interest groups. In section 13.2 we discuss a dynamic version of the common-pool problem formulated in chapter 7. If spending decisions are decentralized, whereas revenues are centralized but residually determined, there is a tendency not only to overspend but also to overborrow. As the property rights to current and future tax revenues are not well defined, all actors have an incentive to spend a lot and to spend soon, in order to appropriate more resources. Public debt accumulation is the equilibrium outcome of a game in which several decision makers with conflicting interests make simultaneous choices in each period. Levhari and Mirman (1980) originally formulated—in the context of natural resources—the idea that a dynamic common-pool problem leads to myopic policies. Velasco (1999) and others applied the idea to government debt. The section closes with a discussion of how appropriate budgetary procedures may contribute to solving the common-pool problem.

In section 3, we then turn to political instability in a two-party system in which governments clearly representing the view of well-defined political majorities make sequential policy choices. We show that in the presence of short-lived governments and unstable political majorities, politicians as well as voters may have an incentive to overaccumulate public debt, even though underaccumulation is also a possibility. This idea is closely related to that in example 3 of chapter 11, in which governments manipulate their debt structure to relax a future incentive constraint and improve their future credibility. We show that governments can use the amount of outstanding public debt strategically to bind the hands of future governments or majorities with different political preferences, in ways first suggested by Alesina and Tabellini (1990) and Persson and Svensson (1989). Furthermore, an incumbent government can also use the debt level to enhance its reelection probability, as suggested by Aghion and Bolton (1990). Our simple two-period example incorporates both of these mechanisms.

In section 13.4 we describe a different idea in the literature, considering not deliberate decisions to borrow, but in contrast, the difficulty of reaching a collective decision on debt stabilization. A consensus to change an unsustainable status quo may not be found, and borrowing is then the only possible course of action. This phenomenon typically arises when players have a veto right. More generally, it may arise when political powers are too dispersed, as in the case of coalition governments or of powerful interest groups having the force to block policy decisions. We follow the approach of Alesina and Drazen (1991), showing how the struggle between powerful groups over who will bear the cost of necessary cuts in spending may lead to a war of attrition delaying the elimination of existing deficits. In this section, as in the others, we reduce the full-blown dynamic models found in the literature to simple two-period examples.

Finally, in section 13.5, we briefly discuss how the politics of intergenerational redistribution may trigger government deficits, as suggested by Cukierman and Meltzer (1989), Tabellini (1991), and others. We also discuss mechanisms that may sustain public debt when we allow for the possibility of outright default.

13.1   A Simple Model of Public Debt

Consider a two-period economy without capital, reminiscent of that in example 1 of chapter 11. Individuals in this economy have identical income and identical preferences over private consumption and leisure. We first describe these individuals' preferences over private economic outcomes and their private economic behavior for a given economic policy, turning then to their policy preferences.

Preferences over private economic outcomes are given by the utility function

$$u = c_1 + c_2 + V(x), \tag{13.1}$$

where we have dropped the superscript ^{i} to simplify notation. Every consumer faces the same constraints. Leisure (x) and labor (l) in period 2 must sum to unity. In period 1, the consumer receives an exogenous endowment, e, that cannot be taxed. Budget constraints are

$$c_1 + b = e$$

$$c_2 = (1 - \tau)l + Rb,$$

where τ is a labor tax rate, ρ the gross interest rate, and b the holding of public debt—the only available form of savings. In period 1, the consumer chooses how much to save, whereas in period 2 he chooses his levels of leisure and consumption.[1] In contrast to example 1 of chapter 11, the government is committed to repaying the debt, which cannot be taxed. Because of the absence of discounting and the linearities in the utility function, an interior equilibrium $b \in [0, e]$ requires $\rho = 1$. Recognizing this, we can write the equilibrium consolidated budget constraint as

$$c_1 + c_2 = e + (1 - \tau)l.$$

Solving the consumer problem leads to the same labor supply function $L(\tau)$ as the one used in previous chapters.

Public spending takes place in both periods. Let g_t denote total per capita public consumption in period t. Using $\rho = 1$, the government budget constraints are

$$g_1 = b$$
$$b + g_2 = \tau l = \tau L(\tau). \tag{13.2}$$

It is useful to reexpress private utility as an indirect utility function defined over the policy variables b and g_2. Private equilibrium utility is a function of only the tax rate τ, and hence of $b + g_2$ (by the period 2 government budget constraint). Thus we can rewrite (13.1) as

$$u = W(b + g_2) \equiv \max [c_1 + c_2 + V(x_2)].$$

This indirect utility function has intuitive properties. Its first derivative, $W_b = W_g < 0$, is the private marginal cost of government spending, which includes the opportunity cost of private consumption as well as the tax distortions. Because the marginal tax distortions are increasing in total spending, we also have $W_{gg} = W_{bb} = W_{gb} < 0$.

Individuals belong to two different groups of equal size, which we label D and R (for, say, Democrats and Republicans, respectively). Group size is normalized to unity. Throughout most of the chapter the groups differ in their preferred allocation of public spending over two types of public consumption: g^D and g^R (in section 13.3 we discuss a case in which they also differ in their preferred size of the public sector). The two types of public consumption each require one unit of output, but they provide different utilities to the two groups. Total government spending in each period is given by $g_t = g_t^D + g_t^R$. For simplicity we assume that individuals belonging to group J care only about g^J, $J = D, R$. Individuals belonging to group J thus have preferences over public policy defined by

$$w^J = W(b + g_2) + H\left(g_1^J\right) + H\left(g_2^J\right), \tag{13.3}$$

where $H(\cdot)$ is the usual concave and well-behaved utility function.

---

1. It would be straightforward to add a labor-leisure choice also in period 1, and doing so would not affect the results of this chapter, though some additional assumptions would be needed in Section 2. The model could also be reinterpreted as referring to a small open economy without capital.

We can derive a normative benchmark by solving the problem of maximizing $(w^D + w^R)$ subject to $g_t = g_t^D + g_t^R$ and to $b = g_1$. The first-order conditions characterizing the optimal policy are

$$2W_b + H_g\left(g_1^J\right) = 0, \qquad J = D, R \qquad\qquad (13.4)$$
$$2W_g + H_g\left(g_2^J\right) = 0, \qquad J = D, R.$$

Since $W_b = W_g$, public consumption is equalized both across periods and across types of public goods: $g_t^D = g_t^R$, $g_1 = g_2$. The optimal policy equates the marginal benefit of public consumption for each group to the social cost. Since taxes can be collected only in period 2, first-period spending is financed through public debt, so as to spread the benefits of public consumption equally in both periods.

13.2 The Dynamic Common-Pool Problem

As in section 7.1, suppose now that each group is free to set public spending on its favored good. This assumption can capture decision making in coalition governments where each spending minister has authority over his own portfolio, or in a weak budget process where spending decisions are de facto decentralized to local governments or public enterprises. Decisions are made sequentially over time. Hence there are two unilateral decisions on public spending, one in each period. In the first period, public debt is residually determined. In the second period, the tax rate is residually determined. To compute the equilibrium, we work backward from the last period.

Consider the decision problem of, say, group J. It maximizes

$$W\left(b + g_2^J + g_2^I\right) + H\left(g_2^J\right)$$

with respect to g_2^J, taking b and g_2^I as given, for $I \neq J$. The resulting first-order condition is

$$W_g\left(b + g_2^J + g_2^I\right) + H_g\left(g_2^J\right) = 0, \qquad J = D, R. \qquad\qquad (13.5)$$

Compared to (13.4), the implied allocation clearly entails overspending. Group I solves a similar problem and behaves identically. As explained in chapter 7, the common-pool problem means that the cost of a public good provided only to one group is shared with other groups, and hence both groups have an incentive to spend more than the optimum. Comparing to (13.4), we see that each group internalizes only half the social cost of raising spending on their own good. Applying the implicit function theorem to the system of equations given by (13.5) and the corresponding expression for the other group, it is easily established that equilibrium spending by both groups is a decreasing function of public debt: $g_2^J = G^J(b)$, with $G_b^J < 0$. Intuitively, because tax distortions are increasing in the tax rate, a higher inherited debt increases the marginal cost of public spending.[2] Thus, overall equilibrium spending in period 2 is also decreasing in debt: $g_2 = G(b) = \sum_J G^J(b)$. These functions are analogous to the equilibrium policy rules discussed in chapter 11 and will act as incentive constraints on period 1 choices.

Next turn to period 1. Both groups take into account the equilibrium outcome of period 2. Thus, group J solves

$$\max_{g_1^J} \left[W(b + G^J(b) + G^I(b)) + H(g_1^J) + H(G^J(b)) \right],$$

subject to $b = g_1^J + g_1^I$, for $I \neq J$. That is, public consumption in period 1 is again set in a decentralized fashion. But now each group takes into account that more spending in period 1 leads to more borrowing, which in turn cuts both groups' period 2 spending. Taking the first-order conditions of this problem and exploiting (13.5) to simplify, we get

$$W_b + W_g G_b^I + H_g(g_1^J) = 0. \tag{13.6}$$

A similar condition applies to group I. The first term on the left-hand side of (13.6), $W_b < 0$, denotes the marginal cost of public debt: more borrowing leads to higher taxes in the following period. The second term, $W_g G_b^I$, is positive (since both its components are negative). That is, from the point of view of group J, the fact that more debt leads to spending cuts by the other group diminishes the cost of borrowing (W_b). Finally, the last term on the left-hand side of (13.6) is the marginal benefit of public consumption.

Using $W_b = W_g$ and (13.5), equation (13.6) can be rewritten as

$$H_g(g_1^J) = H_g(g_2^J)(1 + G_b^I) < H_g(g_2^J), \tag{13.7}$$

where the last inequality follows from $G_b^I < 0$. Hence by concavity of H, in equilibrium $g_1^J > g_2^J$, and similarly for group I. That is, both groups tilt the intertemporal profile of public consumption in favor of period 1. Decentralized spending with a common pool of tax revenues thus entails two distortions: higher spending than optimal in both periods and too much spending in period 1 compared to period 2, and hence too much borrowing. These distortions reflect the same incentive problem: the property rights to tax revenues are not well defined. Both groups have an incentive to spend much, and to spend soon, so as to appropriate more resources for their own benefit. The result is a collective irrationality, departing radically from the cooperative solution.

---

2. Formally, this follows from $H_{gg} < 0$ and $W_{gg}, W_{gb} < 0$.

With more than two groups, the problem becomes even worse, because each group internalizes an even smaller fraction of the future costs of debt issue or of spending in its public good. The model can be generalized to a genuine multiperiod context, as done by Velasco (1999). Velasco's model has richer dynamics than the simple model presented here, with a gradual buildup of debt, and entails the possibility of a delayed endogenous date of stabilization.

Schultz and Sjöström (1997) suggest a related mechanism leading to a debt bias. They show how migration between communities leads to incentives for debt issue: each community can effectively unload some of its debt repayments on others, since every community has to offer the same per capita consumption as the other. Moreover, because policy in Schultz and Sjöström's model is chosen by an elected mayor, voters in each community have an incentive to strategically delegate policy choices to a mayor with a higher than average discount factor and hence stronger incentives to borrow.

The overissue of debt in the model of this section is obviously caused by a flawed government budget process in which each party of the coalition (each group) is given decision-making authority over part of the budget, but nobody is given decision-making authority over the aggregate outcome. Could institutional reforms address this problem?

A natural idea is to centralize decision-making authority completely in one of the groups (or perhaps to reform the electoral system to make majority governments, rather than coalition governments, more likely). If the same party fully controlled all spending decisions, it would indeed appropriately internalize the cost of overspending and of debt issue. Such centralization of decision-making power could be abused, however. In this simple model, group I would spend all the revenue evenly over time on itself, if it had sufficient powers. The allocation of spending across time would thus be optimal, but the allocation across groups would be disastrously uneven. Moreover, in such a world, electoral uncertainty would reintroduce the incentives for debt issue, as we will see in the next section. Institutional checks and balances could mitigate this problem—for instance, by splitting agenda-setting power between the two groups, giving, say, group J agenda-setting power over the budget size and group I agenda-setting power over its allocation, as discussed in chapter 7. Extending the legislative bargaining framework discussed in that chapter to an explicit intertemporal setting is an interesting issue for future research.

The cross-country empirical evidence in von Hagen 1992, von Hagen and Harden 1994, and Alesina, Hommes, Hausmann, and Stein 1996 suggests that certain features of the budget process make it less likely that countries will run into public debt problems. One of the indicators constituting the index of budget stringency in these works is precisely the extent to which power is centralized in the hands of the prime minister or the Treasury minister. Another indicator is whether the budget process entails sequential decision making, with a decision made on the overall budget before the decision on its allocation, as suggested in chapter 7.[3]

Kontopoulos and Perotti (1997, 1999) use a panel data set including both public spending and debt issue in twenty OECD countries from 1960 to 1995. They relate a country's spending and debt to the type and structure of government in that country and find that spending and debt issue correlate positively and significantly with two features. One is the number of coalition partners in government, particularly from the mid-1980s and onward. This finding is broadly consistent with the theoretical results in this section. Interestingly, the other feature correlating with spending and deficits is the number of spending ministers in government, particularly in the subperiod up to the early 1980s. This finding can be interpreted as supporting the idea that special interests influence spending ministers' decisions and that narrower mandates invite interest groups with narrower orientation—and hence higher stakes in policy—to take political action.

13.3   Political Instability

In this section we discuss another feature of the political environment affecting the incentives for public debt issue, namely political instability. In the political system we study, a government, once elected, behaves as a single decision maker. The discussion is therefore most relevant for a two-party system, or a system with two well-defined semipermanent coalitions. The incentive constraint here results from the strategic interaction at different points in time (rather than simultaneously, as in the previous sections). The party deciding on public policy in the current period is aware that with some probability it will not hold office in the next period. This may induce too much borrowing, because the costs in terms of future spending cuts are not fully internalized. An incumbent government may also want to choose debt issue strategically for another reason, however, namely to influence its likelihood of reelection. The ideas in this section have been developed by Alesina and Tabellini (1990), Persson and Svensson (1989), and Aghion and Bolton (1990). As these authors all studied models with partisan politicians, it will be assumed throughout the section that politicians are partisan. As discussed below, however, all results generalize to opportunistic, office-motivated candidates.

Consider, then, a two-party system in which each party cares about the utility of one of the two groups defined in (13.3). The parties and groups are labeled in the same way as

---

3. Hallerberg and von Hagen (1999) argue that countries with majoritarian electoral systems (and thus, those more likely to have one-party governments) have chosen to centralize power in the finance minister in the budget process, whereas countries with proportional electoral systems (those more likely to have coalitions and minority governments) instead have tried to limit their deficits by adopting formal budget targets.

before. Thus the index J can take two values: $J = R, D$. We define p_R as the probability that party R wins, from the viewpoint of period 1. This electoral uncertainty can be due to a random participation rate or to uncertainty about the relative popularity of parties on policy dimensions other than public debt. In section 13.3.3 we suggest an explicit probabilistic voting model for p_R, but we initially treat p_R as exogenous. The economic model is exactly as in section 13.1.

13.3.1 Disagreement over the Composition of Spending

Events in the model unfold as follows: (1) One of the parties holds office in period 1; this party sets public consumption in period 1, financed by issuing debt. Then private economic decisions in period 1 are made. (2) At the start of period 2, elections are held. (3) The elected party takes office and sets public policy for period 2; after that, private economic decisions in period 2 are made.

As before, we characterize the equilibrium by backward induction. Optimal private decisions at stages (1) and (3) are already subsumed in individuals' policy preferences.

Suppose party J holds office in period 2. It chooses g_2^J and g_2^I so as to maximize its objective in (13.3), given outstanding debt, b. The first-order condition for a good of type J is the same as in (13.5) evaluated at $g_2^I = 0$. Thus party J spends only on good J (good $I \neq J$ has only costs and no benefits) and equates the marginal cost of supplying good J to its marginal benefit, from the point of view of group J. Party I, if in office, behaves in a similar fashion with respect to good I. As in section 13.2, this first-order condition defines a reaction function $g_2^J = G(b)$ that is the same for both parties (since only one type of spending is provided in equilibrium, we can omit the J superscript, as the G function also refers to total public spending in period 2). As before, higher debt implies higher period 2 tax distortions; each party is less willing to spend on public goods if it inherits a higher public debt, hence $G_b < 0$.

Next, let us study the period 1 incentives to issue debt at stage (1). (Because the election outcome is (for now) exogenous, there is nothing to be said about stage (2).) The identity of the period 1 incumbent has no impact on the results, but to fix ideas, suppose it is party R. Clearly, this party provides only one type of public good in period 1, namely g_1^R. Thus, $g_1^D = 0$ and $b = g_1^R$. Moreover, its expected payoff, given the expected election outcome, depends on debt, according to the incentive constraint imposed by equilibrium policy choices in period 2:

$$\mathsf{E}[w^R(b)] = W(b + G(b)) + H(b) + p_R H(G(b)).$$

The last term on the right-hand side of this objective function is the expected utility from period 2 public consumption. Since party R loses the election with probability $(1 - p_R)$, in which case $g_2^R = 0$, party R weights the utility of period 2 public consumption with the probability of victory, p_R. The cost of future spending is, however, the same whichever party wins, as both types of government have the same spending in period 2. This explains the first term on the equation's right-hand side.

Given this objective function, optimal debt policy must satisfy

$$W_b + W_g G_b + H_g(g_1) + p_R H_g(g_2)G_b = 0. \tag{13.8}$$

This condition can be rewritten as follows, if we impose the period 2 first-order condition (13.5):

$$H_g(g_1) = H_g(g_2)(1 + (1 - p_R)G_b). \tag{13.9}$$

Condition (13.9) has an intuitive interpretation. To strengthen the intuition, first consider the special case when party R is sure of reelection—that is, $p_R = 1$ for any b. Then (13.9) implies $g_1 = g_2$. In other words, a government that is certain of reelection chooses the efficient debt policy, smoothing public consumption completely over time.

When reelection is not certain, however, other incentives come into play. The larger is the probability that its opponent will win (i.e., the smaller is p_R), the more party R deviates from the efficient debt policy, as is evident from the last term on the right-hand side of (13.9). Because this term is negative, party R sets g_1 above the equilibrium level of g_2 whenever $p_R < 1$, and it sets g_1 farther above g_2 the smaller is p_R. A positive probability of losing the election leads to excessive debt issue and excessive public spending in period 1. Whereas the incumbent government fully internalizes the benefits of borrowing associated with spending in the public good benefiting its constituency, it does not fully internalize the cost of lower public spending in the future, since it bears this cost only if the government is reelected. Thus, the amount of overspending and overborrowing in period 1 is larger, the slimmer is the incumbent government's reelection probability. To express the intuition in an alternative way: it is optimal for the party R government to tie the hands of a prospective party D government through increasing public debt in the current period, because party D will spend on a good that the incumbent, party R, does not value.

It is useful to contrast this incentive to borrow with that which emerges in the dynamic common-pool problem of section 13.2. In both models, everyone fully realizes that more spending today leads to less spending tomorrow. In the common-pool model, the marginal spending cuts affect both types of public good, and hence also a public good not valued by today's decision makers. In the present model, the marginal spending cuts fall instead on one type of public good only, but with some probability, it is the public good not valued by today's decision maker. In both models, although for different reasons, the cost of borrowing in terms of future spending cuts is thus not fully internalized.

Extensions   What happens if disagreement between the two parties is not as extreme as we assumed, so that both parties always spend on both goods, g^D and g^R, although the preferred composition of public spending differs across parties? A higher debt forces future spending cuts in period 2, but which good is cut the most depends on preferences; this determines debt accumulation. Specifically, suppose that party J evaluates public consumption according to $\alpha^J H(g^J) + (1 - \alpha^J) H(g^I)$, with $1 > \alpha^J > \frac{1}{2}$, and similarly for party I, with $\alpha^I = 1 - \alpha^J$. The size of equilibrium debt then depends on the shape of the utility function H. Let $\gamma(g) \equiv -H_{gg}(g)/(H_g(g))^2$ be the concavity index of $H(g)$ (see Debreu and Koopmans 1982). Then Tabellini and Alesina (1990) show that greater political instability leads to greater debt accumulation if $\gamma(g)$ is decreasing in g. Moreover, equilibrium public debt is higher with more-divergent party preferences (the more distant is α^J from $\frac{1}{2}$). Both results are reversed if $\gamma(g)$ is increasing in g.[4] The condition of a decreasing concavity index has an intuitive interpretation, implying that as total spending goes down, both parties choose a more similar composition of g^D and g^R. In other words, it implies that g^D and g^R become closer substitutes at higher levels of spending. In this case, disagreement over the composition of public spending is a luxury: when resources are scarce, we all agree that there are some priorities, such as spending on health and defense, but when resources abound, we can afford to spend in different ways and choose a more divergent mix of public goods. Under this assumption, leaving public debt to the future forces party J to cut g^J (the good about which he cares the most) more than g^I. That is, leaving public debt to the future induces a more equal composition of public goods in the second period. Problem 3 of this chapter deals with a similar condition in the context of a different political model.

Subject to this condition on preferences, the model thus yields the general (unconditional) empirical prediction that countries experiencing political polarization (i.e., sharp disagreement between the majority and the opposition) and political instability (i.e., frequent government turnovers) should accumulate more debt. A more precise (conditional) prediction is that a lower perceived probability of reelection should cause any government to issue more debt, ceteris paribus. If the condition on H does not hold, different political parties should still react in the same way (but by retiring, rather than issuing, debt).

How crucial is the assumption of partisan (outcome-motivated) politicians and postelection politics for these results? Suppose instead that politicians were pure opportunistic office seekers, as in the median-voter or probabilistic voting models of earlier chapters. Could it then be that the voters punish inefficient policies and the myopic bias disappears? The answer is no: the bias toward public debt would resurface even in those models, under equivalent assumptions about political instability. In such models, the voters themselves

---

4. The concavity index is decreasing in g for any constant elasticity of substitution utility function $H(g) = g^\theta/\theta$, with $\theta > 0$.

want myopic policies, for essentially the same reasons as those outlined above. Specifically, consider the Downsian model with identical office-motivated politicians. We know that the equilibrium policy maximizes the median voter's utility. Suppose now, however, that the identity of the median voter changes over time because of shocks to the participation rate or for other exogenous reasons. Then the previously stated results still hold, except that the relevant probability determining debt accumulation refers not to the incumbent's reelection chances, but to the event that the future median voter is an individual with different preferences for public consumption (see Tabellini and Alesina 1990 for a detailed proof).

Alternatively, consider the probabilistic voting model introduced in chapter 3. Here the equilibrium policy in each period would maximize a weighted social welfare function, with weights corresponding to the density of swing voters in all groups. Suppose that these densities change over time because of shocks in the participation rate or the noneconomic (ideological) component of voters' preferences. Then the intertemporal policies again become distorted. A bias toward public debt appears, under conditions similar to the decreasing concavity index for H. This example constitutes problems 1 and 2 of this chapter.

13.3.2 Disagreement over the Size of Spending

If political disagreement concerns the overall size of public spending, rather than its composition, the result that public debt policy is economically inefficient continues to apply. We now consider an adaption of our framework to illustrate this point, which was first made by Persson and Svensson (1989). In this adaption, there is only one type of public spending in each period. Policy preferences of group J are

$$w^J = W(b + g_2) + \alpha^J(H(g_1) + H(g_2)), \qquad J = D, R.$$

We assume that $\alpha^R < \alpha^D$, so we can think of the label R as Republican, or right-wing. Otherwise, the model is exactly the same as before.

Optimal policy in period 2 when party J holds office satisfies

$$W_g(b + g_2) + \alpha^J H_g(g_2) = 0. \tag{13.10}$$

This condition implies that we can write equilibrium period 2 spending as $G^D(b)$ and $G^R(b)$, respectively, with $G^D(b) > G^R(b)$, and $G_b^J < 0$. In words, a D government always outspends an R government, at the same level of debt, and both spend less if the debt is higher.

Suppose that the incumbent in period 1 is an R government. Its objective function can be written as

$$E[w^R(b)] = p_R W(b + G^R(b)) + (1 - p_R)W(b + G^D(b)) + \alpha^R[H(b)$$
$$+ p_R H(G^R(b)) + (1 - p_R)H(G^D(b))].$$

Thus the government evaluates future public spending according to the preferences of its constituency, taking the electoral uncertainty into account. Exploiting (13.10) and doing some rearranging, we can write the first-order condition to this problem as

$$\alpha^R(H_g(g_1) - H_g(G^R(b))) = (1 - p_R)(\alpha^D - \alpha^R)H_g(G^D(b))G_b^D$$
$$+ (1 - p_R)(W_b(b + G^R(b)) - W_b(b + G^D(b))). \quad (13.11)$$

As is evident from (13.11), an R incumbent government chooses a flat spending profile, with $g_1 = g_2$, only if it is certain of reelection, so that $p_R = 1$ and both terms on the right-hand side are zero. The last of these expressions is positive (since $G^R < G^D$ and $W_{bg} < 0$), capturing the fact that future expected tax distortions are higher than what the incumbent would like, as party D will spend more in period 2. The R incumbent adapts to this by spending less and issuing less debt in period 1. The first term on the right-hand side is negative (since $\alpha^D > \alpha^R$ and $G_b^D < 0$). It captures the strategic debt effect: by issuing more debt in period 1, a right-wing incumbent ties the hands of a left-wing successor, making it optimal for a future D government to spend less.

If the strategic debt effect prevails, a right-wing government thus issues more debt than it would absent electoral uncertainty. Furthermore, the effect is stronger the more polarized are the two parties (the larger the distance between α^D and α^R). Conservative governments facing a more liberal opposition have an incentive to borrow more, in order to force future spending cuts if the liberal opposition is elected. In this model, however, the identity of the period 1 government matters. Going through the same steps as above produces a condition for a D incumbent in which p_R enters with the opposite sign. Thus whichever term prevails in (13.11), the incentives for a left-wing government are exactly the opposite.

The empirical implications of this model are thus different from those in the previous subsection. First, there is no general presumption here that governments overissue debt or that greater political instability leads to higher average debt issue. Greater political instability should instead be associated with a more volatile public debt policy. Furthermore, the conditional predictions are different: debt issue should be affected in opposite directions as right-wing and left-wing governments are faced with higher probabilities of electoral defeat.

13.3.3   Endogenous Election Outcomes

Governments also manipulate state variables to increase their chances of reelection. We now modify our model to show how this incentive applies to public debt, illustrating an idea first stressed by Aghion and Bolton (1990), by modeling the voters' behavior along the same lines as in the probabilistic voting model used frequently in earlier parts of the book. Specifically, consider again the model in which groups disagree sharply on the composition of public spending, but suppose that parties and individuals also differ along a second dimension not explicitly modeled. As before, we assume that individual utility depends on the identity of the party holding office, in addition to the public spending it provides. But we allow individuals belonging to the same group to have different preferences over policymakers in this second dimension. Thus we postulate the following overall preferences for individual i in group J, for $J = D, R$:

$$w^{iJ} = W(b + g_2) + H\left(g_1^J\right) + H\left(g_2^J\right) + (\sigma^{iJ} + \delta)K^D, \tag{13.12}$$

where $g_t = \sum_J g_t^J$, and the dummy variable K^D equals 1 if party D holds office in period 2 and 0 if party R holds office. The parameter σ^{iJ} is distributed around a mean value of 0 in the population of each group, according to a uniform distribution with density ϕ^J. In period 1, when the incumbent sets debt policy, the precise value of δ is not known, only its uniform mean-zero distribution with density ψ. The σ^{iJ} parameter thus measures an idiosyncratic ideological (and exogenous) bias in group J for party D, and to the extent that δ is positive, party D enjoys a general popularity advantage. That is, individuals evaluate public consumption according to their group affiliation, and each party cares about its natural constituency.

Voters also trade off the economic benefits obtained from their party, however, against other (exogenous or noneconomic) aspects of public policy, according to the parameters σ^{iJ} and δ. Now group affiliation does not completely determine how individuals vote, so that the vote share of each party is endogenous. Note the difference in assumptions relative to our previous use of the probabilistic voting model. In parts 1–3, we used it as a model of preelection politics, assuming that the two parties were opportunistic (office- or rent-seeking). Here we are dealing with a model of postelection politics in which the parties have partisan preferences, and there is no electoral campaign. The voters perfectly anticipate the policy each party will pursue in period 2, however, and the incumbent party's choice of debt policy b influences these choices.

Consider voter i in group D. She votes for party R if and only if $W(b + G(b)) + H(G(b)) + \sigma^{iD} + \delta < W(b + G(b))$, or if $\sigma^{iD} < -H(G(b)) - \delta$. Thus unless party D is generically unpopular ($\delta < 0$), only group D individuals with a strong idiosyncratic ideological bias against party D vote for party R. Next consider voter i in group R. She votes for party R if and only if $\sigma^{iR} < H(G(b)) - \delta$. This argument is illustrated in figure 13.1 for a realization of $\delta = 0$. The shaded areas denote the vote share of party R in both groups. Not surprisingly, a group R voter is more likely to support party R, since she draws economic benefits from its election.

Combining these conditions and using the uniformity assumption, we get the total vote share for party R as a function of public debt, b, and of popularity, δ:

$$\pi_R(b, \delta) = \frac{1}{2} + H(G(b))\frac{\phi^R - \phi^D}{2} - \phi\delta,$$

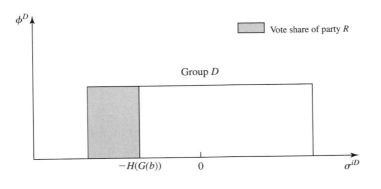

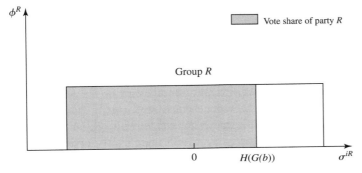

Figure 13.1

where

$$\phi \equiv \frac{\phi^R + \phi^D}{2}$$

is the average density in the population. Before knowing the realization of δ, the probability that R wins is thus

$$p_R = P(b) \equiv \underset{\delta}{\mathrm{Prob}}\left[\pi_R(b, \delta) \geq \frac{1}{2}\right] = \frac{1}{2} + \frac{\psi}{\phi}(\phi^R - \phi^D)H(G(b)). \qquad (13.13)$$

Thus if both groups have the same distribution of ideological preferences (if $\phi^R = \phi^D$), the two parties have the same probability of victory: $p_R = \frac{1}{2}$. Otherwise, the party with more homogeneous supporters (with a higher density ϕ^J) has a higher probability of winning (party D in figure 13.1). The intuition is similar to that of the probabilistic voting model with opportunistic parties. If both parties enacted identical policies, they would each gain 50% of the votes in both groups. Instead, they have partisan preferences, and party J implements

the best policy for group J. Hence the party offering the policy favored by the group with more swing voters gains a higher expected vote share. If the groups had different sizes, clearly the party supported by the larger group would be more likely to win.

How does debt accumulation affect the probability of winning? Differentiating the right-hand side of (13.13), we get

$$\frac{dp_R}{db} \equiv P_b = -H_g G_b \frac{\psi}{\phi}(\phi^D - \phi^R).$$

Because $H_g G_b$ is negative in this equation, its sign is the same as that of the expression in brackets. Higher debt reduces equilibrium spending in period 2. This makes the parties more similar, from an economic point of view. The election outcome therefore depends more on the voters' ideological preferences and less on their economic preferences. As a result, party R loses voters in its natural economic constituency (group R) but gains voters in its opponent constituency (group D). If there are fewer swing voters in group R, therefore, issuing debt increases party R's probability of victory. In terms of figure 13.1, as debt is issued, the identity of the swing voter moves to the left in group R and to the right in group D, by the same horizontal distance. Hence the shaded area increases in size for group D and decreases for group R. If, as drawn, group R has fewer swing voters (if $\phi^D > \phi^R$), party R's expected vote share increases. If the two groups also had different size, then debt accumulation would favor the party whose economic constituency was smaller. The intuition is still the same: debt accumulation enables each party to gain votes *in the opponent's constituency*.

It is now easy to characterize the equilibrium debt issued by an R government, by going through the same steps as in subsection 13.3.1, but with $P(b)$ replacing p_R. The optimality condition for public debt—the analogue of (13.9)—is

$$H_g(g_1) = H_g(g_2)(1 + (1 - P(b))G_b) - P_b H(G(b)) = 0. \qquad (13.14)$$

The first term on the right-hand side of (13.14) is identical to that in (13.9) and has the same meaning. When assessing the future marginal cost of borrowing, the incumbent takes into account the strategic effects of borrowing on its opponent's future spending decisions (captured by $H_g(1 - P(b))G_b$). The last term is new, however, and captures the effect of debt on the reelection probability. We see that if issuing debt enhances the reelection chances for party R, so that $P_b > 0$, this effect adds to the incentives to issue debt, but when $P_b < 0$ (issuing debt decreases party R's chances for reelection) it pulls in the opposite direction. From the previous discussion we know that $P_b > 0$ whenever $\phi^D > \phi^R$. Moreover, from (13.13) $P(b)$ is decreasing in $(\phi^D - \phi^R)$, and a low reelection probability as such pulls in the direction of more debt issue. Hence both effects reinforce each other: the party with fewer swing voters accumulates more debt. The same argument would apply with regard to group size: the party with the smallest economic constituency has stronger incentives to borrow. Stretching the model somewhat, the empirical implication is that governments are more likely to issue debt if their "natural constituency" is small and has a strong ideological attachment. In this case, it is better to appeal to the more mobile swing voters in the opposition party's constituency, the more so the bigger is that constituency. The way to do that in the present model is to issue more debt, as this commits any future government to spending less, thus decreasing the future economic policy differences between the two parties.

The specific positive implications concerning the effect of debt on reelection probabilities are not necessarily robust but depend on the assumptions about voters' preferences in (13.12). But the general idea that public financial policies can also be used to manipulate the two parties' relative popularity, is sound and can be applied to many other issues besides public debt. Clearly, these determinants of economic policy would be even more important if parties were also office-motivated, that is, also cared about staying in office per se. Furthermore, the analysis in this subsection implies that empirical research on strategic debt issue should pay close attention to simultaneity problems. The model illustrates that the chain of causation between debt issue and the probability of reelection may run in both directions.

13.3.4 Discussion

The simple idea that political instability causes government to behave myopically—or strategically, depending on the way you want to look upon it—can be applied in more general models. In fact, the idea of using state variables to "create facts for your successor" is very general and really applies to any intertemporal aspect of public policy, such as the choice of public investment (see Glazer 1989 and chapter 14) or the implementation of tax reforms (see problem 4 of this chapter and Cukierman, Edwards, and Tabellini 1992). Similarly, the idea that governments may want to enhance their reelection probability by "creating a constituency for reelection" is more general than this particular model and has been used to model indexation and central banking reform (Milesi-Ferretti 1994 and 1995b) and privatization (Biais and Perotti 1998).

What about the empirical evidence? The general idea emerging from section 13.3.1, that government turnover is positively associated with debt issue, is consistent with the stylized facts reported in the introduction of the chapter. The model's unconditional predictions have also been taken to the data for developing countries by Ozler and Tabellini (1991) and for U.S. states by Crain and Tollison (1993), who find support for some of them. The more specific conditional predictions regarding the effects of the probability of reelection from sections 13.3.2 and 13.3.3 have been tested by Lambertini (1996) for the United States and for a panel of industrial countries, and by Franzese (1998) for a panel of OECD countries. Neither finds much support for either model. One problem with using time series for a single country is that they have very few observations of political events. On the other hand, proxies for the probability of reelection are bound to be highly imperfect for a wide sample of countries with different electoral systems and political regimes. Indeed, our discussion in part 3 on comparative politics tells us that we should expect the same events to have different consequences in different political systems. Pettersson (1998) has tried to avoid these problems by using a large (eight elections, 275 observation per election) panel from Swedish municipal elections. He finds strong support for the Persson-Svensson model but no support for the Alesina-Tabellini model. According to his results, right-wing governments do issue more debt when facing a higher probability of defeat, whereas left-wing governments do exactly the opposite.

13.4 Delayed Stabilizations

In this section, we focus not on why budget deficits arise, but on why it may take time to get rid of them once they have arisen. Following Alesina and Drazen (1991), we illustrate the likelihood of delayed stabilizations when, out of two parties in a coalition government or two powerful interest groups, each has an incentive to let the other bear the brunt of the necessary adjustment. Asymmetric information about the costs of delaying the stabilization plays a key role in Alesina and Drazen's continuous-time model, which builds on the biological war-of-attrition model of Riley (1980) and the public-good model of Bliss and Nalebuff (1984). Here, we present a related analysis adapted to our simple two-period setting.

Consider the two-group model formulated in section 13.1 with some modifications. Tax revenue can be collected in both periods, but the tax rate τ is now exogenous. It simplifies the notation to make a normalization such that $\tau L(\tau) = \bar{\tau}$. Second, there are two kinds of public goods, g^D and g^R, and aggregate government spending on each good has "gotten stuck" at too high a level. Specifically, the status quo level in period 1 is $g_1^D = g_1^R = \bar{\tau} + \bar{b}$, with $\bar{b} > 0$. Thus, $\bar{b}$ naturally measures the size of the fiscal problem. We study two possible policy outcomes: (1) Stabilization is delayed, in which case $g_1 \equiv g_1^D + g_1^R = 2(\bar{\tau} + \bar{b})$, public debt is $b = 2\bar{b}$, and by the second period budget constraint, $g_2 = 2(\bar{\tau} - \bar{b})$. (2) Stabilization occurs in period 1, in which case aggregate overspending is cut immediately by $2\bar{b}$ and no debt is issued, so that $g_1 = \bar{\tau} = g_2$ and hence $b = 0$. The allocation of spending cuts across the two groups in outcome (2) depends on how stabilization was achieved. We return to this issue below. We are interested in the probability that stabilization is delayed, and what factors make delay more likely.

To simplify the algebra, we now assume that the utility of group J is linear in g_t^J and that the costs of debt policy enter additively in the utility function. They can be interpreted as either a suboptimal spending allocation over time, or other costs associated with debt issue: perhaps part of the deficit is financed through a distortionary inflation tax, or a high debt causes general macroeconomic instability because of an unsustainable budgetary position. We thus write the utility of group J as

$$w^J = W(\bar{\tau}) + g_1^J + g_2^J - \kappa^J b, \tag{13.15}$$

where the first term on the right-hand side is a constant, by the assumption that the tax rate is constant, and the last term denotes the cost of debt for group J, for $J = D, R$. The parameter κ^J measures the cost to group J of postponing the stabilization. A crucial assumption is that this cost is private information to group J. Group $I \neq J$ only knows that κ^J is distributed on the interval $[0, \bar{\kappa}]$ according to the distribution function $F(\kappa^J)$. The corresponding parameter κ^I has the same distribution, but the realizations of κ^J and κ^I are independent.

Each group is represented by a partisan party with the same preferences. All political action takes place at the beginning of period 1, when both parties, simultaneously and non-cooperatively, make a proposal q^I as to whether to stabilize ($q^I = s$) or not ($q^I = n$). If both parties propose n, the stabilization is delayed. But if at least one party proposes s, stabilization takes place. If only one party gives in and proposes s, that party bears the main burden of the necessary cutbacks. Specifically, following Alesina and Drazen (1991), we assume the following:

$$
\begin{aligned}
g_1^J(n, n) &= \bar{\tau} + \bar{b}, \qquad g_2^J(n, n) = \bar{\tau} - \bar{b}, \qquad J = D, R \\
g_t^D(s, n) &= g_t^R(n, s) = \bar{\tau} - \alpha/2, \qquad t = 1, 2 \\
g_t^D(n, s) &= g_t^R(s, n) = \bar{\tau} + \alpha/2, \qquad t = 1, 2 \\
g_t^J(s, s) &= \bar{\tau}, \qquad J = D, R, \qquad t = 1, 2,
\end{aligned}
\tag{13.16}
$$

where $g^J(q^D, q^R)$ denotes how spending on group J depends on the two proposals, and where $\alpha > 0$ measures the advantage of not giving in. Implicit in (13.16) is the idea that the political process gives veto rights to some party or interest group. Thus this model applies to countries ruled by coalition governments or, more generally, to a situation where the executive is weak and faces effective opposition from organized interests with in the legislature or outside of parliament. Note that the model has some features of the dynamic common pool model of section 13.1, in that groups share the cost of delay equally, irrespective of who is responsible for it.

How do parties decide whether to veto the proposed cuts? Consider party J. It compares expected utility when proposing n, denoted by $\mathsf{E}[w^J \mid n]$, and s, denoted by $\mathsf{E}[w^J \mid s]$. Let $p = \mathrm{Prob}\,[q^I = s]$ be the probability that party I proposes s (p is determined in equilibrium). Then (13.15) and (13.16) allow us to compute the expected net gain for J from proposing

n rather than s:

$$\mathsf{E}[w^J \mid n] - \mathsf{E}[w^J \mid s] = \alpha - (1 - p)\kappa^J \bar{b}. \qquad (13.17)$$

Party J proposes s if the expression on the right-hand side of (13.17) is negative, n otherwise. Thus it is more advantageous to propose n if the gains from not giving in are large (α is large), if the costs of deficit finance for group J are low (k^J are low), and if the probability of the opponent's proposing s is high (p is high). Clearly, party J says *no* whenever the cost parameter κ^J is below some critical number K, defined by $K \equiv \alpha/\bar{b}(1 - p)$. Since party I faces an identical decision problem, it also proposes n whenever $\kappa^I \leq K$. Thus it must be the case that $(1 - p) \equiv \text{Prob}\,(q^I = n) \equiv \text{Prob}\,(\kappa^I \leq K) = F(K)$. Using this and setting the expression in (13.17) equal to zero, we can implicitly define the equilibrium value of K by

$$K F(K) = \alpha/\bar{b}.$$

The left-hand side of this expression is increasing in K. Therefore $K = K(\alpha, \bar{b})$, with $K_\alpha > 0$ and $K_{\bar{b}} < 0$.

We can now answer the main questions, namely how often we would observe a delayed stabilization and what factors would make equilibrium delay more likely. Delayed stabilization requires that both groups propose n. Because κ^D and κ^R are independently distributed, the unconditional probability of observing delay is

$$(1 - p)(1 - p) = F(K(\alpha, \bar{b}))F(K(\alpha, \bar{b})).$$

The likelihood of delay is thus increasing in α, the gain from winning the war of attrition when the other party gives in first. If we interpret α as a measure of cohesion in the political system, this result thus says that delayed stabilizations and prolonged deficits are more likely in polarized political systems. Note that if $\alpha = 0$, there is never any delay; postponing adjustment implies only losses for each party. The likelihood of delay is also decreasing in $\bar{b}$, the initial fiscal problem. The model is consistent with the general idea that the worse a fiscal crisis is, the more likely adjustment is; here we get that result because the expected cost of waiting becomes individually larger with a higher $\bar{b}$. Thus the results support the commonly held assumption that financial crises and times of economic distress resulting from budgetary instability act as catalysts of reform and should not be feared too much (Drazen and Grilli 1992). The mechanism causing delay in the model, namely a conflict over how to distribute the losses from cutbacks in government programs, also corresponds well with casual observation. Finally, the model can be used to study the consequences of financial aid to developing countries and conditionality (Casella and Eichengreen 1995). To be effective, external financial aid should not ease the pain of an unsustainable situation (in terms of our model, it should not reduce $\bar{b}$), for this would simply delay the necessary stabilization. Effective financial aid should instead be conditional on a stabilization's taking place and should shrink over time if the stabilization is postponed, to increase the incentives for the rivaling parties to give in early.

Our simple framework in this section shares a major weakness with Alesina and Drazen's framework, though: it does not provide a structural model of the process of reaching agreement on stabilization in a coalition government. A preferable modeling strategy would be to formalize the problem in a fully specified legislative bargaining framework, like that in parts 2–3, but extended to encompass incompletely informed parties.

The idea of delayed reform or, more generally, a bias towards the status quo, also plays an important role in the well-known paper by Fernandez and Rodrik (1991). These authors consider a reform that is socially optimal, in the sense that aggregate gains outweigh aggregate losses. The size of the winning coalition is unknown, however, and individuals are uncertain whether they belong to the winners or the losers. Enacting the reform requires passing two votes, one ex ante and one ex post. Interestingly, the voters reject reforms too often: reforms that would be viable ex post never get a chance, because they are blocked ex ante, and the information that would sustain them (that a majority belongs to the winners) never gets revealed. But the argument relies on the assumption that the gainers cannot compensate the losers. Ideally, this should be a result rather than an assumption. Casting the problem in a more fully specified political model appears, once again, to be a fruitful issue for future research.

13.5   Debt and Intergenerational Politics

The models in this section all focus on how debt redistributes tax distortions, or the benefits of government spending, over time. But they ignore another role of debt: redistribution across generations. They also all assume that any outstanding debt is honored by the government that inherits it. As we have seen in chapter 11, this requires a strong form of commitment. Reputational or institutional forces facilitate commitments, but then they should really be part of the argument; such forces may also not go the entire way toward enforcing commitments.

In conventional representative-agent macroeconomics, debt issue and pay-as-you-go social security are identical policies. Preferences for social security depend, in a predictable way, on age-earning profiles and the population growth rate. Cukierman and Meltzer (1989) analyze budget deficits in a similar way but introduce intergenerational altruism. The degree of altruism varies across households: some households leave positive bequests, whereas others are bequest-constrained. Nonconstrained voters, who can undo any intergenerational redistribution, are concerned only with the general equilibrium effects of the policy and not how it redistributes across generations. But the bequest-constrained voters favor a budget deficit, because it allows them to do something they cannot do privately: redistribute resources toward themselves. In a median-voter equilibrium, the size of the budget deficit depends on the efficiency effects and the number of bequest-constrained voters.

Even though these contributions introduce important aspects of politics, they still hinge on the commitment assumption. As discussed in chapter 6, at any given moment, social security strictly benefits only a minority (the retired) but imposes a cost on a majority (the workers). A similar problem exists for debt. Why then does the majority not repeal the promise to pay social security or to honor the debt? Reputational concerns may help, if honoring the current program enhances the probability that it will be honored in the future. But as discussed in chapter 11, the argument that it does so is not without problems.

Tabellini (1990a, 1991) suggests that one should allow *intra*generational heterogeneity in income, along the same lines as in our discussion about pensions in chapter 6, as well as some form of intergenerational altruism, when thinking about these questions. Pure intergenerational policies rarely exist. Moreover, when generations are altruistically linked, they can undo some of these intergenerational effects within the household, which gives the intragenerational aspects of policy even more strength. Social security programs typically redistribute not only from children to parents but also from rich to poor. Similarly, public debt default has both intergenerational and intragenerational effects (because the rich are likely to hold more of the debt instruments). A policy redistributing across generations may therefore be upheld in equilibrium, without ex ante commitments, by a coalition of voters containing members of different generations who belong to similar income groups. The coalitions forming ex post to support existing social security and outstanding debt are different, however. The old and the children of poor parents support social security, whereas the old and the children of rich parents support honoring outstanding debt. These two intergenerational policies are thus not equal under heterogeneity and lack of commitment. As in chapter 12, incentive constraints in policymaking violate the Modigliani-Miller theorem of government finance.

Dixit and Londregan (1998b) suggest another interesting idea as to why debt might be upheld. If the groups in the population that hold the bulk of the public debt instruments are more politically powerful than other groups, debt may be honored ex post, despite a temptation to renege on it. Dixit and Londregan consider a two-stage model in which heterogenous individuals must in the first stage decide whether to invest their wealth in human capital or public debt, the proceeds of the debt being used to finance public investment. In a second-stage probabilistic voting model, two opportunistic candidates commit to electoral platforms involving how much to tax the population to repay the outstanding debt. There are always equilibria with self-confirming beliefs of full repudiation, similar to the full-expropriation equilibria encountered in chapter 12. If the number of swing voters among the bondholders is large enough, however, there are also better equilibria in which the debt is (partially) honored.

Majority voting is not the only way of thinking about how different generations' policy preferences get aggregated in the political process. In many societies, different age groups—the old, in particular—have well-organized interest groups that lobby and take other political action to support policies benefiting their members. Rotemberg (1990) discusses the repayment of government debt as the outcome of bargaining between living generations. Grossman and Helpman (1998) formulate a dynamic model of intergenerational redistribution in which policy commitments are once more not feasible. In the model, pressure groups of living generations make contributions to the government conditional on the support it gives their members. The model has multiple expectational equilibria, which again are reminiscent of capital taxation examples in chapter 12. It is the expectations of the current government however, about future policy, rather than the expectations of private agents, that introduce the self-fulfilling property. One can easily end up in a very bad equilibrium in which the pressure groups engage in a very stiff and costly competition for policy favors and capital formation suffers.

Mulligan and Sala-i-Martin (1999b) also study a model in which different generations try to influence government policy through lobbying or other activities. They do not model policy formation as an extensive form game. Instead, policy formation is implicit: as in Becker 1983, political activities by organized groups are transformed into policies through a "political pressure function." A central assumption of this model is that political pressure depends on the amount of time organized groups devote to political activities. Because the elderly have more spare time, they have more political influence and manage to direct net government transfers toward themselves.

13.6   Discussion

This chapter studied the determinants of intertemporal fiscal policy. We saw that two features of a political system give rise to myopic policies and inefficiently large public debts. One is what we may call "divided government." In both the dynamic common-pool model of section 13.2 and the delayed-stabilization model of section 13.4, overborrowing arises because decision-making power is too dispersed among different policymakers with conflicting objectives. Debt accumulation does not result from a single centralized decision over a well-defined set of policy instruments but emerges residually from the strategic interaction of several political agents, each having unilateral control over a policy instrument. Centralizing political powers in the hands of a single political agent remedies this political or budgetary failure. Clearly, such centralization may come at the price of allocative distortions.

We may call the second feature leading to debt accumulation "alternating governments," refering to the conflict between alternating policymakers using public debt strategically to influence each other. Political instability is at the core of this failure. Unfortunately, it is difficult to discriminate empirically among these two features, since they often tend to come together: coalition governments are generally short-lived. The empirical evidence, however, does not overwhelmingly favor the alternating-governments model. Inefficiently high debt accumulation may also result from other political forces not discussed (or only marginally mentioned) in this chapter. One was mentioned in the previous section, namely intergenerational redistribution. Another was implicitly discussed in the career-concern model of chapter 4 with regard to electoral business cycles. If voters do not immediately observe the borrowing implications of fiscal policy, electoral cycles may indeed involve larger budget deficits ahead of elections.

If a particular political system leads to inefficiently myopic policies, normative arguments speak in favor of institutional constraints such as balanced budget rules. But since the failure involved has a political origin, a balanced budget constraint must be constitutionally (or supranationally) enforced, for there will always be a simple legislative majority in favor of repealing it. A balanced budget constraint may impose other distortions, however. On the one hand, it may be difficult to incorporate contingencies. Thus the tax-smoothing role of government debt or active stabilization policies may be hampered. On the other hand, when there is more than one government asset or liability, constraining policy myopia over one of these items may aggravate myopia over the others. Peletier, Dur, and Swank (1997) show that a no-borrowing constraint in the political instability model of section 13.3 leads the government to inefficiently cut public investment. Problem 5 of this chapter illustrates this result. Indeed, this result is consistent with the recent behavior of many European states that have cut public investment to cope with the constraints on budget deficits imposed by the Stability Pact.

13.7   Notes on the Literature

An enormous literature deals with the politics of government deficits. Here we refer only to the more recent contributions, which typically study general equilibrium models with rational voters and politicians. A broader survey of the public choice literature than that given here is Mueller 1989; a more recent survey is Alesina and Perotti 1995a. Franzese 1998 gives a broad overview of different hypotheses and confronts many of them with postwar OECD data. Gavin and Perotti 1998 provides a broad description of fiscal policies in Latin America.

The dynamic common-pool problem studied in section 13.2 has a long history. It has been studied in the field of industrial organization, where it refers to dynamic games among oligopolists facing an exhaustible resource, such as an oil field or a fishery (Levhari and Mirman 1980, Benhabib and Radner 1992). In the realm of fiscal policy, it was studied by Tabellini (1987) in a dynamic game of monetary and fiscal policy coordination, and by Velasco (1999) in a setting more similar to that of the model in section 13.2. Chari and Cole (1993) study a related two-period model in which legislators facing a free-rider problem that drives spending too high try to constrain future spending and avoid collective irrationality by issuing more debt.

The ideas underlying the dynamic common-pool problem are also at the core of the more empirically oriented literature on budgetary procedures, such as Alesina and Perotti 1995a, von Hagen and Harden 1994, and Hallerberg and von Hagen 1999. Another interesting (mainly empirical) line of research has investigated how various restrictions affect government borrowing. Most of this literature has studied the variety of institutional arrangements in the U.S. states. See for instance Bohn and Inman 1996, Poterba 1994, and Eichengreen and von Hagen 1996. Kontopoulos and Perotti (1997, 1999) consider panel data from the OECD countries, both on government spending and deficits.

The idea that political instability induces a government to use public debt strategically to influence the future policies of its opponent, was first studied by Alesina and Tabellini (1990) and by Persson and Svensson (1989). The model of section 13.3.1 is related to Alesina and Tabellini 1990, whereas the model in section 13.3.2 is related to Persson and Svensson 1989. Since those two studies were published, many other papers have applied this idea to intertemporal fiscal policy. In particular, Tabellini and Alesina 1990 provides a generalization of these results, Alesina and Tabellini 1989 studies capital flight and external borrowing, Tabellini 1990b looks at these models in the context of international policy coordination, and Glazer 1989 applies the same idea to the choice of duration in public investment. Cukierman, Edwards, and Tabellini (1992) analyze tax reforms from this point of view and provide empirical evidence that political instability is associated with more inefficient tax systems. Roubini and Sachs (1989), Grilli, Masciandaro, and Tabellini (1991), and Ozler and Tabellini (1991) study the general association between different aspects of political instability and debt issue, using cross-national data. Lambertini (1996) and Pettersson (1998) analyze more-specific implications regarding empirical evidence in different panel data sets. The result that public debt policies also affect the incumbent's reelection probability was first studied in this context by Aghion and Bolton (1990). Biais and Perotti (1998) rely on similar ideas to study the determinants of privatizations.

Lizzeri (1996) studies an idea related to the strategic use of debt in a different model of redistribution with opportunistic politicians originally formulated by Myerson (1993b). He considers a two-period economy in which elections are held every period. Candidates can make binding promises before the elections as to how they will redistribute the available resources across voters and over time. Rational voters reward myopic behavior, however, favoring a candidate promising to distribute all resources today, because resources left for the future may be spent on others, by the opponent, if the first-period incumbent is not reelected.

The model of delayed stabilization in section 13.4 is a static simplification of the continuous-time model of Alesina and Drazen (1991), who in turn elaborated on earlier ideas by Riley (1980) and Bliss and Nalebuff (1984). Since then, the model has been extended in several directions by, among others, Drazen and Grilli (1992), Casella and Eichengreen (1995), and Alesina and Perotti (1995b). Fernandez and Rodrik (1991) model the resistance to structural reform in a setting with aggregate certainty but individual uncertainty.

13.8   Problems

1. Preelection politics and government spending when parties are opportunistic

This problem uses the same model as in section 13.3.3 but considers the case in which politicians are purely opportunistic. There are two types of voters: $J \in \{D, R\}$, with indirect utility functions $w^{iJ} = W(b + g_2) + \sum_{t=1}^{2} H(g_t^J) + (\sigma^i + \delta_t) \cdot K_t^D$, with $W_b < 0$, $W_{bb} < 0$. σ^i is an idiosyncratic preference parameter distributed around a zero mean according to a common c.d.f., F_σ, which is not group-specific. δ_t represents the average political preference in favor of party D at date t and follows a c.d.f., F_δ. K_t^D is an indicator variable taking on value 1 if D is elected in period $t = 1, 2$ (in the body of the text, only K_2^D is of importance). Finally, public spending in each period is the sum of the spending on each group $J \in \{D, R\}$. That is, total borrowings, b, will equal first-period total spending: $b = g_1^D + g_1^R$ and $g_2 = g_2^D + g_2^R$.

The timing is as follows: (1) At the beginning of each period, parties announce their platform, that is, a supply of public goods to each group. (2) Then δ_t is realized and voters cast their ballot. (3) The elected party implements its announced platform and payoffs are realized.

a. Compute the optimal provision of public goods when the share of type D voters is $d \in [0, 1]$.

b. Show that opportunistic politicians who either maximize their share of votes or maximize their probability of being elected provide the same—optimal—amount of public goods in the second period.

c. Assume d is constant over time. Show that the level of public expenditures does not affect reelection probabilities. Demonstrate that as a result, politicians also provide the optimal levels of public goods in the first period.

d. Show that if the share of type D voters changes over time, that is, if $d_1 \neq d_2$, whereas individual preferences do not change, the previous result no longer applies: the debt level may be suboptimal.

2. Population structure's influence on dynamic inconsistency

This problem uses the same framework as problem 1 but illustrates how changes in population structure affect the parties' preferences (and therefore equilibrium spending).

a. Consider the case in which $d = .5$, and suppose that the values of σ^i are distributed according to a uniform distribution

$$\mathcal{U}\left[-\frac{1}{2\phi^J}; \frac{1}{2\phi^J}\right],$$

where parameters ϕ^J differ among groups $J \in \{D, R\}$. Show that equilibrium spending will be suboptimal and biased toward the group with the highest ϕ^J in both the first and the second period.

b. Consider the case in which $d = .5$, and suppose that the values of the ϕ^J parameters vary between the first and the second period. Show that first-period spending can be too high or too low compared to the case in which ϕ^J is constant over time.

c. Consider the case in which $\phi^D = \phi^R$ but the value of d changes between the first and the second period because voters change their preferences. Show that in such a case, equilibrium spending is always optimal in both periods. Compare the results with those in question (d) in problem 1 and comment.

3. Overindebtedness

Consider the same framework as in the two previous problems.

a. Suppose that the ϕ parameters are given. Determine the conditions under which the shape of H ensures that a change in d generates an excessive debt level in the first period.

b. Assume now that $d = .5$. Characterize the conditions under which the shape of H ensures that a change in ϕ^J generates an excessive debt level in the first period.

4. Endogenous (in)efficiency of the tax system

This problem draws on Cukierman, Edwards, and Tabellini 1992. Assume a world in which there is neither public debt nor labor. At each period t, consumers have an endowment $e_t = 1$ that can be taxed. The tax system, however, can be inefficient. It is indexed by the parameter θ_{t-1}, which measures the rate of inefficiency: in equilibrium, $g_t = \tau_t =$

$(1 - \theta_{t-1}) \cdot \tau_t^n$, where τ_t^n is the nominal tax rate at time t. Thus $c_t = 1 - \tau_t^n$. At time t, the government selects the time t values of the tax rate, government spending, and tax system inefficiency but knows that this inefficiency will affect tax proceeds only at time $t + 1$. Tax revenues can be spent on two different types of public goods, g_t^J, $J \in \{D, R\}$, entering the utility of group J agents only:

$$w^J = c_1 + c_2 + H\left(g_1^J\right) + H\left(g_2^J\right).$$

As in section 13.3.1, the probability of party R's being in office in period 2 is defined by $p_R \in [0, 1]$. A tax reform consists of lowering θ_t to zero, which can be done at no cost.

a. Derive the optimal tax system, that is, the one maximizing $\sum_J w^J$ with respect to θ.

b. Derive the equilibrium spending in period 2, given the inherited efficiency of the tax system.

c. Show that the equilibrium efficiency of the tax system in period 2 will be suboptimally low if there is too low a probability that the incumbent in period 1 is reelected.

d. Show that the equilibrium efficiency of the tax system in period 2 increases if political polarization decreases. To this end, use the utility function

$$w^J = W\left(\tau_1^n, \tau_2^n\right) + H\left(\min\left[\frac{g_1^J}{\alpha}, \frac{g_1^K}{1-\alpha}\right]\right) + H\left(\min\left[\frac{g_2^J}{\alpha}, \frac{g_2^K}{1-\alpha}\right]\right),$$

with $J, K \in \{D, R\}$, $K \neq J$, and $\alpha \in [1/2, 1)$, where "polarization" is measured by the distance between α and $\frac{1}{2}$.

5. Voting on the budget deficit: Consequences of a balanced budget rule

This problem is based on Tabellini and Alesina 1990 and Peletier, Dur, and Swank 1999. Consider a group of heterogeneous agents in the following two-period model. The group is endowed with one unit of output in each period t and decides, by majority rule, on the consumption of two public goods, g_t and f_t, for $t = \{1, 2\}$. At the beginning of period 1, the group can borrow or lend to the rest of the world at zero interest, and the debt, denoted by b, must be repaid in full at the end of the second period. Agent i's preferences are given by

$$w^i = E\left\{\sum_{t=1}^{2} \alpha^i H(g_t) + (1 - \alpha^i)H(f_t)\right\},$$

where $H(\cdot)$ is strictly increasing and concave and α^i identifies voter i. We assume that the parameter α^i is distributed on $(0, 1)$, and we denote its median value in period t by α_t^m. In other words, the identity of the median voter can change over time.

a. Determine the provision of public goods in the second period. Suppose that the median voter at date 1 is identified by any α_1^m in $(0, 1)$. What is the level of debt issued in period 1 when the median voter at date 1 is certain to be the median voter at date 2? Suppose now that $\alpha_2^m = 1$ with probability π and $\alpha_2^m = 0$ with probability $1 - \pi$. Show that the amount of debt issued in period 1 is positive. How does the level of debt vary with the difference between α_1^m and the expected value of α_2^m?

b. Suppose that b is chosen before the composition of public spending in period 1 is known, that is, at a time when the median voters in both periods 1 and 2 are uncertain. Furthermore, assume that both α_1^m and α_2^m are drawn from the same prior distribution. Show that a balanced budget rule is ex ante efficient. Discuss.

c. Now consider the following variation of the model. At each date, the group can also invest an amount i_t in a stock of public capital, k. Furthermore, this investment remains productive for two periods, that is, $k_1 = i_1$ and $k_2 = i_1 + i_2$. Agent i's preferences are modified in the following way:

$$w^i = E \left\{ \sum_{t=1}^{2} \alpha^i H(g_t) + (1 - \alpha^i) H(f_t) + V(k_t) \right\},$$

where $V(\cdot)$ is strictly increasing and concave.

What investment is selected in period 2 when $\alpha_2^m = 1$ and $\alpha_2^m = 0$? Suppose that $\alpha_2^m = 1$ with probability π and $\alpha_2^m = 0$ with probability $1 - \pi$. Characterize the levels of both investment and debt chosen in period 1 when $\alpha_1^m = 1$. Discuss your results in cases $\pi = 1$ and $\pi < 1$.

d. What is the level of investment when a balanced budget rule is imposed? Compare your findings with the results obtained in question (b) and discuss.

14 Growth

Distorted fiscal policies—such as those emerging from the equilibria in the two previous chapters—are likely to affect a country's economic performance. In fact, political factors and political institutions are correlated with long-run economic growth. Most notably, after controlling for the conventional determinants of growth:

1. Inequality in the distribution of income, wealth, or land is negatively correlated in cross-country data with subsequent growth. On the other hand, the evidence concerning the effect of growth on the distribution of income (the Kuznets curve) is quite mixed, both in cross-sectional and time series data.

2. Political instability, as measured by more-frequent regime changes or political unrest and violence, is negatively correlated with growth in cross-country data.

3. Better protection of property rights is positively correlated with growth. Whereas political rights and the incidence of democracy are strongly correlated with the level of income, findings regarding the effect of democracy on economic growth are not robust.

A recent literature has tried to explain these regularities in a setting in which both economic growth and fiscal policies are endogenous. This chapter provides a selective survey of this literature.

The early literature on endogenous economic growth focused on capital accumulation as the engine of growth (see Barro and Sala-i-Martin 1995). Ultimately, economic growth can be reduced to a private accumulation decision. Any economic policy affecting private returns to investment therefore has effects on growth. Such effects can be permanent or temporary, depending on the specific assumptions made about the productive technology. Two policy instruments naturally affect private rates of return on investment, namely the taxation of capital and the public investment in infrastructures. Some contributions to political economics and growth have emphasized these two policy instruments, asking how the tax rate on capital income or the level of public investment are determined. These models of policy choice are simple adaptations of the models already encountered in the previous chapters of this part. They are presented in sections 14.1, 14.2 and 14.4.

Section 14.1 discusses capital taxation. Here the main idea—as suggested by Alesina and Rodrik 1994 and Persson and Tabellini 1994b—is that income inequality exerts a negative effect on investment and growth, because it provides stronger incentives for redistributive policies, which hurt growth-promoting investment. As in these papers—and a great deal of subsequent work—we rely on a simple median-voter model like that in chapter 6.

Section 14.2 turns to public investment, exploring the idea that political instability can hurt growth because it induces an incumbent government to follow myopic policies, as discussed in the work by Svensson (1998) and Devereux and Wen (1996). The argument is closely related to that concerning strategic debt policy in chapter 13.

Finally, section 14.4 briefly discusses how bad protection of property rights may hurt investment and growth, as noted in Tornell and Velasco 1992 and Benhabib and Rustichini 1996. The underlying ideas are closely related to the dynamic common-pool problem, also discussed in chapter 13.

More recent contributions to research on endogenous growth have emphasized innovation and research activities as the main engine of growth (see Aghion and Howitt 1999). Economic policy can affect technological innovation in many ways besides taxation of aggregate capital: for instance, through regulation in the product and labor markets, trade policy, and patent protection. More generally, economic policies influencing the allocation of resources among alternative sectors or among different technologies are likely to affect the incentives to innovate.

Section 14.3 provides an example of the political determinants of such policies. It illustrates how vested interests may influence policy to protect rents associated with traditional sectors or traditional technologies while discriminating against productive investment in activities with higher growth potential, as discussed in Krusell and Rios-Rull 1996. Formally, we study a model in which lobbying determines sectoral policies, as in the special-interest politics models of chapters 3 and 7.

14.1 Income Inequality and Growth

Consider again a two-period economy inhabited by a continuum of heterogenous agents. Everyone has the same quasi-linear preferences over private consumption in periods 1 and 2 and over government (per capita) consumption in period 2. Consumer i's utility is

$$w^i = U\left(c_1^i\right) + c_2^i + H(g). \tag{14.1}$$

The budget constraints are

$$
\begin{aligned}
c_1^i &= e^i - t - k^i \\
c_2^i &= (1 - \tau_K)A(I)k^i,
\end{aligned} \tag{14.2}
$$

where k^i is private investment, t and τ_K are lump sum and capital taxes raised in periods 1 and 2, respectively, and $A(I)$ is the gross return to private capital, which is increasing in public investment, I. We abstract from credibility problems: the government can commit to these policy instruments before private capital is accumulated. Finally, as in chapters 6 and 12, e^i is the endowment of agent i. Agents' endowments are distributed in the population with mean e and a distribution function for the idiosyncratic part $\mathfrak{F}(e^i - e)$. To proxy empirical income distributions, we assume that the median value of $e^i - e$, labeled $e^m - e$ and defined by $\mathfrak{F}(e^m - e) = \frac{1}{2}$, is negative.

In period 1, the government sets public investment. In period 2, it sets public consumption. We assume a balanced budget in every period. Thus the government budget constraint in per capita terms is

$$I = t$$
$$g = \tau_K A(I)k, \tag{14.3}$$

where, as usual, k denotes per capita (average) capital. Following the approach of chapter 13, we can derive equilibrium private investment from (14.1)–(14.3) as

$$k^i = e - I - U_c^{-1}(A(I)(1 - \tau_K)) + (e^i - e) \equiv K(\tau_K, I) + (e^i - e),$$

where the common investment function satisfies $K_\tau < 0$ and $K_I > 0$. It is again convenient to express the utility from private consumption as an indirect utility function defined over the policy variables:

$$
\begin{aligned}
W^i(\tau_K, I, e^i) &\equiv \max \left[U\left(c_1^i\right) + c_2^i \right] \\
&= U(e - I - K(\tau_K, I)) + (1 - \tau_K)A(I)K(\tau_K, I) + A(I)(1 - \tau_K)(e^i - e) \\
&= W(\tau_K, I) + A(I)(1 - \tau_K)(e^i - e). \tag{14.4}
\end{aligned}
$$

By the envelope theorem, the direct welfare cost of the capital tax, $W_\tau = -A(I)K$, is negative. Moreover, the welfare effect of public investment, $W_I = -U_c + (1 - \tau_K)A_I K$, is monotonically decreasing in I (by $U_{cc} < 0$ and $A_{II} < 0$). Substituting (14.4) into (14.1) and using (14.3), we obtain individual i's policy preferences over the two policy instruments τ_K and I:

$$w^i = W^i(\tau_K, I, e^i) + H(\tau_K A(I)K(\tau_K, I)).$$

These policy preferences are linear in the idiosyncratic variable e^i. They therefore fulfill the intermediate-preference property, in definition 4 of chapter 2, such that the preferred policy of the agent with endowment e^m is a Condorcet winner, even though the policy space is two-dimensional. If we assume that policy decisions are made at the beginning of period 1 in Downsian electoral competition, in which candidates can commit to a policy platform, the winning proposal is the policy this decisive voter prefers. If the second-order conditions are fulfilled, the equilibrium values for I and τ_K thus satisfy:

$$
\begin{aligned}
W_I + H_g \tau_K (KA_I + AK_I) + (e^m - e)(1 - \tau_K)A_I &= 0 \\
W_\tau + H_g A(K + \tau_K K_\tau) - (e^m - e)A &= 0. \tag{14.5}
\end{aligned}
$$

To understand these conditions, first assume that the distribution is symmetric, so that $e^m = e$. Then the third terms in both conditions are zero, and (14.5) characterizes the optimal policy for the average agent, which—by quasi-linear preferences—would also be chosen by a utilitarian planner. The first condition says that it is optimal to provide more public investment than strictly necessary to maximize private indirect utility (i.e., $W_I < 0$), because of the beneficial effects on the future tax base and hence on public spending. (Public debt is not allowed. If it were, this result would be different.) The second condition equates the average private marginal cost of raising revenue ($W_\tau < 0$) with the marginal benefit it generates via public consumption.

But if $e^m < e$, well-known redistributive effects come into play. The decisive voter's capital falls short of average capital by exactly ($e^m - e$). This implies that I is smaller and τ_K is higher than in the hypothetical planning solution, because the decisive voter does not benefit from public investment as much as the average capital holder and does not suffer as much from capital taxes. To see this formally, notice that the third term in the first equation of (14.5) is negative and the third term in the second equation is positive. By the second-order conditions, I must be lower and τ_K must be higher than in the planner's solution.

We thus see that income inequality hampers growth via two different channels. The growth rate from period 1 to period 2, given by $[A(I)K(\tau_K, I)/e] - 1$, is increasing in I (both directly and indirectly) and decreasing in τ_K. Furthermore, the higher is income inequality, as measured by the distance between median and average income, the lower is growth, as equilibrium public investment is smaller and capital taxation—as well as government consumption—is higher.

Alesina and Rodrik (1994) and Persson and Tabellini (1994b) developed this kind of reduced-form prediction in related but explicitly dynamic models. Whereas Persson and Tabellini (as here) focused on the size distribution of income, Alesina and Rodrik focused on the functional distribution of income between labor and capital. Both papers also took the reduced-form prediction to the data—here, Alesina and Rodrik looked at the size distribution of income, as well—and indeed found a strong negative effect of inequality on growth in a cross section of postwar data from a broad sample of countries.[1]

These papers stimulated a body of subsequent work scrutinizing both the empirical and the theoretical argument. Whereas the reduced-form relation from income inequality to growth indeed seems empirically robust, the structural links the theory implies have not always found support in later empirical work.[2] Thus it has been hard to identify both the implied link from inequality to redistribution and the link from redistribution to growth, as

---

1. Persson and Tabellini (1994b) also found a similar relation in a small historical panel of industrialized countries with data going back to the late nineteenth century.

2. Later empirical work based on better data has also questioned an empirical finding by Persson and Tabellini (1994b) that was interpreted as giving indirect support for the theory, namely that the relation between inequality and growth was present only in democracies and not in dictatorships.

emphasized in the recent surveys by Perotti (1996) and Benabou (1996). The model in this section suggests that these links could be pretty subtle, however (with opposite effects of inequality on government consumption and investment, for example, and ambiguous effects on total government spending). Moreover, the failure to find a robust link from tax rates and redistribution to economic growth is a problem for conventional growth theory, not just for political theories of growth. The literature has also searched for other reasons why income inequality and growth may be inversely related. Perotti stresses that one link may run via political instability or via other, nonpolitical, channels such as education. Benabou covers a whole range of recent theoretical work showing that the links between income distribution, policy, and growth may run in different directions. For instance, redistribution may promote growth when agents are credit-constrained or when it promotes education. Problem 2 of this chapter illustrates such an example.

14.2   Political Instability and Growth

We now modify the previous model as follows. First, every private agent has the same first-period endowment: that is, $e^i = e$ and the same average investment function applies for everyone. As in chapter 13, however, agents belong to two different groups, $J = D, R$, and public spending is of either of two types: g^D (benefiting only the D group) or g^R (benefiting only the R group).

Second, and again following chapter 13, policy is set not by majority rule but by an incumbent government acting to maximize the utility of group D agents. The incumbent may be replaced with an alternative government in the future that cares only about group R. For simplicity, we take the reelection probability of the D government $(1 - P)$ as exogenous. It is natural to interpret P as a measure of political instability.

Third, so that a meaningful policy choice is introduced in period 2, policies are chosen sequentially. Thus public investment I is chosen in period 1, before private capital accumulation, and the capital tax rate τ_K is chosen in period 2. To avoid the capital levy problem discussed in chapter 13, we assume that in period 2 the private sector can still avoid some of the tax imposed, though at a cost, by reallocating some of its accumulated capital to a nontaxed asset with a lower return. We could think of this as tax avoidance or capital flight. Specifically, as in section 12.4, we rewrite the period 2 budget constraint as

$$c_2 = (1 - \tau_K)A(I)k + f - M(f),$$

where $M(f)$ is a concave and increasing function of the amount f shielded from taxation and where we have recognized that everybody makes the same savings decision. As in chapter 12, average savings are given by a function $S(\tau_K, I)$ and tax avoidance is given by the function $F(\tau_K, I)$, with $F_\tau > 0$ and $F_I < 0$.[3] The government's tax base can thus be written as a function $K(\tau_K, I) \equiv A(I) S(\tau_K, I) - F(\tau_K, I)$. This function has the same ex ante properties (that is, from the viewpoint of period 1) as before: it is decreasing in τ_K and increasing in I. In period 2, when K and I are given from previous decisions, the ex post tax base $K^2(\tau_K, I)$ is still decreasing in τ_K but with a lesser slope (intertemporal substitution possibilities are eliminated).

The bottom line after these modifications is similar to that in the previous section: we can write the ex ante indirect utility of an agent in group J as

$$w^J = W(\tau_K, I) + H(g^J) = W(\tau_K, I) + H(\tau_K K(\tau_K, I)). \tag{14.6}$$

We can also define ex post indirect utility (for given K and I) as $W^2(\tau_K, I) + H(\tau_K K^2(\tau_K, I))$. Both $W(\tau_K, I)$ and $W^2(\tau_K, I)$ have the same qualitative properties as the corresponding function in section 14.1.

Any government holding power in period 2 spends all revenue on the public good its own constituency favors. The ex post optimal tax rate is therefore given by the condition

$$W_\tau^2 + H_g\big(K^2 + \tau_K K_\tau^2\big) = 0, \tag{14.7}$$

which has the same interpretation as the second condition in (14.5). Thus both prospective governments will set the same tax rate. Condition (14.7) implicitly defines the optimal tax rate as a function of past public investment $\tau_K(I)$ with the slope

$$\frac{d\tau_K(I)}{dI} = -\frac{W_{\tau I}^2 + H_{gg} K_{\tau I}^2}{W_{\tau\tau}^2 + H_{gg} K_{\tau\tau}^2}.$$

Unless H is very concave, $\tau_{KI} > 0$, as the numerator is positive and the denominator is negative (by the second-order condition). Public investment enlarges the tax base, which drives up the optimal tax rate.

The incumbent D government in period 1 chooses I so as to maximize

$$E(w^D) = P W(\tau_K(I), I) + (1 - P)[W(\tau_K(I), I) + H(\tau_K(I) K(\tau_K(I), I))]$$
$$= W(\tau_K(I), I) + (1 - P)[H(\tau_K(I) K(\tau_K(I), I))].$$

We can rewrite the first-order condition for this problem with (14.7), recognizing that $W_\tau^2 = W_\tau$ and $K^2 = K$ at the equilibrium tax rate.[4] Some additional algebra gives

$$W_I + H_g\big[\tau_K K_I + \tau_K \big(K_\tau - K_\tau^2\big)\tau_{KI}\big] - P H_g[\tau_K K_I + \tau_{KI}(K + \tau_K K_\tau)] = 0. \tag{14.8}$$

---

3. The first-order condition for optimal tax avoidance is for the consumer to set $A(I)(1 - \tau_K) - 1 + M_f(f) = 0$. When this condition is inverted, we get the desired tax avoidance function. Note that, in contrast to chapter 12, here there is no investment from abroad in the home country.

4. These equalities follow from rational expectations. The equilibrium savings function (and hence the capital stock) correctly reflects forthcoming tax rates on capital.

Suppose first that D is certain to be reelected: $P = 0$. Then the optimal choice of I boils down to the familiar weighing of private welfare (the first term) against government revenue (the second term), where the latter is fully internalized, as the government is certain to remain in office. The resulting condition is the same as the second condition in (14.5) adjusted for the different timing of tax policy and for the lack of heterogeneity. But when reelection is uncertain, $P > 0$, future government revenue is less valuable and policy myopia sets in. Because the third term in (14.8) is negative, a higher probability P of losing office makes public investment less attractive and reduces it in equilibrium.

In this model, higher instability not only drives down public investment but also reduces growth. Second-period income, $c_2 + g = A(I)K(\tau_K, I) - M(F(\tau_K, I))$, unambiguously goes down as I falls. The direct negative effects of lower public investment and the indirect negative effects of higher waste due to more tax avoidance always outweigh the positive effects of the smaller equilibrium capital tax.

Much of the informal discussion of why political instability is harmful for growth seems to suggest that uncertainty or unpredictability has a direct effect on private investment. We know, however, that uncertainty in returns has ambiguous effects on private investment. Here a different mechanism is at work: political instability induces more-myopic fiscal policies, which in turn reduce public investment and growth. This is related to Svensson 1998, which shows that political instability may make a forward-looking government abstain from improvements in the legal system enforcing private property rights. Svensson's work also finds empirical support for this idea. Political instability (measured as in Alesina, Ozler, Roubini, and Swagel 1996) indeed reduces the protection of private property rights (measured by the same index as in Knack and Keefer 1995) in a wide cross-country sample. Controlling for property rights protection, political instability drops out of a cross-country investment regression.

The theoretical paper by Devereux and Wen (1996) emphasizes a somewhat different mechanism: political instability induces incumbent governments to leave smaller assets to their successors, thereby forcing them to tax capital at a higher rate; the expectation of higher taxes drives down private investment, leaving a smaller tax base for the successor government. Problem 1 of this chapter considers a similar example.

14.3 Special Interests, Rents, and Growth

The previous two sections analyzed how economic policy affects growth by changing the returns on aggregate investment. In this section, we discuss a second channel through which economic policy influences growth: by changing the incentives to innovate. Here the conflict of interest is not between rich and poor or between alternating governments with different preferences for public spending. The central conflict is instead between specific factors of production earning rents in traditional sectors using old technologies and innovators seeking to introduce new productive technologies. According to influential economic historians, this conflict has played an important role throughout the evolution of industrial societies (Mokyr 1990, 1992). Depending on whether the innovators in the dynamic sectors or the vested interests in the traditional sectors are most influential, the government implements policies that promote or stifle economic growth. In this section, we formalize this idea in the context of sectoral policies. We modify the two-period model of the previous sections, adding two sectors and a policy influencing the sectoral allocation of capital and labor. The model adds an explicit political equilibrium to a simple policy example in Persson and Tabellini 1992b. Krusell and Rios-Rull 1996 and chapter 9 of Aghion and Howitt 1999 provide a different economic and political model capturing the same idea but focusing more explicitly on innovation rather than sectoral allocation.

To simplify, we abstract from public consumption and investment and write consumer i's utility function as

$$w^i = U\left(c_1^i\right) + c_2^i.$$

As in section 14.2, every citizen has the same period 1 endowment. But now the endowment can be invested in either of two sectors, T or N. Thus every consumer has the same first-period budget constraint, namely

$$c^i + k^{iT} + k^{iN} = e.$$

In period 2, the same consumption good can be produced with two different technologies associated with the two different sectors of production. In the "new" sector, production requires only capital and takes place according to a linear Ak technology $N = Ak^N$, where k^N is an economy-wide aggregate (average). The "traditional" sector has a well-behaved, constant-returns-to-scale production technology defined over capital k^T and a fixed factor v, namely $T = Q(k^T, v)$. Again, v denotes the economy-wide aggregate (average) amount of the fixed factor. We shall interpret this fixed factor as representing land, but alternative interpretations are also possible where, say, the traditional sector is associated with skills adapted to traditional techniques of production. Here, individuals differ in their land holdings. Specifically, we assume that only a share of the population $\alpha < 1$ owns land. For simplicity, every landowner holds the same amount of land. Thus there are two groups in the population. One is a group of "landowners," of size α, each owning a quantity $\frac{v}{\alpha}$ of land. The other is a group of "capitalists," of size $1 - \alpha$, each owning no land and having a period 2 income only from capital.[5]

---

5. Landowners also earn capital income in period 2, in addition to their rents from land.

We are interested in policies affecting the relative profitability of investment in the two technologies. A host of different policies affect relative profitability, including regulation, patent, industrial, and trade policies. For simplicity, we represent such detailed policies with a sectoral tax, τ_N, levied on the output of the new sector; the per capita tax proceeds $\tau_N k^N$ are distributed as an equal lump sum transfer f to every individual in the economy. The second-period budget constraint can thus be written

$$c_2^i = (1 - \tau_N) A k^{iN} + Q_k k^{iT} + Q_v v^i + f,$$

where we have exploited the condition that the equilibrium reward to each factor equals its marginal product.

Optimal savings and investment decisions by consumers imply

$$U_c(e - k^i) = A(1 - \tau_N) = Q_k(k^T, v). \tag{14.9}$$

Each consumer thus saves the same amount $k^i = k^{iN} + k^{iT}$, irrespective of whether he owns any land. In equilibrium, consumers must be indifferent between the two forms of investment, and their net return must coincide. As U_{cc} is negative, we get our usual savings function, $k^i = K(\tau_N)$, with total savings a declining function of the tax rate. But as $Q_{kk} < 0$, investment in the traditional sector is positively related to the tax on the new sector, $k^T = K^T(\tau_N)$. Moreover, because $Q_{kv} > 0$, the quasi rents to land become an increasing function of the tax $R(\tau_N) = Q_v(K^T(\tau_N), v)$. A tax on the new sector with its capital-intensive technology drives down the marginal return to capital and reduces aggregate investment and growth. Since capital flows to the traditional sector, however, the rents to the fixed factor rise. Thus $R_\tau(\tau_N) = Q_{vk} K_\tau^T > 0$.

Given this structure and some substitution, we can write the indirect utility of individuals belonging to group J as

$$W^J(\tau_N) = W(\tau_N) + R(\tau_N)(v^J - v), \tag{14.10}$$

where v^J denotes per capita holdings of and in group J. Thus in the group of landowners, $v^J = v/\alpha$. In the group of capitalists, $v^J = 0$. The common part in (14.10) satisfies $W(\tau_N) = U(e - K(\tau_N)) + A(K(\tau_N) - K^T(\tau_N)) + Q(K^T(\tau_N), v)$. It is easily shown that the social optimum in this economy, with a utilitarian social welfare function, is to set $\tau_N = 0$. Formally, $W_\tau = 0$ at the point $\tau_N = 0$.[6] Intuitively, the sector-specific tax distorts the allocation

---

6. We have

$$W_\tau = (A - U_c)K_\tau + (Q_k - A)K_\tau^T.$$

From the definition of $W(\tau_N)$, $W_\tau = 0$ at $\tau_N = 0$. One can check that W is concave, so that this defines a unique optimum, under mild conditions on U and Q.

of capital; thus the best policy from a social point of view is to maximize period 2 output and hence economic growth, which calls for a zero tax.

Landowners in the traditional sector have strong interests in protecting their rents, however. It is not implausible to assume that this special-interest group also has the political power to tilt policy in its favored direction. Owners of land or other factors used intensively in traditional sectors often have a disproportionate say in domestic politics. Taking the model less literally, those agents who have acquired a traditional technology become endowed with a fixed factor and have strong incentives to get organized politically to protect the resulting quasi rents. In a new sector, based on a new technology, interest groups may be much harder to form, particularly before the necessary factors or skills have been accumulated.

We illustrate the likely policy bias by adapting the model with probabilistic voting and lobbying introduced in section 3.5 and used in section 7.5. Assume that at the beginning of period 1, two office-seeking parties, A and B, commit to a value of τ_N in the course of the political campaign. The two groups of voters, landowners and capitalists, have the same distribution of ideological preferences for party A versus party B, with uniform density ϕ and mean 0. Party B's average popularity in the population as a whole is given by

$$\delta = \tilde{\delta} + h(C_B - C_A),$$

where $\tilde{\delta}$ is a random variable with a uniform distribution, mean zero, and density ψ. The variable C_P denotes campaign contributions received by party $P = A, B$. Following the steps in those sections of earlier chapters, the swing voter in group J has an ideological bias in favor of B defined by

$$\sigma^J = W^J(\tau_{N,A}) - W^J(\tau_{N,B}) - \delta.$$

Assume that only landowners are organized politically and that their encompassing lobby is the only one to collect and promise campaign contributions. The lobby chooses contributions to the parties so as to maximize the expected utility of its representative member, subject to a quadratic cost, as in section 5.3. Following the same steps as in sections of earlier chapters, we may derive the probability that party A wins the election:

$$p_A = \frac{1}{2} + \psi[W(\tau_{N,A}) - W(\tau_{N,B}) + h(C_A - C_B)].$$

The equilibrium contributions by the landowners' lobby are

$$C_A = \max[0, \alpha \psi h(W^v(\tau_{N,A}) - W^v(\tau_{N,B})]$$
$$C_B = -\min[0, \alpha \psi h(W^v(\tau_{N,A}) - W^v(\tau_{N,B})],$$

where W^v denotes the representative landowner's policy preferences. As before, the land lobby supports only one party, namely the party offering the best policy to its members. As a consequence, the two parties choose the same equilibrium platforms. Using these expressions, (14.10), and our assumption about group size, we can derive an expression characterizing the equilibrium policy:

$$W_\tau = -\frac{\psi h^2}{1 + \alpha \psi h^2} \alpha R_\tau (v^v - v) \equiv -\frac{\psi h^2}{1 + \alpha \psi h^2} v(1 - \alpha) R_\tau < 0. \tag{14.11}$$

Because $R_\tau > 0$, the equilibrium has $W_\tau < 0$. Since W is concave (see note 6), this means that $\tau_N > 0$. Landowners are thus willing to distort the economy to direct scarce capital into the traditional sector, thus raising their own rents. Since landowners are politically more influential, both political parties are willing to bend their policy in the desired direction so as to enhance their probability of winning. Furthermore, (14.11) shows that τ_N is higher, the smaller is α. Thus the more concentrated is land in the population, the larger is the landowners' stake in the policy and the more they are prepared to lobby in favor of distortionary policy.

In this model, aggregate investment, period 2 output, and economic growth are all declining functions of τ_N (for $\tau_N > 0$). The prediction of this simple model is thus consistent with the evidence in Persson and Tabellini 1992b and Alesina and Rodrik 1994 that greater land concentration is associated with lower growth, ceteris paribus. More generally, the model supports the idea that political power of vested interests associated with traditional sectors or traditional technologies can hamper investment and economic growth.

Krusell and Rios-Rull (1996) present a related but much richer argument in a full-fledged overlapping-generations model in which the vested interests are associated with knowledge of how to operate older vintages of technology, obtained through previous human capital accumulation. A simplified version of this model is presented in chapter 9 of Aghion and Howitt 1999. In each period, workers and entrepreneurs of different generations make a political decision whether to permit adoption of the most recent technology. As the authors show, this may very well lead the economy into a growth trap, though equilibrium cycles with accumulation, technology adoption, and growth, followed by standstill, protection, and decline, are also possible equilibrium outcomes.

Boschini (1999) studies how different economies adapt to the opportunities created by skill-biased technical change that requires complementary public investment in infrastructure. How rapidly such investment occurs depends on the income distribution in the economy and the extent of the franchise, but more importantly on the skills of the political elite. Boschini uses the model to investigate nineteenth-century data and finds preliminary evidence in favor of its predictions, namely that a skilled elite and a flat income distribution create the most favorable conditions for industrialization and growth.

J. Svensson (1999) studies an overlapping-generations model in which special interests are capable of earning rents through inefficient public projects with adverse consequences for growth. In analogy with the mechanisms discussed in part 3, he shows that elections can induce greater competition between different special interests. Democracy may therefore increase growth, ceteris paribus, by raising the quality of public spending. Svensson finds preliminary support for this and other predictions of the model in cross-country data.

14.4   Other Political Determinants of Growth

As mentioned in the introduction to this chapter, the data support the idea that poor enforcement of property rights is harmful for investment and growth. The same idea is also derived from some recent theoretical work. Benhabib and Rustichini (1996) study a growth model in which two groups try to redistribute consumption toward themselves at the expense of the economy's capital stock. They show how incentives to obtain such a redistribution may arise at both low and high levels of income, and how greater inequality in the two groups' income may exacerbate these incentives. Their model abstracts from the political mechanism and the channels of redistribution, however.

Tornell and Velasco (1992) focus on redistribution through the fiscal policy process in a linear (Ak) growth model. Their argument, like Benhabib and Rustichini's, is another instance of the common-pool problem discussed in chapters 7 and 13. The common pool in Tornell and Velasco's model is a part of the economy capital stock rather than the government tax base, but the incentive to overexploit this common pool is the same as in the model in this book. Because the redistribution is supposed to take place via the government policy process, the poorly enforced property rights are closely related to weak government. Problem 4 of this chapter illustrates the main idea.

Tornell (1995) studies a related model but allows for endogenous property rights. In particular, property rights in his model can be created and destroyed at a cost. He shows that the economy can go through a cycle with low property rights protection at low and high levels of income. If it does, this pattern is perfectly foreseen and leads to gradually falling growth rates at intermediate levels of income.

Lane and Tornell (1996) show that an exogenous positive shock due to productivity or the terms of trade may actually reduce the growth rate in an economy with powerful interest groups and poorly defined property rights. The mechanism is again a coordination failure between the interest groups, whereby an increase in redistributive transfers more than outweighs the initial increase in the incentives to invest. Svensson (1996) produces a related result in which the interest groups' incentives to hold back on their demand for transfers vary negatively with government income.

14.5   Discussion

This chapter discussed three main ideas. The first is that redistributive politics stifle growth because the resulting tax distortions reduce the incentives to accumulate capital. Hence any political or economic force increasing the size of redistributive transfers, such as greater pretax inequality, is also harmful for growth. As plausible as this idea may be, it receives little support from the data. Even though the negative correlation between inequality and growth may be robust, it is much harder to discern a negative effect of redistributive transfers on growth.

The second idea is that myopic government policies are harmful for growth. Such policy myopia can take more than one form—for instance, too little public investment or too much public debt. It can also have more than one cause: political instability is one, a dynamic common-pool problem resulting from a faulty budgetary process or incomplete property rights is another. In this case, too, the empirical evidence is mixed. Political instability appears to be negatively related to growth, but empirical research has not been closely tied to theoretical work, so the evidence is consistent with more than one theoretical hypothesis. For instance, political instability could lead to unsustainable monetary or fiscal policies, and this, in turn, could have adverse consequences for growth through financial and macroeconomic instability—see Fischer (1991). But other mechanisms of causation cannot be ruled out. As emphasized by Benabou (1996), there is thus scope for new work to provide better theoretical underpinnings for the empirical findings. This task will not be easy, however, given the strong empirical correlations between inequality, instability, and poor enforcement of property rights.

The third idea is that growth reflects microeconomic policies affecting the incentives to innovate, such as regulation or industrial policy. On the one hand, owners of specific factors in traditional sectors trying to preserve their rents often oppose innovation. On the other hand, innovation often entails externalities that open the door for growth-promoting policies. Which policy gets implemented depends on the special-interest politics of the sectors affected. This idea is very appealing, and economic historians have emphasized its relevance; see, in particular, Mokyr 1990. Nevertheless, it has been neglected in the theoretical and empirical literature. Naturally, these three ideas are not mutually inconsistent, and each of them might very well be fruitfully applied to different episodes.

The models summarized in this chapter are all rather simple, even simplistic. Their value added is mainly in their identification of a particular conflict of interest over policies affecting growth. The specific political mechanisms are borrowed from earlier chapters, however. Moreover, reflecting the state of the art when the original contributions were made, these mechanisms pay insufficient attention to political institutions. Given the variety of constitutional forms observed through time and across countries at different stages of development, more careful research on economic growth and comparative politics might have high payoffs.

Finally, all the economic models considered in this chapter focus on policies that directly affect the return on capital, such as capital taxation or public investment. The rate of return on capital depends on many other policies, however, besides those directly affecting capital income. In particular, it may depend on variables affecting the employment rate. This is generally true in standard neoclassical growth models, during the transition to the steady state, and in some models of endogenous growth. Intuitively, the return on capital depends on the capital-labor ratio, and hence anything reducing equilibrium employment may also affect equilibrium growth, temporarily or permanently. Daveri and Tabellini (1997) study this mechanism in a simple model with monopolistic unions, showing that taxes on labor reduce equilibrium growth and investment, because unions manage to shift labor taxation into higher gross real wages, reducing profits. (Problem 3 of this chapter illustrates the argument.) Empirical evidence for industrial countries indicates that this effect may be quantitatively important, particularly for investment. Daveri and Tabellini stop short of making policy endogenous, but their analysis indicates that any policy affecting equilibrium employment or unemployment—such as the labor market regulations or the social security contributions studied in chapter 6—might also affect growth. Combining growth and equilibrium unemployment in a model of endogenous policy thus remains an interesting area for future work.

14.6   Notes on the Literature

There is a very large and still expanding literature on economic growth: see Barro and Sala-i-Martin 1995, and Aghion and Howitt 1999. Many recent contributions pay attention to economic policy and its political determinants. It is beyond the scope of this chapter to adequately survey all of this literature. Here we refer to the publications most closely related to the examples presented in the chapter.

Section 14.1 draws on Alesina and Rodrik 1994 and Persson and Tabellini 1994b, which also documents the negative link between inequality and growth. Early contributions to the theory of income distribution, investment, and growth were also made by Perotti (1993), who studied human capital accumulation and tax-financed subsidies in the presence of borrowing constraints, Bertola (1993), who studied tax policy and the functional distribution of income, Glomm and Ravikumar (1992), who studied private versus public provision of education, and Saint-Paul and Verdier (1993), who also studied redistributive policies that finance public education in a setting with wealth-constrained individuals. Perotti (1996),

Benabou (1996), and Aghion and Howitt (1999) provide additional references to recent theory and empirical work. More recently, Barro (1999) finds evidence of a negative effect of inequality on growth or investment only in the poor segment of a broad panel of countries. A large literature on taxation's effect on growth has generally failed to find robust empirical correlations. See in particular Easterly and Rebelo 1993, and Mendoza, Milesi-Ferretti, and Asea 1997. Caballero and Hammamour (1996) focus on the rents created by factor specificity and how the distribution of those rents affects the incentives to invest.

The negative empirical correlation between political instability and growth is documented by Alesina, Ozler, Roubini, and Swagel (1996) and Barro (1991). Knack and Keefer (1995) discuss the relation between property rights and growth. A survey of the voluminous literature on the links from democracy to growth can be found in Przeworski and Limongi 1993. As stated in the text, few theoretical models spell out the mechanisms whereby political instability is harmful for growth. Two exceptions are Svensson 1998 and Devereux and Wen 1996, from which we draw in section 14.3.

Special-interest politics and growth are analyzed by Persson and Tabellini (1992b) with regard to sectoral policies. Krusell and Rios-Rull (1996) and Aghion and Howitt (1999) study a median-voter model in which the government chooses whether to allow innovation. Mokyr (1990, 1992) documents the relevance of the conflict between traditional sectors and innovative forces in economic history. Boschini (1999) studies the nexus between the distributions of skills and income, the franchise, and industrialization.

14.7 Problems

1. Public debt, political instability, and growth

Consider the following model of public debt, political instability, and growth. There are two periods, with elections held after the first period. The electorate consists of two groups of voters, R and D. Each group has an infinite number of voters and is normalized to size $\frac{1}{2}$. Two public goods, g_t^D and g_t^R, can be provided in each period t, each specific to the corresponding group. The incumbent politician in the first period cares about maximizing the utility of group D. In the second period, he is reelected with exogenous probability p, and with probability $(1-p)$ he is replaced by a politician who cares about maximizing group R's preferences.

The game has the following structure. In the first period the incumbent chooses public spending, g_1^D and g_1^R, and public debt, b, so that the budget constraint is given by

$$\bar{I} + g_1^D + g_1^R + b = \bar{\tau}.$$

Whereas lump sum taxes, $\bar{t}$, and public investment, $\bar{I}$, are exogenously fixed, voters buy public debt with return R_b. Voters also invest in capital to gain a return of R_k. Both R_b and R_k are endogenously determined in the model.

In the second period, the office holder sets proportional taxes on capital, τ, and public goods, g_2^D and g_2^R, so that his budget constraint is satisfied:

$$g_2^j = \tau A(\bar{I})k - R_b b,$$

where $A(\bar{I})$ is the return on capital net of taxes τ. Thus proportional taxes are the government's only source of revenue in period 2. Moreover, the government is obliged to pay voters holding debt a return of R_b.

Voters' utility is given by

$$u^j = U(c_1) + H\left(g_1^j\right) + c_2 + H\left(g_2^j\right).$$

Finally, voters' budget constraints for the two periods are given by

$$c_1 = e - \bar{t} - k - b$$
$$c_2 = (1 - \tau)A(\bar{I})k + Rb,$$

where e is the voters' endowment, k the voters' investment in capital and b their holding of public debt.

a. Write the equilibrium conditions for investment in both capital and public debt to be positive. Calculate the voters' capital investment decision as a function of second-period taxes, $k(\tau)$. Show that this function is decreasing in τ.

b. Calculate the second-period office holder's tax decision as a function of first-period debt, $\tau(b)$. Show that taxes are increasing in debt.

c. Write the expressions for determining the first-period debt decision. Show that if $k_\tau(\tau(b))\tau_b(b) < -1$, then debt is higher when $p < 1$ than when $p = 1$.

d. Discuss political instability's effect on growth in this model.

2. Inequality and growth: Human capital

Consider the following model of the connection between inequality and growth. There are two periods, 1 and 2. Voters live one period and have one child. There are an infinite number of voters, and population size is normalized to one. Voters care about their own consumption, c_{i1}, and are also altruistic in that they care about the child's human capital, h_{i2}:

$$U(c_{i1}, h_{i2}) = c^\alpha h^{1-\alpha}, \quad 0 < \alpha < 1.$$

The human capital of the child, h_{i2}, is transferred from the parents' human capital, h_{i1}, and through education g_1,

$$h_{i2} = (1 - z)\delta h_{i1} + g_1,$$

where $(1 - z)$ is the amount of time parents devote to transferring human capital to children and $\delta \geq 1$ the productivity of this transfer. Initial human capital levels are given by a distribution $F(\cdot)$ on [0, 1] with a median level smaller than the expected level, $h_{m1} < \bar{h}_1$.

The production function in the economy is given by

$$Y_t = H_t$$
$$H_t = z \int_0^1 h_{it}\, dF \equiv z\bar{h}_t.$$

The income of individual i is zh_{it}. Education is produced by the production function $g_t = \delta h'_t$, where h'_t is the amount of human capital devoted to public education. Thus the productivity of public and private education is equal. Public education is financed by a proportional tax, τ_1, decided upon by majority rule in period 1.

a. Show that preferences over taxes derived from the above model imply the existance of a Condorcet winner.

b. Calculate the equilibrium tax rate and show that it is decreasing in $\frac{h_{it}}{\bar{h}_t}$.

c. Write the expression for the growth rate and show that it is increasing in the income inequality of the population.

3. Unions and taxation

The following problem is adopted from Daveri and Tabellini 1997. Consider a two-period overlapping-generations model with a constant population. Individuals have utility on consumption when young and old, c_y and c_o, given by

$$U = \sqrt{c_y} + \sqrt{c_o}.$$

Only young individuals can work. They can be employed, earning $w(1 - \tau^l)$, or unemployed, earning a subsidy of s. τ^l is the labor income tax rate, which is exogenously given. Old individuals earn a return $(1 + (1 - \tau^k)r)$ on their investments in capital when young. τ^k is the tax rate on capital, which is also exogenously given.

Let l stand for the fraction of employed individuals. We can write the government budget constraint as

$$\tau^k rk + \tau^l wl = g + (1 - l)s,$$

where k is the average holding of capital by the current old and g the exogenously determined public spending. Average capital per worker evolves according to

$$k = lk^E + (1 - l)k^U,$$

where subscripts E and U denote the employed and unemployed, respectively.

Production takes place in a large number of identical firms with production functions

$$y = Akl^{1-\alpha}.$$

Firms are competitive in hiring workers and acquiring capital.

a. Given w, τ^k, and τ^l, calculate the demand function for workers and the rate of return on capital.

b. Suppose labor unions set wages. (Unions are assumed to be large enough to set wages but small enough not to affect fiscal policy.) A proportion λ of the labor force are members of labor unions. First, employed individuals become members and then, $\lambda - l$ of the unemployed also become members. Thus assume wages are set by the maximization of

$$\frac{l(k, w)}{\lambda} w(1 - \tau^l) + \frac{\lambda - l(k, w)}{\lambda} s.$$

Compute the equilibrium wage.

c. Show that in this model, employment and growth are positively correlated. What is the explanation for this relation?

4. Growth and the common-pool problem

The following problem demonstrates the effect of the common-pool problem on growth. Suppose that there are two groups, D and R, each with an infinite number of voters and of size 1. The utility of voters in group j is given by

$$u^j = U(c_1) + c_2 + H\left(g_2^j\right).$$

There are two periods. In the first period, voters must decide how much to invest in capital and how much to consume. The budget constraint for voter i is given by

$$e = c_{i1} + k_i,$$

where e is the initial endowment, c_{i1} the first-period consumption, and k_i their investment in capital. The return on capital is assumed to be fixed and equal to $R > 1$.

In the second period, both groups simultaneously choose g^j, and a proportional tax, τ, on capital earnings finances spending. If groups' demands are not compatible with total capital earnings, then no public good is produced. Thus taxes are given by

$$\tau 2kR = \begin{cases} g^D + g^R & \text{if } g^D + g^R \leq 2kR \\ 0 & \text{if } g^D + g^R > 2kR \end{cases}.$$

Throughout, assume that R is large enough so that you get interior solutions.

a. Solve for the choice of g^D and g^R in the second period, given the choices in the first period.

b. Solve for the investment choice in the first period given the choice in the second period.

c. Write the expression for the growth rate in this model.

d. Show that the growth rate would increase if the groups were to coordinate in the second period.

5. Inequality and growth: A specific functional form for $A(I)$

Consider a two-period economy inhabited by a continuum of heterogenous agents. Everyone has the same quasi-linear preferences over private consumption in periods 1 and 2 and over government (per capita) consumption in period 2. Government consumption is endogenous and denoted by g. Consumer i's utility is

$$u^i = U\left(c_1^i\right) + c_2^i + H(g).$$

The consumer's budget constraints are

$$c_1^i = e^i - t - k^i$$

$$c_2^i = (1 - \tau_K)A(I)k^i,$$

where k^i is private investment, t and τ_K lump sum and capital taxes, respectively, and the gross return to private capital is given by

$$A(I) = \begin{cases} \alpha & \text{if } I > \bar{I} \\ 0 & \text{otherwise} \end{cases},$$

where $\alpha > 1$. The government can commit to policy instruments before private capital accumulation. Finally, e^i is the endowment of agent i. Agents' endowments are distributed in the population with mean e and a distribution function for the idiosyncratic part $\mathfrak{F}(e^i - e)$. To proxy empirical income distributions, assume that $\mathfrak{F}$ is skewed to the right: the median value of $e^i - e$, labeled $e^m - e$ and defined by $\mathfrak{F}(e^m - e) = \frac{1}{2}$, is negative. Assuming a balanced budget in every period, the government budget constraint in per capita terms is

$I = t$

$g = \tau_K A(I)\bar{k},$

where $\bar{k}$ denotes per capita (average) capital.

a. Characterize the equilibrium in the model.

b. Show that compared to the symmetric distribution case ($e^m = e$), this equilibrium involves higher taxes and a lower growth rate.

V MONETARY POLITICS

Earlier parts of the book have mostly dealt with economic policy in settings that emphasize long-run allocation and supply side issues. In this final part, however, we focus on inflation, monetary policy, and short-run aggregate demand management. The experience of the OECD countries in the postwar period provides a natural motivation. Empirical evidence can be summarized in the following stylized facts:

1. Inflation rates vary greatly across countries and time. But there is a common time pattern: in most countries, inflation was low in the 1960s, but very high in the 1970s; it came down in the 1980s and 1990s in all countries, though at different speeds and to different extents.[1]

2. Inflation rates are correlated with real variables, such as growth or unemployment, in the short run, but there is little evidence of a systematic correlation over longer periods. Across countries, average inflation and average growth tend to be negatively correlated or not correlated at all.[2]

3. Among industrial countries, there is little evidence of systematic spillover effects between monetary and fiscal policy. Specifically, higher budget deficits are not systematically associated with higher inflation rates.[3]

4. Inflation increases shortly after elections; budget deficits tend to be larger during election years; there is also some (not very strong) evidence that monetary policy is more expansionary before elections. On the other hand, real variables, such as growth or unemployment, are not systematically correlated with election dates.

5. Output displays a temporary partisan cycle just after elections: on average, newly appointed left-wing governments are associated with expansions, right-wing governments with recessions. This cycle tends to occur in the first half of the interelection period and is more pronounced in countries with two-party systems. Inflation displays a permanent partisan cycle: higher inflation is associated with left-wing governments.[4]

6. Average inflation rates correlate negatively with measures of central bank independence: this holds even when controlling for other economic and institutional variables (even though the correlation is less robust). Some evidence indicates that fixed exchange rates are associated with lower inflation. Real variables, on the other hand, are not systematically correlated

---

1. See, for instance, Bordo and Schwarz 1999.

2. See, for instance, Stock and Watson 1999 and Fischer 1991.

3. See, for instance, Grilli, Masciandaro, and Tabellini 1991. This ceases to be true when one considers the interwar period or developing countries. In particular, hyperinflations are typically associated with fiscal problems.

4. The comprehensive study by Alesina, Roubini, and Cohen (1997) suggests statements 4 and 5. Different conclusions are, however, reached by Faust and Irons (1999), who focus only on the United States.

with the monetary regime (although the variance of the real exchange rate is lower under fixed than under floating exchange rates).[5]

These stylized facts will be taken as the starting point of this final part. Fact 1 clearly calls for a positive model of inflation. Fact 2 is not well understood, and the economics profession is still searching for a satisfactory model of the joint determination of nominal and real variables. It suggests, however, that a plausible model would encompass the natural rate hypothesis that the Phillips curve is vertical and monetary policy is neutral in the long run while preserving some scope for aggregate demand policies to affect output in the short run. Fact 3 suggests that abstracting from fiscal policy may not be a bad first approximation. Facts 4 and 5 indicate that political variables might be important ingredients in successful positive models of inflation and macroeconomic policy. Fact 6 suggests that the institutional features of the monetary regime, particularly the statutes regulating the central bank, should also play a role in a successful model. Given the close links between different economies in a world of free trade and free capital movements, international interactions in monetary policymaking and international monetary arrangements deserve explicit attention.

A large literature dealing with these issues has emerged in the last ten to fifteen years. But there are already several good and up-to-date surveys of this literature: see Alesina, Roubini, and Cohen 1997, Drazen 1999, and Walsh 1998, among others. For this reason, we keep the treatment brief and do not always go into the same detail as in the previous chapters. Instead, we concentrate on the main lessons from the literature and attempt to relate these to the material covered so far.

This part differs from earlier parts of the book not only in its subject matter but also in its methodology. Up to this point, we have relied on simple—yet fully specified—general equilibrium models with explicit choice-theoretic foundations on both the economic and the political side. In this part, we rely on social welfare functions directly defined over macroeconomic outcomes and on reduced-form relations between macroeconomic outcomes and policy instruments; at times, we will also be more vague about the underlying political institutions. This lack of microeconomic and micropolitical foundations largely reflects the state of the art of the literature surveyed. But—as further discussed in the concluding chapter—we certainly think there is considerable scope for improvement on the methodological front.

In chapter 15, we formulate and discuss what has been the workhorse model of macroeconomic policy and inflation in much of the recent literature. We use this model, and minor

---

5. See Grilli, Masciandaro, and Tabellini 1991, Cukierman 1992, Jonsson 1995, Eijffinger and de Haan 1996, Mussa 1986, Baxter and Stockman 1989, and Alesina and Summers 1993. The robustness of these findings has been questioned by Posen (1993, 1995) and by Campillo and Miron (1997). See Franzese 1999 for a rebuttal, however.

variations of it, throughout the whole part. In this first chapter of the part, we illustrate how credibility problems may arise in monetary policy and how reputational forces may fully or partially resolve these. Chapter 16 extends the simple model with political institutions and incentives, particularly those associated with elections and partisan politics. We show how political business cycles and partisan cycles, consistent with the stylized facts above, may arise. Institutions designed to tackle the distortions created by credibility problems and political cycles is the topic of chapter 17, which thus deals with central bank independence and other monetary arrangements. Chapter 18, finally, extends the single-country framework of chapter 15 to two countries. There we present some of the ideas in the literature on international coordination of monetary and macroeconomic policy. As in chapter 17, we discuss what kind of institutions—in this case, international institutions—might help implement desirable policies.

15 Credibility of Monetary Policy

This chapter discusses credibility problems in monetary policy. Its theme is familiar from part 4. When monetary policy is chosen sequentially, without binding commitments, the monetary authorities lose control of private expectations. Policy must satisfy an incentive constraint: it must be ex post optimal taking expectations as given. As in part 4, lack of credibility thus forces the policymaker to behave myopically. In part 4, the ex post optimal policy neglected the distorting effects of inflation on money demand (or on savings decisions), and the equilibrium tax structure relied too much on inflation (or on wealth taxes). Here, as well, lack of credibility leads to excessive inflation, but for a different reason. Since expectations are taken as given, the monetary authorities overestimate their ability to boost the economy through expansionary aggregate demand policies. This incentive constraint binds if there is a conflict between the monetary authorities and market forces, so that policy surprises provide the central bank with a valuable additional instrument. The goal of this chapter is to illustrate the nature of this incentive constraint, its origin, and its positive implications. Thus we completely abstract from political issues, which are the topic of chapter 16. Similarly, we make no distinction between the government and the central bank, leaving these important delegation issues to chapter 17. In other words, we can interpret the analysis in the present chapter as applying to a central bank entirely under government control. Finally, we abstract completely from the international aspects of policymaking, which are the topic of chapter 18.

Section 15.1 formulates our static workhorse model, used with minor variations throughout this entire part and in much of the existing literature. It is a simple model of macroeconomic policy and inflation in the spirit of Kydland and Prescott 1977, Fischer 1977, and Barro and Gordon 1983a. Section 15.2 discusses a normative benchmark, namely the ex ante optimal policy under commitment. Section 15.3 derives the celebrated "inflation bias" result: lack of commitment combined with the central bank's ability to temporarily boost the economy may lead to credibility problems, resulting in excessively high equilibrium inflation. Section 15.4 returns to another theme from part 4. It briefly illustrates how reputation may provide full or partial solutions to such credibility problems, drawing on Barro and Gordon 1983b, Backus and Driffill 1985, Canzoneri 1985 and others that in turn borrow heavily from the literature on repeated games. Section 15.5 discusses extensions of our static workhorse model to a dynamic setting. In particular, it introduces a link between current and future policy by allowing persistence in the natural rate of (un)employment, as in Lockwood and Philippopoulus 1994, Jonsson 1997, L. Svensson 1997a, and others.

15.1 A Simple Model of Monetary Policy

The demand side of our static model economy is represented by

$$\pi = m + v + \mu, \tag{15.1}$$

where π is inflation, m is money growth, v is a demand (or velocity) shock, and μ is a "control error" in monetary policy. Letting output enter the implicit money demand function underlying (15.1) complicates the algebra but yields no important additional insights. The supply side of the model assumes that nominal wage setting (unilaterally by firms, unilaterally by labor unions, or bilaterally by bargaining between these actors) aims at implementing an exogenous but stochastic real wage growth target ω.[1] If we let π^e denote rationally expected inflation $\mathsf{E}(\pi)$, nominal wage growth w is given by

$$w = \omega + \pi^e. \tag{15.2}$$

Employment (or output growth), x, satisfies

$$x = \gamma - (w - \pi) - \varepsilon,$$

where γ is a parameter, and ε is a supply shock. Combining this relation with (15.2), we obtain an expectations-augmented short-run Phillips curve

$$x = \theta + (\pi - \pi^e) - \varepsilon, \tag{15.3}$$

where $\theta \equiv \gamma - \omega$ can be interpreted as the stochastic natural rate of employment. We assume that all shocks are white noise, orthogonal to each other, have (unconditionally) expected values of zero, well-defined variances $\sigma_\theta^2, \sigma_\varepsilon^2$, and so on.

The timing of events is as follows: (0) Rules of the monetary regime may be laid down at an institution design stage. (1) Both the private sector and the policymaker observe the value of θ. (2) π^e is formed, given the information about θ. (3) The values of v and ε are observed. (4) The policymaker determines m. (5) μ is realized together with π and x.

The assumed timing captures the following concerns. Some shocks related to the labor market are commonly observable and can therefore be embodied in private-sector wage-setting decisions, here captured by expectations formation. Other shocks can be embodied only in policy. This distinction is best interpreted as reflecting the ease with which monetary policy decisions are made relative to the laborious process of wage setting. It could also reflect a genuine information advantage of the policymaker (which might only be plausible for financial-sector shocks). This advantage allows monetary policy to stabilize the economy. Finally, there is some unavoidable noise in the relation between policy and macroeconomic outcomes.

Clearly (15.1) and the assumed information imply that rationally expected inflation is

$$\pi^e = \mathsf{E}(\pi \mid \theta) = \mathsf{E}(m \mid \theta), \tag{15.4}$$

1. As is well-known, the "surprise supply" formulation we end up with below could also be derived from a model of price-setting firms or from a Lucas-style "island model."

where E is the expectations operator. Substituting (15.1) and (15.4) into (15.3), we have:

$$x = \theta + m - \mathsf{E}(m \mid \theta) + v + \mu - \varepsilon. \tag{15.5}$$

The model thus entails the usual neutrality result: only unanticipated aggregate demand policy affects real variables. When policy responds to shocks, however, it can stabilize employment.

15.2   Ex Ante Optimality

We follow the rational expectations literature in thinking about policy as a rule. A policy rule is an object similar to the policy rules considered in part 4, namely a systematic mapping from the relevant variables observed by the policymaker into policy: $m = \Psi(\theta, v, \varepsilon)$. Suppose society evaluates macroeconomic outcomes according to a quadratic loss function of the form

$$\mathsf{E}[L(\pi, x)] = \mathsf{E}[(\pi - \bar{\pi})^2 + \lambda(x - \bar{x})^2]/2, \tag{15.6}$$

where $\bar{\pi}$ and $\bar{x}$ are society's most preferred values for inflation and employment and λ is the relative weight of fluctuations in these two variables. Since the objective is quadratic in macroeconomic outcomes that in turn are linear in the shocks, the optimal policy rule $m = \Psi(\theta, v, \varepsilon)$ belongs to the class

$$m = \psi + \psi_\theta \theta + \psi_v v + \psi_\varepsilon \varepsilon. \tag{15.7}$$

That is, policy potentially responds, in a linear fashion, to all shocks observable to the policymaker.

   Furthermore, suppose that the policymaker is capable of making a binding commitment to rule (15.7) at the institution design stage (0), that is, before the observation of θ and before the private sector forms its expectations. Clearly, since $\mathsf{E}(v) = \mathsf{E}(\varepsilon) = 0$, this implies private-sector expectations

$$\mathsf{E}(m \mid \theta) = \psi + \psi_\theta \theta. \tag{15.8}$$

By (15.1), (15.5), and (15.7)–(15.8), macroeconomic equilibrium under the rule is given by

$$\pi = \psi + \psi_\theta \theta + (\psi_v + 1)v + \psi_\varepsilon \varepsilon + \mu \tag{15.9}$$

$$x = \theta + (\psi_v + 1)v + \mu + (\psi_\varepsilon - 1)\varepsilon. \tag{15.10}$$

   To find the optimal policy rule, substitute (15.9)–(15.10) into (15.6), take expectations over all shocks, and set the derivatives of the resulting expression with regard to the intercept and the slope coefficients in (15.7) equal to zero. The following results emerge:

1. $\psi = \bar{\pi}$ and $\psi_\theta = 0$. The optimal rule provides an "anchor for inflationary expectations." Expectations are exactly where society wants them to be, namely at the preferred rate of inflation: $\mathsf{E}(\pi \mid \theta) = \bar{\pi}$. The optimal rule is thus conditional neither on the observable shock to the natural rate, θ, nor on society's output target, $\bar{x}$. Such conditionality would be embodied in expectations; it would therefore not contribute to stabilizing employment and only add costly noise to inflation.

2. $\psi_v = -1$. Demand (velocity) shocks are fully stabilized, keeping employment at the natural rate. Because policy operates via aggregate demand, completely stabilizing the demand shocks nullifies their effects on inflation as well as on employment.

3. $\psi_\varepsilon = \lambda/(1+\lambda)$. Supply shocks are stabilized around the natural rate, according to the policymaker's trade-off between inflation and employment fluctuations. The higher the weight on employment, the more actively these shocks are stabilized.

The optimal state-contingent policy rule can thus be written as

$$m = \bar{\pi} - v + \frac{\lambda}{(1+\lambda)}\varepsilon.$$

Macroeconomic outcomes when the rule is followed—indexed by C, for commitment—are

$$\pi^C = \bar{\pi} + \frac{\lambda}{1+\lambda}\varepsilon + \mu \tag{15.11}$$

$$x^C = \theta - \frac{1}{1+\lambda}\varepsilon + \mu. \tag{15.12}$$

Results such as these have exerted—and continue to exert—considerable influence on academic economists' thinking about policy. They suggest that delivering low inflation and stable employment is essentially a technical (not a strategic) problem: clearly announcing a rule aiming at low average inflation can keep inflation low. Demand shocks should be completely stabilized. The inflation and employment consequences of supply shocks should be traded off according to society's preferences. Control errors are unavoidable, but better forecasting or operating procedures in monetary policy might reduce them. Even though this picture may be too rosy for a realistic positive model of macroeconomic policy, it nevertheless provides a useful normative benchmark that can be used for evaluating the outcomes in the positive models to follow.

In most of this part, we simplify the stochastic structure by setting $v = \mu = 0$. Demand shocks, as we saw, present no problem for the policymaker in this class of models, provided that they can be identified in time and that there are no other policy goals such as interest rate smoothing. Control errors do present problems but are unavoidable.[2] With these simplifications, it is no longer meaningful to make a distinction in the model between m and π. For simplicity, we therefore assume that the policymaker sets π directly. Why don't we eliminate the shocks to the natural rate θ, with a similar motivation? The answer is that, whereas such shocks do not affect the solution under commitment, they do affect policy in an interesting way under alternative assumptions about the policymaking process.

15.3 Credibility

Real-world decisions on monetary policy are made sequentially over time, not once and for all. Assuming ex ante commitment to a state-contingent policy rule rhymes badly with this practice. In our static model, an alternative timing captures reality better: policy is chosen under discretion when the policy instruments are set at stage (4) of the above game, after wages have been set (π^e formed) and shocks have been realized. As in part 4, this lack of commitment adds an incentive compatibility constraint to our model: policy must be optimal ex post—when it is, in fact, enacted—taking expectations as given. The additional credibility constraint makes the solution less advantageous for the policymaker (and society).

The policymaker still sets π (that is, m), seeking to minimize the loss in (15.6), but at the new decision stage, all uncertainty has been resolved, so that the expectations operator is redundant. Consider how a marginal monetary expansion affects the loss in (15.6) for given π^e and ε. Using (15.3) and (15.6), we have:

$$\frac{dL(\pi, x)}{d\pi} = L_\pi(\pi, x) + L_x(\pi, x)\frac{dx}{d\pi} = (\pi - \bar{\pi}) + \lambda(\theta + (\pi - \pi^e) - \varepsilon - \bar{x}), \quad (15.13)$$

where a subscript denotes a partial derivative. By (15.13), the benchmark policy rule in (15.11) is not incentive compatible under discretion. To see this, suppose that the realization of the shock is $\varepsilon = 0$ and that wage setters believe in an announcement of that rule implying $\pi^e = \bar{\pi}$. Using the optimal-rules outcome in (15.11)–(15.12) and evaluating the derivative in (15.13) at the point prescribed by the ex ante optimal policy rule, we get

$$\frac{dL(\pi^C, x^C)}{d\pi}\bigg|_{\pi^e = \bar{\pi}} = \lambda(\theta - \bar{x}).$$

2. Abstracting from control errors is innocuous as long as the public can perfectly monitor monetary policy and as long as policymaker competency and effort are exogenous. Below, we comment on where control errors would be of importance. Moreover, in a richer (dynamic) setting with expectations entering the aggregate demand function, demand shocks and control errors may give rise to incentive problems similar to those discussed below (see section 15.5).

If preferred employment (output) exceeds the natural rate, that is, if $\bar{x} > \theta$, an expansion reduces the loss, rendering the ex ante optimal policy rule suboptimal ex post. Once wages have been set, the marginal inflation cost—the first term on the right-hand side of (15.13)—is zero when $\varepsilon = 0$ and is always smaller than the marginal employment benefit—the second term on the right-hand side.[3] Thus the ex post incentive constraint is binding and the low-inflation rule is not credible.

Absent commitment, a credible policy must simultaneously fulfill two conditions, corresponding to the conditions in Definition 4 of an equilibrium without commitment in chapter 11. Specifically, (1) the policy is ex post optimal, that is, $\frac{dL}{d\pi} = 0$, given π^e and ε; and (2) expectations are rational, that is, $\pi^e = \mathsf{E}(\pi \mid \theta)$. In game-theoretic terms, those are the conditions for a Nash equilibrium in a game with many atomistic private wage setters (desiring to minimize the deviation of the realized real wage, $w - \pi^e$, from the targeted real wage, ω) moving before the policymaker.[4] Condition (1) requires the expression in (15.13) to be equal to zero. Taking expectations of that expression, condition (2) can be expressed as $\mathsf{E}(\pi \mid \theta) = \bar{\pi} + \lambda(\bar{x} - \theta)$. Combining the two conditions, we obtain

$$\pi^D = \bar{\pi} + \lambda(\bar{x} - \theta) + \frac{\lambda}{1 + \lambda}\varepsilon, \tag{15.14}$$

where the D superscript stands for "discretion." The employment outcome remains as in (15.12), except that $\mu = 0$, by assumption.

If we assume $\bar{x} - \theta > 0$, the discretionary policy outcome in (15.14) and the commitment outcome in (15.11)–(15.12) illustrate the celebrated "inflation bias" result: equilibrium inflation is higher without commitment to a rule, whereas employment is the same, notwithstanding the policy regime. The bias is more pronounced, the higher is λ (the more valuable is employment on the margin) and the higher is $\bar{x}$ relative to θ (the higher is preferred employment relative to the natural rate); both factors contribute to a greater temptation for the policymaker, once wages are fixed, to exploit his short-run ability to boost employment through expansionary policy. Since the natural rate θ is random, whereas the employment target $\bar{x}$ is presumably constant (or at least more stable than θ), inflation is also more variable under discretion than under the rule. Finally, note that lack of credibility does not affect the response of monetary policy to the ε shocks (those over which the central bank has an information advantage). Thus in this simple static model, lack of credibility does not impair

---

3. To see this most clearly, consider the case when $\varepsilon = 0$, such that the optimal rule prescribes the policy $\pi^R = \bar{\pi}$, implying $x^R = \theta$. Then, by (15.13), the marginal inflation cost is actually zero (to the first order), whereas the marginal employment benefit is positive (if $\bar{x} > \theta$).

4. The equilibrium would also identically apply to a simultaneous game between the government and a single trade union. If the union moved before the government, the equilibrium might differ slightly, but the fundamental incentive problem would not be affected.

the central bank's ability to implement and administer stabilization policies. The optimal stabilization is not a general feature, however, as will be shown in section 15.5, where the natural rate is endogenous due to output persistence.

The inflation bias is due to two key assumptions. First, the timing of the monetary policy decisions. This is familiar from the policy examples in part 4. In chapter 12, for instance, the lack of commitment resulted in a suboptimal tax policy with too high tax rates on capital; here, the result is too high an inflation rate. Second, the assumption that the employment target is higher than the natural rate, that is, $\bar{x} - \theta > 0$. This must be due to a lack of policy instruments: some distortion in the labor or product market keeps employment too low. The government does not remove this distortion, either because it lacks enough policy instruments to do so or because some other incentive problem in the policymaking process keeps the distortion in place. This also corresponds with the earlier analysis; the credibility problems in capital taxation arise because a policymaker, lacking access to a nondistortionary tax instrument, attempts to improve a second-best allocation. Both key assumptions arguably capture important features of monetary policymaking in the real world.

The distortion in the policymaking process can also be described as follows: without commitment, the policymaker (correctly) fails to internalize the mapping from actual to expected policy. He is not being foolish: he really cannot influence private-sector expectations, which is what we mean when we say that policy "lacks credibility." Yet actual policy maps into expected policy in equilibrium when private agents have rational expectations. Under commitment, in contrast, the policymaker internalizes this equilibrium mapping; indeed, announcing the optimal policy rule brings rationally expected inflation down precisely to the preferred rate of inflation. The conclusions are pretty stark. First, a desirable policy rule does not become credible just by being announced; recommending a noncredible policy rule is thus pointless. Second, the inability to commit to a policy rule has obvious costs. Institutional reforms increasing policymakers' commitment ability can thus be desirable.

Critics have subjected this simple model of monetary policy credibility to the plausible objection that "real-world policymakers are not trying to surprise the private sector with unexpected inflation." This criticism misses the point of the analysis, however. The model does not predict that the policymaker tries to generate policy surprises *in equilibrium*. On the contrary, in equilibrium, the policymaker would like to bring inflation down but refrains from doing so, as his lack of credibility would turn any anti-inflationary policy into a recession. In other words, the model predicts that expectations will be subject to inertia with respect to a suboptimally high inflation rate, and that it will be difficult to curb these expectations down to the socially efficient rate. The model does rely, however, on an assumption that the policymaker would want to generate policy surprises *outside equilibrium,* leading to a more favorable outcome. Is this a plausible positive model of inflation? Some observers, like McCallum (1996) and Blinder (1998), do not agree that it is. A convincing rebuttal should address the question already posed by Taylor (1983), who—in a discussion of Barro and Gordon 1983b—asked why society has not found ways around the credibility problem in monetary policy, when it has found ways around the credibility problem of granting property rights to patent holders. This question is best addressed in connection with a closer discussion of the institutions of monetary policymaking, so we return to it in chapter 17.

Cukierman (1988) has extended the generality of the inflation bias result. In a simple paper Cukierman shows that the inflation bias remains present even if the target and natural levels of employment coincide, provided that two conditions are satisfied: there are supply shocks to which the central bank cannot respond (i.e., it has no information advantage over the private sector), and the central bank loss function is asymmetric, with upward deviation of output from target being less costly than downward deviation. Specifically, in terms of our previous notation, suppose that $\theta = \bar{x}$. Moreover, change the timing so that policy is still set after π^e, but before knowing the realization of ε, and is not contingent on ε either. Thus under this timing the central bank loses the ability to stabilize these supply shocks. Finally, suppose that the central bank loss function is asymmetric and that fluctuations of output below $\bar{x}$ are more costly than fluctuations above the target. Then Cukierman shows that the inflation bias remains. The next chapter provides an example of how this asymmetry might arise, with reference to elections and career concerns.

What are the observable implications of the analysis so far? One implication is that when the credibility constraint binds, the central bank reacts to variables such as θ, which enter the private sector's information set (before policy is set). Under commitment, on the other hand, the reaction function does not include such variables. Hence the unconditional variance of inflation is higher under discretion. If a high λ causes the credibility problem, the model indeed predicts a positive correlation between average inflation and the variance of inflation, in conformity with empirical evidence.

The discretionary model also suggests a plausible explanation of the secular trend in inflation experienced by the industrialized countries and mentioned in the introduction to this part. The 1950s and 1960s were a period without serious supply shocks and with a low natural rate of unemployment (low variance of ε, high realizations of θ), which made it easy for countries to keep inflation low. Enter the 1970s with their severe supply shocks (high realizations of ε) that push up the natural rate (this would require serial correlation in employment, as in section 15.5) and inflation; we may then interpret the rise in inflation as the result of policymakers' maintaining their earlier high employment objectives ($\bar{x}$ staying constant, or falling by less than θ). The gradual decline in inflation from the mid-1980s and onward, despite continued high natural rates (in Europe), can be considered as deriving from policymakers' gradually adapting their employment ambitions to structural problems in the labor market ($\bar{x}$ drifting downward over time) and from institutional reforms in central banking arrangements in a number of countries in the last decade. Naturally, learning from past policy mistakes is also likely to have played an important role. Time series implications of this type have received too little attention in the credibility literature so far.[5] Instead, the literature has focused on normative issues of institutional reform and, to some extent, on explaining cross-sectional differences in macroeconomic outcomes for different institutions.

15.4   Reputation

The simple model discussed so far can be criticized for being static and failing to capture the *repeated* nature of policymaking. Specifically, by abstracting from the prospective constraints imposed by repeated interaction with the public, the model ignores reputational forces studied in detail in a branch of the literature. The main result is the same as that demonstrated in the capital taxation example of chapter 12, namely that an expectational link from current observed policy to future expected policy can indeed discipline the policymaker and restore credibility. With repeated interactions, a policymaker operating without commitment still faces an intertemporal trade-off: the future costs of higher expected inflation caused by expansion today may more than outweigh the current benefits of higher employment.

To illustrate this idea, consider the model of section 15.3 repeated over an infinite horizon. The policymaker's intertemporal loss function from the viewpoint of some arbitrary period s can be written

$$\mathsf{E}_s\left[\sum_{t=s}^{\infty}\beta^{t-s}L(\pi_t, x_t)\right],\tag{15.15}$$

where β is a discount factor. To simplify the algebra, we assume the static loss function to be linear, rather than quadratic, in employment:

$$L(\pi, x) = \pi^2/2 - \lambda x.\tag{15.16}$$

With the simpler loss function, the ex ante optimal policy rule is simply to have zero inflation at all times and accept employment $x = \theta - \varepsilon$ (as $\bar{\pi} = 0$ and employment volatility is not

5. See, however, the recent papers by Barro and Broadbent (1997) and Broadbent (1996).

costly), whereas the static equilibrium absent commitment has inflation equal to λ and employment still at $x = \theta - \varepsilon$.

We now show that reputation can indeed create sufficiently strong incentives to enforce zero inflation even under discretion. As an example, assume that wage setters form their expectations in the following way:

$$\pi_t^e = \begin{cases} 0 & \text{iff} \quad \pi_v = \pi_v^e, \quad v = t - 1, \ldots, t - T \\ \lambda & \text{otherwise.} \end{cases} \tag{15.17}$$

This expression shows that wage setters trust a policymaker who sticks with zero inflation in period v to continue with this same policy the following period. If they observe any other policy in period v, however, they lose this trust and instead expect him to pursue a discretionary policy for the next T periods. A policymaker confronted with such expectations formation, in effect, faces a nonlinear incentive scheme: he is rewarded for sticking to the rule but is punished for deviating from it. Consider a policymaker who enjoys the trust of the public (i.e., $\pi_s^e = 0$). When is the punishment strong enough to outweigh the immediate benefit of cheating on the rule?

To answer formally, note that the optimal deviation (found by minimizing the static loss function, given ε and $\pi_s^e = 0$) is simply $\pi_s = \lambda$, implying employment $x_s = \lambda + \theta_s - \varepsilon_s$. After some algebra, the current benefit from cheating can then be expressed as

$$B = L(0, \theta_s - \varepsilon_s) - L(\lambda, \lambda + \theta_s - \varepsilon_s) = \lambda^2/2. \tag{15.18}$$

Because of the simpler loss function, the benefit is independent of the realizations of θ and ε. The punishment comes from having to live with higher expected and actual inflation in the next T periods. Why *higher* actual inflation? As the expectations in (15.17) are consistent with the static Nash equilibrium outcome in section 15.3, it is indeed optimal for the policymaker to bear the punishment, accommodating higher expected inflation, if ever imposed.[6] Thus, the cost of a deviation is

$$C = \mathsf{E}_s \left[\sum_{t=s+1}^{T} \beta^{t-s} (L(\lambda, \theta_t - \varepsilon_t) - L(0, \theta_t - \varepsilon_t)) \right] = \beta \frac{(1 - \beta^T)}{(1 - \beta)} \lambda^2, \tag{15.19}$$

which is clearly stationary if we assume that θ is i.i.d. over time. Obviously the policymaker

---

6. By this argument, the analysis to follow identifies a sequentially rational (subgame-perfect) equilibrium. Note that the punishment this expectations formation mechanism imposes on the policymaker is not the most severe that one can imagine. Other, more severe punishments could be imposed where expectations changed more drastically after a deviation. But unlike this one, these more drastic punishments would not be Nash equilibria of the one-shot game. Thus we would have to impose a separate incentive compatibility constraint on the reputational equilibrium, namely that it indeed be optimal for all players to carry out and bear the punishment after a deviation. This point is illustrated in problem 2 of this chapter and in chapter 3 of Persson and Tabellini 1990.

finds it optimal to stick to the zero-inflation rule as long as $B \leq C$. Inspection of (15.19) and (15.18) reveals that this is more likely the higher the discount factor β and the longer the horizon T for which inflationary expectations increase after a deviation.

Many extensions of this basic framework are feasible, and some have been pursued in the literature. For instance, if we retained the quadratic loss function of the previous section, the benefit of cheating would be an increasing function of the actual realization of θ, whereas the cost would depend on the variance and the expected value of θ. As a result, even with reputation, equilibrium inflation would continue to depend on the actual realization of θ: a high value of θ makes the incentive compatibility condition more binding, because it increases the benefit B but not the cost C. The lowest sustainable inflation rate (defined by the condition that $B = C$) would be an increasing function of θ. Thus, reputation would reduce average inflation but would not change the main positive implications of the model of the previous section. Problem 1 at the end of the chapter discusses this case.

Canzoneri (1985) studied a framework with shocks to inflation that are unobservable to private agents both ex ante and ex post; an example could be the μ shocks in (15.1). If observed inflation exceeds a certain threshold, such monitoring problems give rise to temporary outbreaks of actual and expected inflation, since the public cannot clearly infer whether the high inflation is due to large shocks or to deliberate cheating.

Backus and Driffill (1985), Barro (1986), Tabellini (1985, 1987) and Vickers (1986) studied reputational models of incomplete information in which the private agents are uncertain about the policymaker's "type" (like his λ in the model above). These agents use the information in current observations of policy to learn about the type, and the policymaker optimally sets policy with a view to this private learning process. Such models illustrate how a "dovish" policymaker (someone with a high λ or without access to a commitment technology) can temporarily borrow the reputation of a "hawkish" policymaker (someone with a low λ or with access to a commitment technology). They also illustrate how a hawkish policymaker may have to impose severe output costs on the economy to credibly establish a reputation. This is in contrast to the equilibrium considered above, in which the policymaker merely maintains a reputation he is lucky enough to have. Problem 3 of this chapter provides an example of these reputation mechanisms with asymmetric information and Bayesian learning or signaling.

The central insight of the reputation literature is that ongoing interaction between a policymaker and private agents can mitigate the inflation bias and restore some credibility to a low-inflation monetary policy. Whether this interaction can remove the problem entirely is more controversial, however, and depends on details of the model and the expectations formation mechanism. Even though this insight is important, the reputation literature suffers from several weaknesses. As in the theory of repeated games, there is a multiple-equilibrium problem striking with particular force against a positive model of monetary policy.

Moreover, the problem of explaining how the players somehow magically coordinate on one of the many possible equilibria is worse when the game involves a large number of private agents rather than a few oligopolists. If the model of wage setting is taken seriously, studying wage setting by large trade unions becomes relevant for some countries, which weakens the coordination problem. But al-Nowaihi and Levine (1994) analyze whether it would indeed be in a large trade union's interest to carry out the punishment, by setting higher nominal wages after a government deviation. They find this assumption to be questionable and that at best an inflation rate between the inflation target and the equilibrium under discretion is sustainable.

Finally, the normative implications of the reputational models are somewhat unclear. The fact that reputational equilibria with good outcomes exist is not helpful to a country where inflation is particularly high at a given moment. The lack of suggestions for policy improvements is another reason why researchers have largely turned away from reputational models toward analysis of the policy incentives entailed in different monetary policy institutions. Interesting recent work, however, suggests an institutional interpretation for some of these reputational equilibria: see Jensen 1998, al-Nowaihi and Levine 1996, and Herrendorf 1996. The ideas are related to those in Schotter 1981 and to the view that international institutions may facilitate cooperation in trade policy (see Staiger 1995 for a survey), namely that certain institutions may facilitate sustaining a better outcome through reputational forces.

15.5 Dynamics

The simple static model in this chapter can also be criticized for not allowing dynamic interactions in the economy. For instance, the model does not allow for a paramount feature of short-run fluctuations, namely serial correlation in output and employment. In this final section, we illustrate how the simple model can be extended to allow for this feature of the data.[7] This is done in the simplest possible way, namely by studying a simple two-period model with output persistence. L. Svensson (1997a) deals with the general infinite-horizon case in a variety of institutional settings, including those discussed in chapter 17 (see problem 5 of this chapter). Two related lessons emerge from the analysis. Output persistence raises the systematic inflation bias, and it also introduces a stabilization bias: unlike in the static model, supply shocks are stabilized too much in the discretionary policy regime.

To illustrate these results, consider a two-period version, $t = 1, 2$, of the setup in sections 15.2 and 15.3 (we abstract from control errors, setting $\mu = 0$). The Phillips curve in

---

7. Barro and Gordon (1983a) did allow the natural rate to be persistent but still treated it as exogenous.

each period is the same:

$$x_t = \theta_t + \pi_t - \pi_t^e - \varepsilon_t. \tag{15.20}$$

For simplicity, we assume that the first-period natural rate, θ_1, is now exogenously given and not subject to shocks, but the second-period natural rate satisfies

$$\theta_2 = \rho x_1 + (1 - \rho)\theta_1, \tag{15.21}$$

where ρ measures output persistence. Notice that the period 2 natural rate becomes endogenous and stochastic; to some degree, it incorporates unanticipated period 1 policy shocks and unobservable period 1 supply shocks. Shocks unobservable to wage setters in period 1 thus become publicly observable in period 2. As always, private agents form expectations (set wages) rationally. Finally, society and the central bank have the two-period objective of minimizing

$$\mathsf{E}[L(\pi_1, x_1) + \beta L(\pi_2, x_2)], \tag{15.22}$$

where the static loss function has the same quadratic form as in (15.6).

15.5.1   Ex Ante Optimal Rule

We start with the case in which the government commits once and for all to a state-contingent policy rule before observing any of the shocks. Because of the finite horizon, this rule will be time dependent.[8] We begin with period 2. As this is the last period for a given realization for θ_2, the policy problem in period 2 is exactly the same as in the static model of section 15.2. The optimal period 2 policy rule thus fulfills

$$\pi_2^C = \bar{\pi} + \frac{\lambda}{1 + \lambda}\varepsilon_2,$$

resulting in employment

$$x_2^C = \theta_2 - \frac{1}{1 + \lambda}\varepsilon_2.$$

As before, average (expected) inflation is set at the preferred rate, and supply shocks are stabilized according to the relative weight λ. These expressions can be used to calculate the second-period expected loss, given θ_2, as

$$\mathsf{E}_\varepsilon[L^C(\theta_2)] = \frac{1}{2}\left[\frac{\lambda}{1 + \lambda}\sigma_\varepsilon^2 + \lambda(\bar{x} - \theta_2)^2\right]. \tag{15.23}$$

---

8. The infinite-horizon version of this model in problem 5 of this chapter has equilibrium policy rules that are time-independent.

The optimal period 1 policy rule should thus take into account the impact, through x_1 and θ_2, of period 1 policy on the expected period 2 loss. It should also recognize that the realization of θ_2 depends on ε_1: as noted above, output persistence implies that current supply shocks affect the future natural rate.

The problem of finding the ex ante optimal period 1 policy rule is still linear-quadratic, so we restrict our attention to the following class of linear rules:[9]

$$\pi_1^C = \psi + \psi_\varepsilon \varepsilon_1.$$

The optimal rule can now be found as follows. First, we impose rational expectations: $\pi_1^e = E_\varepsilon(\psi + \psi_\varepsilon \varepsilon_1) = \psi$. Next, we substitute this expression plus the postulated rule into the period 1 Phillips curve (15.20). Then we substitute the resulting period 1 expressions and the expected period 2 loss from (15.23) into the overall objective (15.22), taking account of the persistence relation (15.21). Finally, we minimize the overall loss with regard to ψ and ψ_ε. Carrying out these steps, we get

$$\psi = \bar{\pi}$$
$$\psi_\varepsilon = \frac{\lambda(1 + \rho^2)}{1 + \lambda(1 + \rho^2)}.$$

Average inflation is thus anchored at society's preferred level, as in section 15.2. But because the supply shocks have persistent effects on output, it becomes optimal to pursue a more activist stabilization policy—in the sense of letting π vary more—than in the case with $\rho = 0$. It is easy to verify that ψ_ε is increasing in ρ.

15.5.2   Equilibrium without Commitment

Let us now consider the regime with sequential policymaking, where the timing in each period is the same as in section 15.3. The analysis of period 2 again produces results identical to those in the static model for a given value of θ_2. In other words, we have the equilibrium outcomes

$$\pi_2^D = \bar{\pi} + \lambda(\bar{x} - \theta_2) + \frac{\lambda}{1 + \lambda}\varepsilon_2$$
$$x_2^D = \theta_2 - \frac{1}{1 + \lambda}\varepsilon_2,$$

resulting in the expected loss

$$E_\varepsilon[L^D(\theta_2)] = \frac{1}{2}\left[\frac{\lambda}{1 + \lambda}\sigma_\varepsilon^2 + \lambda(1 + \lambda)(\bar{x} - \theta_2)^2\right].$$

9. We omit time subscripts, but clearly the coefficients of the optimal linear rule refer only to period 1, because with a finite horizon the optimal policy rule cannot be time-invariant.

The new aspect is that the period 2 inflation bias, by its dependency on the period 2 natural rate, now depends on period 1 policy and supply shocks.

Employment persistence affects the government's incentives in period 1. The government still takes period 1 wages, incorporating expectations about current inflation π_1^e, as given. But the government recognizes that the current policy affects future employment as well as its own future policy decisions via its effect on θ_2 and therefore on expectations about future inflation π_2^e.

Consider the period 1 policymaker's problem, namely to minimize

$$L(\pi_1, x_1) + \mathsf{E}_\varepsilon[L^D(\theta_2)],$$

subject to the period 1 Phillips curve (15.20) and the persistence relation (15.21), taking π_1^e as given. As in section 15.3, taking expectations to the first-order condition of that problem allows us to solve for equilibrium π_1^e. Plugging this value back into the first-order condition gives an expression for the equilibrium value of π_1. After straightforward but tedious algebra we can write the solution as

$$\pi_1^D = \bar{\pi} + \frac{(1 + \rho(1 + \lambda))(1 + \lambda(1 + \rho^2(1 + \lambda)))}{1 + \lambda(1 + \rho^2(1 + \lambda))}\lambda(\bar{x} - \theta_1) + \frac{\lambda(1 + \rho^2(1 + \lambda))}{1 + \lambda(1 + \rho^2(1 + \lambda))}\varepsilon_1.$$

$$(15.24)$$

Two conclusions follow. First, not only is average inflation higher than under the rule, but the discretionary inflation bias is more pronounced than without employment persistence. The latter is given by $\lambda(\bar{x} - \theta_1)$, which here is premultiplied by a number larger than unity when $\rho > 0$ in (15.24). The systematic inflation bias is higher because policy today can boost both current and future employment, which makes an expansion more tempting. Second, a stabilization bias appears, whereas in the static model the response to supply shock ε is the same with or without commitment. The coefficient on ε_1 in (15.24) is larger than the response under the optimal rule, given by ψ_ε, because the future inflation bias depends on current employment. To reduce the future inflation bias, the policymaker responds more aggressively to supply shocks under discretion, stabilizing current employment too much. Notice that this stabilization bias is present, even if the inflation bias is absent, that is, when $\bar{x} = \theta_1$.

15.5.3 Discussion

The simple model studied in this section suggests another dimension to the discussion at the end of section 15.3 on the international experience with high inflation in the 1970s and 1980s. Bad supply shocks, such as the oil shocks, may endogenously raise the natural rate of unemployment if employment is persistent. According to the model, such shocks should manifest themselves not only in high average inflation, but also in temporarily high inflation due to an overly activist stabilization policy, particularly in those countries attaching a high relative value to output and employment stabilization. Clearly, for this interpretation to make sense, the employment target $\bar{x}$ must remain constant over time, or at least adjust more slowly than the natural rate.

We have briefly illustrated how to extend the simple model with endogenous persistence in employment and output fluctuations. Another important feature of real-world fluctuations is the slow adjustment to shocks of prices and inflation. The model we have studied implicitly assumes that prices adjust instantaneously to any shock, but this flies in the face of massive evidence of short-run price stickiness and persistence in inflation.

Clarida, Gali, and Gertler (1999) study optimal monetary policy in a model where firms set prices in a staggered way, in the style of Calvo 1983; a subset of firms adjusts its prices in the current period on the basis of expected future economic conditions, including future monetary policy. Clarida et al. show that the inflation bias due to an overambitious output goal arises also in this framework. Commitment to a policy rule is valuable, however, even in the absence of such an inflation bias (i.e., when $\bar{x} = \theta$ in terms of our notation). The ex ante optimal rule internalizes the effect of the rule on current private (price-setting) behavior via expectations of future policy, much as in the examples of chapters 11 and 12. Commitment to the rule prescribes a relatively aggressive policy response to adverse inflationary shocks, which leads to significant downward adjustment by price setters. Absent commitment, the policymaker takes expectations of future policy as given, and price setters rationally expect a less aggressive future policy, which leads to higher realized inflation. In the language of this section: a stabilization bias—which makes inflation fluctuate too much—is present even in the absence of an inflation bias. Clarida et al. also extend the model to include endogenous persistence in inflation. In this case, commitment to a rule implies not only lower inflation but a swifter adjustment of inflation toward its target. Problem 4 of this chapter deals with some of these issues.

15.6   Notes on the Literature

Textbook treatments of the general material in this chapter can be found in Persson and Tabellini 1990, chapters 2–4, and Cukierman 1992, chapters 3, 8–11, and 16, both of which cover the literature up to around 1990, and in Walsh 1998, chapter 8, and Drazen 1999, which also cover the more recent literature. The literature on credibility in monetary policy starts with Kydland and Prescott 1977, which includes a brief section with the basic insights of the static model in section 15.3. Barro and Gordon (1983a) formulate a linear-quadratic version and push its use as a positive model of monetary policy. Parkin (1993) argues that an increase in the natural rate in the kind of model dealt with here can explain the great inflation of the 1970s. Cukierman (1998) discusses the inflation bias that may arise from asymmetric central bank preferences over output when the employment target coincides with the average rate of unemployment.

An inflation bias as well as a stabilization bias can also arise in a static economy if a central bank and a fiscal authority with divergent objectives set fiscal and monetary policy. This point is discussed in Alesina and Tabellini 1987 and Beetsma and Bovenberg 1997.

Barro and Gordon (1983b) started the theoretical literature on reputation in monetary policy, drawing on the work on trigger strategies in repeated games with complete information. Backus and Driffill (1985), Tabellini (1985, 1987), and Barro (1986) develop incomplete-information models of reputation, emphasizing how a dovish policymaker can borrow a reputation from a super-hawkish policymaker who cares about inflation and nothing else. Vickers (1986) in contrast emphasizes how a policymaker who is serious about fighting inflation may have to engage in costly recessionary policies to signal his true identity to an incompletely informed public. Persson and van Wijnbergen (1993) show how income policy may make such signaling cheaper. Grossman and van Huyck (1986) and Horn and Persson (1988) study reputational models of the inflation tax and exchange rate policy, respectively. Al-Nowaihi and Levine (1994) analyze reputation when wages are set by a large trade union. Jensen (1998) and Herrendorf (1996) suggest an institutional interpretation of reputational equilibria. Rogoff (1987) includes an insightful discussion about the pros and cons of the reputational models of monetary policy.

Reputation with imperfect monitoring of monetary policy was first studied by Canzoneri (1985). Ball (1995) develops a model of incomplete information in which the central bank type follows a Markov process and shows how the interaction with temporary supply shocks may produce persistence in the inflation rate. Cukierman and Liviatan (1991) assume that different policymakers differ in their ability to commit rather than in their preferences; they show how the private sector's learning creates an explicit role for monetary policy announcements. Cukierman and Meltzer (1986) study how the public learns about a policymaker's continuously changing weight on inflation relative to employment from observed monetary policy; control errors in policy make learning imperfect, which has important effects on response of macroeconomic outcomes to such preference shocks. Faust and Svensson (1998) extend this analysis.

Dynamic models of the employment motive to inflate were first developed by Lockwood and Philippopoulus (1994), Lockwood, Miller, and Zhang (1998), and Jonsson (1997). See also Barro and Broadbent 1998 and Broadbent 1996. L. Svensson (1997a) provides an exhaustive treatment of monetary policy under employment persistence, including a discussion of different institutional environments to be studied in chapter 17. Clarida, Gali, and Gertler (1999) offer an illuminating discussion of optimal monetary policy in a dynamic neo-Keynesian model with staggered price setting. Cooley and Quadrini (1999) use the methodology of chapter 11 to study optimal and time-consistent monetary policy in a dynamic model with explicit microeconomic foundations in which money and interest rates affect employment via job creation in a search setting.

15.7 Problems

1. Reputation with state-dependent incentives

Consider the following model of monetary policy with reputation: the government controls inflation directly, and its instantaneous loss function is $L(\pi_t, x_t) = \frac{1}{2}(\pi_t^2 + \lambda \cdot x_t^2)$, where $x_t = \theta_t + \pi_t - \pi_t^e$, and π_t denotes inflation, π_t^e expected inflation, and x_t the level of employment. θ_t is random and i.i.d. The intertemporal loss is $\sum_{t=0}^{\infty} \beta^t \cdot L(\pi_t, x_t)$. The government's reputation affects expected inflation and depends on past behavior: $\pi_t^e = \pi^C$ if $\pi_{t-1} = \pi^C$ and $\pi_t^e = \pi^D$ otherwise, where π^C denotes the optimal policy under commitment and π^D under discretion, respectively.

a. Compute the equilibrium policy under commitment and under discretion.

b. Compute the optimal deviation for a government that is expected to play π^C. What are the benefits and the cost of such a deviation? For what values of θ is it optimal for the government to stick to the commitment rule?

2. Optimal punishment rules

This problem is based on Persson and Tabellini 1990, chapter 3. Consider a model with reputation in which the punishment rule is more stringent than in the body of the text:

$$\pi_0^e = 0$$

$$\pi_t^e = \begin{cases} 0 & \text{iff } \pi_v = \pi_v^e, \quad v = t-1, \dots, t-T \\ \kappa \cdot \lambda, \text{ with } \kappa \geq 1 & \text{otherwise.} \end{cases}$$

The instantaneous loss function is given by

$$L(\pi_t, x_t) = \frac{\pi_t^2}{2} - \lambda \cdot x_t,$$

and the intertemporal loss function by $\sum_{t=0}^{\infty} \beta^t \cdot L(\pi_t, x_t)$, with $\beta < 1$. As usual, $x_t = \theta_t - \pi_t^e + \pi_t$, where π_t denotes inflation, π_t^e expected inflation, and x_t the level of employment.

a. In the absence of punishment, what is the optimal deviation if $\pi_t^e = 0$? What is the optimal deviation if $\pi_t^e = \kappa\lambda$?

b. Assume the government is forced to bear the punishment after a deviation, that is, it is forced to set $\pi_{t+v} = \kappa\lambda$ for $v = 1, 2, \ldots, T$ after deviating from π_t^e. What are the cost and benefits of deviating at time t, depending on history (that is, if $\pi_t^e = 0$ or if $\pi_t^e = \kappa\lambda$)?

c. Assume the government is not forced to bear this punishment, but π_t^e still follows the same rule. Would it be rational to expect $\pi_t^e = \kappa\lambda$ after a deviation in $t - 1$ for any value of κ and T? How does the incentive to deviate from high inflation $(\kappa\lambda)$ evolve with κ and T?

d. Draw the graph of equilibrium inflation after a deviation as a function of κ when the government is not forced to bear the punishment after a deviation. If we impose the rational expectations condition $\pi_t^e(\kappa) = \mathsf{E}_{t-1}[\pi_t \mid \kappa]$ after a deviation, how does the incentive to deviate from zero inflation evolve with κ and T?

3. Reputation with incomplete information

This problem is based on Persson and Tabellini 1990, chapter 4. Consider a policymaker i with a policy preference

$$L^i(\pi_t, x_t) = \frac{\pi_t^2}{2} - \lambda^i x_t,$$

where $x_t = \theta_t - \pi_t^e + \pi_t$, and λ^i represents the policymaker's type. The world lasts for two periods, and therefore the intertemporal loss is given by $\sum_{t=1}^{2} \beta^{t-1} \cdot L^i(\pi_t, x_t)$. The actual value of λ^i, however, is private information to the policymaker and hence unknown to the other economic agents. With probability p, the policymaker has a preference $\lambda^i = \lambda^D$ and with probability $(1 - p)$, $\lambda^i = \lambda^R$, with $0 = \lambda^R < \lambda^D$. At the start of the first period, economic agents know only the values of λ^D, λ^R, and p. At the beginning of the second period, they update their beliefs through Bayesian updating, using first-period inflation as an additional piece of information. Note that policymakers cannot precommit to a given inflation rate.

a. Compute the most desired rate of inflation for each type of policymaker.

b. Show that the type D policymaker may want to mimic the behavior of the type R, whereas the opposite is never true.

c. Compute the conditions under which a separating, a semiseparating, or a pooling equilibrium exists. Assume that the updating of beliefs is such that $q = \text{Prob}\,(i = D \mid \pi > \pi_R) = 1$, where q is the posterior probability that the policymaker is of type D.

4. The inflation and stabilization biases

This problem is inspired by Clarida, Gali, and Gertler 1999. Consider an economy in which output depends on realized and prospective inflation: $x_t = \pi_t - E_t[\pi_{t+1}] - \varepsilon_t$, with $\varepsilon_t = \rho \cdot \varepsilon_{t-1} + \hat{\varepsilon}_t$ and $E_t[\hat{\varepsilon}_{t+1}] = 0$. The instantaneous loss function is $L(\pi_t, x_t) = \frac{1}{2}(\pi_t^2 + \lambda \cdot x_t^2)$, and the intertemporal loss is given by $\frac{1}{2}E_t\{\sum_{v=0}^{\infty}\beta^v \cdot L(\pi_{t+v}, x_{t+v})\}$.

a. Compute the first-order condition linking equilibrium inflation and output under discretion.

b. Use this first-order condition to compute the rational expectations equilibrium for inflation one period ahead (employ the Phillips curve to do this). Using this result, compute equilibrium output and inflation under discretion as a function of ε_t.

c. Show that if the policymaker instead has a loss function of the shape $\frac{1}{2}E_t\{\sum_{v=0}^{\infty}\beta^v \cdot [\pi_{t+v}^2 + \lambda \cdot (x_{t+v} - \bar{x})^2]\}$, $\bar{x} > 0$, an inflation bias appears. That is, equilibrium inflation increases, whereas equilibrium output remains unaffected.

d. Compute the optimal inflation and output levels under commitment when x_t^C belongs to the class $x_t^C = -\psi \cdot \varepsilon_t$ (in other words, compute the optimal ψ under commitment, and also set $E_t[\pi_{t+\infty}] = 0$). Show that under commitment, output tends to vary more and inflation to vary less than under discretion, that is, that discretion generates a stabilization bias.

5. Monetary policy with employment persistence and infinite horizon

This problem draws on L. Svensson 1997a. Consider a world with infinite horizons in which the instantaneous loss function is quadratic: $L(\pi_t, x_t; \bar{\pi}, \bar{x}, \lambda) = \frac{1}{2}[(\pi_t - \bar{\pi})^2 + \lambda \cdot (x_t - \bar{x})^2]$. Employment evolves in the same way as in section 15.5: $x_t = \theta_t + \pi_t - \pi_t^e - \varepsilon_t$, where $\theta_t = \rho \cdot x_{t-1}$ (we are setting the natural employment rate to zero for simplicity), and $E_{t-1}[\varepsilon_t] = 0$. Consumers are rational and set expected inflation to $\pi_t^e = E_{t-1}[\pi_t \mid x_{t-1}]$. Policy can be conditioned on x_{t-1} and ε_t. It follows that under a policy rule $\pi_t = \Psi(x_{t-1}, \varepsilon_t)$ and following the notation of chapter 11, the value function is given by $W(x_{t-1}; \Psi) = -E_{t-1}[L(\pi_t, x_t; \bar{\pi}, \bar{x}, \lambda) - \beta \cdot W(x_t; \Psi)]$, where β is the discount rate.

a. Compute the first-order conditions for the maximization of $W^C(x_t; \Psi^C)$ (the value function under commitment) with respect to both π_t and π_t^e subject to the rational expectations condition $\pi_t^e = E_{t-1}[\pi_t]$. (Hint: You must obtain a condition that depends on $W_x^C(x_t; \Psi)$, where the subscript denotes a partial derivative.)

b. The shape of $W(x; \Psi)$ depends on the policy rule the government chooses (see chapter 11). Still, as the loss function is quadratic, we know two things. First, the shape of the welfare function will be $W^C(x) = \omega_0^C + \omega_1^C \cdot x + \frac{\omega_2^C}{2} \cdot x^2$, where the parameters ω_i^C depend on the equilibrium policy rule. Second, the policy rule will be linear: $\pi_t^C = \psi^C + \psi_x^C \cdot x_{t-1} + \psi_\varepsilon^C \cdot \varepsilon_t$. By substituting for $W^C(x)$ and x_t in the first-order condition, show that the equilibrium policy rule is of the type $\pi_t = \bar{\pi} + \psi_\varepsilon^C \cdot \varepsilon_t$. (Hint: Compute ψ_x^C and ψ_ε^C as a function of the parameters ω_i^C.)

c. Compute the value of the parameters ω_i^C (Hint: Use the method of undetermined coefficients.)[10] Compare this rule with the one derived in section 15.2 and comment on the differences.

d. Suppose that the government cannot commit to a policy rule. Without computing the actual value of the new ω_i^D in the value function under discretion, show that there is an inflation bias when $\bar{x} > 0$ and that π^D generally depends on employment, in contrast to π^C.

e. Consider the particular case in which $\bar{x} = 0$, $\rho = 0.1$, $\lambda = 1$, and $\beta = 1$ to compute the commitment and the discretionary policy. Is there an inflation bias? Is there a stabilization bias?

6. Inflation and default

This problem draws on Jahjah 1999. Consider an economy in which the control over inflation and the government budget are in different hands: inflation is set by the central bank and taxes by the government. The central bank can commit to a given inflation rate but is interested in both monetary and financial stability. Here the risk of the government defaulting on its debt represents financial instability. The central bank's loss function is given by $L^B = \frac{\pi^2}{2} - \lambda \cdot (1 - \delta)$, where $\delta \in [0, 1]$ is the government's default rate.

The government's revenue consists of tax revenue, τ, and seignorage revenue (see below). At date 1, the government should repay its debt, together with the interest on it: $(1 + R)D_0$. But the government may decide to default on its debt partly or entirely and shrink this expense to $(1 + R) \cdot (1 - \delta) \cdot D_0$.

The timing is as follows: At time $t = 0$, the central bank first commits to some rule over the inflation rate. Expectations are formed. The government borrows some debt, D_0. At $t = 1$, the central bank implements the inflation rate; and at $t = 2$, the government chooses the default and tax rates. Payoffs are realized.

a. Assuming that money demand is defined by $M_t = P_t$, where M stands for the money base and P for the price level, and knowing that the seignorage revenue of the government is given by $\frac{M_1 - M_0}{P_1}$, compute seignorage as a function of $m_0 = \frac{M_0}{P_0}$ and π. Write down the

---

10. To this end, substitute for π_t^C, the resulting evolution of employment (x_t as a function of x_{t-1} and ε_t), and the quadratic guess of the value function in the original W^C. Then, identifying the appropriate terms with $\omega_2^C/2$ and ω_1^C, compute the exact value function W^C (computing ω_0 is not important).

government's budget constraint as a function of R, D_0, δ, π, τ, and m_0. How does the repayment rate depend on the tax rate?

b. If the government's loss function is given by $L^G = \frac{\tau^2}{2} - \gamma \cdot (1 - \delta)$, what will be the tax rate and the default rate as a function of the initial debt level and the inflation rate?

c. What is the optimal inflation rate in this situation?

d. If lenders demand a fixed *real* return $(1 + R) = \frac{1+\pi^e}{1-\delta^e}$, would the resulting default rate always be zero in equilibrium? Why or why not?

16 Electoral Cycles

Empirical evidence for the democratic OECD countries during the postwar period suggests systematic preelectoral expansionary policies—fact 4 in the introduction to this part—as well as a postelection partisan cycle in real variables and inflation—fact 5. These regularities vary with the country and time period considered, and their robustness has not been checked according to the same standards as, say, in the modern macroeoconometric literature attempting to identify innovations in monetary policy.[1] They are interesting enough, however, to motivate this line of research. Empirical evidence also indicates that retrospective voting is a plausible assumption: the likelihood of election victory for the incumbent government or legislature depends largely on the state of the economy; as expected, a higher growth rate boosts incumbents' reelection probability.[2]

It is tempting to explain fact 4—the "political business cycle"—as the result of opportunistic governments seeking reelection and taking advantage of the voters' irrationality. It is hard, however, to claim that the same individuals act in a rational and forward-looking way as economic agents but become fools when casting their vote. This points to one of the puzzles any rational theory of political business cycles must address: how to reconcile retrospective voting with evidence of systematic policy expansions before elections. We have already indicated a possible answer to this question in chapter 4, when discussing the career concern model: an electoral cycle may arise when voters are rational but imperfectly informed, if performance in office is a signal of the incumbent's talent. In section 16.1, we tell a similar story: higher employment (or growth) is perceived by the voters as indicating a talented incumbent and makes re-appointment more likely. This in turn increases the government's temptation to boost aggregate demand ahead of the elections to appear more talented. Because wage setters (as well as voters) fully understand these incentives, expected inflation also rises before the elections. Thus an electoral cycle takes the form of higher actual and expected inflation but no policy surprises and hence no systematic output effect. In chapter 4 we had assumed that the government was both rent-seeking and office-seeking. Here instead there are no endogenous rents, and the incumbent is office-seeking and outcome-motivated.

Correlations between macroeconomic outcomes and the party in office, fact 5, are simpler to explain, provided that we are willing to assume that policymakers are outcome-seeking and cannot commit to policies ahead of the election. As discussed in chapter 5, policymakers are then motivated by their ideology and, once in office, carry out their own agenda. We are thus in the world of postelection politics with partisan politicians. In the present setting, we obtain a model of "partisan cycles." Section 16.2 briefly summarizes this model.

1. Faust and Irons (1999) criticize the literature on partisan cycles in the United States for failing to control for simultaneity and omitted-variable bias and argue that the support for a partisan cycle in output is much weaker than what a cursory inspection of the data would suggest.

2. See, for instance, Fair 1978.

16.1 Career Concerns and Political Business Cycles

Throughout this section, we exploit a version of the simple monetary policy model of chapter 15, as does most of the literature, but the ideas apply generally to aggregate demand management, including fiscal policy. We study moral hazard as well as adverse selection models, with these labels referring to the informational asymmetry between voters and the elected policymaker.

16.1.1 Moral Hazard

Here, we combine ideas from the career concern model of chapter 4, which in turn builds on Holmström 1982 and Lohmann 1996, whose work builds on Persson and Tabellini 1990. The main insight of this subsection is that elections aggravate the credibility problem of monetary policy, since they raise the benefit of surprise inflation for the incumbent.

Consider a version of the model in section 15.4. Voters are rational, have an infinite horizon, and are all identical. Their preferences are summarized by a loss function defined over inflation and employment identical to (15.15) and (15.16)—we thus make the simplifying assumption that they are linear in employment. Political candidates have the same basic objectives as the voters defined over output and inflation. In addition, however, the ego rents derived during their term in office reduce their loss by R units per period.

As in the career concern model of chapters 4 and 9, candidates differ in their ability to solve policy problems. Elections then become a mechanism for selecting between different policymakers on the basis of their expected competence. One candidate may be particularly able to deal with trade unions and another to deal with an oil price shock, and a third has a better ability to organize his administration. Output growth (employment) reflects this competence: a more competent candidate creates higher growth, ceteris paribus. To capture this, we write the Phillips curve in any given period exactly as in (15.3), except that we set the shock to the natural rate θ to zero:

$$x_t = \left(\pi_t - \pi_t^e\right) - \varepsilon_t. \tag{16.1}$$

We thus consider only ε shocks but change their interpretation. Throughout this section, ε_t captures the incumbent policymaker's competence, not exogenous supply shocks. As in section 4.5, we assume that a specific policymaker's competence follows a simple moving average-process: $\varepsilon_t = -\eta_t - \eta_{t-1}$, where η is an i.i.d. random variable. We assume η has an expected value of 0 (rather than 1) and denote its c.d.f. by $G(\cdot)$ and its density by $\xi(\cdot)$. Note that in this formulation a positive realization of η leads to higher output, thus the higher is η, the more competent is the policymaker. Competence is assumed to be random, since it depends on the salient policy problems, but partially lasting, since the salient policy problems change slowly and since competence may also depend on talent.

This serial correlation forms the basis for retrospective voting: because competence lasts over time, rational voters are more likely to reelect an incumbent who creates a high growth rate just before the elections. In the very first period of this repeated game, we assume $\eta_0 = 0$.

The timing in a given period t is as follows: (1) The previous period's policy instrument and inflation π_{t-1} are observed. (2) Wages (and expected inflation) are determined. (3) The policymaker sets the policy instrument for t. (4) Everybody observes output growth (but the voters do not observe policy until the following period). (5) An election is held if t is an election year, which occurs every other period.

These assumptions warrant a few remarks. Unlike in chapter 15, the policymaker has no informational advantage over private agents: when policy is set at stage (3), the current competence shock η_t is unknown to everyone. Voters face no adverse selection problem in that the policymaker can not deliberately "signal" his competence. This assumption distinguishes the model in Lohmann 1996 from those in Rogoff and Sibert 1988, Rogoff 1990, and Persson and Tabellini 1990. Voters still face a moral hazard problem, however: through his monetary policy action, the incumbent can appear better than he really is. The voters understand these incentives but can do nothing about them, because policy is unobservable. As pointed out in chapters 4 and 9, Holmström (1982) first studied this kind of career concern model in a standard principal-agent setup. The next subsection discusses the alternative (and more complicated) setting in which the policymaker is better informed about his own competence than the voters.

At the time of the elections, voters observe only output growth and wages (expected inflation), not inflation or policy. This assumption is not as unrealistic as it may first appear. Inflation typically lags economic activity. Even though monetary policy instruments are immediately and costlessly observed, they are meaningless unless the voters also observe other relevant information the policymaker has about the state of the economy. To properly understand an expansion of the money supply six months before the elections, voters would have to know the policymaker's forecasts of money demand and other relevant macroeconomic variables. Assuming that policy itself is unobservable is just a convenient shortcut to keeping the voters' signal extraction problem as simple as possible.[3]

Finally, we make two other simplifying assumptions. Once voted out of office, an incumbent can never be reappointed. Also, the opponent in any election is drawn at random from the population and has an unknown preelection competence. Thus, any opponent's expected competence is zero.

---

3. As Lohmann (1996) observes, however, this assumption is not easily made consistent with a surprise supply formulation (as in chapter 15) in which realized real wages determine employment (output growth) in a one-sector setting. Lohmann instead formulates the model as a Lucas-style island model in which firms observe the local inflation but not economy-wide inflation (the policy instrument).

The Equilibrium First, consider wage setters. They have the same information as the policymaker and can thus compute equilibrium policy and perfectly predict inflation. Hence in equilibrium, $\pi_t = \pi_t^e$ in every period. Next, consider voters. By observing output and knowing the shock to competence in the previous period, η_{t-1}, they can correctly infer the incumbent's current competence by using equation (16.1): $\eta_t = x_t - \eta_{t-1}$.[4] The equilibrium voting rule is then immediate. Voters always prefer the policymaker with higher expected competence. Because the opponent has an expected competence of zero, the voters reelect the incumbent with probability 1 if and only if $x_t > \eta_{t-1}$, as in this case $\eta_t > 0$ (if $x_t = \eta_{t-1}$, we can assume that voters randomize, as they are indifferent). To an outside econometrician, observing x_t but not η_{t-1}, this voting rule appears consistent with retrospective voting. The probability of reelection is $\text{Prob}\,[\eta_{t-1} \le x_t] = G(x_t)$, where $G(\cdot)$ is the c.d.f. of η, and it increases with output growth in the election period.

Next, consider the policymaker's optimization problem. In off-election years, he is unable to enhance future reelection probability, because competence shocks last one period only and are observed with the same lag. Hence the equilibrium inflation rate minimizes the static loss in (15.16) with respect to π, subject to (16.1) and taking π^e as given. As in section 15.4, this yields $\pi_t = \lambda$. On-election years entail different incentives: by raising output growth through unexpected inflation, the incumbent policymaker can increase his election probability. In equilibrium, wage setters correctly anticipate these incentives and raise expected inflation accordingly, so that output continues to grow at its natural rate.

To formally derive these results, we first compute the equilibrium probability of reelection from the incumbent's point of view. Recall that he is reelected iff $[x_t > \eta_{t-1}]$, or—by (16.1) and our definition of ε—iff $[\eta_t > \pi_t^e - \pi_t]$. When setting policy, the incumbent has not yet observed η_t. He perceives his probability of reelection as $1 - \text{Prob}\,[\eta_t \le \pi_t^e - \pi_t] \equiv 1 - G(\pi_t^e - \pi_t)$. Clearly, this probability is an increasing function of unexpected inflation.

To proceed, we need some additional notation. Let W^R and W^N be the expected equilibrium continuation values of reappointment or not, respectively, at the point when policy is chosen. Furthermore, let π^E be equilibrium inflation during on-election years, to be derived below. Simple algebra establishes that

$$W^N = \frac{\lambda^2 + \beta(\pi^E)^2}{2(1 - \beta^2)}$$

$$W^R - W^N = -\frac{R(1 + \beta)}{1 - \beta^2(1 - G(0))},$$

(16.2)

---

4. Voters know that $\pi_t = \pi_t^e$. Recall that in period 0 we have, by assumption, set $\eta_0 = 0$. Hence in period 1 $x_1 = \eta_1$, and output fully reveals the policymaker's competence. Knowing η_1, in period 2 voters can infer η_2 from $x_2 = \eta_2 + \eta_1$, and so on.

where $1 - G(0)$ is the equilibrium probability of reelection, as the incumbent perceives it, in all future elections (he recognizes that future inflation surprises are not possible in equilibrium). Intuitively, the incumbent's expected value of winning the elections (the difference $W^R - W^N$) depends on R, the benefits from holding office, but not on the equilibrium policies, λ and π^E, since those are the same irrespective of who is the winner. Furthermore, note that these continuation values do not depend on the policymaker's competence, as competence is not known when policy is set.

We are now ready to formulate an incumbent's problem during an on-election year. Incumbent E takes expected inflation as given and chooses current inflation to minimize

$$\mathsf{E}[L^E] = \frac{\pi_t^2}{2} - \lambda(\pi_t - \pi_t^e) - R + \beta\left[\left(1 - G(\pi_t^e - \pi_t)\right)W^R + G(\pi_t^e - \pi_t)W^N\right]. \quad (16.3)$$

The first two terms in (16.3) capture the expected loss in the current period. The last two terms capture the expected value of future losses, as determined by whether the incumbent is reappointed in the upcoming elections. Taking the first-order condition for a given π_t^e and imposing the equilibrium condition $\pi_t = \pi_t^e$ yields the equilibrium inflation rate during on-election years:

$$\pi^E = \lambda + \beta\xi(0)(W^N - W^R) = \lambda + R\frac{\beta(1+\beta)\xi(0)}{1 - \beta^2(1 - G(0))}, \quad (16.4)$$

where the last equality follows from (16.2). The left-most expression in (16.4) is the marginal cost of inflation (by (16.3) it coincides with actual inflation). The two right-most expressions capture the marginal benefit: λ is the usual benefit of higher output growth, present at all times; the second term is the additional on-election-year benefit that higher output growth increases the incumbent's chance of reelection. This additional benefit of surprise inflation undermines credibility and makes policy more expansionary during on-election years. Thus equilibrium inflation is higher just after an election. Moreover, in such postelection periods it is higher the larger are the benefits from office, as measured by R, and the more surprise inflation raises the probability of reappointment, as measured by the density $\xi(0)$. Finally, because private agents perfectly understand the incentives to inflate before elections, expected inflation is also higher, and equilibrium output growth is not affected. Thus the equilibrium is consistent with stylized fact 4 in the introduction. Elections aggravate the credibility problem, as the incumbent cares even more about output growth during election periods than during nonelection periods.

16.1.2 Adverse Selection

What happens when policy is instead chosen after the incumbent has observed the realization of current competence η_t, but the sequence of events otherwise remains unchanged? In this setting, studied by Rogoff and Sibert (1988), Rogoff (1990), and Persson and Tabellini (1990), the policymaker enjoys an information advantage over wage setters, who do not know the realization of η_t when forming expectations. Output fluctuations can still reveal the policymaker's type, but in a less straightforward fashion: voters must deal with an adverse selection problem, in which an incumbent can use output as a deliberate signal of his competence.

To cope with this more intricate problem, we postulate that in each period, η can take one of only two values, $\overline{\eta} > 0$ and $\underline{\eta} < 0$, with probabilities q and $(1 - q)$, respectively. As before, η is i.i.d. and has an expected value $E(\eta) = q\overline{\eta} + (1 - q)\underline{\eta} = 0$. We refer to an incumbent with a high (low) realization of η as competent (incompetent). The opponent's competence is still unknown to everyone.

In the moral hazard model, all types of incumbents were choosing the same action, since, ex ante, they were all identical. Here the incentives to surprise with higher inflation are stronger for a more competent incumbent. First, a more competent incumbent cares more about winning the elections, since he knows that he can do a better job than his opponent. Second, a more competent incumbent also has a lower cost of signaling his competence through high output growth. Here we only sketch the arguments needed to characterize the equilibrium. A full derivation is provided by Persson and Tabellini (1990, chap. 5) and in problem 1 of this chapter. As a first step, we compute the expected net value of winning the elections:

$$W^R - W^N = \lambda\eta + \frac{(1 + \beta)R}{1 - \beta^2(1 - q)}. \tag{16.5}$$

Comparing (16.5) and (16.2), we note that the net value of winning now depends on the incumbent's competence: a competent incumbent knows that he is more likely to create higher future output growth than his opponent and hence values office more. An incompetent incumbent realizes the converse and is less eager to be reelected.[5] The equilibrium inflation rate trades off this net value of winning against the short run cost of signaling. Both types of incumbent, competent and incompetent, would like to appear competent and are prepared to boost the economy artificially through unexpected inflation to increase their chances of winning. But the competent type can signal at a lower cost: he needs to inflate less to produce any level of output growth. Because the competent type also has a higher

---

5. We assume that R is sufficiently high that even an incompetent incumbent values being reelected. Note also that here, the equilibrium probability of winning future elections coincides with q, the probability of a high realization of η. That is, in equilibrium, a competent incumbent is always reappointed and an incompetent one is not, which is a feature of all separating equilibria discussed below. Some equilibria may exist that do not have this property, that is, that are not separating, but we neglect those here. Persson and Tabellini 1990 contains a more general discussion of this issue.

value of winning, a separating equilibrium generally emerges: rational voters reelect the incumbent only if output growth exceeds a minimum threshold. This threshold is high enough that only a competent incumbent finds it optimal to reach it through unexpected inflation. The incompetent type instead prefers to keep inflation low, knowing he will not be reelected.

Recall that wage setters must form their inflation expectations without knowing which incumbent type they face. Ex post, they will always be wrong, even though their ex ante inflation forecast is rational. If the incumbent is incompetent, he chooses the short-run optimal inflation rate ($\pi = \lambda$ in the model), which is lower than expected; hence the economy goes through a recession. If the incumbent is competent, inflation is higher than expected, and the economy booms.

16.1.3 Discussion

How do the conclusions of the adverse selection model compare with the stylized facts? Clearly, retrospective voting is consistent with the evidence: voters appear to reward pre-electoral booms with reappointment and punish preelectoral recessions. Equilibrium output is not systematically higher before elections; equilibrium inflation is, on average, higher just after the elections, but this cycle is weaker than in the moral hazard model, as only the competent type now raises equilibrium inflation. Overall, the predictions of the adverse selection model are not inconsistent with the stylized facts.

Which model is more satisfactory? The moral hazard model has more clear-cut predictions and makes less-demanding assumptions about the voters' rationality. Moreover, multiplicity of equilibria is an additional problem in the adverse selection model. With enough data, one could discriminate between the two models: output volatility before the elections and inflation volatility after the elections are higher only in the adverse selection model. Note that these two models also have different normative implications. With the moral hazard model, the political cycle is entirely wasteful, whereas it conveys valuable information to voters in the adverse selection model.[6] Note also the contrast with chapter 4, where politicians were rent-seeking. In that case, elections worked as an accountability mechanism: politicians curtailed their rent seeking to impress the voters with their superior competence. Here there are no rents, and accountability is not an issue, but the logic is very similar, and so are the empirical predictions.

---

6. In a closely related adverse selection model of fiscal policy, Rogoff (1990) shows that society may actually be worse off if it tries to curtail preelection signaling through, say, a balanced budget amendment (the loss from not having the information may more than outweigh the gain from eliminating the distortions associated with signaling).

16.2 Partisan Cycles

The prior section relied on two crucial assumptions: voters are all alike and policymakers are opportunistic; their main motivation is reelection to enjoy the rents from office. Elections thus serve one purpose only: to select the most competent policymaker. A substantial part of the book, however, has stressed that voters are not alike. When policymakers cannot commit and are motivated by ideology—their own, or that of the group of voters they represent—electing a specific policymaker indirectly selects a specific policy. Policy outcomes then reflect the elected government's partisan interests. Much of the work on the politics of monetary policy has indeed relied on the kind of partisan models of postelection politics introduced in chapter 5. In monetary policy and, more generally, aggregate demand management, the relative weight assigned to stabilizing output is one crucial concern. For left-wing governments and their constituency, output and employment may weigh more heavily than prices; if so, they will also pursue more expansionary aggregate demand policies than right-wing governments. Elections thus create uncertainty about economic policy. This uncertainty would be greater in a two-party system with very polarized parties than one with parties with ideologies that were closer to one another. In polarized systems, we may observe a postelectoral cycle in the policy instruments and a resulting macroeconomic cycle. We now extend our simple monetary policy model to illustrate these ideas, showing how stylized fact 5 in the introduction to this part can be accounted for. The work on partisan cycles starts with the early adaptive expectations modeling by Hibbs (1977). However, the rational expectations version treated here originates with the work of Alesina (1987, 1988).

16.2.1 The Model

Consider the same model as in section 16.1, except that individual voters differ in their relative evaluation of output and inflation. Voter i's preferences are still described by an intertemporal loss function like (15.16), but voter i's static loss has an idiosyncratic relative weight on employment (output):

$$L^i(\pi, x) = \frac{\pi^2}{2} - \lambda^i x. \tag{16.6}$$

There are two political candidates (or parties), $P = L, R$, modeled as citizen-candidates. That is, they have the same general loss function as the voters, with relative weights $\lambda_L > \lambda_R$. The L candidate thus cares more about output growth and less about inflation than does the R candidate. Everybody knows the candidates' preferences, but the election outcome is uncertain. For simplicity, we abstract from competence or supply shocks: output growth is now described by equation (15.3) but without any ε:

$$x = \theta + \pi - \pi^e. \tag{16.7}$$

The timing of events in each period is as follows: (1) Wages are set. (2) In election years, elections are held; every other period is an election year. (3) The elected candidate sets policy. Thus wage contracts last through half the legislature and cannot be conditioned on the election outcome. Furthermore, there is electoral uncertainty about policy, because of the assumption that candidates set policy once in office. In other words, because binding electoral promises cannot be made, we are in the world of postelection politics, in which policy must be ex post optimal, given the elected policymaker's preferences.

16.2.2   Economic Equilibrium

Under these assumptions, voters are perfectly informed and the state of the economy reveals nothing to them. Hence policymaker P chooses the same inflation rate when in office, notwithstanding whether it is an on- or off-election period. Given the assumed timing, it is easily verified that $\pi_P = \lambda_P$, $P = L, R$. In off-election periods, wage setters anticipate this inflation rate perfectly, and output grows at the natural rate: $x = \theta$. Just before the elections, however, wage setters do not know which policymaker type will win. Suppose they assign probability p_R to the event that R wins. During on-election periods, expected inflation is thus

$$\pi^e = \lambda_R + (1 - p_R)(\lambda_L - \lambda_R).$$

If party R wins, it sets $\pi = \lambda_R < \pi^e$ and causes a recession in the first period of office; output is

$$x = \theta - (1 - p_R)(\lambda_L - \lambda_R).$$

If L wins, the opposite takes place: actual inflation is higher than expected and a boom occurs:

$$x = \theta + p_R(\lambda_L - \lambda_R).$$

Uncertain election outcomes may thus cause economic fluctuations. But this political output cycle occurs after the election and is due to different governments' having different ideologies, in contrast to the previous model, in which the political output cycle is due to signaling and occurs before elections.

Interpreting these ideological differences along a left-right political dimension, we get a possible explanation for stylized fact 5. The model predicts that left-wing governments stimulate aggregate demand and cause higher inflation throughout their tenure, whereas the opposite happens under right-wing governments. The election of a left-wing government creates a temporary boom just after the elections. The victory of the right-wing is instead followed by a recession. These partisan effects are more pronounced under a more polarized political system (i.e., one with large differences between λ_L and λ_R in the model) or, more generally, if the elections identify a clear winner, as in two-party systems. As mentioned above, Alesina, Roubini, and Cohen (1997) find evidence for a rational partisan cycle not only in the United States, but also in the industrial countries characterized by two-party systems. They also report results, based on poll data for the United States, supporting an additional and more precise (conditional) prediction of the model: the partisan cycle after a given election should be stronger, the larger is the uncertainty about the election outcome ahead of that election.

16.2.3   Political Equilibrium

The partisan model focuses on the role of party preferences in elections. Voters anticipate the actions of each party if elected and choose the party whose expected actions will bring the economy closest to their bliss point. Thus fluctuations in the distribution of voters' preferences for the two parties entirely determine each party's probability of winning. Moreover, as electoral promises are not binding and voters are rational and forward-looking, the two candidates' policy platforms do not converge toward the one desired by the median voter.

In the model, voters face a trade-off. If R wins, inflation is lower but output is temporarily higher, whereas the opposite occurs if L wins. How voters evaluate this trade-off depends on their relative weight parameter λ^i. Computing the losses to a generic voter after an R and an L victory, respectively, and taking differences, it is easily verified that voter i strictly prefers R to win if

$$\lambda^i < (1 + \beta)(\lambda_R + \lambda_L)/2. \tag{16.8}$$

The probability p_R of R winning is the probability that the relative weight of the median voter λ^m will satisfy inequality (16.8). Electoral uncertainty thus ultimately relies on the identity of the median voter being unknown. We could make this uncertainty formal by adopting a version of the probabilistic voting model, used in many previous chapters.

16.2.4   Discussion

In this model, right-wing candidates enjoy an electoral advantage, ceteris paribus: because all policymakers suffer from an inflation bias, a high value of λ is a political handicap.[7]

---

7. This observation is related to the argument discussed in chapter 17, about the benefits of appointing a conservative central banker.

Inequality (16.8) implies that a voter whose ideological view is exactly halfway between that of L and R (that is, such that $\lambda^i = (\lambda_R + \lambda_L)/2$) votes for the right-wing candidate. This suggests that an incumbent can act strategically to increase his chances of reelection. Specifically, a right-wing government can make its left-wing opponent less appealing to the voters by increasing the equilibrium inflation bias, perhaps by reducing wage indexation (as discussed by Milesi-Ferretti 1994), by issuing nominal debt (to raise the benefits of surprise inflation), or by creating more monetary policy discretion, via a less disciplining exchange rate regime or weaker legislation regarding central bank independence (as discussed by Milesi-Feretti 1995b). If employment is serially correlated, as in section 15.5, current monetary policy not only influences the incumbent's reelection probability but can also be used to influence the policies of a successor with different preferences (as in Jonsson 1997 and in problem 2 of this chapter). These ideas closely parallel—and indeed have their roots in—the ideas in the literature on strategic public debt policy, discussed extensively in chapter 13.

On the normative side, electoral uncertainty and policy volatility are inefficient, and voters would be better off ex ante by electing a middle-of-the-road government enacting an intermediate policy. In the assumed two-party system, however, there is no way of eliminating this unnecessary volatility. The literature has pointed at circumstances promoting convergence toward the median position. In one such circumstance, studied by Alesina and Cukierman (1990), namely uncertainty about policymaker type, each candidate has an incentive to appear more moderate, so as to raise the probability of winning the next election. In a second such circumstance, studied by Alesina (1987), repeated interactions between the two candidates can sustain self-enforcing cooperative agreements: an incumbent's deviation from a moderate policy would be punished by the opponent reverting to more extreme behavior once in office. Alternatively, the voters could enforce cooperation by punishing a government that enacted extreme policies. Naturally, there is the same problem of multiple equilibria as in the reputational models of section 15.4. Another possible argument for convergence is that the candidates' preferences have been assumed exogenously so that a middle-of-the-road candidate has strong incentives to enter the race. The analysis in chapters 5 and 12 shows that this could indeed happen, but we have also seen that endogenous entry in the citizen-candidate model can still produce two-candidate equilibria with divergent policies.

Institutional checks and balances in the political system can also moderate policy extremism. In a presidential system, for instance, actual policies often result from a compromise between the legislature and the executive. The model of partisan policymakers suggests that voters would take advantage of these institutional checks and balances to moderate the behavior of the majorities. Alesina and Rosenthal (1995) argue that the voters' attempt to moderate policy extremism can explain split-ticket voting in presidential systems (i.e., the same individuals voting for different parties in presidential and congressional elections) and the midterm election cycle (the party who won the last general elections loses the interim election). It would be interesting to spell out the micropolitical foundations behind the reduced-form policy formation function assumed by Alesina and Rosenthal, using the same methodology as in chapters 9 and 10 on legislative bargaining under separation of powers.

The result on policy divergence and partisan cycles hinges on the assumptions about candidate motivations, their ability to commit, and their perception of voting behavior. If the two candidates can make binding commitments to postelection policies in the election campaign, they generally converge to a middle-ground position independent of whether they are outcome- or office-motivated, as we have seen in part 1. What matters for the policy outcome is then the relative timing of the election campaign and the wage setting; see the discussion of the timing of elections relative to capital formation in section 12.3. If wages were set first—in analogy with the assumptions above—the median voter would still prefer inflation above the target, so as to boost employment (assuming that $\lambda^m > 0$), but both candidates would converge to this position, with the result that the partisan cycle was eliminated. As shown by Holub (1999), the extent of the inflation bias in the probabilistic voting model with office-seeking candidates hinges on the number of swing voters in the groups affected differently by monetary policy, such as the employed, the unemployed, and entrepreneurs. If elections were held before wages were fixed, on the other hand, both candidates would converge to the common inflation target $\bar{\pi}$, since this would eliminate all output effects (and hence all sources of disagreement among voters). Problems 3 and 4 of this chapter illustrate some of these issues, contrasting different electoral rules in a probabilistic voting model with partisan politicians.

Other forces that also moderate political cycles appear, however, if we explicitly distinguish between governments and central banks; the central banking institution itself may then insulate monetary policy from political pressure. We will return to this possibility in the next chapter.

16.3   Notes on the Literature

Alesina, Roubini, and Cohen (1997) present existing and new evidence on electoral cycles in OECD countries. They also survey the theoretical work on political cycles in aggregate demand policy. Alesina and Rosenthal (1995) focus on the United States in particular in this context. Faust and Irons (1999) scrutinize the evidence on the U.S. partisan cycle from a time series perspective and suggest that it may result from simultaneity and omitted-variable bias. Mishra (1997) considers OECD country evidence in a similar fashion and finds that it holds up to a larger degree than Faust and Irons found. Fair (1978), Fiorina (1981), and Lewis-Beck (1988) discuss the evidence on retrospective voting in the United States and elsewhere.

The first models of political business cycles with opportunistic government are due to Nordhaus 1975 and Lindbeck 1976. The first model of a partisan political cycle is due to Hibbs 1977. All three of these papers relied on the assumption that private agents are irrational and backward-looking in both their economic and voting decisions.

The model of an opportunistic government and adverse selection with rational voters summarized in section 16.1.2 was developed by Rogoff and Sibert (1988) in the case of fiscal policy and adapted to monetary policy by Persson and Tabellini (1990). Rogoff (1990) generalized the fiscal policy results to two-dimensional signaling by the incumbent. Ito (1990) and Terrones (1989) considered political systems in which the election date is endogenous and chosen by the incumbent himself after having observed his own competence. The moral hazard model studied in section 16.1.1 is very similar to a principal-agent problem with career concerns developed by Holmström (1982). Lohmann (1996) and, in a somewhat different setup, Milesi-Ferretti (1995b) studied this model in the context of monetary policy.

The model of partisan politics with rational voters in section 16.2 is due to Alesina (1987, 1988). Alesina, Londregan, and Rosenthal (1993) and Alesina and Rosenthal (1995) extend this model to allow for ideological parties who also differ in their competence. Milesi-Ferretti (1994) discusses how a right-wing incumbent can increase his popularity by reducing the extent of wage indexation; similar points with regard to nominal debt and the choice of an exchange rate regime were also investigated by Milesi-Ferretti (1995a, 1995b). Jonsson (1997) discusses the strategic manipulation of monetary policy for political purposes when there is autoregression in employment. Alesina and Cukierman (1990) consider uncertainty about the policymaker's ideological type. The role of moderating elections, in theory and in the U.S. data, is studied by Alesina and Rosenthal (1995). Franzese (1999) studies a panel of industrial democracies controlling for central bank independence and a partisan business cycle.

There is also a smaller but interesting empirical literature on electoral cycles in fiscal policy that goes back to Tufte (1978). In a recent paper, Blomberg and Hess (1998) simulate a real business cycle model in which fiscal policy is set according to both a partisan and an opportunistic electoral cycle. The economic and political implications of the model are consistent with U.S. data.

16.4 Problems

1. Timing, moral hazard, adverse selection, and the political business cycle

Consider the model of section 16.1, in which output depends on the policymaker's ability and there is an election every other year. Assume in addition that η_t is uniformly distributed on $[-\frac{a}{2}, \frac{a}{2}]$, with $a > 0$, and that $\beta = 1$.

a. Assume that η_t is not observed by any agent at date t, but only at date $t+1$. Nevertheless, both x_t and π_t are commonly observed immediately after they are realized (before the election, if there is one). Compute equilibrium inflation in on-election years and in off-election years. Show that under this timing there is no political business cycle and explain why not.

b. Change the timing and assume that neither η_t nor π_t are observed at date t, but only at date $t+1$. Only x_t is observed at time t, before the election, if there is one. Compute equilibrium inflation in on-election years and in off-election years. Show that the moral hazard problem of section 16.1 arises.

c. What happens if the incumbent has an informational advantage and is informed about her ability before setting inflation? Show that if the voters' information set is the same as in question (a), equilibrium inflation also remains the same as in question (a) and explain why this is so.

d. Finally, what happens if the policymaker has an informational advantage and voters have the same information as in question (b) (that is, they do not observe inflation before the election)? What inflation rate and output level will an incumbent of type η_t choose in on-election years and in off-election years? (Assume that voters reelect the incumbent only if $x_t > \xi$, where ξ has to be determined.)

2. Partisan political competition and the strategic use of inflation

This problem is based on Jonsson 1997. Let the loss function of an agent J be given by

$$\sum_{t=1}^{2} \frac{\beta^{t-1}}{2} \cdot \left(\pi_t^2 + \lambda \, (x_t - \bar{x}^J)^2\right),$$

where $x_0 = 0$ and $x_t = \rho x_{t-1} + \pi_t - \pi_t^e$, $t = 1, 2$. Notation is the same as in previous problem. Two citizen-candidates, D and R, compete to control policy. Their preferences have the same shape as those of any other agent, with a bliss output level denoted by x^D and x^R, respectively.

a. Compute the equilibrium level of inflation and output if party P is the decision maker for the two periods (and this is common knowledge).

b. Assume now that either party D or party R is in power in the first period (and that this is common knowledge at time 0). At date 2, however, either party can be elected, each with probability $\frac{1}{2}$. Suppose also that $\bar{x}^R = -\bar{x}^D$ and $\bar{x}^D > 0$. If inflation expectations are formed before the election, what will be the equilibrium level of inflation and output in each period? Solve for each type $P = D, R$, being in office in the first and/or the second period.

c. Consider a simplified probabilistic voting model in which the probability that D is elected in the second period is given by some exogenously defined function $p(x_1)$, where p is symmetric around $\frac{1}{2}$ such that $p(x_1) = \frac{1}{2} - p(-x_1)$, $p_x > 0$, for all x_1, and $p_{xx} < 0$ for $x_1 > 0$. Show that endogenous election probabilities add another incentive to manipulate first-period output. Does this reinforce the first-period (dis)inflation bias? (Maintain the same assumptions as in question (b) about the preferences of D and R.)

3. Monetary policy in majoritarian elections

Assume that two parties (A and B) compete to have the right to set monetary policy. The population is composed of three districts J of size $S^J > 0$, $\sum_{J=1}^3 S^J = 1$. Preferences in district J are described by the loss function $L^J(\pi, x) = \frac{\pi^2}{2} - \lambda^J \cdot x$, with $0 = \lambda^1 < \lambda^2 < \lambda^3$. The two parties have ideological preferences $\lambda^A = \lambda^1$ and $\lambda^B = \lambda^3$. The elections are assumed to be majoritarian, that is, a party must collect at least 50% of the votes in at least two districts to win the elections. There is uncertainty about the political support for each party: elector i of district J votes for A instead of B if $L^J(\pi_A, x_A) - \delta - \sigma^i \le L^J(\pi_B, x_B)$, where δ is a nationwide preference component uniformly distributed over $[-\frac{1}{2\psi}, \frac{1}{2\psi}]$ and σ^i is an individual preference component that has a (uniform) distribution that is district-specific: $\sigma^i \sim \mathcal{U}[-\frac{1}{2\phi^J}, \frac{1}{2\phi^J}]$, with $\phi^2 > \phi^1 = \phi^3$. Employment, x, depends only on expected and realized inflation: $x = \pi - \pi^e$. Inflation expectations are formed before the result of the elections is revealed.

Political competition works as follows: after expectations are formed, parties simultaneously announce an inflation rate. This announcement is binding. After the announcement, voters observe their political preferences for each party (σ^i and δ) and decide for which party to vote. The winning party then implements the promised policy for one period.

a. What is the target district for political competition?

b. Compute the first-order conditions for the announced inflation rate. Show that platforms partially converge in equilibrium. Why are they converging here, whereas in section 16.2 they are not?

4. Monetary policy in proportional elections

Consider a country made up of three districts of equal size: $S_1 = S_2 = S_3 = \frac{1}{3}$. The loss functions and the population are in all other respects identical to those of the previous problem. The political system, however, may be different.

a. Would this country gain by choosing a proportional representation system instead of a majoritarian system? Discuss intuitively why inflation would be higher or lower under each electoral system.

b. Assume proportional elections (a party wins if it gets more than 50% of total votes) and that each district has the ability to secede from this "monetary union". After a secession, only politicians from the local district can run in the election, and therefore monetary policy is set at the local (district) level. Which of the districts (1, 2, and/or 3) would gain from this secession? Under what condition would all the three districts agree to build together such a monetary union? Draw a parallel with the location of the European Central Bank.

17 Institutions and Incentives

A significant body of theoretical work on institutions and incentives in monetary policy has developed over the last ten years. In what follows, we give a selective account of some key ideas in that development. We do not follow the actual course of the literature over time but exploit what in retrospect appear to be the logical links between different ideas. The main issue is whether and how appropriate monetary institutions can remedy the incentive problems discussed in chapter 15. Even though we focus on credibility, some results also extend to the political distortions identified in chapter 16.

The last decade has also seen a large number of reforms of real-world monetary regimes in many countries. Many national central banks have been made more independent, like the newly created European Central Bank, and several countries have abandoned earlier intermediate targets, such as money and exchange rates targets, in favor of direct inflation targets. It is not implausible to argue that theoretical and empirical work by academic economists has played a significant role in the design of these reforms.

The ideas in this chapter rely on a common premise: monetary institutions *matter*. A constitutional or institution design stage lays down some fundamental aspects of the rules of the game, which cannot be easily changed. Once an independent central bank has been set up, an international agreement over the exchange rate has been signed, or an inflation target has been explicitly assigned to the central bank, it has some staying power, in the sense that changing the institution ex post is costly or takes time. Some critics question this premise. McCallum (1996) argues that institutional remedies discussed in this section "do not fix the dynamic inconsistency" at the core of this literature, they "merely relocate it." Posen (1998) argues that policymaking institutions themselves are highly endogenous and do not easily lend themselves to manipulation.

These criticisms are correct in claiming that institutions are assumed to enforce a policy that is ex post suboptimal from society's (or the incumbent government's) short-run point of view. Hence there is always a temptation to renege on the institution. Even though institutions do develop over time, however, their staying power need not be very long. In the context of the model dominating the literature, all that is needed is a high cost for changing the institution within the time horizon of existing nominal contracts. Beyond the contracting horizon, expectations would reflect anticipated constitutional change, which removes the distinction between ex post and ex ante optimality. As remarked above, the cost of suddenly changing the institution could also be a loss of reputation, instead of or in addition to a monetary cost. By focusing the political attention on specific issues and commitments, institutions alert private individuals when governments are explicitly reneging on their promises. To pick up the thread from chapter 15, one purpose of successful monetary institutions is to make the commitments in monetary policy as stable as those in patent legislation.

In our view, real-world monetary institutions do have staying power. They can be changed, but the procedures for making these changes often entail delays and negotiations between different parties or groups; furthermore, these delays and negotiations are not random but due to a purposeful design at the time the institution was created. We thus think that the premise of the literature is generally appropriate, but it would be more convincing to derive the institutional inertia as the result of a well-specified noncooperative strategic interaction between different actors, something the literature—so far—has failed to do. Jensen (1998), however, studies a simple model, related to the contracting solution in section 17.3, in which the government can renege on the initial institution at a continuous (non–lump sum) cost. In Jensen's setting, institution design generally improves credibility but cannot completely remove the credibility problem.

The outline of the chapter is as follows. In section 17.1 we discuss simple monetary rules (such as a fixed exchange rate agreement) with escape clauses that allow a country to waive the rules under special circumstances, such as a very large adverse shock. Flood and Isard (1989) first discussed this type of institution, which captures some aspect of the functioning of the European Monetary System (EMS) in the 1980s and early 1990s. Section 17.2 then discusses the pros and cons of delegating monetary policy to an independent and conservative central bank, drawing on the influential contribution by Rogoff (1985a). Finally, section 17.3 asks what is the optimal contract to offer to an independent agency in charge of monetary policy to remedy its incentive problem and shows that such a contract can be interpreted as an inflation target. This result is due to Walsh (1995a) and to Persson and Tabellini (1993).

17.1   Simple Rules and Escape Clauses

Small countries have commonly pegged the value of the exchange rate to gold or to some reserve currency as a device to anchor inflationary expectations, discipline domestic price and wage setting, or prevent political interference in monetary policy. Such attempts have met with mixed success. Among the industrialized countries during the postwar period, the Bretton Woods system and (part of) the EMS experiment were reasonably successful. On the other hand, the unilateral attempts of some European countries to peg their exchange rates in the 1970s and 1980s often ended up in failure: a lack of credibility generating a spiral of repeated devaluations and domestic wages and prices running ahead of foreign inflation. What can explain such differences?

To shed light on this question, let us study a slight modification of the static model in chapter 15. Consider a small open economy, specialized in the production of a single good that the rest of the world also produces. The central bank controls π through its control of the exchange rate, given a foreign inflation rate denoted $\bar{\pi}$. The rest of the model, including the expectations-augmented Phillips curve (15.3), the rational expectations assumption, the policymaker's objective function (15.6), and the timing of events is as in sections 15.2 and 15.3. As in those sections, we assume that θ is stochastic and explicitly assume that θ, as well as $\bar{\pi}$, is known when wages are set (π^e is formed). Note that $\bar{\pi}$ denotes both foreign and target inflation, as pegging the exchange rate to a low-inflation currency can be seen as an explicit or implicit attempt to target a low inflation rate.

Under discretion, the model is formally identical to that in section 15.3 and thus generates the inflation and employment outcomes in (15.12) and (15.14), respectively. As $E(\pi) > \bar{\pi}$, the model is consistent with the idea of a devaluation spiral fueled by low credibility among wage setters and a devaluing exchange rate.

17.1.1 Simple Rules

Consider now the following institution. At the institution design stage (0) society commits to a simple rule of holding the exchange rate fixed (or equivalently, letting it depreciate at a fixed rate ψ). There is commitment, in the sense that the rate of depreciation ψ is chosen at the start of each period and cannot be abandoned until one period later. (Rules with escape clauses are discussed below.) The rule is simple, because it cannot incorporate any contingencies. In practice, multilateral agreements such as the Bretton Woods system or the EMS can enforce simple commitments of this kind, as the short-run interests of other countries are hurt if one country devalues. Policy commitments to complex contingent rules would require implausible assumptions on verifiability and foresight.

What is the optimal rule? Because the depreciation rate is known in advance of wage setting and expectations formation and depreciation cannot be made contingent on the ε shocks, the depreciation rate is neutral with respect to real variables. Hence the optimal rule has $\psi = 0$. Under this simplicity constraint, a fixed exchange rates is thus the optimal commitment and result in the following equilibrium outcome: $\pi^S = \bar{\pi}$, $x^S = \theta - \varepsilon$, where the S superscript stands for "simple" rule.

Whether the simple rule is better than discretion depends on what objective one wants to achieve. The rule creates lower average inflation than under discretion, but employment is more variable. A formal comparison of the two regimes can be made by substituting (15.12), (15.14) and the previous expression for π^S and x^S into (15.6) and taking expectations of the difference in their payoffs. Recalling that $E(\theta) = 0$, this gives

$$E[L(\pi^D, x^D)] - E[L(\pi^S, x^S)] = \frac{\lambda^2}{2}\left[E(\bar{x})^2 + \sigma_\theta^2 - \frac{1}{(1+\lambda)}\sigma_\varepsilon^2\right].$$

The first two terms on the right-hand side capture the benefit of credibility under the simple rule; because the inflation bias is $\lambda(\bar{x} - \theta)$, they measure the squared average bias plus the variance of the bias. The last term is the loss that results from inability to stabilize employment. A simple rule is better than discretion if the gain of credibly low inflation is larger than the loss of stabilization policies. This trade-off between credibility and flexibility is a recurrent theme in the literature on institution design. If, under discretion, the electoral incentives discussed in chapter 16 also distort monetary policy, this further enhances the benefit of the simple rule.

Another simple rule that is often advocated—though harder to enforce—is a commitment to a $\psi\%$ money growth rule. Suppose we add a simple quantity theory equation to our model in which money demand depends on output (or employment) growth, so that $\pi + x = m + v$. The policy instrument is m, as in chapter 15. Under a simple money growth rule, velocity shocks v destabilize employment and prices. A simple exchange rate peg, on the other hand, automatically offsets velocity shocks. From this point of view, a simple money rule is worse than a simple exchange rate peg. On the other hand, a money supply rule could perform better in stabilizing supply shocks; because these shocks destabilize both output and prices, the price response acts as an automatic output stabilizer. In the limit, if $\lambda = 1$, a $\psi\%$ money rule mimics the optimal policy response to a supply shock. Moreover, an exchange rate peg exposes the country to supply shocks originating from abroad. More generally, a simple money rule is likely to perform better than a simple exchange rate rule if supply shocks are more important than financial sector shocks, and vice versa.[1]

17.1.2 Escape Clauses

The assumption that an exchange rate peg, once announced, cannot be abandoned until the following period may be too stark even in this abstract setting. Multilateral exchange rate agreements often have escape clauses: European countries have temporarily left the EMS or, more frequently, realigned their central parities when exceptional circumstances made it difficult to keep the exchange rate within the band. In this subsection, we show how to modify our simple model to capture the bare bones of this kind of policy regime. Here we merely sketch the solution: a full derivation is discussed in problem 1 of this chapter. As we shall see, simple institutional mechanisms exist that allow society to implement a simple rule with an escape clause and thereby strike a better balance between credibility and flexibility.

Throughout the subsection, we temporarily set society's preferred inflation rate $\bar{\pi} = 0$ so as to simplify the algebra. Define *normal times* as a (state-dependent) range of possible realizations of the unobservable supply shock: $\varepsilon \in [\varepsilon^L(\theta), \varepsilon^U(\theta)]$. Inside this interval, the central bank stays committed to the simple rule $\pi^N = 0$. During *exceptional times*, defined by the complementary event $\varepsilon \notin [\varepsilon^L(\theta), \varepsilon^U(\theta)]$, the central bank invokes an escape clause,

---

1. A literature emanating from the closed economy analysis by Poole 1970 has studied these questions in richer models; see Genberg 1989 and Flood and Mussa 1994. More recent contributions to the comparison of exchange rate versus money-based stabilizations of inflation are surveyed by Calvo and Vegh 1999.

abandoning the simple rule and pursuing a discretionary (ex post optimal) policy, given inflationary expectations.

Thus during normal times, employment is

$$x^N = \theta - \pi^e - \varepsilon.$$

Since normal times are defined by the realization of ε, when forming expectations wage setters do not yet know whether a particular time is normal or exceptional. As we shall see, $\pi^e(\theta) = \mathsf{E}(\pi \mid \theta) > 0$, typically. Thus when the rule is followed, not only does the central bank give up on any stabilization policies, but there is an additional employment loss due to the uncertainty about the policy regime. The possibility of invoking the escape clause and abandoning the zero-inflation rule raises expected inflation and creates unexpected deflation (i.e., $\pi < \pi^e$) as long as the rule is followed. This is an instance of a more general phenomenon sometimes called the "peso problem" that is common to all exchange rate pegs with implicit or explicit escape clauses and to other latent regime changes.

What is equilibrium inflation at exceptional times, π^E? Taking $\pi^e(\theta)$ as given and then optimizing with respect to π, it is easy to show that

$$\pi^E = \frac{\lambda}{1 + \lambda}(\bar{x} - \theta + \pi^e(\theta) + \varepsilon). \tag{17.1}$$

Let us also make the simplifying assumption that the interval $[\varepsilon^L(\theta), \varepsilon^U(\theta)]$ is symmetric around zero.[2] In this case, by (17.1) and by $\pi^N = 0$, expected inflation equals

$$\pi^e(\theta) = q(\theta)\mathsf{E}(\pi^E \mid \theta, \varepsilon \notin [\varepsilon^L(\theta), \varepsilon^U(\theta)]) = \frac{q(\theta)\lambda(\bar{x} - \theta)}{1 + \lambda(1 - q(\theta))} > 0, \tag{17.2}$$

where $q(\theta)$ is the probability that the shock ε falls outside the normal-times interval in state θ. Thus quite intuitively, as the interval becomes narrower—that is, as $q(\theta)$ goes up—expected inflation rises, because the escape clause is invoked more often. Combining (17.2) and (17.1), we obtain equilibrium inflation at exceptional times

$$\pi^E = \frac{\lambda(\bar{x} - \theta)}{1 + \lambda(1 - q(\theta))} + \frac{\lambda}{1 + \lambda}\varepsilon. \tag{17.3}$$

Comparing (17.3) with (15.14) and recalling that we have set $\bar{\pi} = 0$, it is easy to see that even at exceptional times and as long as $q(\theta) < 1$, inflation is lower than in the purely discretionary regime of chapter 15, because in some states of the world $\pi = 0$. This increases policy credibility (expected inflation is lower). Hence when the escape clause is invoked,

---

2. Because of the inherent inflation bias, in the model, a symmetric interval is generally not going to be optimal. Furthermore, the optimal degree of the asymmetry is going to depend on the strength of the credibility problem as measured by the parameter θ. The problem in the general case is quite forbidding, however.

optimal inflation is lower than in the purely discretionary regime because monetary policy is more effective.

The peso problem tied to the underlying regime uncertainty thus alters the impact of monetary policy. Employment at exceptional times is

$$x^E = \theta + \pi^E - \pi^e(\theta) - \varepsilon.$$

By (17.3) and (17.2), employment is on average above the natural rate θ: here the peso problem creates positive inflation surprises. The surprise effect in the case of $\varepsilon > \varepsilon^U(\theta)$, say, is tied to both the realization of a high ε and the realization of the exceptional-times regime. As noted above, however, this gain in credibility comes at a price: at normal times, when we stick to zero inflation, we suffer an output loss, both because we do not pursue stabilization policies and because there is unexpected deflation.

Having derived a complete equilibrium solution as a function of the size of the symmetric interval—that is, as a function of $q(\theta)$—one can show that the optimal value of $q(\theta)$ is always strictly positive (problem 1 of this chapter includes the derivation). If the variance of ε is not too large, the optimal value of $q(\theta)$ is also strictly less than 1 (see Persson and Tabellini 1990, Flood and Isard 1989).[3] That is, a rule with an escape clause always dominates a simple rule, and if supply shocks are not too volatile, it also dominates a pure discretion. Choosing the interval size entails a trade-off between credibility and flexibility. But here this trade-off is more favorable than in the choice between simple rules and pure discretion: an escape clause gives the option of retaining flexibility when it is most valuable, namely for extreme realizations of ε.

How can a regime with an escape clause be implemented so as to avoid merely relocating the credibility problem? Any implementation must rely on some delegation of decision-making authority from the government. In a multilateral exchange rate regime, for instance, the government gives up some policy autonomy by subjecting desired realignments of the exchange rate parity to approval by an international body. In this case, a country wishing to devalue would typically face opposition from the other countries in the arrangement (unless the shock was completely asymmetric). The bounds $[\varepsilon^L, \varepsilon^U]$ would then implicitly depend on the devaluing country's bargaining power, which would, in turn, depend on the details of the institution, including the prospective sanctions, the decision-making procedure, and so forth.

In a domestic context, we could suppose that at the institution design stage (before θ is realized), society could delegate to the central bank the mandate of carrying out monetary policy according to a simple rule. When designing the institution, the government would also

---

3. Finding an analytical solution for the optimal value of $q(\theta)$ is generally not feasible, however, even with simplifying assumptions about the distribution of ε. (What causes the complications is that the optimality condition involves the messy conditional variances of π and x.)

set a pair of fixed costs $[c^L(\theta), c^U(\theta)]$ incurred whenever the escape clause is invoked. These costs could capture the public-image loss to the central banker that result from not fulfilling his mandate or the political costs to the government of overriding a central bank committed to the simple rule. They would implicitly define bounds $\varepsilon^L(\theta)$ and $\varepsilon^U(\theta)$ that leave the central bank indifferent between sticking to the simple rule and bearing the cost of no stabilizing policies or paying the cost and invoking the escape clause. In neither of these interpretations, however, is it reasonable to assume that these costs could be calibrated very carefully ex ante. For instance, costs may have to be state independent or symmetric: $c^L(\theta) = c^L$, $c^U(\theta) = c^U$, or $c^U = c^L = c$. Such plausible constraints would prevent society from reaping the full value of the escape clause regime but still generally improve on the discretionary outcome.

Obstfeld (1997b) applies an escape clause model to exchange rate policy in the EMS in a setting with $c^U = c^L = c$ and a fixed value of θ. He observes that such models may generically have multiple rational expectations equilibria for given values of c. Intuitively, we can see that this happens because expected inflation, π^e, depends on how often the escape clause is invoked—it depends on q. At the same time, however, the central bank's ex post decision as to whether to invoke the escape clause also depends on π^e: higher expected inflation makes it optimal to abandon the rule for smaller positive (and larger negative) realizations of ε. Expectations of high inflation (i.e., expectations of frequent exceptions to the rule) can therefore be self-fulfilling. This multiplicity of equilibria is one way to account for the observed speculative attacks on exchange rate regimes that appeared viable until shortly before their collapse. Flood and Marion (1997) point out that preventing multiple equilibria might be an important consideration behind the ex ante choice of c.

These conjectures about implementation may sound plausible, but they stand on quite shaky ground. Analyzing the institution design questions in central banking with the same kind of methodology as the one we used in chapters 9 and 10 on comparative politics would be highly desirable. We will return to this lack of structural, micropolitical foundations later in the chapter.

17.2   Central Bank Independence

The first analytical example of strategic delegation in monetary policy is the independent and conservative central banker suggested by Rogoff (1985a). In this section, we derive and discuss this example in the context of our simple model.

17.2.1   The Conservative Central Banker

To illustrate the idea, we now formalize the distinction between society and its central bank. Society's true preferences take the form of (15.6). At the model's institution design stage

(0), society appoints an independent central banker: once appointed, society can no longer interfere with his decisions. (Towards the end of this subsection, we ask how reasonable this assumption really is.) Prospective central bankers have loss functions of the form (15.6) but differ in their personal values of λ. This suggests a heterogeneity in the population with regard to the relative weight placed on inflation versus employment, from which our formal model abstracts. As discussed in chapter 16, however, we can formally introduce such heterogeneity into the model without any difficulties. Alesina and Grilli (1992) indeed show that strategic delegation of the type to be discussed below would take place endogenously in a model in which heterogenous voters elected the central banker directly. The result is analogous to the endogenous strategic delegation in the context of capital taxation discussed in chapter 12.[4] The appointment thus boils down to the choice of the central banker's λ parameter, which we call λ^B. The private sector observes λ^B and forms its inflationary expectations accordingly.

The appointed central banker sets monetary policy freely according to his own private preferences at stage (4) of the game without commitment in policy, as described in section 15.3. As that section indicates, this choice gives the equilibrium outcomes

$$\pi(\lambda^B, \theta, \varepsilon) = \bar{\pi} + \lambda^B(\bar{x} - \theta) + \frac{\lambda^B}{1 + \lambda^B}\varepsilon \tag{17.4}$$

$$x(\lambda^B, \theta, \varepsilon) = \theta - \frac{1}{1 + \lambda^B}\varepsilon. \tag{17.5}$$

Note that the outcomes depend not only on the realized shocks but also on the banker's preferences. These expressions illustrate a basic trade-off in strategic delegation: a central banker more hawkish on inflation, that is, someone with a lower λ^B, has more credibility in keeping inflation low but is less willing to stabilize supply shocks.

To formally study delegation, consider society's expected-loss function as a function of the central banker type:

$$\mathsf{E}[L(\lambda^B)] = \mathsf{E}[(\pi(\lambda^B, \theta, \varepsilon) - \bar{\pi})^2 + \lambda(x(\lambda^B, \theta, \varepsilon) - \bar{x})^2]/2, \tag{17.6}$$

where the expectation is taken over θ and ε for any λ^B. Next, insert the expressions for equilibrium inflation and employment into (17.6) and take expectations. The derivative of the resulting expression with regard to λ^B is

$$\frac{d\mathsf{E}[L(\lambda^B)]}{d\lambda^B} = \lambda^B(\bar{x}^2 + \sigma_\theta^2) + (\lambda^B - \lambda)\frac{\sigma_\varepsilon^2}{(1 + \lambda^B)^3}. \tag{17.7}$$

---

4. Schultz (1999a) has shown that such delegation may be problematic, however, if done by political parties. In his paper, two parties that have partisan preferences and are better informed than the electorate about the working of the economy make binding appointment promises during the electoral campaign. If political polarization (of the parties) is high, appointments will be partisan, rather than in the interest of the median voter.

The first term is the expected credibility loss from choosing a central banker with a higher λ^B. The second term measures the expected stabilization gain. The optimal appointment involves setting this expression equal to zero. Evaluating this derivative at the extreme points implies that $\lambda > \lambda^B > 0$.[5]

By optimally choosing an independent central banker, society thus strikes a different compromise between credibility and flexibility than in the fixed exchange rate regime. It is still a compromise, however: it is optimal to appoint a central banker who is more conservative on inflation than society itself (to address the inflation bias) yet not ultraconservative (to preserve some of the benefits of stabilization). Note also that fluctuations in the inflation bias arising from observable θ shocks remain. If the λ^B of the optimal central banker could be chosen after the realization of θ, society would want to meet a more serious incentive problem—a smaller θ—with a more hawkish central banker—a smaller λ^B. In practice, the extent of the incentive problem may be serially correlated over time (because of the persistence in the natural rate or in the public debt), so that making appointments at discrete points is probably a good way of dealing with this problem.[6]

17.2.2 Discussion

As in the escape clause model, we could give society or the government the authority to override the central bank's decision in exceptional circumstances. The override option could involve firing the central banker, introducing ad hoc legislation, or an explicit override clause under a prespecified procedure (the latter arrangement is indeed observed in the central bank legislation of many countries). As Lohmann (1992) shows, such an escape clause mitigates the ex post suboptimality of central bank behavior, inducing even a conservative central banker to stabilize extreme supply shocks to the same extent as would society. This option should not be overemphasized, however: escape clauses can hardly be optimally designed ex ante. Moreover, as noted in the introduction to this chapter, if the government has an override option, why does it not use it at all times to get its desired policy ex post?

A few recent papers have extended these results to a setting in which monopolistic unions rather than atomistic agents set wages; see Cukierman and Lippi 1999, Lippi 1998, and Guzzo and Velasco 1999. When wage setters have some market power and act strategically, they take into account the monetary policy response to their actions. A more conservative central bank that accommodates wage pressure to a smaller extent may be counterproductive

---

5. Setting the right-hand side of equation (17.7) to zero yields a fourth-order equation in λ^B that is difficult to solve. As the expression is negative at $\lambda^B = 0$ and positive for all $\lambda^B > \lambda$, and the second-order condition is fulfilled for any λ^B in the interval $(0, \lambda)$, however, we know that the solution must be inside the interval $(0, \lambda)$.

6. The gains from a conservative central banker, in terms of pushing the solution towards the ex ante optimal rule, extend to the dynamic models discussed in section 15.5 with output persistence or forward-looking price setters (see L. Svensson 1997a and Clarida, Gali, and Gertler 1999).

in some situations, because with less monetary accommodation, higher nominal wages are more likely to lead to higher real wages. This in turn may induce trade unions to pursue more aggressive wage policies. The general lesson is that the optimal degree of central bank independence and conservativeness (the optimal value of λ^B) depends on the structure of labor markets. Labor markets in which unions have more monopoly power may make it optimal to reduce the central bank's conservativeness.

Having an independent central bank also protects society from the distortions introduced by the electoral business cycles discussed in chapter 16. In this case, however, independence only is required, and no special emphasis on inflation relative to other macroeconomic goals. Waller (1989) was first to formulate a model of central bank independence under partisan politics; see problems 2 and 3 of this chapter for delegation by political parties. Waller (1992) also studies appointments to a central bank board with overlapping mandates in a two-party system in which the opposition must approve the incumbent government's appointments. Longer terms for the board members, relative to the election period, exert a moderating influence on political cycles by making monetary policy less partisan.

The literal interpretation that society picks a central banker type is not very satisfactory: an individual candidate's priorities or attitudes toward inflation and employment are often unknown and vaguely defined. Although individual attitudes are not unimportant, they are probably less important than the general character and tradition of the institution itself. A better interpretation may be that at the constitutional stage, society drafts a central bank statute spelling out the institution's mission. The parameter λ^B then reflects the priority assigned to price stability relative to other macroeconomic goals. As instrument independence is a necessary condition for delegation to work, we should expect such a strategic setting of goals to work better if combined with institutional and legislative features, granting independence to the central bank and shielding it from short-run political pressures. In this interpretation, the model yields observable implications: countries or time periods in which the central bank statute gives priority to price stability and protects central bank independence should have lower average inflation and higher employment (or output) volatility, for if $\lambda^B < \lambda$, stabilization policies are pursued less vigorously. Moreover, electoral business cycles in inflation or output should be less pronounced with greater central bank independence.

By now, a number of studies have constructed measures of central bank independence based on central bank statutes, also taking into account the priority given to the goal of price stability. Cross-country data for industrial countries show a strong negative correlation between those measures of central bank independence and inflation, but no correlation between output or employment volatility and central bank independence.[7] Thus central

---

7. See, in particular, Bade and Parkin 1988, Grilli, Masciandaro, and Tabellini 1991, Alesina and Summers 1993, Cukierman 1992, and Eijffinger and Schaling 1993.

bank independence seems to be a free lunch: it reduces average inflation at no real cost. Different interpretations of this result have been suggested. Alesina and Gatti (1995) note that an independent central bank could reduce electorally induced output volatility, as would be predicted by the models of chapter 16, and Lippi (1998) provides evidence that could support this proposition.

Posen (1993, 1995) argues that the cross-country correlation between central bank independence and lower inflation is not causal and suggests that society's underlying preferences for low and stable inflation may induce both. Campillo and Miron (1997) also cast doubts on the generality of the findings, using data from a large cross-country sample of 110 countries. Once other possible determinants of inflation are added, central bank independence does not explain low inflation in the full data set, even though it most often does so in the high-income part of the data set. Inflation is instead significantly positively related to outstanding debt and political instability and significantly negatively related to openness (see chapter 18). Franzese (1999), on the other hand, finds stronger empirical support for the idea that central bank independence reduces inflation. He considers a panel of developed democracies, controlling also for the political environment and exploiting both the cross-country and the time series variations in the data.

Finally, Rogoff (1985a) also suggests another interpretation of the model: the conservative central banker might be interpreted as a targeting scheme supported by a set of punishments and rewards. Having a conservative central banker is thus formally equivalent to having an additional term in his loss function, $(\lambda^B - \lambda)(\pi - \bar{\pi})^2$, where $\lambda^B > \lambda$. The central banker therefore has the same objective function as everybody else but faces additional sanctions if actual inflation exceeds the target. In this simple model, a conservative central banker is thus equivalent to an inflation target.[8] A more recent literature has picked up that alternative interpretation, asking which targets are more efficient and, more generally, how a targeting scheme should be designed to shape central bank ex post incentives optimally. The next section discusses that literature.

17.3   Inflation Targets and Contracts

Central banks have traditionally operated with intermediate targets, like money or the exchange rate. In the 1990s, several central banks started to target inflation: whereas some central banks imposed the procedure on themselves, in some cases the governments

---

8. Rogoff (1985a) compares an inflation target to other nominal targets, such as money and nominal income. He shows that strategic concerns of the type considered here can indeed overturn the ranking of intermediate targets, based on parameter values and relative variance of shocks, in the traditional nonstrategic literature on monetary targeting.

have mandated the transition. A substantial literature discusses real-world inflation targeting. Bernanke et al. 1999 offers a useful and broad overview of the experience with inflation targeting so far, including a number of case studies of inflation-targeting countries.[9]

Such targeting schemes have been studied from the point of view of the theory of optimal contracts. Society (or whoever is the principal of the central bank) punishes or rewards its agent, the central bank, conditional on its performance. The question is what constitutes an optimal contract and what kind of behavior it induces on the agent. We illustrate the basic ideas of this recent literature in our simple model of credibility. The optimal contract can easily be modified so as to implement the optimal monetary policy in the presence of the kind of political distortions studied in chapter 16. This extension is not pursued here, however. Much of the discussion in this section is based on results in Walsh 1995a and in Persson and Tabellini 1993.

17.3.1 The Optimal Inflation Contract

In this model, the central bank holds the same quadratic preferences as everybody in society. It sets policy at stage (4) of the game without commitment. At the constitutional stage (0), the government formulates a publicly observable complete contract for the central bank that formulates state-contingent transfers (rewards if positive, punishments if negative) conditional on realized inflation:

$$T(\pi; \theta, \varepsilon) = t_0(\theta, \varepsilon) + t_1(\theta, \varepsilon)\pi + \frac{t_2}{2}(\theta, \varepsilon)\pi^2. \tag{17.8}$$

Our goal is to set optimally the terms $t_i(\theta, \varepsilon)$, $i = 0, 1, 2$, that define the contract. We only include up to second-order terms in the contract, since this is sufficient for our purposes. Units are normalized so that at stage (4), the central bank sets inflation so as to minimize the difference between the loss function and its transfer: $L(\pi, x) - T(\pi; \theta, \varepsilon)$. This formulation implies risk neutrality.

Going through the same steps as in section 15.3 (deriving the central bank optimum condition for inflation, given the contract and expected inflation, solving for rationally expected inflation, and combining the resulting expressions), we get the equilibrium condition:

$$(1 - t_2(\theta, \varepsilon))\pi = \bar{\pi} + t_1(\theta, \varepsilon) + \lambda(\bar{x} - \theta) + \frac{\lambda(1 - t_2(\theta, \varepsilon))}{1 + \lambda - t_2(\theta, \varepsilon)}. \tag{17.9}$$

The benchmark optimum in (15.11) can be implemented by setting $t_2(\theta, \varepsilon) = 0$ and $t_1(\theta, \varepsilon) = t_1(\theta) = -\lambda(\bar{x} - \theta)$. Because the constant $t_0(\theta, \varepsilon)$ affects none of the central bank's marginal incentives, it can be set freely—for instance, it can be set positive enough so that

9. See also Leiderman and Svensson 1995, Haldane 1995, McCallum 1996, Mishkin and Posen 1997, and Almeida and Goodhart 1997.

the participation constraint is satisfied: the central bank leadership finds it attractive enough, in expected terms, to accept the job.

A remarkably simple linear performance contract—imposing a linear penalty on inflation—thus removes the inflation bias completely. The credibility-flexibility trade-off has disappeared: average inflation is brought down to the target at no cost of output volatility. Once the simple contract has been formulated, the central bank has the right incentives to implement the ex ante optimal policy. Note that the optimal contract is not conditional on ε, because the central bank's marginal incentives to stabilize the economy are correct under discretion. (In the terminology of chapter 15, without output persistence, there is an inflation bias but no stabilization bias.) The slope of the penalty for inflation is conditional on θ, however, as the incentive to inflate the economy also varies linearly with θ. To see the intuition for this result, interpret the punishment for inflation as a Pigovian corrective tax. As discussed in chapter 15, we want to address the distortion that the central bank does not internalize the effect of its policy on inflationary expectations when acting ex post. Since expected inflation $E_\varepsilon(\pi \mid \theta)$ is a linear projection of π, a linear penalty for inflation makes the central bank correctly internalize the marginal cost of its policy.[10] To see this formally, we substitute the Phillips curve (15.3) into the objective function (15.6) and calculate the equilibrium marginal cost of expected inflation in state θ as

$$\frac{dE_\varepsilon[L(\pi, x) \mid \theta]}{d\pi^e} = \lambda(\bar{x} - \theta) = -t_1(\theta).$$

17.3.2 Inflation Targets

The absence of a credibility-flexibility trade-off with an optimal contract contrasts with the results in section 17.2, in which we showed that lower expected inflation was associated with distorted stabilization policy. At the end of that section, we pointed to the alternative interpretation of the conservative central result, namely as a quadratic reward inflation target. This solution discussed at the end of the last section is equivalent to an inflation contract with $t_2 = -(\lambda^B - \lambda)$, $t_1 = -(\lambda^B - \lambda)\bar{\pi}$, and $t_0 = -(\lambda^B - \lambda)(\bar{\pi})^2/2$, which clearly gives the central banker incorrect marginal incentives.

Nevertheless, the optimal linear inflation contract can be reinterpreted as being similar to an inflation target. As the intercept can be set freely, we can write the optimal contract as

$$T(\pi; \theta) = \tilde{t}_0 + t_1(\theta)(\pi - \bar{\pi}); \tag{17.10}$$

that is, the central banker is punished linearly, but only for upward deviations from society's preferred inflation rate. Walsh (1995b) shows that the marginal penalty on inflation can be

---

10. Indeed, the optimal contract's linearity is preserved for any general loss functions and not just for the quadratic one.

interpreted as resulting from an arrangement in which the governor of the central bank faces a probability of being fired that increases linearly in inflation. Such an arrangement resembles the Price Targeting Agreement in force in New Zealand since 1990. Other, looser interpretations would be to associate the penalty with altered central bank legislation, a lower central bank budget, or a loss of prestige of the institution and the individuals heading it for failing to deliver on a publicly assigned or self imposed mission. Naturally, it may be impossible to specify the penalty exactly as a linear function of inflation. To approximate an optimal incentive scheme, however, the punishment for upward deviations from an inflation target should increase only gradually with the size of the deviation. In fact, if the central bank is risk-averse, the optimal contract entails a diminishing marginal penalty on inflation (to reintroduce linearity in the incentive scheme).

L. Svensson (1997a) has proposed an alternative interpretation of inflation targets, related to—but somewhat different from—the optimal performance contract interpretation. He assumes that the central bank(er) has no individual preferences over macroeconomic outcomes; instead society can assign a specific objective function to the central bank. Suppose that society manages to assign a loss function with a lower goal for inflation, say $\pi^B(\theta)$ rather than $\bar{\pi}$, to the central bank. Then the optimal goal for inflation is $\pi^B(\theta) = \bar{\pi} - \lambda(\bar{x} - \theta)$. Pursuing this goal would eliminate the inflation bias without abandoning stabilization policies. That is, the lower inflation goal is equivalent to our previous setting with a central bank minimizing $L - T$, where L is the loss function and T is an inflation contract of the form in (17.8), with parameters $t_2 = 0$, $t_1 = -\lambda(\bar{x} - \theta)$ and $t_0 = -[\lambda(\bar{x} - \theta)^2 - 2\pi^*\lambda(\bar{x} - \theta)]/2$. If we are willing to interpret a lower π^B as being associated with greater central bank independence, this representation of an inflation target suggests an alternative explanation for the empirical observation discussed in section 17.2. A lower π^B is associated with lower inflation but not with higher output variability, as in the data.

It is not without problems to associate such a scheme with real-world institutions, however. Suppose that the optimal inflation rate for society, $\bar{\pi}$, is about 2%, and that the average inflation bias, $\lambda(\bar{x} - \theta)$, is about 3% or more (not an outrageous number, given the recent monetary history of many European countries). The central bank should then be given a target, $\pi^B(\theta)$, which is negative—that is, a deflation target. In equilibrium, however, the central bank would not take any action to bring inflation below 2%, which might be problematic to explain to the public. A second, more important, problem relates to enforcement. How can we ensure that the central bank accepts that it must evaluate the costs and benefits of its policy according to the imposed objective function, rather than according to society's preferences? A plausible answer is that the central bank be held accountable for its actions and that there be a performance-based scheme of rewards or punishments that makes the central bank behave in the desired fashion. We have then returned, however, to the performance contract interpretation of inflation targets explicitly suggested by (17.8). If society could really freely impose an objective function on the central bank, the best assignment would be to prescribe the natural rate as the employment target, that is, to set $\bar{x}(\theta) = \theta$, thereby completely eliminating the inflation bias.

A natural question is whether to base the contract or target on inflation or on other measures of performance, such as money, the exchange rate, or nominal income. Persson and Tabellini (1993) show an equivalence result. If the central bank is indeed risk-neutral and faces linear constraints (i.e., the behavioral equations of the economy), as assumed so far, and if the marginal penalties under the contract can be contingent on θ, alternative targets yield the same equilibrium. With relevant nonlinearities in the equations describing the economy, however, an inflation-based contract is simpler; to replicate the ex ante optimal policy with other measures of performance, the contract must be contingent on a larger set of variables, such as shocks to money demand or to the money multiplier. In this sense, an inflation target dominates targeting schemes based on other nominal variables: simplicity implies enhanced accountability and thus easier enforcement. Intuitively, the whole purpose of optimal contracts is to remove an inflation bias, which is most easily done by means of a direct penalty on inflation, rather than in a more roundabout way, by targeting other variables only loosely related to inflation.

In practice, adopting an inflation target means that the central bank is using its own inflation forecast as an intermediate target. L. Svensson (1997b) first modeled this insight formally, in a setting in which current policy has a lagged effect on output and inflation. With such lags, the above logic becomes even stronger. If society's goals are formulated over inflation and output, the inflation forecast is the relevant intermediate target; alternative intermediate targets, such as money, are at best imperfect substitutes for the inflation forecast. L. Svensson (1999a) also provides an illuminating analysis of this point and many other issues in inflation targeting. Interestingly, the empirical evidence on the behavior of the Bundesbank, a very successful central bank, suggests that it has really pursued "inflation targeting in disguise," despite its official monetary target (see Bernanke and Mihov 1997 and Clarida and Gertler 1997).

17.3.3 Simple Contracts

What happens if the contract cannot be made state contingent, so that t_0, t_1, and t_2 in (17.8) each have to be constant across θ? This question and its answer are related to the problem in Herrendorf and Lockwood 1997, which studies delegation in a model with observable shocks, and to that in Beetsma and Jensen 1998, which studies delegation via an optimal contract when the central banker's preferences are uncertain ex ante. To find the optimal incomplete contract in this case, we first insert into the quadratic objective function the solution for π in (17.9) with constant-slope coefficients, as well as the associated solution for x, namely

$$x = \theta - \frac{1 - t_2}{1 + \lambda - t_2} \varepsilon.$$

We then take expectations of the resulting expression over θ and ε and minimize with regard to t_1 and t_2. After tedious but straightforward algebra, we can write the optimality conditions as:

$$t_1 = -\lambda \bar{x} - t_2 \bar{\pi}$$

$$t_2 \frac{(1 - t_2)^3}{(1 + \lambda - t_2)^3} = -\frac{\sigma_\theta^2}{\sigma_\varepsilon^2}. \tag{17.11}$$

These conditions are both intuitive. Using $\mathsf{E}(\theta) = 0$, it is easily shown that the first condition says $\mathsf{E}(\pi) = \bar{\pi}$: unconditionally, expected inflation should coincide with society's preferred rate of inflation. The left-hand side of the second condition is a decreasing function of t_2. As its value is zero at $t_2 = 0$, the condition states that the coefficient on the quadratic term in the contract should be negative. Further, its absolute value should be higher the more important are observable shocks relative to unobservable ones. Thus when a state-contingent linear punishment cannot handle fluctuations in the observable incentives to inflate, the constrained optimum gives up a little bit on (first-best) stabilization to diminish the costly fluctuations in π.

As t_1 contains a term in $\bar{\pi}$, we can rewrite the transfer in the optimal non-state-contingent contract as

$$T(\pi) = t_0 + \bar{t}_1 \pi + t_2 (\pi - \bar{\pi})^2,$$

with $t_2 < 0$ given by (17.11) and $\bar{t}_1 = -\lambda \bar{x} + t_2 \bar{\pi} < 0$. According to this expression, the central bank should be targeting society's preferred rate of inflation and look forward to an extra reward for low inflation. It might not be too far-fetched to interpret the inflation-targeting schemes enacted in the 1990s in many countries as an instance of this arrangement.[11]

17.3.4   Discussion

The simple contracting model discussed in this section has been extended in several directions in the pertinent literature. If some shocks are observable but not verifiable and hence not contractible, the central bank can be required to report the value of these shocks. Persson and Tabellini (1993) show that the optimal contract is related to both the inflation outcome and the central bank announcement; it is structured in such a way as to induce

---

11. In the model of Beetsma and Jensen 1998, with uncertain central bank preferences, the optimal inflation target may instead be above society's target.

optimal behavior as well as truth telling. Policy announcements matter not because they convey information to the private sector (which already observes everything), but because they change central bank incentives, by providing a benchmark against which performance can be assessed ex post.[12] Walsh (1995a) shows that the optimal contract can also handle costly effort by the central bank.

Jonsson (1997), Lockwood (1997), and L. Svensson (1997a) have studied the contract solution when employment is persistent, as in section 15.5. These results are discussed as problems 4 and 5 of this chapter. The ex ante optimal policy is still sustainable, given that the reward can be made contingent on the natural rate of unemployment. This is easily understood from the static analysis in this section, in which we have seen that the optimal contract indeed should be contingent on θ, because the incentive to inflate is decreasing in θ. This is the important point, not whether θ is exogenous, as in this section, or endogenous, as in section 15.5.

Al-Nowaihi and Levine (1998) show how an incentive contract may help eliminate political business cycles in a model in which incumbents have a prospective incentive for preelectoral expansion, as in chapter 16. When the central bank is independent, inflation contracts provide the government with an alternative signaling mechanism, however, eliminating the political business cycle and promoting the election of more-competent governments.

McCallum (1996) and others have argued that the contracting solution makes little sense, since it only replaces one commitment problem with another: who enforces the optimal contract? This question reintroduces the general question about institutional reforms raised at the beginning of this section, although it might apply more forcefully to a more ambitious incentive scheme, such as the optimal contract. As in the case of the fixed exchange rate regimes of section 17.1, enforcement is more likely if agents receive heterogenous ex post benefits of inflation and agents hurt by inflation are given a prominent role in the enforcement. Interestingly, Faust (1996) argues that a desire to balance redistributive interests for and against surprise inflation was a clear objective in the mind of the framers of the Federal Reserve.

As stated before, we also believe that changing institutions takes time. The public image of a policymaker who emphatically announced an inflation target would be severely tarnished if he abandoned it shortly afterward. This is one of the main reasons why inflation targets can alter policymakers' ex post incentives in the real world. The contracting solution's emphasis on accountability and transparency is helpful for analyzing these issues more clearly as well as the trade-offs emerging if the reward scheme cannot be perfectly tailored to mimic the optimal contract. We cannot demand much more than this from simple theoretical models.

---

12. In the reputational model of Cukierman and Liviatan 1991 discussed in chapter 15, in contrast, announcements matter since they convey information about the type of policymaker.

Still, we believe that it is high time for this literature to go beyond alternative variations of the objective function in the simple linear-quadratic problem. As mentioned before, it would be desirable to model the different steps and the incentives in the enforcement procedure as a well-defined extensive form, noncooperative game in which the decision-making authority of the different agents is explicitly modeled. The approach used to discuss checks and balances in the comparative politics part of the book appears particularly promising for tackling this task.

17.4   Notes on the Literature

Persson and Tabellini (1990, chap. 2), Cukierman (1992), Schaling (1995), and Walsh (1998, chap. 8) have surveyed the literature on institutions in monetary policy in textbook form.

The formal theoretical literature on central bank independence starts with Rogoff (1985a), whose analysis of the conservative central banker constitutes the basis of the model in section 17.2, although Barro and Gordon (1983b) suggest the treatment of society's problem as a principal-agent problem in an anticipatory footnote. Waller (1989, 1992) studies equilibrium appointments of central bankers in a context of partisan politics. Waller and Walsh (1996) examine the optimal term length of central bankers in the context of partisan cycles, in which society's objectives may change over time. Fratianni, von Hagen, and Waller (1997), Alesina and Gatti (1995), and Lippi (1998) analyze the role of central bank independence in the absence of a credibility problem but in the presence of electoral incentives. Cukierman and Lippi (1999), Guzzo and Velasco (1999), Lippi (1998), and Franzese and Hall (1998) explore how the optimal central banking arrangement varies with the structure of labor markets.

Giavazzi and Pagano (1988) discuss the commitment ability in multilateral fixed exchange rate regimes, although they carry out their analysis in a richer dynamic framework than the simple model of section 17.1. Flood and Isard (1989) introduce the formal analysis of the rules with escape clauses. Lohmann (1992) discusses the implementation of an escape clause, by costly government override, in a monetary policy model that also includes the delegation to a Rogoff-type central banker. Obstfeld (1997b) applies an escape clause model in his analysis of realignments within the ERM, emphasizing the possibility of multiple equilibria. Bordo and Kydland (1995) argue that the classical gold standard worked like a rule with escape clauses. Flood and Marion (1997) include an insightful discussion of escape clause models and speculative attacks.

The optimal-contract solution to the credibility problem in section 17.3 was developed by Walsh (1995a) and by Persson and Tabellini (1993) and further extended by Beetsma and Jensen (1996) and by Herrendorf and Lockwood (1997); see also the references within the body of the chapter. L. Svensson suggests interpreting an inflation target as an assignment of an objective function (1997a) and analyzes inflation targeting in models with lags between the policy instrument and macroeconomic outcomes (1997b, 1999a).

Insightful general discussions about the appropriate institutional framework for monetary policy can be found in Fischer 1995, McCallum 1996, Goodhart and Viñals 1994, and Blinder 1998. The early real-world experience with inflation targeting is surveyed in Leiderman and Svensson 1995 as well as Haldane 1995, Almeida and Goodhart 1997, and Mishkin and Posen 1996. Bernanke et al. (1999) give an up-to-date overview of the policy experience in inflation-targeting countries. The recent U.K. experience with inflation targeting is discussed by Budd (1998), Bean (1998), and Artis, Mizen, and Kontolemis (1998).

A number of studies—including Bade and Parkin 1988, Alesina 1988, Grilli, Masciandaro, and Tabellini 1991, Cukierman 1992, and Eijffinger and Schaling 1993—have developed empirical measures of central bank independence and studied their relation to inflation and other macroeconomic outcomes in narrow or broad cross sections of countries during the last few decades. Capie, Mills, and Wood (1994) study historical evidence on inflation before and after major central bank reforms in twelve countries since the end of the nineteenth century. Jonsson (1995) uses pooled time series and cross-sectional data from the OECD countries since the early 1960s, finding that the negative relation between central bank independence and inflation is robust to the control of a number of other institutional and economic variables. Posen (1993) criticizes this kind of finding and argues that it is caused by an omitted-variable problem, the causal variable for both independence and inflation being the resistance in the financial community against inflation. Campillo and Miron (1997) find that central bank independence has no effect on inflation once one controls for other determinants of inflation, except perhaps in the industrial countries, whereas Franzese (1999) supports the anti-inflationary benefits of central bank independence in a panel of industrial countries. A survey of different empirical studies is found in Eijffinger and de Haan 1996.

17.5   Problems

1. Escape clauses within a simple rule

This problem is based on Persson and Tabellini 1990, chapter 2. Consider an economy in which the loss function is $L(\pi, x) = \frac{1}{2}[\pi^2 + \lambda \cdot (x - \bar{x})^2]$, with $\bar{x} > 0$ and $x = \pi - \pi^e - \varepsilon$; $\mathsf{E}[\varepsilon] = 0$. As usual, expectations are set before the realization of ε, whereas inflation is chosen afterward.

a. Consider a simple rule in which the central bank is constrained to set inflation at $\pi^S = \bar{\pi}$. What are the levels of inflation and output and the expected loss as a function of $\bar{\pi}$? Compute the optimal value of $\bar{\pi}$. Under what conditions is this simple rule preferred to discretion?

b. Consider a simple rule with an escape clause: if the shock ε belongs to $[-\bar{\varepsilon}, \bar{\varepsilon}]$, the central bank must set $\pi = \bar{\pi}$. This happens with probability $(1 - q)$. Otherwise, if $\varepsilon \notin [-\bar{\varepsilon}, \bar{\varepsilon}]$ (which happens with probability q), the central bank can set inflation to π^E. Compute this value of π^E as a function of $\bar{\pi}$ and ε as well as the resulting expected loss. Compute the optimal value of $\bar{\pi}$ given q. Consider the optimal value of $\bar{\pi}$ and demonstrate that the optimal value of q is strictly between 0 and 1 if σ_ε^2 is not too small.

c. Assume that a penalty c is imposed on the policymaker if he deviates from zero inflation. Assume also that $\lambda = 1$ and that ε is uniformly distributed over $[-\bar{\varepsilon}, \bar{\varepsilon}]$, where $\bar{\varepsilon}$ is close to zero. Show that for some values of c there are multiple equilibria: if economic agents believe either that $\mathsf{E}[\pi] = 0$ or that $\mathsf{E}[\pi] = \bar{x}$, their expectation will be correct (i.e., equilibrium inflation is a self-fulfilling prophecy).

2. Endogenous credibility of the central bank

Consider two parties, R and D, that alternate in power. Each is elected with probability $\frac{1}{2}$. The decision to delegate responsibility for controlling inflation to a central bank has yet to be made. Delegation will be credible, however, only if both parties prefer delegating to a central bank rather than having a 50% chance of being the one that controls inflation— and a 50% chance of seeing the opponent have that control. Each agent has quadratic preferences $L^i[\pi, x] = \pi^2 + \lambda^i \cdot (x - \bar{x})^2$, with $x = \pi - \pi^e - \varepsilon$. There are three types of preferences in the economy: $\lambda^R = 0 < \lambda < \lambda^D = 1$, where λ represents social preferences, λ^R the preferences of the right-wing party and λ^D those of the left-wing party.

a. Assume that $\bar{x} = 0$ and compute the expected loss of having policy made by an agent of type $\lambda^B \in (0, 1)$ for each of the three existing types.

b. Show that both D and R may benefit from delegating to a central bank with preference $\lambda^B \in (0, 1)$, still under the assumption that $\bar{x} = 0$.

c. Consider now the case in which $\bar{x} > 0$. Compare three different equilibria:

1. Policy is delegated to a central banker with preferences $\lambda^B = \lambda$ who operates under commitment (optimal inflation rate).

2. Policy is delegated to a central bank with preferences $\lambda^B \in (0, 1)$ that operates under discretion (suboptimal inflation rate).

3. Policy is set randomly by one of the parties (D or R), who operate under discretion.

Show that there exist cases where parties can agree to switch from equilibrium (3) to (2) but not from (3) to (1).

3. Political competition and optimal delegation

Consider two parties, D and R, who compete for office. In contrast to the other cases we have analyzed, they compete not on the inflation rate, but on the shape of the contract they offer to the central bank. Their platform is binding, and the elected party has to implement the proposed contract. The central bank acts under discretion and has a preference parameter λ, identical to that of the median voter, whose preferences are given by

$$\mathsf{E}_{t-1}\left[L\left(\pi_t, x_t\right)\right] = \mathsf{E}_{t-1}\left[\frac{\pi_t^2}{2} + \frac{\lambda}{2}\left(x_t - \bar{x}\right)^2\right].$$

The feasible contracts belong to the class $T(\pi_t) = t_0 + t_1 \cdot \pi_t$ and cannot be made contingent on shocks. Employment is determined as $x_t = \pi_t - \pi_t^e - \varepsilon_t$, with $\mathsf{E}_{t-1}[\varepsilon_t] = 0$. Once the contract is implemented, the central bank minimizes $L(\pi_t, x_t) - T(\pi_t)$.

a. Compute the platform that a purely opportunistic party would propose to maximize its probability of being elected.

b. Compute the platform that purely ideologist parties with preferences λ^D or λ^R would propose to minimize

$$\mathsf{E}_{t-1}[L^i(\pi_t, x_t)] = \mathsf{E}_{t-1}\left[\frac{\pi_t^2}{2} + \frac{\lambda^i}{2}\left(x - \bar{x}\right)^2\right].$$

Does the result depend on some uncertainty about the median voter's preferences? Discuss the intuition for your result.

c. What would happen with opportunistic parties if they were unable to commit to implementing the contract and instead had a chance to recover direct control on inflation once elected? Would the parties gain by creating such a commitment device?

4. Optimal delegation with persistent output shocks

This problem is inspired by Clarida, Gali, and Gertler 1999. Consider the same economy as in problem 4 in chapter 15: the Phillips curve is given by $x_t = \pi_t - \mathsf{E}_t[\pi_{t+1}] - \varepsilon_t$, with $\varepsilon_t = \rho \cdot \varepsilon_{t-1} + \hat{\varepsilon}_t$ and $\mathsf{E}_t[\hat{\varepsilon}_{t+1}] = 0$. The intertemporal loss function is $\frac{1}{2}\mathsf{E}_t\{\sum_{v=0}^{\infty}\beta^v \cdot [\pi_{t+v}^2 + \lambda \cdot x_{t+v}^2]\}$. In this framework, we have already defined the optimal policy under commitment and under discretion:

$$\pi_t^C = \frac{(1-\rho)\lambda}{1+(1-\rho)^2\lambda}\varepsilon_t, \qquad \pi_t^D = \lambda^B \cdot x^B + \frac{\lambda^B}{1+(1-\rho)\lambda^B}\varepsilon_t,$$

where x^B is the central banker's output target.

a. Show that unless x^B is equal to zero, electing a conservative central banker with $\lambda^B < \lambda$ is not enough to reach the optimal policy under commitment.

b. Can an inflation target or a simple linear contract restore the optimal policy under commitment?

c. Nevertheless, the above value of π_t^C is not the globally optimal policy. Because of error autocorrelation, the globally optimal policy must instead yield $x_t = \delta x_{t-1} - \frac{\beta\delta}{\lambda(1-\beta\delta\rho)}\varepsilon_t$, where

$$\delta = \frac{1 - \sqrt{1 - 4a^2\beta}}{2a\beta}, \qquad a = \frac{\lambda}{(1+\lambda)\beta + \lambda}.$$

Equivalently, this yields a globally optimal inflation rate $\pi_t = \frac{1-\delta\beta}{\beta}\lambda x_{t-1} + \frac{\beta\delta}{1-\beta\delta\rho}\varepsilon_t$. Design the contract that would induce the central bank to implement this globally optimal policy.

5. Optimal delegation when employment is persistent

This problem is based on L. Svensson (1997a). Consider the same framework as in problem 5 in chapter 15: when there is persistence in employment ($x_t = \rho \cdot x_{t-1} + \pi_t - \pi_t^e - \varepsilon_t$) and society has preferences of the shape

$$L(\pi_t, x_t; \bar{\pi}, \bar{x}, \lambda) = \frac{1}{2}\mathsf{E}_0\left\{\sum_{t=0}^{\infty} \beta^v \cdot [(\pi_t - \bar{\pi})^2 + \lambda \cdot (x_t - \bar{x})^2]\right\},$$

the optimal policy under commitment is given by

$$\pi_t^R = \bar{\pi} + \psi_\varepsilon^R \cdot \varepsilon_t = \bar{\pi} + \frac{\lambda}{1 + \lambda - \beta\rho^2} \cdot \varepsilon_t.$$

Under discretion, however, one can show that the equilibrium policy of a government sharing the same preferences as society would be

$$\pi_t^D = \bar{\pi} + \frac{\lambda}{1 - \beta\rho - \beta\psi_x^D} \cdot \bar{x} - \psi_x^D \cdot x_{t-1} + \psi_\varepsilon^D \cdot \varepsilon_t,$$

where

$$\psi_x^D = \frac{1 - \beta\rho^2 - \sqrt{(1 - \beta\rho^2)^2 - 4\lambda\beta\rho^2}}{2\beta\rho},$$

and

$$\psi_\varepsilon^D = \frac{\lambda + \beta \left(\psi_x^D\right)^2}{1 + \lambda - \beta\rho^2 + \beta \left(\psi_x^D\right)^2}.$$

That is, when it exists, the discretionary policy leads (1) to a systematic inflation bias: $\frac{\lambda \bar{x}}{1-\beta\rho-\beta\psi_x^D}$, (2) to a state-contingent inflation bias: $\psi_x^D \cdot x_{t-1}$, that is, the discretionary outcome is inefficiently sensitive to lagged output, and (3) to a stabilization bias: $\psi_\varepsilon^D > \psi_\varepsilon^R$.

a. Show that electing a conservative central banker generally does not allow the optimal policy under commitment to be reached.

b. Show intuitively that a simple linear contract (which imposes an additional penalty that is linear in the inflation level) can eliminate the systematic inflation bias but cannot alter the third and fourth terms of the reaction function π_t^D. (As in problem 5 in chapter 15, you have to use the intertemporal value function to show this.)

c. Show intuitively that imposing an inflation target on the central banker (replacing $\bar{\pi}$ by some other π^B in the loss function) implements the same equilibrium behavior as the simple linear contract.

d. Show intuitively that a more elaborate contract makes it possible to implement the optimal policy under commitment. Consider the case in which the government can appoint a conservative central banker and give her a linear state-contingent inflation target.

18 International Policy Coordination

In a world of free trade and capital mobility, it is unsatisfactory to analyze monetary policy-making in a closed-economy setting. For the major economies, at least, monetary policies become strongly interdependent via international spillover effects on inflation and employment. These interdependencies create strategic interactions in policymaking, a theme fitting well with the main topic of this book. This chapter therefore introduces some of the main ideas from the large literature on international monetary policy coordination, which deals precisely with the strategic aspects of policymaking. This literature is extensively surveyed in Canzoneri and Henderson 1991, Currie and Levine 1993, Ghosh and Masson 1994, and Persson and Tabellini 1995. Accordingly, our choice of topics is highly selective and partly motivated by the desire to indicate parallels with arguments in previous chapters.

The international policy spillovers discussed in this chapter and in much of the literature operate through the exchange rate. Devaluation of a country's currency shifts demand in that country away from foreign goods toward domestically produced goods. This increases employment and inflation at home but has opposite effects abroad. With no coordination, these spillover effects are not internalized. Both countries may thus have an incentive to engage in so-called competitive devaluations to boost domestic employment; their policy responses to supply shocks also become distorted. In the chapter we discuss how these incentive problems interact with lack of domestic credibility and how to design monetary institutions accordingly.

Section 18.1 extends the simple static model of chapter 15 to a two-country setting, borrowing from Persson and Tabellini 1995 and 1996c. The resulting model focuses on international spillovers via the real exchange rate and is consistent with the reduced form of the more extensive models in Rogoff 1985b, or Canzoneri and Henderson 1988, 1991, among others. Each country has a prospective credibility problem in monetary policy of the same type as before, but it also has a latent incentive to engage in competitive devaluations, which implies a conflict over the real exchange rate.

Section 18.2 shows that the equilibrium of this model suffers from two sets of distortions in the absence of mechanisms for inducing international coordination and enhancing credibility. As in chapter 15, lack of domestic credibility implies that inflation is too high and too variable. On top of that, a stabilization bias also shows up as suboptimal fluctuations in real macroeconomic variables; this second distortion is due to individual central banks' failure to internalize international spillovers. We also reproduce a result demonstrated by Rogoff (1985b), namely that monetary policy coordination may be counterproductive if governments lack credibility. The argument appeals to the same kind of second-best reasoning as in chapter 12: coordination removes the second distortion but aggravates the domestic credibility problem.

In section 18.3, we ask how a country can sustain desirable policies. Here we follow the same approach as in chapter 17, highlighting the role of institutions in supporting desirable policies, and show that a pair of optimally chosen inflation targets removes the policy distortions. But we also discuss alternative institutions that may go some way toward implementing desirable policy outcomes. The discussion puts in perspective some historical experiments with multilateral regimes for pegging the exchange rate, such as the Bretton Woods agreement or the EMS.

18.1   A Simple Two-Country Model

Consider a two-country extension of the model used in the earlier chapters of this part. Each of the two countries is specialized in the production of a single good. As before, monetary policy can stabilize the economy in the short run but is subject to a credibility problem. Furthermore, policy has spillover effects abroad, and each country has an incentive to engage in competitive devaluations.

All variables are defined as rates of change. The change in the log of the real exchange rate, z, is defined as

$$z = s + p^* - p, \tag{18.1}$$

where s denotes the rate of nominal depreciation of domestic currency. We let letters without an asterisk denote variables in the "home country" and variables with an asterisk denote variables in the "foreign country." Thus, p and p^* denote producer price inflation rates in the two countries. We start by describing the home country. Consumer price index inflation π is given by

$$\pi = p + \alpha z, \tag{18.2}$$

where α is the share of foreign goods in the home country's consumption basket. Producer price inflation, in turn, satisfies

$$p = m + v. \tag{18.3}$$

As in chapter 15, m is the rate of money growth, and v is a demand, or velocity, shock. Employment x is determined by the same kind of expectations-augmented Phillips curve as in previous chapters,

$$x = \theta + (p - p^e) - \varepsilon, \tag{18.4}$$

the only difference being that the surprise term is now defined over producer price inflation rather than consumer price inflation. Thus p^e is the rationally expected value of p. The natural rate θ is observed by wage setters when wages are set (p^e is formed), whereas the supply shock ε is not. Relative prices of the two goods, z, depend on the relative supply of outside goods, $(x - x^*)$, in relation to the relative demand for each of the two goods. We assume that relative demand is an increasing function of z. The equilibrium real exchange rate satisfies

$$z = \delta(x - x^*) + \phi, \tag{18.5}$$

where $\delta > 0$ is the inverse (relative) demand elasticity of outside goods. A lower supply of home goods (lower x) thus creates relative excess demand for home goods and appreciates the real exchange rate (reduces z). We interpret ϕ as a speculative shock to the nominal exchange rate. By (18.1) and (18.5), the nominal exchange rate satisfies

$$s = \delta[x - x^*] + p - p^* + \phi.$$

The shock ϕ captures all forces moving the nominal exchange rate other than the current output and price fundamentals. In particular, ϕ may reflect expectations of future inflation and devaluations, fear of government defaults, financial crises, or other future events that may induce current capital outflows or inflows. It would thus make sense to relate the shock ϕ to variables determining the systematic incentives to inflate and engage in competitive devaluations. Such variables would be future values of the natural rate θ and of other parameters in the loss function (see below). These links could be made precise in a less stylized, multiperiod model. We assume that the structural shocks v, v^*, ε, ε^*, and ϕ are independently distributed with an expected value of zero.

The home country's central bank chooses the policy instrument m. Policy preferences are given by the loss function

$$L = \frac{1}{2}[\pi^2 + \lambda x^2 + \mu(z - \chi)^2], \tag{18.6}$$

where λ and μ are positive weights. We thus simplify by assuming that the inflation and employment targets are both zero: $\bar{\pi} = \bar{x} = 0$. Assuming that $\mathsf{E}(\theta) < 0$ creates a systematic inflation bias along the lines of that in the previous chapters. We assume that fluctuations in z are costly in their own right, even aside from their possible effects on inflation and employment. This may capture distributional effects, relocation costs, or financial repercussions of unexpected changes in international relative prices that do not show up in macroeconomic performance but nevertheless affect national welfare. It is assumed that the policy target χ for the real exchange rate is observable to wage setters but may be subject to shocks. Assuming that $\mathsf{E}(\chi) > 0$ is a simple (albeit ad hoc) way of introducing a systematic incentive to engage in competitive devaluations. Informally, we can interpret shocks to χ as capturing variations in the clout of the export industry, lobbying for higher profitability through a weaker exchange rate.[1]

The foreign country is modeled in exactly the same way as the home country, with the exception of z entering with an opposite sign. We assume that the parameters α, λ, and μ and the shock θ to the natural rate are identical across countries (that is, we assume $\theta = \theta^*$ throughout).[2] We allow, however, for cross-country differences in the real exchange rate targets ($\chi \neq \chi^*$) and in the variances of all shocks ($\sigma_\varepsilon^2 \neq \sigma_{\varepsilon^*}^2$, say) and for arbitrary covariance across pairs of structural shocks ($\sigma_{\varepsilon\varepsilon^*} \gtrless 0$, say).

Events in the model unfold as follows: (1) Observable shocks collected in the vector $\vartheta = (\theta, \chi, \chi^*)$ are revealed. (2) Private expectations (p^e, p^{*e}) are formed. (3) Structural shocks collected in the vector $\omega = (\varepsilon, \varepsilon^*, v, v^*, \phi)$ are revealed. (4) Policies (m, m^*) are simultaneously set. (5) Macroeconomic outcomes are realized.

18.2   Incentives

In this section, we show how decentralized policymaking may give rise to different policy distortions. To establish a normative benchmark for the analysis, we first study the hypothetical situation in which the two central banks can commit to cooperation ex ante.

18.2.1   Commitment and Cooperation

Suppose that before stage (1) in the model, the two central banks can commit themselves to optimal state-contingent policy rules for m and m^*, minimizing their joint losses, subject to the constraint that private expectations are formed rationally, given available information. Concretely, we thus seek the state-contingent monetary policy rules $(\Psi(\vartheta, \omega))$, $(\Psi^*(\vartheta, \omega))$ minimizing $\mathsf{E}(L + L^*)$, subject to $p^e = \mathsf{E}(p \mid \vartheta)$ and $p^{*e} = \mathsf{E}(p^* \mid \vartheta)$. ($\mathsf{E}(u)$ denotes the unconditional expectation of u, whereas $\mathsf{E}(u \mid \vartheta)$ denotes the conditional expectation of u, given the realization of ϑ.) The first-order condition for the optimal choice of $\Psi(\vartheta, \omega)$ in

---

1. An alternative (but perhaps equally ad hoc) way of modeling the incentive to engage in competitive devaluations would be to let z enter the right-hand side of the supply function (18.4) with a positive sign: a real depreciation would then lead to higher output growth (see Canzoneri and Gray 1985 and Martin 1995). As shown in problem 2 of this chapter, most of the results would apply to this different specification. Note also that a political interpretation of χ (as a result of lobbying by special interests rather than true social welfare) would not change our normative conclusions, because the equilibrium real exchange rate on average is always zero, under all institutional arrangements: this follows from the assumed neutrality of expected policy over real variables.

2. This assumption simplifies the algebra but entails no loss of generality as far as the main results are concerned.

an arbitrary state is obtained in the same way as in chapter 15 and can be expressed as:[3]

$$\pi(\vartheta, \omega) + \lambda(x(\vartheta, \omega) - \theta) + 2\mu\delta z(\vartheta, \omega) + \alpha\delta(\pi(\vartheta, \omega) - \pi^*(\vartheta, \omega)) = 0. \qquad (18.7)$$

As in chapter 15, the optimal policy rule trades off stabilization of domestic inflation around its target (the first term) and prices and employment around the natural rate (the second term). But here it also takes into account the effect of policy on domestic and foreign losses of induced changes in z, both directly (the third term) and indirectly through CPI inflation (the fourth term). Given the corresponding set of first-order conditions for $m^*(\vartheta, \omega)$ and the model structure, we can solve for the optimal policy rule in terms of underlying shocks. Straightforward but tedious algebra gives

$$m = \Psi(\vartheta, \omega) = \psi_\varepsilon \varepsilon - v + \psi_{\varepsilon\varepsilon^*}(\varepsilon - \varepsilon^*) - \psi_\phi \phi, \qquad (18.8)$$

where the ψs are complicated expressions in the model's parameters. As in the closed economy, the central bank thus stabilizes the price and output effects of domestic supply shocks somewhat (one can show that $0 < \psi_\varepsilon < 1$) and domestic demand shocks completely. It also adopts a more restrictive monetary policy, however, to stabilize asymmetric and negative foreign supply shocks, $\varepsilon - \varepsilon^* < 0$. Similarly, it meets speculative shocks against its own currency, $\phi > 0$, through a more contractionary policy to partially offset the real depreciation (one can also show that $\psi_\phi > 0$).

Notice an important aspect of the solution: none of the observable shocks in ϑ enters the optimal policy rule. The reason is familiar from chapter 15. Because these variables are observable, wage setters would anticipate any systematic policy response to them. Furthermore, the real variables in the model are neutral to expected policy. Central banks that indeed have the ability to make a binding commitment to a policy rule are therefore best off by ignoring these shocks, thus keeping expected and actual inflation anchored at zero.

18.2.2 Discretion and Noncooperation

Suppose now, more realistically, that ex ante commitments are infeasible. Furthermore, each central bank chooses its policy ex post, noncooperatively, at stage (4) of the model. The home country's central bank thus minimizes L with respect to $m(\vartheta, \omega)$, taking foreign

---

3. To derive (18.7) we have exploited the fact that in equilibrium and given our assumption that $\theta = \theta^*$, we have

$$\frac{\partial E(L + L^* \mid \vartheta)}{\partial p^e} = -\lambda\theta - \mu\delta(\chi^* - \chi).$$

The first term on the right-hand side is the marginal cost of reducing output below the natural rate; the second term captures the marginal welfare costs of a real depreciation (as p^e rises, z falls). See problem 1 of this chapter for a derivation.

policy $m^*(\vartheta, \omega)$, as well as private expectations $\mathsf{E}(p \mid \vartheta)$ and $\mathsf{E}(p^* \mid \vartheta)$, as given. The first-order condition for $m(\tau, \omega)$ can be written as

$$\pi(\vartheta, \omega) + \lambda(x(\vartheta, \omega) - \theta) + 2\mu\delta z(\vartheta, \omega) + \alpha\delta(\pi(\vartheta, \omega) - \pi^*(\vartheta, \omega))$$
$$= -\lambda\theta + \mu\delta\chi + \mu\delta z(\vartheta, \omega) - \alpha\delta\pi^*(\vartheta, \omega). \qquad (18.9)$$

The condition has been written such that its left-hand side coincides with the expression in (18.7). Thus, the right-hand side of (18.9) captures the forces that induce a deviation from the benchmark optimum. One of these, captured by the first term on the right-hand side of (18.9), is familiar. The credibility (ex post optimality) constraint makes the home central bank ignore the effect of its policy on private expectations formation: the ex post incentive to stimulate growth gives a permanent inflation bias—recall that $\mathsf{E}(\theta) < 0$. The individual rationality constraint associated with noncooperative policymaking also makes the home central bank ignore the spillover effects on the monetary union. The second term on the right-hand side, $\mu\delta\chi$, captures this effect and gives rise to a permanent competitive depreciation bias—recall that $\mathsf{E}(\chi) > 0$. Since the private sector correctly anticipates the incentives to expand employment and depreciate the real exchange rate, the equilibrium rate of expected inflation is higher without any effect on real variables.

To see this result more clearly, consider the following special case. All structural shocks appearing in ω are zero, and the real exchange rate targets coincide in the two countries: $\chi = \chi^* > 0$. In this symmetric situation, it is easy to see that, whatever the policy regime, both countries will pursue the same policies, $m(\vartheta, \mathbf{0}) = m^*(\vartheta, \mathbf{0})$, and have the same realized inflation, $\pi(\vartheta, \mathbf{0}) = \pi^*(\vartheta, \mathbf{0})$. Absent unobservable shocks, policies are perfectly anticipated. Thus inflationary expectations are correct, and by (18.4) employment in each country is at the natural rate $x(\vartheta, \mathbf{0}) = x^*(\vartheta, \mathbf{0}) = \theta$. By (18.5), it follows that the real exchange rate is constant, $z(\vartheta, \mathbf{0}) = 0$. Given these results, it follows immediately from (18.7) that inflation under commitment and cooperation would be zero:

$$\pi^{C,C}(\vartheta, \mathbf{0}) = 0.$$

In the regime of discretion and noncooperation, (18.9) in contrast implies

$$\pi^{D,N}(\vartheta, \mathbf{0}) = \frac{1}{1 + \alpha\delta}(-\lambda\theta + \mu\delta\chi). \qquad (18.10)$$

Inflation in the discretionary noncooperative regime is thus too high and too variable compared to the benchmark optimum. The inflation bias is more pronounced, the larger is the gap between the employment target (of zero) and the natural rate, and the larger is χ governing the incentive for a competitive devaluation.

Inflation is lower the higher is α, the share of foreign goods in the consumption basket, because an expansionary policy depreciates the exchange rate, which adds to the marginal cost of inflation. Thus more-open economies have a smaller incentive to inflate. Romer (1993) used this prediction in his well-known empirical study of the determinants of inflation. He found the prediction to hold. In his broad cross section of countries, larger openness, in the sense of this model, was indeed significantly associated with lower inflation. The result did not hold for the subsample composed of the richest countries, though. The aforementioned and more comprehensive study by Campillo and Miron (1997) subsequently confirmed these results.

The two remaining terms on the right-hand side of (18.9) capture a distorted stabilization of shocks, implying too much volatility not only in inflation but also in employment and real exchange rates. This stabilization bias arises because central bankers do not internalize the international spillover effects of their policies. How this modifies policymaking depends on the shocks.

To clarify the nature of the policy distortion relative to the benchmark, we consider another special case that has received considerable attention in the literature on international policy coordination. This special case assumes that all observable shocks in ϑ are zero, implying that no inflation bias is present. Furthermore, the only structural shocks are symmetric supply shocks $\varepsilon = \varepsilon^*$. Again, in both policy regimes, symmetry implies equal policies, $m(\mathbf{0}, \varepsilon) = m^*(\mathbf{0}, \varepsilon)$, equal employment in the two countries, and an unchanged exchange rate, $z(\mathbf{0}, \varepsilon)$. It follows that producer price inflation and CPI inflation coincide: $\pi(\mathbf{0}, \varepsilon) = p(\mathbf{0}, \varepsilon) = \pi^*(\mathbf{0}, \varepsilon) = p^*(\mathbf{0}, \varepsilon)$. Finally, the absence of an inflation bias means that expected inflation is zero. It follows from the Phillips curve (18.4) that $x(\mathbf{0}, \varepsilon) = x^*(\mathbf{0}, \varepsilon) = \pi(\mathbf{0}, \varepsilon) - \varepsilon$.

With these preliminaries in hand, (18.7) allows us to solve for the inflation rate in the benchmark optimum:

$$\pi^{C,C}(\mathbf{0}, \varepsilon) = \frac{\lambda}{1 + \lambda} \varepsilon.$$

This is exactly the same result as in the closed economy. Suppose we have a negative supply shock, $\varepsilon = \varepsilon^* > 0$. The optimal policy rule trades off the domestic employment benefits of expansionary policy against the domestic inflationary cost at a rate depending on the relative weight of these objectives in the loss function.

Under discretion and noncooperation, (18.9) implies

$$\pi^{D,N}(\mathbf{0}, \varepsilon) = \frac{\lambda}{1 + \lambda + \alpha\delta} \varepsilon.$$

Evidently, the equilibrium policy is not expansionary enough to reach the optimum. The central bank recognizes that expansionary policy has additional inflationary costs at home, because it depreciates the exchange rate. But it does not consider the fact that depreciation induces deflation abroad and thus worsens the trade-off the foreign central bank faces. Each central bank therefore attempts to export some of the necessary adjustments abroad and does not sufficiently stabilize employment. Because the other central bank has similar incentives, however, the effect on the exchange rate is nullified in equilibrium. The end result is thus that policy is too contractionary in both countries. This kind of argument was a common explanation in the monetary policy coordination literature of the early 1980s as to why noncoordinated policy responses in the major countries may have worsened the recession that followed the first two oil shocks.

18.2.3 Discretion and Cooperation

Suppose now that policymakers cannot make ex ante commitments to a policy rule. Nevertheless, they can find a way of enforcing a cooperative policy agreement at the ex post policymaking stage, that is, at stage (4) of the model. It may not immediately be clear why the latter is possible whereas the former is not, as there are also incentives to deviate from the cooperative agreement. Let us postpone that discussion to the next section, though.

Formally, the two policymakers set their policy instruments so as to maximize the sum of their loss functions, taking expected inflation $\mathsf{E}(p \mid \vartheta)$ and $\mathsf{E}(p^* \mid \vartheta)$ as given. The condition for optimal home money growth $m(\vartheta, \omega)$ in this regime of discretion and cooperation is

$$\pi(\vartheta, \omega) + \lambda(x(\vartheta, \omega) - \theta) + 2\mu\delta z(\vartheta, \omega) + \alpha\delta(\pi(\vartheta, \omega) - \pi^*(\vartheta, \omega))$$
$$= -\lambda\theta + \mu\delta(\chi - \chi^*). \tag{18.11}$$

It is obvious that the policy coincides with the benchmark optimum when the inflation bias problem is absent. That is, when $\theta = \theta^* = 0$ and $\chi = \chi^*$, then (18.11) and (18.7) coincide.

The ability to coordinate policy internationally is thus advantageous when the only problem in policymaking is the task of stabilizing structural shocks. The advantages of cooperation are not general, however. To demonstrate this, let us return to the case with symmetric observable shocks and zero structural shocks. Exploiting the symmetry of the solution, namely $x = \theta$, $z = 0$, and $\pi = \pi^*$, we can use (18.11) to write equilibrium inflation as

$$\pi^{D,C}(\vartheta, \mathbf{0}) = -\lambda\theta + \mu\delta(\chi - \chi^*). \tag{18.12}$$

Comparing (18.12) and (18.10), we see that $\pi^{D,C}(\vartheta, \mathbf{0})$ could be higher or lower than $\pi^{D,N}(\vartheta, \mathbf{0})$: under discretion and with no ω shocks, inflation could be higher and more volatile with cooperation than without it. As real output is exactly the same (since we assumed $\omega = \mathbf{0}$) in either case, the outcome under cooperation could be worse for both countries, for a very simple reason. We have seen that noncooperating central banks perceive an additional marginal effect of expanding m. For a given foreign monetary policy, an expansion of m generates a real depreciation of the country's currency. This can be either good or bad: on the one hand, higher prices of imported goods add to CPI inflation; hence, depreciation is costly. On the other hand, a depreciation could take the real exchange rate closer to the target χ, and this would be a benefit. When policymakers cooperate, however, they ignore this effect—or more correctly, they recognize and internalize the cost of the corresponding deflation and appreciation abroad. The perceived cost of expansionary policies could thus be lower than with noncooperation, in which case equilibrium inflation is higher with cooperation.

In other words, if $\pi^{D,N}(\vartheta, \mathbf{0}) < \pi^{D,C}(\vartheta, \mathbf{0})$, perceived exchange rate effects provide a disincentive to inflate: monetary policy without cooperation has a contractionary bias. That bias is a vice when coupled with international conflict over how much to stabilize structural shocks but becomes a virtue when coupled with domestic incentive problems, tied to the temptation of using monetary expansion to boost employment and real exchange rates. This insight is originally due to Rogoff (1985b). The parallels are obvious with our results in chapter 12 regarding the ambiguous benefits of cross-border cooperation in capital taxation.

Naturally, also allowing for the unobservable (structural) shocks, ω, adds to the benefits of cooperation. Cooperation is now also helpful in promoting more-efficient stabilization, though it could still aggravate the domestic credibility (or political) problems. Whether the benefits of cooperation outweigh the cost depends on whether the coordination problem is more serious than the credibility problem. An ex ante assessment of which regime would be preferable would have to rely on comparing the expected value of the loss (18.6) under specific assumptions about the distributions for ϑ and ω. Rogoff (1985b) took this ambiguity to imply that gains from cooperation can be ensured only under appropriate institutions. This point takes us right into the topic of the next section.

18.3 Institutions

Much of the early literature on international policy coordination stopped at the point of making the case for a coordinated policy. It is not enough to demonstrate that the policy outcome under cooperative policymaking is superior, though, as individual countries generally have incentives to deviate from the cooperative policy. The argument is therefore incomplete unless coupled with an argument as to how the suggested solution might be enforced. In his discussion of the main obstacles to successful international policy coordination, Frankel (1988) emphasized precisely the difficulty of enforcing cooperation. The literature has shown that reputational incentives may relax the short-run incentives to deviate from agreed-upon policy when policymakers repeatedly interact over time. The general argument is well-known and has been used earlier in the book. Canzoneri and Henderson 1991, chapters 4–5, and Ghosh and Masson 1994, chapter 8, well summarize its specific application to monetary policy coordination; hence we do not deal with it here. Instead, we follow the same approach as in chapter 17, discussing what institutions might enforce

desirable policy outcomes. We start in the abstract, by showing how a pair of optimal inflation contracts are capable of implementing the optimal policy rule under cooperation and
commitment. Next we discuss variations on this argument, attempting to link the theory to
real-world international monetary arrangements.

18.3.1   Optimal Linear Inflation Contracts

Assume that two central banks set policies independently under discretion at stage (4) in
the model of this chapter. But before stage (1) an "international principal" has the ability
to design institutions, thereby trying to implement a beneficial policy. We show that a
principal who can impose a performance contract on each of the two central banks can
indeed implement the optimal rule under commitment and cooperation.

Specifically, assume that each central bank is faced with a linear but state-contingent
performance contract in realized inflation of the same type as in section 15.3. First, consider
the national central bank. It thus obtains a transfer given by

$$T(\pi(\vartheta, \omega); \vartheta, \omega) = t_0(\vartheta, \omega) - t_1(\vartheta, \omega)\, \pi(\vartheta, \omega). \tag{18.13}$$

As in chapter 17, assume that the central bank minimizes the difference between its loss
function in (18.6) and the transfer in (18.13). It is easily verified that this modifies the
first-order condition under discretion and noncooperation (18.9) at one point only: an extra
term appears on the right-hand side, namely $(1 + \alpha\delta)\, t_1(\vartheta, \omega)$. It then follows directly from
(18.9) and (18.7) that the central bank indeed has the appropriate incentives to implement
the ex ante cooperative policy, if the marginal reward for low inflation is set at:

$$t_1(\vartheta, \omega) = \frac{1}{1 + \alpha\delta}[-\lambda\theta + \mu\delta\chi + \mu\delta z(\vartheta, \omega) - \alpha\delta\pi^*(\vartheta, \omega)], \tag{18.14}$$

where z and π^* are understood to be evaluated at the ex ante optimum. Solving for z and
π^* in the ex ante optimum, the marginal reward can be rewritten in terms of the structural
shocks:

$$t_1(\vartheta, \omega) = \frac{1}{1 + \alpha\delta}[-\lambda\theta + \mu\delta\chi - t_{\varepsilon^*}\varepsilon^* - t_{\varepsilon\varepsilon^*}(\varepsilon - \varepsilon^*) + t_\phi\phi]. \tag{18.15}$$

The coefficients t_{ε^*}, $t_{\varepsilon\varepsilon^*}$, and t_ϕ, like the ψ coefficients in (18.8), are complicated expressions
(with a likely positive sign) in the structural parameters.

The marginal reward in these expressions has an intuitive interpretation. The first two
terms balance the central bank's systematic incentives to expand employment and depreciate
the real exchange rate; the stronger these incentives, the stiffer the optimal penalty. This is
similar to the result in chapter 17 that the reward scheme should be tailored to state-dependent
incentives to inflate. The additional terms correct the stabilization bias deriving from the
failure of the home country's central bank to internalize the foreign spillover effects of its

policy. In particular, the reward should be weaker if the foreign country suffers a negative supply shock (ε^* positive), a less severe asymmetric supply shock (($\varepsilon - \varepsilon^*$) positive), or a speculation against its currency (ϕ negative). In these three cases, the impact of the shock is to generate foreign inflation $\pi^* > 0$ and foreign depreciation (home appreciation) of the real exchange rate $z < 0$. The home country's uncorrected noncooperative policy is then too contractionary, which calls for a weaker marginal reward for low inflation.

The incentive scheme for the foreign central bank should be structured in a similar way: the marginal reward $-t_1^*$ should satisfy

$$t_1^*(\vartheta, \omega) = \frac{1}{1 + \alpha\delta}[-\lambda\theta + \mu\delta\chi^* - t_\varepsilon\varepsilon + t_{\varepsilon\varepsilon^*}(\varepsilon - \varepsilon^*) - t_\phi\phi], \tag{18.16}$$

where $t_\varepsilon = t_{\varepsilon^*}$, and $t_{\varepsilon\varepsilon^*}$, t_ϕ are identical to the coefficients appearing in (18.15). As this expression reveals, the correction of the stabilization bias is symmetric across the two central banks. When it comes to the inflation bias, the country with a worse credibility problem or a stronger incentive to engage in competitive devaluations should face stronger average rewards for approaching its zero-inflation target. In general, the marginal rewards implementing the desired policy thus depend on the sign and size of the shocks.

18.3.2 Optimal Targeting

In the same way as in chapter 17, our linear model implies that state-contingent contracts over any pairs of nominal variables can implement the ex ante optimum policies.[4] As argued in that chapter and in Persson and Tabellini 1993 and 1995, however, complete state-contingent contracting is unlikely to be feasible. Simplicity and verifiability problems may require the penalties and rewards in any central bank incentive scheme to be state independent. One may therefore want to conjecture that the design of international monetary institutions must necessarily tackle a second-best problem, along the lines of the simple contracting solutions discussed in chapter 17. A moment's reflection, however, suggests that this conjecture is not necessarily correct. A recent paper by Jensen (1999) explains why in a model similar to the one in this chapter, except that central banks do not value exchange rate stability as such and do not have the incentives for competitive devaluations.

We can grasp the idea by inspecting the first-order conditions for the ex ante optimal cooperative policy (18.7) and the ex post optimal noncooperative policy (18.9). The stabilization bias, associated with the last two terms on the right-hand side of (18.9), appears because the home central bank sets policy ignoring its effects on the foreign central bank's

---

4. As discussed in chapter 17 and in Persson and Tabellini 1993, this equivalence also remains in more general settings; however, performance contracts written over variables other than π are more informationally demanding if there are nonlinearities in the constraints describing the economy.

loss function via spillover effects on the real exchange rate and foreign inflation. As these terms are linear, an appropriately structured reward that is quadratic in these variables could thus provide the right marginal incentives. Specifically, suppose that the transfer to the home central bank is given by

$$T(\pi, \pi^*, z) = t_0 - [t_\pi(\pi - \pi^B)^2 + t_{\pi^*}(\pi - \pi^*)^2 + t_z z^2]/2. \tag{18.17}$$

Thus, the central bank obtains additional rewards or penalties for stabilizing inflation around an absolute level, π^B, for stabilizing the difference between home and foreign inflation, and for stabilizing the real exchange rate.

Suppose, as before, that when faced with this scheme, the central bank minimizes the difference $L - T(\cdot)$ at stage (4) of the model. The optimal policy is then given by a condition identical to (18.9), except that the following expression also appears on the left-hand side:

$$t_\pi \frac{d\pi}{dm}(\pi - \pi^B) + t_{\pi^*}\left(\frac{d\pi}{dm} - \frac{d\pi^*}{dm}\right)(\pi - \pi^*) + t_z \frac{dz}{dm}$$

$$= -t_\pi(1 + \alpha\delta)\pi^B + (t_\pi(1 + \alpha\delta) + t_{\pi^*}(1 + 2\alpha\delta))\pi - t_{\pi^*}(1 + 2\alpha\delta)\pi^* + t_z\delta z.$$

Suppose further that the domestic incentive problems are not state dependent and are known at the institution design stage, in the sense that $\theta < 0$ and $\chi > 0$ are known constants. We can then find an incentive scheme implementing the ex ante cooperative policy by equating the above expression, term by term, with the expression on the right-hand side of (18.9). Straightforward algebra gives the following solution:

$$t_z = \mu > 0, \quad t_{\pi^*} = \frac{\alpha\delta}{(1 + 2\alpha\delta)} > 0$$

$$t_\pi = -\frac{\alpha\delta}{(1 + \alpha\delta)} < 0, \quad \pi^B = \frac{-\lambda\theta + \mu\delta\chi}{\alpha\delta} > 0. \tag{18.18}$$

The coefficients on relative inflation and the real exchange rate are thus positive, whereas the coefficient on $(\pi - \pi^B)^2$ is negative. That is, the scheme in (18.17) rewards the central bank for targeting foreign inflation, π^* and for achieving stability of the real exchange rate around 0. Because $t_\pi < 0 < \pi^B$, the central bank is also rewarded for deviating from π^B, that is, for keeping inflation below the threshold π^B. The combined effect of t_π and t_{π^*} makes the net marginal rewards independent of the level of π; control of the credibility problem instead relies on the inflation target π^B. The latter observation implies a constant marginal cost of inflation, mimicking the incentives in the optimal linear inflation contract in the same way as in the Svensson solution discussed in section 17.3. Here, however, π^B can be interpreted as an upper threshold, not as a target: the closer we get to π^B, the more the central bank is punished (since $\pi^B > 0$, whereas society's favored inflation rate is zero by assumption).

By the linearity of the model, other targeting schemes could also implement the optimum but are perhaps less intuitive, as they are not related to the underlying policy distortions in the same direct way. If the domestic incentive problem associated with the observable shocks θ and χ is state dependent (in the sense that θ and χ are also random variables), then the state-independent targeting approach discussed here can handle the average distortion associated with $\mathsf{E}(\theta) < 0$ and $\mathsf{E}(\chi) > 0$, although the inflation rate would still be too variable.

18.3.3   International Monetary Arrangements

The discussion above is quite abstract in assuming an institution design stage in which an international principal sets up some mechanism to induce desirable behavior among the central banks of individual countries. Can we think of plausible real-world counterparts to these theoretical constructions? Both the Bretton Woods system and the EMS did indeed grow out of an initial and lengthy period of multilateral negotiations—like the institution design stage of the model above. As already argued in chapter 17, both arrangements also had a codified set of prospective rewards and sanctions tied to the behavior of central banks—like the contractual transfers in the model.[5] Finally, both arrangements amounted to an explicit or implicit policy assignment among the member countries. The U.S. Fed and the German Bundesbank would direct their policies toward a domestic target, providing a nominal anchor to the system. The other central banks would instead have an adjustable exchange rate target vis-à-vis the central currency, whereby they would capture some credibility from the anchor country.

Why would these real-world international monetary arrangements involve the exchange rate as a key intermediate target, rather than a more symmetric arrangement? A possible answer is that the exchange rate is so easily monitored. However, exchange rate stability would work well as a coordination mechanism only if the two countries were subject to symmetric shocks. A classic paper by Canzoneri and Gray (1985) shows that under such circumstances, no international enforcement is needed to reach the cooperative optimum. In the model of this chapter, suppose that the supply shocks are symmetric, $\varepsilon = \varepsilon^*$, and that speculative shocks are absent, $\phi = 0$. Suppose further that the foreign country's central bank faces a strong enough penalty that it always chooses a policy keeping the nominal exchange rate constant, $s = 0$. Suppose finally that the home country has appropriate monetary institutions to take care of any domestic credibility problem. If the home country pursues an optimal noncooperative policy, taking the pegging of the foreign country into account, this

5. Examples were the obligation to inform and consult the International Monetary Fund or other countries before exchange rate changes, the conditional rights to draw on Special Drawing Rights to finance balance-of-payments deficits and the possibility of IMF conditionality, in the case of the Bretton Woods system; and the short-run credit facilities, the ties to other EC institutions like the Common Agricultural Policy, and the practice of not allowing full restoration to parity of overvalued currencies at realignments, in the case of the EMS.

is enough to implement the ex ante cooperative optimum. See Persson and Tabellini 1995 and problem 3 of this chapter for a formal derivation of this result. Problems 4 and 5 of this chapter discuss exchange rate pegs with asymmetric supply shocks.

When the conditions just mentioned are not satisfied, however, international enforcement of exchange rate stability is necessary. In the previous section, we have also seen that asymmetric shocks or speculative shocks call for exchange rate changes, in both the cooperative and the noncooperative solutions. This links well with the discussion in section 17.1. In line with the arguments in that section, it is natural to argue that the Bretton Woods system and the EMS are well described as mechanisms for implementing a simple rule with an escape clause. In normal circumstances, the central-currency country would pursue a restrictive monetary policy, and the exchange rate against the central currency would remain pegged. Temporary slippage of the monetary anchor and realignments would be allowed, however, under exceptional circumstances.[6]

In the model above, an international principal could implement such an escape clause equilibrium by replacing the contracts in (18.18) and (18.16) with a pair of nonlinear, state-independent contracts. Deviations from a fixed exchange rate $s = 0$ and a specific home country money growth rate m would be punished through a pair of noncontingent negative lump sum transfers (c^s, c^m). How often the escape clause would be triggered would depend on (c^s, c^m): the lower their value, the more realizations of ϑ and ω would induce the central banks at stage (4) to break the contract and pursue a decentralized, discretionary policy associated with an exchange rate realignment.

Such a multilateral peg system would be suboptimal relative to the hypothetical benchmark of the ex ante cooperative optimum; just how suboptimal would depend on the properties of the shocks. Frequent realizations of high values of θ, χ, and χ^*, low or negative correlation between ε and ε^*, or a high variance of the speculative shock ϕ would imply a frequent breach of the simple rule. With limited credibility problems of monetary policy, a central country with a great deal of credibility, relatively parallel macroeconomic development in the participating countries, and low capital mobility, however, the incentives to deviate from the simple rule would be small. Describing the 1950s and (most of) the 1960s under the Bretton Woods system as well as the 1980s under the EMS in just those terms is not too far-fetched.

Asymmetric or speculative shocks might make a monetary arrangement creating strong incentives for convergent monetary policies worse than no arrangement at all, however (see problems 4 and 5 of this chapter). Such shocks are therefore especially likely to put a strain on the simple rule and potentially on the whole mechanism. It is interesting to note that the

---

6. The formulation in Article IV of the Bretton Woods agreement, in which devaluations are allowed in situations of "fundamental disequilibrium" only is a classic example of a rule with an escape clause.

asymmetric shocks to the central-currency country indeed preceded eventual breakdowns of both the Bretton Woods system and the EMS: the U.S. fiscal shock in connection with the Vietnam war and Johnson's Great Society program and German unification, respectively. Increasing capital mobility among the relevant countries also preceded the breakdowns: the expansion of the Euromarkets in the late 1960s and the abolishment of capital controls inside the European Community in the late 1980s.

18.4 Discussion

The complete form of monetary policy cooperation would be full monetary union, with a single currency managed by a single central bank. The previous discussion suggests that full monetary union would be a suboptimal arrangement with large asymmetric shocks. If the cooperative optimum under commitment is infeasible, however, we face a second-best institution design problem, namely a choice between different suboptimal alternatives. In the last decade we have witnessed the 1992–1994 turmoil in European markets, followed by the effective breakup of the EMS and the subsequent creation of the European Monetary Union, as well as the Asian and Latin American crises in the late 1990s. We have also seen a very recent trend toward inflation targeting cum floating exchange rates in developing countries. These events suggest that the only relevant choice may be between floating rates (and appropriate domestic institutions) under high capital mobility and full monetary union. Moreover, we have confined our analysis to stabilization policies. Savings on transaction costs (Casella 1992) or microeconomic benefits in other areas of integration (Basevi, Delbono, and Denicoló 1990), may be additional gains from a full monetary union.

Whatever its motivation, a monetary union raises several interesting questions. First, under which circumstances should a single country join a monetary union? To the list that started with Mundell's (1961) high labor mobility and includes the predominant type of macroeconomic shocks, the recent literature on "optimum currency areas" has added the existence of large domestic incentive problems in monetary policy. But there is also an interesting systemic question: how does the design of the common central bank resolve conflicting interests of member countries and shape the union's monetary policy? In keeping with our approach in this book, these positive and normative questions could be productively analyzed by drawing on principal-agent theory and contract theory. A common central bank is an instance of common agency: this common agent serves multiple principals (the member countries) with partly common, partly conflicting interests. The analysis would have the following ingredients: participation constraints must be respected, particularly with asymmetric countries, and the specific collective decision-making mechanism must shape the policy outcome as well as the distribution of costs and benefits. Dixit (1998, 1999b) takes precisely this approach in discussing policymaking by the European Central Bank. Dixit's papers and others mentioned below suggest that the question of how to design a common central bank cannot be analyzed without paying close attention to the broader political and institutional framework in which the member countries interact.

18.5 Notes on the Literature

The model in this chapter has been adapted from Persson and Tabellini 1995 and 1996c, which in turn essentially developed a reduced form of the static models in Canzoneri and Henderson 1988 and 1991. It also encompasses the models in other well-known papers of the traditional policy coordination literature, such as Canzoneri and Gray 1985 and Rogoff 1985b.

Several of the papers in Bryant et al. 1988 discuss the empirical importance of international policy spillovers. Horne and Masson 1988 and Fischer 1988 survey a number of studies attempting to measure the gains from coordination empirically. Most studies seem to find relatively modest gains from coordination, a fact Canzoneri and Henderson 1991 attributes to the nature of the exercise: the studies allow for gains from joint stabilization but not from eliminating permanent conflicts. One might speculate that allowing for domestic incentive problems in empirical studies may give rise to larger prospective gains from coordination, but only to the extent that coordination serves to eliminate first-order losses due to these domestic incentive problems.

Miller and Salmon (1985) derived the Rogoff (1985b) result on the ambiguity of gains from cooperation in a dynamic policy game based on a two-country version of the sticky-price Dornbusch overshooting model. Van der Ploeg (1988) demonstrated the same result in a model in which the private sector in each country is depicted as a forward-looking and intertemporally maximizing representative agent. A related paradox can be found in Frankel and Rockett 1988, which demonstrates that the coordination of monetary policies may lead to worse outcomes than noncoordination if policymakers disagree on how the world economy works. Oudiz and Sachs (1985) found that when policymakers do not cooperate, having access to commitment may not improve the outcome in a model with a truly forward-looking private sector; this is explicated in a two-period model by Canzoneri and Henderson (1991, chap. 5). Similar results can also be found in Levine and Currie 1987 and in Currie, Levine, and Vidalis 1987. International policy cooperation can be counterproductive in the presence of other incentive problems, not just when there is lack of credibility. Tabellini (1990b) considers a model of fiscal policy in which terms-of-trade effects would generate benefits from coordination. See also Chang 1989 on this point. If a domestic political distortion leads to excessive fiscal deficits, however, then international cooperation exacerbates the effects of this distortion and may be counterproductive. Vaubel (1985) makes a similar point in a more general—though less formal—setting.

Obstfeld and Rogoff 1996 summarizes the new microfounded approach to open economy macroeconomics. This approach can be used to discuss proper welfare issues in policy coordination, as suggested by Corsetti and Pesenti (1998) and Ghironi (1998).

The volume edited by Bordo and Eichengreen (1993) contains many useful studies of the Bretton Woods system, analytical as well as descriptive. Useful collections of articles on the EMS and on monetary union in Europe can be found in de Cecco and Giovannini 1989 and Canzoneri, Grilli, and Masson 1992. Martin (1992) compares optimal monetary policy delegation in a monetary union and under flexible exchange rates. Giavazzi and Pagano (1988) discuss the EMS and the incentives created by the practice of not allowing full compensation for inflation differentials at EMS realignments. Cohen and Wyplosz (1989) specifically emphasize the EMS's role as a coordination device.

A large recent literature has studied positive models of monetary policy within the institutional framework of the European Central Bank (ECB). See in particular L. Svensson 1999b and the literature quoted therein. Besides the papers by Dixit (1998, 1999b) quoted above, earlier papers by Casella and Feinstein (1989), Alesina and Grilli (1992), and von Hagen and Süppel (1994) have studied collective decision making inside a common central bank that sets policy for several countries. More recent contributions on the incentive or collective choice problems faced by the ECB include Bottazzi and Manasse 1998, Gruner 1999, Lippi 1999, Muscatelli 1998, Sibert 1998, and Terlizzese 1999.

18.6 Problems

1. Commitment and cooperation

Consider a loss function $L(\pi, \pi^e; \vartheta, \omega)$ in which π denotes inflation (controlled directly by the policymaker), π^e denotes expected inflation (i.e., $\pi^e = \mathsf{E}[\pi \mid \vartheta]$), and ϑ is a vector of random shocks whose realization is observed before expectations are formed. ω is a vector of shocks whose realization is observed after expectations are formed but before π is chosen. Both ϑ and ω are i.i.d. over time (i.e., no autocorrelation).

a. Compute the optimal policy under commitment for this general loss function. To this end, minimize the loss function subject to the constraint $\pi^e = \mathsf{E}[\pi \mid \vartheta]$.

b. Apply this methodology to the loss function used in section 18.2.1 (commitment and cooperation). That is, derive (18.7). How would this result change if both countries were subject to a different observable shock, that is, $\theta \neq \theta^*$?

c. Compute the coefficients of the optimal policy rule in (18.8) under the assumption that $\theta = \theta^*$.

d. Going back to the general loss function, compute the equilibrium policy under discretion, where π^e is taken as given. How can one evaluate the equilibrium value of π^e?

e. Apply this methodology to the loss function used in section 18.2.3 (discretion and cooperation). That is, derive (18.11). How would this result change if $\theta \neq \theta^*$?

f. Apply this methodology to the loss function used in section 18.2.2 (discretion and non-cooperation). That is, derive (18.9). How would this change if $\theta \neq \theta^*$?

2. Output directly dependent on the real exchange rate

This problem is based on Canzoneri and Gray 1985. Consider a version of the model presented in section 18.1 with symmetric shocks $\varepsilon = \varepsilon^*$ and $\theta = \theta^*$, but suppose that $\mu = \phi = v = 0$, and replace the output equation (18.4) with

$$x = \theta + (p - p^e) + \rho z - \varepsilon, \quad \text{with} \quad 0 < \rho < \frac{1}{2}. \tag{18.19}$$

a. Suppose $\varepsilon = 0$ and $\theta < 0$. Show that inflation is zero under commitment and cooperation and positive under discretion and noncooperation (i.e., $\pi^{D,N}(\theta, 0) > \pi^{C,C}(\theta, 0) = 0$). Verify that (1) the inflation bias is more acute the larger is μ—that is, the larger the incentive for a competitive devaluation, and (2) inflation is lower the higher is α (the share of foreign goods in the consumption basket).

b. Suppose central banks coordinate but cannot commit to a policy. If $\varepsilon = 0$ and $\theta < 0$, show that inflation is higher than under no coordination and discretion (i.e., $\pi^{D,C}(\theta, 0) > \pi^{D,N}(\theta, 0)$) iff $\alpha > \rho$.

c. Suppose $\varepsilon > 0$ and $\theta = 0$. Show that the cooperative solution under commitment leads to the same inflation rate as in a closed economy with commitment, or $\pi^{C,C}(\theta, 0) = \lambda\varepsilon/(1+\lambda)$. Show that noncooperative and discretionary policies are too contractionary in equilibrium (i.e., $\pi^{D,N}(\theta, 0) < \pi^{C,C}(\theta, 0)$) iff $\alpha > \rho$.

3. Exchange rate pegs with symmetric supply shocks

Consider a version of the model in section 18.1 in which the countries are subject only to a symmetric supply shock, that is, $\varepsilon^* = \varepsilon$ and $\phi = \theta = \theta^* = v = v^* = 0$. Moreover, set

$\mu = 0$. Before any other event takes place, the home country (but not the foreign country) imposes a nonlinear performance contract on its central bank. The contract is defined over the change in the nominal exchange rate, s:

$$T(s) = \begin{cases} B & \text{if } s = 0 \\ B - c & \text{otherwise,} \end{cases}$$

where c is a positive number and B is chosen so as to satisfy the agent's participation constraint. Thus if the home central bank abandons the pegged exchange rate, it faces a prohibitive cost, provided that c is high enough. The timing of events is as follows: (1) Society commits to a contract in the home country. (2) Expectations m^e and m^{e^*} are formed. (3) The shock ε is realized. (4) The foreign policymaker chooses m^*. (5) The home central bank chooses m. (6) Macroeconomic outcomes are realized.

a. Show that the performance contract will make the home central bank choose the same money growth as the foreign policymaker to keep the exchange rate fixed, that is, $m(\varepsilon) = m^*(\varepsilon)$.

b. Compute the first-best solution (cooperative solution under commitment) $m^C(\varepsilon)$.

c. Show that when the home country commits to the above-mentioned contract $T(s)$, the foreign country implements this first-best cooperative outcome even in the noncooperative Nash equilibrium.

d. Show that the same result holds when employment is also affected by a symmetric observable shock $\theta = \theta^*$ and the foreign central bank can commit ex ante to a policy $m^*(\theta, \varepsilon)$.

4. Exchange rate pegs with asymmetric supply shocks

Suppose that the two countries are hit by common shocks of opposite sign (correlation -1), $\varepsilon = -\varepsilon^* > 0$, and that $\mu = \theta = \theta^* = 0$. The economy is otherwise similar to that in section 18.1.

a. Show that the cooperative equilibrium implements an inflationary policy ($\pi^C > 0$) in the home country and a deflationary policy ($\pi^{*C} < 0$) in the foreign country.

b. Compute the noncooperative equilibrium and show that the policy of the home country is still inflationary but too contractionary ($\pi^C > \pi^D > 0$) whereas that of the foreign country is still deflationary but too expansionary ($\pi^{*C} < \pi^{*D} < 0$).

c. Suppose that the home country imposes an exchange rate peg on its central bank as described in problem 3. Then show, first, that this policy leads to deflation (instead of inflation) in the home country. Next show that the levels of deflation are higher in absolute terms than the inflation in both the cooperative and noncooperative equilibrium ($-\pi^{erp} > \pi^C > \pi^D$). Finally, show that (1) the home country performs worse not only than in the cooperative equilibrium, but also than in the noncooperative equilibrium and (2) the foreign country still deflates, but less than in the cooperative equilibrium ($\pi^{*C} < \pi^{*erp} < 0$). Assume that $\alpha\delta < \frac{1}{2}$ throughout.

5. Endogenous exchange rate pegs

Consider the two-country model with symmetric supply shocks of problem 3 and assume $\mu = 0$. Suppose that the home country can now implement any change it wishes in the nominal exchange rate s by writing a contract $T(s; \hat{s})$:

$$T(s; \hat{s}) = \begin{cases} B & \text{if } s = \hat{s} \\ B - c & \text{otherwise,} \end{cases} \tag{18.20}$$

where c is a positive number and B is chosen so as to satisfy the agent's participation constraint. The foreign country, on the other hand, can implement only a discretionary policy.

a. Show that fixing $\hat{s}$ automatically determines the difference in money growth ($m - m^*$) and the real exchange rate z.

b. Show that the optimal level of $\hat{s}$ is zero if the home country can commit only to a constant exchange rate peg.

c. Assume that the home country can write a contract with its central bank that makes $\hat{s}$ contingent on ε at stage (1) (the timing is defined in problem 3). Under this assumption, show that $\hat{s} = k\varepsilon$, where $k < 0$, that is, the home country enforces a depreciation of its currency when $\varepsilon < 0$ and an appreciation when $\varepsilon > 0$.

d. Show that by making its exchange rate peg conditional on ε, the home country improves upon the cooperative outcome.

19 What Next?

This book has discussed a growing literature that tries to explain economic policy in modern democracies, addressing both the common features of observed policies and their variations across time and place. The importance of this goal is beyond doubt, at least to us. Given the difficulty of this task, the reader can expect to find only preliminary and tentative answers. But is it worth trying? Is the task of explaining economic policy feasible?

As mentioned in chapter 1, we share the first part of the title of our book with Alt and Chrystal 1983. Their book was written at a time when most theorists were quite pessimistic about the research collected under the label *Political Economics,* namely the use of economic methodology for studying policymaking in a democracy (recall the discussion in chapter 2). The ambitious research program already developed by the public choice school was an important exception, but many looked upon this program with skepticism. By now, the tide has changed. New generations of researchers in mainstream economics are less intimidated by negative results in social choice and have absorbed the basic ideas in public choice. Moreover, the methodology of noncooperative game theory has made a solid mark in political science. American congressional politics has come a long way, but similar methods are also penetrating other subfields, such as comparative politics. We are witnessing the beginning of a true integration of different research traditions in economics and political science.

If the task of explaining economic policy is feasible, it is interesting to speculate which way research on political economics might and should go next. This last chapter addresses this question, splitting it into two parts. We first discuss a number of positive questions, pointing out important topics neglected so far on which progress seems to be within reach. Then we review some problems with the analytical methods developed in the book and used in the literature. Even though these problems are difficult and our understanding is limited, we discuss some directions in which progress seems possible.

19.1   Some Positive Questions

The reference list is testimony of a large amount of research developing positive models of economic policy in the last fifteen years. Although some policy areas have received considerable attention, other important topics remain largely unexplored.

19.1.1   Specific Policy Issues

A glaring omission in the literature is the determination of labor market policies and institutions. Regulation of the labor market, the generosity and structure of unemployment insurance, and other labor market programs are certainly major factors behind the widespread unemployment we observe in many parts of the world. Unemployment and labor market programs also differ a great deal across time and place. Furthermore, it is hard to think of a single policy area—with perhaps the exception of capital taxation—that is as strongly associated with politics. Yet very little formal work in political economics attempts to explain those policies and the resulting outcomes. In chapter 6, we pointed to the recent promising work by Saint-Paul (1996) and Hassler et al. (1998). More such work should follow.

Another important topic is economic growth and its interaction with the regulatory environment. A sizeable literature has dealt with the nexus of income distribution, political stability, and economic growth. But other issues of primary importance remain unexplored. Recent contributions in macroeconomics and growth have focused on skill-biased technical change, largely inspired by the information technology (IT) revolution. The importance and consequences of this phenomenon are still in dispute. Some observers argue that its effects differ across countries, contrasting increased unemployment in continental Europe with increased income inequality in Anglo-Saxon countries. Whatever the value of this specific hypothesis, it is clear that large-scale technical change—like the IT revolution, or the introduction of the automobile, and electricity, and steam engines before that—creates great opportunities for societies to raise their standard of living. These opportunities challenge vested interests, however, which want to protect the rents associated with their specific skills or capital. Whether these vested interests succeed in blocking the change by discriminatory regulation or taxation is largely a political issue but has received almost no attention in the formal literature. In chapter 14, we pointed to recent research by Krusell and Rios-Rull (1996) and Aghion and Howitt (1999). More such work should follow.

In analyzing these issues, the few existing papers have taken a very simple view of the political process relying on the median-voter model. This approach, however, obscures the essence of the problem, namely the large stakes associated with the vested interests of "insiders": those with secure jobs or the owners of specific factors of production in traditional sectors with old skills and old technologies. Future work on these issues ought to explore the role of special-interest politics, using some of the tools proposed in this book.

A third area of research with potentially high payoffs is the analysis of economic reform. Even though we have not made this distinction clear, some policy decisions entail radical reforms of the status quo, whereas others require only marginal changes. In practice, this seems to be an important distinction: certain groups or key players often have de facto veto rights, and radical reforms of the status quo are politically feasible only if losing veto players can be compensated. But what is the source of this holdup power? How does it depend on the political system? And how can the losers credibly be promised a compensation? Despite interesting recent research (for instance, Roland 1999 on economies in transition, and the contributions surveyed in Drazen 1999), we have only vague answers to these questions.

19.1.2   Theory and Measurement

The gap between theory and evidence is a final weakness of the existing literature. As we have already indicated throughout the book, there is not a great deal of empirical work on these positive issues, and when there is empirical work, its ties to the underlying theory are often loose. For instance, the empirical analysis of budgetary procedures mentioned in chapter 7, or of central bank independence discussed in chapter 17, has attracted much attention in the academic literature as well as in applied policy debate. But the indicators and tests in this empirical work are not tied well to the extensive form games or theoretical predictions in theoretical work. Ideally, we would like more empirical work "derived from theory" as opposed to "informed by theory."

This may be very hard to achieve because of some inherent difficulties. First of all, it is hard to develop direct, quantitative measures of political institutions. Moreover, as political events are rare, serious time-series studies of a single political jurisdiction are seldom feasible. Pure cross-sectional studies of average outcomes in some time period, on the other hand, run into identification or specification problems. Convincing empirical work requires a combined analysis of time-series and cross-section data. Although economists and political scientists have done plenty of such work, they have not yet taken advantage of the modern estimation techniques for data in the form of dynamic heterogenous panels.[1] Nor has the search for "natural experiments," which has become common practice in one branch of modern labor economics, taken root in political economics.[2]

19.1.3   Comparative Politics

In part 3 we revealed our enthusiasm for a research agenda on comparative politics that would encompass a theory-based search for regularities in the relation between political systems and policy outcomes. Political constitutions are viewed as incomplete contracts laying down the rules for how to appoint political decision makers on behalf of the voters and how to allocate decision-making authority, or control rights, among them. Different extensive form games can then capture the essence of these rules.

A possible argument against this kind of research parallels the critique of modern game theory applied to industrial organization: "the possible assignments of control rights is infinite, and you can prove anything with extensive form game theory." We do not find this criticism too damaging for a positive theory of policy.[3] Constitutional rules are well

---

1. See, for instance, Baltagi 1995, Pesaran and Smith 1995, and Phillips and Moon 1999.

2. See, however, Besley and Case 1995a, Levitt and Snyder 1997, and Pande 1999.

3. A normative approach to institutional reform would be more problematic, however. Before suggesting the design of institutions, a clear stance must be taken on the source of the contractual incompleteness. Laffont 1999 advocates an alternative approach, more solidly based on implementation games.

established, both legally and historically. Different democracies display rich variation in how they carry out elections and allocate political control. A wealth of historical, descriptive, and legal studies document these differences. In other words, the rules—for proposing, amending, or vetoing policy proposals, for forming or dissolving governments, or for electing political representatives—that define a particular extensive form game need not rely on the researchers' imagination. They can and should be given a solid empirical foundation.

Political scientists have done a great deal of analytical work on comparative politics, theoretical as well as empirical. But that work is typically confined to consequences or correlations within the domain of the political system: certain electoral systems are associated with a larger or smaller number of "effective parties," presidential systems create weaker incentives for party discipline compared to parliamentary systems, and certain rules for dissolving governments may be more prone to generate minority governments, for example. In parts 2, 4, and 5, we mentioned some work by economists on institutions and economic policy, for example, on the correlation between budget processes, electoral systems, and the propensity to run budget deficits.

What is lacking is a systematic investigation of how commonly adopted constitutional arrangements shape policy choices. In part 3, we focused on how different electoral rules and different political regimes, in their crudest form, might manifest themselves in different levels and compositions of government spending, including wasteful spending that benefits only politicians. We also hinted at the possibility that different electoral rules might give different incentives for electoral cycles. This kind of investigation sets a very interesting agenda for future research.

Part 3 was confined to the government-spending side of public finance. Similar tensions between broad versus narrow benefits in the electorate and benefits for the politicians also arise in tax and regulatory policy, for example. Moreover, electoral rules and political regimes differ in finer dimensions than the crude classifications made in part 3. This suggests more-specific questions of great importance. Does the recently adopted presidential line item veto in the United States reduce or increase special interests' power to extract policy favors? Could appropriate electoral reform address the lack of political accountability that seems evident in countries like Japan, Italy, and Belgium? Would different rules for government dissolution or formation give more stability and longer horizons for policymakers in those parliamentary systems plagued by recurrent government crises? What constitutional reform in Russia and some Latin American countries could break the current stalemate between different political actors and at the same time allow the voters to better control widespread corruption?

It is essential that new research on comparative politics be not only empirically *motivated,* but also empirically *oriented.* Preliminary empirical results are encouraging. We mentioned the cross-sectional study by Persson and Tabellini (1999b) that discovered that presidential regimes have much smaller governments than parliamentary regimes, exactly as in the theory of chapter 10. Do these findings extend to the growth of government in panel data? Can empirical support also be found for the other predictions of the same theory regarding the composition of spending? Only more research can tell. Convincing evidence also requires new and extensive data collection regarding political institutions from which to construct empirical counterparts of theoretical concepts, as with measures of separation of powers and legislative cohesion across political systems.

19.2 Analytical Issues

The main subject of this book is not empirical work, however. We have tried to provide a comprehensive theoretical treatment of economic policymaking in a number of areas, relying on a set of common tools. As described in chapter 1, however, these tools are associated with very different modeling strategies. Partly this reflects the fact that policy issues are inherently different: in chapter 2 we spelled out an argument for the obvious conclusion that one must adapt the modeling to the policy problem at hand. Mainly, however, the different modeling strategies just reflect our ignorance about the best way of thinking about a number of difficult issues. In the following, we outline some of the problems where our ignorance reveals itself most clearly.

19.2.1 Pre- versus Postelection Politics

In the book, we have intermittently dealt with models of preelection politics, in which the candidates make binding policy choices during the course of the electoral campaign, and models of postelection politics, in which incumbents make policy choices once in office. From the perspective of realism, the latter model is most plausible: most policies are designed and decided upon by incumbent administrations and legislatures. Equally clearly, however, promises in the electoral campaign often manifest themselves in subsequent policy choices and constrain what actions elected officials are willing to take. Empirical work on this subject is difficult to do but available studies indicate that perhaps 30–40% of electoral promises are kept (see Harrington 1992).

It is thus somewhat schizophrenic to study either extreme: where promises have no meaning or where they are all that matter. To bridge the two models is an important challenge. Two possible channels through which preelection promises may interact with postelection choices are information transmission and reputation.

With asymmetric information, preelectoral announcements could play a role in information transmission, as in models of regulatory agencies (Baron and Myerson 1982, Laffont and Tirole 1993). Harrington (1993) studies a model in which politicians are office-motivated and voters are asymmetrically informed about the politicians' intended policies. His model has equilibria in which politicians find it optimal to reveal information truthfully to voters about their type (intended policies), as this enhances their chances of reelection. Moreover, if elected, politicians stick to these promises. Schultz (1999b) studies a similar problem with partisan politicians and uninformed voters. There are no electoral announcements, but the incumbent's policy choice becomes a signal of his knowledge before an upcoming election.

Austen-Smith and Banks (1989) instead consider a two-period model of electoral accountability under moral hazard. Even though there is no asymmetric information, in some equilibria the voters' strategy of reelecting the incumbent depends on the observed policy outcome relative to the platform upon which the incumbent was initially elected. This reputational mechanism disciplines the incumbent and creates an incumbency effect, despite all politicians' being identical.

These approaches make strong assumptions about the voters' sophistication and rationality. Nevertheless, they contain interesting ideas and certainly deserve further attention. Both may lack an essential ingredient, however: neither makes any distinction between individual candidates and political parties. This is a common feature of practically all the formal analysis of political equilibria, but it is an unfortunate one. Take the reputational mechanism, for example. The important aspect of reputation building might apply to the party's collective reputation, rather than to the politician's individual reputation. This is certainly the case in most parliamentary regimes, and especially in those with proportional elections. A serious study of these issues in the context of policymaking requires a model of parties' internal organization that can be embedded in a broader model of policy choice.

A more careful study of political parties may thus be a crucial step in political economics, perhaps even more crucial than the step in microeconomics of developing a theory of the firm. Some promising papers have recently been written on this topic. Roemer 1999 formulates an interesting model in which the party decisions reflect the internal struggle between three groups of party members with different goals, namely reformists, militants, and opportunists. Caillaud and Tirole 1998 and 1999 see the party as an intermediary, providing information to uninformed voters. According to this approach, for instance, the party's credibility in the voters' eyes depends on its internal governance structure and in particular on the internal balance of power between ideological and opportunistic party members.

19.2.2 Opportunistic versus Partisan Politicians

We have also entertained different assumptions about the politicians' motives. Most often, we have assumed politicians to be self-interested and opportunistic, but we have frequently taken their objectives to be partisan and indistinguishable from those of specific groups of voters. Again, it is not satisfactory to leap back and forth between such different assumptions. From a methodological point of view, we prefer the former assumption. Yet the partisan model also captures an important feature. The tension between opportunism and partisanship reflects our imperfect understanding of ideology in politics. Ideology is obviously important, but it is far from clear how this concept relates to formal models of policy choice. To say that ideology is a feature of voters' preferences and that legitimate policy choices must therefore be made in accordance with these preferences is somewhat too simplistic.

One possibility is to view ideology as a specific set of beliefs about how the world operates, say, with regard to the consequences of policy. Piketty (1995) follows this approach: he studies an imperfect-information model of redistributive policy in which all citizens agree on the goal of policy but learn about the disincentive effects of taxation from their immediate environment. Interestingly, the economy may converge to an equilibrium with different self-confirming ideologies (beliefs) in different groups.

Another possibility is to view ideology as a "brand name" that facilitates delegation when there is uncertainty about upcoming policy issues. In particular, the brand name could be a coordination device simplifying the task of a set of politicians offering a credible coalition to the voters in the electoral campaign, when policy is to be decided by postelection bargaining. Morelli (1998) pursues this approach in a citizen-candidate model with a party formation stage among partisan politicians followed by legislative bargaining among the parties represented in the legislature. Cox's (1987b) idea of the "efficient secret" also suggests a link between ideology, brand name, and coalition formation. Cox's fascinating book accounts for the conversion of the English Parliament in the mid-nineteenth century from a set of individual politicians, catering to splintered local interests, to national parties, offering clear policy platforms for alternative governments. These are powerful ideas. Once more, they lead to the conclusion that we need a workable theory of the party and its internal organization.

19.2.3 Voters

We have made sharp assumptions not only about politicians but also about voters. Empirically oriented political scientists have studied voting behavior extensively. It is far from clear whether our modeling is consistent with their results. Typically, we have assumed voters to be selfish, considering only their own economic well-being when casting their vote. This may be the wrong starting point, however, and it seems to confront us head on with the paradox of voting (Downs 1957). Why do these selfish voters bother to vote at all? If voters are not selfish when expressing their vote and instead act on the basis of their ideology or a sense of justice, many of the results discussed in this book could be questioned and the distinction between partisan and opportunistic politicians may lose some relevance.

We must cling to the hope that even though we do not fully understand the motives for voting, our analysis is still valid when it comes to the voters' marginal choices. The argument is analogous to applications of price theory (see Grofman 1996 for a similar argument). As economists, we may not be well equipped to understand why people consume alcoholic beverages, but we may still be able to predict accurately what happens to the consumption of wine versus beer when their relative price changes. Furthermore, a strong idelogical component may very well determine whether and how citizens vote; this component could well differ across different groups of voters. The probabilistic voting model used so extensively in the book can be interpreted precisely in this way, allowing for different turnout rates and different ideological attachments within different groups of voters. It clearly needs better microfoundations, however. Such microfoundations might be built by facing up to the challenges outlined above, namely by studying ideology as a coordination device among voters and political parties alike. Coordination among voters is likely to be particularly important when there are more than two parties. This is indeed the view taken in Cox's (1997) comprehensive analysis of strategic voting under different electoral rules.

We have also typically assumed voters to be well informed about candidates and policy alternatives they face, even though this flies in the face of extensive evidence that some voters ignore even the most basic political facts. In some contexts, as in chapters 3, 7, and 14, we have allowed for uninformed voters who are impressionable and can easily be swayed by the candidates' political campaign messages. Although this modeling is suggestive, it too suffers from incomplete microfoundations. How do voters obtain their information? And why are some voters informed while others are not? An obvious answer to the first question is that voters obtain their information from the media. Strömberg (1998a) sets up a formal model of politics and the media. He then shows that the interaction between electoral competition and competition between profit-maximizing media provides an answer to the second question. Optimal behavior by the media tends to bias the information—and hence, the policy outcome—toward groups that are attractive for advertisers. This is a promising approach warranting further research. More generally, neglecting the information aggregation aspect of politics may be a serious omission (see Piketty 1999 for a survey).

19.2.4   Interest Groups

Throughout the book, the activities and behavior of organized interest groups have received much attention. In the models we have studied, lobbies attempt to influence policy or the outcome of elections through their contributions. Interest groups engage in other political activities, however, that are neglected in this book and in much of the literature.

One important role interest groups play is to provide information to policymakers or voters. Austen-Smith (1997) surveys the literature regarding the former, whereas Grossman and Helpman (1999) show that interest groups can influence uninformed voters by endorsing candidates or policies. Another role for interest group endorsements is to induce voters to coordinate their votes on the same party. This may be particularly important in contexts involving many parties, some of which may risk losing all their seats because of a minimum threshold requirement. A convincing modeling of these issues probably requires a workable model of interest groups' internal structure, however.

Interest groups also influence policy through organized protests and strikes. This important form of political participation is not well understood in the formal literature. Why do voters at large often sympathize with interest groups who disrupt social and economic activities? Why would a government attempting to restrain such disruptive activities risk its popularity rather than strengthen it? One possible answer is, once more, related to ideology. Another answer might be that protests signal the intensity of group preferences, and other groups want to retain the possibility of signaling their own discontent in the future if and when their interests are badly hurt. Whatever the answer, this issue clearly deserves more attention than it has received (see, however, Lohmann 1994 and 1998).

Less formal work exists on the interaction between lobbying and other types of political activity. In chapter 7, we gave an example of how lobbies attempt to influence the outcome of legislative bargaining by interacting with individual legislators. This is a difficult problem but one deserving further study. It may help us understand the seemingly very different patterns of interest group activity in different political systems. In the United States, for example, lobbying is quite fragmented, as interest groups interact mainly with individual lawmakers. In Europe, on the other hand, interest groups are generally larger and have more symbiotic relations with political parties. This pattern could reflect the differences across political regimes emphasized in chapter 10: presidential-congressional regimes have greater separation of proposal powers among individual legislators, whereas the institutions of parliamentary regimes produce legislative cohesion in the form of stable coalitions within and across parties. The recent work by Bennedsen and Feldmann (1999) takes an approach in this direction.

Finally, an obvious but fundamental question is how interest groups solve their internal free-rider problem and why some economic interests are better organized than others. Despite the importance of this question, the formal literature has made little progress since Olson raised it a long time ago (1965). One interesting possibility is that the government itself helps groups solve this free-rider problem through regulation or other policy actions that involve the interest groups actively in the design of the resulting programs. Mulligan and Sala-i-Martin (1999b) formalize this conjecture in the context of pensions and early retirement legislation (see chapter 6). This idea suggests other interesting questions. What do politicians gain from the formation of active pressure groups? And how can politicians preserve the loyalty of interest groups once they have been formed? Once more, we are led to a nexus of the issues raised above, about the meaning of ideology, the motivation of politicians, and the role of political parties.

19.3   Concluding Remarks

Much remains to be done in the coming years, but we are convinced that the research agenda sketched out above is a feasible one. In the last few years, different research programs in political economics have begun to converge. As researchers are being exposed to other traditions, they are acquiring a broader outlook and a more versatile set of analytical tools. The sharp boundary that used to exist between economics and political science is becoming fuzzier, as researchers on both sides learn from each other. But although the political economics—rational choice—approach is becoming more mainstream in economics as well as in political science, a considerable number of skeptics remain within the more traditional camps of both fields.

A good way of convincing these skeptics is to show persuasive evidence in favor of tightly specified models. Another is to show that theory-based research helps discover new empirical regularities. Examples of regularities discovered in the last fifteen years include the partisan cycle in output, the negative correlation between central bank independence and inflation, the negative effect of inequality on growth, and the stark difference in the size of government across different political regimes. Even though the robustness of these findings and their ultimate explanations are still subject to debate, they have drawn the attention to important economic phenomena and their interaction with political and social issues.

The task ahead is to demonstrate that the approach of political economics holds water, theoretically and empirically. The jury is still out, and a unanimous verdict is lacking. As advocates of the approach, we are confident that it will ultimately win approval. A strong sense of optimism is indeed one of our reasons for writing this book. Many of the remaining problems are certainly difficult, but then, easy problems are rarely exciting. A sense of excitement for the task is another of our reasons for writing this book. We hope that whoever has read this far also has gotten a sense of optimism and enthusiasm. If such a reader is induced to think hard about some of the remaining problems, we have achieved our goal.

References

Aghion, P., and Bolton, P. 1990. "Government domestic debt and the risk of a default: A political-economic model of a strategic role of debt." In R. Dornbusch and M. Draghi, eds., *Public Debt Management: Theory and History*. Cambridge: Cambridge University Press.

Aghion, P., and Bolton, P. 1998. "Incomplete social contracts." University College, London. Mimeographed.

Aghion, P., and Howitt, P. 1999. *Endogenous Growth Theory*. Cambridge: MIT Press.

Aidt, T. 1998. "Political internalization of economic externalities and environmental policy." *Journal of Public Economics* 69: 1–16.

Alesina, A. 1987. "Macroeconomic policy in a two-party system as a repeated game." *Quarterly Journal of Economics* 102: 651–78.

Alesina, A. 1988. "Credibility and political convergence in a two-party system with rational voters." *American Economic Review* 78: 796–805.

Alesina, A., and Bayoumi, T. 1996. "The costs and benefits of fiscal rules: Evidence from U.S. states." Working paper no. 5614, National Bureau of Economic Research, Cambridge, Mass.

Alesina, A., and Cukierman, A. 1990. "The politics of ambiguity." *Quarterly Journal of Economics* 105: 829–50.

Alesina, A., and Drazen, A. 1991. "Why are stabilizations delayed?" *American Economic Review* 81: 1170–88.

Alesina, A., Easterly, W., and Baqir, R. 1997. "Public goods and ethnic divisions." Working paper no. 6009, National Bureau of Economic Research, Cambridge, Mass.

Alesina, A., and Gatti, R. 1995. "Independent central banks: Low inflation at no cost?" *American Economic Review Papers and Proceedings* 85: 196–200.

Alesina, A., and Grilli, V. 1992. "The European central bank: Reshaping monetary politics in Europe." In M. Canzoneri, V. Grilli, and P. Masson, eds., *Establishing a Central Bank: Issues in Europe and Lessons from US*. Cambridge: Cambridge University Press.

Alesina, A., Hommes, R., Hausmann, R., and Stein, E. 1996. "Budget deficits and budget procedures in Latin America, Interamerican Development Bank." Washington, D.C. Unpublished manuscript.

Alesina, A., Londregan, J., and Rosenthal, H. 1993. "A model of the political economy of the United States." *American Political Science Review* 87: 12–33.

Alesina, A., Ozler, S., Roubini, N., and Swagel, P. 1996. "Political Instability and economic growth." *Journal of Economic Growth* 1: 189–212.

Alesina, A., and Perotti, R. 1995a. "The political economy of budget deficits." *IMF Staff Papers* (March): 1–37.

Alesina, A., and Perotti, R. 1995b. "Budget deficits and budget institutions." Working paper no. 5556, National Bureau of Economic Research, Cambridge, Mass.

Alesina, A., Prati, A., and Tabellini, G. 1990. "Public confidence and debt management: A model and a case study of Italy." In R. Dornbusch and M. Draghi, eds., *Public Debt Management: Theory and History*. Cambridge: Cambridge University Press.

Alesina, A., and Rodrik, D. 1994. "Distributive politics and economic growth." *Quarterly Journal of Economics* 109: 465–90.

Alesina, A., and Rosenthal, H. 1995. *Partisan Politics, Divided Government and the Economy*. Cambridge: Cambridge University Press.

Alesina, A., Roubini, N., and Cohen, G. 1997. *Political Cycles and the Macroeconomy*. Cambridge: MIT Press.

Alesina, A., and Spolaore, E. 1997. "On the number and size of nations." *Quarterly Journal of Economics* 112: 1027–56.

Alesina, A., Spolaore, E., and Wacziarg, R. 1997. "Economic integration and political disintegration." Harvard University. Mimeographed.

Alesina, A., and Summers, L. 1993. "Central bank independence and macroeconomic performance: Some comparative evidence." *Journal of Money, Credit and Banking* 25: 151–62.

Alesina, A., and Tabellini, G. 1987. "Rules and discretion with noncoordinated monetary and fiscal policy." *Economic Inquiry* 25: 619–30.

Alesina, A., and Tabellini, G. 1989. "External debt, capital flight and political risk." *Journal of International Economics* 27: 199–220.

Alesina, A., and Tabellini, G. 1990. "A positive theory of fiscal deficits and government debt." *Review of Economic Studies* 57: 403–14.

Alesina, A., and Wacziarg, R. 1998. "Openness, country size and government." *Journal of Public Economics* 69: 305–21.

Almeida, A., and Goodhart, C. 1997. "Does the adoption of inflation target affect central bank behavior?" *Banca Nazionale de Lavoro Quarterly Review* (March): 19–108.

al-Nowaihi, A., and Levine, P. 1994. "Can political monetary cycles be avoided?" *Journal of Monetary Economics* 42: 525–45.

al-Nowaihi, A., and Levine, P. 1996. "Independent but accountable: Walsh contracts and the credibility problem." University of Surrey, UK. Mimeographed.

al-Nowaihi, A., and Levine, P. 1998. "Can reputation solve the monetary policy credibility problems?" *Journal of Monetary Economics* 33: 355–80.

Alt, J. E., Carlsen, F., Heum, P., and Johansen, K. 1999. "Asset specificity and the political behavior of firms: Lobbying for subsidies in Norway." *International Organization* 53: 96–116.

Alt, J., and Chrystal, A. 1983. *Political Economics*. Berkeley and Los Angeles: University of California Press.

Aragones, E., and Postlewaite, A. 1999. "Ambiguity in election games." Universitat Pompeu Fabra. Barcelona, Spain. Mimeographed.

Arrow, K. 1951. *Social Choice and Individual Values*. New York: John Wiley and Sons. (Rev. ed., 1963.)

Artis, M., Mizen, P., and Kontolemis, Z. 1998. "Inflation targeting: What can the ECB learn from the recent experience of the Bank of England?" *Economic Journal* 108: 1810–25.

Atkinson, A. 1999. "The economic consequences of rolling back the welfare state." Center for Economic Studies. Nuffield College, Oxford, UK. Mimeographed.

Austen-Smith, D. 1987. "Interest groups, campaign contributions and probabilistic voting." *Public Choice* 54: 123–39.

Austen-Smith, D. 1997. "Interest groups: Money, information, and influence." In D. C. Mueller, ed., *Perspectives on Public Choice,* 296–321. New York: Cambridge University Press.

Austen-Smith, D., and Banks, J. S. 1988. "Elections, coalitions and legislative outcomes." *American Political Science Review* 82: 405–22.

Austen-Smith, D., and Banks, J. S. 1989. "Electoral accountability and incumbency." In P. C. Ordeshook, ed., *Models of Strategic Choice in Politics*. Ann Arbor: University of Michigan Press.

Austen-Smith, D., and Wright, J. R. 1992. "Competitive lobbying for a legislator's vote." *Social Choice and Welfare* 9: 229–57.

Azariadis, C., and Galasso, V. 1997. "Fiscal constitutions and the determinacy of intergenerational transfers." Working Paper no. 97-71, Universidad Carlos III de Madrid.

Backus, D., and Driffill, J. 1985. "Inflation and reputation." *American Economic Review* 75: 530–38.

Bade, R., and Parkin, M. 1988. "Central bank laws and inflation: A comparative analysis." University of Western Ontario, London, Ontario. Mimeographed.

Ball, L. 1995. "Time consistent policy and persistent changes in inflation." *Journal of Monetary Economics* 36: 329–50.

Baltagi, B. 1995. *Economic Analysis of Panel Data*. New York: Wiley.

Banks, J., and Sundaram, R. 1993. "Adverse selections and moral hazard in a repeated elections model." In

W. Barnett, M. Hinich, and N. Schofield, eds., *Political Economy: Institutions, Information, Competition and Representation.* New York: Cambridge University Press.

Banks, J., and Sundaram, R. 1996. "Electoral accountability and selection effects." University of Rochester, Rochester, N.Y. Mimeographed.

Baqir, R. 1999. "Districts, spillovers, and government overspending." University of California, Berkeley. Mimeographed.

Baron, D. 1991. "Majoritarian incentives, pork barrel programs and procedural control." *American Journal of Political Science* 35: 57–90.

Baron, D. 1993. "A theory of collective choice for government programs." Research paper no. 1240, Graduate School of Business, Stanford University, Stanford, Calif.

Baron, D. 1994. "Electoral competition with informed and uninformed voters." *American Political Science Review* 88: 33–47.

Baron, D. 1998. "Comparative dynamics of parliamentary governments." *American Political Science Review* 92: 593–609.

Baron, D., and Diermeier, D. 1999. "Dynamics of parliamentary cycles: Elections, governments, and parliaments." Stanford University, Stanford, Calif. Mimeographed.

Baron, D., and Ferejohn, J. 1989. "Bargaining in legislatures." *American Political Science Review* 83: 1181–1206.

Baron, D., and Myerson, R. (1982). "Regulating a monopolist with unknown costs." *Econometrica* 50: 911–30.

Barro, R. 1973. "The control of politicians: An economic model." *Public Choice* 14: 19–42.

Barro, R. 1979. "On the determination of public debt." *Journal of Political Economy* 87: 940–47.

Barro, R. 1986. "Reputation in a model of monetary policy with incomplete information." *Journal of Monetary Economics* 17: 1–20.

Barro, R. 1991. "Economic growth in a cross section of countries." *Quarterly Journal of Economics* 106: 407–43.

Barro, R. 1999. "Inequality, growth and investment." Working paper no. 7038, National Bureau of Economic Research, Cambridge, Mass.

Barro, R., and Broadbent, B. 1997. "Central bank preferences and macroeconomic equilibrium." *Journal of Monetary Economics* 39: 17–43.

Barro, R., and Gordon, D. 1983a. "A positive theory of monetary policy in a natural rate model." *Journal of Political Economy* 91: 589–610.

Barro, R., and Gordon, D. 1983b. "Rules, discretion and reputation in a model of monetary policy." *Journal of Monetary Economics* 12: 101–21.

Barro, R., and Sala-i-Martin, X. 1995. *Economic Growth.* New York: McGrawHill.

Basevi, G., Delbono, F., and Denicoló, V. 1990. "International monetary cooperation under tariff threat." *Journal of International Economics* 28: 1–23.

Baumol, W. J. 1967. "The macroeconomics of unbalanced growth: The anatomy of the urban crisis." *American Economic Review* 57: 415–26.

Baxter, M., and Stockman, A. 1989. "Business cycles and the exchange rate regime: Some international evidence." *Journal of Monetary Economics* 23: 377–400.

Bean, R. 1998. "The new UK monetary arrangements: A view from the literature." *Economic Journal* 108: 1795–1809.

Becker, G. S. 1983. "A theory of competition among pressure groups for political influence." *Quarterly Journal of Economics* 98: 371–400.

Becker, G. S. 1985. "Public policies, pressure groups and deadweight costs." *Journal of Public Economics* 28: 330–47.

Becker, G. S., and Mulligan, C. B. 1998. "Deadweight costs and the size of government." Working paper no. 6789, National Bureau of Economic Research, Cambridge, Mass.

Beetsma, R., and Bovenberg, L. 1997. "The interaction of fiscal and monetary policy in a monetary union: Credibility and flexibility." In A. Razin and E. Sadka, eds., *Globalization: Public Economics Perspectives.* Cambridge: Cambridge University Press.

Beetsma, R., and Jensen, H. 1998. "Inflation targets and contracts with uncertain central bank preferences." *Journal of Money, Credit and Banking* 30: 384–403.

Benabou, R. 1996. "Inequality and growth." In B. Bernanke and J. Rotemberg, eds., *NBER Macroeconomics Annual,* 11–74. Cambridge, Mass.: National Bureau of Economic Research.

Benhabib, J., and Radner, R. 1992. "The joint exploitation of a productive asset: A game-theoretic approach." *Economic Theory* 2: 155–90.

Benhabib, J., and Rustichini, A. 1996. "Social conflict and growth." *Journal of Economic Growth* 1: 125–39.

Bennedsen, M. 1998. "Vote buying through resource allocation in government controlled enterprises." University of Copenhagen. Mimeographed.

Bennedsen, M. Forthcoming. "Political ownership." *Journal of Public Economics.*

Bennedsen, M., and Feldmann, S., 1999. "Lobbying legislatures." University of Chicago. Mimeographed.

Bensaid, B., and Jeanne, O. 1997. "The instability of fixed exchange rate systems when raising the nominal interest rate is costly." *European Economic Review* 41: 1461–78.

Bergstrom, T. C., and Goodman, R. P. 1973. "Private demands for public goods." *American Economic Review* 63: 280–96.

Bernanke, B., Laubach, T., Mishkin, F., and Posen, A. 1999. *Inflation Targeting: Lessons from the International Experience.* Princeton: Princeton University Press.

Bernanke, B., and Mihov, I. 1997. "What does the Bundesbank target?" *European Economic Review* 41: 1025–53.

Bernheim, D., and Whinston, M. 1986. "Menu auctions, resource allocation, and economic influence." *Quarterly Journal of Economics* 101: 1–31.

Bertola, G. 1993. "Factor shares and savings in endogenous growth." *American Economic Review* 83: 1184–98.

Bertola, G. 1999. "Microeconomic perspectives on aggregate labor markets." In O. Ashenfelter and D. Card, eds., *Handbook of Labor Economics* III.

Besley, T., and Case, A. 1995a. "Incumbent behavior: Vote-seeking, tax-setting, and yardstick competition." *American Economic Review* 85: 25–45.

Besley, T., and Case, A. 1995b. "Does electoral accountability affect economic policy choices? Evidence from gubernatorial term limits." *Quarterly Journal of Economics* 110: 769–98.

Besley, T., and Coate, S. 1997. "An economic model of representative democracy." *Quarterly Journal of Economics* 112: 85–114.

Besley, T., and Coate, S. 1998a. "Sources of inefficiency in a representative democracy: A dynamic analysis." *American Economic Review* 88: 139–56.

Besley, T., and Coate, S. 1998b. "Centralized vs. decentralized position of local public goods: A political economy analysis." London School of Economics. Mimeographed.

Besley, T., and Coate, S. 1999. "Lobbying and welfare in a representative democracy." London School of Economics. Mimeographed. Forthcoming, *Review of Economic Studies.*

Biais, B., and Perotti, E. 1998. "Machiavellan privatization." Forthcoming, *American Economic Review.*

Bingham Powell Jr., G. 1982. *Contemporary Democracies: Participation, Stability, and Violence.* Cambridge: Harvard University Press.

Black, D. 1948. "On the rationale of group decision making." *Journal of Political Economy* 56: 23–34.

Blais, A., Blake, D., and Dion, S. 1993. "Do parties make a difference? Parties and the size of government in liberal democracies." *American Journal of Political Science* 37: 40–62.

Blanchard, O. 1998. "European unemployment: The role of shocks and institutions." Baffi Lecture, October, Rome.

Blinder, A. S. 1998. *Central Bank in Theory and Practice.* Cambridge: MIT Press.

Bliss, C., and Nalebuff, B. 1984. "Dragon-slaying and ballroom dancing: The private supply of a public good." *Journal of Public Economics* 25: 1–12.

Blomberg, B. S., and Hess, G. 1998. "Is the political business cycle for real?" Ohio State University. Mimeographed.

Boadway, R., and Wildasin, D. 1989a. "A median voter model of social security." *International Economic Review* 30: 307–28.

Boadway, R., and Wildasin, D. 1989b. "Voting models of social security determination." In B. A. Gustafsson and N. A. Klevmarken, eds., *The Political Economy of Social Security.* Amsterdam: North-Holland.

Bohn, H. 1990. "Tax smoothing with financial instruments." *American Economic Review* 80: 1217–30.

Bohn, H., and Inman, R. 1996. "Balanced-budget rules and public deficits: Evidence from the U.S. states." *Carnegie Rochester Conference Series on Public Policy* 45: 13–76.

Boldrin, M., and Montes Alonso, A. 1998. "Intergenerational transfer institutions: Public education and public pensions." Universidad Carlos III de Madrid. Mimeographed.

Boldrin, M., and Rustichini, A. 1996. "Equilibria with social security." *Review of Economic Dynamics,* forthcoming.

Bolton, P., and Roland, G. 1997. "The breakup of nations: A political economy analysis." *Quarterly Journal of Economics* 112: 1057–90.

Bordignon, M., and Brusco, S. 1999. "Optimal secession rules." Catholic University of Milan. Mimeographed.

Bordignon, M., Manasse, P., and Tabellini, G. 1997. "Optimal regional redistribution under asymmetric information." Discussion papers no. 1347, Centre for Economic Policy Research, London. Forthcoming, *American Economic Review.*

Bordo, M., and Eichengreen, B. 1993. *A Retrospective on the Bretton Woods System.* Chicago: University of Chicago Press.

Bordo, M., and Kydland, F. 1995. "The gold standard as a rule: An essay in exploration." *Explorations in Economic History* 32: 423–64.

Bordo, M., and Schwarz, A. 1999. "Policy regimes and economic performance: The historical record." In J. Taylor and M. Woodford, eds., *Handbook of Macroeconomics.* Amsterdam: Elsevier.

Boschini, A. 1999. "Skills, franchise and industrialization." Stockholm University. Mimeographed.

Boskin, M. J., Kotlikoff, L. J., Puffert, D. J., and Shoven, J. B. 1987. "Social security: A financial appraisal across and within generations." *National Tax Journal*: 40.

Bottazzi, L., and Manasse, P. 1998. "Bankers' vs. workers' Europe: Asymmetric information in EMU." Working paper no. 127. Innocenzo Gasparini Institute for Economic Research, Milan.

Boylan, R.T. 1995. "An optimal auction perspective on lobbying." Mimeographed.

Brams, S., and Merrill, S. 1983. "Equilibrium strategies for final-offer arbitration: There is no median convergence." *Management Science* 29: 927–41.

Brennan, G., and Buchanan, J. M. 1980. *The Power to Tax: Analytical Foundations of a Fiscal Constitution.* Cambridge: Cambridge University Press.

Brennan, G., and Hamlin, A. 1994. "A revisionist view of the separation of powers." *Journal of Theoretical Politics* 6: 345–68.

Breton, A. 1974. *The Economic Theory of Representative Government.* Chicago: Aldine.

Breton, A. 1991. "The organization of competition in congressional and parliamentary governments." In A. Breton, G. Galeotti, P. Salmon, and R. Wintrobe, eds., *The Competitive State.* 13–38. Dordrecht: Kluwer Acedemic Publishers.

Broadbent, B. 1996. "Monetary policy regimes and the cost of discretion." Harvard University. Mimeographed.

Bronars, S., and Lott Jr., J. 1995. "Do campaign donations alter how a politician votes?" University of Chicago. Mimeographed.

Browning, E. 1975. "Why the social insurance budget is too large in a democracy" *Economic Inquiry* 22: 373–88.

Bryant, R., Henderson, D., Holtham, G., Hooper, P., and Symansky, S. 1988. *Empirical Macroeconomics for Interdependent Economies.* Washington, D.C.: Brookings Institution.

Buchanan, J. M., and Faith, R. L. 1987. "Secession and the limits of taxation: Toward a theory of internal exit." *American Economic Review* 77: 1023–1031.

Buchanan, J. M., and Tullock, G. 1962. *The Calculus of Consent: Logical Foundation of Constitutional Democracy.* Ann Arbor: University of Michigan Press.

Budd, A. 1998. "The role and operations of the Bank of England monetary policy committee." *Economic Journal* 108: 1783–94.

Bulow, J., and Rogoff, K. 1989. "Sovereign debt: Is to forgive to forget?" *American Economic Review* 79: 43–50.

Buti, M., Pench, L. R., and Sestito, P. 1998. "European unemployment: Contending theories and institutional complexities." Policy paper, European University Institute, Florence, Italy.

Caballero, R., and Hammamour, M. 1996. "The macroeconomics of specificity." Working paper no. 5757, National Bureau of Economic Research, Cambridge, Mass.

Caillaud, B., and Tirole, J. 1998. "Parties as political intermediaries." Institute of Industrial Economics. Mimeographed.

Caillaud, B., and Tirole, J. 1999. "Party governance and ideological bias." *European Economic Review* 43: 779–89.

Calvert, R. 1985. "Robustness of the multi-dimensional voting model: Candidate motivations, uncertainty, and convergence."*American Journal of Political Science* 29: 69–95.

Calvert, R. 1986. *Models of Imperfect Formation in Politics.* Chur, Switzerland: Harwood Academic Publishers.

Calvo, G. 1978. "On the time consistency of optimal policy in a monetary economy." *Econometrica* 46: 1411–28.

Calvo, G. 1983. "Staggered prices in a utility maximizing framework." *Journal of Monetary Economics* 12: 383–98.

Calvo, G. 1988. "Servicing the public debt: The role of expectations." *American Economic Review* 78: 647–61.

Calvo, G., and Guidotti, P. 1990. "Indexation and maturity of government bonds: An exploratory model." In R. Dornbusch and M. Draghi, eds., *Public Debt Management: Theory and History.* Cambridge: Cambridge University Press.

Calvo, G., and Vegh, C. 1999. "Inflation stabilization and BOP crises in developing countries." In J. Taylor and M. Woodford, eds., *Handbook of Macroeconomics.* Amsterdam: Elsevier Science.

Cameron, D. R. 1978. "The expansion of the public economy: A comparative analysis." *American Political Science Review* 72: 1203–61.

Campillo, M., and Miron, J. 1997. "Why does inflation differ across countries?" In C. Romer and D. Romer, eds. *Reducing Inflation: Motivation and Strategy.* Chicago: University of Chicago Press.

Canzoneri, M. 1985. "Monetary policy games and the role of private information."*American Economic Review* 75: 1056–70.

Canzoneri, M., and Gray, J. 1985. "Monetary policy games and the consequences of noncooperative behavior." *International Economic Review* 26: 547–64.

Canzoneri, M., Grilli, V., and Masson, P., eds., 1992. *Establishing a Central Bank: Issues in Europe and Lessons from the U.S.* Cambridge: Cambridge University Press.

Canzoneri, M., and Henderson, D. 1988. "Is sovereign policy making bad?" *Carnegie Rochester Conference Series* 28: 93–140.

Canzoneri, M., and Henderson, D. 1991. *Monetary Policy in Interdependent Economies: A Game-Theoretic Approach.* Cambridge: MIT Press.

Capie, F., Mills, T., and Wood, G. 1994. "Central bank independence and inflation performance: An exploratory data analysis." In P. Siklos, ed., *Varieties of Monetary Reforms: Lessons and Experiences on the Road to Monetary Union.* Dordrecht, Netherlands: Kluwer Academic Publishers.

Caplin, A., and Nalebuff, B. 1988. "On 64%-majority rule." *Econometrica* 56: 787–814.

Caplin, A., and Nalebuff, B. 1991. "Aggregation and social choice: A mean voter theorem." *Econometrica* 59: 1–23.

Carillo, J., and Mariotti, T. 1999. "Electoral competition and politicians' turnover." European Centre for Advanced Research in Economics, Brussels. Mimeographed.

Casella, A. 1992. "On markets and clubs: Economic and political integration of regions with unequal productivity." *American Economic Review Papers and Proceedings* 87: 115–21.

Casella, A., and Eichengreen, B. 1995. "Can foreign aid accelerate stabilization." Discussion paper no. 961, Centre for Economic Policy Research, London.

Casella, A., and Feinstein, J. 1989. "Management of a common currency." In M. de Cecco and A. Giovannini, eds., *A European Central Bank?* Cambridge: Cambridge University Press.

Casella, A., and Feinstein, J. 1990. "Public goods in trade: On the formation of markets and political jurisdictions." Working paper no. 3554, National Bureau of Economic Research, Cambridge, Mass.

Chamley, C. 1986. "Optimal taxation of capital income in general equilibrium with infinite lives." *Econometrica* 54: 607–22.

Chang, R. 1988. "International coordination of fiscal deficits?" *Journal of Monetary Economics* 25: 347–66.

Chang, R. 1998. "Credible monetary policy in an infinite horizon model: Recursive approaches." *Journal of Economic Theory* 81: 431–61.

Chari, V., Christiano, L., and Eichenbaum, M. 1996. "Expectation traps and discretion." Northwestern University, Evanston, Ill. Mimeographed.

Chari, V., Christiano, L., and Kehoe, P. 1992. "Optimal fiscal and monetary policy: Some recent results." In A. Cukierman, Z. Hercowitz, and L. Leiderman, eds., *Political Economy, Growth and Business Cycles*. Cambridge: MIT Press.

Chari, V., and Cole, H. 1993. "Why are representative democracies fiscally irresponsible?" Staff report no. 163, Federal Reserve Bank of Minneapolis.

Chari, V., Jones, L. E., and Marimon, R. 1997. "The economics of split-ticket voting in representative democracies." *American Economic Review* 87: 957–76.

Chari, V., and Kehoe, P. 1990. "Sustainable plans." *Journal of Political Economy* 98: 617–36.

Chari, V., and Kehoe, P. 1993. "Sustainable plans and mutual default." *Review of Economic Studies* 60: 175–96.

Clarida, J., Gali, J., and Gertler, M. 1999. "The science of monetary policy." *Journal of Economic Literature*. Forthcoming.

Clarida, J., and Gertler, M. 1997. "How the Bundesbank conducts monetary policy." In C. Romer and D. Romer, eds., *Reducing Inflation: Motivation and Strategy*, 363–406. Chicago: University of Chicago Press.

Coase, R. H. 1960. "The problem of social cost." *Journal of Law and Economics* 3: 1–44.

Coate, S. 1997. "Distributive policy making as a source of inefficiency in representative democracy." University of Pennsylvania, Philadelphia. Mimeographed.

Cogan, J. 1994. "The dispersal of spending authority and federal budget deficits." In J. Cogan, T. Murris, and A. Schick, eds., *The Budget Puzzle: Understanding Federal Spending*. Stanford, Calif.: Stanford University Press.

Cohen, D. 1999. "Welfare differentials across French and US labour markets: A general equilibrium interpretation." Discussion paper no. 2114, Centre for Economic Policy Research, London.

Cohen, D., and Michel, P. 1988. "How should control theory be used to calculate a time-consistent government policy?" *Review of Economic Studies* 55: 263–74.

Cohen, D., and Wyplosz, C. 1989. "European monetary union: An agnostic evaluation." In R. Bryant, D. Henderson, G. Holtham, P. Hooper, and S. Symanski, eds., *Macroeconomic Policies in an Interdependent World*. Washington D.C.: Brookings Institution.

Cole, H., and Kehoe, P. 1994. "Reputation spillover across relationships with enduring and transient benefits: Reviving reputation models of debt." Working paper no. 534, Federal Reserve Bank of Minneapolis.

Cole, H., and Kehoe, T. 1996a. "Self-fulfilling debt crises and capital flight." Federal Reserve Bank of Minneapolis. Mimeographed.

Cole, H., and Kehoe, T. 1996b. "Self-fulfilling debt crises." Staff report no. 211, Federal Reserve Bank of Minneapolis.

Conesa, J. C., and Krueger, D. 1999. "Social security reform with heterogeneous agents." *Review of Economic Dynamics* 2: 757–95.

Cooley, T., and Quadrini, V. 1999. "How the Fed should react: Optimal monetary policy in a Phillips-curve world." Mimeograph, New York University.

Cooley, T., and Soares, J. 1999. "A positive theory of social security based on reputation." *Journal of Political Economy* 107: 135–60.

Corsetti, G., and Pesenti, P. 1998. "Welfare and macroeconomic interdependence." Yale University. Mimeographed.

Coughlin, P. 1992. *Probabilistic Voting Theory*. Cambridge. Cambridge University Press.

Coughlin, P., and Nitzan, S. 1981. "Electoral outcomes with probabilistic voting and Nash social welfare maxima." *Journal of Public Economics* 15: 113–21.

Cox, G. W. 1987a. "Electorial equilibria under alternative voting institutions." *American Journal of Political Science* 31: 82–108.

Cox, G. W. 1987b. *The Efficient Secret*. Cambridge: Cambridge University Press.

Cox, G. W. 1990a. "Centripetal and centrifugal incentives in electoral systems." *American Journal of Political Science* 34: 903–35.

Cox, G. W. 1990b. "Multicandidate spatial competition." In J. M. Enelow and M. J. Hinch, eds., *Advances in the Spatial Theory of Voting*. Cambridge: Cambridge University Press.

Cox, G. W. 1997. *Making Votes Count: Strategic Coordination in the World's Electoral Systems*. New York: Cambridge University Press.

Cox, G. W., and McCubbins, M. 1986. "Electoral politics as a redistributive game." *Journal of Politics* 48: 370–89.

Crain, M., and Tollison, R. 1993. "Time inconsistency and fiscal policy: Empirical analysis of U.S. states, 1969–89." *Journal of Public Economics* 51: 153–59.

Crémer, J., and Palfrey, T. R. 1996a. "Political confederation." Institute of Industrial Economics, University of Toulouse, France. Mimeographed.

Crémer, J., and Palfrey, T. R. 1996b. "In or Out? Centralization by majority vote." Institute of Industrial Economics, University of Toulouse, France. Mimeographed.

Cukierman, A. 1992. *Central Bank Strategy, Credibility and Independence—Theory and Evidence*. Cambridge: MIT Press.

Cukierman, A. 1998. "The inflation bias result revisited." Tel-Aviv University, Tel-Aviv, Israel. Mimeographed.

Cukierman, A., Edwards, S., and Tabellini, G. 1992. "Seignorage and political instability." *American Economic Review* 82: 537–55.

Cukierman, A., and Lippi, F. 1999. "Central bank independence, centralization of wage bargaining, inflation and unemployment: Theory and some evidence." *European Economic Review* 43: 1395–1434.

Cukierman, A., and Liviatan, N. 1991. "Optimal accommodation by strong policymakers under incomplete information." *Journal of Monetary Economics* 27: 99–127.

Cukierman, A., and Meltzer, A. 1986. "A theory of ambiguity, credibility and inflation under discretion and asymmetric information." *Econometrica* 54: 1099–1128.

Cukierman, A., and Meltzer, A. 1989. "A political theory of government debt and deficits in a Neo-Ricardian framework." *American Economic Review* 79: 713–48.

Cukierman, A., and Meltzer, A. 1991. "A political theory of progressive income taxation." In A. H. Meltzer, A. Cukierman, and S. Richard, eds., *Political Economy*. Oxford: Oxford University Press.

Currie, D., and Levine, P. 1993. *Rules, Reputation and Macroeconomic Contracts*. Cambridge: Cambridge University Press.

Currie, D., Levine, P., and Vidalis, N. 1987. "International cooperation and reputation in an empirical two-bloc model." In R. Bryant and R. Portes, eds., *Global Macroeconomics: Policy Conflict and Cooperation.* London: Macmillan Press.

Daveri, F. 1998. "EFU after EMU?" Innocenzo Gasparini Institute for Economic Research, Milan. Mimeographed.

Daveri, F., and Tabellini, G. 1997. "Unemployment, growth and taxation in industrial countries." Working paper no. 122, Innocenzo Gasparini Institute for Economic Research, Milan.

Davis, O. A., de Groot, M., and Hinich. M. J. 1972. "Social preference orderings and majority rule." *Econometrica* 40: 147–57.

de Cecco, M., and Giovannini, A., eds. 1989. *A European Central Bank?* Cambridge: Cambridge University Press.

Debreu, G., and Koopmans, T., 1982. "Additively decomposed quasi-convex functions," *Mathematical Programming* 24: 1–38.

Denzau, A., and Munger, M. 1986. "Legislators and interest groups: How unorganized interests get represented." *American Political Science Review* 80: 89–106.

Devereux, M., and Wen, J. F. 1996. "Political uncertainty, capital taxation and growth." University of British Columbia, Vancouver, Canada. Mimeographed.

Dewatripont, M., Jewitt, I., and Tirole, J. 1999a. "The economics career concerns, part I: Comparing information structures." *Review of Economic Studies* 66: 183–98.

Dewatripont, M., Jewitt, I., and Tirole, J. 1999b. "The economics of career concerns, part II: Application to missions and accountability of government agencies." *Review of Economic Studies* 66: 199–217.

Dewatripont, M., and Maskin, E. 1995. "Credit and efficiency in centralized and decentralized economies." *Review of Economic Studies* 62: 541–55.

Diermeier, D., and Feddersen, T. 1998. "Cohesion in legislatures and the vote of confidence procedure." *American Political Science Review* 92: 611–21.

Diermeier, D., and Merlo, A. 1998. "Government turnover in parliamentary democracies." New York University. Mimeographed.

Diermeier, D., and Merlo, A. 1999. "An empirical investigation of coalition bargaining procedures." Northwestern University, Evanston, Ill. Mimeographed.

Dixit, A. 1996a. *The Making of Economic Policy: A Transaction-Cost Politics Perspective.* Cambridge: MIT Press.

Dixit, A. 1996b. "Special interest politics and endogenous commodity taxation." *Eastern Economic Journal* 22: 375–88.

Dixit, A. 1997. "Power of incentives in private vs. public organizations." *American Economic Review* 87: 378–82.

Dixit, A. 1998. "Equilibrium contracts for the European central bankers." Princeton University, Princeton, N.J. Mimeographed.

Dixit, A. 1999a. "Some lessons for transactions-cost politics for less-developed countries." Princeton University, Princeton, N.J. Mimeographed.

Dixit, A. 1999b. "A repeated game model of monetary union." Princeton University, Princeton, N.J. Mimeographed.

Dixit, A., Grossman G., and Gul, F. 1999. "A theory of political compromise." *Journal of Political Economy*, forthcoming.

Dixit, A., Grossman, G., and Helpman, E. 1997. "Common agency and coordination: General theory and application to government policy making." *Journal of Political Economy* 105: 752–69.

Dixit, A., and Londregan, J. 1996. "The determinants of success of special interests in redistributive politics." *Journal of Politics* 58: 1132–55.

Dixit, A., and Londregan, J. 1998a. "Ideology, tactics, and efficiency in redistributive politics." *Quarterly Journal of Economics* 113: 497–529.

Dixit, A., and Londregan, J. 1998b. "Political power and the credibility of government debt." *Journal of Economic Theory*, forthcoming.

Downs, A. 1957. *An Economic Theory of Democracy*. New York: Harper and Row.

Drazen, A. 2000. *Political Economy in Macroeconomics*. Princeton, N.J.: Princeton University Press, forthcoming.

Drazen, A., and Grilli, V. 1992. "The benefit of crisis for economic reform." Manuscript, Birkbeck College, London.

Easterly, W., and Rebelo, S. 1993. "Fiscal policy and growth." *Journal of Monetary Economics* 32: 417–58.

Eaton, J., and Fernandez, R. 1995. "Sovereign debt." In G. Grossman and K. Rogoff, eds., *Handbook of International Economics,* Vol. 3. Amsterdam: Elsevier.

Edwards, S., and Tabellini, G. 1994. "Political instability, political weakness and inflation: An empirical analysis." In C. Sims, ed., *Advances in Economic Theory—Proceedings of the 1990 World Meetings of the Econometric Society*. Cambridge: Cambridge University Press.

Eichengreen, B. 1990. "The capital levy in theory and practice." In R. Dornbusch and M. Draghi, eds., *Public Debt Management: Theory and History*. Cambridge: Cambridge University Press.

Eichengreen, B., and von Hagen, J. 1996. "Federalism, fiscal restraints and European monetary union." *American Economic Review Papers and Proceedings* 86: 135–38.

Eijffinger, S., and de Haan, J. 1996. *The Political Economy of Central Bank Independence*. Special Papers in International Economics no. 19, Princeton University, Princeton, N.J.

Eijffinger, S., and Schaling, E. 1993. "Central bank independence in twelve industrial countries." *Banca Nazionale del Lavoro* 184: 1–41.

Enelow, J. M., and Hinich, M. J. 1982. "Ideology, issues and the spatial theory of elections." *American Political Science Review* 76: 493–501.

Enelow, J. M., and Hinich, M. J. 1984. *The Spatial Theory of Voting: An Introduction*. Cambridge: Cambridge University Press.

Epple, D., and Riordan, M. 1987. "Cooperation and punishment under repeated majority voting." *Public Choice* 55: 41–73.

Evans, P., Jacobsen, H., and Putnam, R. 1993. "Double-edged diplomacy." In *International Bargaining and Domestic Policies*. Berkeley and Los Angeles: University of California Press.

Fair, R. 1978. "The effect of economic events on votes for president." *Review of Economics and Statistics* 60: 159–73.

Faust, J. 1996. "Whom can we trust to run the Fed? Theoretical support for the founders' views." *Journal of Monetary Economics* 37: 267–83.

Faust, J., and Irons, J. 1999. "Money, politics and the post-war business cycle." *Journal of Monetary Economics* 43: 61–89.

Faust, J., and Svensson, L. 1998. "Transparency and credibility." Institute for International Economic Studies, Stockholm University. Mimeographed.

Feldstein, M. 1988. "Distinguished Lecture on Economics in Govenment: Thinking about international economic coordination." *Journal of Economic Perspectives* 2: 3–13.

Feldstein, M., ed. 1998. "Privatizing social security." National Bureau of Economic Research project report. Chicago: University of Chicago Press.

Ferejohn, J. 1986. "Incumbent performance and electoral control." *Public Choice* 50: 5–26.

Ferejohn, J., Fiorina, J. M., and McKelvey, R. D. 1987. "Sophisticated voting and agenda independence in the distributive politics settings." *American Journal of Political Sciences* 31: 169–94.

Ferejohn, J., and Krehbiel, K. 1987. "The budget process and the size of the budget." *American Journal of Political Sciences* 31: 296–320.

Fernandez, R., and Rodrik, D. 1991. "Resistance to reform: Status quo bias in the presence of individual specific uncertainty." *American Economic Review* 81: 1146–55.

Fershtman, C., and Judd, K. 1987. "Equilibrium incentives in oligopoly." *American Economic Review* 77: 927–40.

Fershtman, C., Judd, K., and Kalai, E. 1991. "Observable contracts: Strategic delegation and cooperation." *International Economic Review* 32: 551–59.

Fiorina, M. 1977. *Congress: Keystone of the Washington Establishment.* New Haven, Conn.: Yale University Press.

Fiorina, M. 1981. *Retrospective Voting in American National Elections.* New Haven, Conn.: Yale University Press.

Fischer, S. 1977. "Long-term contracts, rational expectations and the optimal money supply rule." *Journal of Political Economy* 85: 163–90.

Fischer, S. 1980. "Dynamic inconsistency, cooperation, and the benevolent dissembling government." *Journal of Economic Dynamics and Control* 2: 93–107.

Fischer, S. 1988. "International macroeconomic policy coordination." In M. Feldstein, ed., *International Economic Cooperation.* Chicago: University of Chicago Press.

Fischer, S. 1991. "Growth, macroeconomics and development." *NBER Macroeconomics Annual 1991.* Cambridge: MIT Press.

Fischer, S. 1995. "The unending search for monetary salvation." *NBER Macroeconomics Annual 1995.* Cambridge: MIT Press.

Flood, R., and Isard, P. 1989. "Monetary policy strategies." *IMF Staff Papers* 36: 612–32.

Flood, R., and Marion, N. 1997. "Perspectives on the recent currency crisis literature." International Monetary Fund. Washington, D.C. Mimeographed.

Flood, R., and Mussa, M. 1994. "Issues concerning nominal anchors for monetary policy." Working paper no. 4850, National Bureau of Economic Research, Cambridge, Mass.

Frankel, J. 1988. "Obstacles to international macroeconomic policy coordination." International Finance Section paper, Princeton University, Princeton, N.J.

Frankel, J., and Rockett, K. 1988. "International macroeconomic policy coordination when policy-makers disagree on the model." *American Economic Review* 78: 318–40.

Franzese, R. 1998. "The positive political economy of public debt: An empirical examination of the OECD postwar experience." Ann Arbor: University of Michigan. Mimeographed.

Franzese, R., 1999. "Partially independent central banks, politically responsive governments, and inflation." Forthcoming in *American Journal of Political Science.*

Franzese, R., and Hall, P. 1998. "Mixed signals: Central bank independence, coordinated wage-bargaining and European monetary union." *International Organization* 52: 505–36.

Fratianni, M., von Hagen, J., and Waller. C. 1997. "Central banking as a principal agent problem." *Economic Inquiry* 35: 378–93.

Frenkel, J., Razin, A., and Sadka, E. 1991. *International Taxation in an Integrated World.* Cambridge: MIT Press.

Frey, B. S. 1983. *Democratic Economic Policy—A Theoretical Introduction.* Oxford: Martin Robertson & Company Ltd.

Friedman, D. 1977. "A theory of the size and shape of nations." *Journal of Political Economy* 85: 59–77.

Fudenberg, D., and Tirole, J. 1993. *Game Theory.* Cambridge: MIT Press.

Galasso, V. 1998. "The US social security: A financial appraisal for the median voter." Universidad Carlos III de Madrid. Mimeographed.

Galasso, V., and Conde Ruiz, J. I. 1999. "Positive arithmetic of the welfare state." Universidad Carlos III de Madrid. Mimeographed.

Gans, J. S., and Smart, M. 1996. "Majority voting with single-crossing preferences." *Journal of Public Economics* 59: 219–37.

Gavin, M., and Perotti, R. 1998. "Fiscal policy in Latin America." In B. Bernanke and J. Rotemberg, eds., *NBER Macroeconomic Annual 1997.* Cambridge: MIT Press.

Genberg, H. 1989. "Exchange rate management and macroeconomic policy: A national perspective." *Scandinavian Journal of Economics* 91: 439–69.

Ghironi, P. 1998. "U.S.-Europe economic interdependence (I): Positive analysis." University of California, Berkeley. Mimeographed.

Ghosh, A., and Masson, P. 1994. *Economic Cooperation in an Uncertain World*. Oxford: Blackwell.

Giavazzi, F., and Pagano, M. 1988. "The advantage of tying one's hands: EMS discipline and central bank credibility." *European Economic Review* 32: 1055–75.

Giavazzi, F., and Pagano, M. 1990. "Confidence crises and public debt management." In R. Dornbusch and M. Draghi, eds., *Public Debt Management: Theory and History*. Cambridge: Cambridge University Press.

Gibbard, A. 1973. "Manipulation of voting schemes: A general result." *Econometrica* 41: 587–601.

Gilligan, T. V., and Krehbiel, K. 1989. "Organization of informative committees by a rational legislature." *American Journal of Political Science* 34: 531–64.

Giovannini, A., Hubbard, G., and Slemrod, J. 1993. *Studies in International Taxation*. Chicago and London: University of Chicago Press.

Glazer, A. 1989. "Politics and the choice of durability." *American Economic Review* 79: 1207–14.

Glomm, G., and Ravikumar, B. 1992. "Public versus private investment in human capital endogenous growth and income inequality." *Journal of Political Economy* 100: 813–34.

Goldbe, P., and Maggi, G. 1997. "Protection for sale: An empirical investigation." Working paper no. 5942, National Bureau of Economic Research, Cambridge, Mass.

Goodhart, C., and Viñals, J. 1994. "Strategy and tactics of monetary policy." In J. Fuhrer, ed., *Goals, Guidelines and Constraints Facing Monetary Policymakers*. Boston: Federal Reserve Bank of Boston.

Gordon, R. 1983. "An optimal taxation approach to fiscal federalism." *Quarterly Journal of Economics* 98: 567–86.

Grandmont, J.-M. 1978. "Intermediate preferences and the majority rule." *Econometrica* 46: 317–30.

Grilli, V., Masciandaro, D., and Tabellini, G. 1991. "Political and monetary institutions and public financial policies in the industrial countries." *Economic Policy* 13: 342–92.

Grillo, M., and Polo, M. 1993. "Political exchange and allocation of surplus: A model of two-party competition." In A. Breton, G. Galeotti, P. Salmon, and R. Wintrobe, eds., *Preferences and Democracy*. Norwell, MA: Kluwer Academic Publishers.

Grofman, B. 1996. "Political economy: Downsian perspectives." In R. Goodin and H.-D. Klivyemann, eds., *A New Handbook of Political Science*. Oxford: Oxford University Press.

Groseclose, T., and Snyder, J. 1996. "Buying supermajorities." *American Political Science Review* 90: 303–15.

Grossman, G., and Helpman, E. 1994. "Protection for sale." *American Economic Review* 84: 833–50.

Grossman, G., and Helpman, E. 1995. "The politics of free-trade agreements." *American Economic Review* 85: 667–90.

Grossman, G., and Helpman, E. 1996. "Electoral competition and special interest politics." *Review of Economic Studies* 63: 265–86.

Grossman, G., and Helpman, E. 1998. "Intergenerational redistribution with short-lived governments." *Economic Journal* 108: 1299–1329.

Grossman, G., and Helpman, E. 1999. "Competing for endorsements." *American Economic Review* 89: 501–24.

Grossman, H. 1991. "A general equilibrium model of insurrections." *American Economic Review* 81: 912–21.

Grossman, H. 1994. "Production, appropriation, and land reform." *American Economic Review* 84: 705–12.

Grossman, H. 1999. "Kleptocracy and revolutions." *Oxford Economic Papers* 51: 267–83.

Grossman, H., and Kim, I. 1996a. "Predation and production." In M. R. Garfinkel and S. Skaperdas, eds., *The Political Economy of Conflict and Appropriation*. Cambridge: Cambridge University Press.

Grossman, H., and Kim, I. 1996b. "Predation and accumulation." *Journal of Economic Growth* 1: 333–51.

Grossman, H., and van Huyck, J. 1986. "Inflation, seignorage and reputation." *Journal of Monetary Economics* 18: 20–32.

Grossman, H., and van Huyck, J. 1988. "Sovereign debt as a contingent claim: Excusable default, repudiation, and reputation." *American Economic Review* 78: 1988–97.

Gruner, H. 1999. "On the role of conflicting national interests in the ECB Council." Discussion paper no. 2192, Centre for Economic Policy Research, London.

Guzzo, V., and Velasco, A. 1999. "The case of a populist central banker." *European Economic Review* 43: 1317–44.

Haldane, A. G., ed. 1995. *Targeting Inflation: A Conference of Central Banks on the Use of Inflation Targets, Organized by the Bank of England.* London: Bank of England.

Hallerberg, M., and von Hagen, J. 1999. "Electoral institutions, cabinet negotiations, and budget deficits within the European Union." In J. Poterba and J. von Hagen, *Fiscal Rules and Fiscal Performance.* Chicago: University of Chicago Press.

Hamada, K. 1974. "Alternative exchange rate systems and the interdependence of monetary policies." In R. Aliber, ed., *National Monetary Policies and the International Financial System.* Chicago: University of Chicago Press.

Hamada, K. 1976. "A strategic analysis of monetary interdependence." *Journal of Political Economy* 84: 677–700.

Harrington, J. E. 1992. "The revelation of information through the electoral process: An exploratory analysis." *Economics and Politics* 4: 255–75.

Harrington, J. E. 1993. "The impact of re-election pressures on the fulfillment of campaign promises." *Games and Economic Behavior* 5: 71–97.

Hart, O. 1995. *Firms, Contracts and Financial Structure.* Oxford: Oxford University Press.

Hassler, J., and Rodriguez Mora, J. V. 1999. "Employment turnover and unemployment insurance." *Journal of Public Economics* 73: 55–83.

Hassler, J., Rodriguez Mora, J. V., Storesletten, K., and Zilibotti, F. 1998. "Equilibrium unemployment insurance." Seminar paper no. 665, Institute for International Economic Studies.

Helpman, E., and Persson, T. 1998. "Lobbying and legislative bargaining." Mimeographed.

Herrendorf, B. 1996. "Inflation targeting as a way of precommitment." University of Warwick, U.K. Mimeographed.

Herrendorf, B., and Lockwood, B. 1997. "Rogoff's 'conservative' central banker restored." *Journal of Money, Credit and Banking* 29: 476–95.

Hettich, W., and Winer, S. L. 1988. "Economic and political foundations of tax structure." *American Economic Review* 78: 701–12.

Hettich, W., and Winer, S. L. 1997. "The political economy of taxation." In D. Mueller, ed., *Perspectives on Public Choice,* 481–505. New York: Cambridge University Press.

Hibbs, D. A. 1977. "Political parties and macroeconomic policy." *American Political Science Review* 71: 1467–78.

Hillman, A. 1989. *The Political Economy of Protection.* Chur, Switzerland: Harwood Academic Publishers.

Hinich, M. J. 1977. "Equilibrium in spatial voting: The median voter result is an artifact." *Journal of Economic Theory* 16: 208–19.

Hinich, M. J., Ledyard, J. O., and Ordershook, P. C. 1972. "Nonvoting and the existence of equilibrium under majority vote." *Journal of Economic Theory* 44: 144–53.

Holmström, B. 1982. "Managerial incentive problems—A dynamic perspective." In *Essays in Economics and Management in Honor of Lars Wahlbeck.* Helsinki: Swedish School of Economics; reprinted in *Review of Economic Studies* 66 (1999): 169–82.

Holmström, B., and Milgrom, P. 1988. "Common agency and exclusive dealing." Yale University. Mimeographed.

Holsey, C. M. and Borcherding, T. E. 1997. "Why does government's share of national income grow? An assessment of the recent literature on the U.S." In D. Mueller, ed., *Perspectives on Public Choice,* 562–89. New York: Cambridge University Press.

Holub, T. 1999. "A swing voter model of the inflation bias." London School of Economics. Mimeographed.

Horn, H., and Persson, T. 1988. "Exchange rate policy, wage formation and credibility." *European Economic Review* 32: 1621–36.

Horne, J., and Masson, P. 1988. "Scope and limits of international economic cooperation and policy coordination." *International Monetary Fund Staff Papers* 35: 259–96.

Hotelling, H. 1929. "Stability in competition." *Economic Journal* 39: 41–57.

Huber, J. D. 1996. "The vote of confidence in parliamentary democracies." *American Political Science Review* 90(2): 269–82.

Husted, T. A., and Kenny, L. W. 1997. "The effect of the expansion of the voting franchise on the size of government." *Journal of Political Economy* 105: 54–82.

Inman, R. P. 1987. "Markets, government and the 'new' political economy." In A. J. Auerbach and M. Feldstein, eds., *Handbook of Public Economics,* vol. 2. Amsterdam: North-Holland.

Inman, R. P., and Rubinfeld, D. L. 1997. "The political economy of federalism." In D. Mueller, ed., *Perspectives on Public Choice*, 73–105. New York: Cambridge University Press.

Inter-American Development Bank. 1997. *Economic and Social Progress Report 1997*. Part 3. Washington, D.C.

Ito, T. 1990. "The timing of elections and political business cycles in Japan." *Journal of Asian Economics* 1: 135–46.

Jahjah, S. 1999. "Inflation, debt and default." International Monetary Fund, Washington, D.C. Mimeographed.

Jensen, H. 1996. "The advantage of international fiscal cooperation under alternative monetary regimes." *European Journal of Political Economy* 12: 485–504.

Jensen, H. 1998. "Credibility of optimal monetary delegation." *American Economic Review* 87: 303–25.

Jensen, H. 1999. "Optimal monetary policy cooperation through state-independent contracts with targets." Forthcoming in *European Economic Review*.

Jonsson, G. 1995. "Institutions and macroeconomic outcomes—The empirical evidence." *Swedish Economic Policy Review* 2: 181–212.

Jonsson, G. 1997. "Monetary politics and unemployment persistence." *Journal of Monetary Economics* 39: 303–25.

Kalandrakis, T. 1999. "General political equilibrium in parliamentary democracies." University of California, Los Angeles. Mimeographed.

Kau, J. B., and Rubin, P. H. 1981. "The size of government." *Public Choice* 37: 261–74.

Keen, M. 1993. "Structure of the fiscal and social changes according to their degree of mobility." University of Essex, U.K. Mimeographed.

Kehoe, P. 1989. "Policy cooperation among benevolent governments may be undesirable." *Review of Economic Studies* 56: 289–96.

King, M., and Fullerton, D., eds. 1984. *The Taxation of Income from Capital: A Comparative Study of the United States, United Kingdom, Sweden, and West Germany*. Chicago: University of Chicago Press.

Klein, P., and Rios-Rull, V. 1999. "Time-consistent optimal fiscal policy." Institute for International Economic Studies, Stockholm University, Stockholm, Sweden. Mimeographed.

Knack, S., and Keefer, P. 1995. "Institutions and economic performance: Cross-country tests using alternative institutional measures." *Economics and Politics* 7: 207–27.

Kontopoulos, Y., and Perotti, R. 1997. "Fragmented fiscal policy." Columbia University, New York. Mimeographed.

Kontopoulos, Y., and Perotti, R. 1999. "Government fragmentation and fiscal policy outcomes: Evidence from the OECD countries." In J. Poterba, and J. von Hagen, eds., *Fiscal Institutions and Fiscal Preference*. Chicago: University of Chicago Press.

Kotlikoff, L., Persson, T., and Svensson, L. 1988. "Social contracts as assets: A possible solution to the time-consistency problem." *American Economic Review* 78: 662–77.

Kramer, G. H. 1972. "Sophisticated voting over multidimensional choice spaces." *Journal of Mathematical Sociology* 2: 165–80.

Krehbiel, K. 1987. "Why are congressional committees powerful?" *American Political Science Review* 81: 929–35.

Krehbiel, K. 1991. "Information and Legislative Organization." Ann Arbor: University of Michigan Press.

Krusell, P., Quadrini, V., and Rios-Rull, V. 1997. "Politico-economic equilibrium and economic growth." *Journal of Economic Dynamics and Control* 21: 243–72.

Krusell, P., and Rios-Rull, V. 1996. "Vested interests in a positive theory of stagnation and growth." *Review of Economic Studies* 63: 601–31.

Krusell, P., and Rios-Rull, V. 1999. "On the size of the U.S. government: Political economy in the neoclassical growth model." *American Economic Review*.

Kydland, F., and Prescott, E. 1977. "Rules rather than discretion: The inconsistency of optimal plans." *Journal of Political Economy* 85: 473–90.

Kydland, F., and Prescott, E. 1980. "Dynamic optimal taxation, rational expectations, and optimal control." *Journal of Economic Dynamics and Control* 2: 78–91.

Laffont, J.-J., 1999. *Incentives and Political Economy: 1997 Clarendon Lectures*. Oxford University Press. Forthcoming.

Laffont, J.-J., and Martimort, D. 1999. "Collusion and delegation." *Rand Journal of Economics*, 30: 2: 232–62.

Laffont, J.-J., and Tirole, J.-J. 1993. *A Theory of Incentives in Procurement and Regulation*. Cambridge: MIT Press.

Lambertini, L. 1996. "Are budget deficits used strategically?" University of California at Los Angeles. Mimeographed.

Lambertini, L., and Azariadis, C. 1998. "The fiscal politics of big governments: Do coalitions matter?" University of California at Los Angeles. Mimeographed.

Lane, P., and Tornell, A. 1996. "Power, growth and the voracity effect." *Journal of Economic Growth* 1: 213–41.

Laver, M., and Shepsle, K. 1990. "Coalitions and cabinet government." *American Political Science Review* 81: 873–90.

Laver, M., and Shepsle, K. 1996. *Making and Breaking Governments: Cabinets and Legislatures in Parliamentary Democracies*. New York: Cambridge University Press.

Ledyard, J. O. 1981. "The paradox of voting and candidate competition: A general equilibrium analysis." In A. L. Roth and J. Kagel, eds., *The Handbook of Experimental Economics*, 777–94. Princeton, N.J.: Princeton University Press.

Ledyard, J. O. 1984. "The pure theory of large two-candidate elections." *Public Choice* 44: 7–41.

Leiderman, L., and Svensson, L. 1995. *Inflation Targets*. London: Centre for Economic Policy Research.

Levhari, D., and Mirman, L. 1980. "The great fish war: An example using the Cournot-Nash solution." *Bell Journal of Economics* 11: 322–34.

Levine, P., and Currie, D. 1987. "Does international macroeconomic policy coordination pay and is it sustainable? A two country analysis." *Oxford Economic Papers* 39: 38–74.

Levitt, S., and Poterba, J. 1994. "Congressional distributive politics and state economic performance." Working paper no. 4721, National Bureau of Economic Research, Cambridge, Mass.

Levitt, S., and Snyder, J. 1997. "The impact of federal spending on house election outcomes." *Journal of Political Economy* 105: 30–53.

Lewis-Beck, M. 1988. *Economics and Elections: The Major Western Democracies*. Ann Arbor: University of Michigan Press.

Liebert, U. 1995. "Parliamentary lobby regimes." In H. Döring, ed., *Parliaments and Majority Rule in Western Europe*. Frankfurt: Campus-Verlag.

Lijphart, A. 1984. *Democracies*. New Haven, Conn.: Yale University Press.

Lijphart, A., ed. 1992. *Parliamentary versus Presidential Government*. Oxford: Oxford University Press.

Lijphart, A. 1994. *Electoral Systems and Party Systems: A Study of Twenty-Seven Democracies 1945–1990*. Oxford: Oxford University Press.

Lindbeck, A. 1976. "Stabilization policies in open economies with endogenous politicians." *American Economic Review Papers and Proceedings* 66: 1–19.

Lindbeck, A., and Weibull, J. 1987. "Balanced-budget redistribution as the outcome of political competition." *Public Choice* 52: 273–97.

Lindbeck, A. and Weibull, J. 1993. "A model of political equilibrium in a representative democracy." *Journal of Public Economics* 51: 195–209.

Lindert, P. 1994. "The rise of social spending, 1880–1930." *Explorations in Economic History* 31: 1–36.

Lindert, P. 1996. "What limits social spending?" *Explorations in Economic History* 33: 1–34.

Lippi, F. 1998. "On central bank independence and the stability of policy targets." *Scandinavian Journal of Economics* 100: 495–512.

Lippi, F. 1999. "Median voter preferences, central bank independence and conservatism." Discussion paper, Banco d'Italia, Rome.

Lizzeri, A. 1996. "Budget deficits and redistributive politics." Princeton University, Princeton, N.J. Mimeographed.

Lizzeri, A., and Persico, N. 1998. "The provision of public goods under alternative electoral incentives." University of Toulouse, Toulouse, France. Mimeographed.

Lockwood, B. 1997. "The allocation of powers in federal and unitary states: A contractarian approach." Mimeographed.

Lockwood, B. 1998. "Distributive politics and the benefits of decentralization." University of Warwick, UK. Mimeographed.

Lockwood, B., Miller, M., and Zhang, L. 1998. "Designing monetary policy when unemployment persists." *Economica* 65: 327–45.

Lockwood, B., and Philippopoulus, A. 1994. "Insider power, unemployment and mutiplier inflation equilibria." *Economica* 61: 59–77.

Loewy, M. 1988. "Equilibrium policy in an overlapping generations economy." *Journal of Monetary Economics* 22: 485–500.

Lohmann, S. 1992. "The optimal degree of commitment: Credibility and flexibility." *American Economic Review* 82: 273–86.

Lohmann, S. 1994. "Information aggregation through costly political auction." *American Economic Review* 84: 518–30.

Lohmann, S. 1996. "Democracy and inflation." University of California at Los Angeles. Mimeographed.

Lohmann, S. 1998. "An informational rationale for the power of special interests." *American Political Science Review* 92: 809–27.

Lowry, R., Alt, J., and Ferree, K. 1998. "Fiscal policy outcomes and electoral accountability in American states." *American Political Science Review* 92: 759–74.

Lucas, R. E. Jr. 1990. "Supply-side economics: An analytical review." *Oxford Economic Papers* no. 42: 293–316.

Lucas, R. E., and Stokey, L. 1983. "Optimal fiscal and monetary policy in an economy without capital." *Journal of Monetary Economics* 12: 55–94.

Magee, S. P., Brock, W. A., and Young, L. 1989. *Black Hole Tariffs and Endogenous Policy Theory: Political Economy in General Equilibrium*. Cambridge: Cambridge University Press.

Martin, P. 1992. "Choosing central bankers in Europe." Graduate Institute of International Studies, Geneva. Mimeographed.

Martin, P. 1995. "Free riding, convergence and two speed monetary unification in Europe." *European Economic Review* 39: 1345–64.

Maskin, E., and Xu, C. 1999. "Soft budget constraint theories: From centralization to the market." Harvard University, Cambridge, Mass. Mimeographed.

Mátyás, L., and Sevestre, P., eds. 1996. *The Econometrics of Panel Data*. Boston: Kluwer Academic Publishers.

Mazza, I., and van Winden, F. 1995. "Two-tier lobbying." University of Amsterdam. Mimeographed.

Mayhew, D. R. 1974. *Congress: The Electoral Connection*. New Haven, Conn.: Yale University Press.

McCallum, B. 1996. "Crucial issues concerning central bank independence." Working paper no. 5597, National Bureau of Economic Research, Cambridge, Mass.

McCubbins, M., Noll, R., and Weingast, B. 1987. "Administrative procedures as instruments of political control." *Journal of Law, Economics and Organization* 3: 243–79.

McKelvey, R. D. 1976. "Intransitivities in multidimensional voting models and some implications for agenda control." *Journal of Economic Theory* 12: 472–82.

McKelvey, R. D. 1986. "Covering, dominance, and institution-free properties of social choice." *American Journal of Political Science* 30: 283–314.

McKelvey, R. D., and Riezman, R. 1991. "Seniority in legislatures." *American Political Science Review* 86: 951–65.

Meltzer A., and Richard, S. 1981. "A rational theory of the size of government." *Journal of Political Economy* 89: 914–27.

Meltzer, A., and Richard, S. 1983. "Tests of a rational theory of the size of government." *Public Choice* 41: 403–18.

Meltzer, A., and Richard, S. 1985. "A positive theory of in-kind transfers and the negative income tax." *Public Choice* 47: 231–65.

Mendoza, E., Milesi-Ferretti, G.-M., and Asea, P. 1997. "On the ineffectiveness of tax policy in altering long-run growth: Harberger's superneutrality conjecture." *Journal of Public Economics* 66: 99–126.

Mendoza, E., Razin, A., and Tesar, L. 1994. "Effective tax rates in macroeconomics: Cross-country estimates of tax rates on factor incomes and consumption." *Journal of Monetary Economics* 34: 297–323.

Milesi-Ferretti, G.-M. 1994. "Wage indexation and time consistency." *Journal of Money, Credit and Banking* 26: 941–50.

Milesi-Ferretti, G.-M. 1995a. "Do good or do well? Public debt management in a two-party economy." *Economics and Politics* 7: 58–74.

Milesi-Ferretti, G.-M. 1995b. "The disadvantage of tying their hands: On the political economy of policy commitments." *Economic Journal* 105: 1381–1402.

Milesi-Ferretti, G.-M., Perotti, R., and Rostagno, M. 1999. "Electoral systems and the composition of public spending." Columbia University, New York. Mimeographed.

Miller, M., and Salmon, M. 1985. "Policy coordination and dynamic games." In W. Buiter and R. Marston, eds., *International Economic Policy Coordination*. Cambridge: Cambridge University Press.

Mishkin, F., and Posen, A. 1996. "Experiences with inflation targeting as a strategy for the conduct of monetary policy." Federal Reserve Bank of New York. Mimeographed.

Mishkin, F., and Posen, A. 1997. "Inflation targeting: Lessons from four countries." *Federal Reserve Bank of New York Economic Policy Review* 3: 9–110.

Mishra, D. 1997. "An unbiased reexamination of political cycle in OECD countries." University of Maryland, College Park. Mimeographed.

Missale, A., and Blanchard, O. 1994. "The debt burden and debt maturity." *American Economic Review* 84: 309–19.

Mokyr, J. 1990. *The Lever of Riches: Technological Creativity and Economic Progress*. New York: Oxford University Press.

Mokyr, J. 1992. "Is economic change optimal?" *Australian Economic History Review* 32: 3–23.

Morelli, M. 1999. "Equilibrium party structure and policy outcomes under different electoral systems." Iowa State University, Ames. Mimeographed.

Mortensen, D. T., and Pissarides, C. A. 1998. "New developments in models of search in the labor market." Northwestern University. Mimeographed.

Moser, P. 1997. "Legislative institutions and their impact on public policy: A survey." Discussion paper no. 9708, University of St. Gallen, Switzerland.

Mudambi, R., Navarra, P., and Nicosia, C. 1996. "Plurality versus proportional representation: An analysis of Sicilian elections." *Public Choice* 86: 341–57.

Mudambi, R., Navarra, P., and Sobbrio, G. 1998. "Changing the rules: Political party competition under plurality and proportionality." Forthcoming in *European Journal of Political Economy.*

Mueller, D. C. 1989. *Public Choice II.* Cambridge: Cambridge University Press.

Mueller, D. C., ed., 1997. *Perspectives on Public Choice: A Handbook.* New York: Cambridge University Press.

Mueller, D. C., and Stratmann, T. 1999. "The economic effects of democractic participation." University of Vienna. Mimeographed.

Mulligan, C., and Sala-i-Martin, X. 1999a. "Social security in theory and practice (I): Facts and political theories." Working paper no. 7118, National Bureau of Economic Research, Cambridge, Mass.

Mulligan, C., and Sala-i-Martin, X. 1999b. "Social security in theory and practice (II): Efficiency theories, narrative theories, and implications for reform." Working paper no. 7119, National Bureau of Economic Research, Cambridge, Mass.

Mundell, R. 1961. "A theory of optimum currency areas." *American Economic Review* 51: 657–65.

Muscatelli, A. 1998. "Optimal inflation contracts and inflation targets with uncertain central bank preferences: Accountability through independence?" *Economic Journal* 108: 529–42.

Mussa, M. 1986. "Nominal exchange rate regimes and the behavior of real exchange rates." *Carnegie Rochester Series on Public Policy* 25: 117–214.

Myers, G., and Sengupta, A. 1997. "Equilibrium constitutions in a federal system." University of Waterloo, Waterloo, Ontario. Mimeographed.

Myerson, R. 1993a. "Effectiveness of electoral systems for reducing government corruption: A game theoretic analysis." *Games and Economic Behavior* 5: 118–32.

Myerson, R. 1993b. "Incentives to cultivate favored minorities under alternative electoral systems." *American Political Science Review* 87: 856–69.

Myerson, R. 1995. "Analysis of democratic institutions: Structure, conduct and performance." *Journal of Economic Perspectives* 9(1): 77–89.

Myerson, R. 1999. "Theoretical comparison of electoral systems: 1998 Schumpeter Lecture." *European Economic Review* 43: 671–97.

Nickell, S. and Layard, R. 1999. "Labour market institutions and economic performance." In O. Ashenfelter and D. Card, eds., *Handbook of Labor Economics*, vol. 3.

Niskanen, W. A. 1971. *Bureaucracy and Representative Government.* New York: Aldine-Ahterton.

Nordhaus, W. 1975. "The political business cycle." *Review of Economic Studies* 42: 169–90.

North, D. C. 1985. "The growth of government in the United States: An economic historian's perspective." *Journal of Public Economics* 28: 383–99.

North, D. C., and Weingast, B. 1989. "Constitutions and commitment: The evolution of institutions governing public choice in seventeenth-century England." *Journal of Economic History* 69: 803–32.

Oates, W. E. 1972. *Fiscal Federalism.* New York: Harcourt, Brace and Jovanovich.

Obstfeld, M. 1997a. "Dynamic seigniorage theory: An exploration." *Macroeconomic Dynamics* 3: 588–614.

Obstfeld, M. 1997b. "Destabilizing effects of exchange rate escape clauses." *Journal of International Economics* 43: 61–77.

Obstfeld, M., and Rogoff, K. 1996. *Foundations of International Macroeconomics.* Cambridge: MIT Press.

Olofsgård, A. 1999. "Secessions and nationalism in a model with size externalities and imperfect mobility." Institute for International Economic Studies. Stockholm, Sweden. Mimeographed.

Olson, M. 1965. *The Logic of Collective Action: Public Goods and the Theory of Groups.* Cambridge: Harvard University Press.

Ordeshook, P. C. 1986. *Game Theory and Political Theory: An Introduction.* Cambridge: Cambridge University Press.

Ordeshook, P. C. 1997. "The spatial analysis of elections and committees: Four decades of research." In D. C. Mueller, ed., *Perspectives on Public Choice,* 247–70. New York: Cambridge University Press.

Osborne, M. J. 1995. "Spatial models of political competition under plurality rule: A survey of some explanations of the number of candidates and the positions they take." *Canadian Journal of Economics* 28: 261–301.

Osborne, M. J., and Slivinsky, A. 1996. "A model of political competition with citizen-candidates." *Quarterly Journal of Economics* 111: 65–96.

Oudiz, G., and Sachs, J. 1985. "International policy coordination in dynamic macroeconomic models." In W. Buiter and R. Marston, eds., *International Economic Policy Coordination.* Cambridge: Cambridge University Press.

Ozler, S., and Tabellini, G. 1991. "External debt and political instability." Working paper no. 3772, National Bureau of Economic Research, Cambridge, Mass.

Pande, R. 1999. "Minority representation and policy choices: The significance of legislator identity." Columbia University, New York. Mimeographed.

Panizza, U. 1998. "Income inequality and economic growth: Evidence from the American data." Inter-American Development Bank. Washington, D.C. Mimeographed.

Panizza, U. 1999. "On the determinants of fiscal centralization: Theory and evidence." *Journal of Public Economics* 74: 97–140.

Parkin, M. 1993. "Inflation in North America." In Shigehara, K. ed., *Price Stabilization in the 1990s.* Basingstoke: Macmillan.

Partridge, M. 1997. "Is inequality harmful for growth? Comment." *American Economic Review* 97: 1019–32.

Patton, C. 1978. "The politics of social security." In M. Boskin, ed., *The Crisis in Social Security.* San Francisco, California: Institute for Contemporary Policy Studies.

Peletier, D., Dur, R., and Swank, H. 1997. "Voting on the budget deficit: Comment." Forthcoming in *American Economic Review.*

Peltzman, S. 1980. "The growth of government." *Journal of Law and Economics* 19: 211–40.

Peltzman, S. 1992. "Voters as fiscal conservatives." *Quarterly Journal of Economics* 107: 329–61.

Perotti, R. 1993. "Political equilibrium, income distribution and growth." *Review of Economic Studies* 60: 755–76.

Perotti, R. 1996. "Growth, income distribution and democracy: What the data say." *Journal of Economic Growth* 1: 149–88.

Persson, M., Persson, T., and Svensson, L. 1987. "Time consistency of fiscal and monetary policy." *Econometrica* 55: 1419–31.

Persson, M., Persson, T., and Svensson, L. 1996. "Debt, cash flow and inflation incentives: A Swedish example." Working paper no. 5772, National Bureau of Economic Research, Cambridge, Mass.

Persson, T. 1998. "Economic policy and special interest politics." *Economic Journal* 108: 310–27.

Persson, T., Roland G., and Tabellini, G. 1997. "Separation of powers and political accountability." *Quarterly Journal of Economics* 112: 1163–1202.

Persson, T., Roland, G., and Tabellini, G. 1998a. "Comparative politics and public finance." Forthcoming in *Journal of Policical Economy.*

Persson, T., Roland, G., and Tabellini, G. 1998b. "Towards micropolitical foundations of public finance." *European Economic Review* 42: 685–94.

Persson, T., and Svensson, L. 1984. "Time consistent fiscal policy and government cash flow." *Journal of Monetary Economics* 14: 365–74.

Persson, T., and Svensson, L. 1986. "International borrowing and time-consistent fiscal policy." *Scandinavian Journal of Economics* 88: 273–95.

Persson, T., and Svensson, L. 1989. "Why a stubborn conservative would run a deficit : Policy with time-inconsistency preferences." *Quarterly Journal of Economics* 104: 325–45.

Persson, T., and Tabellini, G. 1990. *Macroeconomic Policy, Credibility and Politics.* Chur, Switzerland: Harwood Academic Publishers.

Persson, T., and Tabellini, G. 1992a. "The politics of 1992: Fiscal policy and European integration." *Review of Economic Studies* 59: 689–701.

Persson, T., and Tabellini, G. 1992b. "Growth, distribution and politics." *European Economic Review* 36: 593–602.

Persson, T., and Tabellini, G. 1993. "Designing institutions for monetary stability." *Carnegie-Rochester Conference Series on Public Policy* 39: 53–89.

Persson, T., and Tabellini G., eds. 1994a. *Monetary and Fiscal Policy. Vol I: Credibility. Vol II: Politics.* Cambridge: MIT Press.

Persson, T., and Tabellini, G. 1994b. "Is inequality harmful for growth?" *American Economic Review* 84: 600–21.

Persson, T., and Tabellini, G. 1994c. "Representative democracy and capital taxation." *Journal of Public Economics* 55: 53–70.

Persson, T., and Tabellini, G. 1994d. "Does centralization increase the size of government?" *European Economic Review* 38: 765–73.

Persson, T., and Tabellini, G. 1995. "Double-edged incentives: Institutions and policy coordination." In G. Grossman and K. Rogoff, eds., *Handbook of International Economics.* Vol. 3. Amsterdam: North-Holland.

Persson, T., and Tabellini, G. 1996a. "Federal fiscal constitutions: Risk sharing and moral hazard." *Econometrica* 64: 623–46.

Persson, T., and Tabellini, G. 1996b. "Federal fiscal constitutions: Risk sharing and moral hazard." *Journal of Political Economy* 104: 979–1009.

Persson, T., and Tabellini, G. 1996c. "Monetary cohabitation in Europe." *American Economic Review Papers and Proceedings* 86: 111–16.

Persson, T., and Tabellini, G., 1998. "Political economics and public finance." Forthcoming in A. Auerbach and M. Feldstein, eds., *Handbook of Public Economics.* Amsterdam: North-Holland.

Persson, T. and Tabellini, G. 1999a. "Political economics and macroeconomic policy." In J. Taylor and M. Woodford, eds., *Handbook of Macroeconomics.* Amsterdam: North-Holland.

Persson, T., and Tabellini, G. 1999b. "The size and scope of government: Comparative politics with rational politicians. 1998 Marshall Lecture." *European Economic Review* 43: 699–735.

Persson, T., and van Wijnbergen, S. 1993. "Signalling, wage controls and monetary disinflation policy." *Economic Journal* 103: 79–97.

Pesaron, H., and Smith, R. 1995. "Estimating long-run relationships from dynamic heterogeneous panels." *Journal of Econometrics* 68: 79–113.

Pettersson, P. 1998. "An empirical investigation of the strategic use of debt." Institute for International Economic Studies. Stockholm, Sweden. Mimeographed.

Phillips, P. C. B., and Moon, H. R. 1999. "Linear regression limit theory for non-stationary panel data." *Econometrica* 67: 1057–1111.

Piketty, T. 1995. "Social mobility and redistributive politics." *Quarterly Journal of Economics* 110: 551–84.

Piketty, T. 1999. "The information-aggregation approach to political institutions." *European Economic Review* 43: 791–800.

Pissarides, C. A. 1990. *Equilibrium Unemployment Theory.* Oxford: Blackwell.

Pissarides, C. A. 1998. "The impact of employment tax cuts on unemployment and wages: The role of unemployment benefits and tax structure." *European Economic Review* 42: 155–83.

Plott, C. R. 1967. "A notion of equilibrium and its possibility under majority rule." *American Economic Review* 57: 787–806.

Polo, M. 1998. "Electoral competition and political rents." Innocenzo Gasparini Institute for Economic Research, Milan. Mimeographed.

Pommerehne, W. W., and Frey, B. S., 1978. "Bureaucratic behaviour in democracy: A case study." *Public Finance* 33: 98–112.

Poole, K. T. 1970. "Optimal choice of monetary policy instruments in a simple stochastic model." *Quarterly Journal of Economics* 84: 197–216.

Poole, K. T., and Romer, T. 1985. "Patterns of PAC contributions to the 1980 campaigns for the US House of Representatives." *Public Choice* 47: 63–112.

Poole, K. T., and Rosenthal, H. 1991. "Patterns of congressional voting." *American Journal of Political Science* 35: 228–78.

Posen, A. 1993. "Why central bank independence does not cause low inflation: There is no institutional fix for politics." Harvard University. Mimeographed.

Posen, A. 1995. "Declarations are not enough: Financial sector services of central bank independence." In B. Bernanke and J. Rotemberg, eds., *NBER Macroeconomics Annual 1995*. Cambridge, MA: MIT Press.

Posen, A. 1998. "Do better institutions make better policy?" *International Finance* 1: 173–205.

Poterba, J. 1994. "State responses to fiscal crises: 'Natural Experiments' for studying the effects of budgetary institutions." *Journal of Political Economy* 102: 799–821.

Poterba, J., and von Hagen, J., eds. 1999. *Fiscal Rules and Fiscal Performance*. Chicago: University of Chicago Press.

Potters, J., and van Winden, F. 1992. "Lobbying and asymmetric information." *Public Choice* 74: 269–92.

Przeworski, A., and Limongi, F. 1993. "Political regimes and economic growth." *Journal of Economic Perspectives* 7: 51–70.

Putnam, R. 1989. "Diplomacy and domestic politics: The logic of two-level games." *International Organization* 42: 427–60.

Qian, Y., and Roland, G. 1998. "Federalism and the soft budget constraint." *American Economic Review* 88: 1143–62.

Rama, M., and Tabellini, G. 1998. "Lobbying by capital and labor over trade and labor market policies." *European Economic Review* 42: 1295–1316.

Rasmusen, E. 1993. "Lobbying when the decisionmaker can acquire independent information." *Public Choice* 77: 899–913.

Razin, A., and Sadka, E. 1991. "International fiscal policy coordination and competition: An exposition." Working paper no. 3779, National Bureau of Economic Research, Cambridge, Mass.

Renström, T. 1997. "Endogenous taxation in dynamic economies." Oxford University. Mimeographed.

Riezman, R., and Wilson, J. D. 1997. "Political reform and trade policy." *Journal of International Economics* 42: 67–90.

Riker, W. H. 1962. *The Theory of Political Coalitions*. New Haven, Conn.: Yale University Press.

Riker, W. H. 1982. *Liberalism against Populism: A Confrontation between the Theory of Democracy and the Theory of Social Choice*. San Francisco: Freeman.

Riley, J. 1980. "Strong evolutionary equilibrium and the war of attrition." *Journal of Theoretical Biology* 82: 383–400.

Rivière, A. 1998. "Strategic voting and electoral systems." European Centre for Advanced Research in Economics, Brussels. Mimeographed.

Rivière, A. 1999. "Citizen candidacy, party formation and Duverger's law." European Centre for Advanced Research in Economics, Brussels. Université Libre de Bruxelles. Mimeographed.

Roberts, K. 1977. "Voting over income tax schedules." *Journal of Public Economics* 8: 329–40.

Rodriguez, F. 1997. "Taking power seriously: A new approach to the politics of redistribution." Harvard University. Mimeographed.

Rodrik, D. 1995. "Political economy of trade policy." In G. Grossman and K. Rogoff, eds., *Handbook of International Economics*. Vol. 3. Amsterdam: North-Holland.

Rodrik, D. 1998. "Why do more open economies have bigger governments?" *Journal of Political Economy* 106: 997–1032.

Rodrik, D., and van Ypersele, T. 1999. "Capital mobility, distributive conflict and international tax consideration." Working paper no. 7150, National Bureau of Economic Research, Cambridge, Mass.

Roemer, J. 1994. "A theory of policy differentiation in single issue electoral politics." *Social Choice and Welfare* 11: 355–80.

Roemer, J. 1997. "Political-economic equilibrium when parties represent constituents: The unidimensional case." *Social Choice and Welfare* 14: 479–502.

Roemer, J. 1999. "The democratic political economy of progressive income taxation." *Econometrica* 67: 1–20.

Rogers, C. 1986. "The effects of distributive goals on the time inconsistency of optimal taxes." *Journal of Monetary Economics* 17: 251–70.

Rogers, C. 1987. "Expenditure taxes, income taxes, and time-inconsistency." *Journal of Public Economics* 32: 215–30.

Rogoff, K. 1985a. "The optimal degree of commitment to an intermediate monetary target." *Quarterly Journal of Economics* 100: 1169–90.

Rogoff, K. 1985b. "Can international monetary policy coordination be counterproductive?" *Journal of International Economics* 18: 199–217.

Rogoff, K. 1987. "A reputational constraint on monetary policy." *Carnegie Rochester Conference Series on Public Policy* 24: 115–65.

Rogoff, K. 1990. "Equilibrium political budget cycles." *American Economic Review* 80: 21–36.

Rogoff, K., and Sibert, A. 1988. "Elections and macroeconomic policy cycles." *Review of Economic Studies* 55: 1–16.

Roland, G. 1999. *Politics, Markets, and Firms: Transition and Economics*. Cambridge: MIT Press, forthcoming.

Romer, D. 1993. "Openness and inflation: Theory and evidence." *Quarterly Journal of Economics* 107: 869–903.

Romer, T. 1975. "Individual welfare, majority voting and the properties of a linear income tax." *Journal of Public Economics* 7: 163–68.

Romer, T., and Rosenthal, H. 1978. "Political resource allocation, controlled agendas and the status quo." *Public Choice* 33(4): 27–43.

Romer, T., and Rosenthal, H. 1979. "Bureaucrats versus voters: On the political economy of resource allocation by direct democracy." *Quarterly Journal of Economics* 93: 563–87.

Rosenthal, H. 1990. "The setter model." In J. Enelow and M. J. Hinch (eds.). *Advances in the Spatial Theory of Voting*, 199–234. Cambridge: Cambridge University Press.

Rotemberg, J. 1990. "Constituencies with finite lives and the valuation of government bonds." Massachusetts Institute of Technology. Mimeographed.

Rothstein, P. 1990. "Order restricted preferences and majority rule." *Social Choice and Welfare* 7: 331–42.

Roubini, N., and Sachs, J. 1989. "Political and economic determinants of budget deficits in the industrial democracies." *European Economic Review* 33: 903–33.

Saint-Paul, G. 1993. "On the political economy of labor market flexibility." *NBER Macroeconomics Annual*. Cambridge, MA: MIT Press.

Saint-Paul, G. 1996. "Exploring the political economy of labor market institutions." *Economic Policy* 23: 265–315.

Saint-Paul, G. 1999. "The political economy of employment protection." University Pompeu Fabra. Barcelona. Mimeographed.

Saint-Paul, G., and Verdier, T. 1993. "Education, democracy and growth." *Journal of Development Economics* 42: 399–407.

Sappington, D. 1982. "Optimal regulation of research and development under imperfect information." *Bell Journal of Economics* 13: 354–68.

Satterthwaite, M. A. 1975. "Strategy-proofness and Arrow's conditions: Existence and correspondence theorems for voting procedures and social welfare functions." *Journal of Economic Theory* 10: 187–217.

Schaling, E. 1995. *Institutions and Monetary Policy: Credibility, Flexibility, and Central Bank Independence.* Aldershot: Edward Elgar Publishers.

Schattschneider, E. E. 1935. *Politics, Pressures and the Tariff.* Englewood Cliffs, N.J.: Prentice Hall.

Schofield, N. 1993. "Party competition in a spatial model of coalition formation." In W. Barnett, M. J. Hinch and N. Schofield, eds., *Political Economy: Institutions, Competition and Representation,* 135–174. Cambridge: Cambridge University Press.

Schofield, N. 1997. "Multiparty electoral politics." In D. Muller, ed., *Perspectives on Public Choice.* Cambridge: Cambridge University Press.

Schotter, A. 1981. *The Economic Theory of Social Institutions.* Cambridge: Cambridge University Press.

Schultz, C. 1999a. "Monetary policy, delegation and polarization." *Economic Journal* 109: 164–79.

Schultz, C. 1999b. "Political competition and polarization." University of Copenhagen. Mimeographed.

Schultz, C., and Sjöström, T. 1997. "Elections, public debt and migration." University of Copenhagen. Mimeographed.

Seabright, P. 1996. "Accountability and decentralization in government: An incomplete contracts model." *European Economic Review* 40: 61–89.

Shepsle, K. A. 1979. "Institutional arrangements and equilibrium in multi-dimensional voting models." *American Journal of Political Science* 23: 27–59.

Shepsle, K. A. 1989. "Studying institutions: Some lessons from the rational choice approach." *Journal of Theoretical Politics* 1: 131–48.

Shepsle, K. A. 1999. "From generation to generation: A formal analysis of intertemporal strategic interaction." Harvard University. Mimeographed.

Shepsle, K. A., and Weingast, B. R. 1981. "Structure-induced equilibrium and legislative choice." *Public Choice* 37: 503–19.

Shields, T. G., and Goidel, R. K. 1997. "Participation rates, socioeconomic classes and congressional elections." *American Journal of Political Science* 41: 683–91.

Shleifer, A., and Vishny, R. 1999. *The Grabbing Hand: Government Pathologies and their Cures.* Cambridge: Harvard University Press.

Shugart, M. S., and Carey, J. M. 1992. *Presidents and Assemblies: Constitutional Design and Electoral Dynamics.* New York: Cambridge University Press.

Sibert, A. 1998. "The reputation of the European central bank." Paper presented at workshop, "The Euro and its Effects on the Spanish Economy," Donostia–San Sebastian, November 26–27, 1998.

Siebert, H., ed. 1998. Redesigning social security. Tübingen: Instituet fuer Weltwirtschaft an der Universitaet Kiel.

Snyder, J. 1991. "On buying legislatures." *Economics and Politics* 3: 93–110.

Sørensen, P. B. 1991. "Coordination of capital income taxes and monetary union: What needs to be done?" Institute of Economic, Copenhagen University. Mimeographed.

Staiger, R. 1995. "International rules and institutions for cooperative trade policy." In G. Grossman and K. Rogoff, eds., *Handbook of International Economics.* Vol. 3. Amsterdam: North-Holland.

Stenmark, K. 1999. "Government structure and fiscal policy." Stockholm University. Mimeographed.

Stigler, G. J. 1970. "Director's law of public income distribution." *Journal of Law and Economics* 13: 1–10.

Stigler, G. J. 1971. "The theory of economic regulation." *Bell Journal of Economics and Management Science* 2: 3–21.

Stigler, G. J. 1972. "Economic performance and political competition." *Public Choice* 13: 91–106.

Stock, J., and Watson, M. 1999. "Business cycle fluctuations in U.S. macroeconomic time series." In J. Taylor and M. Woodford, eds., *Handbook of Macroeconomics*. Amsterdam: Elsevier.

Strömberg, D. 1996. "Demography, voting, and local public expenditures: Theory and evidence from Swedish municipalities." Mimeographed. Princeton University.

Strömberg, D. 1998a. "Mass-media competition, political competition, and public policy." Mimeographed. Princeton University.

Strömberg, D. 1998b. "Radio's impact on New Deal spending." Institute for International Economic Studies, Stockholm. Mimeographed.

Strömberg, D. 1999. "The Lindbeck-Weibull model in US federal structure." Institute for International Economic Studies, Stockholm. Mimeographed.

Stuart, C., and Hansson, I. 1989. "Social security as trade among living generations." *American Economic Review* 79(5): 1182–95.

Sturzenegger, F., and Tommasi, M. 1998. *The Political Economy of Reform*. Cambridge: MIT Press.

Svensson, J. 1996. "Collusion and interest groups: Foreign aid and rent dissipation." The World Bank. Washington, D.C. Mimeographed.

Svensson, J. 1997. "The control of public policy: Electoral competition, polarization and primary elections." The World Bank. Washington, D.C. Mimeographed.

Svensson, J. 1998. "Investment, property rights and political instability: Theory and evidence." *European Economic Review* 42: 1317–41.

Svensson, J. 1999. "Democracy, government spending and growth." The World Bank. Washington, D.C. Mimeographed.

Svensson, L. 1997a. "Optimal inflation targets, 'conservative' central bankers and linear inflation contracts." *American Economic Review* 87: 98–114.

Svensson, L. 1997b. "Inflation forecast targeting: Implementing and monitoring inflation targets." *European Economic Review* 41: 1111–46.

Svensson, L. 1999a. "Inflation targeting as a monetary policy rule." *Journal of Monetary Economics* 43: 607–54.

Svensson, L. 1999b. "Monetary policy issues for the Eurosystem." Discussion paper no. 2197, Centre for Economic Policy Research, London.

Taagepera, R., and Shugart, M. S. 1989. *Seats and Votes: The Effects and Determinants of Electoral Systems*. New Haven, Conn.: Yale University Press.

Tabellini, G. 1985. "Accommodative monetary policy and central bank reputation." *Giornale Degli Economisti* 44: 389–425.

Tabellini, G. 1987. "Money, debt and deficits in a dynamic game." *Journal of Economic Dynamics and Control* 10: 427–42.

Tabellini, G. 1990a. "A positive theory of social security." Working paper no. 3272, National Bureau of Economic Research, Cambridge, Mass.

Tabellini, G. 1990b. "Domestic politics and the international coordination of fiscal policies." *Journal of International Economics* 28: 245–65.

Tabellini, G. 1991. "The politics of intergenerational redistribution." *Journal of Political Economy* 99: 335–57.

Tabellini, G., and Alesina, A. 1990. "Voting on the budget deficit." *American Economic Review* 80: 37–39.

Tanzi, V., and Davoodi, H. 1997. "Corruption, public investment, and growth." Working paper no. 97/139, International Monetary Fund, Washington, D.C.

Tanzi, V., and Schuknecht, L. 1995. "The growth of government and the reform of the state in industrial countries." Working paper no. 95/130, International Monetary Fund, Washington, D.C.

Taylor, J. 1983. "Rules, discretion and reputation in a model of monetary policy: Comments." *Journal of Monetary Economics* 12: 123–25.

Terlizzese, D. 1999. "A note on lexicographic ordering and monetary policy." Bank of Italy, Rome. Mimeographed.

Terrones, M. 1989. "Macroeconomic policy choices under alternative electoral structures." University of Wisconsin. Mimeographed.

Tirole, J. 1994. "The international organization of government." *Oxford Economic Papers* 46: 1–29.

Tirole, J. 1999. "Incomplete contracts: Where do we stand?" *Econometrica.* 67: 741–81.

Tornell, A. 1995. "Economic growth and decline with endogenous property rights." Harvard University. Mimeographed.

Tornell, A., and Velasco, A. 1992. "The tragedy of the commons and economic growth: Why does capital flow from poor to rich countries." *Journal of Political Economy* 100: 1208–31.

Tsebelis, G. 1995. "Decisionmaking in political systems: Presidentialism, parliamantarism, multicameralism, and multipartism." *British Journal of Political Science* 25: 289–325.

Tufte, E. R. 1978. *Political Control of the Economy.* Princeton: Princeton University Press.

Tullock, G. 1959. "Some problems of majority voting." *Journal of Political Economy* 67: 571–79.

Tullock, G. 1988. "Future directions of rent-seeking research." In K. Rowley, R. Tollison, and G. Tullock, eds., *The Political Economy of Rent-Seeking.* Boston: Kluwer.

van der Ploeg, F. 1988. "International policy coordination in interdependent monetary economies." *Journal of International Economics* 23: 1–23.

Vaubel, R. 1985. "International collusion or competition for macroeconomic policy coordination." *Recherches Economiques de Louvain* 51: 223–40.

Velasco, A. 1994. "Are balance of payment crisis rational?" Working paper, New York University, New York.

Velasco, A. 1999. "A model of endogenous fiscal deficit and delayed fiscal reforms." In J. Poterba and J. von Hagen, eds., *Fiscal Rules and Fiscal Performance.* Chicago: University of Chicago Press.

Verbon, H. 1988. *The Evolution of Public Pension Schemes.* Berlin and Heidelberg: Springer-Verlag.

Vickers, J. 1985. "Delegation and the theory of the firm." *Economic Journal* 95: 138–47.

Vickers, J. 1986. "Signalling in a model of monetary policy with incomplete information." *Oxford Economic Papers* 38: 443–55.

Volkerink, B., and de Haan, J. 1999. "Political and institutional determinants of the tax mix: An empirical investigation for OECD countries." Research report, Systems, Organisation and Management, University of Groningen, Netherlands.

von Hagen, J. 1992. "Budgeting procedures and fiscal performance in the European communities." Economic papers no. 96, European Commission, Brussels.

von Hagen, J. 1998. "Budgeting institutions for aggregate fiscal discipline." Policy paper no. B98-01 (February), Zentrum fur Europeische Integrationsforschung, Bonn.

von Hagen, J., and Harden, I. 1994. "National budget processes and fiscal performance." *European Economy Reports and Studies* 3, EU, Brussels.

von Hagen, J., and Harden, I. 1996. "Budget processes and commitment to fiscal discipline" Working paper, International Monetary Fund, Washington, D.C.

von Hagen, J., and Süppel, R. 1994. "Central bank constitutions for federal monetary unions." *European Economic Review* 38: 774–82.

Wagner, A. 1893. *Grundlegung der Politischen Oekonomie.* (Foundations of Political Economy) 3d ed. Leipzig, Germany: C. F. Winter.

Waller, C. 1989. "Monetary policy games and central bank politics." *Journal of Money, Credit and Banking* 21: 422–31.

Waller, C. 1992. "A bargaining model of partisan appointments to the central bank." *Journal of Monetary Economics* 29: 411–28.

Waller, C., and Walsh, C. 1996. "Central bank independence, economic behavior, and optimal term limits." *American Economic Review* 96: 1139–53.

Wallis, J. J., and Oates, W. E. 1988. "Does economic sclerosis set in with ages? An empirical study of the Olson hypothesis." *Kyklos* 41: 397–417.

Walsh, C. 1995a. "Optimal contracts for central bankers." *American Economic Review* 85: 150–67.

Walsh, C. 1995b. "Is New Zealand's Reserve Bank Act of 1989 an optimal central bank contract?" *Journal of Money, Credit and Banking* 27: 1179–91.

Walsh, C. 1998. *Monetary Theory and Policy.* Cambridge: MIT Press.

Weingast, B. R., and Marshall, W. 1988. "The industrial organization of congress, or, Why legislatures, like firms, are not organized as markets." *Journal of Political Economy* 96: 132–63.

Weingast, B. R., Shepsle, K., and Johnsen, C. 1981. "The political economy of benefits and costs: A neoclassical approach to distributive politics." *Journal of Political Economy* 89: 642–64.

Williamson, O. E. 1985. *The Economic Institutions of Capitalism.* New York: Free Press.

Wilson, J. 1987. "Trade, capital mobility and tax competition." *Journal of Political Economy* 95: 835–56.

Wilson, J. 1989. *Bureaucracy—What Government Agencies Do and Why They Do It.* New York: Basic Books.

Wittman, D. 1977. "Candidates with policy preferences: A dynamic model." *Journal of Economic Theory* 14: 180–89.

Wittman, D. 1983. "Candidate motivation: A synthesis of alternative theories." *American Political Science Review* 77: 142–57.

Wittman, D. 1986. "Final-offer arbitration." *Management Science* 32: 1551–61.

Wittman, D. 1989. "Why democracies produce efficient results." *Journal of Political Economy* 97: 1395–1424.

Wittman, D. 1995. *The Myth of Democratic Failure: Why Political Institutions Are Efficient.* Chicago: University of Chicago Press.

Wright, R. 1986. "The redistributive roles of unemployment insurance and the dynamics of voting." *Journal of Public Economics* 31: 377–99.

Author Index

Subject Index